Optimal Pricing, Inflation, and the Cost of Price Adjustment

Optimal Pricing, Inflation, and the Cost of Price Adjustment

edited by Eytan Sheshinski and Yoram Weiss

The MIT Press
Cambridge, Massachusetts
London, England

338.52
062

This book was set in Times Roman by Asco Trade Typesetting Ltd., Hong Kong, and was printed and bound in the United States of America.

Library of Congress Cataloging-in-Publication Data

Optimal pricing, inflation, and the cost of price adjustment / edited
  by Eytan Sheshinski and Yoram Weiss.
        p.   cm.
    Includes bibliographical references and index.
    ISBN 0-262-19332-9
    1. Pricing.   2. Inflation (Finance)   I. Sheshinski, Eytan.
  II. Weiss, Yoram.
  HF5416.5.067   1993
  338.5′2—dc20   92-35198
                                                    CIP

TP

Contents

Preface   vii

Contributors   xiii

I   NOMINAL RIGIDITIES: MICROECONOMIC   1
EVIDENCE AND MACROECONOMIC
IMPLICATIONS

1   **Inflation and Price Adjustment: A Survey of Findings**   3
from Micro-Data
Yoram Weiss

2   **Individual Inertia and Aggregate Dynamics**   19
Andrew Caplin

II   TOOLS OF ANALYSIS: MATHEMATICAL   47
THEORY OF INVENTORY CONTROL

3   **The Optimality of (S, s) Policies in the Dynamic**   49
Inventory Problem
Herbert Scarf

4   **Quasi-Variational Inequalities and Impulse Control**   57
Agnès Sulem

5   **A Simplified Treatment of the Theory of Optimal**   97
Regulation of Brownian Motion
Avinash Dixit

III   OPTIMAL PRICING POLICIES UNDER   115
INFLATION

6   **Inflation and Costs of Price Adjustment**   117
Eytan Sheshinski and Yoram Weiss

7   **Optimum Pricing Policy under Stochastic Inflation**   143
Eytan Sheshinski and Yoram Weiss

8   **Staggered and Synchronized Price Policies under**   169
Inflation: The Multi-product Monopoly Case
Eytan Sheshinski and Yoram Weiss

IV   AGGREGATION AND THE EFFECTS OF   215
MONEY ON AGGREGATE OUTPUT

9   Menu Costs and the Neutrality of Money   217
Andrew S. Caplin and Daniel F. Spulber

10   Dynamic (S, s) Economies   241
Ricardo J. Caballero and Eduardo M.R.A. Engel

11   State-Dependent Pricing and the Dynamics of Money   277
and Output
Andrew Caplin and John Leahy

V   SEARCH AND THE WELFARE COSTS OF   303
INFLATION

12   Search, Price Setting, and Inflation   305
Roland Benabou

13   Inflation and Efficiency in Search Markets   341
Roland Benabou

14   Search, Sticky Prices, and Inflation   385
Peter Diamond

VI   PRICING POLICIES UNDER INFLATION: The   407
EMPIRICAL EVIDENCE

15   Why Are Prices Sticky? Preliminary Results from an   409
Interview Study
Alan S. Blinder

16   The Frequency of Price Adjustment: A Study of   423
Newsstand Prices of Magazines
Stephen G. Cecchetti

17   The Behavior of Prices and Inflation: An Empirical   445
Analysis of Disaggregated Price Data
Saul Lach and Daniel Tsiddon

18   Inflation and Relative Prices: Evidence from Argentina 485
Mariano Tommasi

Index   513

Preface

The chapters in this volume provide an analysis of nominal price rigidities in an inflationary environment. A basic observation, which is in the background of this work, is that economic decisions are often characterized by periods of inaction followed by an abrupt change. Thus, in an inflationary economy, firms change nominal prices intermittently. The frequency and size of price changes by each firm and the degree of synchronization among different firms determine the aggregate dynamics of the economy. The common methodological feature is that firms follow rather simple pricing policies in which the real price floats freely between two predetermined bounds and action is triggered only if one of the bounds is reached. Such S-s policies yield tractable models of dynamic adjustment. The main purpose of the analysis is to evaluate the effects of inflation on aggregate output and on welfare.

The volume begins with two introductory surveys that are intended to motivate the collection. Yoram Weiss surveys the empirical studies of pricing policies by individual firms. His chapter documents the prevalence of nominal rigidities and the systematic impact of inflation on the size and frequency of price changes. Andrew Caplin's contribution surveys the theoretical efforts to integrate the nominal rigidities at the micro level into macro relationships. He provides a unified treatment of the aggregation issues within a simple framework. Taken together, these two surveys provide a strong case for the research agenda followed by the authors included in this collection. It is possible to formulate a tractable model of aggregate adjustments in which nominal and real variables interact and which is founded on plausible micro foundations. Moreover, the model has testable implications at both the micro and the macro levels.

The second part of the book treats the general problem of optimal dynamic adjustment in the presence of convex costs of adjustment. The chapter by Herbert Scarf provides the classical treatment of inventory adjustment under uncertain demand, including a proof of the optimality of S-s policies. The chapter by Agnès Sulem surveys the mathematical methods of impulse control. This technique provides a characterization of the optimal policy in terms of a system of inequalities and differential equations that the value function must satisfy. The necessary conditions have a direct economic interpretation. During a period of inaction the value is governed by the external forces (such as inflation), and it is maximized when an action is taken. Action is triggered if the difference between the current value and the maximal value exceeds the (lump-sum) cost of adjustment. The analytical problem is to find the values of the state at which an action is triggered and the size of the adjustment. The chapter by Sulem contains applications to the single commodity and to the two-commodity inventory problems, in which explicit solutions are derived. The chapter by Avinash Dixit provides a more heuristic exposition of the same methods, including a diagrammatic interpretation.

The third part includes applications of the inventory models to the case of nominal price adjustment by an individual firm. The three chapters by Eytan Sheshinski and Yoram Weiss provide a general framework and yield some comparative static results. In particular, they show that an increase in the rate of inflation widens the bounds within which real prices float. Therefore, firms are pushed further from their maximal profits position. This illustrates how inflation affects the welfare (profits) of individual firms. An important methodological feature of this work is that the optimal policy is characterized in terms of a *state* variable, which is the real (relative) price of the firm at any point in time. The time pattern of price changes, rather than being prespecified, is an endogenous outcome of the model. For instance, it is shown by the authors that inflation may increase or decrease the frequency of price changes, depending on the concavity of the profit function in the log of the real price. In a later chapter they show that a monopoly that sells *two* goods will prefer to synchronize (stagger) the price changes of its products if the two prices interact positively (negatively) in the profit function.

The fourth part addresses the question of aggregation. What is the behavior of the aggregate price level and aggregate output in an economy populated by firms following an S-s pricing policy? Andrew Caplin and Daniel Spulber show that a nominal price rigidity at the level of the firm need not carry to the aggregate. They first argue that with a "one-sided" inflationary process, in which shocks can only be positive, the only time-invariant distribution of relative prices is the *uniform* distribution. If there is a monetary shock of size Δ, then $\Delta/(S$-$s)$ of the firms will be induced to raise their price by $(S$-$s - \Delta)$, and the remaining $(S$-$s - \Delta)/(S$-$s)$ of the firms will maintain their nominal price and suffer a real reduction of size Δ. The aggregate effect on the average *real* price is zero. This means that the aggregate price level follows the money stock and that monetary changes will have no real effects (assuming that aggregate output is fully determined by the real money stock). Ricardo Caballero and Eduardo Engel strengthen these results by showing that the price distribution *con-*

verges to the uniform distribution from any initial distribution, provided that idiosyncratic shocks are added to the common inflationary shocks. The crucial assumptions for this result are continuity and monotonicity of the inflationary process.

The neutrality of monetary policy fails if the monetary shocks can be both negative and positive, that is, if inflation is "two-sided." In this case, the limiting distribution is triangular (or piecewise exponential) rather than uniform, since firms return to the same target both from the upper and from the lower trigger. Following a positive inflationary shock, the price increase by firms at the bottom does not offset the reduction in the real price of firms in the middle and top of the distribution. Hence the average real price declines and aggregate output rises. Thus, nominal rigidities at the level of the firm translate into aggregate rigidities. Andrew Caplin and John Leahy illustrate this principle in the context of a special case that allows them to trace the output dynamics.

The fifth part introduces active search by consumers. This option puts further constraints on the distribution of relative prices, in addition to the invariance imposed by consistent aggregation. Roland Benabou develops a general equilibrium framework in which each consumer's search policy depends on the price variability created by the S-s pricing policies of firms and each firm chooses its S-s bounds based on the reservation strategy of searchers. He shows that a higher inflation rate, in addition to widening the S-s bounds, reduces the level of both S and s. This is caused by the fact that inflation increases the incentive to search and encourages competition among firms. In a subsequent chapter he shows that if one takes into account *all* the components—reduced profits, reduced prices, higher costs of nominal price changes, and higher costs of search—inflation may increase or decrease welfare. Peter Diamond, who assumes that nominal prices are "stamped" at production and can be changed only when a new product is introduced, obtains a stronger result: as inflation increases, welfare initially increases, then declines. In this model each firm sets an initial price that is equal to the consumer's reservation price.

Inflation has two opposing effects on the reservation price and, therefore, on welfare. On the one hand, it raises the variance of relative prices, which increases the reservation price. On the other hand, it reduces profits and causes firms to exit. This implies a longer waiting period until a purchase occurs, which reduces the reservation price. The first factor dominates at low levels of inflation and the second dominates at higher rates.

The sixth and last part of the book is devoted to empirical analysis of nominal price rigidities. Alan Blinder summarizes the results of interviews in which companies report the frequency of price changes and the causes for price rigidity. The chapter by Stephen Cecchetti analyzes the nominal price adjustments of newspapers in the United States. Saul Lach and Daniel Tsiddon analyze the price adjustments of a group of products during two inflationary episodes in Israel. Mariano Tommasi provides a similar analysis for Argentina. All these studies find a substantial amount of nominal rigidities and systematic effects of inflation on the frequency and size of price adjustments.

Our objective in gathering all these works within a single volume is twofold. First, we wish to give a sense of the scope of recent efforts to explicitly incorporate *frictions* in economic models. Second, by providing easy access to some of the main works, we hope to promote further research on an elusive but important question: What are the real effects of inflation?

Acknowledgments

Some of the chapters in this volume have previously appeared elsewhere, and are reprinted here with permission. In Part II, Chapter 3, "The Optimality of (S, s) Policies in the Dynamic Inventory Problem," was published in K. Arrow, S. Karlin, P. Suppes, eds., *Mathematical Methods in Social Sciences*, Stanford University Press, 1959: 196–202. Chapter 5, "A Simplified Treatment of the Theory of Optimal Regulation of Brownian Motion," appeared in *Journal of Economic Dynamics and Control*, 1991, vol. 15, 657–673.

In Part III, the following articles have been reprinted from the *Review of Economic Studies*: Chapter 6, "Inflation and Costs of Price Adjustment," 1977, vol. 44, 287–303; Chapter 7, "Optimum Pricing Policy Under Stochastic Inflation," 1983, vol. 50, 513–529; and Chapter 8, "Staggered and Synchronized Price Policies Under Inflation: The Multi-product Monopoly Case," 1992, vol. 59, 331–359.

In Part IV, Chapter 9, "Menu Costs and the Neutrality of Money," was previously published in *Quarterly Journal of Economics*, 1987, vol. 102, 703–726. Chapter 10, "Dynamic $(S\text{-}s)$ Economies," appeared in *Econometrica*, 1991, vol. 59, 1659–86, and is used here with the permission of The Econometric Society. Chapter 11, "State Dependent Pricing and the

Dynamics of Money and Output," appeared in *Quarterly Journal of Economics*, 1991, vol. 106, 683–708.

Part V consists of articles that previously appeared in *Review of Economic Studies*: Chapter 12, "Search, Price Setting and Inflation," 1988, vol. 55, 353–373; Chapter 13, "Inflation and Efficiency in Search Markets," 1992, vol. 59, 299–329; Chapter 14, "Search, Sticky Prices and Inflation," 1993, vol. 60, 53–68.

In Part VI, Chapter 15, "Why Are Price Sticky? Preliminary Results from an Interview Study," appeared in *American Economic Review*, 1991, vol. 81, 89–96. Chapter 16, "The Frequency of Price Adjustment," was published in *Journal of Econometrics*, 1986, vol. 31, 255–274. Chapter 17, "The Behavior of Prices and Inflation: An Empirical Analysis of Disaggregated Price Data," appeared in the *Journal of Political Economy*, University of Chicago Press, 1992, vol. 100, 349–389.

Contributors

Roland Jean-Marc Benabou
Department of Economics
MIT
Cambridge, MA

Alan S. Blinder
Department of Economics
Princeton University
Princeton, NJ

Ricardo J. Caballero
Department of Economics
MIT
Cambridge, MA

Andrew Caplin
Department of Economics
Columbia University
New York, NY

Stephen G. Cecchetti
Department of Economics
Ohio State University
Columbus, OH

Peter A. Diamond
Department of Economics
MIT
Cambridge, MA

Avinash Dixit
Department of Economics
Princeton University
Princeton, NJ

Eduardo M.R.A. Engel
Department of Economics
MIT
Cambridge, MA

Saul Lach
Department of Economics
The Hebrew University of
Jerusalem
Jerusalem, Israel

John Leahy
Department of Economics
Harvard
Cambridge, MA

Herbert E. Scarf
Cowles Foundation
and Department of Economics
Yale University
New Haven, CT

Eytan Sheshinski
Department of Economics
The Hebrew University of
Jerusalem
Jerusalem, Israel

Daniel F. Spulber
Department of Economics
Northwestern University
Evanston, IL

Agnès Sulem
I.N.R.I.A.
Cedex, France

Mariano Tommasi
Department of Economics
UCLA
Los Angeles, CA

Daniel Tsiddon
Department of Economics
The Hebrew University of
Jerusalem
Jerusalem, Israel

Yoram Weiss
Department of Economics
Tel Aviv University
Tel Aviv, Israel

I NOMINAL RIGIDITIES: MICROECONOMIC EVIDENCE AND MACROECONOMIC IMPLICATIONS

1 Inflation and Price Adjustment: A Survey of Findings from Micro-Data

Yoram Weiss

Introduction

The purpose of this survey is to summarize the empirical findings that are in the background of the theoretical chapters in this volume. To capture the complex interactions between theory and evidence, I provide an almost historical account of recent developments in this area. First came the realization of a potentially important empirical regularity, namely, nominal price changes occur in discrete jumps. Since firms can change the size and frequency of price changes, old issues such as whether prices are "administrated," "rigid," or "flexible" can be put in a *dynamic* context where rigidities are matter of degree and are in principle measurable. By definition, nominal rigidities affect real variables. The question is whether these effects are in any way systematic. The second discovery was that inflation, combined with nominal rigidities at the level of the firm, indeed affects the *distribution* of relative prices in a clear way. As inflation rises, the variance of relative prices across products and sellers increases.

Based on these regularities, it appears that a question that has eluded economists for many years—What are the welfare costs of inflation?—can perhaps be resolved. The missing step to be filled in is an economic model that would explain the nominal rigidities, link the pricing policies of different firms in a consistent way, and identify the interactions between consumers' and firms' behavior. The chapters in this volume are only a small, nonrepresentative selection of this research effort.

The theoretical challenge is substantial. In particular, economists versed with the importance of real variables are puzzled by the absence of indexation. Although the role of prices is to provide information on opportunity costs in terms of other goods (rather than money), indexation makes sense only if many firms adopt it. The "public good" aspect of pricing rules suggests that if firms act independently, there will be multiple equilibria, some with and some without indexation (see Ball and Romer [1991]). A shift between such equilibria requires *coordination*. Indeed, collective bargaining often leads to explicit wage indexation. In some markets, indexation is achieved in a nonorganized fashion. For instance, since the sharp inflation in 1983–1984, real estate transactions in Israel are denominated in U.S. dollars, although only Israeli shekels change hands.

However, for most goods, sellers and customers are only casually related and, therefore, have to rely on standard modes of transaction.

A model that yields, as an equilibrium outcome, a standard pricing mode in which firms post *nominal* prices and *maintain* them sufficiently long to allow consumers to make comparisons has not yet been constructed. Instead, there are various models that use shortcuts consistent with nominal rigidities but do not fully explain them. For example, the introduction of cost of price adjustment is an attempt to capture, at the level of the firm, the informational costs imposed on consumers by too frequent price changes. The general approach is to focus on relatively simple pricing rules and to examine their sensitivity to market structure and macro changes. These simple models generated testable implications and spawned new empirical work. One can discern the development of two distinct but complementary lines of research. The first is the formulation of models with testable implications at the level of the pricing unit (a firm or a store). The second is the formulation of models with testable implications at the level of the industry or the economy at large.

Following these developments, I first survey evidence on individual price paths, inflation, and price variability. I then describe some tests concerning time-dependent and state-dependent pricing policies of individual firms and conclude with a description of findings related to aggregate behavior. The focus of this survey is exclusively on micro data. For related surveys, dealing with the macro evidence, the reader is referred to Gordon [1990] and Ball, Mankiw, and Romer [1988]. The survey is further tilted toward relatively recent studies. The reader would perhaps not be surprised to learn that the empirical regularities of relative price dispersion and inflation (or deflation) have been known for many years (see, in particular, Mills [1927] and Lange [1932]). A comprehensive discussion of this earlier literature would be useful and relevant, but is outside the scope of this survey.

Nominal Prices Change in Discrete Jumps

Individual firms do not change prices continuously. *Nominal* prices of narrowly defined goods are held constant during time intervals that are sufficiently long to contain observable changes in circumstances or "fundamentals." The frequency of price changes is highly sensitive to macroeconomic variables, in particular to the rate of inflation. Generally, a higher

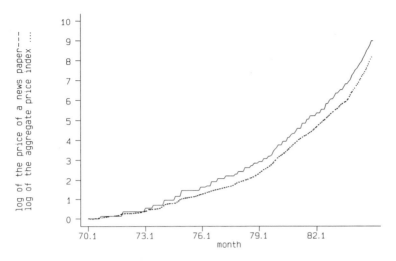

Figure 1.1
Nominal price of a daily newspaper and the aggregate price level: Israel, 1970–1984

rate of inflation leads to more frequent price changes. Yet nominal price rigidities are observed even under sharp inflation, causing substantial erosion of real prices. Figures 1.1 and 1.2 illustrate these general points. They record the price path of a single product, a daily newspaper in Israel, in comparison with the aggregate price path. Observations were taken monthly. As the inflation rate rises from 1 percent to 10 percent a month, the duration of the fixed price intervals is reduced from eight months to one month (or less). Figure 1.3 records the prices of two daily newspapers in Germany during the hyperinflation of 1921–1923. Except for some isolated cases, where the two firms raised their price on the same day, we can note lack of synchronization. The (relative) size of price changes differs, too. Consequently, during any short interval, such as a week, the rates of price change differ. Similar patterns have been recorded in many studies (Sheshinski, Tishler, and Weiss [1981]; Cecchetti [1985], [1986]; Kashyap [1991]; Lach and Tsiddon [1991]; Hanoch and Galyam [1984]; and Tommasi [1991]). They all point to the same empirical regularity.

An immediate implication of nominal rigidity is that the price of any given product, relative to the aggregate of all other products, varies over time. Even if fully predictable, these changes may cause welfare costs as

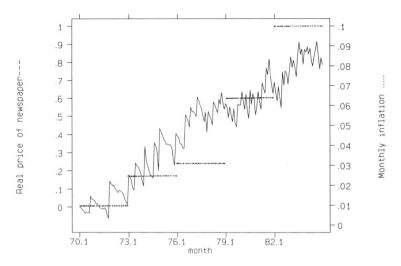

Figure 1.2
Real price of a daily newpaper (logs) and monthly inflation (three years averages)

they force each firm to diverge from the optimal real price at any given moment. A question of interest is whether a higher inflation rate increases or decreases this variation over time. This depends on the adjustments in the two main aspects of the pricing policy: frequency and size of price changes. Lach and Tsiddon [1991] compare two inflationary episodes in Israel. They find that in the period with higher inflation, there was higher frequency and a wider variation in real prices between nominal price changes. Real prices eroded by about 10 percent prior to a nominal price increase. Kashyap [1991] performed a similar experiment, using U.S. data, and found no systematic effect of inflation on the size of price changes. Note that the two studies differ substantially in the inflation rates within their sample periods (2.5–7.5 percent annual rates in the United States vs. 4–9 *monthly* rate in Israel).

Inflation and Relative Price Dispersion

Among the important observable consequences of nominal price rigidities are the effects on relative price variability. That is, different sellers vary in the timing and size of nominal price changes. Consequently, there is vari-

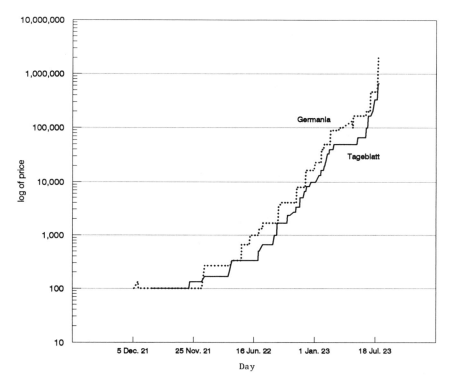

Figure 1.3
Index of daily prices of German newspapers

ability in the price level across identical products at a point in time, and in addition the rates of change in the prices of identical products may vary when measured over a relatively short period. Similar effects can be expected across different products. The emergence of a cross-section dispersion in the prices of identical (or similar) products and the different rates of change in the real price of identical (or similar) products affect the incentives for search, and may have important welfare implications. Generally speaking, variability over time implies an erosion in search capital of consumers who engage in repeat purchases and is, therefore, harmful. However, variability across sellers may be beneficial if increased search promotes competition (see Benabou [1991a]).

With the aid of some additional assumptions on the inflationary process and the pricing policies of individual firms, one can obtain a reduced form relationship where an increase in the inflation rate leads to increased variability *both* across product and across time. This outcome is obtained if an increase in inflation does not raise the frequency or the correlation of price changes too sharply. This means that the relationship between inflation and relative price variability is a matter for empirical investigation. If a systematic positive relationship can be established, we have taken the first step toward the measurement of the welfare costs of inflation (see Jaffe and Kleiman [1977]; Danziger [1988]).

The links between inflation and relative price variability have been studied extensively. Generally, an increase in inflation leads to higher variability (see Vining and Elwertowski [1976]; Parks [1978]; Fischer [1981], [1982]; and Domberger [1987]). However, at very high rates of inflation the relationship is reversed, and an increase in inflation reduces the variance (see Tommasi [1991]; Van Hoomissen [1988]; and Danziger [1987]). These findings can be stated somewhat differently, as follows: At moderate rates of inflation an increase in inflation raises the relative *size* of each price increase; in addition, the degree of synchronization is rather low, so that within a short period only a few firms change prices (see Kashyap [1991, Table 2] and Tommasi [1991, Table 6]). Hence, the variability in price levels and price changes tends to increase. At high rates of inflation, and within a short period, most firms raise prices and at more similar rates (see Tommasi [1991, Table 6] and Lach and Tsiddon [1991, Table 4]. Therefore, variability is reduced.

It should be noted that as the rate of inflation increases, its variance (over time) increases (see Engle [1983] and Taylor [1981]). Hence, the observed changes in price variability can also be linked to changes in the variability (or predictability) of the inflation rate itself. One possible link is through the increased divergence of inflationary expectations across economic agents (Cukierman and Wachtel [1979]). One indication of the increased uncertainty is the large number of price *reductions* during periods of high inflation. Tommasi [1991] reports that 35 percent of all nominal price changes in Argentina were price reductions. Lach and Tsiddon [1991] report that 12 percent of all price changes in Israel were price reductions. In both samples inflation was high and variable. One may incorporate inflationary uncertainty explicitly and use a forecasting equation for the inflationary process to separate expected and unexpected inflation. Generally, *both* expected and unexpected inflation raise the variability in price changes (see Parks [1978]; Fischer [1981], [1982]; Lach and Tsiddon [1991]). An exception is Blejer and Leiderman [1982], who report that only unexpected inflation matters.

The inflationary process is rarely smooth. It turns out that even during periods of general inflation there are occasional instances of deflation. Mills [1927, p. 285] observed that "dispersion is affected by the degree, or violence, of the change [in the price level] not the direction of the change." This suggests the use of the absolute value (or the square) of the price change, in addition to the inflation rate, as explanatory variables for relative price variation. Fischer [1981], Hercowitz [1981], Domberger [1987], and Tommasi [1991] found support for Mill's claim.

A special case of inflationary shock is one that simultaneously affects many sectors. The energy shock of 1973 is an example. In principle, such common shocks may reduce price dispersion; however, Fischer [1981] and Cukierman and Padoaa-Schioppa [1986] report that the 1973 food and energy shock led to an increase in relative price variability.

The evidence on the relationship between the aggregate inflation and relative price variability is generally consistent with nominal rigidities but can be explained by a variety of other models. Important alternative models are based on different adjustments in different "localized markets" (see Hercowitz [1981]) or increased divergence in expectations (see Cukierman and Wachtel [1982]). In special cases, one can use reduced form predictions to discriminate among these models. For instance, the finding that a large energy shock led to higher variability is better explained by the local market model than by price rigidity. In general, one cannot assess the importance of nominal rigidities simply from reduced form relationships. Let us turn, therefore, to more structural tests.

Testing Simple Models of Pricing

Consider the behavior of economic agents who operate in an inflationary environment. Suppose these agents have some control over the price of a product or an input. Since the general price level increases, the single unit is *forced* to react. The question is what pricing policy a firm should adopt.

One class of models stipulates a set time period with fixed, or otherwise predetermined, nominal prices—the "contract period." The question then is what determines the length of the contract, the behavior of real prices within the contract period, and the extent to which successive contracts are linked (see Gray [1978]; Danziger [1983]; Dye [1985]). These types of models were tested mainly in the labor market. For instance, Ehrenberg, Danziger, and San (1984) and Cecchetti [1987] report *no* relationship between contract duration and inflation. The apparent reason is that longer contracts usually have better indexation provisions. In fact, Hendricks and Kahn [1986] show that longer contracts provide *better* protection against inflationary uncertainty. These findings are consistent with the theoretical predictions (see Danziger [1983]). Card [1990] finds that "mistakes" carry over across contracts. If real wages go down during the contract period, due to unanticipated inflation, then the negotiated initial wage in the subsequent contract will be lower. Thus, unanticipated shocks are distributed over a rather long period.

Another class of models stipulates adjustment costs for nominal price changes. The timing of price changes is then derived endogenously. If inflation is constant and all other aspects of the firm's decision problem are stationary, then one can show that the real price of the firm will fluctuate between two predetermined bounds that remain *constant* over time. A similar policy will be adopted if inflation follows a memoryless stochastic process, in which the future path of prices depends only on the curent real price (see Sheshinski and Weiss [1977] [1983]). Following the inventory literature, these pricing policies are called *S-s* policies. This class of models appears to be more appropriate for price adjustments of goods in which no explicit "contract period" is used. A difficulty in applying these models is that the cost of price adjustment is not observable. The same difficulty appears in other duration models (e.g., search), however, and can be overcome.

A more serious problem is that it is not clear how the model should be applied to nonstationary situations. Yet researchers tend to apply the model as if stationary conditions hold. Thus, a typical test is to examine whether variations in expected inflation broaden the *S-s* bounds, as predicted by a comparative statics analysis of Sheshinski and Weiss [1977]. Cecchetti [1986] rejects this prediction, but he used only price data and ignored the potential role of changes in production costs. Correcting for (presumably permanent) changes in costs, Sheshinski, Tishler, and Weiss [1981] find that the initial real price in each price cycle and the final real price tend to increase. The latter is contrary to the prediction of the *S-s* model, which implies that the terminal real price should decline. The upshot of these findings is that, relative to the predictions of a stationary

S-s model, as inflation rises, the frequency of price changes increase "too much."

A study by Dahlby [1992] includes, in addition to costs, some information on demand. Using data on car insurance rates in Canada, she compares the *S-s* model with a "myopic" model that ignores future inflation, and finds that the two models fit equally well. Examining the reduced form equation, she finds that expected inflation had no effect on the probability of a nominal price change, given the current real price, the costs of production, and the demand indicators. Note, however, that the inflation rates during the sample period were rather low, about 8 to 12 percent per year.

Kashyap [1991] and Carlton [1986] mention the presence of many small price changes as a possible refutation of an *S-s* model with fixed costs of adjustment. It should be noted that both small and large price *reductions* are consistent with the model. If the firm finds itself with a real price above *S*, it may either postpone the price change or change immediately, in which case a small or a large price reduction is possible (see Sheshinski, Tishler, and Weiss [1981]; Sheshiski and Weiss [1992]; and Tsiddon [1981]). It is true, however, that the stationary model is not consistent with small price *increases* within an inflationary period. It is always better to let inflation erode the real price and then make a large price increase, thus striking a balance between costs of price adjustment and suboptimal profits. Small price increases can occur in a nonstationary environment in which demand or costs of production change.

It is often questioned whether costs of price change are empirically significant. A study by Slade [1991] on pricing of a single product (crackers) by groceries in an American city provides some estimates of the implied magnitude of the costs of price adjustment. In her sample, the average store's revenue from this item is about $17 per week. A nominal price change in a week occurs with a probability of .18 and costs about $5 dollars, of which $4 are fixed costs. Thus, the (expected) costs of price adjustment constitute 4 percent of weekly sales, a figure which is quite large. Clearly, such estimates are subject to many potential errors. The main point, however, is that with a well-specified model, costs of price adjustment can be *estimated* from the data.

I will mention some further findings that do not test a particular model of price setting but still can be interpreted within these models. Tommasi [1991] found that an increase in the inflation rate reduces the *correlation* over time between the *real* prices charged by the same store. Hanoch and Galyam [1984] found that inflation reduces the correlation between the nominal price increases in successive months. These findings, which are consistent with either the *S-s* or the "contract period" model, show quite directly the erosion of search capital of consumers who plan a repeat purchase in a particular store. Also common to both types of models is the prediction that larger price increases should be associated with longer fixed-price intervals. Findings by Lach and Tsiddon [1991] and Carlton [1986] support this prediction, but in the data of Kashyap [1991, fig. 3A], duration and size appear to be independent.

Sheshinski and Weiss [1992] extend the stationary *S-s* model to a multiproduct firm. There, a key question is whether a firm will change all its prices simultaneously or in a staggered fashion. In some of the disaggregated studies it is not at all clear which decision unit determines prices. In particular, is it the producer or the retailer? To the extent that decisions are made at the store level, it is quite clear from the data reported in Tommasi [1991, table 7] that not all prices are changed simultaneously. Only at the highest rates of inflation are all prices are raised. Lieberman and Zilberfarb [1985] record prices of products produced by different firms within the same retail chain. They, too, report that firms do *not* increase all their prices simultaneously. Of firms producing ten or more goods, only 16 percent raised their prices together.

General Equilibrium

One can go beyond the single firm and examine the determination of pricing policies within an equilibrium context. The added ingredients are the introduction of many interacting sellers who offer the same good and face many consumers who search for the lowest price (see Benabou [1988], [1991] and Fishman [1992]). The models generate an equilibrium distribution of prices and times of price change, and can be used to assess the welfare implications of inflation in equilibrium. The general equilibrium is much more difficult to analyze, and the models are of necessity more stylized. It is, therefore, somewhat premature to discuss testable implications of such models. Instead, I will survey empirical findings that bear on the *assumptions* of these models. Again, one may separately discuss models based on a "contract period" and models based on costs of adjustment.

Taylor [1980] has shown that the time structure of wage contracts can have important implications for the dynamic behavior of *aggregate* wages and output. Blanchard [1987] extends the approach to the analysis of prices. Generally, a larger degree of staggering slows down the adjustments in these aggregates to macroeconomic shocks. Several authors have followed with equilibrium models designed to determine endogenously the extent of staggering (see Fethke and Policiano [1986]; Ball and Cecchetti [1988]; Ball and Romer [1989]). However, for simplicity, they all assume unrealistic time structures in which all firms choose the same contract length. Taylor [1983] provides data on the time pattern of union wage contracts in the United States. He notes that 72 percent of union workers are employed under three-year contracts, 16 percent under two-year contracts, and 12 percent under one-year contracts. Irrespective of length, these contracts tend to expire and renew within the second and third quarters. The three-year contracts appear to be synchronized. Yet even within a "busy" quarter only 18 percent of all wage contracts are renewed. Thus, staggering is caused more by the coexistence of contracts of different lengths than by different timings for a standard contract. Benabou and Bismut [1987] use a bargaining model to tie the behavior of wages over time to the distribution of contract lengths. The implied distribution is quite different from the data reported by Taylor [1983], with less weight on the long contracts.

One attraction of the *S-s* pricing models is that they can be aggregated in a consistent fashion. As shown by Caplin and Spulber [1987], Bertola and Caballero [1990], and Caballero and Engel [1991], there is an invariant distribution of relative prices that supports a steady-state equilibrium for the industry (economy). This distribution will be uniform if the inflationary process is one-sided (aggregate prices can only move upward) and triangular or piecewise exponential if inflation is two-sided. Moreover, because of the positive drift, more firms adjust their prices upward and the steady-state distribution is thus skewed to the right. Lach and Tsiddon [1991] report that relative prices of identical goods are distributed in a unimodal way and are *not* uniform, with a weak tendency toward right skewness. Slade [1991] reports negative skewness. Again, the difference in results is due the fact that in Slade's sample there is almost no inflation.

Caballero and Engle [1991] show that under a suitable transformation of variables, heterogeneity in the width of the *S-s* band does not affect

the form of the steady-state distribution. However, the observed untrans-
formed price distribution is affected by differences across firms in costs of
price adjustment and other parameters. Indeed, the duration of the fixed-
price intervals varies widely across and within products (Carlton [1986]).
Part of the variation is explained by differences in the degree of competitiveness. Apparently, longer intervals are associated with higher concentration (Carlton [1986]). Dahlby [1992] reports that a higher market
share *reduces* the probability of a price change. One may perhaps argue
that costs of price adjustment are higher if each firm controls a larger
share of the market. However, this interpretation seems inconsistent with
the findings of Domberger [1987] that the effect of inflation on price
variability is *weaker* in industries that are more highly concentrated.
Domberger [1987] interprets his findings as suggesting lower costs of
search in concentrated industries. Indeed, one of the main messages of the
equilibrium approach is that in examining equilibrium outcomes, equal
attention should be given to supply-side considerations (costs of price
adjustment) and to demand-side considerations (costs of search). Following this approach, Benabou [1992] reports that inflation tends to reduce
markups (i.e., prices relative to costs). He interprets this as an indication of
increased search activity caused by the higher inflation rates.

Conclusions

The findings from micro data suggest that nominal rigidities abound and
that they display systematic patterns. Not surprisingly, much of the evidence comes from a few countries that have recently experienced sharp
inflation, and is derived from relatively small samples. The next step will
be to assess further the robustness of the findings, using more countries,
longer periods, and richer sets of data. There is already some evidence that
results differ in countries that have experienced low inflation, such as
Canada and the United States, and countries that have experienced high
inflation, such as Israel and Argentina.

At this early stage of the research, the connections between the data and
theory are rather loose. The available models for dynamic pricing policies
are too simplistic and have not been structurally tested. Techniques for
structural estimation of dynamic decision rules are now available and
have been applied in a variety of fields. Thus, in principle one may esti-

mate some key parameters to be used in simulations of the optimal policies under varying conditions. This research agenda requires the incorporation of *all* relevant information at the level of the firm, including costs and demand data.

In many ways it seems simpler to direct the research to the equilibrium implications at the level of the industry or the economy. Data on the observed distributions of real prices (wages) and the timing of price (wage) changes, together with information on their shifts due to inflation and other causes, can be used effectively in the analysis of aggregate dynamics. However, unless one gets better underpinning for the individual decision process, I doubt whether the welfare implications of the aggregate patterns can be assessed.

References

Ball, L., and Cecchetti, S. (1988). "Imperfect Information and Staggered Price Setting." *American Economic Review*, 78, pp. 999–1018.

Ball, L., Mankiw, G., and Romer, D. (1988). "The New Keynesian Economics and the Output Inflation Trade-off." *Brookings Papers on Economic Activity*, 1, pp. 1–82.

Ball, L., and Romer, D. (1989). "The Equilibrium and Optimal Timing of Price Changes." *Review of Economic Studies*, 56, pp. 179–198.

Ball, L. and Romer, D. (1991). "Sticky Prices as Coordination Failure." *American Economic Review*, 81, pp. 539–552.

Benabou, R. (1988). "Search, Price Setting and Inflation." *Review of Economic Studies*, 55, pp. 353–373.

Benabou, R. (1991). "Inflation and Efficiency in Search Markets." *Review of Economic Studies*, 59, 299–330.

Benabou, R. (1992). "Inflation and Markups: Theories and Evidence from the Retail Sector." *European Economic Review*, 36, pp. 566–574.

Benabou, R., and Bismut, C. (1987). "Wage Bargaining and Staggered Contracts: Theory and Estimation." Mimeo, CEPREMAP, Paris.

Bertola, G., and Caballero, R. (1990). "Kinked Adjustment Costs and Aggregate Dynamics." *N.B.E.R. Macroeconomics Annual*, pp. 237–288.

Blanchard, O. (1987). "Individual and Aggregate Price Adjustments." *Brookings Papers on Economic Activity*, 1, pp. 57–122.

Blejer, M., and Leiderman, L. (1982). "Inflation and Real Price Variability in the Open Economy." *European Economic Review*, 18, pp. 387–402.

Caballero, R., and Engel, E. (1991). "Dynamic S-s Economies." *Econometrica*, 59, 1659–1686.

Caplin, A., and Spulber, D. (1987). "Menu Costs and the Neutrality of Money." *Quarterly Journal of Economics*, 102, pp. 703–725.

Card, D. (1990). "Unexpected Inflation, Real Wages and Determination of Union Contracts." *American Economic Review*, 80, pp. 669–688.

Carlton, D. (1986). "The Rigidity of Prices." *American Economic Review*, 76, pp. 637–658.

Cecchetti, S. (1985). "Staggered Contracts and the Frequency of Price Changes." *Quarterly Journal of Economics*, 100, pp. 935–959.

Cecchetti, S. (1986). "The Frequency of Price Adjustment." *Journal of Econometrics*, 31, pp. 255–274.

Cecchetti, S. (1987). "Indexation and Incomes Policy: A Study of Wage Adjustments in Unionized Manufacturing." *Journal of Labor Economics*, 5, pp. 391–412.

Cukierman, A., and Padoaa-Schioppa, F. (1986). "Relative Price Variability, Inflation and the Price of Energy." Mimeo, Tel Aviv University, Department of Economics.

Cukierman, A., and Wachtel, P. (1979). "Differential Inflationary Expectations and the Variability of the Rate of Inflation: Theory and Evidence." *American Economic Review*, 69, pp. 595–609.

Cukierman, A., and Wachtel, P. (1982). "Relative Price Variability and Non Uniform Inflationary Expectations." *Journal of Political Economy*, 90, pp. 146–157.

Dahlby, B. (1992). "Price Adjustments in the Automobile Insurance Market: A Test of the Sheshinski-Weiss Model." *Canadian Journal of Economics*, 25, pp. 564–583.

Danziger, L. (1983). "On the Frequency of Wage Indexation." *European Economic Review*, 22, pp. 297–304.

Danziger, L. (1987). "Inflation, Fixed Costs of Adjustment and Measurement of Relative Price Variability: Theory and Evidence." *American Economic Review*, 77, pp. 704–713.

Danziger, L. (1988). "Costs of Price Adjustment and the Welfare Economics of Inflation and Disinflation." *American Economic Review*, 78, pp. 633–646.

Domberger, S. (1987). "Relative Price Variability and Inflation: A Disaggregated Analysis." *Journal of Political Economy*, 95, pp. 547–566.

Dye, R. (1985). "Optimal Length of Labo Contracts." *International Economic Review*, 26, pp. 251–270.

Ehrenberg, R., Danziger, L., and San, G. (1984). "Cost of Living Adjustment Clauses in Union Contracts." *Research in Labor Economics*, 6, pp. 1–63.

Engle, R. (1983). "Estimates of the Variance of U.S. Inflation Based upon ARCH Model." *Journal of Money, Credit and Banking*, 15, pp. 287–301.

Fethke, G., and Policiano, A. (1986). "Will Wage Setters Stagger Decisions?" *Quarterly Journal of Economics*, 101, pp. 867–897.

Fischer, S. (1981). "Relative Shocks, Relative Price Variability, and Inflation." *Brookings Papers on Economic Activity*, 2, pp. 381–431.

Fischer, S. (1982). "Relative Price Variability and Inflation in the United States and Germany." *European Economic Review*, 18, pp. 171–196.

Fishman, A. (1992). "Search, Technology, Staggered Price Setting and Price Dispersion." *American Economic Review*, 82, pp. 287–298.

Gordon, R. (1990). "What Is New-Keynesian Economics?" *Journal of Economic Literature*, 28, pp. 1115–1171.

Gray, J. (1978). "On Indexation and Contract Length." *Journal of Political Economy*, 86, pp. 1–18.

Hanoch, G., and Galyam, Z. (1984). "An Empirical Model of Price Adjustment in an Inflationary Environment." Bank of Israel discussion paper.

Hendricks, W., and Kahn, L. (1987). "Contract Length, Wage Indexation, and Ex-ante Variability of Real Wages." *Journal of Labor Research*, 8, pp. 221–236.

Hercowitz, Z. (1981). "Money and Dispersion of Relative Prices." *Journal of Political Economy*, 89, pp. 328–356.

Jaffe, D., and Kleiman, E. (1977). "The Welfare Implications of Uneven Inflation." In E. Lundbeck, ed., *Inflation Theory and Anti-Inflation Policy*. London: Macmillan.

Kashyap, A. (1991). "Sticky Prices: New Evidence from Retail Catalogs." Mimeo, University of Chicago, Graduate School of Business.

Lach, S. and Tsiddon, D. (1991). "The Behavior of Prices and Inflation: An Empirical Analysis of Disaggregated Price Data." *Journal of Political Economy*, 100, pp. 349–389.

Lange, O. (1932). *Die Preisdispersion als Mittel zur statistischen Messung wirtschaftlicher Gleichgewichtsstorungen*. Leipzig: Hans Buske Verlag.

Liberman, Y., and Zilberfarb, B. (1985). "Price Adjustment Strategy Under Conditions of High Inflation: An Empirical Examination." *Journal of Economics and Business*, 37, pp. 193–205.

Mills, F. (1927). *The Behavior of Prices*. New York: N.B.E.R.

Parks, R. (1978). "Inflation and Relative Price Variability." *Journal of Political Economy*, 86, pp. 79–96.

Sheshinski, E., Tishler, A., and Weiss, Y. (1981). "Inflation, Costs of Price Adjustments and the Amplitude of Real Price Changes: An Empirical Analysis." In J. Flanders and A. Razin, eds., *Development in an Inflationary World*. New York: Academic Press.

Sheshinski, E., and Weiss. Y. (1977). "Inflation and Costs of Price Adjustment." *Review of Economic Studies*, 44, pp. 287–303.

Sheshinski, E., and Weiss, Y. (1983). "Optimum Pricing Policy Under Stochastic Inflation." *Review of Economic Studies*, 50, pp. 513–529.

Sheshinski, E., and Weiss, Y. (1992). "Staggered and Synchronized Price Policies Under Inflation: The Multi-Product Monopoly Case." *Review of Economic Studies*, 59, pp. 331–360.

Slade, M. (1991). "Sticky Prices in a Dynamic Oligopoly." Mimeo. University of British Columbia, Department of Economics.

Taylor, J. (1980). "Aggregate Dynamics and Staggered Contracts." *Journal of Political Economy*, 88, pp. 1–24.

Taylor, J. (1981). "On the Relation Between the Variability of Inflation and the Average Inflation Rate." *Carnegie-Rochester Conference Series on Public Policy*, 15, pp. 57–86.

Taylor, J. (1983). "Union Wage Settlements During Disinflation." *American Economic Review*, 73, pp. 981–993.

Tommasi, A. (1991). "Inflation and Relative Prices: Evidence from Argentina." Mimeo, U.C.L.A., Department of Economics (ch. 18 in this volume).

Tsiddon, D. (1991). "On the Stubbornness of Sticky Prices." *International Economic Review*, 32, pp. 69–75.

Van Hoomissen, T. (1988). "Price Dispersion and Inflation: Evidence from Israel." *Journal of Political Economy*, 96, pp. 1303–1314.

Vining, R., and Elwertoski, T. (1976). "The Relationship Between Relative Prices and the General Price Level." *American Economic Review*, 66, pp. 699–708.

2 Individual Inertia and Aggregate Dynamics

Andrew Caplin

1. Overview

Many economists believe that prices are sticky in the short run, so that shocks to nominal variables have real effects on the economy. It is very difficult to provide microeconomic underpinnings for this view. Even if one believes that individual nominal prices are sticky, it is not clear what implications this has for the dynamics of the aggregate price level. This chapter surveys a recent literature exploring the connections between the microeconomics and the macroeconomics of sticky prices.

The standard approach used by macroeconomists to model individual inertia is to assume that agents lack flexibility within some exogenously set period, and that they regain freedom of action only at the end of the period. This is not very satisfactory, especially in the context of price-setting, where there is no natural counterpart to the period of forced inflexibility. It is clearly of interest to see what happens when one builds frictional models of economic aggregates in which each agent's decision on when to act is endogenized. This is precisely the challenge that is faced in the literature on aggregation that is the subject of this survey.

The aggregation literature has a broader objective than simply to increase our understanding of price dynamics. One of the main goals of macroeconomics in general is to explain how exogenous shocks influence such aggregates as the price level, the level of employment, capital investment, and expenditure on consumer durables. In each case, the underlying individual decisions involve elements of inertia. In the case of employment, for example, both hiring and laying off workers involve fixed costs, as do plant openings and plant closings. The broad objective of the aggregation literature is to increase our understanding of the linkages between individual inertia and aggregate dynamics. While the literature is still at a very early stage, there are encouraging signs that the techniques being developed in the pricing context may usefully be applied to other areas of macroeconomics.

The remainder of the survey is structured as follows. Section 2 presents a very brief description of the microeconomic models with fixed price adjustment costs. Section 3 describes the method of aggregation in the deterministic case. Sections 4 through 7 form the heart of the survey, and focus on the known techniques of aggregation in stochastic settings. The major results on one-sided and two-sided aggregation are illustrated with some simple examples. Section 8 concludes with a discussion of some directions of current and future research.

2. Optimal Pricing Strategies

Sheshinski and Weiss [1977] develop the fundamental deterministic model of nominal price rigidity in the face of inflation. A monopolistic firm producing a nonstorable good faces an exogenous demand function and a fixed real cost structure. There is a deterministic and constant rate of inflation. There is also assumed to be a fixed real cost associated with nominal price adjustment. With this price adjustment cost, the form of the optimal strategy is to adjust the log of the real price to an upper level S as soon as it hits a lower trigger s. Sheshinski and Weiss characterize the optimal price trigger and target, and demonstrate that increases in the rate of inflation and the price adjustment cost increase the proportionate price adjustment, S-s.

Stochastic variants of the model have been investigated by Sheshinski and Weiss [1983], Danziger [1983], and Caplin and Sheshinski [1987]. These models share with the original Sheshinski-Weiss model the assumption that there is no deflation. This places the models in the same analytic class as the one-sided (S, s) inventory model of Arrow, Harris, and Marschak [1951]. With two-sided inflationary shocks, the optimal pricing policy is generally of the two-sided (S, s) variety, with an upper trigger, a lower trigger, and a target. Barro [1972] provides a pioneering study of two-sided pricing policies, and an up-to-date treatment can be found in Caplin and Leahy [1992a].

The most important common element among the stochastic models of nominal price stickiness is the state dependence of the optimal pricing strategy. It is always the current real price and inflationary prospects, rather than calendar time per se, that trigger price adjustment. This distinction is hidden in deterministic models, where the optimal price adjustment policy can be described equivalently in terms either of the optimal time or of the optimal real price erosion between price adjustments. It is the state dependence of the optimal pricing policy that accounts for the distinctive branch of macroeconomics based on costs of price adjustment.

One fundamental microeconomic issue is whether it is possible to provide a deeper explanation for firms' apparent reluctance to change their nominal prices. Of course there are many possible explanations for infrequent changes of pricing strategy, ranging all the way from the purely mechanical tasks of reprinting catalogs and price stickers to such issues as how to get consensus on change inside the political structure of a firm. It is unfortunate that so little attention has been given to characterizing the circumstances that give rise to high and low levels of nominal price inertia. Progress in this dimension calls for more detailed empirical work and for increased understanding of the manner in which corporations actually arrive at pricing decisions. (Carlton [1986]; Cecchetti [1986]; Kashyap [1991]; and Lach and Tsiddon [1992] provide some empirical insights.) Until there has been more structured work along these lines, researchers will continue to work with models that give a fundamental role to an unobservable cost parameter.

3.   Deterministic Aggregation

Even in the deterministic case, there is a fundamental issue of aggregation when one moves to the macroeconomic level. The firms in the Sheshinski-Weiss model treat inflation as exogenous, but their optimal choices determine prices endogenously. In order for the macroeconomic formulation to be consistent, it must be confirmed that firms' optimal choices generate the inflation process that they take as given in making their choices. In the deterministic case, the heart of the aggregation procedure is first to solve for optimal (S, s) price bounds against an exogenous inflation rate, and then to assume that the cross-sectional distribution of the log of real prices is uniformly distributed between these bounds. The key observation is that in this case the cross-sectional distribution remains forever uniform. Aggregate consistency then follows from the fact that continuous changes in the exogenous price level induce precisely the same change in an endogenous price index.

The simplest issue to address in aggregative menu cost models is the connection between inflation, the average level of output across firms, and relative price variability. Rotemberg [1982], Danziger [1983], and Benabou and Konieczny [1991] analyze these issues. Taking the form of firms' profit functions as exogenous, these authors discuss the effects of changes in the inflation rate on the level of output. Within this framework, the impact of inflation on average output depends crucially on curvature properties of the profit function. But by working with an exogenous profit function, these studies rule out possible feedback effects from the price distribution onto demand and profits. This feedback is particularly relevant if consumer search is involved on the demand side, since in this case one needs to know far more than the average price in order to pin down the level of demand. The simultaneity of pricing strategies and demand when consumers face search costs and firms face price adjustment costs is explored in Benabou [1988].

Benabou considers a market that receives a constant (unit) flow of new consumers in each period. Each consumer searches for a unit of a single produced good, which is sold by a continuum of monopolistically competitive suppliers. Each search takes τ units of labor. It takes c units of labor to produce each unit of output, and β units to change the nominal price of the good, where price adjustment is triggered by inflation at constant rate g. The goal of each searcher is to minimize the expected labor input used in the combination of search and purchase. The goal of the firms is to maximize the expected discounted value of profits, using the constant discount factor δ. There is a continuum of consumers per firm; the mass of consumers per firm is denoted m. The model is closed with the assumption that there is free entry of firms.

Given firms' technologies and objectives, the Sheshinski-Weiss model shows that firms will pursue (S, s) pricing strategies where it is convenient to measure prices in terms of labor units. With initial log prices uniformly distributed between s and S, it follows from the self-replicating nature of the uniform distribution that all consumers will face the identical price distribution when they enter the market. In equilibrium, the values of S and s constitute a fixed point. The equilibrium bounds on the real price are best responses to the optimal search behavior that is generated when log prices are uniformly distributed between them. In addition, the equilibrium mass of consumers per firm must be such that the zero profit condition is met.

One condition for an optimal pricing strategy is that the flow of profits at price s must equal the interest available on the value of the optimal strategy given immediate price adjustment. With free entry, this implies that the flow profit at the lower price bound must be zero, so that $e^s = c$. With s fixed in this manner, the assumption of optimal consumer search can be used to determine S. The key observation is that in equilibrium, the representative consumer must have a reservation price of S, the highest price that firms charge. Given such a reservation price, no firm will charge more because it would then get zero demand, while a lower price would involve voluntarily forgone profits. Straightforward computation of the reservation price yields the equation

$$S(e^S - \tau) = e^S - c, \tag{2.1}$$

which has a unique solution. Finally, the given values of S and s combined with the mass of consumers per firm determine the present value of the optimal strategy to firms. The equilibrium mass m is determined by setting this value to zero.

The comparative static properties of the Benabou model with free entry are radically different from those of the Sheshinski-Weiss model. One of the main findings of Sheshinski and Weiss is that increased inflation widens the optimal range of the real price. But in the free entry version of the Benabou model, the effects of increased inflation are entirely absorbed by a change in the mass of firms. The real price bounds S and s depend only on the consumer search costs. While the irrelevance of inflation is special to the case of costless entry, the result does help to highlight the potentially important role of general equilibrium conditions in aggregation models.

One of the most important issues that can be addressed in models of inflation and search is the impact of inflation on welfare. The results of Benabou [1992] and Diamond [1992] indicate a complex set of effects of inflation on welfare. On the one hand, increases in inflation stimulate search, which tends to depress the average price and reduce monopoly distortions. On the other hand, high rates of inflation increase both the direct resource costs of frequent price adjustment and the indirect costs stemming from additional search activity.

4. Stochastic Aggregation: A Simple Framework

Macroeconomic interest in the implications of price adjustment costs was stimulated by the static monopoly models of Akerlof and Yellen [1985], Mankiw [1985], and Parkin [1986]. Blanchard and Kiyotaki [1985] develop a variant of this model with monopolistically competitive firms.

They consider the impact of a monetary shock on an economy with price adjustment costs in which all firms begin with optimally set prices. They show that in the face of a nominal contraction, monopolistically competitive firms derive only a very small proportion of the social benefit that they provide by cutting prices. Each firm may find it optimal to maintain a fixed nominal price despite potentially great social gain from price cuts: small price adjustment costs may lead to far larger social costs. This follows from the fact that there is an aggregate demand externality in a monopolistically competitive economy, so that demand contractions tend to move the economy even further from the competitive optimum.

An immediate question is whether the simple "menu cost" insight survives to a dynamic setting in which the distribution of prices is endogenized. Exploring this issue calls for novel approaches to aggregation, in which the state dependence of the decision on when to adjust prices plays a key role. In the remainder of this section, we develop the simplest framework in which it is possible to analyze state-dependent aggregation. This is followed in Sections 5 and 6 by a detailed analysis of the two best-understood special cases. In Section 7, we consider what happens when some of the most restrictive aspects of the framework are relaxed. The approach to aggregation outlined below draws heavily on the work of Caplin [1985], Caplin and Spulber [1987], Caballero and Engel ([1991a] and [1992a]), and Caplin and Leahy [1992a].

There is a continuum of monopolistically competitive firms indexed by $i \in [0, 1]$. The (log) nominal price of firm i in period t is $p_i(t)$, and the aggregate price index $p(t)$ is simply the geometric average of these individual prices, $p(t) = \int p_i(t)$. Each firm faces a real price adjustment cost, and therefore allows its nominal price to diverge from its optimal level, $\hat{p}_i(t)$. All firms are assumed to have identical real profit functions that have as their argument the deviation of the firm's nominal price from its optimal level,

$$d_i(t) \equiv p_i(t) - \hat{p}_i(t). \tag{2.2}$$

Exogenous shocks to the optimal price derive both from common monetary disturbances and from idiosyncratic real distribances,

$$\Delta \hat{p}_i(t) = \Delta m(t) + \varepsilon_i(t), \tag{2.3}$$

where $\Delta x(t) \equiv x(t + 1) - x(t)$.

Equation (2.3) implies that the direct impact of monetary shocks is felt in a one-for-one influence on firms' optimal prices: the effect of a monetary shock is therefore independent of whether the shock impacts prices or output. Since the idiosyncratic shocks average out to zero, the average optimal price, $\hat{p}(t) = \int \hat{p}_i(t)\,di$, is driven completely by the common monetary shock,

$$\Delta \hat{p}(t) = \Delta m(t). \tag{2.4}$$

To capture the potential impact of monetary shocks on the real economy, we assume that the velocity of money is constant,

$$m(t) = p(t) + y(t), \tag{2.5}$$

where the variables have the standard interpretation and are all measured in logs. In combination equations (2.2)–(2.5) reveal that the study of output dynamics in this framework reduces to the analysis of the time path of the average deviations,

$$\Delta y(t) = \Delta m(t) - \Delta p(t) = -\int_0^1 \Delta d_i(t)\,di. \tag{2.6}$$

Equations (2.2)–(2.6) clarify the three stages involved in analyzing output dynamics. First, the exogenous processes driving money and the idiosyncratic elements must be specified. Second, each firm's initial price and optimal pricing strategy must be identified, so that the contingent path of deviations $d_i(t)$ can be characterized. Finally, these dynamic processes must be aggregated across the different firms $i \in [0, 1]$ so that the dynamics of the aggregate deviation, and therefore output, can be characterized. Unfortunately, the two conceptually straightforward tasks of individual optimization and aggregation present formidable technical difficulties. It has proved necessary to identify and work with very special stochastic descriptions of money and the idiosyncratic shocks in order to make analytic progress. Fortunately, these special cases have already provided some intriguing insights.

In order to present the results in the simplest possible setting, we work in the next two sections with discrete examples in which the increment to each firm's optimal nominal price during any period can take on only one of two values,

$$\Delta \hat{p}_i(t) \in \{a, b\}, \qquad a > b.$$

With this assumption, the impact of a common monetary shock is felt only in the *proportion* of the firms that face the larger of the two increases in their optimal prices. We further restrict attention to cases in which the money shock itself can take only one of two values. Specifically, there are two equiprobable states of monetary expansion, $\theta(t) = h, l$. In the high growth state a proportion $0.5 + q$ of the firms faces the larger increase in their optimal nominal price, $\Delta\hat{p}_i(t) = a$, while in periods of low money growth the proportion facing such increases is $0.5 - q$.[1]

The parameter $q \in [0, 0.5]$ measures the importance of common shocks relative to idiosyncratic shocks to firms' optimal prices. With $q = 0.5$, all firms in the economy face the same shock to their optimal nominal price in any given period. This case therefore involves no idiosyncratic influences whatever on optimal prices, so that the common monetary shock is the only forcing process. As q shrinks to zero, so the contemporaneous correlation between the optimal price shocks faced by distinct firms approaches zero. In the limit with $q = 0$, the optimal price dynamics are independent across firms and the monetary shock is therefore irrelevant. In the next two sections, we show the qualitative behavior of the macroeconomy depends on the three parameters, $\{a, b, q\}$ of this elementary framework.

5. One-Sided Aggregation and Neutrality

A central determinant of the qualitative impact of money on the economy is whether shocks are one-sided, in that they always induce price changes in the same direction. To consider the one-sided case, it is natural to focus on an inflationary environment, in which optimal prices never fall. We analyze the simplest possible case, with $\Delta\hat{p}_i(t) \in \{0, 1\}$. In a period of high money growth, a proportion $(0.5 + q)$ of the firms face unit increases in their optimal nominal price while the others have an unchanged optimum. In periods of low money growth the proportions are reversed.

The central result for the one-sided case is that in the long run, money is neutral. This is a subtle result. As equation (2.6) shows, in order to understand the impact of money growth in any period t, we must study the change in the deviation averaged across all firms in the economy. In order to understand the neutrality result, we must therefore first understand the dynamic behavior of the *cross-sectional* distribution of prices. What makes this so tricky is that we may expect the common monetary shock to produce correlations in the levels of the deviation at distinct firms. The special feature of the one-sided (S, s) aggregation model is that even in the presence of common shocks, we are able to provide a complete and simple analysis of the dynamics of the cross-sectional distribution. We prepare for the analysis of the cross section by making as much progress as we can on the basis of time-series analysis of the individual firms.

Individual Behavior and Average Neutrality

While the response of the economy to monetary shocks in any given period t depends on the behavior of the entire cross-sectional distribution of prices, the *average* effects of a given monetary shock over the long run can be computed simply by analyzing the time-series behavior of the deviation at an individual firm. The precise thought experiment involved in computing the average effect of monetary growth over the long run is to measure the empirical distribution of the change in output in periods of high and low money growth. High money growth may be characterized as having an expansionary effect *on average* if in this long sequence of observations the average of the empirically observed changes in output is positive,

$$E[\Delta y|\theta = h] > 0. \tag{2.7}$$

The expectation in equation (2.7) is taken across periods t in which there is high money growth. Note that equation (2.9) implies that low money growth is contractionary, since expected output is constant over time.

With equation (2.6) we know that the time-series average change in output can be computed simply by studying the equivalent time-series average at the level of the individual firm,

$$E[\Delta y|\theta = h] = -E[\Delta d_i|\theta = h]. \tag{2.8}$$

Furthermore, in our simple framework the only direct impact of a monetary shock is to influence the mass of firms that face increases in their optimal nominal prices in the period. Therefore large monetary shocks expand output on average if and only if an increase in an individual firm's optimal nominal price is expected to lower the deviation, by causing a less than one-for-one average response in terms of upward price adjustment,

$$E[\Delta y|\theta = h] \sim -E[\Delta d_i|\Delta \hat{p}_i = 1], \tag{2.9}$$

where the relation $x \sim y$ means the expressions x and y are always of the same sign.

Equation (2.9) motivates our interest in the long-run behavior of an individual firm's deviation. Given the one-sided independent shocks to the firm's optimal price and the cost of price adjustment, we know that the optimal pricing policy is of the one-sided (S, s) variety: the deviation is increased to some level S the instant it hits the lower limit of s. Combining the independent shocks and the simple strategy, we obtain a complete description of the deviation as a Markov process. In fact, the long-run structure of the one-sided (S, s) model is particularly simple, since the stationary distribution of deviations is uniform over the ergodic set $[s + 1, S]$. What this means in empirical terms is that if an individual firm is observed over a long period of time, the proportion of the time that it spends in each state in $[s + 1, S]$ will head toward $\frac{1}{D}$.

One immediate implication of the long-run uniformity of individual prices is that in terms of the relevant long-run average, the deviation of a firm is unaffected when its optimal nominal price increases,

$$E[\Delta d_i | \Delta \hat{p}_i = 1] = E[\Delta d_i | \Delta \hat{p}_i = 0] = 0. \tag{2.10}$$

Here, the average is taken across time at a given firm i. To demonstrate equation (2.10), note that if $\Delta \hat{p}_i = 1$, then the deviation diminishes by one unit if the firm has an initial deviation in any one of the states $[s + 2, S]$, and increases by $D - 1$ units if the initial deviation is $s + 1$. But the uniformity of the long-run average empirical distribution implies that the firm has an initial deviation of $s + 1$ in a proportion $\frac{1}{D}$ of the periods. The long-run average effect of the monetary shock can therefore be computed as

$$E[\Delta d_i | \Delta \hat{p}_i = 1] = \frac{D - 1}{D}(1) + \frac{1}{D}(-D + 1) = 0,$$

confirming equation (2.10). Equations (2.9) and (2.10) together imply that the monetary shock is neutral in terms of its long-run average effect.

It is important to understand that the average neutrality result does not answer the question of whether monetary shocks can have systematic effects on the economy: it only says that inasmuch as there are periods in which high money growth expands output, there must also be periods in which high money growth causes output to contract. For example, average neutrality is entirely consistent with the representative agent case, in which shocks are perfectly correlated and all firms have the same initial price. In the representative agent case, the level of output changes dramatically over time as the average price deviation moves over the range $[s + 1, S]$. Here an increase in the money supply has a small expansionary influence, provided the deviation is in the range $[s + 2, S]$. However it has a large contractionary influence if the deviation is $s + 1$. The result on average neutrality points out only that the unconditional average of these effects is zero. There may still be scope for a long-run effect of monetary shocks on output, although the sign of the effect may depend on the level of current output. In order to go beyond this and explore the realized pattern of responses to monetary shocks, we must study aggregate dynamics. As equation (2.6) demonstrates, the impact of money on the economy in any given period t depends on the change that it produces in the cross-sectional distribution of deviations. In order to make further progress in understanding the impact of monetary shocks, we must therefore turn our attention to analyzing the dynamic behavior of the cross-sectional distribution of deviations.

Cross-Sectional Behavior and Long-Run Neutrality

We first consider distributional dynamics in the trivial case in which the shocks to optimal prices are independent across firms. It is easy to confirm that in this case, firms' price deviations head toward independence, so that the cross-sectional distribution approaches the uniform distribution, which is the steady-state distribution for each firm considered in isolation. Note that once the cross-sectional distribution of deviations is close to uniform, the expansionary effect of an increase in the optimal nominal price on firms with $d_i(t) \in [s + 2, S]$ will approximately counterbalance the contractionary effect for firms with deviation $d_i(t) = s + 1$. This implies that once enough time has passed, the distribution of deviations will become invariant to monetary shocks. Here it would be accurate to say that in the long run, monetary shocks have no influence on output. We refer to this as *long-run neutrality*.

The remarkable feature of the one-sided aggregation model is that the tendency toward cross-sectional uniformity that characterizes the independent case is present in all cases except for the pure representative agent case. This implies that long-run neutrality is the rule in these models, not the exception. The representative agent case in which there is some long-run effect of money on output is a false limit.

To indicate why this is true, we change perspective and view the dynamic behavior of the cross-sectional distribution of prices as the object of probabilistic analysis. Consider the vector of deviations for two arbitrary firms $i, j \in I$. The Markov transition matrix is recorded for a special case with $S = 1$ and $s = -2$:

$$
\begin{array}{ccccc}
 & (1,1) & (1,0) & (0,1) & (0,0) \\
(1,1) & \begin{bmatrix} 0.25 + q^2 & 0.25 - q^2 & 0.25 - q^2 & 0.25 + q^2 \\ (1,0) & 0.25 - q^2 & 0.25 + q^2 & 0.25 + q^2 & 0.25 - q^2 \\ (0,1) & 0.25 - q^2 & 0.25 + q^2 & 0.25 + q^2 & 0.25 - q^2 \\ (0,0) & 0.25 + q^2 & 0.25 - q^2 & 0.25 - q^2 & 0.25 + q^2 \end{bmatrix}
\end{array}
$$

To understand this, note, for example, that both firms face unit increases in their optimal prices with probability $0.5[(0.5 + q)^2 + (0.5 - q)^2] = 0.25 + q^2$: the first term is the probability of two unit increases in the high money growth state and the second term is the probability of two unit increases in the low money growth state. The key observation is that the transition matrix is doubly stochastic (both row and column sums are unity), and that therefore the unique stationary distribution is uniform, for $q \in (0, 0.5)$. This means that in the long run the price deviations of the firms are independent even when the shocks are highly correlated. The independence result in the example generalizes to the case of any finite number of firms, and to more general descriptions of the monetary shock (Caplin [1985]).

The independence result suggests that the tendency toward uniformity of the cross-sectional distribution that is present when there is no common shock will also be present when there is a common monetary shock, provided only that there is still some idiosyncratic component to the shocks. To demonstrate this, we move to the third level of aggregation and study the dynamics of the entire distribution of deviations as a Markov process.

Consider again the simple case above with $S = 1$ and $s = -2$ so that the state space for an individual firm's deviation is $\{1, 0, -1\}$. To work out the transition function for the distribution of deviations, assume that the proportion of firms in each state in period t is given by the vector $p(t) = (p_1(t), p_0(t), p_{-1}(t)) \in S^2$. In the high money expansion state, a proportion $0.5 + q$ of the population faces increases in optimal price, while $0.5 - q$ faces an unchanging optimal price. In this case, the proportions of the population in each state in period $t + 1$ are

$$p(t + 1) = (0.5 - q)p(t) + (0.5 + q)(p_{-1}(t), p_1(t), p_0(t)). \tag{2.11}$$

In the case with the low money shock, the probabilities $(0.5 + q)$ and $(0.5 - q)$ are simply reversed.

The key observation is that the distribution heads monotonically to uniformity from any initial condition. To see this, note that the difference between the proportions in distinct states in period $(t + 1)$ can be expressed as a weighted average of the differences from the previous period, with the weights adding up to $0.5 + q$. For example, in the high money growth state,

$$p_1(t + 1) - p_0(t + 1) = (0.5 - q)[p_{-1}(t) - p_0(t)] + 2q[p_{-1}(t) - p_1(t)].$$

This implies that the maximum difference between state occupancy probabilities shrinks geometrically over time at rate $0.5 + q$, so that the distribution approaches uniformity at this rate. Note that while there may be output oscillations and systematic effects of monetary shocks along an adjustment path, and convergence may be very slow (particularly as the idiosyncrasies shrink), the price distribution heads inevitably toward the uniform steady state. The study of the path to uniformity is due to Caballero and Engel ([1991a] and [1992a]).

These results show the remarkably simple structure of one-sided models of (S, s) aggregation. For long-run purposes, the cross-sectional distribution of prices can be treated as beginning in the uniform steady state, as in Caplin and Spulber [1987]. This implies that in the most natural stochastic model of aggregation in the presence of costs of price adjustment, monetary shocks have no effect on output since they simply rotate the uniform distribution. It turns out that these conclusions can alter dramatically when we allow for two-sided monetary shocks. To illustrate the distinction between the one-sided and the two-sided cases, we develop a special symmetric model in which increases and decreases in money are equally likely.

6.   Two-Sided Aggregation and Nonneutrality

We amend the model in the simplest way to allow for two-sided symmetric shocks. In the money growth state $(\theta(t) = h)$, a proportion $(0.5 + q)$ of the firms have a unit increase in their optimal prices and a proportion $(0.5 - q)$ have a unit decrease. In the equiprobable money contraction state ($\theta(t) = l$), a proportion ($0.5 + q$) have a unit increase and ($0.5 - q$) have a decrease. As in the one-sided case, as q increases from 0 to 0.5, the extent of the common shock relative to the idiosyncratic shock increases.

At the level of the individual firm, the shock to the optimal price in each period is equally likely to be a unit increase or a unit decrease. If we add in the assumption that the profit function is symmetric in the deviation, then we conclude that each firm optimally pursues a symmetric two-sided (S, s) strategy in which the deviation is adjusted to zero each time it hits symmetrically placed upper and lower barriers at D and $-D$, respectively. To increase our understanding of output dynamics in the symmetric case, we begin with a simple special case.

A Three-State Example

We consider the special case with $D = 2$ and $D = -2$ so that the state space for any firm is $\{1, 0, -1\}$. In this case, there is a simple periodic structure to the dynamic behavior of the price deviation. If $d_i(t) = 0$, then the deviation in the following period is either $d_i(t + 1) = -1$ or $d_i(t + 1) = 1$. In either case, the deviation deterministically returns to the value $d_i(t + 2) = 0$. The deviation therefore alternates between periods in state 0 and periods in one of the other two states. This implies that in the long run, the firm spends 50 percent of the time in state $d_i = 0$, and 25 percent in each of the states $d_i = 1, -1$. The stationary distribution of the deviations for each firm is triangular rather than the uniform distribution of the one-sided case.

The fact that the long-run distribution is triangular immediately implies that, in contrast with the one-sided case, there are average nonneutralities. An increase in a firm's optimal price leads to a decrease in the deviation for the firm unless it has the lowest deviation of -1, in which case it raises the deviation back to zero. But over the long run, the proportion of periods that the firm starts with the lowest deviation level is 0.25. The increase in the optimal price therefore systematically tends to lower the firm's deviation,

$$E[\Delta d_i(t) | \Delta \hat{p}_i(t) = 1] = -\tfrac{1}{2}.$$

According to equation (2.9), this result demonstrates that there is on average an expansionary effect of monetary growth on output in the two-sided model. Symmetric reasoning shows that there is on average a contractionary effect of reductions in the money supply.

The average non-neutrality result is uninfomative concerning the precise form of the nonneutralities that are present. As in the one-sided case, the only way to understand the response of the economy as a whole to a monetary shock is to study the dynamics of the cross-sectional distribution of deviations. It turns out that this is far more complex in the two-sided case than in the one-sided case. Recall that the key simplifying feature of the one-sided case is that the deviations of distinct firms approach independence in the long run, even when the shocks are correlated across firms. In contrast, in the two-sided case the correlation in shocks across firms implies a corresponding correlation in the deviation levels across firms. This implies that the triangular distribution that defines the time-series behavior of a single firm is inadequate to summarize cross-sectional behavior, even in the long run.

Before studying the complex dynamics of the cross-sectional distribution, it is useful to get rid of the periodicity in the behavior of the deviation. This is accomplished by perturbing the stochastic environment to allow for a small probability $\varepsilon > 0$ that any firm has an unchanged nominal price in any given period. In the money growth state, a proportion $(0.5 + q - \frac{\varepsilon}{2})$ have a unit increase in their optimal prices and a proportion $(0.5 - q - \frac{\varepsilon}{2})$ have a unit decrease. These proportions are reversed in the money contraction state.

Let $p(t) = (p_1(t), p_0(t), p_{-1}(t))$ denote the proportion of firms with each deviation level in period t. In the money expansion state, the next period's distribution is

$$p(t + 1) = \varepsilon p(t) + \left((0.5 - q - \frac{\varepsilon}{2}) p_0(t), \right.$$

$$(1 - \varepsilon)(p_1(t) + p_{-1}(t)), \quad \left. \left(0.5 + q - \frac{\varepsilon}{2} \right) p_0(t) \right).$$

In the case with monetary contraction, the probabilities $(0.5 - q - \frac{\varepsilon}{2})$ and $(0.5 + q - \frac{\varepsilon}{2})$ are simply reversed. We now explore certain qualitative aspects of the dynamic behavior of the distribution induced by this law of motion.

Note first that in contrast with the one-sided case, there is no tendency for the distribution to settle down even in the long run. After a series of monetary expansions there are more firms with deviation $d_i(t) = -1$ than with deviation $d_i(t) = 1$, and vice versa. The fact that there are such long-run fluctuations in the distribution of deviations greatly complicates the pattern of output dynamics. Fortunately, there are two observations that open the door to a qualitative analysis of output fluctuations in the long run.

The first useful observation is that the proportion of firms with deviation level $d_i(t) = 0$ settles down to 0.5 in the long-run

$$\lim_{t\to\infty} p_0(t) = \lim_{t\to\infty} (p_1(t) + p_{-1}(t)) = 0.5.$$

To prove this, note that regardless of the shock realization,

$$[p_1(t + 1) + p_{-1}(t + 1)] - p_0(t + 1) = [p_0(t)(1 - \varepsilon) + \varepsilon(p_1(t) + p_{-1}(t))]$$
$$- [(1 - \varepsilon)(p_1(t) + p_{-1}(t)) + \varepsilon p_0(t)]$$
$$= (1 - 2\varepsilon)(p_0(t) - (p_1(t) + p_{-1}(t))),$$

so that the absolute difference shrinks geometrically to zero, and convergence is confirmed. This result implies that for purposes of long-run analysis, one can set $p_0(0) = 0.5$. In this case the law of motion in the money expansion state simplifies to

$$p(t + 1) = \left[\varepsilon p_1(t) + 0.5\left(0.5 - q - \frac{\varepsilon}{2}\right), 0.5, \varepsilon p_1(t) + 0.5\left(0.5 + q - \frac{\varepsilon}{2}\right) \right].$$

$$(2.12)$$

As before, the probabilities $(0.5 - q - \frac{\varepsilon}{2})$ and $(0.5 + q - \frac{\varepsilon}{2})$ are simply reversed in the money contraction state.

Analysis of equation (2.12) produces the second qualitative insight into distributional dynamics. Consider the absolute difference between the proportion of firms with $d_i = 1$ and the proportion with $d_i = -1$,

$$|p_1(t + 1) - p_{-1}(t + 1)| = |\varepsilon[p_1(t) - p_{-1}(t)] + q| \geq q - \varepsilon.$$

Note that as the common shock comes to dominate the idiosyncratic shocks (i.e., as $q \nearrow 0.5$ and $\varepsilon \searrow 0$), so the absolute difference increases to 0.5. This means that when the common shock predominates, the distribution tends to fluctuate between periods with almost all firms having $d_i \in \{0, 1\}$, and periods with almost all firms having $d_i \in \{-1, 0\}$.

Both the observation that $p_0(t) \to 0.5$ and the observation that $|p_1(t) - p_{-1}(t)| \to 0.5$ when common shocks predominate have counterparts in a more general symmetric model with an arbitrary value of D. The fact that $p_0(t) \to 0.5$ has as its general counterpart a tendency to "modulo uniformity" in the distribution of deviations. This means that when states are paired into modulo D equivalence classes by combining states j and $j - D$, $1 \le j \le D - 1$, each such class heads toward equal population,

$$\lim_{t \to \infty} p_0(t) = \lim_{t \to \infty} [p_j(t) + p_{j-D}(t)] = \frac{1}{D}.$$

The reason for this result is that the symmetric model with states grouped according to modulo equivalence is formally equivalent to the one-sided model in Section 4. For example, when the states are grouped into modulo equivalence classes, the law of motion is Markovian, the resulting transition matrix is doubly stochastic, and the stationary distribution is uniform.

The general counterpart to the fact that $|p_1(t) - p_{-1}(t)| \to 0.5$ with dominant common shocks is that in such cases, "most" of the firms will be within $D - 1$ of one another "almost" all the time (the precise limit result is in Caplin and Leahy [1992a]). The idea behind this result is that after D successive monetary realizations of the same sign, almost all of the firms will be in the same half of the state space. From this point on, the vast bulk of the firms will typically be within $D - 1$ of one another, since almost all of them face the same change in their optimal price, and each time the price is adjusted, the deviation is set back to $d = 0$, which is within $D - 1$ of everyone. The limited tendency to drift apart due to idiosyncratic shocks will almost always be quickly overcome by the pull of the common shock.

The combination of the limit on the range of deviations and the uniformity of the distribution when using modulo D equivalence classes has a dramatic influence in pinning down distributional dynamics. The only distributions on $[-D + 1, D - 1]$ that are both modulo uniform and have a range of no more than $D - 1$ are the distributions that are uniform on $[x - D + 1, x]$ for some $x \in [0, D - 1]$. It is this fact that informs the symmetric two-sided model of Caplin and Leahy [1992a]. They explore a limit version of the symmetric model in which there are no idiosyncratic shocks. They argue that in order for the model to be an appropriate limiting case, the initial distribution of deviations should be uniform on some range of length $D - 1$. This assumption leads to a simple characterization of output dynamics, to which we now turn.

A Limit Case

The special properties of the model of Caplin and Leahy [1992a] are that all shocks are common ($\varepsilon = 0$ and $q = 0.5$), and that the initial distribution of deviations is uniform on $[x(0) - D + 1, x(0)]$ for some $x(0) \in [0, D - 1]$. The property that makes this case so tractable is that this class of distributions is self-replicating: if the initial distribution is uniform on an interval of length $D - 1$, then monetary shocks in either direction cause it to remain within the class. This is geometrically clear, as illustrated in the "elevator" picture of Caplin and Leahy, reproduced here as Figure 2.1.

The initial distribution of the deviations can be represented as an elevator of height $D - 1$ moving inside an elevator shaft of height $2(D - 1)$, as in Figure 2.1(a). The elevator starts at a random position in the shaft. Until the elevator has either risen to the top or fallen to the base of the shaft, the nominal prices of all firms remain unchanged. During this time the elevator moves precisely with the money supply. Only when the elevator seeks to go through the top or the base of the shaft is its motion constrained. If the money supply increases when the elevator is at the base, firms are simply rotated around the range $[-D + 1, 0]$. The *distribution* of the deviations is unchanged, as in the one-sided model of Caplin and Spulber [1987]. The firms that raise their price simply fill in the space vacated by firms pulled below the origin, as in Figure 2.1(b).

The implication is that the limit version of the model has a simple one-parameter structure. The complete cross-sectional distribution at any time t can be characterized by the single parameter $x(t) \in [0, D - 1]$ defining the maximal value of the deviation in the uniform distribution.

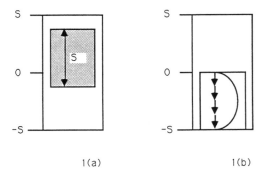

1(a)   1(b)

Figure 2.1

Given the "random walk" shock process that is driving it, the stochastic process followed by $x(t)$ is known as the random walk "regulated" at 0 and $D - 1$ (the terminology is due to Harrison [1985]). This structure makes it straightforward in principle to study the evolution of prices and output. From equation (2.6), output moves as the inverse of the average deviation. With the uniformity result, the mean is simply the midpoint of the distribution, which moves one-for-one with $x(t)$. To follow the output process, it is therefore sufficient to keep track of the midpoint of the price distribution.

It is instructive to explore the statistical relationship between money and output in this limit version of the symmetric model. Note first that the effect of money on the economy is closely tied to the level of output. As Figure 2.2 shows, money growth is less expansionary when current output is high than when it is low. In geometric terms, this corresponds to the monotonic reduction in the difference between the paths of output corresponding to the high and low levels of initial output as time passes.

A second general point to note is the sharp asymmetry between the minimal effects on output of continuations in existing monetary trends, and the large effect of reversals. To consider this issue formally, we must weigh the various possible levels of output according to the stationary distribution of the regulated random walk, which has $x(t)$ uniformly distributed over $[0, D - 1]$. This means that the expected change in output given a single positive monetary shock is $\frac{1}{D-1}$, since after the shock $x(t + 1)$ takes each value in the range $[1, D - 2]$ with probability $\frac{D-1}{D}$, and takes value $D - 1$ with probability $\frac{2}{D}$. The expected change in output following a second positive monetary shock is only $\frac{1}{D-2}$ as $x(t + 2)$ takes each value in the range $[2, D - 2]$ with probability $\frac{1}{D}$, and value $D - 1$ with probability $\frac{3}{D}$. The effect of more shocks in this same direction continues to dimin-

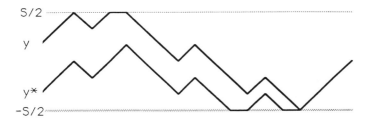

Figure 2.2

ish. After there have been D such shocks in a row, further increases in the money supply have no effect on output. In contrast, a contraction in the money supply after D positive shocks is fully reflected in a reduction in output.

Unfortunately, the sample path dependence of the two-sided model makes the relationship between the level of output and net monetary expansion quite intricate. Distinct monetary paths between two periods 0 and $t > 1$ can lead to very different output levels, even if there is no net change in the money supply. For example, if the money supply falls for the first D periods, and then increases for the next D periods, then output is at its minimal level in period $t = 2D$. If instead the money supply rises for the first D periods, and then falls for the next D periods, output is at its minimal level. Despite this, it turns out that there is a well-behaved statistical relationship between monetary expansion and output in discretely observed data, in that higher rates of net money growth are associated with higher expected levels of final output. The statistical argument is provided in Caplin and Leahy [1992b], in which the existence of a positive correlation between inflation and output is also established.

7. Relaxing the Assumptions

We briefly consider the potential impact of two different types of amendment of the model. For the first set of amendments, we maintain the basic structure of the model in equations (2.2)–(2.6) and consider what happens under more general stochastic mechanisms than the one-sided and symmetric two-sided cases so far discussed. The second amendment involves allowing for endogeneity of the processes that determine optimal nominal prices.

The simplest amendment to the model is to consider asymmetric two-sided variants of the model. In this case, optimal pricing strategies are of the two-sided (S, s) variety. While precise results are hard to provide for these cases, there are certain correlations that can be understood in broad qualitative terms.

Consider a case in which there is a positive drift in the money supply, $\mu > 0$. In this case the ergodic distribution of an individual firm's price concentrates on values of the deviation in the lower portion of the state space. This asymmetry becomes more and more noticeable as the mean inflation rate increases. In the limit as the mean increases, the steady-state distribution of an individual firm's deviation gradually becomes uniform on the lower portion of the state space.

The case with high mean inflation is useful as it highlights the asymmetry properties of the aggregation model. When there has been a long period of rapid monetary expansion, the cross-sectional distribution of deviations will begin to approach the uniform distribution, as in the purely one-sided case. This means that further monetary expansion has only a small effect on output. On the other side, there is great potential for reductions in money to reduce output, as the deviations move into a previously unoccupied region of the state space.

Caballero and Engel [1991b] provide further qualitative insights into the real effects of monetary shocks as a function of the mean and variance of the monetary process. One important topic that they address is how the money-output correlation depends on the monetary process. They show that there is a subtle dependence in which the effects of increased variance of inflation depend on the mean level of inflation. If there is no drift in the money supply, increases in the variance of money generally serve to reduce the correlation between monetary shocks and output: additional monetary variability tends to make output more noisy, and the resulting reversion to the mean reduces the association. But another factor becomes important as the rate of inflation increases. With very high average inflation, the neutrality result becomes relevant, so that the correlation between money and output falls to zero. In this case the effect of increased noise may be entirely the opposite: by making the model more two-sided, it may actually increase the correlation between money and output.

Another qualitatively important amendment to the model is to allow for a broader class of shock processes. The simplest example is to consider a process in which there is at some time t a change from one monetary process to another. It is an important characteristic of the aggregation models that they are capable of producing quite radical responses at such turning points. If both upper and lower adjustment barriers expand at t, then there will be a long period of inaction. If both barriers contract, then there will be a period of very rapid adjustment, although the net effect on output will depend on the state of the system before the shock. Overall, the endogenous response of the strategies has the potential to radically influence the response of the economy to shocks.

So far we have treated all stochastic processes as fully exogenous. Not only does this rule out feedback rules for money, but it also involves a very special assumption in which the effect on a firm's optimal nominal price of an increase in real balances is precisely the same as the effect of a decrease in the real price. Allowing for differences between these effects enables us to consider the impact of strategic complementarity on the relation between money and output. We therefore consider what happens when the model is amended by replacing equation (2.4) with equation (2.4'),

$$\Delta \hat{p}_i(t) = \Delta y(t) + b \Delta p(t) + \varepsilon_i(t), \tag{2.4'}$$

With $b > 1$, the goods are strategic complements, and with $b < 1$ they are strategic substitutes.

This apparently minor change has a radical effect on the complexity of the analysis. Note that in equation (2.4'), the variables influencing optimal strategies are endogenous: the quantity theory constrains only the sum $\Delta y(t) + \Delta p(t)$, not the individual components. The fact that the forcing processes are endogenous raises a fundamental issue of consistency. Do the stochastic properties of the endogenously generated price index mimic the properties of the process used to determine the optimality of the strategies?

Given the complexity of the interdependence, it is not surprising that attention has been limited to very special cases. The best-understood example is the symmetric two-sided case studied by Caplin and Leahy [1992a]. They exploit the very special nature of the symmetric framework to derive output dynamics that are qualitatively very similar to those for the symmetric case with one state variable. However, the additional state variable opens the door to the analysis of strategic complementarity. The main qualitative effect of increasing the degree of strategic complementarity is to make output fluctuations larger and to shrink the range of relative price variation. The reason is straightforward: when goods are strategic complements, firms care more about keeping their relative price close to unity than they do about maintaining a tight relationship between their price and the level of real balances.

8.   Conclusions

We conclude by taking a more general perspective on the topic of aggregation when there are microeconomic frictions. First, we point out some of the weaknesses of the aggregation framework outlined above. We then explain why, despite these weaknesses, the conceptual framework developed in the pricing context may be applicable to other topics in macroeconomics. We conclude by outlining some directions of current and future research.

One difficulty with the class of models is that while there is methodological advance in the technique of aggregation, very little attention is given to equilibrium analysis. For example, in the pricing models used in analyzing stochastic aggregation, the profit function is treated as exogenous. The work of Benabou on the deterministic search model suggests that this is inappropriate. The more general theoretical issue is the lack of attention to such deep parameters as utility functions and the technology of price adjustment. In addition there is the unanswered question of exactly what money is doing in these models in the first place. This raises two key questions. First, accepting that the aggregation models are seriously incomplete, what evidence is there that they are nevertheless worthy of attention? Second, are there any approaches that will allow us to combine the insights of the aggregation literature with those of the dynamic general equilibrium theorists?

The goal of the aggregation literature is to understand frictions in general: the pricing example is chosen as much for its arithmetic as its economic properties (the quantity theory is the main simplifying assumption). The general issue is that in any model with fixed adjustment costs at the microeconomic level, individuals allow the variables under their control to drift away from their statically optimal levels. In all such models, aggregate dynamics are therefore driven in part by the behavior of the deviations. In the face of common shocks, there is no reason for the deviations to average out to zero: the behavior of the deviations may be an important part of the behavior of the aggregates. This is relevant not only to price dynamics but also to the dynamics of employment, the demand for consumer durables and other investment goods, and asset demands. In this context, the aggregation literature has both highlighted weaknesses in existing approaches to frictional analysis and provided distinctive insights.

On the destructive side, one of the main implications of the aggregation models is that frictional models based on a fictional representative agent can be very misleading: the neutrality result with one-sided shocks is an extreme example. When one aggregates appropriately, connections between individual behavior and aggregate dynamics are subtle. Caballero

[1991b] explores this point in the context of employment dynamics. Empirical investigation shows that the cyclic behavior of job dynamics is driven more by job destruction than by job creation. This has been connected by some to a supposed asymmetry at the microeconomic level, where there may be more scale economies in closing down than in opening up employment opportunities. Caballero demonstrates that there is only a tenuous connection between the microeconomic asymmetry and its supposed macroeconomic counterpart. He also shows how to construct a coherent aggregation story that encompasses the stylized behavior at both the microeconomic and the macroeconomic levels.

On the constructive side, one of the main achievements of the simple aggregation models is that they have identified some important qualitative features of frictional dynamics. For example, one of the central features of the state-dependent models is the stark contrast between one-sided and two-sided models. Other noteworthy effects are the state dependence in the effects of shocks, sharp asymmetries between continuations and reversals of trend, and the potentially dramatic effects of changes in strategy. More generally, the models provide clear evidence that the economic impact of a given shock depends crucially on the overall nature of the stochastic process generating the shocks.

Since the aggregation models appear to have distinctive statistical properties, it is especially important to take them to the data. Empirical work on models of state-dependent aggregation is at an early stage, but the work on durables (Bertola and Caballero [1990] and Caballero [1991a]) and pricing suggests that the area has much promise. Caballero and Engel [1992b] are pursuing a promising new empirical approach to the aggregation problem. They relax the rigid (S, s) aggregation framework and adopt instead a "semistructural" approach. In this approach, the spirit of the models is stressed rather than the precise microeconomic foundations. Caballero and Engel capture the spirit of the models by conjecturing that those with large deviations are more prone to adjust than those that are close to where they would like to be. This is tested using data on job creation and destruction, and appears to be confirmed. They show that this "increasing hazard model" gives rise to a significant improvement over the partial adjustment model in the understanding of job creation and destruction. The improvement is particularly important at cyclical turning points, which is consonant with the qualitative predictions of the aggregation models. In future, it will be important to carry out empirical studies at the various levels of aggregation, a process that has been initiated by Eberly [1991].

While the empirical work strongly suggests that the insights derived from the aggregation literature are worth pursuing, this does not mean that increased attention to equilibrium considerations is unwarranted. In fact, future theoretical progress in modeling these issues will surely call for the development of sophisticated nonrepresentative agent models of equilibrium dynamics in the presence of frictions. The work of such authors as Hopeyhahn and Rogerson [1991] on entry and exit shows that there is no contradiction between general equilibrium dynamics and progress in understanding distributional dynamics.

On one level, one might expect the addition of general equilibrium effects to modify, rather than overturn, the findings of the current partial equilibrium models of aggregation. But on another level, the adoption of the equilibrium viewpoint may have a far more radical influence. Adopting the general equilibrium viewpoint focuses attention on whether there are any macroeconomic inefficiencies associated with individual frictions (except in the obvious case of monopoly pricing). One natural candidate is an information externality. Microeconomic frictions imply that inaction is optimal in many circumstances. Inasmuch as agents learn from the actions that others take, the presence of inertia therefore acts as a barrier preventing the smooth transmission of information. This means that when an individual overcomes inertia and takes a costly action, a great deal of previously hidden information may be released to outsiders. The fact that information may be released through infrequent changes of behavior can have radical implications for aggregate dynamics, and may rationalize rapid changes in market mood and outcome due to contagion effects (see Caplin and Leahy [1992c] for an introduction to this issue).

Overall, the approach to aggregation inspired by models of state-dependent pricing has already produced valuable insights into price dynamics. It has also influenced research into issues such as the demand for consumer durables and labor market dynamics. By forcing us to investigate nonrepresentative agent approaches to macroeconomics, the literature has taken macroeconomists into largely uncharted territory. Rather than providing microeconomic foundations for macroeconomics, the goal of the research is to rebuild portions of macroeconomics from the ground up.

Notes

David Canning and John Leahy provided valuable comments on this survey article.

1. Note that discretizing the model in this way necessarily violates the spirit of equation (2.3), which presupposes independence between the common monetary shock and the idiosyncratic shocks at the level of the individual firm. But since neither the idiosyncratic shock nor the monetary shock is deterministic, independence implies that as their sum, $\Delta p_i(t)$ should be able to take at least three distinct values. Fortunately the results do not change in any essential way if we enlarge the stage space, so that the additional simplicity we gain by limiting attention to only two possible values of $\Delta \hat{p}_i(t)$ is costless.

References

Akerlof, G., and J. Yellen. (1985). "Can Small Deviations from Rationality Make a Significant Difference to Economic Equilibria?" *American Economic Review*, LXXV, 708–720.

Arrow, K. J., T. Harris, and J. Marschak. (1951). "Optimal Inventory Policy." *Econometrica*, XIX, 250–272.

Barro, R. (1972). "A Theory of Monopolistic Price Adjustment." *Review of Economic Studies*, XXXIV, 17–26.

Benabou, R. (1988). "Search, Price Setting and Inflation." *Review of Economic Studies*, LV, 353–376.

Benabou, R. (1992). "Inflation and Efficiency in Search Markets." *Review of Economic Studies*, LIX, 299–330.

Benabou, R., and J. Konieczny. (1991). "On Inflation and Output with Costly Price Changes: A Simple Unifying Result." Mimeo.

Bertola, G., and R. Caballero. (1990). "Kinked Adjustment Costs and Aggregate Dynamics." *NBER Macroeconomics Annual*, 237–295.

Blanchard, O., and N. Kiyotaki. (1987). "Monopolistic Competition and the Effects of Aggregate Demand." *American Economic Review*, LXXVII, 647–666.

Blinder, A. (1981). "Retail Inventory Investment and Business Fluctuations." *Brookings Papers on Economic Activity*, 2, 443–505.

Caballero, R. (1991a). "Durable Goods: An Explanation for Their Slow Adjustment." *Journal of Political Economy*, forthcoming.

Caballero, R. (1991b) "A Fallacy of Composition." *American Economic Review*, forthcoming.

Caballero, R., and E. Engel. (1991a). "Dynamic S-s Economies." *Econometrica*, LXI, 1659–1686.

Caballero, R., and E. Engel. (1991b). "The Output-Inflation Tradeoff Revisited." Mimeo.

Caballero, R., and E. Engel. (1992a). "The S-s Economy: Aggregation, Speed of Convergence and Monetary Policy Effectiveness." *Review of Economic Studies*, forthcoming.

Caballero, R., and E. Engel. (1992b). "Beyond the Partial Adjustment Model." *American Economic Review*, LXXXII, 360–364.

Caplin, A. (1985). "The Variability of Aggregate Demand with (S, s) Inventory Policies." *Econometrica*, LIII, 1395–1410.

Caplin, A., and J. Leahy. (1991). "State Dependent Pricing and the Dynamics of Money and Output." *Quarterly Journal of Economics*, CVI, 683–708.

Caplin, A., and J. Leahy. (1992a). "Aggregation and Optimization with State Dependent Pricing." Columbia University Discussion Paper 599.

Caplin, A., and J. Leahy. (1992b). "Statistical Properties of the Regulated Brownian Motion." Harvard University Discussion Paper 1596.

Caplin, A., and J. Leahy. (1992c). "Business as Usual, Market Crashes, and Wisdom After the Fact." Columbia University Discussion Paper 602.

Caplin, A., and E. Sheshinski. (1987). "Optimality of (S, s) Pricing Policies." Mimeo.

Caplin, A., and D. Spulber. (1987). "Menu Costs and the Neutrality of Money." *Quarterly Journal of Economics*, CII, 703–725.

Carlton, D. (1986). "The Rigidity of Prices." *American Economic Review*, LXXVI, 637–658.

Cecchetti, S. (1986). "The Frequency of Price Adjustment: A Study of the Newsstand Price of Magazines." *Journal of Econometrics*, XXXI, 255–274.

Danziger, L. (1983). "Price Adjustments with Stochastic Inflation." *International Economic Review*, XXIV, 699–707.

Diamond, P. (1992). "Search, Sticky Prices, and Inflation." *Review of Economic Studies*, forthcoming.

Dixit, A. (1989). "Entry and Exit Decisions Under Uncertainty." *Journal of Political Economy*, XCVII, 620–638.

Dixit, A. (1991). "Analytic Approximations in Models of Hysteresis." *Review of Economic Studies*, LVIII, 1141–1151.

Eberly, J. (1991). "Adjustment of Consumers' Durables Stocks: Evidence from Automobile Purchases." Wharton School Working Paper 22.

Grossman, S., and G. Laroque. (1990). "Asset Pricing and Optimal Portfolio Choice in the Presence of Illiquid Durable Consumption Goods." *Econometrica*, LVIII, 28–51.

Harrison, J. M. (1985). *Brownian Motion and Stochastic Flow Systems*. New York: Wiley.

Hopeyhahn, H., and R. Rogerson. (1991). "Job Turnover and Policy Analysis: A General Equilibrium Analysis." Mimeo.

Kashyap, A. (1991). "Sticky Prices: New Evidence from Retail Catalogs." Mimeo, University of Chicago, Graduate School of Business.

Lach, S., and D. Tsiddon. (1992). "The Behavior of Prices and Inflation: An Empirical Analysis of Disaggregated Price Data." *Journal of Political Economy*, C, 349–389.

Mankiw, N. G. (1985). "Small Menu Costs and Large Business Cycles: A Macroeconomic Model of Monopoly." *Quarterly Journal of Economics*, C, 529–539.

Rotemberg, J. (1982). "Monopolistic Price Adjustment and Aggregate Output." *Review of Economic Studies*, IL, 517–531.

Sheshinski, E., and Y. Weiss. (1977). "Inflation and the Costs of Price Adjustment." *Review of Economic Studies*, XLIV, 287–303.

Sheshinski, E. and Y. Weiss. (1983). "Optimum Pricing Policy Under Stochastic Inflation." *Review of Economic Studies*, L, 513–529.

Tsiddon, D. (1988). "On the Stubbornness of Sticky Prices." Hebrew University Working Paper no. 174.

II TOOLS OF ANALYSIS: MATHEMATICAL THEORY OF INVENTORY CONTROL

3 The Optimality of (S, s) Policies in the Dynamic Inventory Problem

Herbert Scarf

1. Introduction

An elaborate discussion of the history and general features of the inventory problem may be found in [2]. We shall content ourselves here with a brief description of the type of model introduced in [1] and discussed by a number of subsequent authors ([2], [3], [4]).

A sequence of purchasing decisions is made at the beginning of a number of regularly spaced intervals. These purchases contribute to a build-up of inventories which are then depleted by demands during the various intervals. We shall assume the demands to be independent observations from a common distribution function, though varying distributions may be treated by the same technique.

Various costs are charged during the successive periods, and the objective is to select the purchasing decisions so as to minimize the expectation of the discounted value of all costs. There are, generally speaking, three types of costs: a purchasing or ordering cost $c(z)$, where z is the amount purchased; a holding cost $h(\cdot)$, which is a function of the excess of supply over demand at the end of the period; and a shortage cost $p(\cdot)$, which is a function of the excess of demand over supply at the end of the period. Holding or shortage costs are charged at the end of every period, and ordering costs are charged when a purchase is made. We shall assume initially that purchases are made only at the beginning of the period and that delivery is instantaneous. In Section 3 the case of a time lag in delivery will be discussed.

If the stock level immediately after purchases are delivered is y, then the expected holding and shortage costs to be charged during that period are given by

$$
L(y) = \begin{cases} \displaystyle\int_0^y h(y - \xi)\varphi(\xi)\,d\xi + \int_y^\infty p(\xi - y)\varphi(\xi)\,d\xi & y \geq 0. \\[2ex] \displaystyle\int_0^\infty p(\xi - y)\varphi(\xi)\,d\xi & y < 0, \end{cases}
\tag{3.1}
$$

where φ is the density of the demand distribution.

Let us assume that the inventory problem has a horizon of n periods and that the problem is begun with an initial inventory of x units. Let

$C_n(x)$ represent the expected value of the discounted costs during this n-period program if the provisioning is done optimally. (The discount factor will be denoted by α, and will be between 0 and 1.) Then it is easy to see that $C_n(x)$ satisfies the functional equation

$$C_n(x) = \min_{y \geq x} \left\{ c(y - x) + L(y) + \alpha \int_0^\infty C_{n-1}(y - \xi)\varphi(\xi)\,d\xi \right\}, \tag{3.2}$$

and that if $y_n(x)$ is the minimizing value of y in (3.2), then $y_n(x) - x$ represents the optimal initial purchase. The purpose of this chapter will be to show that under surprisingly weak conditions the optimal policy will be of a very simple type.

Let us begin by reviewing some of the work that has been done on the one-period problem ($n = 1$, and $C_0 \equiv 0$). The single-period problem is essentially a problem in the calculus and a considerable amount is known about it, in distinction to the sequential problem [2, chap. 8]. The simplest case is when the ordering cost is linear, i.e., $c(z) = c \cdot z$. In this case the optimal policy for the single-period model is frequently defined by a single critical number $\bar{x}$, as follows: If $x < \bar{x}$, buy $\bar{x} - x$, and if $x > \bar{x}$, do not buy. Analogous results frequently hold in the sequential problem, the optimal policy being defined by a sequence of critical numbers $\bar{x}_1, \bar{x}_2, \ldots$; see [3]. A sufficient condition for these results to hold is that $L(y)$ be convex, a condition which obtains when the holding and shortage costs are each convex increasing functions which vanish at the origin. A number of other sufficient conditions for the one-period model and the dynamic model are given by Karlin in [2, chaps. 8 and 9, respectively].

The situation is considerably more complex when the ordering cost is no longer linear. We shall concentrate on the simplest type of non-linear cost:

$$c(z) = \begin{cases} 0 & z = 0, \\ K + c \cdot z & z > 0. \end{cases} \tag{3.3}$$

K is usually described as the reorder cost.

With this type of ordering cost the optimal policy in the single-period model is frequently defined by a pair of critical numbers (S, s) as follows: If $x < s$, order $(S - x)$, and if $x > s$, do not order. There are examples in the single-period model in which such a policy is not optimal. However, if the holding and shortage costs are linear functions of their arguments [$h(u) =$

$h \cdot u$ and $p(u) = p \cdot u$], or more generally if $L(y)$ is convex, then the optimal policy for the single-period model is (S, s) [2, chap. 8].

However, even with the assumption of linear holding and shortage costs, the literature is very meager on the properties of optimal policies for the dynamic model. Bratten has shown (see [2, chap. 9]) that if the density of demand is decreasing, the optimal policy for the dynamic model is defined by a sequence of pairs of critical number $(S_1, s_1), (S_2, s_2), \ldots$. The only other result is due to Karlin [2], viz.: if φ has a monotone likelihood ratio, if the holding and shortage costs are linear, and if $c + h > \alpha p$, then the optimal policy is of the same sort. Both of these results are rather restrictive, the former because it requires a decreasing density, and the latter because of the severe constraint on the costs.

In this chapter we shall show that when the holding and shortage costs are linear, or more generally when $L(y)$ is convex, and the ordering cost is as described above, the optimal policy in the dynamic problem is *always* of the (S, s) type *without* any additional conditions.

The two results mentioned above are based on a study of the functions

$$G_n(y) = cy + L(y) + \alpha \int_0^\infty C_{n-1}(y - \xi)\varphi(\xi)\,d\xi. \tag{3.4}$$

It is optimal to order from x if and only if there is some y larger than x, with $G_n(x) > K + G_n(y)$; and if we do order from x, it is to that $y > x$ which minimizes $G_n(y)$. [See (2).] When either Bratten's condition or Karlin's condition is assumed, it may be shown that $G_n(y)$ decreases to a minimum and subsequently increases. If the minimizing value of y is denoted by S_n and if s_n is defined by

$$G_n(s_n) = G_n(S_n) + K, \tag{3.5}$$

then the policy defined by (S_n, s_n) is indeed optimal. However, a few numerical calculations are sufficient to show that the functions G_n do not always have this regular behavior; they may actually have a number of maxima and minima. The idea of the proof given in this chapter is that although G_n may have a large number of maxima and minima, the oscillations are never sufficiently large to cause a deviation from the (S, s) policy.

Explicitly, what we shall demonstrate is that if $L(y)$ is convex, the following inequality holds: Let $a \geq 0$; then

$$K + G_n(a + x) - G_n(x) - aG_n'(x) \geq 0. \tag{3.6}$$

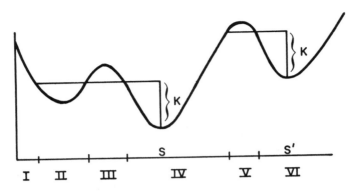

Figure 3.1

To see that (3.6) implies that the optimal policy is (S, s), let us examine the accompanying graph of $G_n(x)$, which illustrates a typical case in which more complex policies are to be expected. With this type of graph for G_n, we would order in interval I to the point S, not order in interval II, order in III to S, not order in IV, order in V to S' and not order in VI. But if (3.6) is correct, this sort of graph is impossible; for let $x + a = S$ and x be the point in III at which the relative maximum is attained. For this value of x, $G'_n(x) = 0$, and (3.6) implies that $K + G_n(S) - G_n(x) \geq 0$, which contradicts the graph. The same argument may be applied to the point S'.

2. The Case of Zero Time Lag

In this section we consider the case in which delivery of orders is instantaneous. It will be shown that if $L(x)$ is convex and the ordering costs are given by (3.3), the optimal policies are of the (S, s) type.

In order to demonstrate (3.6), we shall make use of the following definition:

DEFINITION. *Let $K \geq 0$, and let $f(x)$ be a differentiable function. We say that $f(x)$ is K-convex if*

$$K + f(a + x) - f(x) - af'(x) \geq 0, \text{ for all positive a and all x.} \tag{3.7}$$

If differentiability is not assumed, then the appropriate definition of K-convexity would be

$$K + f(a + x) - f(x) - a\left[\frac{f(x) - f(x - b)}{b}\right] \geqq 0. \tag{3.8}$$

Inasmuch as our applications will be to differentiable functions, we shall use (3.7) rather than (3.8). It may be shown that (3.7) implies (3.8), and of course (3.8) implies (3.7) if $f(x)$ is differentiable.

There are a number of simple properties of K-convex functions which will be of some use to us:

(i) 0-convexity is equivalent to ordinary convexity.

(ii) if $f(x)$ is K-convex, then $f(x + h)$ is K-convex for all h.

(iii) If f and g are K-convex and M-convex, respectively, then $\alpha f + \beta g$ is $(\alpha K + \beta M)$-convex when α and β are positive. This property may be extended to denumerable sums and integrals whenever the interchange of limits is permissible.

Now let us turn our attention to a proof of (3.6). We shall show inductively that each of the functions $G_1(x)$, $G_2(x)$, ... are K-convex. G_1 is clearly K-convex, since $G_1(x)$ equals $cx + L(x)$, which is 0-convex and therefore K-convex. Let us assume that $G_1, \ldots, G_n$ are K-convex. If we examine (3.4), we see that in order to demonstrate the K-convexity of $G_{n+1}(x)$, it is sufficient to show that

$$\int_0^\infty C_n(x - \xi)\varphi(\xi)\,d\xi$$

is K-convex, and by properties (ii) and (iii) above, it is sufficient to show that $C_n(x)$ is K-convex.

The K-convexity of $C_n(x)$ may be shown as follows. We first notice that the argument of Section 1 demonstrates, as a consequence of the K-convexity of $G_n(x)$, that the optimal policy for the n-period problem is (S, s). In other words, if S_n is the absolute minimum of $G_n(x)$, and if s_n is defined as the value of $x < S_n$ satisfying $K + G_n(S_n) = G_n(s_n)$, then the optimal policy is to order to S_n if $x < s_n$ and otherwise not to order. Therefore

$$C_n(x) = \begin{cases} K + c(S_n - x) + C_n(S_n) = K - cx + G_n(S_n) & x < s_n, \\ -cx + G_n(x) & x > s_n. \end{cases} \tag{3.9}$$

We shall use (3.9) to demonstrate the K-convexity of $C_n(x)$. We distinguish three cases, using the notation of (3.7).

Case 1. $x > s_n$.

In this region $C_n(x)$ is equal to a linear function plus a K-convex function and is therefore K-convex.

Case 2. $x < s_n < x + a$.

In this case

$$K + C_n(x + a) - C_n(x) - aC_n'(x) = K + C_n(x + a) - C_n(x) + ac,$$

and this is positive since

$$C_n(x) = \min_{y > x} \left\{ K + c(y - x) + L(y) + \alpha \int_0^\infty C_{n-1}(y - \xi)\varphi(\xi)\,d\xi \right\}$$

$$\leq K + ca + L(x + a) + \alpha \int_0^\infty C_{n-1}(x + a - \xi)\varphi(\xi)\,d\xi$$

$$= K + ca + C_n(x + a).$$

(We use the fact that $x + a > s_n$, and therefore it is optimal not to order from $x + a$.)

Case 3. $x + a < s_n$.

In this region $C_n(x)$ is linear and therefore K-convex. This completes the induction, and demonstrates the optimality of (S, s) policies for the case considered in this section.

3.   The Case of a Time Lag in Delivery

When there is a time lag in delivery, the character of optimal policies is very much dependent upon whether excess demand is backlogged or expedited; see [2, chap. 10]. If excess demand is backlogged, it is known that the optimal policy is a function of stock on hand plus stock ordered but not yet delivered, whereas if excess demand is expedited, the optimal policy never has this simple form. We shall restrict ourselves to the backlog case.

Let the time lag be denoted by λ, so that an order placed at the beginning of a period is delivered λ periods later at the beginning of the period. Consider a problem with a horizon of n periods. Let x represent current stock, x_1 stock to be delivered at the beginning of the next period, and generally speaking, x_j stock to be delivered j periods later, where $j = 1, 2, \ldots, \lambda - 1$. Let $C_n(x, x_1, \ldots, x_{\lambda-1})$ be the minimum expected cost for such a program. Then it is easy to see that this function satisfies an equation analogous to (3.2), namely

$$C_n(x, x_1, \ldots, x_{\lambda-1})$$

$$= \min_{z \geq 0} \left\{ c(z) + L(x) + \alpha \int_0^\infty C_{n-1}(x + x_1 - \xi, x_2, \ldots, z) \varphi(\xi) \, d\xi \right\}, \quad (3.10)$$

and that the minimizing value of z in this equation represents the optimal purchase.

We shall next demonstrate that if $L(x)$ is convex and the purchase costs are given by (3.3), the optimal policy is described by two numbers S_n and s_n as follows: If $x + x_1 + \cdots + x_{\lambda-1} > s_n$, do not order; if $x + x_1 + \cdots + x_{\lambda-1} < s_n$, order up to S_n.

The proof begins with a repetition of the argument in [2, p. 159]. It follows from (3.10) that C_n may be written in the following form (for $n \geq \lambda$):

$$C_n(x, x_1, x_2, \ldots, x_{\lambda-1})$$

$$= L(x) + \alpha \int_0^\infty L(x + x_1 - \xi) \varphi(\xi) \, d\xi$$

$$+ \cdots + \alpha^{\lambda-1} \int_0^\infty \cdots \int_0^\infty L\left(x + \cdots + x_{\lambda-1} - \sum_{i=1}^{\lambda-1} \xi_i\right) \varphi(\xi_1) \cdots \varphi(\xi_{\lambda-1}) \, d\xi_1 \cdots d\xi_{\lambda-1}$$

$$+ f_n(x + x_1 + \cdots + x_{\lambda-1}), \quad (3.11)$$

where $f_n(u)$ satisfies the functional equation

$$f_n(u) = \min_{z \geq 0} \left\{ c(z) + \alpha^\lambda \int_0^\infty \cdots \int_0^\infty L\left(u + z - \sum_{i=1}^{\lambda} \xi_i\right) \varphi(\xi_1) \cdots \varphi(\xi_\lambda) \, d\xi_1 \cdots d\xi_\lambda \right.$$

$$\left. + \alpha \int_0^\infty f_{n-1}(u + z - \xi) \varphi(\xi) \, d\xi \right\}. \quad (3.12)$$

It follows also from (3.10) that the minimizing value of z gives the optimal purchase if

$$x + \sum_{j=1}^{\lambda-1} x_j = u.$$

(The initial conditions are $f_1(u) = \cdots = f_\lambda(u) = 0$.) If we write $y = u + z$, then (3.12) is identical with (3.2), except for the fact that $L(y)$ has been replaced by

$$\alpha^\lambda \int_0^\infty \cdots \int_0^\infty L\left(y - \sum_{i=1}^\lambda \xi_i\right) \varphi(\xi_1) \cdots \varphi(\xi_\lambda) \, d\xi_1 \cdots d\xi_\lambda.$$

However, if $L(y)$ is convex, then its replacement is also convex, and this is all that is necessary to repeat the argument of Section 2. This concludes the proof of the optimality of (S, s) policies in the time-lag case.

Note

This work was supported in part by the Office of Naval Research.

References

[1] Arrow, K. J., T. Harris, and J. Marschak. "Optimal Inventory Policy," *Econometrica*, 19 (1951), 250–72.

[2] Arrow, K. J., S. Karlin, and H. Scarf. *Studies in the Mathematical Theory of Inventory and Production*, Stanford, Calif.: Stanford University Press, 1958.

[3] Bellman, R., I. Glicksberg, and O. Gross. "On the Optimal Inventory Equation," *Management Science*, 2 (1955), 83–104.

[4] Dvoretzky, A., J. Kiefer, and J. Wolfowitz. "The Inventory Problem, I. Case of Known Distributions of Demand," *Econometrica*, 20 (1952), 187–222.

[5] Dvoretzky, A., J. Kiefer, and J. Wolfowitz. "On the Optimal Character of the (S, s) Policy in Inventory Theory," *Econometrica*, 21 (1953), 586–96.

4 Quasi-Variational Inequalities and Impulse Control Problems

Agnès Sulem

Stochastic control and impulse control theory have numerous applications in management. Typical fields of application are inventory and production, finance, and investment planning. Indeed, management problems deal with dynamic systems subject to stochastic evolution, and decisions have to be taken in order to optimize an economic value function.

In continuous control theory, the control variable is a process whose value can be decided at every time t in terms of the available informations at time t, and it appears in the evolution equation of the system. In this case, the optimal value function is solution of a nonlinear partial differential equation, called a Hamilton-Jacobi-Bellman (HJB) equation. This equation can be obtained heuristically by using an argument based on the optimal principle of dynamic programming.

In the case of impulse control theory, the state of the system is subject at some times (the "impulse times") to jumps (the "impulses"). The impulse times, the number of impulses, and the intensity of the impulses are decision variables that constitute an impulse control. An important feature of impulse control is that in general there is a cost associated with each impulse. A. Bensoussan and J. L. Lions [6] have developed a general methodology for solving impulse control problems, based on the concept of quasi-variational inequalities (QVIs). The QVIs can be considered as special cases of dynamic programming equations for discrete control variables, the decision variable being the choice of exerting an impulse.

We shall proceed as follows: in section 1 we formulate the impulse control problem in continuous time and derive the QVI satisfied by the value function by using dynamic programming methodology. An analogy with the continuous control problem is given. Section 2 is devoted to existence, uniqueness, and regularity theorems for solution of the QVIs. We shall consider finite and infinite horizon problems in both stochastic and deterministic cases. Application of impulse control theory to inventory control problems is studied in section 3. Two examples are given: the first considers a stochastic one-product inventory system; the second, a two-dimensional deterministic system subject to economies of joint ordering. In both cases, explicit solution of the QVI governing the optimal cost leads to the determination of the optimal ordering policy.

1 Continuous Control and Impulse Control Theory

1.1 The Model

We consider dynamic systems and denote by $y(t) \in \mathbb{R}^n$ the state of the system at time t, where n is the number of state variables. We suppose here that time is continuous, although the analysis can be done in discrete time as well.

Let us first consider the evolution of the system in the absence of control; in the deterministic case, $y(t)$ is the solution of a differential equation:

$$\frac{dy(t)}{dt} = b(y(t), t), \quad y(0) = y_0. \tag{1.1}$$

In the stochastic case, we suppose that a zero-mean random term is added to the r.h.s. of (1.1). More precisely, we suppose that $y(t)$ is governed by the following Ito stochastic differential equation:

$$dy(t) = b(y(t), t)\, dt + \sigma(y(t), t)\, dW(t) \tag{1.2}$$

where $W(t)$ is a n-dimensional Wiener process, that is, a nondifferentiable continuous Gaussian process with independent increments.

In the standard setup (strong solution), one assumes Lipschitz properties with respect to the space variables, for the given functions b and σ.

The process $y(t)$, solution of equation (1.2), is a continuous Markov process, called a diffusion process, where b is the drift and σ the diffusion term. We refer to [12] and [25] for a discussion of (1.2).

Equations (1.1) and (1.2) describe free evolution models, without control variables. In order to model the dependence of the state evolution on the control, we consider two cases: the continuous and the impulse control.

In the case of continuous control, we suppose in general that the drift term b and the diffusion σ depend on a control term v, the value of which can be decided at every time t. In general, $v(t)$ has to satisfy contraints: $v(t) \in \mathcal{U}_{ad}$. If the evolution of $y(t)$ can be observed in the course of time, the observation is said to be complete; otherwise, the observation is partial.

Equation (1.2) is thus written

$$dy(t) = b(y(t), v(t), t) + \sigma(y(t), v(t), t)\, dW(t). \tag{1.3}$$

In the impulse control case, the state of the system is submitted to jumps at some impulse times $0 \le \theta_1 < \theta_2 < \cdots < \theta_i < \cdots$. The decision variables consist of these impulse times θ_i and the size of the impulses ξ_i. The sequence $V = (\theta_i, \xi_i)_{i>0}$ is termed an impulse control.

The state evolution is then given by

$$dy(t) = b(y(t), t) dt + \sigma(y(t), t) dW(t) + \sum_{i \geq 1} \xi_i \delta(t - \theta_i),$$

$$y(0) = y_0, \tag{1.4}$$

where δ denotes the Dirac measure.

More explicitly, relation (1.4) means that between times θ_i and θ_{i+1}, the evolution of the system is given by

$$dy(t) = b(y(t), t) dt + \sigma(y(t), t) dW(t), \quad \theta_i < t < \theta_{i+1},$$

$$y(\theta_i) = y(\theta_i^-) + \xi_i, \tag{1.5}$$

$$y(0) = y_0,$$

where

$$y(\theta_i^-) = y(\theta_{i-1}) + \int_{\theta_{i-1}}^{\theta_i} b(y(t), t) dt + \int_{\theta_{i-1}}^{\theta_i} \sigma(y(t), t) dW(t) \tag{1.6}$$

and $\theta_0 = 0$.

The impulse times θ_i and the quantities ξ_i are random in general. The events $\{\theta_i \leq t\}$ depend on the information available up to time t, and the value of ξ_i depends on the information available up to time θ_i. The impulse times are stopping times, using the probability theory terminology.

1.2 The Economic Value Function

We now set the optimization problem. For the continuous control problem, the functional to optimize over the set of admissible controls can be written in general as

$$J(v) = E\left(\int_0^T e^{-\alpha t} f(y(t), v(t), t) dt + h(y(T)) e^{-\alpha T} \right), \tag{1.7}$$

where E denotes expectation, α is the discount rate, and T is the horizon (which can be infinite). The integral cost $\int_0^T e^{-\alpha t} f(y, v, t)$ is attached to the evolution of the system, and $h(y(T)) e^{-\alpha T}$ is the final cost.

For the impulse control problem, the cost function to optimize over all possible impulse controls $V = (\theta_i, \xi_i)_{i>0}$ is

$$J(V) = E\left(\int_0^T e^{-\alpha t} f(y(t), t)\, dt + \sum_i c(\xi_i) e^{-\alpha \theta_i} + h(y(T)) e^{-\alpha T}\right) \tag{1.8}$$

where $c(\xi_i)$ is the cost for each impulse.

We suppose $c(\xi_i) \geq k > 0$, which means that each time the system is controlled, a fixed setup cost k is incurred. The presence of this fixed cost prevents the system from being controlled in a continuous fashion.

1.3 Dynamic Programming

We shall now characterize the optimal cost function (or value function) as a solution of a partial differential equation associated with the control problem. The derivation of these equations is easily justified, via Ito's formula, if we know a priori that the value function is C^2, that is, twice continuously differentiable (or continuously differentiable for the deterministic control problem). It is not the case in general, but we shall show later how these equations always characterize the value function under general conditions.

In order to derive formally the partial differential equation satisfied by the value function, we assume below all the necessary regularity for the solution and use the optimality principle of dynamic programming. This principle, due to Bellman [4], is one of the main tools in the study of optimal control problems involving solutions of ordinary or stochastic differential equations. It states that no matter how one has reached the present state, all decisions from that point forward should be optimal.

a. Continuous Control. We first consider the continuous control case with complete observation, and we assume that the state domain is $\mathbb{R}^n$.

We denote by $\Phi(x, t)$ the minimized expected total cost from t to T, discounted to time t and conditional on the level $y(t) = x$:

$$\Phi(x, t) = \inf_{v(\cdot)} E\left(\int_t^T e^{-\alpha(s-t)} f(y(s), v(s), s)\, ds + h(y(T)) e^{-\alpha(T-t)}\right). \tag{1.9}$$

We shall express the value function at time t in terms of the value function at time $t + \delta$, through dynamic programming. Suppose that a control $v(s)$ is applied on the interval $(t, t + \delta)$, and that we know the optimal policy $u(s)$ to apply from time $t + \delta$ on, the state of the system being $y(t + \delta)$ at time $t + \delta$.

Let us call $\tilde{v}(s)$ the following control:

$$\tilde{v}(s) = \begin{cases} v(s) & on \ (t, t + \delta), \\ u(s) & for \ s > t + \delta. \end{cases} \tag{1.10}$$

We have

$$J_{x,t}(\tilde{v}(\cdot)) = E\left(\int_t^{t+\delta} e^{-\alpha(s-t)} f(y(s), v(s), s) \, ds + e^{-\alpha\delta} \Phi(y(t + \delta), t + \delta)\right). \tag{1.11}$$

We derive from the optimality principle that if $v(s)$ on $(t, t + \delta)$ is chosen in order to optimize (1.11), we obtain the optimal value function; in other words, the optimal policy on (t, T) can be decomposed into $u(s)$, $s \in (t, t + \delta)$ and $u(s)$, $s \in (t + \delta, T)$. The latter is also the optimal policy for a problem starting at time $t + \delta$ in the state $y(t + \delta)$. We thus obtain

$$\Phi(x, t) = \inf_{v(t, t+\delta)} E\left(\int_t^{t+\delta} e^{-\alpha(s-t)} f(y(s), v(s), s) \, ds + e^{-\alpha\delta} \Phi(y(t + \delta), t + \delta)\right). \tag{1.12}$$

We then expand the r.h.s of (1.12) to the first order in δ. Applying Ito's formula, using the property $E(W(t + \delta) - W(t))^2 = \delta$ of the Wiener process, we get

$$E\Phi(y(t + \delta), t + \delta) = \Phi(x, t) + \delta\nabla\Phi \cdot b(x, v, t) + \delta\frac{\partial\Phi}{\partial t}$$

$$+ \delta \sum_{i,j} \frac{\partial^2\Phi}{\partial x_i \partial x_j} a_{ij}(x, v, t) + o(\delta), \tag{1.13}$$

where the matrix $a = (a_{ij})_{i,j=1\cdots n}$ is defined by

$$a = \tfrac{1}{2}\sigma \cdot \sigma^T, \tag{1.14}$$

$\nabla\Phi$ is the gradient of Φ, and σ^T denotes the transposed matrix of σ.

When δ goes to zero, we obtain the following nonlinear partial differential equation for $\Phi(x, t)$, called the HJB or dynamic programming equation:

$$\frac{\partial\Phi}{\partial t} + \inf_{v \in \mathcal{U}_{ad}} \{A(v)\Phi + f(v)\} = 0 \tag{1.15}$$

with

$$A(v)\Phi = \sum_{i,j} a_{ij}(x, v, t) \frac{\partial^2 \Phi}{\partial x_i \partial x_j} + b(x, v, t) \cdot \nabla\Phi - \alpha\Phi. \tag{1.16}$$

Moreover, we have the final condition

$$\Phi(x, T) = h(x) \tag{1.17}$$

which comes from the definition of Φ.

b. Impulse Control. Let us now turn to the impulse control problem. The evolution of the system is given by (1.4) and the economic functional by (1.8). We have to adapt the dynamic programming argument to have the analytic problem satisfied by the value function: at time t, one can either decide to exert an impulse to the system immediately or to wait for a certain period of time δ. The resulting costs are estimated by assuming that the subsequent decisions are optimal.

(i) If an impulse is exerted at time t, the state jumps from x to an optimal level $x + \xi$ and the resulting cost is $c(\xi) + \Phi(x + \xi, t)$.

By definition of Φ, we get

$$\Phi(x, t) - \inf_{\xi} (c(\xi) + \Phi(x + \xi, t)) \le 0. \tag{1.18}$$

(ii) If we let the system evolve freely during δ, the optimal cost is bounded from above by the sum of the running cost from t to $t + \delta$, and of the optimal cost from time $t + \delta$ on:

$$\Phi(x, t) \le E\left(\int_t^{t+\delta} f(y(s)) e^{-\alpha(s-t)} \, ds + \Phi(y(t + \delta), t + \delta) e^{-\alpha\delta} \right). \tag{1.19}$$

We expand the r.h.s. of (1.19) using (1.13). We obtain

$$\Phi(x, t) \le \Phi(x, t) + \delta A\Phi + \delta \frac{\partial \Phi}{\partial t} + \delta f(x) + o(\delta) \tag{1.20}$$

where

$$A\Phi = \sum_{i,j} a_{ij}(x, t) \frac{\partial^2 \Phi}{\partial x_i \partial x_j} + b(x, t) \cdot \nabla\Phi - \alpha\Phi. \tag{1.21}$$

Taking the limit when δ goes to zero, we get

$$\frac{\partial \Phi}{\partial t} + A\Phi + f \geq 0. \tag{1.22}$$

Since once of the two possible decisions has to be taken, one of the inequalities (1.18) or (1.22) should be an equality.

It follows that the value function obeys the following parabolic equation, the QVI:

$$\min\left(\frac{\partial \Phi}{\partial t} + A\Phi + f, M\Phi - \Phi\right) = 0 \quad \text{in } \mathbb{R}^n \tag{1.23}$$

with

$$M\Phi(x, t) = \inf_{\xi} \left(c(\xi) + \Phi(x + \xi, t)\right) \tag{1.24}$$

and A is defined in (1.21).

Moreover, the final condition (1.17) has to be satisfied.

In the infinite horizon model, the optimal cost function $\Phi(x)$ from 0 to ∞, conditional on the level $y(0) = x$, is the solution of the elliptic QVI:

$$\min(A\Phi + f, M\Phi - \Phi) = 0. \tag{1.25}$$

In the deterministic case ($\sigma = 0$), the operator A reduces to the first-order operator

$$A\Phi = b \cdot \nabla\Phi - \alpha\Phi. \tag{1.26}$$

1.4 Boundary Conditions

When the matrix σ is not degenerated (i.e., $\sigma\sigma^T \geq \lambda I$, where $\lambda > 0$ and I is the identity matrix), the state process $y(t)$ can take any value in $\mathbb{R}^n$. If $y(t)$ is constrained to be in a specific domain $\mathcal{O} \subset \mathbb{R}^n$, we have two possibilities:

(i) Either keep the state equation (1.2) or (1.4) but replace the horizon T with $T \wedge \tau$ in (1.7) or (1.8), where τ is the first exit time of the domain, and add a stopping cost $(g(y(\tau))e^{-\alpha\tau})\chi_{\tau < T}$ (e.g., in some financial problems, τ can be interpreted as a bankruptcy time).

In the case of continuous control, the value function is then the solution of equations (1.15)–(1.17) in $\mathcal{O}$ with the Dirichlet boundary condition

$$\Phi(x, t) = g \qquad \text{for } x \in \partial\mathcal{O} \tag{1.27}$$

where $\partial\mathcal{O}$ is the boundary of the domain $\mathcal{O}$.

In the case of impulse control, the boundary condition for the QVI (1.25) is

$$\min(\Phi - g, M\Phi - \Phi) = 0 \qquad \text{on } \partial\mathcal{O}. \tag{1.28}$$

(ii) Or model the state $y(t)$ as a reflected diffusion process

$$dy(t) = b(y(t), t) \, dt + \sigma(y(t), t) \, dW(t) + v(y(t)) \, d\xi(t) \tag{1.29}$$

where $v(x)$ is the inner normal vector of $\mathcal{O}$ at point x and $\xi(t)$ is an increasing scalar process ($d\xi \geq 0$), strictly increasing on the boundary of $\mathcal{O}$. In other words, when $y(t)$ reaches the boundary, it is reflected inside $\mathcal{O}$ in the direction of v. In this case, a penalizing cost of the form $\int_t^T \rho(y(s), s) \, d\xi(s)$ has to be added to the cost function (1.7) or (1.8). The value function for the continuous control problem is then the solution of equations (1.15)–(1.17) with the Neumann boundary condition

$$\rho + v \cdot \nabla\Phi = 0 \qquad \text{on } \partial\mathcal{O}. \tag{1.30}$$

For the impulse control problem, the boundary condition for the QVI (1.23) or (1.25) is expressed by

$$\min(\rho + v \cdot \nabla\Phi, M\Phi - \Phi) = 0 \qquad \text{on } \partial\mathcal{O}. \tag{1.31}$$

1.5 Determination of the Optimal Policy

We now have to explain how the optimal policy is obtained. At every time t, the value of the optimal control has to be given as a function of the available information. At time t, the available data are the values of the state and control variables up to time t. A control is called Markovian or obtained by "feedback" if the optimal control value at time t only depends on the state at time t. One basic result of the stochastic control theory is the existence of an optimal control which is Markovian, in the case of complete information [11].

There is a fundamental distinction between deterministic and stochastic control in the role of feedback. In deterministic control, feedback controllers give no lower cost than open-loop controls (which can be obtained by the theory of Pontryagin's maximum principle), but in the stochastic case, we do better by using feedback controls [11].

In the case of continuous control, we define $V(x, t)$ as the function that realizes the infimum in eq. (1.15). The optimal control is thus given by

$$v(t) = V(y(t), t) \tag{1.32}$$

and is Markovian.

For the impulse control problem, we must decide at every time t whether an impulse has to be exerted, and if necessary, the size of the impulse.

We define the continuation set as

$$\mathscr{C} = \left\{ (x, s), \Phi(x, s) < \inf_{\xi} (c(\xi) + \Phi(x + \xi, s)) \right\}.$$

Let us denote by $\hat{\xi}(x, s)$ a function that realizes the infimum in the above expression, for fixed (x, s), that is,

$$\inf_{\xi} (c(\xi) + \Phi(x + \xi, s)) = c(\hat{\xi}(x, s)) + \Phi(x + \hat{\xi}(x, s), s). \tag{1.33}$$

The optimal impulse control is constructed as follows. Let us start at point $(y(t), t)$. Two situations are possible:

(i) If $(y(t), t) \in \mathscr{C}$, the optimal policy is to let the system evolve freely. Let θ_1 be the first time the trajectory reaches the boundary of the continuation set. This is the first impulse time. The state is then $y(\theta_1^-)$. The size of the impulse is given by $\hat{\xi}(y(\theta_1^-), \theta_1)$. Hence

$$y(\theta_1) = y(\theta_1^-) + \hat{\xi}(y(\theta_1), \theta_1). \tag{1.34}$$

Note that the point $(y(\theta_1), \theta_1)$ is back in the continuation set.

The same procedure is carried over from now on. We can define in this way, by induction, the sequence of optimal (θ_i) and (ξ_i), $i \geq 1$.

(ii) If $(y(t), t) \notin \mathscr{C}$, an impulse of size $\hat{\xi}(y(t), t)$ has to be exerted immediately. We then proceed as above.

1.6 Remarks

1. Note that the QVI (1.23) or (1.25) is no more than the dynamic programming equation with a control variable v belonging to the discrete set $\{0, 1\}$. If $v = 1$, an impulse is exerted; if $v = 0$, the system evolves as a pure diffusion process. It follows that the numerical algorithms for solving the HJB equations can be easily adapted to QVIs.

2. The main problem in the formulation of optimal control problems in continuous time is the regularity of solutions. In general, the value function Φ is not C^2, and straightforward application of Ito's formula in (1.13)

is not mathematically rigorous. The theory of viscosity solutions [9] has filled this regularity gap: although the value function Φ does not in general have the desired regularity, it is always characterized as a generalized solution, called viscosity solution, of the associated partial differential problem in some weak sense, and is uniquely determined. In the next section, existence, uniqueness, and regularity results for the solutions of the QVIs associated with impulse control problems are stated.

Note that the continuous problem can be interpreted as a limit of discrete problems of control of Markov chains. This is the usual approach for numerical analysis of dynamic programming equations. The important concept is then the "maximum principle."

2 Study of the QVIs Associated with Impulse Control Problems

2.1 Historical Comments

The formulation of impulse control problems in terms of QVIs is given by Bensoussan and Lions [6]. The terminology comes from an analogy with the variational inequality (VI) problem, which can be stated as follows:

$$\min(Au + f, \psi - u) = 0 \quad \text{in } \mathcal{O} \subset \mathbb{R}^n \text{ (or } \mathcal{O} \times \,]0, T[\text{ in the evolution case),}$$
$$(2.1)$$

where A is a second-order differential operator (elliptic or parabolic) and ψ is called an obstacle.

The VIs were first introduced to solve problems of potential theory and mechanical problems, and then extended to the treatment of optimal stopping time problems. In the latter case, ψ represents a cost attached to the stopping of the system. Consider now the QVI

$$\min(Au + f, Mu - u) = 0 \quad \text{in } \mathcal{O},$$
$$(2.2)$$

with boundary conditions of Neumann or Dirichlet type, depending on whether the process is reflected or stopped on the boundary $\partial \mathcal{O}$. Here, the obstacle is Mu, where M is a nonlinear increasing operator. The obstacle is thus implicit, since it depends on the solution. This explains the terminology of QVIs.

Two kinds of methods have been used in the study of QVI (2.2):

(i) The classical variational approach used by Bensoussan and Lions [6], which leads to a weak formulation of the QVI (2.2) and requires less regularity for the solution. Let $a(u, v)$ be the continuous bilinear form associated to the operator A, defined on an appropriate Hilbert space V. The variational formulation of (2.2) is

Find $u \in V$ such that $u \leq Mu$,

$$a(u, v - u) + \int_{\mathcal{O}} f \cdot (v - u) \, dx \leq 0, \qquad \forall v \in V, v \leq Mu. \tag{2.3}$$

The methods consists in finding a fixed point of a map defined by a VI by using the monotonicity properties of the operator M:

$M\varphi_1 \geq M\varphi_2$ whenever $\varphi_1 \geq \varphi_2$ (pointwise).

Indeed, let $\psi = T(\varphi)$ be the solution of the VI

$$a(\psi, v - \psi) + \int_{\mathcal{O}} f \cdot (v - \psi) \, dx \leq 0, \qquad \forall v \in V, v \leq M\varphi, \psi \leq M\varphi. \tag{2.4}$$

The solution u of the QVI (2.3) is a fixed point of the map T. The next step is the study of the regularity of the weak solution u.

(ii) The more recent approach of search of "viscosity solutions." The main properties that motivate the introduction of viscosity solutions are the stability and the uniqueness of these solutions, and the direct link with the control problem. They were introduced for first-order HJB equations by Crandall and Lions [10] and extended to first-order QVIs in Barles [2]; indeed, viscosity solutions need not be differentiable everywhere and thus are not sensitive to the classical problem of the crossing of characteristics. The only regularity required is continuity. The concept of viscosity solutions was extended to second-order QVIs in [14, 20, 9], and used to establish uniqueness and existence theorems for a wide class of HJB equations and QVIs.

2.2   Some Definitions of Functional Spaces

Let $\mathcal{O}$ be an open set of $\mathbb{R}^n$ endowed with the Lebesgue measure dx. We recall some useful definitions of functional spaces [7]:

$$L^p(\mathcal{O}) = \left\{ u \text{ measurable on } \mathcal{O} \text{ and } \int_{\mathcal{O}} |u|^p \, dx < \infty \right\}, \qquad 1 \leq p < \infty.$$

$$L^\infty(\mathcal{O}) = \{ u \text{ measurable on } \mathcal{O} \text{ and } \exists C > 0, |u(x)| \leq C \text{ a.e. in } \mathcal{O} \}.$$

$$C^k(\mathcal{O}) = \{ k\text{-times continuously differentiable functions on } \mathcal{O} \}, \qquad k \in N.$$

$C(\mathcal{O}) = \{\text{continuous functions on } \mathcal{O}\}.$

$$C^{0,\alpha}(\overline{\mathcal{O}}) = \left\{ u \in C(\mathcal{O}), \ \sup_{x \neq y \in \mathcal{O}} \frac{|u(x) - u(y)|}{|x - y|^\alpha} < \infty \right\}, \qquad 0 < \alpha < 1.$$

$C^{k,\alpha}(\overline{\mathcal{O}}) = \{ u \in C^k(\mathcal{O}), \ D^j u \in C^{0,\alpha}(\overline{\mathcal{O}}), \ \forall j, \ |j| \leq k \}.$

where

$$D^\alpha u = \frac{\partial^{\alpha_1 + \alpha_2 + \cdots + \alpha_n}}{\partial^{\alpha_1} x_1 \cdot \partial^{\alpha_2} x_2 \cdot \cdots \cdot \partial^{\alpha_n} x_n} u, \qquad |\alpha| = \sum_{i=1}^n \alpha_i.$$

Moreover, we shall use the Sobolev spaces:

$$W^{1,p}(\mathcal{O}) = \left\{ u \in L^p(\mathcal{O}), \frac{\partial u}{\partial x_i} \in L^p(\mathcal{O}), \forall i = 1, 2, \ldots, n \right\}, \quad 1 \leq p \leq \infty$$

$$W^{2,p}(\mathcal{O}) = \left\{ u \in L^p(\mathcal{O}), \frac{\partial u}{\partial x_i} \in L^p(\mathcal{O}), \frac{\partial^2 u}{\partial x_i \partial x_j} \in L^p(\mathcal{O}), \forall i, j = 1, \ldots, n \right\},$$
$$1 \leq p \leq \infty.$$

2.3 Second Order Elliptic QVIs

Here we present some existence, uniqueness and regularity results for the solutions of elliptic QVIs and then give the interpretation of the solution as the optimal cost function of an associated impulse control problem.

2.3.1 Elliptic QVIs in $\mathbb{R}^n$. We consider the QVI

$$\min(Au + f, Mu - u) = 0 \qquad \text{in } \mathbb{R}^n \tag{2.5}$$

where A is a second-order differential operator defined by

$$Au = \sum_{i,j=1}^n a_{ij}(x) \frac{\partial^2 u}{\partial x_i \partial x_j} + \sum_{i=1}^n b_i(x) \frac{\partial u}{\partial x_i} - \lambda(x) u, \tag{2.6}$$

and M is an operator given by

$$Mu(x) = k + \inf_{\xi \geq 0} \{ C_0(\xi) + u(x + \xi) \} \tag{2.7}$$

where $k > 0$ is fixed, and $\xi \geq 0$ means $\xi = (\xi_1, \ldots, \xi_n)$ with $\xi_i \geq 0$.

The main result is that in the case of nondegenerate diffusion processes —that is, when the operator A is uniformly elliptic—equation (2.5) has a unique solution in $W^{2,\infty}(\mathbb{R}^n)$, that is, the solution has its first and second derivatives bounded and satisfies the QVI (2.5) almost everywhere in $\mathbb{R}^n$. A consequence is that the solution is continuously differentiable. This is proved in [18] under a set of assumptions that are detailed below.

THEOREM 1. *Suppose that*

- $a_{ij}, b_i, \lambda,$ *and* $f \in W^{2,\infty}(\mathbb{R}^n)$, $\qquad$ (2.8)

- $\exists v > 0, \sum_{i,j=1}^{n} a_{ij}\xi_i\xi_j \geq v|\xi|^2, \forall \xi \in \mathbb{R}^n$ *(ellipticity condition)*, $\qquad$ (2.9)

- $\exists \lambda_0 > 0, \forall x \in \mathbb{R}^n, \lambda(x) \geq \lambda_0$, $\qquad$ (2.10)

   C_0 *is a continuous, nonnegative function such that* $C_0(0) = 0$,

- *Moreover* C_0 *is subadditive, that is,* $\qquad$ (2.11)

   $C_0(\xi_1 + \xi_2) \leq C_0(\xi_1) + C_0(\xi_2), \forall \xi_1, \xi_2 \in \mathbb{R}^{n+}$.

Then the QVI (2.5) has a unique solution in $W^{2,\infty}(\mathbb{R}^n)$.

2.3.2 The Dirichlet Problem for the Elliptic QVI. Consider now the QVI

$$\min(Au + f, Mu - u) = 0 \qquad \text{in } \mathcal{O} \qquad (2.12)$$

where $\mathcal{O}$ is a bounded, connected, and smooth open set of $\mathbb{R}^n$, with the Dirichlet boundary condition

$$u/\partial\mathcal{O} = \Phi \qquad (2.13)$$

or

$$u/\partial\mathcal{O} = \min(\Phi, Mu). \qquad (2.14)$$

The operator M is defined by

$$Mu(x) = k + \inf_{\substack{\xi \geq 0 \\ x+\xi \in \overline{\mathcal{O}}}} \{C_0(\xi) + u(x + \xi)\}. \qquad (2.15)$$

We suppose that

$$\exists \alpha \in \,]0, 1[, \, a_{ij} \in C^{2,\alpha}(\overline{\mathcal{O}}), \, b_i \in C^{0,\alpha}(\overline{\mathcal{O}}), \, \lambda \in C^{0,\alpha}(\overline{\mathcal{O}}), \, f \in C^{0,\alpha}(\overline{\mathcal{O}}). \qquad (2.16)$$

In order to get the $W^{2,\infty}(\mathcal{O})$ regularity of the solution up to the boundary, we have to make some additional assumptions on the domain $\mathcal{O}$ and the boundary data. Namely, we suppose

$$C_0(\xi) \in W^{2,\infty}(\mathbb{R}^n), \tag{2.17}$$

$$\Phi \in C^{2,\alpha}(\partial \mathcal{O}). \tag{2.18}$$

Moreover, we set

$$M_0 \Phi(x) = k + \inf_{\substack{\xi \geq 0 \\ x+\xi \in \partial \mathcal{O}}} \{C_0(\xi) + \Phi(x + \xi)\} \tag{2.19}$$

and assume that

$$M_0 \Phi \in W^{2,\infty}(\mathcal{O}). \tag{2.20}$$

THEOREM 2. *We suppose* (2.9), (2.10), (2.11), (2.16), (2.17), (2.18), *and* (2.20). *Then, the solution u of the QVI* (2.12)–(2.14) *is unique and belongs to* $W^{2,\infty}(\mathcal{O})$.

As a consequence, u is continuously differentiable. The assumption (2.20) may be automatically satisfied if the domain $\mathcal{O}$ has some geometric properties—for example, if $\mathcal{O}$ is strictly convex [20].

Remark 1. In general, the QVI (2.2) with the boundary condition (2.13) has no solution because we do not know a priori whether $Mu \geq \Phi$ on $\partial \mathcal{O}$. We thus have to assume the existence of a subsolution $\underline{u}$ satisfying $M\underline{u} \geq \Phi \geq \underline{u}$ on $\partial \mathcal{O}$. In this case, the QVI (2.12)–(2.13) has a unique solution in $W^{2,\infty}(\mathcal{O})$.

Remark 2. In the case of a Neumann boundary condition, we have the local regularity result: $u \in W_{loc}^{2,p}(\mathcal{O})$, $\forall p \geq 2$, $p < \infty$ (see [2] and [9]). This also implies that the solution is continuously differentiable.

2.3.3 The Degenerate Case in $\mathbb{R}^n$. Since many applications of optimal stochastic control concern degenerate problems, we consider now the QVI (2.5) in the general situation of a possibly degenerate diffusion process—that is, when the condition (2.9) is not satisfied [19]. We suppose that λ is a positive constant.

THEOREM 3. *Suppose that*

$$a_{ij}, b_i, f \text{ belong to } W^{2,\infty}(\mathbb{R}^n) \text{ and are bounded in } W^{2,\infty}(\mathbb{R}^n). \tag{2.21}$$

Then, $\exists \lambda_0$ such that if $\lambda > \lambda_0$,

(i) *the solution u of the QVI (2.5) is semiconcave, that is, u is continuous and* $u(x) - \frac{1}{2}C|x|^2$ *is concave for some constant* $C > 0$ *and*

(ii) $Au \in L^\infty(\mathbb{R}^n)$.

Remark 3. The constant λ_0 is computed explicitly in [14].

2.4 The Associated Stochastic Impulse Control Problem

The purpose here is to give the stochastic interpretation of u, the solution of the QVI (2.12)–(2.13), in terms of control of diffusion processes. Let $(\Omega, \mathcal{F}, \mathcal{F}_t, P, W_t)$ be a standard space composed by a probability space $(\Omega, \mathcal{F}, P)$ with a right-continuous increasing filtration of complete sub-σ algebra $\mathcal{F}_t$ and a Brownian motion W_t in $\mathbb{R}^n$, $\mathcal{F}^t$-adapted. (It is important to think of $\mathcal{F}^t$ as measuring the information available at time t).

For any sequence $\theta_0 = 0 < \theta_1 < \theta_2 < \cdots < \theta_i < \cdots$, $\theta_i \to_{i \to \infty}^{+\infty}$ of $\mathcal{F}^t$-stopping times and $\xi_1, \ldots, \xi_i, \ldots$ of $\mathcal{F}^{\theta_i}$-measurable random variables with values in $\mathbb{R}^{n+}$, we can define by induction

$$\begin{cases} dy_x^i(t) = b(y_x^i(t)) \, dt + \sigma(y_x^i(t)) \, dW_t & \text{for } \theta_{i-1} \le t \le \theta_i, \\ y_x^i(\theta_{i-1}) = y_x^{i-1}(\theta_{i-1}) + \xi_{i-1}, \\ y_x^0(0) = x, \, \xi_0 = 0, \end{cases} \tag{2.22}$$

where

$$b = (b_i)_{i=1\cdots n} \quad \text{and} \quad \tfrac{1}{2}\sigma\sigma^T = a \quad (\text{matrix } (a_{ij})_{i,j=1\cdots n}). \tag{2.23}$$

We set

$$y_x(t) = y_t = y_x^i(t), \qquad \theta_i \le t < \theta_{i+1}. \tag{2.24}$$

We shall say that a control $V = (\theta_i, \xi_i)_{i \ge 1}$ is admissible if $y_x(\theta_i) \in \bar{\mathcal{O}}$ whenever $y_x^{i-1}(\theta_i) \in \bar{\mathcal{O}}$. We then define the cost function

$$J_x(V) = E^x \left(\int_0^\tau f(y_x(t)) e^{-\lambda t} \, dt + \sum_{\substack{i \ge 1 \\ \theta_i \le 2}} (k + C_0(\xi_i)) e^{-\lambda \theta_i} + \Phi(y_x(\tau)) e^{-\lambda \tau} \right)$$

$$\tag{2.25}$$

where τ is defined by

$$\tau = \inf\{t \ge 0, \, y_x(t) \notin \bar{\mathcal{O}}\}. \tag{2.26}$$

We thus have the main result:

THEOREM 4. *The solution of the* QVI (2.12)–(2.13) *is the optimal cost function*

$$u(x) = \inf_{V \text{ adm.}} J_x(V).$$ (2.27)

Moreover, there is an optimal impulse control.

Note that the change of boundary data from (2.13) to (2.14) does not induce any change on the optimal cost function (see [21]).

Remark 4. The case of a vanishing discount factor α is studied in [17, 15, 23, 22]. As usual in control theory, the asymptotic behavior of αu when α goes to 0 is related to the optimal ergodic cost.

2.5 Parabolic QVIs

We now turn to the evolution case of parabolic QVIs. The additional difficulty arises from the dependence on t of the unknown function u. The treatment of this problem can be found in [6] and [9].

Consider the parabolic QVI

$$\begin{cases} \min\left(\dfrac{\partial u}{\partial t} + Au + f, \, Mu - u\right) = 0 & \text{in } Q = \mathcal{O} \times \,]0, T[, \\[2mm] u/\partial\mathcal{O} = 0, \\[2mm] u(T) = 0, \end{cases}$$ (2.28)

where A and M are given by (2.6) and (2.7).

THEOREM 5. *Suppose that the functions a_{ij}, b_i, λ, C_0 are time-independent and satisfy (2.16) and (2.9). Moreover, suppose*

- $f(\cdot, t) \in C^{0,\alpha}(\overline{\mathcal{O}})$,

- $f(x, \cdot) \in C^{0,\alpha/2}([0, T]))$, (2.29)

- $f(x, t + h) \leq f(x, t), \, \forall h \geq 0$,

- $\gamma(x) \in W^{2,\infty}(\mathcal{O})$, (2.30)

where

$$\gamma(x) = k + \inf_{\substack{\xi \geq 0 \\ x + \xi \in \overline{0}}} C_0(\xi), \qquad x \in \overline{\mathcal{O}}.$$ (2.31)

Then, there exists a unique solution u of the parabolic QVI *(2.28) such that* $u \in W^{2,1,p}(Q)$, $\forall p$, $p \geq 2$, $p < \infty$ *and* $\frac{\partial u}{\partial t} + Au \in L^{\infty}(Q)$.

(In $W^{2,1,p}(Q)$, the first superscript refers to the state variable and the second to the time variable.)

Moreover, the solution of the QVI (2.28) can be interpreted as above, as the optimal cost function of an impulse control problem over a finite horizon.

2.6 First-Order QVIs and Deterministic Impulse Control Problems

Let us now turn to the study of first-order QVIs that are related to deterministic impulse control problems [2], [16].

We consider the first-order QVI

$$\min(H(x, u, \nabla u), Mu - u) = 0 \qquad \text{in } \mathbb{R}^n \tag{2.32}$$

where

$$H(x, u, \nabla u) = b \cdot \nabla u - \lambda u + f \tag{2.33}$$

and

$$Mu(x) = k + \inf_{\xi \geq 0} \{C_0(\xi) + u(x + \xi)\}. \tag{2.34}$$

We suppose

$$(b_i)_{i=1 \cdots n}, f \in W^{1,\infty}(\mathbb{R}^n) \tag{2.35}$$

where b_i is the ith component of the drif term b.

The deterministic impulse control problem associated with (2.32) is defined as follows:

The state of the controlled system is given by

$$\begin{cases} \dfrac{dy_x}{dt}(t) = b(y_x(t)) & \text{for } t \in]\theta_i, \theta_{i+1}[\quad \text{for all } i \in \mathbb{N}, \\[2mm] y_x(0) = x, \\[2mm] y_x(\theta_i) = y_x(\theta_i^-) + \xi_i, \end{cases} \tag{2.36}$$

where $\theta = (\theta_i)_{i \in \mathbb{N}}$ is a nondecreasing sequence of positive reals satisfying $\theta_i \to +\infty$ when $i \to +\infty$ and $(\xi_i)_{i \in \mathbb{N}}$ is a sequence of elements of $\mathbb{R}^{n+}$.

The Lipschitz property of b implies the existence and uniqueness of a solution $y_x(t)$ of (2.36). The optimal cost function u is defined by

$$u(x) = \inf_{(\theta_i, \xi_i)_{i \in \mathbb{N}}} \int_0^\infty f(y_x(t)) e^{-\lambda t} \, dt + \sum_{i \in \mathbb{N}} (k + C_0(\xi_i)) e^{-\lambda \theta_i}. \tag{2.37}$$

2.6.1   Viscosity Solutions for First-Order QVIs   In general, QVI (2.32) has no continuously differentiable solution, and we shall thus use here the concept of "viscosity solution," since the only regularity required for these functions is continuity. The optimal cost function (2.37) is then characterized as the unique viscosity solution of the QVI (2.32).

We recall that a function u from $\mathcal{O}$ to $\mathbb{R}$ is differentiable at $y_0 \in \mathcal{O}$ and that $Du(y_0) = p_0 \in \mathbb{R}^n$ if we have

$$u(y) = u(y_0) + p_0 \cdot (y - y_0) + o(|y - y_0|). \tag{2.38}$$

Obviously (2.38) is the conjunction of the two relations

$$\limsup_{y \to y_0} (u(y) - u(y_0) - p_0 \cdot (y - y_0))(|y - y_0|)^{-1} \leq 0 \tag{2.39}$$

and

$$\liminf_{y \to y_0} (u(y) - u(y_0) - p_0 \cdot (y - y_0))|y - y_0|^{-1} \geq 0. \tag{2.40}$$

If u is continuous, it may fail to be differentiable at every $y_0 \in \mathcal{O}$. Nevertheless, there are many choices of $(y_0, p_0) \in \mathcal{O} \times \mathbb{R}^n$ for which inequality (2.39) or (2.40) holds.

Then the superdifferential (resp. the subdifferential) of u at point y_0 is the set, denoted by $D^+ u(y_0)$ (resp. $D^- u(y_0)$) of $p_0 \in \mathbb{R}^n$ such that (2.39) (resp. 2.40) holds.

We denote by $BUC(\mathbb{R}^n)$ the space of bounded and uniformly continuous functions on $\mathbb{R}^n$.

DEFINITION. $u \in BUC(\mathbb{R}^n)$ *is a viscosity solution of the* QVI (2.32) *if*

$$\forall y \in \mathbb{R}^n, \forall p \in D^+ u(y), \min(H(y, u(y), p), Mu - u) \geq 0,$$
$$\forall y \in \mathbb{R}^n, \forall p \in D^- u(y), \min(H(y, u(y), p), Mu - u) \leq 0. \tag{2.41}$$

Let us give another definition that is more practical in particular to show uniqueness results.

PROPOSITION. $u \in BUC(\mathbb{R}^n)$ *is a viscosity solution of the* QVI (2.32) *if and only if the two following properties hold:*
If $\forall \Phi \in C^1(\mathbb{R}^n)$, at each local maximum point x_0 of $u - \Phi$, we have

$$\min(H(x_0, u(x_0), D\Phi(x_0)), Mu(x_0) - u(x_0)) \geq 0, \qquad (2.42)$$

If $\forall \Phi \in C^1(\mathbb{R}^n)$, at each local minimum point x_0 of $u - \Phi$, we have

$$\min(H(x_0, u(x_0), D\Phi(x_0)), Mu(x_0) - u(x_0)) \leq 0. \qquad (2.43)$$

We have the following theorem:

THEOREM 6.   *Suppose that assumptions (2.11) and (2.35) are satisfied. Then there exists a unique viscosity solution of the problem (2.32) in* $\mathrm{BUC}(\mathbb{R}^n)$.

Remark 5.   The concept of viscosity solution gives a notion of a generalized solution of (2.32) that is requested to be only continuous in $\mathcal{O}$. Moreover, this notion is stable with respect to the topology of uniform convergence over compact sets. If u is C^1 (i.e., continuously differentiable), then the viscosity solution coincides with the usual strong solution.

The definition of viscosity solutions can easily be extended to problems with unbounded data, since only local properties are used here.

2.6.2   Characterization of the Optimal Cost Function   We have the following main result [2]:

THEOREM 7.   *Under assumptions (2.11) and (2.35), the optimal cost function $u(x)$ defined in (2.37) is the unique viscosity solution of the QVI (2.32) in* $\mathrm{BUC}(\mathbb{R}^n)$.

Regularity and asymptotic properties of the optimal cost function

• $\exists \lambda_0 > 0$ such that if $\lambda > \lambda_0$, then $u \in W^{1,\infty}(\mathbb{R}^n)$ and satisfies the QVI (2.32) almost everywhere in $\mathbb{R}^n$. (The constant λ_0 is given in [2].)

This is a consequence of the fact that the QVI (2.32) holds at each differentiability point of u.

• Suppose $C_0(\xi) \to +\infty$ when $|\xi| \to +\infty$ and $f(x) \to l$ when $|x| \to +\infty$. Then $u(x) \to \frac{l}{\lambda}$ when $|x| \to +\infty$.

• The optimal cost $u(x)$ can also be characterized as the maximal subsolution of the QVI (2.32) [16].

3   Explicit Solution of QVIs Arising in Inventory Control Problems

Inventory control theory provides typical examples of application of impulse control theory. In this section, we formulate the inventory control problem in terms of an impulse control problem and give two examples to illustrate the use of quasi-variational techniques. The first example concerns a one-product inventory system subject to a demand modelized by a diffusion process. The second example deals with a deterministic two-product system subject to economies of joint ordering. The optimal (s, S) policy is obtained in the one-dimensional case. In the two-dimensional problem, the exact construction of the boundary of the continuation set leads to the optimal ordering policy. In both cases, the method consists in solving the QVI satisfied by the optimal cost and requiring maximal regularity for the solution.

3.1   The Inventory Control Problem

We analyze the optimal ordering policy for a n-product inventory system. We denote by $D(s, t)$ the cumulative demand over the period (s, t) and we model $D(s, t)$ as

$$D(s, t) = \int_s^t g(\theta) \, d\theta - \int_s^t \sigma(\theta) \, dW(\theta) \tag{3.1}$$

where W is a n-dimensional Wiener process and σ is an $n \times n$ diagonal matrix. The function g represents the deterministic trend, and the stochastic integral models the random part of the demand.

We assume that we can observe the evolution of the process $W(t)$, which is the only source of uncertainties of the problem. The ordering times $\theta_1 \le \theta_2 \le \cdots \le \theta_i \le \cdots$ are stopping times with respect to the filtration $\mathscr{F}^t = \sigma(W(s), s \le t)$, and the corresponding orders ξ_i are $\mathscr{F}^{\theta_i}$-measurable. The set V formed by the sequence of θ_i and ξ_i is an impulse control. We restrict ourselves here to the case of positive controls ξ_i.

We denote by $c(\xi)$ the ordering cost for a quantity of stock ξ. We suppose that delivery is instantaneous. The case of time lag in delivery is studied in [24] in the case of discrete time and in [1] in the case of continuous time.

We suppose that unfilled demand is backlogged, and that there are no constraints on the state variable $y(t)$, ($y(t) \in \mathbb{R}^n$). The inventory level $y(t)$ is thus solution of the stochastic differential equation

$$dy(s) = -g(s) \, ds + \sigma(s) \, dW(s) + \sum_{i \ge 1} \xi_i \delta(s - \theta_i), \quad y(0) = x. \tag{3.2}$$

We seek an ordering policy $V = (\theta_i, \xi_i)_{i \ge 1}$ that minimizes the expected discounted total cost $J(V)$ over an infinite horizon, where future costs are discounted at interest rate $\alpha > 0$. This cost functional is the sum of an integral cost attached to the evolution of the stock and the ordering costs:

$$J(V) = E\left(\int_0^\infty e^{-\alpha s}f(y(s))\,ds + \sum_{i \geq 1} c(\xi_i)e^{-\alpha\theta_i}\right) \tag{3.3}$$

The function $f(y)$ represents either the storage or the shortage penalty cost rate, depending on the sign of the components of y. We suppose that the function f is convex.

We know that the value function

$$u(x) = \inf_V \{J(V), y(0) = x\} \tag{3.4}$$

is the solution of the QVI

$$\min(Au + f, Mu - u) = 0 \quad \text{in } \mathbb{R}^n \tag{3.5}$$

where

$$Au = \tfrac{1}{2}tr(D^2u\sigma\sigma^T) - g\cdot\nabla u - \alpha u, \tag{3.6}$$

and

$$Mu = \inf_\xi \{c(\xi) + u(x + \xi)\}. \tag{3.7}$$

(D^2u denotes the matrix of the second derivatives of u.)

Remark. The treatment of excess demand is important. When excess demand is lost, the evolution of the inventory level can be modeled by a reflected diffusion process. We have the constraint $y(t) \in \bar{\mathcal{O}}$, where $\mathcal{O}$ is a open set of $\mathbb{R}^n$, and the evolution of $y(t)$ is given by

$$dy(s) = -g(s)\,ds + \sigma(s)\,dW(s) + v(y(s))\,d\eta(s) + \sum_{i \geq 1} \xi_i\delta(s - \theta_i). \tag{3.8}$$

The term $v(y(s))$ can be interpreted as the lost demand at time s. The cost functional is then

$$J(V) = E\left(\int_0^\infty e^{-\alpha s}f(y(s))\,ds + \sum_{i \geq 1} c(\xi_i)e^{-\alpha\theta_i} + \int_0^\infty e^{-\alpha s}p(y(s))\,d\eta(s)\right) \tag{3.9}$$

where $\rho(y(s))\,d\eta(s)$ is the penalizing cost resulting from lost demand in a time period ds.

In this case, the value function is the solution of the QVI (3.5) with the Neumann boundary condition

$$\min(\rho + v \cdot \nabla u, Mu - u) = 0. \tag{3.10}$$

The inventory state space is divided into two regions: the continuation set $\mathscr{C} = \{x \in \mathbb{R}^n, u(x) < Mu(x)\}$, where the system evolves freely according to the equation $Au + f = 0$, and its complement $\Omega = \{x \in \mathbb{R}^n, u(x) = Mu(x)\}$, which corresponds to the states where an order is placed. As long as the system evolves in the continuation set, no order should be made. When the system reaches the boundary of the continuation set, it is the right time to order.

We are facing here a free-boundary problem because the boundary of $\mathscr{C}$ is one of the unknowns of (3.5). This boundary is reduced to one point in the one-dimensional problem, and to a curve in $\mathbb{R}^2$ for the two-product case.

3.2 A One-Dimensional Diffusion Inventory System

We consider the one-product case, $y \in \mathbb{R}$. We suppose that the ordering cost consists of a fixed setup cost $k > 0$ and a constant unit purchase cost $C \geq 0$ proportional to the amount ordered. The storage and penalty cost rate is given by $-px$ if $p \leq 0$ and qx if $q \geq 0$. We suppose that the mean demand g and the diffusion term σ in (3.2) are positive constants.

In this model, the optimal ordering policy is of the (s, S) form: when the stock level decays below a critical level s, an order is placed that brings the stock up to an optimal level S. As long as the stock exceeds s, no order is placed (see [26]).

The existence of an optimal ordering policy of the (s, S) type was proved by Scarf [24] for a discrete time model and by Constantidines and Richard [8] in the case of continuous time. Here the aim is to compute this policy explicitly by solving the QVI

$$\min(Au + f, Mu - u) = 0 \qquad \text{in } \mathbb{R} \tag{3.11}$$

where A and M are given by

$$Au(x) = \frac{1}{2}\sigma^2 \frac{d^2u}{dx^2} - g\frac{du}{dx} - \alpha u, \tag{3.12}$$

$$Mu(x) = k + \inf_{\xi \geq 0} (C\xi + u(x + \xi)). \tag{3.13}$$

3.3 Solution of the QVI

In Ω that is, for $x \leq s$,

$$u(x) = k + \inf_{\xi \geq 0} (C\xi + u(x + \xi)) \tag{3.14}$$

$$= k + C(S - x) + u(S). \tag{3.15}$$

We look for a continuously differentiable solution of the QVI (3.11). Continuity of the derivative of u at the boundary point s is expressed by

$$du(s)/dx = -C. \tag{3.16}$$

Integration of the equation $Au + f = 0$ with the boundary condition (3.16) then leads to the expression of u in the continuation set in terms of its value $u(s)$ on the boundary:

$$u(x) = \frac{1}{\lambda_1 - \lambda_2} \left[\frac{2}{\sigma^2} \int_s^x f(t)(e^{-\lambda_1(x-t)} - e^{-\lambda_2(x-t)}) \, dt \right.$$

$$\left. + (C - \lambda_2 u(s))e^{-\lambda_1(x-s)} - (C - \lambda_1 u(s))e^{-\lambda_2(x-s)} \right] \quad \text{with} \tag{3.17}$$

$$\lambda_1 = ((g^2 + 2\alpha\sigma^2)^{1/2} - g)/\sigma^2 \quad \text{and} \tag{3.18}$$

$$\lambda_2 = (-(g^2 + 2\alpha\sigma^2)^{1/2} - g)/\sigma^2. \tag{3.19}$$

In addition, the following conditions must be satisfied:

(i) the infimum in (3.14) is achieved at S:

$$du(S)/dx = -C. \tag{3.20}$$

(ii) u is continuous at s:

$$u(S) = u(s) - k - C(S - s). \tag{3.21}$$

(iii) u grows linearly when $x \to +\infty$:

$$\lim_{x \to +\infty} \frac{u(x)}{f(x)} < +\infty. \tag{3.22}$$

Note that s is strictly negative; otherwise, equations (3.20)–(3.22) would imply $s = S$, or equivalently $k = 0$, which contradicts the assumptions.

Equations (3.17) and (3.22) give the optimal cost in terms of s:

For $x \geq 0$,

$$u(x) = \frac{-q}{\alpha}\left(\frac{g}{\alpha} - x\right) + \frac{1}{\lambda_1}\left(C - \frac{p}{\alpha}\right)e^{-\lambda_1(x-s)} + \frac{p+q}{\alpha(\lambda_1 - \lambda_2)}\left(e^{(\lambda_1 - \lambda_2)s} - \frac{\lambda_2}{\lambda_1}\right)e^{-\lambda_1 x}.$$

$$(3.23)$$

For $s \leq x \leq 0$,

$$u(x) = \frac{p}{\alpha}\left(\frac{g}{\alpha} - x\right) + \frac{1}{\lambda_1}\left(C - \frac{p}{\alpha}\right)e^{-\lambda_1(x-s)}$$

$$+ \frac{p+q}{\alpha(\lambda_1 - \lambda_2)}e^{-\lambda_2 s}\left(e^{-\lambda_1(x-s)} - \frac{\lambda_1}{\lambda_2}e^{-\lambda_2(x-s)}\right).$$

$$(3.24)$$

Since x is unbounded from above, the term in $e^{-\lambda_2 x}$ vanishes in the expression of $u(x)$ for $x \geq 0$ in order to satisfy (3.22).

THEOREM. *When S is positive, the optimal policy (s, S) is solution of the system*

$$\begin{cases} S = ((-p + C\alpha)s + \lambda_2^{-1}(p + q)(1 - e^{-\lambda_2 s}) - k\alpha)/(q + C\alpha), \\ e^{\lambda_1 S} = [(-p + C\alpha)e^{\lambda_1 s} + (\lambda_1 - \lambda_2)^{-1}(p + q)(\lambda_1 e^{(\lambda_1 - \lambda_2)s} - \lambda_2)]/(q + C\alpha), \end{cases}$$

$$(3.25)$$

which admits a unique solution if and only if

$$p - \alpha C > 0.$$

$$(3.26)$$

Sketch of the proof. Equations (3.25) are derived from (3.20)–(3.21) where $u(S)$ and $u(s)$ are respectively given by equation (3.23) at the point S and equation (3.24) at the point s.

We define the functions:

$$M(x) = ((-p + C\alpha)x + \lambda_2^{-1}(p + q)(1 - e^{-\lambda_2 x}) - k\alpha)/(q + C\alpha), \qquad (3.27)$$

$$N(x) = ((-p + C\alpha)e^{\lambda_1 x} + (\lambda_1 - \lambda_2)^{-1}(p + q)(\lambda_1 e^{(\lambda_1 - \lambda_2)x} - \lambda_2))/(q + C\alpha),$$

$$(3.28)$$

$$F(x) = e^{\lambda_1 M(x)} - N(x).$$

$$(3.29)$$

Equations (3.25) are thus rewritten in the form $F(s) = 0$. When $p - \alpha C > 0$, the function F is extremal at the points $x_0 = \frac{-1}{\lambda_2} \ln \frac{p - \alpha C}{p + q}$ and $x_1 = \frac{1 - e^{-\lambda_2 x_1}}{\lambda_2} -$

$\frac{k\alpha}{p+q}$ and is negative at these points. Moreover $\lim_{x \to -\infty} F(x) = +\infty$ and $F(0) < 0$. Consequently F has a unique root $s < 0$. We can show that

$$s \leq x_0. \tag{3.30}$$

When $p - \alpha C$ goes to zero, the boundary point s of the continuation set goes to $-\infty$. That means that when the storage cost becomes very small, the entire demand is kept in backlog.

Let us now check the inequalities $Au + f \geq 0$ for $x < s$ and $Mu - u > 0$ for $x \geq s$.

We assume that the necessary condition (3.26) for existence of a solution (s, S) is satisfied. For $x \leq s$, the inequality $Au + f \geq 0$ is equivalent to

$$(p - \alpha C)(s - x) + \frac{p + q}{\lambda_2} e^{-\lambda_2 s} - \frac{p}{\lambda_2} - \frac{C\alpha}{\lambda_1} + Cg \geq 0, \tag{3.31}$$

which is readily obtained from (3.26) and (3.30).

To prove the inequality $Mu - u > 0$ for $x \geq s$, we consider the second derivative of u. Equations (3.23), (3.24), and (3.30) imply $d^2u/dx^2 \leq 0$ for $s \leq x \leq 0$ and $d^2u/dx^2 \geq 0$ for $x \geq 0$.

Consequently, using (3.16) and (3.20), we have $du/dx \leq -C$ for $s \leq x \leq S$ and $du/dx \geq -C$ for $x \geq S$. The infimum in the expression of $Mu(x)$ is thus achieved at the point $\xi = S - x$ for $s \leq x \leq S$ and at $\xi = 0$ for $x \geq S$. This gives

$$Mu(x) = k + C(S - x) + u(S) \quad \text{for } s \leq x \leq S \quad \text{and} \tag{3.32}$$

$$Mu(x) = k + u(x) \quad \text{for } x \geq S. \tag{3.33}$$

The function $Mu - u$ is thus increasing from 0 to k on the interval (s, S) and is equal to the constant k for $x \geq S$. It follows that the strict inequality $Mu - u > 0$ is satisfied for $x > s$. Therefore $u(x)$ is the optimal cost function.

The optimal cost is displayed in Figure 4.1 for $\alpha = 10^{-2}$, $g = 0.2$, $\sigma = 0.6$, $c = 0.85$, $p = 0.12$, $q = 0.08$, $k = 0.14$.

3.3.1 Special Cases

—Deterministic demand. When the demand is determinstic ($\sigma = 0$), the optimal cost u_d in the continuation set is given by

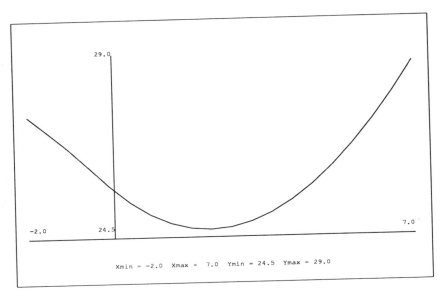

Figure 4.1
Optimal cost as a function of the inventory level

$$u_d(x) = u_d(0)e^{-\alpha x/g} + \frac{r}{\alpha}x + \frac{rg}{\alpha^2}(e^{-\alpha x/g} - 1) \quad \text{with} \tag{3.34}$$

$$r = \begin{cases} q & \text{for } x \geq 0, \\ -p & \text{for } x < 0, \end{cases} \tag{3.35}$$

and

$$u_d(0) = \frac{q + \alpha C}{\alpha^2} \exp\left(\frac{\alpha S_d}{g}\right) - \frac{qg}{\alpha^2}. \tag{3.36}$$

The optimal policy (s_d, S_d) satisfies the following system derived from (3.16), (3.20), and (3.21):

$$\begin{cases} (q + \alpha C)\exp\left(\frac{\alpha S_d}{g}\right) + (p - \alpha C)\exp\left(-\frac{\alpha(q + \alpha C)S_d + \alpha^2 k}{g(p - \alpha C)}\right) - (p + q) = 0, \\ s_d = -\frac{(q + \alpha C)S_d + \alpha k}{p - \alpha C}. \end{cases} \tag{3.37}$$

There exists a unique solution of (3.37) if and only if $p - \alpha C > 0$. Moreover, $S_d > 0$ and $s_d < 0$.

—Limit case of a zero discount factor.

PROPOSITION 1. *When the discount factor α goes to zero, the optimal cost function u solution of the QVI (3.11) behaves like $\mu/\alpha + u_0$. The constant μ represents the optimal average cost per unit time with no discounting of future costs:*

$$\mu = \inf_{(\theta_i, \xi_i)_{i \geq 1}} \lim_{T \to +\infty} \frac{1}{T} E\left(\int_0^T f(x(t)) \, dt + \sum_{\theta_i \leq T} (k + C\xi_i) \right) \tag{3.38}$$

and the function u_0 defined within an additive constant satisfies the QVI

$$\min(\tilde{A}u_0 + f, Mu_0 - u_0) = 0 \quad \text{in } \mathbb{R} \tag{3.39}$$

with

$$\tilde{A}u_0 = \frac{1}{2}\sigma^2 \frac{d^2 u_0}{dx^2} - g\frac{du_0}{dx} - \mu \tag{3.40}$$

and Mu_0 defined in (3.13).

Proof. Proceeding as above, we solve the QVI (3.39) associated with the zero discount factor problem. We obtain a continuously differentiable solution $u_0(x)$ and a constant μ, defined by

$$\mu = qS_0 + \frac{q\sigma^2}{2g} + Cg, \tag{3.41}$$

for $x \leq s_0$,

$$u_0(x) = u_0(s_0) + C(s_0 - x), \tag{3.42}$$

for $s_0 \leq x \leq 0$,

$$u_0(x) = u_0(s_0) - \frac{p}{2g}(x^2 - s_0^2)$$

$$- \frac{\sigma^2}{2g}\left(\frac{\mu}{g} + \frac{p\sigma^2}{2g^2} - C + \frac{ps_0}{g}\right)\left(1 - \exp\left(\frac{2g}{\sigma^2}(x - s_0)\right)\right)$$

$$- \frac{1}{g}\left(\mu + \frac{p\sigma^2}{2g}\right)(x - s_0),$$

for $x \geq 0$,

$$u_0(x) = u(s_0) + \frac{q}{2g}x^2 - \frac{1}{g}\left(\mu - \frac{q\sigma^2}{2g}\right)x + \frac{ps_0^2}{2g} + \frac{1}{g}\left(\mu + \frac{p\sigma^2}{2g}\right)s_0$$

$$+ \frac{\sigma^4}{4g^3}(p + q)(1 - e^{2gs_0/\sigma^2}), \tag{3.44}$$

where the critical levels (s_0, S_0), which define the optimal policy associated with (3.39), are given by

$$\begin{cases} S_0 = \frac{ps_0}{q} - \frac{(p + q)\sigma^2}{2gq}(1 - \exp(2gs_0/\sigma^2)), \\[2mm] (\exp(2gs_0/\sigma^2))\left(\frac{(p + q)\sigma^2}{4g}\exp(2gs_0/\sigma^2) - (p + q)s_0 - \frac{p\sigma^2}{2g}\right) \\[2mm] \quad + \frac{pgs_0^2}{\sigma^2} + ps_0 + \frac{\sigma^2(p - g)}{4g} - \frac{2g^2qk}{(p + q)\sigma^2} = 0. \end{cases} \tag{3.45}$$

Let us now make a Taylor expansion as α goes to zero of the solution $u(x)$ of the QVI (3.11), given by (3.15), (3.23), and (3.24), and of the optimal policy (s, S) defined by the system (3.25). We obtain

$$\lim_{\alpha \to 0} \alpha\mu = \mu \tag{3.46}$$

$$\lim_{\alpha \to 0} s = s_0 \tag{3.47}$$

$$\lim_{\alpha \to 0} S = S_0 \tag{3.48}$$

where μ, s_0, and S_0 are given by (3.41) and (3.45).

If, in addition, the demand is deterministic ($\sigma = 0$), then (3.41) and (3.45) reduce to

$$\mu = Cg + \left(\frac{2pgqk}{p + q}\right)^{1/2}, \tag{3.49}$$

$$S_0 = \left(\frac{2pgk}{q(p + q)}\right)^{1/2}, \qquad s_0 = -\left(\frac{2qgk}{p(p + q)}\right)^{1/2}. \tag{3.50}$$

The inventory problem without discounting of future costs is also studied in Bather [3].

3.4 Explicit Solution of a Deterministic Two-Product Inventory Problem

3.4.1 The Model We analyze now the optimal ordering policy of a deterministic two-product inventory system $X = (x_1, x_2)$ where x_i denotes the level of product i ($i = 1$ or 2). The system is subject to constant demand rates $G = (g_1, g_2)$ and the stock levels can be increased at any time by any desired amount of product 1 or 2. An order placed at time θ_j entails a fixed setup cost $k^{(j)} > 0$ equal to K when both products are jointly ordered and to $k_i \leq K$ when only the product i is ordered. We assume economies of joint ordering, a condition expressed by $K < k_1 + k_2$.

We suppose that the inventory storage and shortage costs are linear and determined by the function $f(X)$:

$$f(X) = f_1(x_1) + f_2(x_2) \tag{3.51}$$

where

$$f_i(x_i) = \begin{cases} -p_i x_i & \text{for } x_i \leq 0, \\ q_i x_i & \text{for } x_i \leq 0, \end{cases} \qquad p_i, q_i > 0, \quad i = 1, 2. \tag{3.52}$$

The optimal cost function u is given by the solution of the QVI

$$\min(Au + f, Mu - u) = 0 \qquad \text{in } \mathbb{R}^2, \tag{3.53}$$

where

$$Au = -G \cdot \nabla u - \alpha u, \tag{3.54}$$

$$Mu = \min(M_0 u, M_1 u, M_2 u), \tag{3.55}$$

and

$$M_0 u(x_1, x_2) = K + \inf_{\substack{\xi_1 \geq 0 \\ \xi_2 \geq 0}} u(x_1 + \xi_1, x_2 + \xi_2), \tag{3.56}$$

$$M_1 u(x_1, x_2) = k_1 + \inf_{\xi_1 \geq 0} u(x_1 + \xi_1, x_2), \tag{3.57}$$

$$M_2 u(x_1, x_2) = k_2 + \inf_{\xi_2 \geq 0} u(x_1, x_2 + \xi_2). \tag{3.58}$$

The purpose here is to obtain a smooth solution of the QVI (3.53) and to determine the regions in which no product, a single product, and both products are ordered in optimal quantities (see [27]).

3.4.2 Evolution of the Inventory System and Expression of the Optimal
Cost   In the continuation set, the system follows the characteristics of the equation

$$G \cdot \nabla u + \alpha u = f, \tag{3.59}$$

which are straight lines of slope g_2/g_1. When integrated along these characteristics, equation (3.59) gives the expression of the optimal cost function u in the continuation set:

$$u(X) = u(\eta)e^{-\alpha t} + \int_0^t f(\eta + Gs)e^{-\alpha(t-s)} \, ds \tag{3.60}$$

where $X = \eta + Gt \in \mathscr{C}$, and t is the time required to go from X to the point η of the boundary $\partial\mathscr{C}$.

The complement of the continuation set $\Omega = \{X \in \mathbb{R}^2, u(X) = Mu(X)\}$ is constituted by three subspaces: Ω_0, where both products are jointly ordered, and the Ω_i's ($i = 1, 2$), where only the product i is ordered. We denote by (γ_i) ($i = 0, 1, 2$) the boundaries of $\mathscr{C}$ with the Ω_i's. Note that since we are looking for at least continuous solution u, Ω is a closed set.

In Ω_0,

$$u(X) = M_0 u = K + u(S), \tag{3.61}$$

which is a constant denoted by a.

S is the point reached after an optimal joint ordering of both products. The cost u is minimal at S and satisfies

$$\nabla u(S) = 0. \tag{3.62}$$

In Ω_2,

$$u(x_1, x_2) = M_2 u(x_1, x_2) = k_2 + u(x_1, \Gamma_2(x_1)), \tag{3.63}$$

where $(x_1, \Gamma_2(x_1))$ represents the point reached after an order of product 2 placed at the point (x_1, x_2).

$\Gamma_2(x_1)$ satisfies

$$\partial_2 u(x_1, \Gamma_2(x_1)) = 0. \tag{3.64}$$

In Ω_1,

$$u(x_1, x_2) = M_1 u(x_1, x_2) = k_1 + u(\Gamma_1(x_2), x_2). \tag{3.65}$$

The straight lines ($x_i = x_i^0$) define the boundaries between Ω_0 and Ω_i.

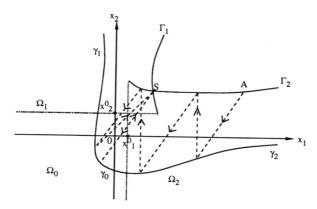

Figure 4.2
Typical evolution of the system

The curves $\Gamma_2 = \{(x_1, \Gamma_2(x_1)), x_1 \geq x_1^0\}$ and $\Gamma_1 = \{(\Gamma_1(x_2), x_2), x_2 \geq x_2^0\}$ represent the set of inventory levels reached after an order of product 1 and 2, respectively. They intersect at the point S. The value of x_1^0 (resp. x_2^0) is obtained by writing the continuity of u in (x_1^0, x_2) for all x_2.

Figure 4.2 displays typical evolution of the system when the initial inventory state is a point A of the curve Γ_2.

3.4.3 Determination of the Boundary of the Continuation Set

—Construction of the boundary γ_0. The boundary γ_0 is obtained by requiring that u is continuously differentiable across this line; u being constant in Ω_0, the gradient ∇u vanishes on γ_0, and (3.59) then reduces to

$$f_1(x_1) + f_2(x_2) = a\alpha. \tag{3.66}$$

As f_1 and f_2 are piecewise linear, the boundary γ_0 consists of three segments when x_i^0 ($i = 1, 2$) are positive (see Figure 4.3):

$$(\gamma_{01}): x_2 = \frac{p_1}{q_2} x_1 + \frac{a\alpha}{q_2}, \tag{3.67}$$

$$(\gamma_{02}): x_2 = \frac{q_1}{p_2} x_1 - \frac{a\alpha}{p_2}, \tag{3.68}$$

$$(\gamma_{03}): x_2 = -\frac{p_1}{p_2} x_1 - \frac{a\alpha}{p_2}. \tag{3.69}$$

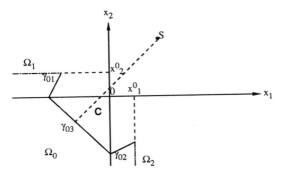

Figure 4.3
The boundary γ_0 between the continuation set and the region Ω_0 where the two products are jointly ordered up to the optimal level S

—Recursive construction of the boundary γ_2 and the curve Γ_2. We restrict ourselves here to the construction of Γ_2 and γ_2. The curves Γ_1 and γ_1 are obtained similarly. We denote the equation of the boundary γ_2 by $x_2 = \gamma_2(x_1)$. The curves Γ_2 and γ_2 consist of elements D_n and D'_n obtained by a recursive procedure.

D_1 is the set of inventory levels of Γ_2 that reach the boundary segment γ_{03} by free evolution. The element D_1 is then constructed by following back the characteristics from γ_{03} to the curve Γ_2 (Figure 4.4). To each point $(x_1, \Gamma_2(x_1))$ of D_1 we associate a boundary point $(x_1, \gamma_2(x_1))$ defined as follows: when an order of product 2 is placed at the point $(x_1, \gamma_2(x_1))$, the inventory reaches the level $(x_1, \Gamma_2(x_1))$. We call D'_1 the set of these points. We obtain

$$D'_1 = \left\{ \left(x_1, -\frac{q_2}{p_2} x_2 - \frac{\alpha k_2}{p_2} \right) \in \mathbb{R}^2, \text{ with } (x_1, x_2) \in D_1 \right\}. \tag{3.70}$$

The elements D_2 and D'_2 are constructed from D'_1 and D_2, respectively, in the same way that D_1 and D'_1 are obtained from γ_{03} and D_1. We iterate the procedure to obtain the elements D_n and D'_n ($n \geq 3$) of the curves Γ_2 and γ_2: D_n is obtained by following back the characteristics of (3.59) from D'_{n-1} to the curve Γ_2.

Similarly, two sequences d_n and d'_n of elements of the curves Γ_2 and γ_2 can be obtained by following back the characteristics from the boundary segment γ_{02} to the curve Γ_2.

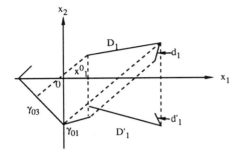

Figure 4.4
The element D_1 of the curve Γ_2 and the associated boundary element D_1'

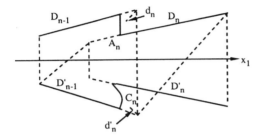

Figure 4.5
Recursive procedure of construction and matching of the elements D_n and D_n'

There may exist several possible choices for the size of the order to be placed at a point of Ω_2. Indeed, the procedure we have used to obtain the curve Γ_2 provides local minima of $\inf_{\xi_2 \geq 0} u(x_1, x_2 + \xi_2)$ in the expression of $M_2 u$. We must now compare them to get the global minimum. For α small, the cost on d_n is larger than the cost on D_n, and thus nonoptimal. Let us denote by $x_2 = \Gamma_{2,n}(x_1)$ the equation of D_n and by u_n the cost u on D_n.

There exists a sequence of points $A_n = (x_{1n}, \Gamma_{2,n}(x_{1n})) \in D_n$ such that

$$\begin{cases} u_{n-1}(x_{1n}, \Gamma_{2,n-1}(x_{1n})) = u_n(A_n^-), \\ (u_{n-1}(x_1, \Gamma_{2,n-1}(x_1)) - u_n(x_1, \Gamma_{2,n}(x_1)))(x_1 - x_{1n}) > 0 \quad \text{for } x_1 \neq x_{1n}. \end{cases} \tag{3.71}$$

The cost is thus optimal on D_{n-1} for $x_1 \leq x_{1n}$ and on D_n for $x_1 \geq x_{1n}$. A unique determination of $\Gamma_2(x_1)$ can then be defined, for $x_1 \geq x_1^0$ (Figure 4.5).

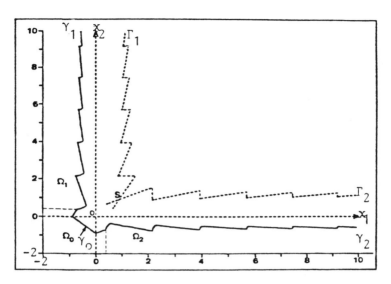

Figure 4.6
Optimal ordering policy

The elements $D'_n(D'_0 \equiv \gamma_{02})$ of the boundary are matched by curves C_n in a way that makes u continuous everywhere (Figure 4.5).

This completes the construction of the boundary γ_2 between the continuation set and Ω_2 (see [27]). This boundary is piecewise continuously differentiable.

The optimal ordering policy is displayed in Figure 4.6 for a vanishing discount factor, $p_1 = p_2 = 2$, $q_1 = q_2 = 1$, $g_1 = g_2 = 1$, $K = 1.2$, $k_1 = k_2 = 1$. The continuous line represents the boundary $\partial \mathscr{C} = \gamma_0 \cup \gamma_1 \cup \gamma_2$ of the continuation set. The dotted line ($\Gamma_1 \cup \Gamma_2$) represents the set of states reached after an order of one product.

3.4.4 Asymptotic Properties and Regularity

—Behavior of the system when one of the product levels goes to infinity. When the level x_1 of product 1 goes to infinity and the level x_2 of product 2 remains finite, the curves Γ_2 and γ_2 converge to straight lines:

$$\lim_{x_1 \to +\infty} \Gamma_2(x_1) = \bar{S}_2, \tag{3.72}$$

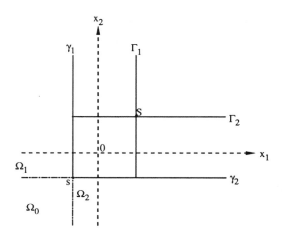

Figure 4.7
Decomposition of the system when $K = k_1 + k_2$ (no coupling)

$$\lim_{x_1 \to +\infty} \gamma_2(x_1) = \frac{-\alpha k_2 - q_2 \bar{S}_2}{p_2} = \bar{s}_2, \tag{3.73}$$

where $(\bar{s}_2, \bar{S}_2)$ is the optimal (s, S) policy of an inventory consisting of the single product 2 [27].

—Evolution of the system in terms of the coupling between the products. We have studied here the case of a strong coupling. When the coupling decreases—namely, when K tends to $k_1 + k_2$—the boundary γ_0 between the continuation set and Ω_0 is shrunk. It is reduced to a single point s when there is no coupling ($K = k_1 + k_2$). The inventory system is then decomposed into two independent one-dimensional systems (Figure 4.7).

—Limit case of a zero discount factor. When α vanishes, we have an ergodic result similar to Proposition 1 in section 3.1.

—Regularity. We have given here a recursive procedure of construction of the smoothest possible solution of the QVI (3.53). This solution is continuous but is not continuously differentiable (in particular, it is not continuously differentiable on the elements C_n of the boundary). This solution is the viscosity solution of QVI (3.53), as defined in the previous section. In particular, we check that (2.42) and (2.43) hold at the points where u is not continuously differentiable.

3.4.5   Remarks on the n-Product System   Let us extend some previous results to a n-product inventory system $X = (x_1, x_2, \ldots, x_n)$ subject to economies of joint ordering in the limit case of a zero discount factor. The complexity of the problem grows with the number of products, but we can nevertheless determine for any n the region Ω_0 of the n-dimensional state space where all products are jointly ordered, the point S of minimal cost reached after a joint ordering of all products, and the optimal average cost μ per unit time.

We denote by K the fixed cost for a joint order of all products, and we assume that the shortage and storage cost rate functions of each product are independent and linear: $f(X) = \sum_{i=1}^{n} f_i(x_i)$ where f_i $(i = 1, \ldots, n)$ is defined in (3.52).

Proceeding as in two dimensions, we determine the following:

—the boundary γ_0 between the continuation set and the region Ω_0:

$$(\gamma_0): f(X) = \mu. \tag{3.74}$$

—the optimal average cost μ per unit time and the point $S = (S_1, \ldots, S_n)$ of minimal cost:

$$\mu = \left(2K \left(\sum_{k=1}^{n} p_k g_k - \sum_{k=1}^{n} \frac{p_k^2 g_k}{p_k + q_k} \right) \right)^{1/2}, \tag{3.75}$$

$$S_i = \frac{p_i g_i}{p_i + q_i} \left(\frac{2K}{\sum_{k=1}^{n} p_k g_k - \sum_{k=1}^{n} p_k^2 g_k (p_k + q_k)^{-1}} \right)^{1/2}, \qquad i = 1, \ldots, n. \tag{3.76}$$

As in the two-dimensional case, we can foresee that the boundary of the continuation set has the shape of a damping sawtooth converging at infinity.

Appendix.   Probability Theory Definitions

A *probability space* $(\Omega, \mathscr{F}, P)$ is defined by a set Ω, a σ-algebra $\mathscr{F}$, and a probability measure P. $\mathscr{F}$ is a set of subsets of Ω such that

$\forall A_i, i \in I$ countable, $A_i \in \mathscr{F}$, then $\bigcap_i A_i, \bigcup_i A_i \in \mathscr{F}$,

if $A \in \mathscr{F}, C_A \in \mathscr{F}$,

$\varnothing, \Omega \in \mathscr{A}$.

A *random variable* f is a measurable map $\Omega \xrightarrow{f} \mathbb{R}$.

If f_k, $k \in K$, are random variables, there is a smallest σ-algebra denoted by $\sigma(f_k, k \in K)$ for which all the maps f_k are measurable.

A *filtration* $\mathscr{F}^t$ is an increasing family of sub σ-algebra of $\mathscr{F}$, (i.e., $\mathscr{F}^s \subset \mathscr{F}^t$ if $s \leq t$).

A positive random variable $T(\omega)$ is an $\mathscr{F}^t$-*stopping time* if $\forall t$, $\{\omega, T(\omega) \leq t\} \subset \mathscr{F}^t$.

Consider a filtration that is continuous to the right (i.e., $\mathscr{F}^t = \bigcap_{s > t} \mathscr{F}^s$) and $\mathscr{F}^t$ complete—that is, it contains all subsets of Ω with probability 0. A stochastic process $W(t)$ with values in $\mathbb{R}^n$ is an $\mathscr{F}^t$-Wiener process if it is adapted to $\mathscr{F}^t$ (i.e., $W(t)$ is $\mathscr{F}^t$-measurable for all t) and satisfies

$W(t)$ is continuous, $W(0) = 0$,

$E[W(t) - W(s)/\mathscr{F}^s] = 0, \forall t \geq s$,

$E\{[W(t) - W(s)][W(t) - W(s)]^T/\mathscr{F}^s\} = I(t - s), \forall t \geq s$,

where I stands for the identity matrix, and E for the expectation. As a consequence, a Wiener process is a Gaussian process.

A fundamental result of stochastic differential calculus is *Ito's formula*: Let ξ be a process defined by the stochastic differential form:

$$d\xi(t) = a(t) \, dt + b(t) \, dW(t), \qquad \xi(0) = \xi_0$$

where $a(t)$ and $b(t)$ are processes adapted to $\mathscr{F}^t$. Let $\psi(x, t): \mathbb{R}^n \times [0, T] \to \mathbb{R}$ be twice differentiable in x and once in t. Then, we have

$$\psi(\xi(t), t) = \psi(\xi_0, 0) + \int_0^t \left(\frac{\partial \psi}{\partial t} + \frac{\partial \psi}{\partial x} \cdot a(s) + \frac{1}{2} tr \frac{\partial^2 \psi}{\partial x^2} bb^T(s) \right)(\xi(s), s) \, ds$$

$$+ \int_0^t \frac{\partial \psi}{\partial x}(\xi(s), s) \cdot b(s) \, dW(s).$$

We recall that the trace of a matrix M, $(tr \, M)$, is the sum of its diagonal elements. Notice that this calculus differs from ordinary differential calculus by the second-order term.

References

[1] Bar-Ilan, A., and Sulem, A. (1991). Explicit solution of inventory problems with delivery lags. *Preprint*.

[2] Barles, G. (1985). Quasi-variational inequalities and first-order Hamilton-Jacobi equations. *Nonlinear Analysis. Theory, Methods and Applications*. Vol. 9, no. 2, pp. 131–148.

[3] Bather, J. A. (1966). A continuous time inventory model. *J. Appl. Probab*. 3, 538–549.

[4] Bellman, R. (1957). *Dynamic programming*. Princeton University Press, Princeton, N.J.

[5] Bensoussan, A. (1982). *Stochastic control by functional analysis methods*. North-Holland, Amstersam.

[6] Bensoussan, A., and Lions, J. L. (1982). *Contrôle impulsionnel et inéquations quasi-variationnelles*. Dunod, Paris.

[7] Brezis, H. (1983). *Analyse fonctionnelle. Théorie et applications*. Masson, Paris.

[8] Constantinides, G., and Richard, S. (1978). Existence of optimal simple policies for discounted-cost inventory and cash management in continuous time. *Oper. Res*. 26, 620–636.

[9] Crandall, M. G., Ishii, H., and Lions, P. L. (1992). User's guide to viscosity solutions of second order partial differential equations. *Bull. Amer. Math. Soc*. 27, 1–67.

[10] Crandall, M. G., and Lions P. L. (1983). Viscosity solutions of Hamilton-Jacobi equations. *Trans. Amer. Math. Soc*., 277, 1–42.

[11] Fleming, W. H., and Rishel, R. W. (1979). *Deterministic and stochastic optimal control*. Springer, New York.

[12] Ikeda, N., and Watanabe, S. (1981). *Stochastic differential equations and diffusion processes*. North-Holland, Amsterdam.

[13] Lions, P. L. (1982). *Generalized solutions of Hamilton-Jacobi equations*. Pitman, London.

[14] Lions, P. L. (1983). Optimal control and H. J. B. equations. Parts 1 and 2. *Comm. in P.D.E*. 8, 1101–1174, 1229–1276. Part 3, in *Nonlinear partial differential equations and applications*, College de France Seminar, Vol. V. Pitman, London.

[15] Lions, P. L., and Perthame, B. (1986). Quasi-variational inequalities and ergodic impulse control. *SIAM J. Control Optim*. 24, 604–615.

[16] Menaldi, J. L. (1982). Le problème de contrôle impulsionnel déterministe et l'inéquation quasi-variationnelle du premier ordre associée. *J. Applied Math. Optim*. 8, no. 3, 223–243.

[17] Menaldi, J. L., Perthame, B., and Robin, M. (1990). Ergodic problem for optimal stochastic switching. *J. Math. Anal. and Appl*. 147, no. 512–530.

[18] Perthame, B. (1983). Inéquations quasi-variationnelles et équations de Hamilton-Jacobi-Bellman dans $\mathbb{R}^n$. *Ann. Toulouse*, 5, 237–257.

[19] Perthame, B. (1984). Continuous and impulsive control of diffusion processes in $\mathbb{R}^n$. *Nonlinear Analysis*, T.M.A., 8, no. 10, 1227–1239.

[20] Perthame, B. (1985). On the regularity of the solutions of quasi-variational inequalities. *Funct. Anal*. 64, 190–208.

[21] Perthame, B. (1985). Some remarks on quasi-variational inequalities and the associated impulse control problem. *Ann. Inst. Henri Poincaré, Analyse non linéaire*, 2, no. 3, 237–260,

[22] Perthame, B. (1988). Vanishing impulse cost in the quasi-variational inequality for ergodic impulse control. *Asymp. Anal*. 1, 13–21.

[23] Robin, M. (1983). Long term average cost control problems for continuous time Markov process: A survey. *Acta Appl. Math*. 1, 281–299.

[24] Scarf, H. (1960). The optimality of (S, s) policies in the dynamic inventory problem. In *Mathematical methods in the social sciences*. K. J. Arrow, S. Karlin, and P. Suppes (eds.), pp. 196–202. Stanford University Press, Stanford, Cal.

[25] Strook, D. W., and Varadhan, S. R. S. (1979). *Multidimensional diffusion processes*. Springer Verlag, Berlin.

[26] Sulem, A. (1986). A solvable one-dimensional model of a diffusion inventory system. *Math. Oper. Res.* 11, 125–133.

[27] Sulem, A. (1986). Explicit solution of a two-dimensional deterministic inventory problem. *Math. Oper. Res.* 11, 134–146.

5 A Simplified Treatment of the Theory of Optimal Regulation of Brownian Motion

Avinash Dixit

Introduction

Optimal regulation of Brownian motion is a topic in the theory of stochastic optimal control that is finding several economic applications. Two of the most prominent ones will motivate my formulation.

Inventory Policy

In Scarf's (1960) famous (S, s) model, the stock X of inventories fluctuates in response to a random flow of sales, and can be replenished by incurring a lump-sum cost of ordering [in addition to the cost of purchasing or carrying, which is linear in the amount $(S - s)$ ordered]. No action is taken until X reaches a lower barrier s, when enough is ordered to raise the stock to a level S. In the case of cash management, where random income flows add to the stock just as random expenditure requirements deplete it, a similar policy can be added at the upper end. If X grows to a level r, it can be reduced to R by paying a lump-sum transaction cost, and receiving a reward—a higher interest rate—that is linear in the size $(r - R)$ of the transaction.

Other examples of two-sided (S, s) policies include a consumer's decision to change the size of a durable such as a house or a car when his wealth fluctuates [Grossman and Laroque (1990)] and a firm's decision to change its price given random inflation and menu costs [Caplin and Leahy (1991)].

Irreversible Investment

Pindyck (1988) and Bertola (1988) model the irreversible investment decision of a firm facing uncertain demand or cost. New capital is purchased at a constant (possibly random) price, so the cost of adjusting the stock is linear in the amount of the adjustment. The optimal policy is to regulate the marginal revenue product of capital at an upper barrier r. No investment is made unless this barrier is hit, when just enough is invested to keep the marginal revenue product from rising any higher. If the marginal revenue product can go negative, or if investment is partially reversible, then a similar policy should be employed at a lower barrier s.

Other economic models of this kind include employment decisions with hiring and firing costs [Bentolila and Bertola (1990)], entry and exit decisions of firms in foreign markets [Dixit (1989a)], and real international investment [Dumas (1988)].

The mathematical theory of stochastic optimal control is highly developed. Well-known textbooks include Fleming and Rishel (1975), Krylov (1980), and Karatzas and Shreve (1988). For the two classes of economic applications mentioned above, the papers by Harrison and Taksar (1983) and Harrison, Sellke, and Taylor (1983) are particularly useful. But the mathematics is quite formidable, and most users in economics would benefit from a simpler albeit less rigorous treatment. In financial economics, the theory of option pricing benefited from a simple treatment based on a discrete approximation to Brownian motion developed by Cox and Ross (1976) and Cox, Ross, and Rubinstein (1979). In this chapter I offer a similar simplification for the optimal regulation problem. I recast it into a discrete Markov chain framework. Then an extension of a diagram from Constantinides and Richard (1978) and Harrison, Sellke, and Taylor (1983) leads to the results very quickly.

As an incidental benefit, I am able to clarify the role of the 'smooth pasting' condition pertaining to the first derivative of the value function that appears in this literature. This is usually derived as a part of the necessary conditions for optimality. Krugman (1988) pioneered its use in a macroeconomic application that involved no optimization. His idea has been taken up by many others including Froot and Obstfeld (1989) and Miller and Weller (1988), but the formal basis of his analysis has not been clear. Dumas (1991) resolved this question. With lump-sum costs or discrete adjustments, the smooth pasting condition holds only for the optimum policy; with linear costs it holds for any given barrier control, and a second-order smooth pasting condition replaces it at the optimally chosen barrier. Once again, my analysis provides a somewhat easier understanding of this issue.

My focus will be on the first-order necessary conditions for the optimum choice of the control parameters s, S, r, and R. I shall not discuss the existence of an optimum, nor prove that the optimum policy has the assumed parametric form, nor examine sufficiency. All these issues are important, but they are treated in the literature, and a simplified exposition of the necessary conditions is valuable in itself.

The Problem and Its Markov Chain Representation

If no control is exercised, the state variable X follows a Brownian motion:

$$dX = \mu\, dt + \sigma\, dz, \tag{5.1}$$

where dz is the increment of the standard Wiener process. The actual control policy allows this process to go on over an open interval (s, r). Controls are applied only if X hits s or r. Two cases are considered. The first occurs when there is a lump-sum component to the cost, as in the inventory problem. The control moves the state variable in a jump to an interior point of the range (s, r); this ensures that the lump-sum cost is not incurred too frequently. In the second case there is no lump-sum component, and the minimum amount of control is exercised to keep the state variable from going outside the range. The names for the cases are those used by Harrison and his co-authors (1983).

Impulse Control

If X hits s, it is instantaneously moved to S within the range (s, r) at a cost C_s that is a combination of a lump-sum and a linear component,

$$C_s = a_s + b_s(S - s). \tag{5.2}$$

If X hits r, it is similarly moved to $R \in (s, r)$ at cost

$$C_r = a_r + b_r(r - R). \tag{5.3}$$

Instantaneous or Barrier Control

If x hits s, it is moved up by an infinitesimal amount ds at cost

$$dc_s = b_s\, ds. \tag{5.4}$$

Likewise, if x hits r, it is moved down by an infinitesimal amount dr at cost

$$dc_r = b_r\, dr. \tag{5.5}$$

In both these cases, b_r can be negative, for example credit for return of inventories or proceeds from resale of capital. But there must be some irreversibility, that is, $b_s + b_r > 0$.

There is a flow reward function $f(x)$ and a discount rate ρ. Define the expected present value of the net benefit, starting at $x \in (s, r)$ and pursuing a policy of the kind described above:

$$F(x) = E\left\{\int_0^\infty e^{-\rho t} f(x_t)\, dt - \text{regulation costs} | x_0 = x\right\}. \tag{5.6}$$

The aim is to evaluate $F(x)$ for given s, S, r, and R in the case of impulse control or s and r in the case of instantaneous control, and then to choose the values of these parameters to maximize $F(x)$.

In the discrete approximation to this problem, we divide time into small intervals of length τ, and the state space into steps of size ξ. The state variable now ranges over a discrete set of values X_i, such that

$$X_{i+1} - X_i = \xi \quad \text{for all } i. \tag{5.7}$$

Absent control, the state variable would execute a random walk. Starting at X_i, time τ later it would be at

$$\begin{cases} X_{i-1} & \text{with probability } p, \\ X_{i+1} & \text{with probability } q = 1 - p. \end{cases}$$

These probabilities, and the discrete time interval τ and space step ξ, must be compatible with the law governing the original Brownian motion. Comparing the means, we have

$$\mu\tau = q\xi + p(-\xi).$$

Using $p + q = 1$, this gives

$$q = \tfrac{1}{2}(1 + \mu\tau/\xi), \qquad p = \tfrac{1}{2}(1 - \mu\tau/\xi). \tag{5.8}$$

Turning to the variances, we need

$$\begin{aligned}
\sigma^2\tau &= q(\xi - \mu\tau)^2 + p(\xi + \mu\tau)^2 \\
&= (q + p)\xi^2 - 2(q - p)\xi\mu\tau + (q + p)\mu^2\tau^2 \\
&= \xi^2 - \mu^2\tau^2.
\end{aligned}$$

Keeping only the leading term on the right-hand side, we set

$$\sigma^2\tau = \xi^2. \tag{5.9}$$

In the limit as τ and ξ go to zero while preserving the relation (5.9), our discrete random walk converges to the continuous Brownian motion. For more details on this, see Cox and Ross (1976).

Now introduce control. Let l, L, M, and m be the indices corresponding to s, S, R, and r, that is,

$$X_l = s, \qquad X_L = S, \qquad X_M = R, \qquad X_m = r. \tag{5.10}$$

The random walk is allowed to go on from the initial points in the range $i = l + 2, \ldots, m - 2$. Starting at $i = l + 1$, if the next step is to the right, again no action is taken. But if the next step is to l, it is instead moved instantaneously to L. Thus the transitions starting at X_{l+1} are

$$\begin{cases} X_L & \text{with probability } p, \\ X_{l+2} & \text{with probability } q = 1 - p. \end{cases}$$

Likewise, starting at X_{m-1}, the transitions are

$$\begin{cases} X_{m-2} & \text{with probability } p, \\ X_M & \text{with probability } q = 1 - p. \end{cases}$$

The transition probabilities over two or more basic time intervals are given by the appropriate powers of the matrix A.

Therefore the state variable behaves as a Markov chain in the range $i = l + 1, \ldots, m - 1$. The transition matrix A is given below. The rows and columns are identified along the left and top borders. The element in the ith row and the jth column is the transition probability of going from state X_i to X_j in the basic time interval τ.

$$A = \begin{array}{c} \\ l+1 \\ l+2 \\ \vdots \\ m-2 \\ m-1 \end{array} \begin{array}{c} \begin{array}{ccccccccccc} l+1 & l+2 & l+3 & \ldots & L & \ldots & M & \ldots & m-3 & m-2 & m-1 \end{array} \\ \left[\begin{array}{ccccccccccc} 0 & q & 0 & \ldots & p & \ldots & 0 & \ldots & 0 & 0 & 0 \\ p & 0 & q & \ldots & 0 & \ldots & 0 & \ldots & 0 & 0 & 0 \\ \vdots & \vdots & \vdots & \ddots & \vdots & \ddots & \vdots & \ddots & \vdots & \vdots & \vdots \\ 0 & 0 & 0 & \ldots & 0 & \ldots & 0 & \ldots & p & 0 & q \\ 0 & 0 & 0 & \ldots & 0 & \ldots & q & \ldots & 0 & p & 0 \end{array} \right] \end{array}. \tag{5.11}$$

The control exercised at the lower barrier moves the state variable from l to L. The discrete version of (5.2) shows the cost of this to be

$$C_s = a_s + b_s \xi (L - l). \tag{5.12}$$

Instantaneous control follows as a special case of this. We interpret the minimum amount of control as moving the state variable by one step, that is, $L = l + 1$. Since $a_s = 0$ for the case of instantaneous control, (5.12) becomes

$$dc_s = b_s \xi, \tag{5.13}$$

which is just the discrete version of (5.4).

Similarly, at the upper barrier we have

$$C_r = a_r + b_r \xi (m - M), \tag{5.14}$$

and the special case of instantaneous control, interpreted as $M = m - 1$ and $a_r = 0$, yields

$$dc_r = b_r \xi. \tag{5.15}$$

The Value Function for Any Given Control

Now suppose the control parameters s, S, R, and r, or their discrete equivalents l, L, M, and m, are given. Define

$$f = (f_i | i = l + 1, \ldots, m - 1) \tag{5.16}$$

as the column vector of the flow rewards, net of the adjustment costs that can arise when $i = l + 1$ and $m - 1$. Thus

$$f_i = f(X_i)\tau \quad \text{for} \quad i = l + 2, \ldots, m - 2. \tag{5.17}$$

For $i = l + 1$, the flow payoff always accrues, but additionally with probability p the state variable hits the lower barrier, the control is exercised, and its cost is paid. Therefore,

$$f_{l+1} = f(X_{l+1})\tau - p[a_s + b_s \xi (L - l)]. \tag{5.18}$$

Similarly at the upper barrier,

$$f_{m-1} = f(X_{m-1})\tau - q[a_r + b_r \xi (m - M)]. \tag{5.19}$$

Let F be the column vector corresponding to the value function $F(x)$. Its ith component is $F(X_i)$, the expected present value of the flow rewards minus control costs starting from state i. Successive application of the transition matrix at once gives

$$F = \sum_{k=0}^{\infty} e^{-k\rho\tau} A^k f. \tag{5.20}$$

Let $B = e^{-\rho\tau}A$, then

$$F = \sum_{k=0}^{\infty} B^k f = (I - B)^{-1}f$$

or

$$(I - B)F = f. \tag{5.21}$$

This equation has a familiar interpretation. If we write it as

$$F = f + BF,$$

it is a dynamic programming decomposition of the state valuation F into the current period's flow f and the expected discounted valuation BF at the end of the period. Alternatively, we could express it as the sum of the dividend and the expected capital gain being equal to the normal return.

I shall write out (5.21) in more detail and then proceed to the limit as τ and ξ go to zero in the right proportions. This needs to be done separately for the interior states from $(l + 2)$ to $(m - 2)$, and the extreme states $l + 1$ and $m - 1$. The calculation for the interior states gives us a differential equation, and that for the extreme states yields its boundary conditions.

For an interior state i, (5.21) becomes

$$-e^{-\rho\tau}pF(X_{i-1}) + F(X_i) - e^{-\rho\tau}qF(X_{i+1}) = f(X_i)\tau. \tag{5.21'}$$

Multiply by $e^{\rho\tau}$ and rearrange terms:

$$[e^{\rho\tau} - 1]F(X_i) - p[F(X_{i-1}) - F(X_i)] - q[F(X_{i+1}) - F(X_i)] = e^{\rho\tau}f(X_i)\tau.$$

Next expand this using a Taylor series, and remembering that ξ^2 is of order τ. The right-hand side is just

$$\tau f(X_i) + o(\tau),$$

where $o(\tau)$ collects all terms that go to zero faster than τ. The left-hand side becomes

$$\rho\tau F(X_i) - p[-F'(X_i)\xi + \tfrac{1}{2}F''(X_i)\xi^2] - q[F'(X_i)\xi + \tfrac{1}{2}F''(X_i)\xi^2] + o(\tau)$$

$$= \rho\tau F(X_i) - F'(X_i)(q - p)\xi - \tfrac{1}{2}F''(X_i)(q + p)\xi^2 + o(\tau)$$

$$= \rho\tau F(X_i) - \mu\tau F'(X_i) - \tfrac{1}{2}\sigma^2\tau F''(X_i) + o(\tau).$$

In deriving the last line, I have used the formula (5.8) for q and p, and the relation (5.9) between τ and ξ. Now reunite the two sides, divide by τ, and proceed to the limit. At the same time replace X_i by X. This yields the differential equation

$$\tfrac{1}{2}\sigma^2 F''(X) + \mu F'(X) - \rho F(X) + f(X) = 0. \tag{5.22}$$

As the calculation was done for $i = l + 2, \ldots, m - 2$, the equation is valid for $s < X < r$.

This is a linear differential equation, so its general solution can be expressed as the sum of two parts, the general solution of the homogeneous equation omitting $f(X)$ (the complementary function), and any particular solution of the full equation.

The complementary function is

$$C_1 e^{\alpha_1 X} + C_2 e^{\alpha_2 X}.$$

where C_1, C_2 are constants to be determined from boundary conditions and α_1, α_2 are the roots (which are real and of opposite signs) of the characteristic equation in z:

$$\tfrac{1}{2}\sigma^2 z^2 + \mu z - \rho = 0. \tag{5.23}$$

A very convenient particular solution of (5.22) is the expected discounted flow payoff

$$V(X) \equiv E\left\{ \int_0^\infty e^{-\rho t} f(X_t)\, dt \,\middle|\, X_0 = X \right\}, \tag{5.24}$$

calculated *ignoring all barriers and controls on the process* X. To see that (5.24) satisfies the differential equation (5.22), revert to the discrete approximation. Starting from X_i, the flow payoff in the first time interval of length τ is $f(X_i)\tau$. Since the barriers are being ignored and no control is exercised, the state variable moves to X_{i-1} with probability p and to X_{i+1} with probability q. The discounted flow payoffs starting at the new state are once again given by the V function. Thus,

$$V(X_i) = f(X_i)\tau + e^{-\rho\tau}[pV(X_{i-1}) + qV(X_{i+1})].$$

This is exactly like (5.21'), replacing F by V. Therefore it can be expanded in a Taylor series and simplified as above, leading to the conclusion that V satisfies (5.22).

The general solution of (5.22) is then the sum of the complementary function and the particular solution,

$$F(X) = C_1 e^{\alpha_1 X} + C_2 e^{\alpha_2 X} + V(X). \tag{5.25}$$

This can be interpreted as follows. $V(X)$ is the expected present value payoff when the X process is allowed to proceed without regulation, while $F(X)$ is the same when the process is regulated using the *impulse* or the *instantaneous* form of control as described above. Therefore the first two terms in (5.25) must represent the additional value of the control.

Likewise, the boundary conditions corresponding to the control give us the information to fix the constants of integration C_1 and C_2. At $i = l + 1$, (5.21) gives

$$-e^{-\rho\tau}pF(X_L) + F(X_{l+1}) - e^{-\rho\tau}qF(X_{l+2}) = f(X_{l+1})\tau - p[a_s + b_s\xi(L - l)]$$

or

$$e^{\rho\tau}F(X_{l+1}) - pF(X_L) - qF(X_{l+2}) = e^{\rho\tau}f(X_{l+1})\tau - e^{\rho\tau}p[a_s + b_s\xi(L - l)].$$

This simplifies differently in the cases of impulse and instantaneous control.

For impulse control, the left-hand side expands to

$$[1 + \rho\tau + o(\tau)][F(s) + \xi F'(s) + o(\xi)] - \tfrac{1}{2}(1 - \mu\xi/\sigma^2)F(S)$$

$$- \tfrac{1}{2}(1 + \mu\xi/\sigma^2)[F(s) + 2\xi F'(s) + o(\xi)]$$

$$= -\tfrac{1}{2}[F(S) - F(s)] + O(\xi),$$

where $O(\xi)$ denotes terms such that $O(\xi)/\xi$ stays bounded above as $\xi \to 0$. [Note that τ is $o(\xi)$.] The right-hand side becomes

$$\tau[1 + \rho\tau + o(\tau)][f(s) + \xi f'(s) + o(\xi)]$$

$$- \tfrac{1}{2}(1 - \mu\xi/\sigma^2)[1 + \rho\tau + o(\tau)][a_s + b_s(S - s)]$$

$$= -\tfrac{1}{2}[a_s + b_s(S - s)] + O(\xi).$$

When the two sides are brought together and ξ is allowed to go to zero, we have

$$F(S) - F(s) = a_s + b_s(S - s). \tag{5.26}$$

In words, the gain in value from exercising the control is exactly equal to the cost of doing so. This is the value matching condition.

For instantaneous control, the terms independent of ξ disappear and the expansion has to be carried one step further. We have $a_s = 0$ and

$L = l + 1$. The left-hand side expands to

$$[1 + \rho\tau + o(\tau) - \tfrac{1}{2}(1 - \mu\xi/\sigma^2)][F(s) + \xi F'(s) + o(\xi)]$$
$$- \tfrac{1}{2}(1 + \mu\xi/\sigma^2)[F(s) + 2\xi F'(s) + o(\xi)]$$
$$= -\tfrac{1}{2}\xi F'(s) + o(\xi).$$

The right-hand side is

$$\tau[1 + \rho\tau + o(\tau)][f(s) + \xi f'(s) + o(\xi)]$$
$$- [1 + \rho\tau + o(\tau)][\tfrac{1}{2}(1 - \mu\xi/\sigma^2)]\xi b_s$$
$$= -\tfrac{1}{2}b_s\xi + o(\xi).$$

Equating the two sides, dividing by ξ, and taking limits as $\xi \to 0$, we get

$$F'(s) = b_s. \tag{5.27}$$

The derivative of the value function equals the derivative of the linear control cost function. This is called the smooth pasting condition, and usually arises as an optimality condition. But we see that in the case of instantaneous control it holds for arbitrarily fixed, not necessarily optimal, barriers.

Similarly, at the upper barrier we have for the case of impulse control the value matching condition

$$F(R) - F(r) = a_r + b_r(r - R), \tag{5.28}$$

while in the case of instantaneous control we have the smooth pasting condition

$$F'(r) = -b_r. \tag{5.29}$$

In any case, there are two boundary conditions that fix the constants C_1 and C_2 in (5.25), thus completing the solution for $F(X)$ for any given control parameters.

Conditions for Optimal Control

Here I find the additional conditions that hold when the control parameters are chosen optimally. I begin with the case of impulse control. That of instantaneous control can be derived from it by a limiting argument, or by an independent but similar chain of reasoning.

First use the parametric form of the solution (5.25) to write out the value matching conditions (5.26) and (5.28):

$$C_1[e^{\alpha_1 S} - e^{\alpha_1 s}] + C_2[e^{\alpha_2 S} - e^{\alpha_2 s}] + [V(S) - V(s)]$$

$$= a_s + b_s(S - s) \tag{5.26'}$$

and

$$C_1[e^{\alpha_1 R} - e^{\alpha_1 r}] + C_2[e^{\alpha_2 R} - e^{\alpha_2 r}] + [V(R) - V(r)]$$

$$= a_r + b_r(r - R). \tag{5.28'}$$

Differentiate (5.26') with respect to r,

$$\frac{\partial C_1}{\partial r}[e^{\alpha_1 S} - e^{\alpha_1 s}] + \frac{\partial C_2}{\partial r}[e^{\alpha_2 S} - e^{\alpha_2 s}] = 0.$$

Since $S > s$ and α_1 and α_2 are of opposite signs, the two bracketed expressions on the left-hand side are of opposite signs. Therefore $\partial C_1/\partial r$ and $\partial C_2/\partial r$ are of the same sign. The same argument applies to the derivatives of C_1 and C_2 with respect to the other three parameters.

Now consider the effect of the parameters on $F(X)$ for any fixed X. For example, with respect to r we have

$$\frac{\partial F(X)}{\partial r} = \frac{\partial C_1}{\partial r}e^{\alpha_1 X} + \frac{\partial C_2}{\partial r}e^{\alpha_2 X}.$$

Since the two derivatives on the right-hand side have the same sign and the two exponentials are always positive, the sign of this expression is the same for all X. In other words, a change in r either shifts the whole function $F(X)$ up or the whole of it down. The same goes for the other three parameters.

Then the first-order condition for the optimal choice of r can be written unambiguously as $\partial F(X)/\partial r = 0$ or

$$\frac{\partial C_1}{\partial r} = \frac{\partial C_2}{\partial r} = 0.$$

Differentiating (5.28') with respect to r and using these conditions, we have

$$-C_1\alpha_1 e^{\alpha_1 r} - C_2\alpha_2 e^{\alpha_2 r} - V'(r) = b_r.$$

But this is simply $F'(r) = -b_r$. Again, similar arguments hold for the other parameters.

This gives the conditions for optimal control at the lower barrier,

$$F'(s) = b_s = F'(S), \tag{5.30}$$

and those at the upper barrier,

$$F'(r) = -b_r = F'(R). \tag{5.31}$$

In other words, optimality of impulse control requires the smooth pasting conditions. The value matching conditions (5.26) and (5.28) and the smooth pasting conditions (5.30) and (5.31) contain six equations that fix the optimal values of the four control parametes s, S, R, and r, and the two constants C_1 and C_2 in the solution for the value function.

A simple diagram adapted from Constantinides and Richard (1978) or Harrison, Sellke, and Taylor (1983) shows the whole solution at once. Note that in the general solution (5.25), the particular integral $V(X)$ is the expected present value of the flow rewards that would accrue if no control at all is exercised. In a well-behaved problem, $V(x)$ is concave.[1] Since the optimal control should do better, the parameters C_1 and C_2 should be positive. Then the two terms that multiply these parameters by exponentials are both convex functions. The one with the positive root dominates as X goes to ∞, and the other dominates as X goes to $-\infty$. Thus, in general, $F(X)$ is convex [$F'(X)$ is increasing] for X near $\pm\infty$, and $F(X)$ is concave [$F'(X)$ is decreasing] in a middle range. Therefore the general appearance of

$$F'(X) = C_1\alpha_1 e^{\alpha_1 X} + C_2\alpha_2 e^{\alpha_2 X} + V'(X), \tag{5.32}$$

is as shown in Figure 5.1.

The smooth pasting conditions (5.30) and (5.31) tell us that at the points s and S, the height of the curve $F'(x)$ is b_s, and the height at r and R is $-b_r$. Then the value matching conditions say that the area (shown shaded) trapped by the $F'(X)$ curve and the horizontal line at height b_s between the points s and S is just the lump-sum component of the cost of control, a_s. Similarly a_r is the area shown shaded at the upper barrier. This suggests a graphical way of solving the problem. Draw the curve $F'(X)$ as defined by (5.32) and two horizontal lines at heights b_s and $-b_r$. Vary the parameters

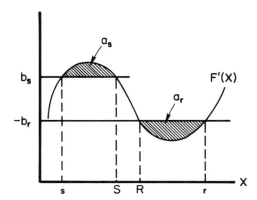

Figure 5.1
Optimal impulse control

C_1 and C_2 until the two shaded areas equal a_s and a_r, respectively. The four points of intersection then define the optimal values of the four parameters.

The case of instantaneous control can now be derived as the limit where a_s and a_r go to zero. In Figure 5.1, the two shaded areas shrink to zero. The points s and S for the lower barrier control merge, as do the points r and R for the upper barrier control. Figure 5.2 shows the limit. If the state variable tries to cross the lower barrier s, the instantaneous control simply brings it back to the barrier. Similarly at the upper barrier.

In this limit, the curve $F'(X)$ becomes tangential to the horizontal lines at heights b_s and b_r at s and r, respectively. The matching of the values of the derivatives is already captured in the smooth pasting conditions (5.27) and (5.29) that hold for instantaneous control without any consideration of optimality. The additional conditions of tangency that hold at the optimum are

$$F''(s) = 0 \tag{5.33}$$

and

$$F''(r) = 0. \tag{5.34}$$

At the optimally chosen barriers for instantaneous control, we have a match between the second-order derivatives of the value function and those of the linear control cost function, namely zero. Dumas (1988) calls this the

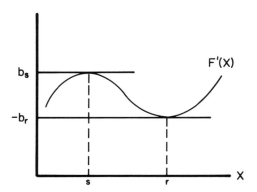

Figure 5.2
Optimal instantaneous control

super contact condition. Now (5.27), (5.29), (5.33), and (5.34) are four equations to determine the two optimal control barriers s, r and the two constants C_1, C_2.

To sum up, we have the following results. With a lump-sum component to the cost of control, the zeroeth-order (no derivatives) value matching conditions (5.26) and (5.28) hold for arbitrarily fixed control parameters, and the first-order smooth pasting conditions (5.30) and (5.31) hold when the parameters are chosen optimally. With no lump-sum cost, the first-order smooth pasting conditions (5.27) and (5.29) hold for arbitrarily fixed instantaneous control barriers, and the second-order super contact conditions (5.33) and (5.34) apply when the barriers are optimized.

Instead of obtaining the optimal instantaneous control policy as the limit of the optimal impulse control policy when the lump-sum component of the control cost goes to zero, we could have derived it by a parallel but independent argument. This means writing the smooth pasting conditions (5.27) and (5.29) that hold at arbitrary barriers in terms of the parametric form (5.25) of the solution. Then one establishes that the derivatives of C_1 and C_2 with respect to the control barrier s have the same sign, and likewise with respect to r. Optimality then requires that these derivatives be zero. Differentiating (5.27) and (5.29) with respect to the parameters and using this requirement, we get (5.33) and (5.34).

One other special case is worth pointing out. In the impulse control problem, if there is only a lump-sum cost, b_s and b_r are both zero. Then the two horizontal lines in Figure 5.1 coincide and $S = R$. This is shown in

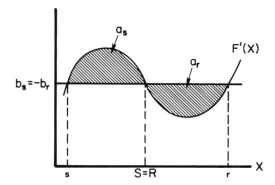

Figure 5.3
Pure lump-sum cost case

Figure 5.3. When either the lower barrier s or the upper barrier r is hit, the control moves the state to the same interior point. The same thing happens more generally if $b_s = -b_r$, for example, in the inventory problem when there is a lump-sum cost of orders but any returns earn full credit.

Extensions and Applications

The general framework described above can easily be adapted or modified to handle many related problems. Here are just a few examples.

Geometric Brownian Motion

If X is a variable like a price that is better modelled as following a geometric Brownian motion,

$$dX/X = \mu\,dt + \sigma\,dz,$$

then by Itô's Lemma $x = \ln X$ follows an arithmetic Brownian motion,

$$dx = (\mu - \tfrac{1}{2}\sigma^2)\,dt + \sigma\,dz,$$

which is just like (5.1) with μ redefined.

Mixed and One-sided Controls

The two barriers in the analysis of the two preceding sections involved the same kind of control problem, either both instantaneous or both impulse. But it is perfectly easy to treat a model where there is one of each kind; just let one shaded area in Figure 5.1 go to zero. It is almost equally easy to handle cases of one-sided control. If X must be prevented from going too low, but there is no reason to stop it from rising as high as it likes, then the lower barrier parameters (S, s) are obtained from the same analysis as above, while some other economic argument such as convergence must be invoked to provide a boundary condition for the differential equation (5.22) as X goes to infinity.

Stopping Problems

Instantaneous and impulse controls share the feature that they change the state variable and then allow the Brownian motion to continue (subject to the same control rule as before). In some problems, the whole motion is stopped when the state variable reaches a barrier level. The decision to scrap a machine when demand falls or costs rise to a certain level is a case in point. Suppose that stopping when the state is X yields a terminal one-time payoff $G(X)$. Examples are the scrap value of capital or the firing cost (negative payoff) for labor. Going through the same steps as in sections 3 and 4, it is possible to show that for a given barrier level s, we have the value matching condition

$$F(s) = G(s), \tag{5.35}$$

while the optimally chosen barrier additionally satisfies the smooth pasting condition

$$F'(s) = G'(s). \tag{5.36}$$

More General Stochastic Processes

Finally, and most importantly, the Markov chain approach seems well suited to extensions that embed the individual optimization problem treated above into a general equilibrium framework, where the X process is an endogenous outcome of similar decision problems solved by individuals with rational expectations.

Note

I thank Bernard Dumas for valuable discussions and comments on an earlier draft, the referees for useful suggestions, and the National Science Foundation for financial support under grant SES-8803300.

1. Establishing the exact conditions on $f(X)$ to make $V(x)$ concave is of course the essence of the work of Scarf (1960); remember that I am leaving aside these questions and concentrating on the characterization of (S, s) type solutions.

References

Bentolila, Samuel and Giuseppe Bertola, 1990, Firing costs and labor demand: How bad is Eurosclerosis?, Review of Economic Studies 57, 381–402.

Bertola, Giuseppe, 1988, Irreversible investment, Working paper (Princeton University, Princeton, NJ).

Caplin, Andrew and John Leahy, 1991, State-dependent pricing and the dynamics of money and output, Quarterly Journal of Economics, 106, 683–708.

Constantinides, George M. and Scott F. Richard, 1978, Existence of optimal simple policies for discounted-cost inventory and cash management in continuous time, Operations Research 26, 620–636.

Cox, John C. and Stephen A. Ross, 1976, The valuation of options for alternative stochastic processes, Journal of Financial Economics 3, 145–166.

Cox, John C., Stephen A. Ross, and Mark Rubinstein, 1979, Option pricing: A simplified approach, Journal of Financial Economics 7, 229–263.

Dixit, Avinash, 1989a, Hysteresis, import penetration, and exchange rate pass-through, Quarterly Journal of Economics 104, 205–228.

Dixit, Avinash, 1989b, Entry and exit decisions under uncertainty, Journal of Political Economy 97, 620–638.

Dumas, Bernard, 1988, Pricing physical assets internationally, Working paper no. 2569 (National Bureau of Economic Research, Cambridge, MA).

Dumas, Bernard, 1991, Super contact and related optimality conditions, Journal of Economic Dynamics and Control 15, 675–685.

Fleming, W. H. and R. W. Rishel, 1975, Deterministic and stochastic optimal control (Springer-Verlag, Berlin).

Froot, Kenneth A. and Maurice Obstfeld, 1989, Exchange-rate dynamics under stochastic regime shifts: A unified approach, Working paper no. 2998 (National Bureau of Economic Research, Cambridge, MA).

Grossman, Sanford J. and Guy Laroque, 1990, Asset pricing and optimal portfolio choice in the presence of illiquid durable consumption goods, Econometrica 58, 25–51.

Harrison, J. Michael and Michael I. Taksar, 1983, Instantaneous control of Brownian motion, Mathematics of Operations Research 8, 439–453.

Harrison, J. Michael, Thomas M. Sellke, and Allison J. Taylor, 1983, Impulse control of Brownian motion, Mathematics of Operations Research 8, 454–466.

Karatzas, Ioannis and Steven E. Shreve, 1988, Brownian motion and stochastic calculus (Springer-Verlag, Berlin).

Krugman, Paul, 1988, Target zones and exchange rate dynamics, Working paper no. 2481 (National Bureau of Economic Research, Cambridge, MA).

Krylov, N. V., 1980, Controlled diffusion processes (Springer-Verlag, Berlin).

Miller, Marcus and Paul Weller, 1988, Target zones, currency options and monetary policy, Working paper (University of Warwick, Coventry).

Pindyck, Robert S., 1988, Irreversible investment, capacity choice, and the value of the firm, American Economic Review 78, 969–985.

Scarf, H., 1960, The optimality of (S, s) policies in the dynamic inventory problem, in: Kenneth J. Arrow, Samuel Karlin, and Patrick Suppes, eds., Mathematical methods in the social sciences (Stanford University Press, Stanford, CA).

III OPTIMAL PRICING POLICIES UNDER INFLATION

6 Inflation and Costs of Price Adjustment

Eytan Sheshinski and Yoram Weiss

1 Introduction

How much? Companies that sell through catalogs run into a pricing problem.

Fast rising prices threaten to make catalog quotes out of date. Montgomery Ward & Co. which bought cautiously for its winter catalog, says it is "keeping its fingers crossed" that prices won't surge much in the near future. An official of Oak Supply & Furniture Co., Chicago, complains that the company's catalogs have been obsolete in terms of prices before they got into customers' hands the past two years. Basco Inc., Cherry Hill, N.J. mailed its latest catalog just a few weeks ago but already is reviewing some prices.

J. C. Penney Co. says it stands behind prices during the approximately seven-month life of its semiannual catalogs. Like other companies, it gets guarantees from many vendors that they won't raise their prices for specified periods. But more catalog sellers tell customers prices are subject to change. Jewelcor Inc. puts such a warning on its catalog's jewelry pages.

Some companies, such as Basco, consider putting out catalogs more frequently to keep up with prices. For the last two years Sears Roebuck has issued some 20 special catalogs twice rather than once a year. (*Wall Street Journal*—10/31/74).

As the above quotation indicates, price adjustments are not costless. There are real costs associated with the transmission of price information to the consumers and with the decision process itself. Price changes may be required either because of structural shifts in demand or due to a change in the general price level. The magnitude of the adjustment costs depends critically on whether these changes are anticipated. In principle, if inflation were perfectly anticipated, costs of adjustment could presumably be avoided by a pre-announced formula for price changes. For this reason, the recent literature on monopolistic price adjustment (Barro [2] and Bewley [3]), has focused on the choice of price policies under conditions of random changes in demand or costs. These studies have ignored, however, the role of inflationary expectations in the formation of these policies. The purpose of this chapter is to evaluate these effects.

We consider a monopolistic firm that produces a non-storable product whose demand depends on its price relative to the price of rival commodities, considered as an aggregate. The firm expects the aggregate price level and its costs of production to increase at a certain given rate. In the absence of adjustment costs the optimal policy would be to increase its own price continuously at the same rate. We assume, however, that a fixed real charge is associated with each price change. Consequently, the optimal policy is characterized by a sequence of finite intervals during which *nominal* price is held constant, followed by discrete price adjustments. Our analysis focuses on the effect of the expected rate of inflation on the frequency and the magnitude of these price changes.

For reasons of simplicity, the model is purely deterministic. Specifically, the aggregate rate of inflation is perfectly anticipated. Furthermore, the real costs of price adjustment are assumed to be independent of the expected rate of inflation. Nevertheless, they may be interpreted as reflecting the costs which are required to eliminate the uncertainty on behalf of consumers concerning changes in *relative* (in contrast to aggregate) prices.

The main results of the chapter can be briefly summarized. In terms of real prices, the firm is shown to follow a policy whereby the nominal price is fixed over intervals of constant duration, with proportionately fixed adjustments between periods. The real price thus fluctuates between two fixed bounds, decreasing continuously over each interval. Formally, identical results were obtained for models in which costs of adjustment are associated with quantities of inputs or outputs (Scarf [5] and Srinivasan [6]).

The focus of this chapter is on the effects of changes in various parameters on the optimal policy:

(1) An increase in the rate of inflation is shown to increase the initial price and to decrease the terminal price in each period, thereby increasing the magnitude of each price change. However, its effect on the frequency of price changes is shown to be ambiguous. One expects intuitively that an increase in the rate of inflation will lead to an increase in the frequency of price changes, but we provide a counter example to this conjecture. A sufficient condition for this outcome is that *the effect of a nominal price increase on real profits be non-decreasing as the real price decreases.*

(2) An increase in the level of real adjustment costs leads to a reduction in the frequency of price changes and consequently to larger adjustments in prices.

(3) An increase in the real rate of interest decreases both the initial and the terminal real prices in each interval. The effect on the frequency of price changes is generally ambiguous. This change is shown to depend on a condition analogous to *risk-dominance* in the theory of choice under uncertainty.

(4) The imposition of a specific excise-tax on the firm's output is shown to increase both the initial and the terminal real prices in each

period. Again, the effect on the frequency of price changes is shown to depend on a condition identical to risk-dominance.

We also discuss briefly the welfare implications of the problem. In the presence of costs of price adjustment, the socially optimum policy, defined in terms of maximizing consumer's surplus, also calls for an (s, S) price adjustment policy, although in a different range than the one chosen by the monopoly. This would provide an interesting measure for the "costs of inflation" (Bailey [1]).

The plan of this chapter is as follows. Section 2 presents the model and derives the optimal policy. A formal proof of the recursive solution is given in an Appendix. Sections 3 and 4 derive and discuss the effects of changes in the rate of inflation, Section 5 the effects of changes in the costs of adjustment and Section 6 the effects of changes in the real rate of interest. Section 7 analyses the effects of taxes on the firm's policy. Section 8 provides some numerical examples which show that conditions laid out in previous sections to ensure unambiguous results for the effects of some parameter changes are not redundant. Section 9 discusses the welfare implications.

2   A Model of Price Adjustment

Notation
p_t = nominal price charged by the firm at time t.
g = rate of inflation (constant).
$\bar{p}_t = e^{gt}$ = general price level at time t (by normalization $\bar{p}_0 = 1$).
$z_t \equiv p_t/\bar{p}_t$ = real price charged by the firm at time t.
$q_t = f(z_t)$ = quantity demanded of the firm's output at time t (f invariant over time).
$c(q_t)$ = real unit costs of production at time t (c invariant over time).
$F(z_t) \equiv [z_t - c(f(z_t))]f(z_t)$ = real profits at time t.[1]
β = real costs of nominal price adjustment ($\beta \geq 0$ constant).
r = real rate of interest ($r > 0$ constant).
V_0 = present discounted value of real profits at time 0.

Suppose that at time $t_0 = 0$ the firm plans to adjust its nominal price at the points of time $0 \leq t_1 < t_2 < t_3 < \cdots < t_\tau < t_{\tau+1} < \cdots$. Denote the nominally fixed price in the interval $[t_\tau, t_{\tau+1})$ by p_τ. Then $p_\tau e^{-gt}$ is the real price at any t in this interval. Accordingly, total real profits of the firm during this period, including the costs of price adjustment at time $t_{\tau+1}$, discounted to time 0, are given by

$$\int_{t_\tau}^{t_{\tau+1}} F(p_\tau e^{-gt})e^{-rt}\,dt - \beta e^{-rt_{\tau+1}}. \tag{6.1}$$

Summing (6.1) over τ,

$$V_0 = \sum_{\tau=0}^{\infty}\left[\int_{t_\tau}^{t_{\tau+1}} F(p_\tau e^{-gt})e^{-rt}\,dt - \beta e^{-rt_{\tau+1}}\right], \tag{6.2}$$

where the initial price, p_0, is assumed to be given, and $t_0 = 0$.

The objective of the firm is to choose the sequences $\{t_\tau\}$ and $\{p_\tau\}$, $\tau = 1$, $2, \ldots$, that maximize V_0.

We assume that $F(\ )$ is differentiable almost everywhere, strictly quasi-concave, that there exists a number $s^* > 0$ such that $F(s^*) > 0$, and at any z for which $F'(z)$ exists

$$F'(z) \gtreqless 0 \quad \text{as} \quad z \lesseqgtr s^*. \tag{6.3}$$

Thus, $F(z)$ attains a unique maximum at s^*. Further assumptions are required in order to insure that $V_0 \geqq 0$ at the optimum, i.e., that the firm makes non-negative profits. Specifically, the adjustment costs β should be small relative to $F(s^*)$.[2]

Assuming that an interior maximum exists, the first-order conditions are:

$$\frac{\partial V_0}{\partial t_\tau} = [-F(p_\tau e^{-gt_\tau}) + F(p_{\tau-1}e^{-gt_\tau}) + \beta r]e^{-rt_\tau} = 0, \quad \tau = 1, 2, \ldots \tag{6.4}$$

$$\frac{\partial V_0}{\partial p_\tau} = \int_{t_\tau}^{t_{\tau+1}} F'(p_\tau e^{-gt})e^{-(r+g)t}\,dt = 0 \quad \tau = 1, 2, \ldots \tag{6.5}$$

Examining these conditions, it is immediately seen from (6.5) that when $g = 0$, there will be a unique optimal price p^*, such that $F'(p^*) = 0$, which holds for all τ. Consequently, $\partial V_0/\partial t_\tau > 0$ for any τ, which means that it is never optimal to change price. It can similarly be seen that if $\beta = 0$, the nominal price will change continuously so as to keep the real price constant. The subsequent analysis will thus focus on the non-trivial case $g \neq 0$ and $\beta > 0$.

It is proved in the Appendix that for any initial price p_0, a solution to the system (6.4)–(6.5) must have a *periodic* (or recursive) form:

$$p_\tau = p_{\tau-1} e^{g\varepsilon} \quad \text{and} \quad t_{\tau+1} = t_\tau + \varepsilon, \quad \tau = 1, 2, \ldots, \tag{6.6}$$

where $\varepsilon > 0$ is a constant. This property follows directly from the independence of the real optimal policy (after the first price change) evaluated at any τ, of initial conditions. Due to the recursive nature of the solution, the real price in each period, z_t, is seen to move between two *fixed* values (s, S), where $S = se^{g\varepsilon}$. Changing variables by the transformation $z = p_t e^{-gt}$, conditions (6.4)–(6.5) can be expressed in terms of real prices (z) instead of time (t):

$$F(s) - F(S) + r\beta = 0 \tag{6.4'}$$

$$\int_s^S F'(z) z^{r/g} \, dz = 0. \tag{6.5'}$$

Conditions (6.4')–(6.5') are two equations to determine the bounds (s, S) on the real price movement.

The value of discounted real profits just prior to the first price change, V_1, is thus given by[3]

$$V_1 = \frac{1}{1 - e^{-r\varepsilon}} \left[\int_0^\varepsilon F(p_1 e^{-gt}) e^{-rt} \, dt - \beta \right]. \tag{6.7}$$

Using the same transformation as above, (6.7) can also be expressed in terms of s and S,

$$V_1 = \frac{1}{g(S^{r/g} - s^{r/g})} \left[\int_s^S F(z) z^{(r/g)-1} \, dz - \beta g S^{r/g} \right]. \tag{6.8}$$

Differentiating (6.8) partially w.r.t. S and s and equating to zero, we obtain the first-order conditions

$$F(S) - rV_1 - r\beta = 0 \tag{6.9}$$

$$-rV_1 + F(s) = 0, \tag{6.10}$$

which are equivalent to (6.4') and (6.5'), as can be seen by integrating the latter by parts. We also find that at any point (s, S) which satisfies conditions (6.9)–(6.10),

$$\frac{\partial^2 V_1}{\partial s^2} = \frac{-F'(s) s^{(r/g)-1}}{g(S^{r/g} - s^{r/g})} < 0, \quad \frac{\partial^2 V_1}{\partial S^2} = \frac{F'(S) S^{(r/g)-1}}{g(S^{r/g} - s^{r/g})} < 0, \quad \frac{\partial^2 V_1}{\partial S \partial s} = 0, \tag{6.11}$$

where by (6.3) and (6.5'), $F'(S) < 0$ and $F'(s) > 0$. Thus, at any stationary point, the second-order conditions are satisfied. This implies that the solution to (6.9)–(6.10) is *unique*.[4] Note also that if there exists a solution to (6.9)–(6.10) with $F(s) > 0$ then, in view of (6.10), $V_1 > 0$ at the optimum. Conversely, any solution to (6.9)–(6.10) which entails $F(s) < 0$ cannot be globally optimal.

The interpretation of these equations and the properties of the optimal plan are straightforward. The nominal price is held fixed over an interval ε. The real price drifts continuously from the initial level S to the level s at the end of the period, at which point a *jump* occurs and the real price is set again at S. This pattern repeats itself over time. The gains from postponing a price change are the profits just prior to the change, $F(s)$, and the interest saved on the adjustment costs, $r\beta$. The loss from such postponement is the profits just after the change, $F(S)$. Condition (6.4') states that at the optimum these gains and losses should be equal. Equation (6.5') states that the nominal price should be set at such a level that the *marginal profits* due to the change in real prices will average to zero. In view of (6.3), we have from (6.5') that $s < s^* < S$, i.e. the firm operates initially with negative marginal profits, and with positive marginal profits towards the end of each period (Figure 6.1). Clearly, as implied by (6.4')–(6.5'), in the absence of adjustment costs ($\beta = 0$), the monopoly would continuously operate at the maximum profits point s^*.

Let us make two additional observations. First, due to discounting there is an asymmetry in the solution. The level of real profits after a price increase exceeds by $r\beta$ the level of real profits just before the price change.

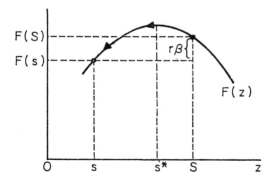

Figure 6.1

Therefore $s*$ is in general not the simple mean of s and S, even if the profit function is symmetric (e.g., quadratic).

Second, equation (6.5') can be interpreted as stating that if real prices are distributed randomly with a power density function $z^{r/g}$, *expected* marginal profits should be equal to zero. We shall find this analogy with uncertainty useful in the interpretation of the comparative-statics results.

We now turn to an analysis of the dependence of the optimal solution on the parameters g, r and β. There are two aspects of the optimal policy which are of interest: the relative magnitude of price changes, $S/s = e^{g\varepsilon}$; and the *frequency* of price changes, i.e., $\varepsilon = (\ln S - \ln s)/g$.

3 Changes in the Rate of Inflation

Differentiating the system (6.4')–(6.5') totally with respect to g, we obtain:

$$\frac{dS}{dg} = \frac{rF'(s)}{g^2\Delta} \int_s^S F'(z)z^{r/g} \ln z \, dz \qquad (6.12)$$

$$\frac{ds}{dg} = \frac{rF'(s)}{g^2\Delta} \int_s^S F'(z)z^{r/g} \ln z \, dz \qquad (6.13)$$

where

$$\Delta \equiv F'(S)F'(s)(S^{r/g} - s^{r/g}). \qquad (6.14)$$

Since $F'(s) > 0$ and $F'(S) < 0$, it follows that $\Delta < 0$. We now have the following proposition:

PROPOSITION 1. $dS/dg > 0$, $ds/dg < 0$.

Proof.   We shall prove that when (6.5') is satisfied then

$$\int_s^S F'(z)z^{r/g} \ln z \, dz < 0.$$

Let $B(z) \equiv \int_s^z F'(x)x^{r/g} \, dx$. By (6.5'), $B(s) = B(S) = 0$. Also, by (6.3), $B(z) > 0$ for all $s < z < S$. Integrating by parts,

$$\int_s^S F'(z)z^{r/g} \ln z \, dz = \int_s^S B'(z)\ln z \, dz$$

$$= B(z)\ln z \Big|_s^S - \int_s^S \frac{B(z)}{z} \, dz = -\int_s^S \frac{B(z)}{z} \, dz < 0. \qquad (6.15)$$

Now, by (6.12), (6.13), and (6.15),

$$-\operatorname{sgn}\frac{dS}{dg} = \operatorname{sgn}\frac{ds}{dg} = \operatorname{sgn}\int_s^S F'(z)z^{r/g}\ln z \, dz < 0. \quad \|$$
(6.16)

Proposition 1 establishes that a higher rate of inflation leads to larger nominal price adjustments in each period. This can be seen by observing that, by (6.6), $S/s = P_\tau/P_{\tau-1} = e^{g\varepsilon}$ for any τ. It should be emphasized that this result holds independently of whether the frequency of price changes increases or decreases with the rate of inflation.

Somewhat surprisingly, the effect on ε of an increase in the rate of inflation is, in general, ambiguous. It is quite easy to identify the source of this ambiguity. An increase in the rate of inflation has two opposite effects on the net gain from postponement of a price change. On the one hand, it decreases the terminal *real* price, $P_1 e^{-g\varepsilon}$, and hence the benefit from postponement, which is the level of real profits just prior to the price change. On the other hand, the costs of postponing a price change, rV, also decrease. This is seen from (6.10) and Proposition 1,

$$\frac{\partial V_1}{\partial g} = \frac{F'(s)F'(S)}{g^2\Delta}\int_s^S F'(z)z^{r/g}\ln z \, dz < 0.$$
(6.17)

Obviously $\partial V_1/\partial g = dV_1/dg$ at the optimum. As one would expect, in the presence of adjustment costs, an increase in the rate of inflation reduces the monopoly's real profits.

In order to establish the effect of a change in the rate of inflation on ε, one has to impose a restriction on the profit function. The condition is that the effect on real profits of a change in the (fixed) nominal price (i.e., $F'(p_1 e^{-gt})e^{-gt}$) be a non-decreasing function of time. We state this formally in terms of changes in real prices.[5]

Monotonicity (M). $F'(z)$ is non-increasing in z.

We now have the following:

PROPOSITION 2.   *Under Condition* (M), $d\varepsilon/dg < 0$.

Proof.   By definition,

$$\frac{d\varepsilon}{dg} = \frac{1}{g}\left[\frac{1}{S}\frac{dS}{dg} - \frac{1}{s}\frac{ds}{dg} - \varepsilon\right] = \frac{1}{g}\left[\frac{d\ln S}{dg} - \frac{d\ln s}{dg} - (\ln S - \ln s)\right].$$
(6.18)

Substituting from (6.12), (6.13), and (6.14)

$$\frac{d\varepsilon}{dg} = \frac{1}{g^2}\left[\frac{r}{g\Delta}\left(\frac{F'(s)}{S} - \frac{F'(S)}{s}\right)\int_s^S F'(z)z^{r/g}\ln z\,dz - (\ln S - \ln s)\right]$$

$$= \frac{r}{g^3\Delta}\int_s^S G(z)z^{(r/g)-1}\,dz, \tag{6.19}$$

where, upon substitution from (6.9),[6]

$$G(z) \equiv \left(\frac{F'(s)}{S} - \frac{F'(S)}{s}\right)F'(z)z(\ln z - \ln S) - F'(S)F'(s)(\ln S - \ln s). \tag{6.20}$$

Define a function $H(z)$:

$$H(z) \equiv \frac{F'(s)}{S}F'(z)z(\ln s - \ln S). \tag{6.21}$$

It is easy to verify that $G(s) = H(s)$ and $G(S) = H(S)$. Further, we want to show that $G(z) - H(z) > 0$ for all $s < z < S$. It is easy to see that $G(s^*) - H(s^*) > 0$. Consider the case when $s < z < s^*$. From (6.19) and (6.20),

$$G(z) - H(z) = \frac{F'(s)}{S}F'(z)z(\ln z - \ln s) - \frac{F'(S)}{s}[F'(s)s(\ln S - \ln s)$$

$$- F'(z)z(\ln S - \ln z)]. \tag{6.22}$$

The first term on the R.H.S. of (6.16) is positive since $F'(z) > 0$ for $z < s^*$. By assumption, $F'(s)s \geq F'(z)z$. Hence the second term in (6.16) is non-negative.

This proves that $G(z) - H(z) > 0$ for $s < z < s^*$. Now, when $s^* < z < S$, write

$$G(z) - H(z) = [F'(z)z - F'(S)S]\frac{F'(s)}{S}(\ln S - \ln s)$$

$$+ \left(\frac{F'(s)}{S} - \frac{F'(S)}{s}\right)F'(z)z(\ln z - \ln S). \tag{6.23}$$

By assumption, $F'(z)z \geq F'(S)S$. Thus, in (6.17), the first term in brackets is non-negative. Since $F'(z) < 0$ for $s^* < z < S$, the second term is positive.

We have shown that $G(z) - H(z) > 0$ for all $s < z < S$. Hence, by (6.20) and (6.5')

$$\int_s^S G(z)z^{(r/g)-1}\, dz > \int_s^S H(z)z^{(r/g)-1}\, dz = 0 \tag{6.24}$$

from which it follows, by (6.19), that $d\varepsilon/dg < 0$. $\quad\|$

In order to show that Condition (M) is not redundant, we provide in Section 8 an example which illustrates that if this condition is not satisfied then $d\varepsilon/dg$ may be positive.

4 Discussion

The role of Condition (M) in establishing the effect of a change in g on ε is best seen by re-examining the first-order conditions (6.4)–(6.5). Due to the recursive nature of the solution, these equations can be expressed in terms of the initial nominal price set by the firm, p_1, and the length of the interval, ε, during which the price is held fixed.

$$g \int_0^\varepsilon F'(p_1 e^{-gt})p_1 e^{-gt}\, dt - r\beta = 0 \tag{6.4''}$$

$$\int_0^\varepsilon F'(p_1 e^{-gt})p_1 e^{-(r+g)t}\, dt = 0. \tag{6.5''}$$

Consider the effect of an increase in g on p_1, holding ε constant. Let p_1 be adjusted so as to satisfy condition (6.5″). Using (M) we will show that after such an adjustment, the L.H.S. of (6.4″) will be positive, which calls for a reduction in ε.

Note first that under (M), an increase in g raises, for given p_1 and ε, the L.H.S. of (6.5″). To restore equality, p_1 must be increased. Thus, initially real price is higher. Due to (M), however, it must be the case that the new final real price is lower. This is illustrated in Figures 6.2(a) and 6.2(b).

These figures describe the real price and the effect of a change in p_1 on real profits as functions of time, for two alternative rates of inflation, g_0 and g_1 ($> g_0$). By (M), the curves in Figure 6.2(b) must be non-decreasing in t. Furthermore, the difference between these curves has an opposite sign to the difference between the real price curves in Figure 6.2(a). Hence if a higher rate of inflation leads to uniformly higher real prices, the curves in 6.2(b) would not intersect, and condition (6.5″) could not be satisfied.

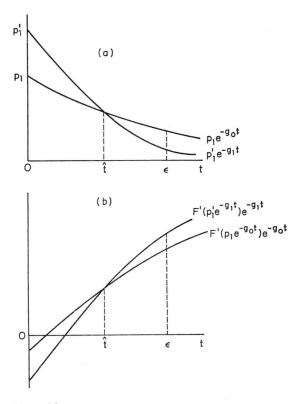

Figure 6.2

By (6.5″), the discounted area under both curves in 6.2(b) is equal to zero. Therefore, the *undiscounted* area under the marginal profit curve with the higher rate of inflation, g_1, must be larger than the corresponding area for the curve with g_0. Hence the L.H.S. of (6.4″) must be higher for g_1. This means that the difference $F(S) - F(s)$, which is the cost of postponing a price change, increases. It thus becomes profitable to reduce ε so as to satisfy this condition.

5 Changes in Adjustment Costs

To find the effects of a change in price adjustment costs, we differentiate (6.4′)–(6.5′) totally w.r.t. β, which yields

$$\frac{dS}{d\beta} = -\frac{r}{\Delta} F'(s)s^{r/g} > 0 \tag{6.25}$$

$$\frac{ds}{d\beta} = -\frac{r}{\Delta} F'(S)S^{r/g} < 0. \tag{6.26}$$

Hence, by definition

$$\frac{d\varepsilon}{d\beta} = \frac{1}{g}\left(\frac{1}{S}\frac{dS}{d\beta} - \frac{1}{s}\frac{ds}{d\beta}\right) > 0. \tag{6.27}$$

As expected, higher adjustment costs lead to less frequent and to larger price changes.

6 Changes in the Real Rate of Interest

One expects a relation between the rate of inflation and the real rate of interest, depending on the effect of inflation on the level of real savings and investment. It is therefore of interest to study the effects of a change in the real rate of interest on the optimal price adjustment policy in the presence of inflation.

To find the effects of a change in r, we differentiate (6.4')–(6.5') totally, yielding:

$$\frac{dS}{dr} = \frac{-F'(s)}{g\Delta}\left[\int_s^S F'(z)z^{r/g}\ln z\, dz + \beta g s^{r/g}\right] \tag{6.28}$$

substituting for β from (6.4') and integrating, using (6.5'),

$$= \frac{-F'(s)}{g\Delta}\int_s^S [F'(z)z\ln z + F(z) - F(S)]z^{(r/g)-1}\, dz.$$

Similarly,

$$\frac{ds}{dr} = \frac{-F'(S)}{g\Delta}\left[\int_s^S F'(z)z^{r/g}\ln z\, dz + \beta g S^{r/g}\right]$$

$$= \frac{-F'(S)}{g\Delta}\int_s^S [F'(z)z\ln z + F(z) + F(s)]z^{(r/g)-1}\, dz. \tag{6.29}$$

Observe first that, by (6.8) and (6.5') we have

$$\frac{dV_1}{dr} = \frac{-1}{rg(S^{r/g} - s^{r/g})} \int_s^S [F'(z)z \ln z + F(z)]z^{(r/g)-1} \, dz. \tag{6.30}$$

Hence, by (6.10),

$$V_1 + r\frac{dV_1}{dr} = \frac{-1}{g(S^{r/g} - s^{r/g})} \int_s^S [F'(z)z \ln z + F(z) - F(s)]z^{(r/g)-1} \, dz. \tag{6.31}$$

In view of (6.31), (6.29) may be rewritten

$$\frac{ds}{dr} = \frac{1}{F'(s)}\left(V_1 + r\frac{dV_1}{dr}\right). \tag{6.32}$$

Also, from (6.31) and (6.4'), (6.28) may be rewritten

$$\frac{dS}{dr} = \frac{1}{F'(S)}\left(V_1 + r\frac{dV_1}{dr} + \beta\right). \tag{6.33}$$

Thus, the sign of ds/dr is the same as the sign of $V_1 + r(dV_1/dr)$, which is the change in rV_1 (the "permanent real profit") w.r.t. an increase in r. Note that $V_1 + r(dV_1/dr) < 0$ is a *necessary* condition for $d\varepsilon/dr = ((1/S)\,ds/dr - (1/s)\,ds/dr)/g > 0$, because otherwise, by (6.32) and (6.33), $ds/dr > 0$ and $dS/dr < 0$. We shall now prove that this condition is always satisfied.

PROPOSITION 3. $ds/dr < 0$ *and* $dS/dr < 0$.

Proof. Let $B(z) = \int_s^z F'(x)x^{r/g} \, dx$. Then, integrating by parts

$$\int_s^S [F'(z)z \ln z + F(z)]z^{(r/g)-1} \, dz = \int_s^S [F(z)z^{r/g} - B(z)]\frac{1}{z}dz. \tag{6.34}$$

Integrating $B(z)$ by parts

$$B(z) = F(z)z^{r/g} - F(s)s^{r/g} - \frac{r}{g}\int_s^z F(x)x^{(r/g)-1} \, dx. \tag{6.35}$$

Substituting (6.35) in (6.34),

$$\int_s^S [F'(z)z \ln z + F(z)]z^{(r/g)-1} \, dz$$

$$= \int_s^S \left[F(s)s^{r/g} + \frac{r}{g}\int_s^z F(x)x^{(r/g)-1} \, dx\right]\frac{1}{z}dz. \tag{6.36}$$

From (6.29) and (6.36),

$$\frac{ds}{dr} = \frac{-F'(S)}{g\Delta} \int_s^S \left[F(s)(s^{r/g} - z^{r/g}) + \frac{r}{g} \int_s^z F(x)x^{(r/g)-1}\, dx \right] \frac{1}{z}\, dz$$

$$= \frac{-rF'(S)}{g^2\Delta} \int_s^S \int_s^z [F(x) - F(s)]x^{(r/g)-1}\, dx\, \frac{1}{z}\, dz < 0, \tag{6.37}$$

since $F(x) > F(s)$ for all $s < x \leq S$, $F'(S) < 0$, and $\Delta < 0$.

Now it follows from (6.36) and (6.28) that

$$\frac{dS}{dr} = \frac{-F'(s)}{g\Delta} \int_s^S \left[F(s)s^{r/g} - F(S)z^{r/g} + \frac{r}{g} \int_s^z F(x)x^{(r/g)-1}\, dx \right] \frac{1}{z}\, dz$$

$$= \frac{-F'(s)}{g\Delta} \int_s^S \frac{G(z)}{z}\, dz, \tag{6.38}$$

where

$$G(z) \equiv (F(s) - F(S))s^{r/g} + \frac{r}{g} \int_s^z (F(x) - F(S))x^{(r/g)-1}\, dx \tag{6.39}$$

using (6.5′),

$$= \frac{r}{g} \left[\int_s^z (F(x) - F(S))x^{(r/g)-1}\, dx - \int_s^S (F(x) - F(S))x^{(r/g)-1}\, dx \right]$$

$$= -\frac{r}{g} \int_z^S (F(x) - F(S))x^{(r/g)-1}\, dx.$$

Clearly, $G(S) = 0$. Also,

$$G(s) = -\frac{r}{g} \int_s^S (F(x) - F(S))x^{(r/g)-1}\, dx = (F(s) - F(S))s^{r/g} < 0. \tag{6.40}$$

Furthermore,

$$G'(z) = \frac{r}{g}(F(z) - F(S))z^{(r/g)-1}, \tag{6.41}$$

which changes sign once, being negative for small and positive for large values of z. It follows that $G(z) < 0$ for all $s \leq z < S$. Since $F'(s) > 0$ and $\Delta < 0$, (6.38) implies that $dS/dr < 0$. ‖

Since over a typical cycle, real marginal profits are first negative and then positive, the net effect of an increase in the rate of interest is to reduce the present value of marginal profits. Therefore the firm's response is to increase the relative weight of the positive marginal profits by decreasing the upper and lower real prices. The sign of $d\varepsilon/dr$ is in general ambiguous. In Section 8 an example is provided in which $d\varepsilon/dr$ has *opposite* signs for alternative values of the parameters. However, we can provide a sufficient condition which determines the sign of $d\varepsilon/dr$.

From (6.28)–(6.29) and the definition of ε, we have

$$
\frac{d\varepsilon}{dr} = \frac{1}{g^2\Delta sS}\left[(F'(S)S - F'(s)s)\int_s^S F'(z)z^{r/g}\ln z\,dz + \beta g(F'(S)S^{(r/g)+1}\right.
$$
$$
\left. - F'(s)s^{(r/g)+1})\right] \tag{6.42}
$$

using (6.4') and (6.5')

$$
= \frac{1}{g^2\Delta sS}\left[(F'(s)s - F'(S)S)\int_s^S \frac{1}{z}\int_s^z F'(x)x^{r/g}\,dx\,dz\right.
$$
$$
\left. + \frac{g}{r}\int_s^S F'(x)\,dx(F'(S)S^{(r/g)+1} - F'(s)s^{(r/g)+1})\right]
$$
$$
= \frac{[F'(s)s - F'(S)S]\beta}{g\Delta sS}\int_s^S [\varphi(z) - \psi(z)]z^{r/g}\,dz
$$

where

$$
\phi(z) = \frac{r}{g}\frac{z^{-(r/g)-1}\int_s^z F'(x)x^{r/g}\,dx}{\int_s^S F'(x)\,dx}, \quad \psi(z) = \frac{F'(z) + zF''(z)}{\int_s^S [F'(z) + zF''(z)]\,dz}. \tag{6.43}
$$

Using (6.5'), it can be verified that $\int_s^S \phi(z)\,dz = \int_s^S \psi(z)\,dz = 1$. Furthermore, $\phi(z) \geq 0$ and under Condition (M), $\psi(z) \geq 0$ for all $s \leq z \leq S$, wherever they exist.

The sign of $d\varepsilon/dr$ is thus seen to be determined by the difference in the expected value of the discount factor $z^{r/g}$ under the distributions $\phi(z)$ and $\psi(z)$. This fact suggests the application of a "*risk-dominance*" criterion (Hadar and Russell [4]). Condition (M) prevents a direct application of this criterion to expression (6.42) in its present form. However, a transformation of (6.42) into time units leads to the desired condition.

Let

$$\hat{\phi}(z) \equiv g\phi(z)z \quad \text{and} \quad \hat{\psi}(z) = g\psi(z)z. \tag{6.44}$$

Also, recall that $z = p_1 e^{-gt}$. We now state:

PROPOSITION 4.   *If $\hat{\phi}(z)$ is risk-dominant to $\hat{\psi}(z)$, then $d\varepsilon/dr > 0$ and vice versa.*

Proof.   Using the above transformation for z, it is seen that $\hat{\phi}(z) \geqq 0$, $\hat{\psi}(z) \geqq 0$, and $\int_0^\varepsilon \hat{\phi}(z)\,dt = \int_0^\varepsilon \hat{\psi}(z)\,dt = 1$. Furthermore, (6.42) can be rewritten

$$\frac{d\varepsilon}{dr} = \frac{[F'(s)s - F'(S)S]\beta}{g\Delta sS} \int_0^\varepsilon [\hat{\phi}(z) - \hat{\psi}(z)]z^{r/g}\,dt. \tag{6.45}$$

Now, integrating by parts

$$\int_0^\varepsilon [\hat{\phi}(z) - \hat{\psi}(z)]z^{r/g}\,dt = r \int_0^\varepsilon z^{r/g} \int_0^t [\hat{\phi}(z) - \hat{\psi}(z)]\,dx\,dt. \tag{6.46}$$

Thus, a sufficient condition for $d\varepsilon/dr > 0$ is that $\int_0^t [\hat{\phi}(x) - \hat{\psi}(x)]\,dx < 0$ for all $0 < t \leqq \varepsilon$. That is, $\hat{\phi}$ is risk-dominant to $\hat{\psi}$. Clearly, $d\varepsilon/dr < 0$ if $\hat{\psi}$ is risk-dominant to $\hat{\phi}$.   ‖

It should be noted that risk-dominance is sufficient, but not necessary, to determine the sign of $d\varepsilon/dr$.

The appearance of distribution functions should not be surprising. Both the effect of a change in the rate of interest and the effect of a change in the initial nominal price are *spread* throughout the price cycle. The distributions ϕ and ψ describe the change in S, holding S/s (and thus ε) constant, required to equilibrate conditions (6.4′) and (6.5′), respectively. Their difference will determine the direction of the optimal change in ε.

It is interesting to compare the difference between the effects of an increase in β to the effects of an increase in r. Generally, one expects their effects to be similar. However, an increase in r is seen to decrease prices unambiguously while an increase in β raises initial prices and decreases terminal prices (thus increasing the amplitude of price changes). Similarly, the change in the length of the price cycle is ambiguous in the former case, and positive in the latter. These differences are due to the fact that an increase in β increases only the benefits of further postponing a price change, while an increase in r also reduces the marginal profitability of a nominal price increase.

7 The Effects of Taxes

For policy purposes it is important to be able to predict the effects of excise taxes on the firm's price adjustment policy. In general, such taxes will affect both the level and the frequency of price changes.

Consider first a specific tax, levied at a fixed real level of $\theta \geq 0$ per unit sold. Real after tax profits, $G(z, \theta)$, are given by

$$G(z, \theta) = F(z) - \theta f(z), \tag{6.47}$$

where $f(z)$ is the quantity demanded and z is the real price facing the consumer. We assume that $G(z, \theta)$, as $F(z)$, is strictly quasi-concave and has a unique maximum. Given this assumption, the general nature of the solution remains unchanged. The first-order conditions for a maximum are now given by (6.7) with $G(z, \theta)$ replacing $F(z)$. Using the definition of $G(\ )$, these may be written

$$F(s) - F(S) + \theta[f(S) - f(s)] + r\beta = 0 \tag{6.48}$$

$$\int_s^S [F'(z) - \theta f'(z)] z^{r/g} \, dz = 0. \tag{6.49}$$

Differentiating (6.48)–(6.49) w.r.t. θ, we have

$$\frac{dS}{d\theta} = \frac{G_z(s, \theta)}{\Delta} \int_s^S f'(z)(z^{r/g} - s^{r/g}) \, dz > 0 \tag{6.50}$$

$$\frac{ds}{d\theta} = \frac{G_z(S, \theta)}{\Delta} \int_s^S f'(z)(z^{r/g} - S^{r/g}) \, dz > 0, \tag{6.51}$$

where $\Delta = G_z(S, \theta) G_z(s, \theta)(S^{r/g} - s^{r/g}) < 0$, and $G_z(\ )$ is the partial derivative w.r.t. z. We assume a regularly shaped demand function with $f'(z) < 0$.

As one would expect, the effect of the tax is uniformly to increase the real price paid by consumers. The effects of the tax on the frequency of price adjustments depend on further assumptions. By (6.50), (6.51) and the definition of ε, we have

$$\frac{d\varepsilon}{d\theta} = \frac{1}{g\Delta sS} \int_s^S f'(z)[G_z(s, \theta)s(z^{r/g} - s^{r/g}) - G_z(S, \theta)S(z^{r/g} - S^{r/g})] \, dz$$

$$= \frac{\int_s^S f'(z) \, dz \int_s^S [G_z(z, \theta) + z G_{zz}(z, \theta)] \, dz}{g\Delta sS} \int_s^S [\phi(z) - \psi(z)] z^{r/g} \, dz, \tag{6.52}$$

where

$$\phi(z) = \frac{G_z(z,\theta) + zG_{zz}(z,\theta)}{\int_s^S [G_z(z,\theta) + zG_{zz}(z,\theta)]\, dz}, \quad \psi(z) = \frac{f'(z)}{\int_s^S f'(z)\, dz}. \tag{6.53}$$

Clearly, $\int_s^S \phi(z)\, dz = \int_s^S \psi(z)\, dz = 1$. Furthermore, under Condition (M) and the assumption $f' < 0$, $\phi(z) \geqq 0$ and $\psi(z) \geqq 0$. Thus $\phi(z)$ and $\psi(z)$ can be regarded as density functions, and one may apply the results from the theory of "risk-dominance." Specifically, it can be seen from (6.52) that $d\varepsilon/d\theta$ has the opposite sign to

$$\int_s^S [\phi(z) - \psi(z)]z^{r/g}\, dz = z^{r/g} \int_s^z [\phi(x) - \psi(x)]\, dx \Big|_s^S$$

$$- \frac{r}{g} \int_s^S z^{(r/g)-1} \int_s^z [\phi(x) - \psi(x)]\, dx\, dz$$

$$= -\frac{r}{g} \int_s^S z^{(r/g)-1} \int_s^z [\phi(x) - \psi(x)]\, dx\, dz. \tag{6.54}$$

Hence $d\varepsilon/d\theta$ will be positive or negative depending upon whether $\psi(\varepsilon)$ is *risk-dominant* or *risk-inferior* to $\phi(z)$.

As seen from (6.53), $\phi(z)$ reflects the relative change in $zG_z(z)$, while $\psi(z)$ reflects the relative change in $f(z)$, with respect to an increase in real price. In principle, their difference may go either way.

A similar analysis can be applied to the case of an *ad valorem* tax, levied as a fixed percentage of sales. If the tax rate is θ ($0 \leq \theta < 1$), then after tax real profits are given by $G(z,\theta) = F(z) - \theta z f(z)$. The expressions for $dS/d\theta$ and $ds/d\theta$ are the same as (6.50) and (6.51) with $f(z) + zf'(z)$ replacing $f'(z)$. This term is the marginal revenue w.r.t. a price increase, and it is negative or positive depending upon whether demand elasticity is larger or smaller than unity. Unlike the standard monopoly case, the firm need not operate exclusively at prices associated with positive marginal revenue. Nevertheless, the first-order conditions impose a constraint on the "average" marginal revenue. Using the first-order conditions, equations (6.50) and (6.51) can be rewritten as:

$$\frac{dS}{d\theta} = \frac{G_z(s,\theta)}{\Delta(1-\theta)} \left[\int_s^S m(z)(z^{r/g} - s^{r/g})\, dz - r\beta s^{r/g} \right] \tag{6.55}$$

$$\frac{ds}{d\theta} = \frac{G_z(S,\theta)}{\Delta(1-\theta)} \left[\int_s^S m(z)(z^{r/g} - S^{r/g})\, dz - r\beta S^{r/g} \right], \tag{6.56}$$

where $m(z) = d[c(f(z))f(z)]/dz$ is the marginal cost w.r.t. a price increase. Clearly $m(z) < 0$ since $f'(z) < 0$ and marginal costs w.r.t. output increases can be assumed to be positive. It is seen that $dS/d\theta > 0$. As in the case of a specific tax, the firm increases the initial real price as a result of a tax increase. However, the sign of $ds/d\theta$ as well as $d\varepsilon/d\theta$ appears to be ambiguous. The source of the difference between the results in these two cases is that with an *ad valorem* tax, tax payments increase with revenue, which provides an incentive for the firm to allow some reduction in prices.

8 Some Numerical Examples

Our purpose in this section is to provide counter examples to two presumably intuitive notions. First, that in the presence of price adjustment costs, an increase in the expected rate of inflation will lead to a higher frequency of price changes. Second, that an increase in the real rate of interest will lead to a lower frequency of price changes. The examples can also provide some insight to the potential importance of price adjustment costs.

Suppose that $F(z)$ is piecewise linear:

$$F(z) = \begin{cases} az, & z \leq s^* \\ (a + b)s^* - bz, & z > s^*, \end{cases} \tag{6.57}$$

where $a > 0$ and $b > 0$ are constants.[7] Conditions (6.4')–(6.5') are in this case

$$-a(s^* - s) + b(S - s^*) + r\beta = 0 \tag{6.58}$$

$$-b(S^{(r/g)+1} - s^{*(r/g)+1}) + a(s^{(r/g)+1} - s^{*(r/g)+1}) = 0. \tag{6.59}$$

Let the parameters be: $s^* = 1$, $a = 0.5$, $b = 15$, $r = 0.05$ and $\beta = 0.85$. Then the relation between alternative values of g and ε can be calculated from (6.58)–(6.59):

Rate of inflation (%)	0.14	0.18	0.22	0.26	0.30	0.34	0.38	0.42	0.46	0.50
Frequency of price change (ε years)	7.16	6.66	6.37	6.21	6.15	6.19	6.33	6.61	7.09	8.03

It is seen that at inflation rates above 30 per cent, increases in the inflation rate lead to an increase in ε, i.e. to a reduction in the frequency of price change. Notice that the function (6.57) violates Condition (M) for $z < s^*$. Accordingly, the example was chosen with a negatively skewed function $(b > a)$, so as to increase the length of time spent in this region. For the same purpose, the adjustment costs were set at a relatively high level (higher than the maximum profit flow), which explains the unrealistically long intervals between price changes.

This counter example may suggest that instances of reduced frequency of price changes, though theoretically possible, are not likely to be met in practice. For short intervals, the firm is in the neighbourhood of s^*, where Condition (M) is satisfied.[8]

The profit function (6.57) can also be used to show that increases in the rate of interest may increase ε, i.e., increase the frequency of price changes.

Let $s^* = 1, a = 0.5, b = 0.001, g = 0.1$ and $\beta = 0.0001$. Then the relation between r and ε is:

Rate of interest (%)	0.04	0.06	0.08	0.10	0.12	0.14	0.16	0.18	0.20	0.30
Frequency of price change (ε years)	1.341	1.336	1.330	1.324	1.314	1.313	1.308	1.302	1.297	1.270

It is seen that the "anomalous" case occurs for fairly realistic intervals between price changes. It must be noted, however, that a high degree of positive skewness, with the firm spending most of the time at the range of negative marginal profits, was required to produce the example.

Finally, we would like to report that numerical experiments with a quadratic profit function (which, in the absence of production costs, is obtained from a linear demand function) give high intevals between price changes (1–2 years) even with very low adjustment costs. This is due to the fact that, unlike (6.57), the loss in profits from any price $z \neq s^*$ in the neighborhood of s^* is relatively small.

9 Concluding Remarks

In the presence of costs of adjustment, even a fully anticipated inflation entails a real cost. For the firm this is reflected in a reduction in real discounted profits as the rate of inflation increases. However, we would like to inquire whether the reduction in profits is also a social cost to the economy. The question arises since the monopoly tends to choose lower real prices (and hence larger quantities) over the last part of each period in which the nominal price is fixed, which may increase net social welfare.

A standard criterion which may be applicable in the present partial equilibrium context is that of *consumer's surplus*. Thus, let $G(z)$ be net consumer's surplus associated with a real price z,

$$G(z) = F(z) + \int_z^\infty f(z)\,dz. \tag{6.60}$$

The socially optimal policy is defined as the sequence of nominal prices and dates that maximizes (6.7) with $G(z)$ replacing $F(z)$ in the objective function. If we assume that G, as F, is strictly quasi-concave, then the socially optimum policy will have the same qualitative properties as the monopoly's optimum policy, the difference being that real prices vary around the competitive price which is equal to real marginal costs.

A natural measure for the "social costs of inflation" would be the difference between the discounted value of consumer's surplus in the absence of inflation and the discounted value of consumer's surplus minus the costs of price adjustment in the presence of inflation. This difference can be evaluated under alternative market organizations. In particular, it may be evaluated under the socially optimal (s, S) policy and under the monopoly (s, S) policy.

Another question of interest concerns the measure of monopoly costs under inflation. This would involve the difference in the level of the social welfare function under the socially optimal and under the monopoly's (s, S) policies for a given expected rate of inflation. One would like to investigate the effect of changes in the expected rate of inflation on this measure.

Two other extensions seem to be of interest. First would be the introduction of inventory decisions on behalf of the firm and the consumers. For example, if consumers can store the commodity, then price differences cannot exceed storage costs.[9] Another application of the analysis is to input decisions, particularly with respect to the duration of wage contracts, since changes in wage contracts may also entail real costs.

The analysis can also be extended to a multi-product firm. A natural question is whether the optimal frequency of price changes will be uniform across products. Returns to scale in the provision of information may lead the firm to announce all price changes simultaneously.

Finally, some macroeconomic implications of the analysis can be noted. According to the analysis, with a constant rate of inflation, prices will increase on the average at the rate of inflation. More importantly, if the timing of firms' price adjustments is independent, then we would observe a variance of price changes across products or firms which increases with the rate of inflation. This implies that informational costs exist even with a steady aggregate rate of inflation. Furthermore, if, as the analysis suggests, firms adjust prices more frequently as the rate of inflation increases unexpectedly, then one would expect to observe a larger initial adjustment in the average price, the larger the rate of inflation.

Price adjustment policies of the kind described in this chapter are particularly visible with respect to the rate of exchange. Differences in rates of inflation on the one hand and informational costs adjustment on the other hand induce many countries to engage in periodic exchange rate adjustments. Our analysis could be applicable to the analysis of optimal rate of exchange policies.

Costs of adjustment have recently become a central issue in taxation policies. Inflation continuously erodes the basis of various taxes (such as the property tax). In view of the considerable costs of asset revaluation, standard practice is periodic reassessment. It would be of interest to investigate the dependence of the optimal frequency of such revaluatons and of the optimal tax rates on the expected rate of inflation.

Appendix

The firm looks for a pair of sequences $\{t_\tau\}$ and $\{p_\tau\}$, $\tau = 1, 2, 3, \ldots$, that maximize the present discounted value of real profits at time $t_0 = 0$:

$$V_0 = \sum_{\tau=0}^{\infty} \left[\int_{t_\tau}^{t_{\tau+1}} F(p_\tau e^{-gt}) e^{-rt} \, dt - \beta e^{-rt_{\tau+1}} \right]. \tag{6A.1}$$

Denote an optimal pair of such sequences by $\{t_\tau^*\}$ and $\{p_\tau^*\}$. We assume that such solutions exist with $V_0 \geq 0$ at the optimum (since no production is always feasible). We now have the following:

THEOREM.   *For any solution $\{t_\tau^*\}$ and $\{p_\tau^*\}$, there exists a unique $\varepsilon > 0$, such that $t_{\tau+1}^* = t_\tau^* + \varepsilon$ and $p_{\tau+1}^* = p_\tau^* e^{g\varepsilon}$.*

Proof.   By the principle of optimality we know that if $\{t_\tau^*\}$ and $\{p_\tau^*\}$ maximize V_0, they also maximize the discounted real profits at the points of time $t_1^*, t_2^*, \ldots$, and so on, which we denote $V_1, V_2, \ldots$. Specifically,

$$V_1 = \sum_{\tau=1}^{\infty} \left[\int_{t_\tau}^{t_{\tau+1}} F(p_\tau e^{-gt}) e^{-r(t-t_1^*)}\, dt - \beta e^{-r(t_{\tau+1}-t_1^*)} \right] \tag{6A.2}$$

$$V_2 = \sum_{\tau=2}^{\infty} \left[\int_{t_\tau}^{t_{\tau+1}} F(p_\tau e^{-gt}) e^{-r(t-t_2^*)}\, dt - \beta e^{-r(t_{\tau+1}-t_2^*)} \right] \tag{6A.3}$$

changing the summation index

$$= \sum_{\tau=1}^{\infty} \left[\int_{t_{\tau+1}}^{t_{\tau+2}} F(p_{\tau+1} e^{-gt}) e^{-r(t-t_2^*)}\, dt - \beta e^{-r(t_{\tau+2}-t_2^*)} \right].$$

Using the transformation $u = t - t_1^*$, rewrite (6A.2)

$$V_1 = \sum_{\tau=1}^{\infty} \left[\int_{t_\tau - t_1^*}^{t_{\tau+1}-t_1^*} F(p_\tau e^{-gt_1^*} e^{-gu}) e^{-ru}\, du - \beta e^{-r(t_{\tau+1}-t_1^*)} \right]. \tag{6A.4}$$

Similarly, using $u = t - t_2^*$, rewrite (6A.3) as

$$V_2 = \sum_{\tau=1}^{\infty} \left[\int_{t_{\tau+1}-t_2^*}^{t_{\tau+2}-t_2^*} F(p_{\tau+1} e^{-gt_2^*} e^{-gu}) e^{-ru}\, du - \beta e^{-r(t_{\tau+2}-t_2^*)} \right]. \tag{6A.5}$$

We observe that the variables to be determined in V_1 are

$$\{t_\tau - t_1^*\} = \{0, t_2 - t_1^*, t_3 - t_1^*, \ldots\} \text{ and } \{p_\tau e^{-gt_1^*}\} = \{p_1^* e^{-gt_1^*}, p_2 e^{-gt_1^*}, \ldots\}.$$

In V_2 they are $\{t_{\tau+1} - t_2^*\} = \{0, t_3 - t_2^*, t_4 - t_2^*, \ldots\}$ and $\{p_{\tau+1} e^{-gt_2^*}\} = \{p_2^* e^{-gt_2^*}, p_3 e^{-gt_2^*}, \ldots\}$. The functions V_1 and V_2 are *identical* in the corresponding variables. Hence

$$t_2^* - t_1^* = t_3^* - t_2^* = \cdots = \varepsilon$$

and

$$p_1^* e^{-gt_1^*} = p_2^* e^{-gt_2^*} = \cdots$$

or

$$p_2^* = p_1^* e^{g(t_2^* - t_1^*)} = p_1^* e^{g\varepsilon}, \text{ etc.} \quad \|$$

We have shown that any solution to (6A.1) has a recursive form. In the text we show that the recursive solution is *unique*.

Notes

This work was supported in part by National Science Foundation Grant SOC74-11446 at the Institute for Mathematical Studies in the Social Sciences at Stanford University, and in part by the Alfred P. Sloan Foundation. We would like to thank Frank Fisher and Peter Hammond for helpful comments.

1. This formulation assumes that output is always identical to sales. It was pointed out to us by Edi Karni that in the presence of costs of price adjustment a monopoly may prefer not to satisfy demand. The general definition of real profits should be:

$$F(z_t) = \max_{q_t \leq f(z_t)} \ [(z_t - c(q_t))q_t].$$

A sufficient condition for the maximum to be attained at $q_t = f(z_t)$ is that $c(q_t)$ be independent of q_t.

2. Clearly, if F were non-negative for all $z \geq 0$, a policy of no price change would ensure $V_0 > 0$. This, however, does not seem to be an acceptable assumption.

3. Note that the definition of V_1 includes the cost of the first price change. To simplify notation, and without loss of generality, we assume hereon that $t_1 = 0$, so that $p_1 e^{-gt_1}$ is p_1.

4. Conditions (6.9)–(6.10) can be replaced by the equivalent conditions

$$F(S) - F(s) - r\beta = 0 \tag{6.9'}$$

and (6.10). For any S, if there exists an s, such that $0 \leq s < S$, which satisfies (6.9'), this solution must be unique. This follows from the strict quasi-concavity of F. Furthermore, these solutions define a differentiable function $s = g(S)$, over an interval of S (which obviously contains all the possible solutions). Consider the function $H(S) \equiv V_1(s, S) = V_1(g(S), S)$, which is continuously differentiable in S. Clearly $H'(S) = 0$ is a necessary condition for an optimum and is equivalent to conditions (6.9)–(6.10). To show that the maximum is unique, it is sufficient that $H'(S) = 0 \Rightarrow H''(S) < 0$. Now, $H''(S)$ evaluated at the optimum has the opposite sign of the Jacobian of (6.9)–(6.10) which, by (6.11) is positive.

5. If $F(z)$ is twice differentiable, Condition (M) is equivalent to $F'(z) + F''(z)z < 0$ for all z. This is clearly stronger than the assumption that $F(z)$ be strictly concave, i.e. $F''(z) < 0$.

6. Note that a term $[(F'(s)/S - F'(S)/s]F'(z)z \ln S$ has been added in the definition of $G(z)$. But this addition to (6.14) is, in view of (6.5'), equal to zero.

7. If production costs were zero $(c = 0)$, $F(z) = zf(z)$. Thus, (6.57) would imply that

$$f(z) = \begin{cases} a, & z \leq s^* \\ \dfrac{(a + b)s^*}{z} - b, & z > s^* \end{cases}$$

i.e. the quantity demanded increases as the real price decreases to s^*, while any further price decrease leaves the quantity demanded unchanged.

8. Strictly speaking, this is true only for functions which are continuously differentiable.

9. In fact, more than non-storability is required. In our model demand depends only on the current price charged by the firm. It is assumed that while consumers have firm expectations with respect to the general price level, they ignore (due, presumably, to informational costs) the time pattern of future prices of any particular commodity. If consumers could in fact predict all prices with perfect foresight, they would obviously go on a buying spree just before the anticipated price increase. More generally, if substitution across time is admitted, demand will depend on the whole price cycle of each firm.

References

[1] Bailey, M. J. "The Welfare Cost of Inflationary Finance," *Journal of Political Economy*, 64 (1956), 93–110.

[2] Barro, R. J. "A Theory of Monopolistic Price Adjustment," *Review of Economic Studies*, 39 (1972), 17–26.

[3] Bewley, T. "A Theoretical Study of Optimal Price Adjustment," Discussion Paper No. 403, Harvard Institute of Economic Research (1975).

[4] Hadar, J. and Russell, W. R. "Rules for Ordering Uncertain Prospects," *American Economic Review*, 59 (1969), 25–34.

[5] Scarf, H. "The Optimality of (s, S) Policies in the Dynamic Inventory Problem," in Arrow, K., Karlin, S. and Suppes, P. (eds.), *Mathematical Methods in the Social Sciences* (Stanford University Press, 1959).

[6] Srinivasan, T. N. "Geometric Rate of Growth of Demand", in Manne, A. (ed.), *Investments for Capacity Expansion: Size, Location, and Time-Phasing* (MIT Press, 1967).

7 Optimum Pricing Policy under Stochastic Inflation

Eytan Sheshinski and Yoram Weiss

1 Introduction

In this chapter we consider pricing policies of individual firms in an inflationary environment. Each firm expects the general price level to increase and must determine the rate of increase of its own price. It is assumed that the firm incurs an adjustment cost when it changes its nominal price. Consequently, firms choose to change prices occasionally rather than continuously.

Our purpose is to analyse the dependence of the magnitude and the frequency of nominal price changes on the inflationary process. This problem has been analysed by Sheshinski and Weiss (1977, 1979) for the case of a fixed and certain rate of increase in the aggregate price level. This chapter extends the analysis to the case of uncertainty.[1]

The dependence of price policies of individual firms on the aggregate price level implies a relation between relative price dispersion and the inflation rate. This link is an important source of the real costs of inflation as pointed out by Okun (1971). Extensive empirical research has established the existence of a positive relation between the rate of inflation and its variability and relative price dispersion (surveyed by Gordon (1981), Fischer (1981) and Taylor (1981)).

We consider an inflationary stochastic process in which the rate of change of the price level can be positive or zero. The times spent in each state are of random duration. This class of processes includes Two-State Markov Chains and Renewal Processes as special cases.

The optimal policy is shown to be (S, s). That is, each firm changes its nominal price whenever its real price falls below some predetermined level, s. The new nominal price is chosen to attain a predetermined real price, S. The duration of the period with fixed nominal price is thus random.

The main result of the chapter is that for the class of stochastic processes analysed, the optimal policy is the same as the one obtained under certainty for some specific rate of inflation. This certainty-equivalence rate of inflation depends on characteristics of the stochastic process but is independent of firm-specific attributes. It always exceeds the expected rate of inflation by a risk premium which depends on the real interest rate and on the parameters of the stochastic process. One can therefore utilize results obtained by Sheshinski and Weiss (1977) for the certainty case to analyse the effects of changes in the parameters of the inflationary process. It is shown that a mean-preserving increase in spread leads to an increase in the amplitude of real price variations and decreases the expected frequency of nominal price changes. A spread-preserving increase in the expected rate of inflation increases the bounds within which real prices vary only if the variability of expected future prices is small. Thus, the main empirical implication of Sheshinski and Weiss (1977) that a higher expected rate of inflation increases the amplitude of real price changes need not hold under more general circumstances. This corresponds to the empirical findings mentioned in Taylor (1981), suggesting a stronger link between relative price dispersion and the variance of the aggregate inflation rate than with its mean.

2   The Inflationary Process

Consider a price process which can move between two states, denote 0 and 1. Each state is associated with a fixed rate of change in the price level. The duration of times (sojourn times) in each state are random variables which are independently and identically distributed. We assume that in state 0 the price level is unchanged while in state 1 it changes at a rate g, $g > 0$. We further assume that the sojourn times in state 1 are identically, exponentially distributed with intensity $\lambda_1 > 0$. The distribution of sojourn times in state 0, whose density is denoted $q(t)$, is unrestricted. We denote the sojourn times in state 0 and 1 by η_i and ζ_i, $i = 0, 1, \ldots$ respectively.

Let $T_i(t)$, $i = 0, 1$, be the total time spent in state i in the interval $[0, t]$. By definition $T_0(t) + T_1(t) = t$. The price level, p_t, is governed by

$$\log p_t = g T_1(t) \tag{7.1}$$

where $p_0 = 1$.

For large t, the asymptotic mean of $x_t \equiv \log p_t$ is linear in time:

$$E(x_t) = \left(\frac{g}{1 + \lambda_1 E(\eta)} \right) t \tag{7.2}$$

where $E(\eta) = \int_0^\infty t q(t)\, dt$. We may interpret $g/(1 + \lambda_1 E(\eta))$ as the *expected rate of inflation*. This rate depends positively on the rate of growth of prices in state 1, g, and on the expected fraction of time spent in state 1 which, in turn, is inversely related to $\lambda_1 E(\eta) = E(\eta)/E(\zeta)$, the ratio of expected sojourn times in states 0 and 1, respectively.

3   The Optimal Pricing Policy

We follow Sheshinski and Weiss (1977) and consider a price-setting firm whose real profits depend on the real price of its product, i.e. the ratio of its own nominal price to the price level. The underlying simplifying assumptions are that at each time consumers' demand is a function of the current real price (thus excluding storage and substitution over time). Other factors which may affect demand, such as real incomes, are constant. Similarly, costs adjust instantaneously to the price level.

There are fixed costs associated with nominal price changes and thus the firm will keep its price constant over finite intervals of time. Consequently, real price and real profits are random variables. The distribution of these variables depends on the pricing policy of the firm.

The firm is assumed to be risk neutral and to observe the price level instantaneously. Its objective is to maximize the present value of expected real profits over an infinite horizon. Due to the assumed monotonicity and stationarity of the inflationary process, the problem becomes analogous to the classical inventory problem (Scarf (1959), Denardo (1982, 135–156)). In particular, the policy is of the (S, s) form. That is, in terms of the log of real prices, the firm chooses a critical value s such that whenever the log of its real price falls to s, it adjusts its nominal price so as to attain a real price S. Under this policy, the firm changes price only in state 1. There is a minimal time-interval between successive price changes $\hat{t}, \hat{t} = (1/g)(S - s)$, while the actual duration between price changes is random (see Figure 7.1). The precise conditions for the optimality of the (S, s) policy are provided in Appendix A.

This characterization of the optimal policy relies heavily on the assumed properties of the inflationary process. Specifically, the assumptions that the process is monotone with only one state of positive growth and one state of zero growth are required for two bounds only to describe the optimal policy.[2]

Given this policy, the value of the objective function is determined by the choice of (S, s). We shall first specify the relation between these parameters and the objective function and then characterize their optimal choice.

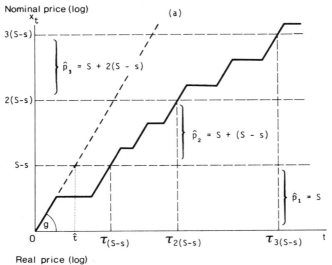

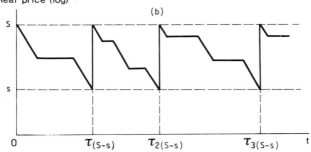

$\hat{p}_1, \hat{p}_2, \hat{p}_3, \ldots$ = Firm's nominal prices (log).

$\tau_{S-s}, \tau_{2(S-s)}, \tau_{3(S-s)}, \ldots$ = Dates of firm's price changes.

Figure 7.1

In order to calculate the expected profits of the firm we have to use the probability distribution of the price level conditioned on being in state 1 at time 0. It can be shown (see Karlin and Taylor (1975), p. 233) that[3]

$$H(x,t) \equiv Pr\{T_1(t) \geq x | \text{state 1 at } t = 0\}$$

$$= Pr\{\tau_x \leq t | \text{state 1 at } t = 0\}$$

$$= \sum_{n=0}^{\infty} G_n(t - x) \frac{(\lambda_1 x)^n}{n!} e^{-\lambda_1 x}, \qquad 0 \leq x \leq t, \qquad (7.3)$$

where τ_x is the waiting-time for x and $G_n(u)$ is the n-th convolution of the distribution of sojourn time in state 0.

The density of T_1 for a given t is thus

$$-\frac{\partial H(x,t)}{\partial x} \equiv -H_x(x,t)$$

and, similarly, the density of τ_x is

$$\frac{\partial H(x,t)}{\partial t} \equiv H_t(x,t).$$

Consider the firm at a time of a price change. Due to the assumptions of infinite horizon and the time independence of the interarrival times of the inflationary shocks, the firm's future is independent of the chronological time at which the price change occurs.

Let V denote maximal expected discounted real profits net of price adjustment costs, evaluated at the time of a price change. The following recursive formula holds:

$$V = -\beta + \int_0^{\hat{\imath}} e^{-rt} \left[e^{-\lambda_1 t} F(S - gt) + \int_0^t - H_x(x,t) F(S - gx)\, dx \right] dt$$

$$+ \int_{\hat{\imath}}^{\infty} e^{-rt} \int_0^{\hat{\imath}} - H_x(x,t) F(S - gx)\, dx\, dt$$

$$+ V \int_{\hat{\imath}}^{\infty} e^{-rt} H_t(\hat{\imath}, t)\, dt + V e^{-(r+\lambda_1)\hat{\imath}} \qquad (7.4)$$

where

β = fixed real adjustment costs

r = fixed real interest rate

$F(\cdot)$ = real profits as a function of the log of real price.

Since we observe the firm at a point of a price change, adjustment costs are subtracted with certainty and without discounting. The first integral represents expected profits until $\hat{t}$, which is the earliest feasible time of the next price change. In calculating the expected profit at a given t notice that in calculating expected values we take into account the concentration of probability mass at $T_1(t) = t$. Starting in state 1 at time 0, the probability of staying in the same state up to time t is $e^{-\lambda_1 t}$.

The second integral represents expected profits after $\hat{t}$, assuming that the change in the log of the price level since the last nominal change has not reached $S - s$. The last two terms represent expected discounted profits following a price change which occurs when $S - s$ is reached.

It is shown in Appendix B that (7.4) can be rewritten in the form

$$V = -\beta + \int_0^{\varepsilon_u} F(S - g_u x)e^{-rx}\, dx + Ve^{-r\varepsilon_u} \tag{7.5}$$

where

$$g_u = \frac{gr}{\lambda_1(1 - \mathscr{L}_q(r)) + r}, \tag{7.6}$$

$$\varepsilon_u = \frac{1}{g_u}(S - s), \tag{7.7}$$

and

$$\mathscr{L}_q(r) = \int_0^\infty e^{-rt} q(t)\, dt \tag{7.8}$$

is the Laplace Transform of $q(\cdot)$.

Form (7.5) of the recursive relation enables us now to state a basic certainty equivalence result.

4 Certainty Equivalence

In Sheshinski and Weiss (1977) we have shown that with a certain and constant rate of inflation the optimal policy is (S, s) with fixed time intervals between successive price changes. The recursive formula for V in that case can be written as

$$V = -\beta + \int_0^{\varepsilon_c} F(S - g_c t)e^{-rt}\, dt + Ve^{-r\varepsilon_c} \tag{7.9}$$

where g_c is the *certain* rate of inflation and $\varepsilon_c = (1/g_c)(S - s)$ is the fixed time-interval between successive price changes.

Let the inflationary stochastic process be specified by a vector of parameters, ω, and denote the solution to the recursive equation (7.5) by $V_u(S, s, r, \beta, \omega)$. Similarly, denote the solution to equation (7.9) by $V_c(S, s, r, \beta, g_c)$.

DEFINITION 1. *A certainty-equivalence rate of inflation, g_u, is a real-valued function $g_u(r, \omega)$ such that*

$$V_u(S, s, r, \beta, \omega) = V_c(S, s, r, \beta, g_u(r, \omega))$$

for all values of S, s, r, β and ω.

Note that we require g_u to depend only on parameters of the inflationary process, ω, and on the rate of interest, r. Parameters which vary across firms, such as adjustment costs, β, or parameters which characterize the profit function are excluded. This allows us, in analogy to the certainty case, to derive results which are not firm-specific.[4]

Comparing expressions (7.5) and (7.9), the following theorem is immediate:

THEOREM 1. *For the class of stochastic processes defined by (7.9), there exists a certainty-equivalence rate of inflation, $g_u(r, \omega)$, given by (7.6).*

Definition (7.6) provides a constructive method to calculate the certainty-equivalence rate of inflation. It is seen to depend on r, g, λ_1, and on the parameters of the density $q(t)$. It seems surprising that the concavity of the profit function has no bearing on the calculations. This is due to the fact that the optimum policy under certainty already takes into account such considerations (Sheshinski and Weiss (1977)).

A natural question is the relation between the certainty-equivalence rate and the expected aggregate rate of inflation, $g/(1 + \lambda_1 E(\eta))$. The following definition and proposition address this issue.

DEFINITION 2. $R(r, \omega) \equiv g_u(r, \omega) - g/(1 + \lambda_1 E(\eta))$ *is the risk-premium associated with a rate of interest r and a stochastic inflationary process parametrized by ω.*

PROPOSITION 1. $R \Rightarrow 0$ where $r \Rightarrow 0$, and $dR/dr > 0$.

Proof.   Using definition (7.6),

$$R = g\left[\frac{1}{1 + (\lambda_1/r)(1 - \mathscr{L}_q(r))} - \frac{1}{1 + \lambda_1 E(\eta)}\right]. \tag{7.10}$$

Expanding $\mathscr{L}_q(r)$ by a Taylor's series around $r = 0$,

$$1 - \mathscr{L}_q(r) = E(\eta)r - \frac{E(\eta^2)}{2}r^2 + \frac{E(\eta^3)}{3!}r^3 - \cdots. \tag{7.11}$$

Substituting in (7.10),

$$R = g\left[\frac{1}{1 + \lambda_1 E(\eta) - \dfrac{E(\eta^2)}{2}\lambda_1 r + \dfrac{E(\eta^3)}{3!}\lambda_1 r^2 - \cdots} - \frac{1}{1 + \lambda_1 E(\eta)}\right] \geqq 0. \tag{7.12}$$

Thus, $R \Rightarrow 0$ when $r \Rightarrow 0$. Furthermore, for $r > 0$

$$\frac{d}{dr}\left(\frac{1 - \mathscr{L}_q(r)}{r}\right) = \frac{1}{r^2}\int_0^\infty e^{rt}(rt - e^{-rt} + 1)q(t)\,dt < 0. \tag{7.13}$$

Hence $dR/dr > 0$ for $r > 0$.

It should be noted that when a certainty equivalence exists, the optimal (S, s) values chosen under uncertainty converge to their values under certainty (and $V_c - V_u$ tends to zero) as r approaches zero. The reason is that for given (S, s), different time-paths of the real price have the same effect on real profits. In addition, the expected frequency of price changes will be the same. When $r > 0$, the timing of the realization of various real prices is relevant.

5   Inflation as a Renewal Process

The stochastic process used in Section 2 to describe inflation is closely related to the well-known class of *Renewal Processes*. This specification views the inflationary process as a sequence of randomly spaced shocks which are independently and identically distributed:

$$x_t \equiv \log p_t = \sum_{i=1}^{N_t} y_i \tag{7.14}$$

where N_t is a *renewal counting process*, i.e. the duration of the periods between successive shocks is i.i.d. with density $q(t)$ (Parzen (1962)), Chapter 5). The shocks, y_i, are non-negative, $y_i \geq 0$, with common density $h(y)$.

For large t, the asymptotic mean, $E(x_t)$, and variance, $\text{Var}(x_t)$, are (Parzen (1962), p. 180),

$$E(x_t) = \frac{E(y)}{E(\eta)} t \tag{7.15}$$

and

$$\text{Var}(x_t) = \left(\frac{\text{Var}(y)}{E(\eta)} + \frac{\text{Var}(\eta)E(y)^2}{E(\eta)^3} \right) t \tag{7.16}$$

where $E(y)$ and $\text{Var}(y)$ are the mean and variance of the shock size, y, respectively, and $E(\eta)$ and $\text{Var}(\eta)$ are the mean and variance of the inter-arrival time, η. Equations (7.15) and (7.16) hold for *all* t when $q(t)$ is exponential, i.e. when (7.14) is a Compound Poisson Process.

As before, we may interpret $E(y)/E(\eta)$, i.e. the product of the average size of shocks and the intensity of shocks as the expected rate of inflation.

We shall now show that the process described in Section 2 converges to a renewal process in which the distribution of shock size, $h(y)$ is exponential, i.e. $h(y) = \alpha e^{-\alpha y}$, $\alpha > 0$ constant.

We can rewrite (7.3) as follows:

$$\Pr\{T_1(t) \geq x | \text{state 1 at } t = 0\} = \sum_{n=0}^{\infty} G_n(t - x)(F_n(x) - F_{n+1}(x))$$

$$= \sum_{n=0}^{\infty} F_n(x)(G_n(t - x) - G_{n-1}(t - x)) \tag{7.17}$$

where $F_n(x)$ is the n-th convolution of the sojourn time in state 1, and $G_{-1}(x) = 0$, $G_0(x) = 1$, $F_0(x) = 1$, for all $x \geq 0$.

Accordingly,

$$\Pr\{x_t \geq x | \text{state 1 at } t = 0\} = \sum_{n=0}^{\infty} F_n\left(\frac{x}{g}\right)\left(G_n\left(t - \frac{x}{g}\right) - G_{n-1}\left(t - \frac{x}{g}\right)\right). \tag{7.18}$$

Using the assumption that the sojourn-times in states 1 are exponentially distributed, we can write

$$F_n\left(\frac{x}{g}\right) = \int_0^{x/g} f_n(u)\, du = \lambda_1 \int_0^{x/g} e^{-\lambda_1 u} \frac{(\lambda_1 u)^{n-1}}{(n-1)!}\, du$$

$$= \frac{\lambda_1}{g} \int_0^x e^{-(\lambda_1/g)y} \frac{\left(\dfrac{\lambda_1}{g} y\right)^{n-1}}{(n-1)!}\, dy \qquad n = 1, 2, \ldots. \tag{7.19}$$

Define $\alpha = \lambda_1/g$ and let λ_1 and $g \to \infty$ holding α constant. From (7.17) we now obtain that

$$\Pr\{x_t \geqq x | \text{state 1 at } t = 0\} = 1 + \sum_{n=1}^{\infty} \alpha \int_0^x e^{-\alpha y} \frac{(\alpha y)^{n-1}}{(n-1)!}\, dy(G_n(t) - G_{n-1}(t)). \tag{7.20}$$

Hence,

$$\Pr\{x_t \leqq x | \text{state 1 at } t = 0\} = \sum_{n=1}^{\infty} \alpha \int_0^x e^{-\alpha y} \frac{(\alpha y)^{n-1}}{(n-1)!}\, dy(G_{n-1}(t) - G_n(t)). \tag{7.20}$$

The term in brackets can be recognized as the probability of having $n - 1$ shocks in $(0, t]$ when the waiting time between shocks has density $q(t)$. The integral will be recognized as the probability that the log of the price level, x_t, after n shocks (the first occurring at $t = 0$) does not exceed x, when the distribution of shock, $h(y)$, is exponential.

This result raises the question whether the certainty-equivalence result proved in Theorem 1 can be extended to renewal processes in which the shock size is not distributed exponentially. In order to answer this question it is necessary to examine the nature of the optimal policy for this class of general renewal processes.

Using the same arguments as in Appendix A it is easy to show that the firm will change prices only upon the occurrence of a shock in the price level. However, due to the discontinuity of the price level, the real price at such points is not well-defined. In particular, it is not clear what is the nominal price necessary to attain S and how does the firm ascertain that s has been reached.

The most natural formulation appears to be one in which the firm chooses its nominal price just after the shock (ex-post). For this case, the optimality of (S, s) policies can be proved. However, a certainty-equivalence does not exist.[5]

An alternative, which may be termed a precommitment policy, would be to announce prior to the shock critical values for the price level which will generate a price change and the chosen nominal prices for the firm. For this class of policies one can show that if the policy is of the (S, s) type then a certainty-equivalence exists if and only if $h(y)$ is exponential and that an (S, s) is optimal if and only if $h(y)$ is exponential (see Sheshinski and Weiss (1982)). Thus, the precommitment policy can be interpreted as the limit of the policy described in Section 2 when the rate of growth in state 1, g, increases while the expected sojourn time in this state, $1/\lambda_1$, becomes shorter, keeping the combined effect on the price level, g/λ_1, unchanged.

6   Expected Frequency of Price Changes

Another variable of interest is the time between successive price changes by the firm. In contrast to the certainty case, under uncertain inflation this is a random variable. We shall calculate here only the expected time between successive price changes.

From (7.3),[6]

$$E(\tau_x) = x + \int_x^\infty \left[1 - \sum_{n=0}^\infty G_n(t - x) \frac{(\lambda_1 x)^n}{n!} e^{-\lambda_1 x} \right] dt$$

$$= x + \int_x^\infty \left[1 - \sum_{n=0}^\infty G_n(t - x)(F_n(x) - F_{n+1}(x)) \right] dt$$

$$= x + \int_x^\infty \sum_{n=1}^\infty F_n(x)(G_{n-1}(t - x) - G_n(t - x)) \, dt$$

$$= x + E(\eta) \sum_{n=1}^\infty F_n(x)$$

$$= (1 + \lambda_1 E(\eta)) x. \tag{7.22}$$

Recall that $x_t = g T_1(t)$, hence expected waiting time to reach a particular level for x_t, say $S - s$, is given by

$$\frac{(1 + \lambda_1 E(\eta))(S - s)}{g}. \tag{7.23}$$

Under the (S, s) policy this is the expected time between price changes by the firm. Comparing (7.23) and (7.2) we see that for large t,

$$E(\tau_{S-s}) = \frac{t(S - s)}{E(x_t)} \tag{7.24}$$

which is "Wald's Identity" (Feller (1971), p. 397).

7 Comparative Statics

In this section we wish to investigate the effect of changes in the parameters of the inflationary process on the choice of (S, s) and on the expected time between successive price adjustments by the firm.

For empirical applications of the model, it is useful to separate two aspects of the inflationary process: the mean rate of inflation and its variance. These aspects can be directly identified in a sub-class of the processes described in Section 2. This is the class of Two-State Markov Chains (see Parzen (1962) and Cohen (1979)). In this case the sojourn-time distribution in both states is assumed exponential. Thus,

$$q(t) = \lambda_0 e^{-\lambda_0 t}. \tag{7.25}$$

For large, t, the asymptotic mean and variance of $x_t \equiv \log p_t$ are again linear in time (Parzen (1962), pp. 294–295),

$$E(x_t) = \left(\frac{\lambda_0 g}{\lambda_0 + \lambda_1}\right) t \tag{7.26}$$

$$\mathrm{Var}(x_t) = \left(\frac{2\lambda_0 \lambda_1 g^2}{(\lambda_0 + \lambda_1)^3}\right) t. \tag{7.27}$$

Letting $\lambda_1, g \to \infty$ while $\lambda_1/g = \alpha$ constant, we obtain as a special case of the above formulas

$$E(x_t) = \frac{\lambda_0}{\alpha} t \tag{7.28}$$

and

$$\mathrm{Var}(x_t) = \frac{2\lambda_0}{\alpha^2} t \tag{7.29}$$

which can be recognized as the expectation and variance of a Compound Poisson Process (Parzen (1962), p. 130) and holds for *all* t.

We shall exploit the certainty-equivalence result (Theorem 1) to perform the comparative statics. Using (7.25) and definition (7.6), g_u becomes in our case

$$g_u = \frac{(\lambda_0 + r)g}{\lambda_0 + \lambda_1 + r}. \tag{7.30}$$

It has been shown in Sheshinski and Weiss (1977) that under certainty an increase in the rate of inflation increases S and decreases s thus increasing the amplitude of real price variations.

The effects of the parameters of the inflationary process on the optimum (S, s) can therefore be inferred from their effect on the certainty-equivalence rate $g_u(r, \lambda_0, \lambda_1, g)$.

An increase in the rate of growth of the price level when in state 1, g, or in the probability of staying in this state (reduction in λ_1) is seen to increase g_u and hence will increase S and decrease s. An increase in the probability of staying in state 0 with no price level changes (reduction in λ_0), decreases g_u and has the opposite effect on (S, s). Each of these cases involves simultaneous changes in the mean and variance of the price level. It is, however, possible to separate these effects. In view of (7.26)–(7.27), a mean-preserving increase in the variance of the price level is attained by decreasing λ_0 and λ_1 in the same proportion, holding g constant. As seen from (7.30), such a change increases g_u. We thus draw the important conclusion that an increase in the variability of the price level unambiguously leads to an increase in the amplitude of the firm's real price.

Adapting equation (7.24) to our case

$$E(\tau_{S-s}) = \frac{(\lambda_0 + \lambda_1)(S - s)}{\lambda_0 g}. \tag{7.31}$$

Hence, the increase in the bounds, $S - s$, within which real price is allowed to fluctuate will also lead to an increase in the expected time interval between price changes, i.e. reduces the expected frequency of price changes.

Spread preserving changes may lead to ambiguous results depending on the measure of the spread. Increasing the mean holding the variance constant (via an equally proportional increase in λ_0, λ_1, and g^2) will increase g_u if

$$\frac{(\lambda_0 + r)(\lambda_0 + \lambda_1 + r)}{r\lambda_1} > \frac{1}{2}$$

which holds for large λ_0, i.e. when uncertainty is small. However, holding the coefficient of variation constant and increasing the mean (via increasing g) will lead to larger S and smaller s, as in the certainty case.

Also, as in the certainty case, the relation between the expected rate of inflation and $E(\tau_{S-s})$ is ambiguous. For instance, increasing g, holding λ_0 and λ_1 constant, increases $S - s$ and the denominator in (7.31), with an indeterminate effect on $E(\tau_{S-s})$.

8 Interactions Across Firms

So far we have examined the behaviour of a representative firm in isolation. The inflationary process was treated as exogenous rather than an outcome of the actions of individual firms. Nor did we discuss the source of the aggregate disturbances. These could be demand shifts or cost (input-price) induced changes, firm-specific or industry-wide. None of these specifications is necessarily suggested by the model. A detailed analysis of these issues is beyond the scope of this chapter. Nevertheless, we would like to outline a possible framework for such an analysis.

Suppose the economy consists of two sectors: a competitive sector of price-takers and a monopolistic sector of price setters. Assume that exogeneous shocks in costs or in demand affect the competitive sector. Since competitive firms cannot adopt independent price policies, this sector will adjust its price immediately. The resulting change in relative prices will induce a change in the demand facing firms in the monopolistic sector. In this sector price changes in general do not occur immediately. On average, however, monopolistic firms adjust their price at the same rate as competitive firms. The aggregate outcome is therefore consistent with the expectations of each firm. Whenever a firm changes its nominal price, it increases it by the rate of $S - s$ and keeps it constant for an average duration of $E(\tau_{S-s})$. As seen from (7.33), optimal behaviour implies that the rate of price change per unit time of each firm is on average equal to the expected rate of inflation.

A stronger test of consistency would require fulfillment of expectations at any moment in time and not only on average. Under certainty, conditions for such consistency can be easily described. If the dates of price changes by firms are uniformly distributed, then the aggregate price level will increase continuously at a constant rate, as expected by firms, even though every firm in isolation follows a discontinuous price policy. Indeed, no exogeneous shocks are needed to generate this process as firms's price policies will follow each other indefinitely. In contrast, the process which we have described cannot be sustained without outside shocks since in periods with no price change, *all* firms will choose to keep their own price unchanged and there will be no cause for further price increases. Moreover, under uncertainty we can no longer assume that the distribution of the dates of price changes is invariant over time. Suppose for example, that all firms are identical in their (S, s) policies and that exogeneous shocks transmitted from the competitive sector, occur randomly. Suppose further that firms are initially uniformly distributed with respect to the timing of their price adjustment. If the size of the exogeneous shock is relatively small and if the shocks are widely spaced over time, one may observe an initial period of gradual price level adjustment in which a fixed fraction of firms change prices at each instant followed by a period of no price change. The duration of each adjustment period will depend on the size and duration of the exogeneous shocks. In general, we cannot expect the distribution of the dates of price changes to be invariant over time since large or/and closely spaced shocks may lead to synchronization and hence change the distribution.[7] There is thus no simple correspondence between the process of exogeneous shocks and the process followed by the aggregate price level.

Appendix A

The purpose of this appendix is to prove the optimality and uniqueness of (S, s) policies for the class of stochastic processes specified in equations (7.3) and (7.21). Without loss of generality we assume that in state 1 the price level changes at a rate of unity, i.e. $g = 1$.

The proof proceeds in two steps. We first provide conditions which ensure that firms will change prices only when the aggregate price level increases (state 1). We then prove that the optimal policy is (S, s), i.e. when the firm's real price reaches (or falls below) a critical level, s, its nominal price is adjusted discretely so as to attain a real price, S $(> s)$.

THEOREM 1A. *Let the firm be in state* 0 *at time* t_0. *Then, if the density of waiting-time to the next shock conditioned on being in state* 0 *up to time* $t_0 + x$,

$$q_{t_0}(x) = \frac{q(t_0 + x)}{1 - Q(t_0 + x)},$$

is a monotone non-increasing function of x, *it is never optimal to change prices in state* 0.

Proof. Let the firm's real price at t_0 be z_0 and let t_1, $t_1 > t_0$, be a time such that the firm is still in state 0 (i.e. no shock has occurred in $(t_0, t_1]$). Suppose that at t_1 it is optimal to change the real price to z_1. This change is profitable if

$$\int_0^\infty \left(F(z_1)\frac{1}{r}(1 - e^{-rt}) + W(z_1)e^{-rt} \right) q_{t_1}(t)\, dt - \beta$$

$$> \int_0^\infty \left(F(z_0)\frac{1}{r}(1 - e^{-rt}) + W(z_0)e^{-rt} \right) q_{t_1}(t)\, dt. \qquad (7.1a)$$

where $W(z)$ is the value of the optimal policy at a transition to state 1, conditioned on a real price of z. Now, take $t_2 \in (t_0, t_1)$. Due to the monotonicity assumption, $q_{t_2}(t) \geqq q_{t_1}(t)$, $\forall t \geqq 0$. Thus, replacing $q_{t_1}(t)$ with $q_{t_2}(t)$ in (7.1a) retains the inequality. Hence it would be profitable for the firm to choose the same nominal (and real) price as in t_1 and hold it fixed until the next shock including t_1. By a similar argument, if the firm contemplates additional changes in its nominal price between t_1 and the next shock, one can show that it is profitable to choose the same price as t_1 somewhat earlier and to follow the same pattern of price changes thereafter. This includes *not* changing the price at t_1. An optimal price choice at t_2 can only increase this gain. It follows that a price change cannot occur in state 0. ‖

Since price changes are costly, the firm will avoid price adjustments in the absence of a change in the current or expected aggregate price level. In state 0 the current price level is unchanged and the expectation for a price shock decreases due to the monotonicity assumption. In these circumstances, additional information only decreases the incentive for a price change. Note that the Poisson process, $q(t) = \lambda e^{-\lambda t}$, and, more generally, the Gamma density,

$$q(t) = \frac{\lambda^{\alpha} t^{\alpha-1}}{\Gamma(\alpha)} e^{-\lambda t},$$

with $0 < \alpha \leq 1$ (see Barlow and Proschan's discussion of the Hazard-Rate (1975, Chapter 3)), satisfy the condition of Theorem 1A.

THEOREM 2A. *If* (a) *the conditions of Theorem 1A are satisfied;* (b) *the density of waiting time in state 1 is exponential and* (c) *the profits function, $F(z)$, is strictly quasi-concave in z, then the optimal policy is (S, s).*

Proof. Suppose that nominal price changes can occur in short intervals of fixed length, h. Denote by $W_h(z)$ the value of the firm's optimal plan conditioned on being in state 1 with a real price z. Due to assumption (b), $W_h(z)$ is independent of the time of entry into state 1.

Let

$$\Omega_h(z) = \lambda_1 \int_0^h e^{-\lambda_1 t} \left[\int_0^t e^{-ru} F(z - u) \, du + e^{-rt} W_h^0(z - t) \right] dt$$

$$+ e^{-\lambda_1 h} \left[\int_0^h e^{-ru} F(z - u) \, du + e^{-rh} W_h(z - h) \right], \qquad (7.2a)$$

where

$$W_h^0(z) = \int_0^\infty q(t) \left[\int_0^t F(z) e^{-ru} \, du + e^{-rt} W_h(z) \right] dt. \qquad (7.3a)$$

The function $\Omega_h(z)$ is the expected value of discounted real profits associated with a real price z in the time interval $(0, h]$ and conditioned on being in state 1 at time 0. It accounts for the possibility of leaving state 1 sometime prior to h. The possibility of more than one switch across states is of second order and hence disregarded for small h. The function $W_h^0(z)$ is the expected value of discounted real profits evaluated upon entry to state 0. The calculation makes use of Theorem 1A, which implies that z remains constant in state 0.

With the above definitions we can define $W_h(z)$ recursively as follows:

$$W_h(z) = \text{Max}[\Omega_h(z), \text{Max}_{z_1} \Omega_h(z_1) - \beta]. \qquad (7.4a)$$

We wish to investigate the properties of $W(z) = \lim_{h \to 0} W_h(z)$. For a given h, consider the set $Z_h = \{z | \Omega_h(z) > \text{Max}_{z_1} \Omega_h(z_1) - \beta\}$. Let $Z = \lim_{h \to 0} Z_h$. For any $z \in Z$, we have, using (7.3a),

$$W_h(z) = \lambda_1 \int_0^h e^{-\lambda_1 t} \left[\left[\int_0^t e^{-ru} F(z-u)\, du + e^{-rt} \left(\frac{F(z-t)}{r}(1 - \mathscr{L}_q(r)) \right) \right. \right.$$

$$\left. + W_h(z-t)\mathscr{L}_q(r)) \right] dt + e^{-\lambda_1 h} \left[\int_0^h e^{-ru} F(z-u)\, du + e^{-rh} W_h(z-h) \right]$$

(7.5a)

where

$$\mathscr{L}_q(r) = \int_0^\infty e^{-rt} q(t)\, dt \tag{7.6a}$$

is the Laplace Transform of $q(\cdot)$. Subtracting $W_h(z)$ from both sides of (7.5a), dividing by h and passing to the limit as $h \to 0$, we obtain

$$0 = \frac{\lambda_1}{r} F(z)(1 - \mathscr{L}_q(r)) + \lambda_1 W(z)\mathscr{L}_q(r) + F(z) - (r + \lambda_1)W(z) - W'(z). \tag{7.7a}$$

Now let $\hat{z}$ be a boundary point of Z. At such a point there is a switch to z_1^*, the solution to $\text{Max}_{z_1} \Omega(z_1)$ (where $\Omega(z) = \lim_{h \to 0} \Omega_h(z)$), which is independent of z. Thus, $W'(\hat{z}) = 0$. Rearranging (7.7a) at $\hat{z}$, we have

$$F(\hat{z}) = rW(\hat{z}). \tag{7.8a}$$

Also,

$$W''(\hat{z}) = F'(\hat{z})(\lambda_1(1 - \mathscr{L}_q(r)) + r). \tag{7.9a}$$

Since z_1^* is independent of z, $W(\hat{z}) = \Omega(z_1^*) - \beta$ for *any* switch point. Due to assumption (c), (7.8a) has either two or no solution. Assuming that β is sufficiently small for the existence of a solution, we distinguish two possible points, $\hat{z}_1$ and $\hat{z}_2$ (see Figure 7.2).

If for any $z < \hat{z}_1$ or $z > \hat{z}_2$, $W(z) > \Omega(z_1^*) - \beta$ then there must be an additional switch point, which by (7.8a) will contradict assumption (c). Due to (7.9a), clearly $\hat{z}_1 < z_1^* < \hat{z}_2$. In view of the *monotonicity* of the price level, once z_1^* is chosen, z can only move downwards. Thus, after the first switch, only $\hat{z}_1$ is relevant. Accordingly, we denote $\hat{z}_1 = s$ and $z_1^* = S$ which completes the proof.

We have shown that s is unique. We now provide conditions for the uniqueness of S.

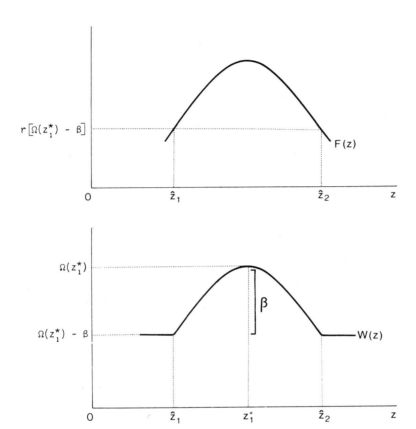

Figure 7.2

Denote the value of the firm's plan, $W(z)$, evaluated at $z = s$, by $V(S, s)$. This function will satisfy the recursive equation (7.5) which implies

$$V(S, s) = \frac{-\beta + \int_0^{\varepsilon_u} F(S - g_u x) e^{-rs} \, dx}{1 - e^{-r\varepsilon_u}} \qquad (7.10a)$$

where

$$\varepsilon_u = \frac{1}{g_u}(S - s)$$

and

$$g_u = \frac{gr}{\lambda_1(1 - \mathcal{L}_q(r)) + r}.$$

The first-order conditions for an interior maximum of V w.r.t. S and s can be written

$$F(s) - rV = 0, \tag{7.11a}$$

and

$$\int_0^{\varepsilon_u} F'(S - g_u x)e^{-rx}\,dx = 0. \tag{7.12a}$$

Integrating (7.12a) using (7.11a), this equation can be rewritten

$$F(S) - F(s) - r\beta = 0. \tag{7.12'a}$$

Equations (7.11a) and (7.12'a) are the same first-order conditions obtained in Sheshinski and Weiss (1977), equations (9)–(10). The second-order conditions are

$$F'(s) > 0 \quad \text{and} \quad F'(S) < 0, \tag{7.13a}$$

which in view of the strict quasi-concavity of $F(\cdot)$ and (7.12a) are seen to be satisfied at the optimum. Hence, the optimum (S, s) is unique.   ∥

Appendix B

The purpose of this Appendix is to prove that (7.4) can be rewritten in the form (7.5).
   Define

$$\hat{H}_x(x, t) \equiv \begin{cases} -H_x(x, t) & \text{if } x \leq t \\ 0 & \text{otherwise.} \end{cases} \tag{7.1b}$$

Using (7.1b), one can verify the following equalities:

$$\int_0^i e^{-rt} \int_0^t -H_x(x, t)F(S - gx)\,dx\,dt + \int_i^\infty e^{-rt} \int_0^i -H_x(x, t)F(S - gx)\,dx\,dt$$

$$= \int_0^i e^{-rt} \int_0^i H_x(x, t)F(S - gx)\,dx\,dt + \int_i^\infty e^{-rt} \int_0^i \hat{H}_x(x, t)F(S - gx)\,dx\,dt$$

$$= \int_0^\infty e^{-rt} \int_0^{\hat{\imath}} \hat{H}_x(x,t) F(S - gx) \, dx \, dt$$

$$= \int_0^{\hat{\imath}} \int_0^\infty e^{-rt} \hat{H}_x(x,t) F(S - gx) \, dt \, dx$$

$$= \int_0^{\hat{\imath}} \int_x^\infty - e^{-rt} H_x(x,t) F(S - gx) \, dt \, dx \tag{7.2b}$$

Using (7.3) to calculate $H_x(x,t)$, we obtain

$$-\int_x^\infty e^{-rt} H_x(x,t) \, dt = \frac{\lambda_1}{r} e^{-(r+\lambda_1)x} + \sum_{n=1}^\infty \int_x^\infty e^{-rt} g_n(t-x) \frac{(\lambda_1 x)^n}{n!} e^{-\lambda_1 x} \, dt$$

$$+ \lambda_1 \sum_{n=1}^\infty e^{-\lambda_1 x} \int_x^\infty e^{-rt} G_n(t-x) \frac{(\lambda_1 x)^n}{n!} \, dt$$

$$- \lambda_1 \sum_{n=1}^\infty \int_x^\infty e^{-rt} G_n(t-x) \frac{(\lambda_1 x)^{n-1}}{(n-1)!} e^{-\lambda_1 x} \, dt.$$

Similarly,

$$\int_{\hat{\imath}}^\infty e^{-rt} H_t(\hat{\imath}, t) \, dt = \sum_{n=1}^\infty \int_{\hat{\imath}}^\infty e^{-rt} g_n(t - \hat{\imath}) \frac{(\lambda_1 \hat{\imath})^n}{n!} e^{-\lambda_1 \hat{\imath}} \, dt. \tag{7.4b}$$

Performing the integrations and summations in (7.3b) and (7.4b), we obtain

$$-\int_x^\infty e^{-rt} H_x(x,t) \, dt = \frac{\lambda_1}{r} e^{(\lambda_1 \mathscr{L}_q(r) - \lambda_1 - r)x} - \frac{\lambda_1}{r} \mathscr{L}_q(r) e^{(\lambda_1 \mathscr{L}_q(r) - \lambda_1 - r)x}$$

$$+ e^{(\lambda_1 \mathscr{L}_q(r) - \lambda_1 - r)x} - e^{-(\lambda_1 + r)x} \tag{7.5b}$$

and

$$\int_{\hat{\imath}}^\infty e^{-rt} H_t(\hat{\imath}, t) \, dt = e^{(\lambda_1 \mathscr{L}_q(r) - \lambda_1 - r)\hat{\imath}} - e^{-(\lambda_1 + r)\hat{\imath}} \tag{7.6b}$$

where we make use of the fact that

$$\int_x^\infty e^{-rt} g_n(t - x)\, dt = e^{-rx} \int_0^\infty e^{-ru} g_n(u)\, du \tag{7.7b}$$

$$= e^{-rx} \mathscr{L}_q^n(r). \tag{7.7b}$$

Substituting in (7.4) in the text, one obtains

$$V = -\beta + \int_0^{\hat{t}} F(S - gx)\left(\frac{\lambda_1(1 - \mathscr{L}_q(r)) + r}{r}\right) e^{-(\lambda_1(1 - \mathscr{L}_q r)) + r)x}\, dx$$

$$+ \, V e^{-(\lambda_1(1 - \mathscr{L}_q(r)) + r)\hat{t}}. \tag{7.8b}$$

Changing variables in the integral in (7.8b)

$$u = \left(\frac{\lambda_1(1 - \mathscr{L}_q(r)) + r}{r}\right) x$$

and using $\hat{t} = (1/g)(S - s)$, one obtains (7.5).

Notes

Partial financial support from the Center for Research on Organizational Efficiency at Stanford University NSF Grant BNS 76-22943 and from the Department of Economics at New York University at Stony-Brook is gratefully acknowledged. When writing the paper, the first author was a Fellow at the Center for Advanced Study in the Behavioral Sciences at Stanford, on leave from the Hebrew University in Jerusalem. The second author was visiting at the Department of Economics and Visiting Scholar at the Hoover Institution at Stanford University, on leave from Tel-Aviv University. The authors would like to thank Joel Cohen, Joseph Rinott and David Siegmund for helpful discussions.

1. Extensions of the Sheshinski and Weiss (1977) model to the case of uncertainty have been made in unpublished works by Padan (1981), Danziger (1981) and Roberds (1979). The present work has benefited from our direct interaction with Padan and Danziger.

2. Non-monotone processes require three or four parameters to describe the optimal policy. See, for example, Frenkel–Jovanovicz (1980) in the context of firms' optimum cash management and Harrison, Sellke and Taylor (1981). The monotonicity allows us to obtain results analogous to the certainty case discussed in Sheshinski and Weiss (1977).

With more than one possible positive growth rate, again there will be more than two parameters since the (S, s) values will depend on the state, i.e. on the slope of the price level profile and not only on the level.

3. The formula follows from the observation that

$$\Pr\{T_0(t) \leq x\} = \Pr\{\theta(t - x) \leq x\}$$

where

$$\theta(t) = \eta_1 + \eta_2 + \cdots + \eta_{N_1(t)},$$

η_i is the sojourn time spent in state 0 and $N_1(t)$ is the renewal process generated by the sojourn time in state 1.

4. Definition 1 is equivalent to the requirement that S and s will be the same *functions* of g under certainty and g_u under uncertainty. This is necessary for the equivalence of the comparative statics. A weaker definition will equate the value of the optimal solution (evaluated, possibly, at different (S, s) values).

5. Denote by $P_n(t)$ the probability of n shock in the interval $(0, t]$. Then,

$$P_n(t) = \Pr\{N(t) = n\} = \Pr\{\eta_1 + \eta_2 + \cdots + \eta_n \leq t\} - \Pr\{\eta_1 + \eta_2 + \cdots + \eta_{n+1} \leq t\},$$
$$n = 1, 2, \ldots$$

where η_1 is concentrated at 0 and η_i, $i = 2, 3, \ldots$ are i.i.d. the precommitment and ex-post policies are, respectively,

(a) $$V = -\beta + \int_0^\infty e^{-rt} \sum_{n=1}^\infty P_n(t) \int_0^{S-s} F(S - x) h_n(x)\, ds\, dt$$

$$+ V \int_0^\infty e^{-rt} \frac{\partial}{\partial t} \sum_{n=1}^\infty P_n(t) \int_{S-s}^\infty h_n(x)\, dx\, dt + V \int_{S-s}^\infty h_1(x)\, dx$$

(b) $$V = -\beta + \int_0^\infty e^{-rt} \sum_{n=2}^\infty P_n(t) \int_0^{S-s} F(S - x) h_n(x)\, dx\, dt$$

$$+ V \int_0^\infty e^{-rt} \frac{\partial}{\partial t} \sum_{n=2}^\infty P_n(t) \int_{S-s}^\infty h_n(x)\, dx\, dt + F(S) \int_0^\infty e^{-rt} P_1(t)\, dt$$

where $h_n(x)$ is the n-th convolution of $h(y)$:

$$h_n(x) = \int_0^x h_{n-1}(x - y) h(y)\, dy \qquad n = 2, 3, \ldots$$

and $h_1(y) = h(y)$.

The difference between (a) and (b) is that after the choice of S there is a positive probability weight associated with no further shocks, in which case the real price remains S. This is represented by the last term on the R.H.S. of (b). On the other hand, there is zero weight associated with s. This asymmetry causes the non-existence of certainty-equivalence.

6. In the following we use the relationship

$$\int_x^\infty (G_{n-1}(t - x) - G_n(t - x))\, dt = \int_0^\infty [(1 - G_n(u)) - (1 - G_{n-1}(u))]\, du$$

$$= E(\eta_1 + \eta_2 + \cdots + \eta_n) - E(\eta_1 + \eta_2 + \cdots + \eta_{n-1}) = E(\eta)$$

and

$$F_n(x) = \int_0^x \frac{(\lambda_1 y)^{n-1}}{(n - 1)!} e^{-\lambda_1 y}\, dy.$$

7. For some discussion of the transmission mechanism across firms and the effects of aggregate shocks see Blanchard (1982) and Parkin (1982).

References

Barlow, R. and Proschan, F. (1975) *Statistical Theory of Reliability and Life Testing* (Holt, Rinehart and Winston).

Blanchard, O. (1983), "Price Asynchronization and Price Level Inertia" in Dornbusch, R. and Simonsen, M. (eds.) Inflation, Debt and Indexation (MIT Press).

Cohen, J. (1979), "Random Evolutions in Discrete and Continuous Time," *Stoch. Processes Appl.*, 2, 245–251.

Danziger, L. (1981), "Uncertain Inflation and the Optimal Policy of Price Adjustments" (Working Paper 27–81, Foerder Institute, Tel-Aviv University).

Denardo, E. V. (1982) *Dynamic programming models and applications* (Prentice Hall).

Feller, W. (1971) *An Introduction to Probability Theory and its Applications* Vol. II (Wiley).

Fischer, S. (1981), "Relative Shocks, Relative Price Variability and Inflation," *Brookings Economic Papers* No. 2, pp. 381–431.

Frenkel, J. and Jovanovicz, B. (1980), "On Transactions and Precautionary Demand for Money," *Quarterly Journal of Economics*, 96, 25–44.

Gordon, R. (1981), "Output Fluctuations and Gradual Price Adjustments," *Journal of Economic Literature*, 19, 493–530.

Harrison, M., Sellke, T. and Taylor, A. (1981), "Impulse Control of Brownian Motion" (Stanford University, mimeo).

Karlin, S. and Taylor, H. (1975) *A First Course in Stochastic Processes* (Academic Press).

Okun, A. (1971), "The Mirage of Steady Inflation," *Brookings Papers in Economic Activity*, 2, 435–498.

Padan, O. (1981), "Optimal Pricing Policy for a Monopolistic Firm Under Conditions of Uncertain Inflation" (unpublished Ph.D. dissertation, The Hebrew University, Jerusalem).

Parkin, M. (1982), "The Output Inflation Tradeoff when Prices are Costly to Change" (Research Report No. 8209, Department of Economics, University of Western Ontario).

Parzen, E. (1962) *Stochastic Processes* (Holden-Day).

Roberds, W. (1979), "Dynamic Monopoly Pricing with Uncertainty and Fixed Costs of Price Adjustment" (unpublished manuscript, Carnegie-Mellon).

Scarf, H. (1959), "The Optimality of (S, s) Policies in the Dynamic Inventory Problem" in Arrow, K., Karlin, S. and Suppes, P. (eds.) *Mathematical Methods in the Social Sciences* (Stanford University Press).

Sheshinski, E. and Weiss, Y. (1977), "Inflation and Costs of Price Adjustment," *Review of Economic Studies*, 54, 287–303.

Sheshinski, E. and Weiss, Y. (1979), "Demand for Fixed Factors, Inflation and Adjustment Costs," *Review of Economic Studies*, 56, 31–45.

Sheshinski, S. and Weiss, Y. (1982), "Optimum Pricing Policy Under Stochastic Inflation" (Technical Report No. 363, Institute for Mathematical Studies in the Social Sciences, Stanford University).

Taylor, J. (1981), "On the Relation Between the Variability of Inflation and the Average Inflation Rate," *Journal of Monetary Economics*, Carnegie-Rochester Conference Series on Public Policy, 15, 57–86.

Addendum

It was pointed out to us by Andrew Caplin that Theorem 1A in Appendix A only establishes that a firm would never *delay* a price change in the state with zero inflation but does not exclude the possibility of a price change *immediately* upon entry into this state. Intuitively, with a sufficiently low exit rate from the state with zero inflation, the firm would prefer to raise or reduce the price instantaneously rather than stay locked in a suboptimal state. Thus, in general, the optimal policy would be characterized by two distinct (S, s) pairs: one pair (S_0, s_0) is associated with the state of zero inflation, and another pair (S_g, s_g) is associated with positive inflation. In the zero inflation case, the firm would aim to place itself closer to the profit maximizing price, s^*. One may, therefore, conjecture that $S_0 - s_0 < S_g - s_g$.

The problem with the one-sided inflationary process analysed in this chapter is that the current real price is not a sufficient statistic for the prediction of future prices. Some additional information is contained in the immediate past (i.e., in the derivative) of the price path. By assuming that price changes occur only in state g and that the sojourn times in this state are exponential, we effectively made the problem memoryless, which led to a simple (S, s) policy. One way to justify this assumption is to argue that the costs of price adjustment also depend on the rate of inflation, and that it is more costly to change nominal prices when there is no aggregate inflation. Alternatively, if the exit rate from the state with zero inflation is sufficiently high, then the simple (S, s) policy analysed in the chapter is probably a close approximation to the optimal one.

8 Staggered and Synchronized Price Policies under Inflation: The Multiproduct Monopoly Case

Eytan Sheshinski and Yoram Weiss

1. Introduction

The microeconomic background of an inflationary process is characterized by discrete jumps in individual prices. This observation has led to several studies on the aggregation of discrete pricing policies into a smooth time path for the aggregate price level. The feasibility of such aggregation is necessary for the overall consistency of individual pricing policies (Caplin and Spulber (1987)). A crucial issue for such an analysis is the interaction among individual price policies. If all firms follow identical real price cycles that are uniformly spread over time, then consistent aggregation is feasible (Sheshinski and Weiss (1977)). There may, however, be important reasons why such uniformity may not emerge as an equilibrium outcome. In oligopolistic markets, where each firm takes into account the actions of its rivals, pricing policies will be interdependent. In multiproduct monopolies, there is a further source for interdependence, namely, increasing returns in the costs of price adjustment. Even under competitive conditions, bunching over time may be caused by aggregate shocks, while idiosyncratic shocks are needed to maintain the spread.

Apart from the issue of consistent aggregation, the time pattern of individual price policies has important implications for the real costs of inflation. If individual price paths are staggered, then temporary shocks may be propagated over long periods. Synchronized price policies, on the other hand, may accelerate the adjustment process (see Blanchard (1983), Blanchard and Fischer (1989, Chapter 8), and Taylor (1980)). In addition, non-synchronized price policies lead to price variations across products and thereby to search costs incurred by consumers (Benabou (1988), Fishman (1987)).

In this chapter we analyze the optimal price policy of a single profit-maximizing decision maker, i.e. a multiproduct monopoly. This policy may be interpreted as the cooperative outcome of a duopoly game. Indeed, we view this analysis as a first step in the investigation of various non-cooperative equilibria of dynamic Bertrand duopoly games with differentiated products.

The main object of our chapter is the determination of the conditions that lead to staggered or synchronized pricing policies, when the timing of price changes is endogenous.[1] Two aspects of the multiproduct monopoly decision problem influence this choice. First, the interaction in the profit function between the prices of the two goods. Generally, positive interactions enhance synchronization while negative interactions lead to staggering. Second, the form of the price adjustment costs. Here one may distinguish between *"menu costs"* and *"decision costs"*. Under menu costs, costs are independent of the number of items in the price list. This extreme form of increasing returns to scale ("economies of scope") leads to synchronization. Under decision costs, we consider a constant returns to scale technology, whereby each price change requires an adjustment cost. This provides an incentive for staggering, namely, the saving on the additional adjustment costs associated with joint price changes.

In this chapter we devote our attention to the case of positive interactions and constant returns to scale in the costs of price adjustment. This choice is motivated by our interest in the duopoly problem, where these assumptions are likely to hold. A longer version (Sheshinski and Weiss (1989)) treats menu costs and negative or zero interactions.

Special consideration is given to steady-state (repetitive) pricing policies where the *same* real price is chosen at each adjustment. In staggered steady states, price adjustments alternate. In a synchronized steady state, prices are adjusted simultaneously.

Our main results can be summarized as follows:

(1) The synchronized steady state and the symmetric staggered steady state are unique.

(2) A positive rate of interest is required to sustain both types of equilibria under positive interactions. In particular, for the class of quadratic profit functions, when the rate of interest approaches zero, a staggered steady state is optimal if, and only if, the two prices are strategic substitutes, while a synchronized steady state is optimal if, and only if, prices are strategic complements.

(3) The synchronized steady state is locally stable. Specifically, if initial real prices are sufficiently close to each other, then a synchronized steady state is attained after the first price change. In addition, there is a broad class of initial conditions that lead to an immediate change in both prices, followed by a synchronized steady state.

(4) We prove a necessary and sufficient condition for the local stability of the staggered steady state. For the class of quadratic profit functions,

we show that the staggered steady state is locally unstable. Moreover, under no circumstance will a joint price change be followed by a staggered steady state. That is, a staggered steady state can be reached only asymptotically (Sheshinski and Weiss (1989)).

(5) We derive explicit solutions for the case of quadratic profit functions when the rate of interest approaches zero. As in the single good case, we find that an increase in the costs of adjustment or a reduction in the rate of inflation reduce the frequency of price changes. A stronger positive price interaction reduces the frequency of price changes in the synchronized steady-state.

The analysis in this chapter applies beyond the price adjustment problem to other multiproduct inventory models. From this point of view, we extend the work of Bensoussan and Proth (1982) and Sulem (1986) who analyzed an optimal reordering policy in a multiproduct case. Our work differs from theirs by allowing for interactions in demands. However, Sulem discusses a more general cost of adjustment structure.

2. The Model

Consider an economy subject to an inflationary trend where the aggregate price level grows at a constant rate, g $(g > 0)$. We analyze a monopoly which sells two related products whose demands depend on the current *real* prices of the two goods. The monopoly controls the *nominal* price of each good and there is a fixed real cost of nominal price adjustments.

Let $z_i(t)$ denote the log of the real price of good i at time t, $t \in [0, \infty)$. The real profit function of the monopoly, denoted by $F(z_1, z_2)$, is assumed to be continuous, time invariant and symmetric in its arguments, $F(a, b) = F(b, a)$. In addition, it is assumed to be strictly quasi-concave and twice-differentiable for all (z_1, z_2) for which $F(z_1, z_2) > 0$. We denote partial derivatives by subscripts (e.g. $F_{ij} = \partial^2 F / \partial z_i \partial z_j$). Naturally, we assume that $F(z_1, z_2) > 0$ for *some* (z_1, z_2). However, there exist $\underline{z}$ and $\bar{z}$ $(\bar{z} > \underline{z})$, such that $F(z_1, z_2) \leq 0$ for all (z_1, z_2) *not* satisfying $\underline{z} \leq z_i \leq \bar{z}$, $i = 1, 2$.[2] These assumptions imply the existence of a unique maximum for $F(z_1, z_2)$, which, by symmetry, satisfies $z_1 = z_2 = \bar{S}$ and $F(\bar{S}, \bar{S}) > 0$. The assumption that positive profits are attained on a compact set of real prices is intended to ensure the existence of a well-defined pricing policy. Observe that the set of prices for which profits are non-positive need not be compact. The reason is that the firm has the option of not producing at prices below variable costs. The class of functions satisfying all of these conditions is denoted $\mathscr{F}$.

The problem facing the monopoly is a choice of price paths, $(z_1^*(t), z_2^*(t))$, which maximize the present value of real profits over an infinite horizon, given some initial condition $(z_1(0), z_2(0))$.

The salient feature of our model is the discontinuous pattern of nominal price adjustments. This widely observable phenomenon is generated in our model by the presence of non-convex costs of price adjustment: any nominal price change, no matter how small, requires non-negligible costs of adjustment. Specifically, the real cost of any nominal price change is assumed to be a constant denoted by β ($\beta > 0$).

The main question which the chapter addresses is the following: will the monopoly adopt a *synchronized* policy of price adjustments, whereby both prices are changed simultaneously, or a *staggered* policy whereby the two nominal prices are changed at different points in time.

Any pricing policy can be described by two pairs of sequences, $\{S_\tau^i\}_{\tau=0}^\infty$ and $\{t_\tau^i\}_{\tau=0}^\infty$, $i = 1, 2$, where S_τ^i is the real price of good i set at time t_τ^i by adjusting the nominal price of good i, keeping it unchanged during the interval $[t_\tau^i, t_{\tau+1}^i)$. Special attention will be given to repetitive price paths satisfying

$$S_{\tau+1}^i = S_\tau^i \quad \text{and} \quad t_{\tau+1}^i = t_\tau^i + \varepsilon^i, \qquad \tau = 0, 1, 2, \ldots \tag{8.1}$$

where ε^i ($\varepsilon^i > 0$), $i = 1, 2$, are constants denoting the time intervals between subsequent price changes. Thus, on such paths, the real prices chosen at the beginning of each interval and the duration until the next price change remain constant. We shall refer to such paths as steady states. A *symmetric* steady state is defined by the additional restriction

$$S_\tau^1 = S_\tau^2 = S \quad \text{and} \quad \varepsilon^1 = \varepsilon^2 = \varepsilon, \qquad \tau = 0, 1, 2, \ldots \tag{8.2}$$

where S ($S > 0$) and ε ($\varepsilon > 0$) are constants. Along such a path, the real price of each good follows the *same* cycle. Among the symmetric steady states we can identify a *synchronized* steady state by the added requirement that

$$t_0^1 = t_0^2, \tag{8.3}$$

that is, the prices of both goods are always changed at the same time. Finally, a (symmetric) *staggered steady-state* is defined by

$$|t_0^1 - t_0^2| = \frac{\varepsilon}{2}, \tag{8.4}$$

that is, the prices of the two goods are changed alternately and the time distance between *any* two price changes is equal.

The time-pattern of the monopolist's optimal price policy, in particular whether price changes will be synchronized, depends crucially on two features of the model. The first relates to the technology of price adjustments, and the second to the form of the profit function. One issue of concern is the degree of returns to scale in the costs of price adjustment when both prices are changed simultaneously. Under constant returns to scale the monopoly incurs a cost of 2β whenever prices are changed jointly. Under increasing returns to scale these costs will be less than 2β, possibly as low as β. The degree of returns to scale depends on the distinction between "*menu costs*" and "*decision costs*" of price adjustment. By menu costs we refer to costs such as advertising and updating of price lists. By decision costs we refer to costs of acquiring information on the production and demand of different products and to costs related to the organization and computation of coordinated price changes in multiproduct firms. If the costs of price adjustment are interpreted as menu costs, one would expect these costs to be β, independently of the number of items in the menu. If, however, these costs are interpreted as decision costs, one would expect that the complexity of the choice, and thus the costs, will depend on the number of items involved, suggesting that constant returns to scale is the more appropriate assumption. Indeed, a typical organizational solution to this problem is decentralization, whereby separate divisions are allowed to follow separate pricing policies, maximizing objective functions set by the centre. The overall outcome of this process is that adjustment costs for the monopoly are the sum of the costs incurred by the separate "price centres". A similar distinction in the inventory adjustment context was made by Sulem (1986).[3]

The other issue of concern is the interaction in demand and possibly in the production of the two goods. In general, an increase in one price may increase or decrease the marginal profitability of an increase in the other price. For instance, in the absence of costs, a positive (negative) interaction arises when an increase in one price raises (reduces) both the quantity demanded and the slope of the demand curve for the other good. One would expect that if the goods are *strategic complements*, i.e. raising z_i

increases the marginal profits of z_j, $j \neq i$, then synchronization is more likely, and *vice versa*.

The focus of this chapter is on the case of constant returns to scale in the costs of adjustment and positive price interactions. These assumptions and symmetry appear to be more appropriate for the duopoly case. We retain them in the analysis of the multiproduct monopoly to support the interpretation of this model as a cooperative duopoly equilibrium. Specifically, we assume

ASSUMPTION A1.   *Complementarity.*   For any (z_1, z_2),

$$F_{ij}(z_1, z_2) > 0, \qquad i \neq j, \quad i, j = 1, 2. \tag{8.5}$$

An additional assumption that will be used in subsequent analysis is:

ASSUMPTION A2.   *Non-reversibility.*   For any (z_1, z_2) and x $(x > 0)$,

$$F_i(z_1, z_2) > 0 \quad \Rightarrow \quad F_i(z_1 - x, z_2 - x) > 0, \qquad i = 1, 2. \tag{8.6}$$

Assumption A2 imposes the natural requirement that if a price increase is profitable at (z_1, z_2), then it is also profitable after these real prices are eroded by inflation to $(z_1 - x, z_2 - x)$.

In some cases we will need a stronger version of A2:

ASSUMPTION A3.   *Monotonicity.*   For any (z_1, z_2),

$$F_{ii}(z_1, z_2) + F_{ij}(z_1, z_2) < 0, \qquad i \neq j, \quad i, j = 1, 2 \tag{8.7}$$

Assumption A3 in conjunction with Assumption A1, ensures that over any time-interval with fixed nominal prices, the profitability of a price increase rises with time. Observe also that Assumptions A1 and A3 imply that $F(z_1, z_2)$ is strictly concave. On the other hand, Assumptions A1 and A2 do not imply concavity.

3.   Characterization of the Optimal Policy and the Associated Value Function

Let $V(z_1, z_2)$ be the value function associated with an optimal policy starting at real prices (z_1, z_2) at time 0. The existence of such a function is guaranteed by our assumption that $F(z_1, z_2)$ has a well-defined maximum and by assuming that the real interest rate, r, is positive. The value function is defined recursively:[4]

$$V(z_1, z_2) = \text{Max}_{t \geq 0} \left\{ \int_0^t e^{-rx} F(z_1 - gx, z_2 - gx) \, dx \right.$$

$$+ e^{-rt} \text{Max}[\text{Max}_{S_1, S_2} V(S_1, S_2) - 2\beta, \text{Max}_{S_1} V(S_1, z_2 - gt)$$

$$\left. - \beta, \text{Max}_{S_2} V(z_1 - gt, S_2) - \beta] \right\}. \tag{8.8}$$

where t is the time of the subsequent price change and (S_1, S_2) are the real prices chosen at that time (i.e. nominal prices are set so as to attain these real prices). If the optimal t is $t = 0$, then a price change occurs immediately; otherwise the current nominal prices will be kept unchanged, with real prices decreasing at the rate of inflation, g, over the interval $[0, t)$. Because of our assumption that $F(z_1, z_2)$ is non-positive outside a finite box, a price change is optimal after a finite lapse of time. That is, the R.H.S. of (8.8) actually achieves the maximum (see Appendix A).

We begin our analysis by stating some properties of the value function which will be used subsequently:

(i) $$\frac{1}{1 - e^{-r(\bar{z} - \underline{z})/g}} \left[\int_0^{(\bar{z} - \underline{z})/g} e^{-rx} F(\bar{z} - gx, \bar{z} - gx) \, dx - 2\beta \right]$$

$$\leq V(z_1, z_2) \leq \frac{F(\bar{S}, \bar{S})}{r},$$

(ii) $V(z_1, z_2)$ is symmetric,

(iii) $V(z_1, z_2)$ is continuous,

(iv) $V(z_1, z_2)$ is differentiable, except possibly at some boundary points.

The upper and lower bounds on $V(z_1, z_2)$ can be easily demonstrated. The upper bound is the present discounted value of the flow of maximum profits, $F(\bar{S}, \bar{S})$, which would be attained in the absence of adjustment costs, $\beta = 0$. The lower bound is the present discounted value of a feasible repetitive policy where real prices vary between $\bar{z}$ and $\underline{z}$. (Recall that outside these bounds profits are non-positive.) We assume throughout that costs of price adjustment are relatively small, specifically, that $\int_0^{(\bar{z} - \underline{z})/g} e^{-rx} F(\bar{z} - gx, \bar{z} - gx) \, dx - 2\beta > 0$. This ensures that for any initial condition, $V(z_1, z_2) > 0$.

Symmetry of $V(z_1, z_2)$ follows directly from the assumed symmetry of the profit function, $F(z_1, z_2)$. Starting from $z_1 = a$ and $z_2 = b$ or $z_1 =$

b and $z_2 = a$, the monopoly can obtain the same present value of future profits simply by exchanging the optimal price sequences of the two products.

Continuity of $V(z_1, z_2)$ can be established by noting that (8.8) is a fixed point of a contraction mapping which maps continuous functions into continuous functions (see Stokey and Lucas (1989, Chapter 3, pp. 49–55)).

Differentiability of $V(z_1, z_2)$ can be established whenever the choice of the controls in (8.8) is unique and thus continuous in (z_1, z_2). In Appendix A we show that after the first price change, the time of the subsequent price increase and the value of the real prices chosen at that time are uniquely determined.

Let

$$M(z_1, z_2) = \text{Max}\{V^* - 2\beta, \text{Max}_{S_1} V(S_1, z_2) - \beta, \text{Max}_{S_2} V(z_1, S_2) - \beta\}$$
(8.9)

where $V^* = \text{Max}_{S_1, S_2} V(S_1, S_2)$.

Since it is always feasible to change prices immediately, that is, to set $t = 0$ in (8.8), we have

$$V(z_1, z_2) \geqq M(z_1, z_2).$$
(8.10)

Similarly, since it is always feasible not to change any price in the time interval $[0, t)$, we must have for all $t \geqq 0$,

$$V(z_1, z_2) \geqq \int_0^t e^{-rx} F(z_1 - gx, z_2 - gx)\, dx + e^{-rt} V(z_1 - gt, z_2 - gt).$$
(8.11)

Since there are only two possibilities: change some price immediately or keep both prices fixed for a while, *either* (8.10) *or* (8.11) must hold as an equality for all t satisfying $\delta \geqq t \geqq 0$, for *some* $\delta > 0$.

If $V(z_1, z_2)$ is differentiable, we can expand the R.H.S. of (8.11) by a Taylor expansion, rearrange and divide by gt, taking the limit as $t \to 0$, to obtain

$$F(z_1, z_2) \leqq gV_1(z_1, z_2) + gV_2(z_1, z_2) + rV(z_1, z_2),$$
(8.12)

where $V_i = \partial V / \partial z_i$, $i = 1, 2$. The inequalities (8.10) and (8.12) are related by the complementary slackness condition (see Sulem (1986) and Bensoussan, Crouhy and Proth (1983)):

$$[V(z_1,z_2)-M(z_1,z_2)][gV_1(z_1,z_2)+gV_2(z_1,z_2)+rV(z_1,z_2)-F(z_1,z_2)]=0.$$
$$(8.13)$$

The solution of the monopoly's problem is now described with the aid of four distinct sets:

$$C = \{z_1,z_2 | V(z_1,z_2) > M(z_1,z_2)\}.$$

$$T_0 = \{z_1,z_2 | V(z_1,z_2) = M(z_1,z_2) = V^* - 2\beta\}.$$

$$T_1 = \{z_1,z_2 | V(z_1,z_2) = M(z_1,z_2) = \text{Max}_{S_1} \, V(S_1,z_2) - \beta\}.$$

$$T_2 = \{z_1,z_2 | V(z_1,z_2) = M(z_1,z_2) = \text{Max}_{S_2} \, V(z_1,S_2) - \beta\}.$$

$$(8.14)$$

The set C is the *continuation set*, where no price change occurs. The set T_0 *triggers a change in both prices*, while T_i, $i = 1$, 2, is the set which *triggers a change in the price of good i only*.

Condition (8.13) implies that for $(z_1,z_2) \in C$, we have

$$rV(z_1,z_2) = F(z_1,z_2) - gV_1(z_1,z_2) - gV_2(z_1,z_2).$$
$$(8.15)$$

Equation (8.15) can be interpreted as an asset pricing formula. The imputed value of a state which does not generate a price change, $rV(z_1,z_2)$, is given by the current flow of profits, $F(z_1,z_2)$, less the depreciation caused by the inflationary erosion in real prices, $gV_1(z_1,z_2) + gV_2(z_1,z_2)$. In subsequent analysis we shall refer to equation (8.15) as the *"valuation formula"*.

Although the valuation formula (8.15) is stated in terms of the derivatives of the value function, it is not necessary to assume differentiability for this purpose. In Appendix A we prove that along any path satisfying the first-order conditions, a closely related formula must hold. For instance, if the optimal path is such that prices are raised alternately, first good 1, then good 2, then good 1 again, and so on, then

$$rV(z_1,z_2) = F(z_1,z_2) - g\int_0^{t_1^*} e^{-rx} F_1(z_1 - gx, z_2 - gx)\,dx$$

$$- g\int_0^{t_1^*} e^{-rx} F_2(z_1 - gx, z_2 - gx)\,dx$$

$$- g\int_{t_1^*}^{t_2^*} e^{-rx} F_2(S_1^* - g(x - t_1^*), z_2 - gx)\,dx,$$
$$(8.16)$$

where t_i^*, $i = 1, 2$, is the time when the price of good i is changed and S_1^* is the real price chosen for good 1 at time t_1^*.

Equation (8.16) states that the imputed value of a given state equals the current flow of profits, $F(z_1, z_2)$, minus the reduction in profits which is caused by keeping the nominal price of good 1 fixed until the date t_1^* and the reduction in profits caused by keeping the nominal price of good 2 unchanged until t_2^*. All future information is incorporated in the choice of t_1^*, t_2^*, and S_1^*. It is shown in Appendix A that when $V(z_1, z_2)$ is differentiable, then $gV_1(z_1, z_2)$ equals the first integral on the R.H.S. of (8.16), and $gV_2(z_1, z_2)$ is the sum of the second and third integrals. In other words, the partial derivatives of V are equal to the cumulative change in profits until the next price change.

With each point in the trigger sets T_0, T_1 and T_2 is associated a choice of an optimal pair of new real prices. Specifically, for any $(z_1, z_2) \in T_i$, $i = 1, 2$, there is a *unique* real price chosen for good i, S_i^*, whose value depends on z_j, $j \neq i$. We write $S_i^* = S(z_j)$, $j \neq i$, $i, j = 1, 2$. These "*reaction functions*" are symmetric and stationary (see Appendix A). In contrast, for $(z_1, z_2) \in T_0$, in view of the symmetry imposed by our assumptions, if (S_1^*, S_2^*) is an optimal choice, so is (S_2^*, S_1^*). Hence, in general, uniqueness cannot be expected. It is, however, easy to show that with *positive* interactions, $F_{12} > 0$, any point $(z_1, z_2) \in T_0$ triggers a unique action $S_1^* = S_2^* = S_a^*$. To see this, observe that for a symmetric profit function with positive interactions

$$F(z_1, z_2) < \tfrac{1}{2} F(z_1, z_1) + \tfrac{1}{2} F(z_2, z_2) = f(z_1) + f(z_2) \tag{8.17}$$

for all (z_1, z_2), such that $z_1 \neq z_2$ where $f(z_i) \equiv \tfrac{1}{2} F(z_i, z_i)$, $i = 1, 2$.[5] That is, a mixture of the profits at the extremes exceeds profits at any midpoint. Hence, the value of the optimal programme associated with an additive profit function of the form $f(z_1) + f(z_2)$ provides an upper bound for the optimal value of the programme associated with $F(z_1, z_2)$. An optimum for an additive profit function is attained when an (S, s) policy is followed for each of the two goods (see Sheshinski and Weiss (1989)). When the initial conditions are subject to choice, the firm can attain this upper bound by selecting at time 0 the same real price, S_a^*, for both goods, followed by a synchronized (S, s) policy for both goods thereafter.

The chosen pair of real prices triggered by $(z_1, z_2) \in T_0$, must be in the interior of C. Clearly, an immediate subsequent price change cannot be optimal since the same outcome can be obtained without incurring the additional adjustment cost. For the same reason, with $(z_1, z_2) \in T_i$, $i = 1$, 2, the chosen prices cannot be in T_i. Nor can the chosen prices be in T_j, $j \neq i$, unless (z_1, z_2) is also in T_0, in which case a joint change into C is triggered. Moreover, at the chosen point, $V(z_1, z_2)$ is differentiable. This follows from the fact that the subsequent optimal date of price adjustment, $t^*(z_1, z_2)$, and the real prices chosen at that time are uniquely determined (see Appendix A). Accordingly, setting $V_1(S_a^*, S_a^*) = V_2(S_a^*, S_a^*) = 0$ in the "valuation formula", (8.15), we obtain the following equation:

$$rV(S_a^*, S_a^*) = F(S_a^*, S_a^*). \tag{8.18}$$

At the time of a joint price change, current profits reflect the full imputed value of the new state, since depreciation is locally negligible.

However, when only one price is chosen optimally, the depreciation of the other price has to be taken into account. Specifically, we have

$$rV(S_1^*, z_2) = F(S_1^*, z_2) - gV_2(S_1^*, z_2), \tag{8.19}$$

and

$$rV(z_1, S_2^*) = F(z_1, S_2^*) - gV_1(z_1, S_2^*). \tag{8.20}$$

Equations (8.19) and (8.20) are obtained from (8.15) by setting $V_1(S_1^*, z_2) = 0$ and $V_2(z_1, S_2^*) = 0$, respectively.

Recall that points in the trigger sets are related to the corresponding chosen points via the relationship $V(z_1, z_2) = M(z_1, z_2)$. Thus, if (z_1, z_2) is in the interior of, say, T_1, we have $V(z_1, z_2) = V(S(z_2), z_2) - \beta$.

Since this relationship holds for all (z_1, z_2) in the interior of T_1, we can differentiate to obtain

$$V_1(z_1, z_2) = 0, \tag{8.21}$$

and

$$V_2(z_1, z_2) = V_2(S(z_2), z_2). \tag{8.22}$$

Thus, using equation (8.12) and (8.19), we obtain

$$F(z_1, z_2) \leq F(S(z_2), z_2) - r\beta \quad \text{for } (z_1, z_2) \in T_1. \tag{8.23}$$

By a similar argument:

$$F(z_1, z_2) \leq F(z_1, S(z_1)) - r\beta \quad \text{for } (z_1, z_2) \in T_2, \tag{8.24}$$

$$F(z_1, z_2) \leq F(S^*, S^*) - 2r\beta \quad \text{for } (z_1, z_2) \in T_0. \tag{8.25}$$

The economic interpretation of equations (8.23)–(8.25) is clear. The R.H.S. of each equation is the cost of a delay in a price change, consisting of foregone profits at the *new* real prices net of adjustment costs, while the L.H.S. is the benefit of such delay, consisting of profits at the *old* prices. To trigger an immediate price change it is *necessary* (though not sufficient) for a short delay to be unprofitable.

Figure 1 describes the continuation and trigger sets and the corresponding choice (reaction) functions, $S(z)$. Observe, first, that T_0 consists of four distinct subsets: for all $(z_1, z_2) \in T_0^{++}$, a price-increase of *both* goods to (S_a^*, S_a^*) is triggered. For all $(z_1, z_2) \in T_0^{--}$, a *reduction* of both prices is triggered, while for $(z_1, z_2) \in T_0^{-+}$ (or $\in T_0^{+-}$), one price is increased and the other decreased. Similarly, each T_i, $i = 1, 2$, consists of two regions, one, denoted by T_i^+, calls for a price increase in good i, while T_i^- calls for an immediate price reduction.

Generally, a joint price change is triggered whenever both real prices are distant from the level, $(\bar{S}, \bar{S})$, which yields maximum profits. A single price change is triggered whenever one price is distant from $\bar{S}$ while the other is close. Continuation occurs when both prices are close to $(\bar{S}, \bar{S})$.

Having assumed a positive inflation, $g > 0$, price reductions can occur only once, at the outset ($t = 0$). (See Appendix A, Lemma 1.) In contrast, the regions T_0^{++} and T_i^+, $i = 1, 2$, are reachable from C after some delay and revisited periodically. At any point on the boundaries of T_i^+ and T_0^{++}, which are reachable from the reaction curves $S(z_1)$ and $S(z_2)$, $V(z_1, z_2)$ is differentiable. As shown in Appendix A, following a price increase, the timing and the prices chosen for the subsequent change are uniquely determined, which implies that V is differentiable along a path starting at any point on $S(z_1)$ or $S(z_2)$. Using the "valuation formula", (8.15), it follows that (8.23)–(8.25) hold with equality at points where such paths reach the boundaries between C and the trigger sets. This observation helps to determine the boundaries between the continuation and the trigger sets. For instance, at the boundary between C and T_1^+, where an increase in the price of good one is triggered, the firm is indifferent between holding nominal prices unchanged, obtaining the current level of profits, $F(z_1, z_2)$, and raising the price of good one to $S(z_2)$, obtaining $F(S(z_2), z_2) - r\beta$. The term $r\beta$ is the imputed interest on adjustment costs. We denote by $s(z_i)$ the boundary points between C and T_j^+, i.e. points which trigger an immediate increase in z_j, $j \neq i$, $i, j = 1, 2$ (see Figure 1).

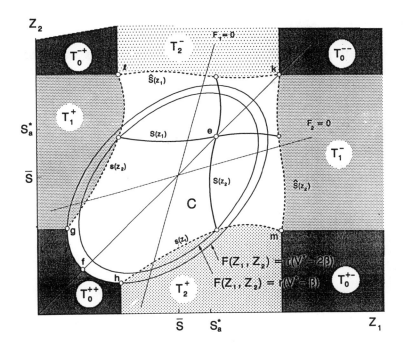

Figure 8.1

Somewhat different considerations apply to price reductions. For instance, at the boundary between T_0^{--} and C, point k in Figure 8.1, the firm is indifferent between an immediate price reduction to (S_a^*, S_a^*) and holding both prices unchanged until their real values erode to point f on the boundary between C and T_0^{++}. This indeterminacy in the action leads to non-differentiability of $V(z_1, z_2)$ at point k. On the diagonal above point k, $V_1(z, z) = V_2(z, z) = 0$. However, on the diagonal just below this point, the gradient must be strictly negative.[6] Let $\hat{S}(z_i)$ denote the boundary points between C and T_j^-, i.e. points which trigger an immediate decrease in z_j, $j \neq i$, $j = 1, 2$. Generally, $V(z_1, z_2)$ is not differentiable along this boundary.

We now turn to a description of the boundary between C and T_0^{++}. This boundary is determined by the condition $F(z_1, z_2) = F(S_a^*, S_a^*) - 2r\beta$. That is, the firm is just indifferent between raising both prices to (S_a^*, S_a^*) and holding them unchanged instantly. In particular, consider point h in

Figure 1, whose coordinates are $(z_1, s(z_1))$. This point is on the boundary of C, T_0^{++} and T_2^+. At such a point, changing only z_2 to $S(z_1)$ is equivalent to changing both prices to (S_a^*, S_a^*). Consistency requires that $S(z_1) = S_a^*$ and, in addition, following the change in z_2, the firm should be willing to change z_1 immediately. That is, the best response to $(z_1, s(z_1))$ is (z_1, S_a^*), which in turn has to be a point in T_1^+. Furthermore, (z_1, S_a^*) must be on the boundary of C and T_1^+, for otherwise points in the interior of T_2^+ would also lead to a joint price increase. Thus,

$$F(z_1, s(z_1)) = F(z_1, S_a^*) - r\beta, \tag{8.26}$$

and

$$F(z_1, s(z_1)) = F(S_a^*, S_a^*) - 2r\beta, \tag{8.27}$$

which implies that

$$F(z_1, S_a^*) = F(S_a^*, S_a^*) - r\beta. \tag{8.28}$$

Under the assumption of positive interactions, $F_{12} > 0$, and using the quasi-concavity of $F(z_1, z_2)$, conditions (8.26) and (8.28) imply that $z_1 > s(z_1)$. That is, point h must be strictly to the right of the diagonal. Consequently, there is a non-degenerate segment (gh) on the boundary between C and T_0^{++}, where a joint price increase is strictly preferable to a single price increase. This feature is special to the case of positive interactions. The segment gh degenerates to a single point when $F_{12} = 0$ and disappears when $F_{12} < 0$ (see Sheshinski and Weiss (1989)). Intuitively, under positive interactions, when the two prices are not too far from their maximum profit position, an anticipated change in the price of good j at some future date, $t^*(z_1, z_2)$, creates an incentive to postpone the change in the price of good i, $i \neq j$, to that same date.

It can be shown that with positive interaction in the profit function, the reaction curves must have a positive slope in the neighbourhood of (S_a^*, S_a^*). That is, an increase in z_i leads to a higher chosen real price for good j, i.e., $S'(S_a^*) > 0$.[7] Finally, it can be shown that $S'(z) < 1$ for all z, and that whenever $V(z_1, z_2)$ is differentiable at the boundary, $s(z)$, then $s'(z) < 1$.[8] The former is the local stability condition in the static Bertrand model. The latter is consistent with the requirement that any path emanating from $S(z)$ intersects a trigger set once.

Any path satisfying the first-order conditions can be portayed by a trajectory which moves smoothly inside the continuation set where both

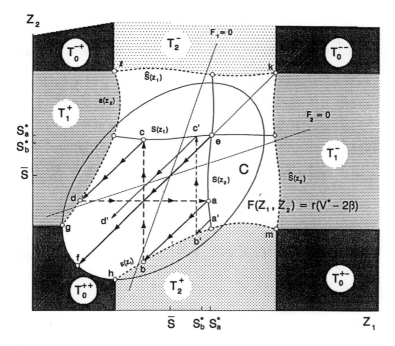

Figure 8.2

real prices erode at the same rate, g, and then jumps to the reaction curves whenever the corresponding trigger sets are met. In Figure 8.2 we present three such paths. Consider first the repetitive paths, indicated by (e, f) and (a, b, c, d). The first represents a synchronized steady state and the latter a (symmetric) staggered steady state.

The conditions determining these repetitive paths are as follows. A synchronized steady state is characterized by a pair, (S_a^*, ε), satisfying:

$$F(S_a^*, S_a^*) = rV(S_a^*, S_a^*)$$

$$= \frac{r}{1 - e^{-r\varepsilon}}\left[\int_0^\varepsilon e^{-rx}F(S_a^* - gx, S_a^* - gx)\,dx - 2\beta e^{-r\varepsilon}\right], \quad (8.30)$$

and

$$F(S_a^* - g\varepsilon, S_a^* - g\varepsilon) - F(S_a^*, S_a^*) + 2r\beta = 0, \quad (8.31)$$

where S_a^* is the initial level of real prices at the beginning of a cycle and ε is the duration of each cycle.

The first equality in condition (8.30) follows, using the "valuation formula", (8.15), from the maximization of V w.r.t. the chosen initial prices. The second equality is derived from the definition of V, (8.7), under a stationary policy. Condition (8.31) is necessary for the optimality of the timing of a price change.

Similarly, a symmetric staggered steady stage is characterized by a pair (S_b^*, t) satisfying

$$F(S_b^*, S_b^* - gt) = rV(S_b^*, S_b^* - gt) + gV_2(S_b^*, S_b^* - gt)$$

$$= \frac{r}{1 - e^{-rt}} \left[\int_0^t e^{-rx} F(S_b^* - gx, S_b^* - gt - gx) \, dx - \beta e^{-rt} \right]$$

$$+ g \int_0^t e^{-rx} F_2(S_b^* - gx, S_b^* - gt - gx) \, dx, \tag{8.32}$$

and

$$F(S_b^* - 2gt, S_b^* - gt) - F(S_b^*, S_b^* - gt) + r\beta = 0, \tag{8.33}$$

where S_b^* is the level of the real price chosen when only one price is raised and t is the time-interval between successive price changes (i.e. the duration between subsequent price changes of the same good is $2t$).

Using integration by parts, (8.30) and (8.31) imply

$$\int_0^\varepsilon e^{-rx} F_1(S_a^* - gx, S_a^* - gx) \, dx = 0. \tag{8.34}$$

Similarly, (8.32) and (8.33) imply

$$\int_0^t e^{-rx} F_1(S_b^* - gx, S_b^* - gt - gx) \, dx + \int_t^{2t} e^{-rx} F_1(S_b^* - gx, S_b^* + gt - gx) \, dx = 0. \tag{8.35}$$

The above conditions can be easily interpreted: in steady-state, the discounted value of marginal profits over a typical cycle is zero. In addition, at a point of price change, marginal benefits and losses from postponing the price adjustment are equal.

Under Assumptions A1 and A2, it follows from equations (8.34) and (8.35), that marginal profits, F_i ($i = 1, 2$), are negative at the beginning and positive at the end of each price interval. Thus, a typical price cycle starts at a price which exceeds the level which maximizes profits and terminates at a price below that level. Such oscillations strike a balance between the loss in profits and the costs of price adjustment. It can be shown that the same pattern also obtains outside steady-state (Sheshinski and Weiss (1989, Lemma 2)).

It is easy to check that both paths (e, f) and (a, b, c, d) satisfy the first-order conditions at all times, provided that the initial state is on one of these paths. That is, the staggered and synchronized steady states, defined in Section 2, provide a solution of the first-order conditions for *some S, ε* and *t*. In Appendix B we prove the following:

PROPOSITION 1.   *There is at most one optimal synchronized steady state. Under Assumption* A1 *and* A2, *there is at most one optimal symmetric staggered steady state.*

The proof of uniqueness of the two steady states relies on the assumption that these are optimal. Thus, in addition to (8.30)–(8.33), we assume that the appropriate second-order conditions hold. Proposition 1 does not establish the existence of optimal paths of this form. In Appendix A we state explicitly the sequence of first-order conditions which an optimal path must satisfy. It is easy to verify that a pair (S_a, ε) or (S_b, t) which satisfy equations (8.30)–(8.31) or (8.32)–(8.33), respectively, satisfy these first-order conditions. Hence, the question of existence of a steady-state path which satisfies the first-order conditions can be reduced to whether equations (8.30)–(8.31) or (8.32)–(8.33) have a solution. We do not attempt to provide general conditions for existence. In a subsequent section we calculate explicit solutions for some specific examples. This is not sufficient, however, to establish the existence of an optimal path of the required form. In addition, one has to verify that the second-order conditions are satisfied.

4. Stability Analysis

We have identified two repetitive paths which satisfy the necessary conditions for an optimum, provided the initial conditions are on one of these paths. For other initial conditions, the optimal path is, in general, non-repetitive. That is, different real prices are chosen at sucessive points of price change and the time intervals between such changes also vary. This dynamic adjustment reflects *history-dependence*. That is, the optimal level for the new price of good i depends on the real price of good j, $j \neq i$. Of course, history does not matter if it is optimal to change *both* prices.

It is thus natural to inquire whether such dynamic paths converge asymptotically to a steady-state. We restrict our inquiry to paths that initiate in the neighbourhood of the two symmetric steady states and provide two *local-stability* results.

PROPOSITION 2. *Under positive interactions, $F_{12} > 0$, the synchronized steady state is locally stable.*

Proof. Starting in the neighbourhood of the synchronized steady-state path, it is seen in Figure 8.1 that the trajectory reaches a point on the boundary of T_0^{++} on the non-degenerate segment gh. This triggers a joint price increase to the synchronized steady state at point e. ‖

In Appendix C we provide a necessary and sufficient condition for local stability of the staggered steady-state. This condition depends, in general, on the values of (S_b^*, t) which solve equations (8.32)–(8.33). For specific profit functions, however, these conditions can be verified *a priori*. In particular, consider the class of (symmetric) quadratic profit functions:

$$F(z_1, z_2) = a(z_1 + z_2) - b(z_1^2 + z_2^2) + cz_1 z_2, \qquad (8.36)$$

where, to guarantee strict quasi-concavity, we set $b > 0$ and $4b^2 - c^2 > 0$. For this important class of functions we prove the following:

PROPOSITION 3. *If $F(z_1, z_2) \in \mathcal{F}$ is quadratic, given by (8.36), then, with positive interactions, $F_{12} = c > 0$, the staggered steady state is locally unstable.*

Proof. Appendix C. ‖

The path $a'b'c'd'$ in Figure 8.2 illustrates the local instability of the staggered steady state. Starting at an initial point near the staggered steady-state path, a', the optimal trajectory converges to the synchronized steady state.

Propositions 2 and 3 present a sharp contrast between the two types of steady state. For positive interactions, $F_{12} > 0$, the staggered steady state path is followed only if the initial price configuration is on this path. On the other hand, the synchronized steady state is attained from a wide range of initial conditions, i.e. an immediate jump to the synchronized steady-state path occurs whenever the two prices are far away from their maximum profits level. If prices are not too far from that point and from each other, then it is optimal to postpone the jump to the synchronized steady state. In contrast, if only one price is far away from its profit-maximizing level, then this price will be changed immediately, but a steady state does *not* follow. Instead, the firm will adopt a nonrepetitive path. We have seen that that with quadratic profits, this path does not converge to a staggered steady state. Thus, it remains to be determined whether it converges to the synchronized steady state. This is a question of *global stability*.

The analysis of a global stability requires a complete solution for the value function. An approximate solution can be obtained from the knowledge of $V(z_1, z_2)$ around the staggered and synchronized steady states (see Sheshinski and Weiss (1989)).

5. An Example

In this section we derive, for certain cases of our model, explicit solutions to the steady-state values in terms of the underlying parameters of the model and provide some comparative statics. For this purpose we use two simplifying assumptions common to the related literature on optimal inventory policy (e.g. Constantinides and Richard (1978) and Sulem (1986)).

The first assumption is a quadratic instantaneous profit function, of the form (8.36). The second assumption is the maximization of average profits per price cycle, which is equivalent to the limit of discounted real profits in steady-state when the rate of interest approaches zero.

Consider a synchronized steady-state path satisfying equations (8.30)–(8.31). These necessary conditions implicitly define S_a^* and ε as functions of the rate of interest, r. The limit of these values as $r \to 0$ must satisfy

$$a - (2b - c)\left(S_a^* - g\frac{\varepsilon}{2}\right) = 0, \tag{8.37}$$

and

$$\varepsilon = \left[\frac{12\beta}{g^2(2b - c)}\right]^{1/3}. \tag{8.38}$$

These equations are obtained by taking the limits of (8.30)–(8.31) as $r \to 0$. The limit of $rV(S_a^*, S_a^*)$ as $r \to 0$, denoted by μ_1, is

$$\mu_1 = \frac{1}{\varepsilon} \left[\int_0^\varepsilon F(S_a^* - gx, S_a^* - gx)\, dx - 2\beta \right], \qquad (8.39)$$

where $F(z_1, z_2)$ is given by (8.36). The R.H.S. of (39) is seen to be the average profits associated with the limit price cycle.

Similarly, consider a staggered steady-state path satisfying equations (8.32)–(8.33). As $r \to 0$, the solution, (S_b^*, t), approaches a limit satisfying

$$a - (2b - c)(S_b^* - gt) = 0, \qquad (8.40)$$

and

$$t = \left[\frac{3\beta}{g^2(4b + c)} \right]^{1/3}. \qquad (8.41)$$

The corresponding limit of $rV(S_b^*, S_b^* - gt)$ as $r \to 0$, denoted by μ_2, is

$$\mu_2 = \frac{1}{t} \left[\int_0^t F(S_b^* - gx, S_b^* - gt - gx)\, dx - \beta \right], \qquad (8.42)$$

where $F(z_1, z_2)$ is given by (8.36).

As we have already indicated in Section 3, conditions (8.30)–(8.31) and (8.32)–(8.33) are necessary but, in general, *not* sufficient for optimality. To determine the optimality of (S_a^*, ε) and (S_b^*, t), we shall refer to:

PROPOSITION 4. *If $F(z_1, z_2) \in \mathscr{F}$ is a quadratic function given by (8.36), then*

$$\mu_1 - \mu_2 \gtrless 0 \quad \Leftrightarrow \quad F_{12} = c \gtrless 0. \qquad (8.43)$$

Proof. Appendix D. ‖

Proposition 4 implies that with positive interactions, $F_{12} = c > 0$, average profits associated with a synchronized price policy exceed average profits associated with a staggered policy. It follows that in this case, whenever a price change is contemplated, a move to the synchronized steady state which costs 2β, will dominate a move to the staggered steady state, which costs only β. The reason is that the undiscounted difference between the value of the two programmes exceeds any finite β. We therefore conclude:

COROLLARY 1. *For a quadratic profit function, (8.36), with positive interactions, $F_{12} = c > 0$, the staggered steady state is never optimal in the limit where $r \to 0$.*

Corollary 1 is not true if $r > 0$, since in this case the gain from moving to the synchronized steady state may be outweighed by the additional costs of adjustment.

Expressions (8.37)–(8.38) and (8.40)–(8.41) provide a convenient framework for comparative statics. It is seen that in both steady states, an increase in the costs of adjustment, β, or a reduction in the rate of inflation, g, increase the duration between successive price changes. For the synchronized steady state, an increase in the concavity of the profit function, i.e. an increase in $2b - c$, decreases the duration of fixed nominal price intervals. The reason is that as profits decline faster around the maximum it becomes more costly to keep the nominal price unchanged. It is seen from (8.38) that a stronger positive interaction, i.e. higher c, reduces the frequency of price changes in the synchronized steady state. On the other hand, as seen from (8.41), a stronger positive interaction reduces the frequency of price changes in the staggered steady state. The loss in profits caused by keeping nominal prices constant diminishes with c if prices are kept equal but increases in c if the two prices are kept apart. The effects on the initial real price, S_a^* and S_b^*, are generally in the same direction as the effect on duration, as seen in equations (8.37) and (8.40). This is also true with regard to the effect of an increase in g on initial prices. This is because the elasticities determined by (8.38) and (8.41) are less than unity. The terminal prices, $S_a^* - g\varepsilon$ and $S_b^* - 2gt$ in the synchronized and staggered steady states, respectively, change in opposite direction to ε or t.

For a additive profits, $c = 0$, (8.38) and (8.41) imply that $\varepsilon = 2t$ and, using (8.37) and (8.40), that $S_a^* = S_b^*$. Thus, the synchronized and the symmetric staggered steady states have the same upper and lower bounds on real prices. Along the staggered path, price adjustments occur alternately at a frequency twice as high as that of joint price adjustments in the synchronized steady state.

6. Conclusions and Their Robustness to Alternative Assumptions

The main finding of this paper is that, with positive interactions, it is unlikely that a multiproduct monopoly will adopt a staggered price policy. In this section we examine the sensitivity of this result to our assumptions concerning the costs of price adjustment and the interactions of the two prices in the monopolist's profit function.

Increasing returns to scale in the costs of price adjustment, e.g. menu costs, would further strengthen the tendency for synchronization of price changes. In fact, as shown in Sheshinski and Weiss (1989), in the menu costs case, the monopolist's optimal pricing strategy is fully synchronized following the first price change. In this case, the optimal policy for two goods reduces to the one-good case analysed in Sheshinski and Weiss (1977).

In the absence of positive price interactions in the profit function, the likelihood of a staggered policy increases substantially. In the case of additive profits (zero interactions) there is a continuum of non-synchronized steady-states, all with the same (S, s) values for both goods, which differ in the timing of the price change of the goods. The value of each steady-state increases as the difference between the time of price adjustment of the different goods decreases (see Sheshinski and Weiss (1989)). Thus, the synchronized steady state is the best. Nevertheless, for a wide range of initial conditions, it is preferable to change only *one* of the two prices, thereby saving on the costs of price adjustment.

Negative price interactions in the profit function fully exclude a synchronized price policy (Sheshinski and Weiss (1989)). This has been illustrated in the example discussed in Section 5. For a positive interest rate and non-negative interactions either one or the other steady state may be optimal depending on initial conditions. However for the special case of quadratic profits, we have shown that in the limit, when the rate of interest approaches zero, a sharp classification exists: positive interactions eliminate staggering while negative interactions eliminate synchronization.

The important role of the interactions in determining the timing of price changes, can be explained intuitively. Recall that the gain from postponing a price change is the sum of current flow of profits $F(z_1, z_2)$ and the interest gained on the delay in adjustment costs, $r\beta$. The loss from postponing a price change is the flow of profits evaluated at the new real price, S_1^*. Hence, the difference $F(z_1, z_2) + r\beta - F(S_1^*, z_2)$ is the net gain from postponing a price change of good 1. If the price of good 2 is to be raised now, then, with positive interactions, $F_{12} > 0$, the gains from postponing the price increase of good 1 diminish. This creates an incentive for synchronization. Conversely, if $F_{12} < 0$, then staggering is enhanced.

To further explore the role of different assumptions on the nature of the optimal programme we use some numerical analysis. We restrict our attention to synchronized and staggered steady states which can be solved using equations (8.30)–(8.31) or (8.32)–(8.33).

In table 8.1 we present such solutions for the case of a quadratic profit function. The Table highlights the following points.

(1) The synchronized steady state provides a higher value than the staggered steady state whenever $c > 0$. This pattern is reversed for negative interactions. Although not presented in the table, the synchronized steady state still dominates at zero and small negative interactions.

(2) The staggered steady state may be optimal even if it is dominated by the synchronized steady state since it costs β to move from one steady state to the other. The asterisks in Table I indicate cases where such a move is profitable. It is seen that optimality of the staggered steady state is enhanced by high costs of price adjustment in conjunction with weak positive (or negative) interactions.

(3) Although the staggered steady stage appears to be optimal under mild positive interactions, it is not locally stable (as stated in Proposition 3). For all the simulations in Table I we have verified that the stability test fails if $c > 0$ and passes if $c < 0$.

(4) With positive interactions the staggered steady state involves more frequent price changes and smaller price increases for each of the two goods. This is in addition to the fact that one of the goods is changed every *half* period. With negative interactions, price changes for each product are less frequent in the staggered steady state.

(5) As noted in our previous work, small costs of price adjustment are sufficient to generate time intervals with fixed nominal prices whose duration seems plausible. In the upper panel of Table I we use costs of adjustment which are one permill of the current flow of profits, $\beta = 0.001$. We see that at an inflation rate of 20% a year, prices are raised jointly every 8 months in a synchronized steady state and, in the staggered steady state (with $c = 1$), each price is raised every 6 months. The values of the optimal programmes, however, differ from the upper bound, $F(\bar{S}, \bar{S})/r$, by only half of one percent. This reflects the flatness of the value function around its maximum (see Akerlof and Yellen (1985)).

Table 8.1
Comparison of steady states for different rates of inflation, different costs of adjustment and different interactions[1]

Cost of price adjustment β	inflation rate g	Synchronized steady state[2]				Staggered steady states[2]											
						c = 1				c = 0.025				c = −0.25			
		S_a^*	s_a	ε	rV_a	S_b^*	s_b	$2t$	rV_b	S_b^*	s_b	$2t$	rV_b	S_b^*	s_b	$2t$	rV_b
0.001	0.05	1.041	0.957	1.687	0.9983	1.029	0.967	1.243	0.9976*	1.041	0.957	1.667	0.9982	1.048	0.950	1.973	0.9985
	0.10	1.052	0.946	1.063	0.9973	1.038	0.960	0.783	0.9962*	1.051	0.947	1.050	0.9972	1.061	0.937	1.243	0.9977
	0.20	1.066	0.932	0.669	0.9956	1.048	0.950	0.493	0.9940*	1.065	0.933	0.661	0.9955*	1.077	0.923	0.783	0.9962
	0.30	1.076	0.923	0.511	0.9943	1.058	0.943	0.376	0.9921*	1.075	0.924	0.505	0.9941*	1.089	0.909	0.598	0.9950
	0.50	1.093	0.909	0.363	0.9918	1.066	0.932	0.263	0.9888*	1.089	0.910	0.359	0.9917*	1.106	0.893	0.425	0.9930
0.1	0.05	1.171	0.778	7.856	0.9708	1.110	0.821	5.782	0.9518*	1.168	0.780	7.760	0.9655	1.208	0.748	9.193	0.9717
	0.10	1.227	0.733	4.939	0.9486	1.154	0.773	3.637	0.9217*	1.222	0.736	4.879	0.9430	1.271	0.694	5.778	0.9527
	0.20	1.295	0.673	3.108	0.9131	1.207	0.749	2.290	0.8735*	1.291	0.677	3.891	0.9070	1.350	0.623	3.637	0.9225
	0.30	1.342	0.630	2.372	0.8832	1.243	0.719	1.747	0.8329*	1.337	0.634	2.343	0.8767	1.404	0.572	2.774	0.8967
	0.50	1.410	0.566	1.687	0.8320	1.295	0.673	1.243	0.7634*	1.406	0.571	1.666	0.8248	1.483	0.497	1.973	0.8528

Notes:

1. The interest rate is set at r = 0.1. The profit function is $F(Z_1, Z_2) = a(Z_1 + Z_2) - b(Z_1^2 + Z_2^2) + cZ_1 \cdot Z_2$. Throughout the table we set a = 1 and 2b − c = 1. The normalization implies that the maximal profits, 1, are attained at $Z_1 = Z_2 = 1$.

2. Subscripts a and b indicate synchronized and staggered steady states, respectively. S_i^* is the real price of each good just after a price increase; s_i is the real price of each good just before a price increase; rV_i is the imputed flow value of the optimal programme, $i = a, b$. The time interval over which the nominal price of each good is held fixed is ε and $2t$, respectively; t is the time between price change of different goods at the staggered steady state.

* The staggered steady state is suboptimal.

(6) The loss of potential profits due to adjustment costs increases with the rate of inflation. There is a magnification effect where even minute adjustment costs translate into a non-negligible loss of profits. This is due to the accumulation of two effects: as the rate of inflation increases, price adjustments occur more frequently and the firm is away from the maximal profits point for a longer period. For instance, with $g = 0.50$, $c = 1$, we see, in the upper panel of Table I, that at a staggered steady state an adjustment cost of 0.001 translates into a loss of profits of 0.011. In the lower panel of Table I, the numbers are 0.1 and 0.237, respectively.

(7) The reduction in profits due to increased inflation is more pronounced on the staggered steady-state paths than on the synchronized paths. The reason is that the distance between the prices of the two goods along the staggered steady-state path increases with the rate of inflation. With positive interaction, this is an additional cause for the reduction in profits.

(8) In all the cases presented in Table I, an increase in the inflation rate g, or a reduction in β cause more frequent price adjustments and larger variation in real prices. A larger c increases the frequency of price changes in the staggered steady state. These patterns are consistent with the analysis discussed in Section 5.

Staggered price policies have been assumed in support of consistent aggregation (i.e. a continuous aggregate price level associated with discrete price changes by individual firms). From this point of view, it is natural to ask whether the results of the multiproduct monopoly extend to other industrial structures such as duopoly or competition. If price changes are controlled by different firms, the likelihood of a staggered price policy increases. This is a consequence of two considerations: first, in the absence of cooperation, returns to scale in the costs of price adjustment cannot be exploited. Second, the monopoly, who internalizes all interactions, would change both prices even if this is not optimal for each duopolist separately. If the number of firms increases to the point where interactions become negligible, firms will adopt independent (S, s) policies, where the timing of price changes by each firm depends only on its initial conditions. Hence, a large common shock would place all firms within T_0, which leads to a synchronized policy thereafter. This is the reason why idiosyncratic shocks are required to sustain staggering (see Sheshinski and Weiss (1983) and Ball and Romer (1989)).

Appendix A

The purpose of this appendix is to establish some basic features of the optimal pricing policy and its associated value function. First, we show that there exists an optimal programme where $V(z_1, z_2)$, defined in (8.7), attains a maximum. Second, following the first price change, the timing of subsequent price increases and the associated real prices are uniquely determined. Finally, we note that uniqueness implies that $V(z_1, z_2)$ is differentiable at all (z_1, z_2) reachable after a price increase.

The optimal policy is a member of a class of policies which can be described as sequences of nominal prices for each of the two goods and time-intervals over which each nominal price prevails. This characterization follows from the existence of positive costs of adjustment for nominal price changes.

Let us define

$$\{\mu_\tau\}_{\tau=1}^{\infty} = \{t_\tau, S_{1\tau}, S_{2\tau}\}_{\tau=1}^{\infty}, \tag{A.1}$$

where t_τ are the dates of *nominal* price changes (for at least one good) and $S_{j\tau}$, $j = 1, 2$, are the logs of the *real* prices chosen at these dates. Clearly, $S_{j\tau} \in R$ and $t_\tau \in R^+$, $t_{\tau+1} \geq t_\tau$ and $t_1 \geqq 0$. Without loss of generality, we can assume $t_{\tau+1} > t_\tau$. Due to the fixed costs of adjustment, the price of the same good will not be raised twice within a short interval. If two different prices are raised within a short interval, we can treat that as a simultaneous raise of two prices. We denote the set of all sequences satisfying the above restrictions by U.

To each sequence $\{\mu_\tau\}_{\tau=1}^{\infty} \in U$, we can associate the present discounted value of real profits

$$J(z_1, z_2, \{\mu_\tau\}_{\tau=1}^{\infty}) = \int_0^{t_1} e^{-rx} F(z_1 - gx, z_2 - gx)\, dx + \beta e^{-rt_1} \sum_{j=1}^{2} \delta(S_{j1} - z_j + gt_1)$$

$$+ \sum_{\tau=1}^{\infty} \left\{ \int_{t_\tau}^{t_{\tau+1}} e^{-rx} F(S_{1\tau} - g(x - t_\tau), S_{2\tau} - g(x - t_\tau))\, dx \right.$$

$$\left. + \beta e^{-rt_{\tau+1}} \sum_{j=1}^{2} \delta(S_{j\tau+1} - S_{j\tau} + g(t_{\tau+1} - t_\tau)) \right\}, \tag{A.2}$$

where

$$\delta(y) = \begin{cases} 0 & \text{if } y = 0 \\ -1 & \text{if } y \neq 0. \end{cases} \tag{A.3}$$

By definition (A.3), costs of adjustment are avoided if there is no nominal price change. That is, if the real price chosen at time t_τ coincides with the real price induced by the nominal price chosen at time $t_{\tau-1}$.

The value function is defined as

$$V(z_1, z_2) = \text{Sup}_{\{\mu_\tau\}_{\tau=1}^\infty \in U} J(z_1, z_2, \{\mu_\tau\}_{\tau=1}^\infty). \tag{A.4}$$

Observe that $J(z_1, z_2, \{\mu_\tau\}_{\tau=1}^\infty)$ is *upper semi-continuous*.

Recall that under our assumptions, profits are positive only within a finite box, $\underline{z} \leq z_i \leq \bar{z}, i = 1, 2$. Charging at some t_τ an initial price for good j, $S_{j\tau}$, which exceeds $\bar{z}$, yields non-positive profits for a period of $t_S = (S_{j\tau} - \bar{z})/g$. The value of the programme associated with this choice is at most $e^{-rt_S} F(\bar{S}, \bar{S})/r$. On the other hand, the firm can obtain immediately

$$\frac{1}{1 - e^{-r(\bar{z}-\underline{z})/g}} \left[\int_0^{(\bar{z}-\underline{z})/g} e^{-rx} F(\bar{z} - gx, \bar{z} - gx) \, dx - 2\beta \right].$$

By assumption, this value is positive. Hence, for a sufficiently large $S_{j\tau}$ (and t_S), the policy of repetitive adjustments from $\bar{z}$ to $\underline{z}$ dominates. Setting $S_{j\tau}$ below $\underline{z}$ or postponing the nominal price changes until some real price erodes below $\underline{z}$ is also sub-optimal. Any such path can be replaced by a path which differs only in the initial phase but yields positive profits via continuous price adjustments. It follows that, without loss of generality, we can select the optimal policy from a *compact* subset of U.

We can now apply *Weierstrass' Theorem* which states that an upper semi-continuous function defined on a compact subset (of a normed linear space) achieves its maximum. We conclude:

PROPOSITION I. *There exists an optimal policy, $\{\mu_\tau^*\}_{\tau=1}^\infty \in U$, for which $V(z_1, z_2)$, defined in (A.4), attains its maximum.*

Any path which maximizes $V(z_1, z_2)$ must satisfy a sequence of necessary first-order conditions. For example, consider a pair (z_1, z_2) where the optimal sequence is such that prices are raised alternately, first good 1, then good 2, then good 1 again, and so on. In this case the value function becomes

$$V(z_1, z_2) = \int_0^{t_1^*} e^{-rx} F(z_1 - gx, z_2 - gx)\, dx - \beta e^{-rt_1^*}$$

$$+ \int_{t_1^*}^{t_2^*} e^{-rx} F(S_{11}^* - g(x - t_1^*), x_2 - gx)\, dx - \beta e^{-rt_2^*}$$

$$+ \int_{t_2^*}^{t_3^*} e^{-rx} F(S_{11}^* - g(x - t_1^*), S_{22}^* - g(x - t_2^*)) - \beta e^{-rt_3^*}$$

$$+ \int_{t_3^*}^{t_4^*} e^{-rx} F(S_{13}^* - g(x - t_3^*), S_{22}^* - g(x - t_2^*)) - \beta e^{-rt_4^*}$$

$$+ \cdots \qquad\qquad\qquad\qquad\qquad\qquad\qquad\qquad\qquad (A.6)$$

corresponding first-order conditions are

$$F(z_1 - gt_1^*, z_2 - gt_1^*) \leqq F(S_{11}^*, z_2 - gt_1^*) - r\beta, \text{ with equality if } t_1^* > 0,$$

$$F(S_{11}^* - g(t_2^* - t_1^*), z_2 - gt_2^*) = F(S_{11}^* - g(t_2^* - t_1^*), S_{22}^*) - r\beta$$

$$F(S_{11}^* - g(t_3^* - t_1^*), S_{22}^* - g(t_3^* - t_2^*)) = F(S_{13}^*, S_{22}^* - g(t_3^* - t_2^*)) - r\beta$$

$$\vdots \qquad\qquad\qquad\qquad\qquad\qquad\qquad \vdots \qquad\qquad (A.7)$$

and

$$\int_{t_1^*}^{t_2^*} e^{-rx} F_1(S_{11}^* - g(x - t_1^*), z_2 - gx)\, dx$$

$$+ \int_{t_2^*}^{t_3^*} e^{-rx} F_1(S_{11}^* - g(x - t_1^*), S_{22}^* - g(x - t_2^*))\, dx = 0$$

$$\int_{t_2^*}^{t_3^*} e^{-rx} F_2(S_{11}^* - g(x - t_1^*), S_{22}^* - g(x - t_2^*))\, dx$$

$$\vdots$$

$$+ \int_{t_3^*}^{t_4^*} e^{-rx} F_2(S_{13}^* - g(x - t_3^*), S_{22}^* - g(x - t_2^*))\, dx = 0 \qquad (A.8)$$

$$\vdots$$

Multiplying both sides of (A.6) by r, integrating by parts each integral in the sequence, and using the first-order conditions (A.7) and (A.8), one obtains

$$rV(z_1, z_2) = F(z_1, z_2) - g \int_0^{t_1^*} e^{-rx} F_1(z_1 - gx, z_2 - gx) dx$$

$$- g \int_0^{t_1^*} e^{-rx} F_2(z_1 - gx, z_2 - gx) dx$$

$$- g \int_{t_1^*}^{t_2^*} e^{-rx} F_2(S_{11}^* - g(x - t_1^*), z_2 - gx) dx. \tag{A.9}$$

Equation (A.9) (which is the same as (8.16) in the text) establishes the "valuation formula" in its integral form. It is important to note that no differentiability assumptions on $V(z_1, z_2)$ are required to derive this result. Similarly, equations (8.30) and (8.34) in the text, which identify the staggered steady state, can be derived directly from equations (A.7)–(A.9), without the assumption that $V(z_1, z_2)$ is differentiable.

Differentiability of the value function is closely associated with the uniqueness of the optimal controls, $\{\mu_\tau^*\}_{\tau=1}^\infty$, for a given initial condition, (z_1, z_2). We cannot establish such uniqueness for all possible pairs of initial conditions. However, we can show that following the *first* price change, all subsequent choices of dates and real prices are uniquely determined.

To establish this fact, we first need to narrow down the possible patterns which constitute a solution to the optimization problem. This is done in the following two lemmata.

LEMMA 1. *It is not optimal to delay a price reduction, i.e. if a price reduction occurs it must occur once, at time $t = 0$.*

LEMMA 2. *If only one price is raised, it must be the price of the good with the lower real price.*

Proof of Lemma 1. Suppose that for some (z_1, z_2), $t_1^* > 0$ and $S_{11}^* < z_1 - gt_1^*$, i.e. a reduction in z_1 occurs after a delay. The value of such policy can be written as

$$\int_0^{t_1^*} e^{-rx} F(z_1 - gx, z_2 - gx) dx + e^{-rt_1^*} [V(S_{11}^*, z_2 - gt_1^*) - \beta].$$

Now consider a feasible alternative programme where the price of good 1 is reduced at time 0 to $S_{11}^* + gt_1^*$ and kept unchanged up to t_1^*. The value of this alternative path is

$$-\beta + \int_0^{t_1^*} e^{-rx}F(S_{11}^* + gt_1^* - gx, z_2 - gx)\,dx + e^{-rt_1^*}V(S_{11}^*, z_2 - gt_1^*).$$

We want to show that it exceeds the value of the original programme. That is,

$$\int_0^{t_1^*} e^{-rx}[F(S_{11}^* + gt_1^* - gx, z_2 - gx)\,dx - F(z_1 - gx, z_2 - gx)]\,dx$$

$$> \beta(1 - e^{-rt_1^*}). \tag{A.10}$$

By the assumption that $S_{11}^* + gt_1^* < z_1$, we have under monotonicity, (8.7), that the integrand in (A.10) is strictly monotone decreasing in x. Since t_1^* is a maximizer, we have by (A.7) that

$$F(S_{11}^*, z_2 - gt_1^*) - F(z_1 - ft_1^*, z_2 - gt_1^*) \geq r\beta.$$

Hence,

$$F(S_{11}^* + gt_1^* - gx, z_2 - gx) - F(z_1 - gx, z_2 - gx) > r\beta.$$

for all $x \in [0, t_1^*)$, which establishes (A.10)   ‖

Proof of Lemma 2. Suppose that $z_2 > z_1$, and z_2 is raised at $t = 0$. That is, $t_1^* = 0$, $S_{21}^* > z_2$ and $S_{11}^* = z_1$. By (A.7),

$$F(z_1, S_{21}^*) - r\beta \geq F(z_1, z_2), \tag{A.11}$$

because otherwise the firm would postpone the increase in z_2. By quasi-concavity and $S_{21}^* > z_2$, it follows that $F_2(z_1, z_2) > 0$. Suppose that at t_2^*, the price of z_1 is raised to S_{12}^*. Write the value of the proposed programme:

$$\int_0^{t_2^*} e^{-rx}F(z_1 - gx, S_{21}^* - gx)\,dx + e^{-rt_2^*}[V(S_{12}^*, S_{21}^* - gt_2^*) - \beta].$$

Consider now an alternative feasible programme in which z_1 is raised at time 0 to S_{21}^*, and at time t_2^*, the price of z_2 is raised to S_{12}^*, yielding

$$\int_0^{t_2^*} e^{-rx}F(S_{21}^* - gx, z_2 - gx)\,dx + e^{-rt_2^*}[V(S_{21}^* - gt_2^*, S_{12}^*) - \beta].$$

By symmetry, $V(S_{12}^*, S_{21}^* - gt_2^*) = V(S_{21}^* - gt_2^*, S_{12}^*)$.

We want to show that

$$\int_0^{t_2^*} e^{-rx}[F(S_{21}^* - gx, z_2 - gx) - F(z_1 - gx, S_{21}^* - gx)]\,dx$$

$$= (z_2 - z_1)\int_0^{t_2^*} e^{-rx}F_2(S_{21}^* - gx, \xi - gx)\,dx > 0 \qquad (A.12)$$

where $z_1 \leqq \xi \leqq z_2$. By complementarity, (8.5), $F_2(z_1, z_2) > 0 \Rightarrow F_2(S_{21}^*, z_2) > 0$, since $S_{21}^* > z_2 > z_1$. By monotonicity, (8.7), (and thus concavity of $F(z_1, z_2)$),

$$F_2(S_{21}^*, z_2) > 0 \Rightarrow F_2(S_{21}^*, \xi) > 0 \Rightarrow F_2(S_{21}^* - gx, \xi - gx) > 0$$
$$\text{for all } x \in [0, t_2^*].$$

Hence (A.12) holds, which implies that the alternative programme is superior. ∥

We are now ready to establish the following proposition:

PROPOSITION II. *Following the first price change, the date of subsequent price changes is* unique.

Proof. Assume that at time 0 the price of good 1 has changed and set at S_{11}^* and suppose that there are two dates, t_2^* and t_2^{**} ($> t_2^*$) which are both optimal dates for subsequent price changes. With each of these dates there is an associated future sequence of prices. Clearly, both sequences must satisfy the necessary conditions for a local maximum, (A.7)–(A.8), and must yield the same value of V. We do not need to specify these sequences, since one can use the "valuation formula", (A.9), to evaluate each alternative, based only on actions taken in the next round.

There are several cases to consider depending on the pattern of price changes. In the first case, the price of good 2 is raised both at t_2^* and at t_2^{**}. Setting $t_1^* = 0$ in (A.9), we have

$$rV(S_{11}^*, z_2) = F(S_{11}^*, z_2) - g\int_0^{t_2^*} e^{-rx}F_2(S_{11}^* - gx, z_2 - gx)\,dx$$

$$= F(S_{11}^*, z_2) - g\int_0^{t_2^{**}} e^{-rx}F_2(S_{11}^* - gx, z_2 - gx)\,dx. \qquad (A.13)$$

It follows that

$$\int_0^{t_2^*} e^{-rx}F_2(S_{11}^* - gx, z_2 - gx)\,dx = \int_0^{t_2^{**}} e^{-rx}F_2(S_{11}^* - gx, z_2 - gx)\,dx.$$

(A.14)

Under the F.O.C. (A.7), we have

$$F(S_{11}^* - gt_2^*, S_{22}^*) - F(S_{11}^* - gt_2^*, z_2 - gt_2^*) - r\beta \geq 0,$$

(A.15)

where S_{22}^* is the choice of z_2 at t_2^*. By Lemma 1, $S_{22}^* > z_2 - gt_2^*$ and therefore (A.15) and quasi-concavity imply that $F_2(S_{11}^* - gt_2^*, z_2 - gt_2^*) > 0$, i.e. marginal profits from raising the price of good 2 are positive just prior to the price increase. Under the irreversibility assumption, it follows that $F_2(S_{11}^* - gx, z_2 - gx) > 0$ for all $x \in [t_2^*, t_2^{**}]$. Hence, two integrals in (A.14) can be equal only if $t_2^* = t_2^{**}$, which establishes uniqueness for this case.

A similar proof applies to the cases in which the price of good 1 is raised together with the price of good 2 and to the case in which the price of good 1 is raised at both t_2^* and t_2^{**}. The cases in which two *different* prices are raised at t_2^* and t_2^{**} are excluded by Lemma 2. Thus, the date of the subsequent price change is unique. ‖

It remains to be shown that at the time of price change a unique action is taken.

PROPOSITION III. *Following the first price change, subsequent chosen real prices are unique.*

Proof. Consider first the case where only the price of good 1 is raised at t_2^*. Assume, contrary to the Proposition, that there are two choices, say, S_{12}^* and S_{12}^{**}.

By the F.O.C., (A.7), setting $t_1^* = 0$, we must have

$$F(S_{11}^* - gt_2^*, S_{21}^* - gt_2^*) = F(S_{12}^*, S_{21}^* - gt_2^*) - r\beta$$

$$= F(S_{12}^{**}, S_{21}^* - gt_2^*) - r\beta.$$

(A.16)

Hence,

$$F(S_{12}^*, S_{21}^* - gt_2^*) = F(S_{12}^{**}, S_{21}^* - gt_2^*).$$

(A.17)

Let $S_{12}^* > S_{12}^{**}$. Then, by quasi-concavity, $F_1(S_{12}^{**}, S_{21}^* - gt_2^*) > 0$, which under irreversibility, (A.1), contradicts the F.O.C. (A.8).

Finally, consider the case in which both prices are raised at t_2^*. As explained in the text, under positive interaction, the best choice, starting from $(z_1, z_2) \in T_0$ is to select a synchronized steady state. In Appendix B we shall prove that the synchronized steady state is unique. ‖

Having established uniqueness, differentiability of the value function follows. First we note that uniqueness implies continuity of the optimal choice with respect to variations in the initial state. Now, let $\{\mu_\tau\}_{\tau=1}^\infty$ be an optimal choice for (z_1, z_2) and $\{\mu_\tau^h\}_{\tau=1}^\infty$ be an optimal choice for $(z_1, z_2 + h)$, where $h > 0$. By definition

$$J(z_1, z_2, \{\mu_\tau\}_{\tau=1}^\infty) \geqq J(z_1, z_2, \{\mu_\tau^h\}_{\tau=1}^\infty), \tag{A.18}$$

$$J(z_1, z_2 + h, \{\mu_\tau^h\}_{\tau=1}^\infty) \geqq J(z_1, z_2 + h, \{\mu_\tau\}_{\tau=1}^\infty), \tag{A.19}$$

or

$$J(z_1, z_2 + h, \{\mu_\tau^h\}_{\tau=1}^\infty) - J(z_1, z_2, \{\mu_\tau^h\}_{\tau=1}^\infty)$$

$$\geqq J(z_1, z_2 + h, \{\mu_\tau^h\}_{\tau=1}^\infty) - J(z_1, z_2, \{\mu_\tau\}_{\tau=1}^\infty)$$

$$\geqq J(z_1, z_2 + h, \{\mu_\tau\}_{\tau=1}^\infty) - J(z_1, z_2, \{\mu_\tau\}_{\tau=1}^\infty). \tag{A.20}$$

Consider a point (z_1, z_2) in the interior of C where, in (A.2), $\delta(S_{j1} - z_j + gt_j) = 0$, $j = 1, 2$. In this neighborhood, $J(z_1, z_2, \{\mu_\tau\}_{\tau=1}^\infty)$ is differentiable w.r.t. z_1 and z_2. Dividing both sides of (A.20) by h, letting h approach zero and using the continuity of $\{\mu\}$ in z, we see that the first and last expressions in (A.20) both converge to $\partial/\partial z_2 J(z_1, z_2, \{\mu_\tau\}_{\tau=1}^\infty)$. Therefore, the limit of the middle term exists. This limit is, by definition, $\partial V(z_1, z_2)/\partial z_2$. This yields the usual envelope relationship.

$$\frac{\partial V(z_1, z_2)}{\partial z_2} = \frac{\partial}{\partial z_2} J(z_1, z_2, \{\mu_\tau\}_{\tau=1}^\infty). \tag{A.21}$$

A similar proof applies to the other partial derivatives.

Having established differentiability along the reaction curves $S(z_1)$ and $S(z_2)$, it is easy to show that $V(z_1, z_2)$ is also differentiable at any $(z_1, z_2) \in C$ which is reachable from these curves. This follows from the observation that at any such point, subsequent choices are consistent with those made at the origin. In addition, $V(z_1, z_2)$ is also differentiable at any point in the interior of C on a path reaching a point on $S(z_i)$, $i = 1, 2$, which is in the interior of C. This follows from the relation between the value function at these two points. That is, $V(z_1, z_2)$ at the origin of the path is equal to the integral of discounted profits until $S(z_i)$ is reached, plus the discounted value of V at that point.

Appendix B

Proof of Proposition 1.   We first prove that the synchronized steady state is unique. Any maximizer of V must be in the interior of C. Otherwise an additional cost of β would be incurred to obtain the same value, V^*. By the results of Appendix A, V is differentiable at this point. Using (8.15) we obtain

$$rV(S_1, S_2) = F(S_1, S_2) \tag{B.1}$$

where $(S_1, S_2) \in \mathrm{argmax}_{z_1, z_2} V(z_1, z_2)$.

Now suppose that $S_1 \neq S_2$. Then, by symmetry, the points (S_1, S_2) and (S_2, S_1) are both maximizers of $V(z_1, z_2)$, yielding the same value V^*.

$$S_1^\gamma = \gamma S_1 + (1 - \gamma)S_2,$$
$$S_2^\gamma = \gamma S_2 + (1 - \gamma)S_1. \tag{B.2}$$

Using recursive equation (8.7), the value associated with $V(S_1, S_2)$ is

$$V(S_1, S_2) = \int_0^{t^*} e^{-rx}F(S_1 - gx, S_2 - gx)\,dx + e^{-rt^*}[V^* - 2\beta], \tag{B.3}$$

where $t^* = t^*(S_1, S_2)$ is the optimal time for the subsequent price change and V^* is the maximum value of V realized at t^*. Starting at (S_1^γ, S_2^γ), the same choices are still feasible. Hence,

$$V(S_1^\gamma, S_2^\gamma) \geqq \int_0^{t^*} e^{-rx}F(S_1^\gamma - gx, S_2^\gamma - gx)\,dx + e^{-rt^*}[V^* - 2\beta]. \tag{B.4}$$

By strict quasi-concavity, $F(S_1 - gx, S_2 - gx) < F(S_1^\gamma - gx, S_2^\gamma - gx)$ for all x, $t^* \geqq x \geqq 0$. Thus, equations (B.3) and (B.4) imply that $V(S_1^\gamma, S_2^\gamma) > V(S_1, S_2)$, which contradicts the assumption that (S_1, S_2) maximizes V. This proves that $S_1 = S_2 = S$. To prove that S is unique we use again the quasi-concavity of F together with the "valuation formula", (8.15).

Suppose there are two pairs, (S^a, S^a) and (S^b, S^b), $S^a \neq S^b$, that maximize V. Let $S^\theta = \theta S^a + (1 - \theta) S^b$, $0 < \theta < 1$. Then,

$$F(S^\theta, S^\theta) > F(S^a, S^a) = F(S^b, S^b) = rV^* \geq rV(S^\theta, S^\theta). \tag{B.5}$$

Inequality (B.5) and the "valuation formula", (8.15), imply that for θ in the neighbourhood of 0 or 1, we must have

$$gV_1(S^\theta, S^\theta) + gV_2(S^\theta, S^\theta) > 0. \tag{B.6}$$

But (B.6) implies that V can be increased in the neighbourhood of (S^a, S^a) or (S^b, S^b), contrary to the assumption that these are local maxima.

We shall now prove the uniqueness of the symmetric staggered steady state, (S_b^*, t). For brevity, we write $S_b^* = S$. Consider the point $(S, \hat{z}) \in C$, where the price of the first good has just been changed, and let t_2 be the timing of the subsequent price change and S_2 the value of the subsequent real price. The F.O.C. satisfied at that point are:

$$V_2(S - gt_2, S_2) = 0 \tag{B.7}$$

and

$$F(S - gt_2, \hat{z} - gt_2) - r(V(S - gt_2, S_2) - \beta) - gV_1(S - gt_2, S_2) = 0. \tag{B.8}$$

At a symmetric steady state, $S_2 = S$, $t_2 = t$ and $\hat{z} = S - gt$. Evaluating the second-order conditions at this point, we have the requirement that the matrix A,

$$A = \begin{bmatrix} V_{22}(S - gt, S) & -gV_{12}(S-gt, S) \\ -gV_{12}(S - gt, S) & -g[(F_1(S-gt, S-2gt) + F_2(S-gt, S-2gt) + g[rV_1(S-gt, S) + gV_{11}(S-gt, S)]] \end{bmatrix} \tag{B.9}$$

be negative-definite. Now consider the system

$$V_2(S - gt, S) = 0 \tag{B.10}$$

and

$$F(S - gt, S - 2gt) - r(V(S - gt, S) - \beta) - gV_1(S - gt, S) = 0 \tag{B.11}$$

as two equations in the unknowns S and t.

To prove uniqueness, we shall show that the Jacobian, B,

$$B = \begin{bmatrix} V_{12}(S-gt,S) + V_{22}(S-gy,S) & -gV_{12}(S-gt,S) \\ F_1(S-gt,S-2gt) + F_2(S-gt,S-2gt) - rV_1(S-gt,S) & -g[F_1(S-gt,S-2gt) + 2F_2(S-gt,S-2gt) \\ -gV_{11}(S-gt,S) - gV_{12}(S-gt,S) & +g[rV_1(S-gt,S) + gV_{11}(S-gt,S-2gt)] \end{bmatrix}$$

(B.12)

is negative-definite. The first diagonal term is, under Assumption A1 and A2,

$$b_{11} = V_{12} + V_{22} = \frac{1}{g} F_2(S - gt, S) < 0.$$

(B.13)

The other diagonal term, b_{22}, is equal to the lower-diagonal term in (B.9), a_{22} minus $gF_2(S - gt, S - 2gt)$. By Assumption A2, F_2 just prior to a price change has to be positive. Thus, the whole term is negative. The determinant condition can be written in the form

$$b_{11}(-gF_2(S - gt, S - 2gt)) + |A| > 0. \quad \|$$

(B.14)

Appendix C

The purpose of this appendix is to analyse the stability of the staggered steady state.

We begin by calculating the *slope* of the reaction curves $S_i^* = S(z_j)$, $i \neq j, i, j = 1, 2$, evaluated at $S_i^* = S_b^*$ and $z_j = S_b^* - gt$, where S_b^* and t are determined by equations (8.32) and (8.33). To save on notation we shall omit again the superscript and subscript, writing S instead of S_b^*.

Suppose that z_1 has just been raised to S and that $z_2 = S - gt$. At this point we have

$$V_1(S, z_2) = 0,$$

(C.1)

$$gV_{11}(S, z_2) + gV_{21}(S, z_2) = F_1(S, z_2),$$

(C.2)

and

$$V_2(S, z_2) = \int_0^t e^{-rx} F_2(S - gx, z_2 - gx) \, dx, \tag{C.3}$$

where (C.2) follows from the valuation formula (8.15) and (C.1). Differentiating (C.1) we obtain

$$S'(z_2) = \frac{V_{12}(S, z_2)}{V_{11}(S, z_2)}. \tag{C.4}$$

Using (C.2) to eliminate V_{11},

$$gV_{12}(S, z_2) = \frac{S'(z_2)F_1(S, z_2)}{S'(z_2) - 1}. \tag{C.5}$$

Differentiating (C.3) we have

$$V_{21}(S, z_2) = \int_0^t e^{-rx} F_{21}(S - gx, z_2 - gx) \, dx + e^{-rt} F_2(S - gt, z_2 - gt) \frac{\partial t}{\partial z_1}. \tag{C.6}$$

To find $\partial t / \partial z_1$, we note that in steady state,

$$(S, t) = \operatorname{argmax}_{S_2, t_2} \left\{ \int_0^{t_2} e^{-rx} F(S - gx, z_2 - gx) \, dx + e^{-rt_2} [V(S - gt_2, S_2) - \beta] \right\}. \tag{C.7}$$

Differentiating the F.O.C. for the maximation in (C.7), we obtain

$$\begin{bmatrix} -g[F_1(S - gt, z_2 - g) + F_2(S - gt, z_2 - gt) - rV_1(S - gt, S) - gV_{11}(S - gt, S)] & -gV_{12}(S - gt, S) \\ -gV_{21}(S - gt, S) & V_{22}(S - gt, S) \end{bmatrix} \begin{bmatrix} \partial t / \partial z_1 \\ \partial S / \partial z_1 \end{bmatrix}$$

$$= \begin{bmatrix} -F_1(S - gt, z_2 - gt) + rV_1(S - gt, S) + gV_{11}(S - gt, S) \\ -V_{21}(S - gt, S) \end{bmatrix} \tag{C.8}$$

The second-order conditions for maximization require that the matrix in (C.8) be negative-definite. Using the valuation formula, we have

$$rV_1(S - gt, S) + gV_{11}(S - gt, S) = F_1(S - gt, S) - gV_{12}(S - gt, S). \tag{C.9}$$

Also,

$$V_{22}(S - gt, S) = -\frac{V_{12}(S - gt, S)}{S'(S - gt)}. \tag{C.10}$$

Substituting (C.9)–(C.10) into (C.8), we can solve for $\partial t/\partial z_1$ in terms of $S'(S - gt)$, to obtain:

$$g\frac{\partial t}{\partial z_1} = \frac{F_1(S - gt, z_2 - gt) - F_1(S - gt, S) - F_2(S - gt, S)S'(S - gt)}{F_1(S - gt, z_2 - gt) + F_2(S - gt, z_2 - gt) - F_1(S - gt, S) - F_2(S - gt, S)S'(S - gt)}. \tag{C.11}$$

The denominator on the R.H.S. of (C.11) is positive by second-order conditions. Combining (C.5), (C.6) and (C.11) and using symmetry, we obtain

$$\frac{S'(z_2)}{S'(z_2) - 1} = C + D\frac{A - S'(S - gt)}{B - S'(S - gt)}, \tag{C.12}$$

where

$$A = \frac{F_1(S - gt, z_2 - gt) - F_1(S - gt, S)}{F_2(S - gt, S)},$$

$$B = A + \frac{F_2(S - gt, z_2 - gt)}{F_2(S - gt, S)}, \tag{C.13}$$

$$C = \frac{g\int_0^t e^{-rx}F_{12}(S - gx, z_2 - gx)\,dx}{F_2(S - gt, S)},$$

and

$$D = e^{-rt}\frac{F_2(S - gt, z_2 - gt)}{F_2(S - gt, S)}.$$

Equation (C.12) determines the slope of the reaction curve for the first good in terms of the slope of the second good's reaction curve evaluated at the *subsequent* price change. Setting $z_2 = S - gt, S'$ at this point is unknown, satisfying the non-linear difference equation:

$$\frac{x_n}{x_n - 1} = C + D\frac{A - x_{n+1}}{B - x_{n+1}}. \tag{C.14}$$

The optimality of the staggered path requires convergence of the sequence defined by (C.14) when solved forwards.

To analyse the behaviour of the solutions to (C.14), we rewrite it as

$$x_n = \frac{CB + DA - (C + D)x_{n+1}}{CB + DA - B + (1 - C - D)x_{n+1}} \equiv f(x_{n+1}). \tag{C.15}$$

Note first that the condition $x_n = x_{n+1} = x$ defines a quadratic equation which has at most two roots. In general, one root is characterized by $f'(x) < 1$ and the other by $f'(x) > 1$. The second, being unstable, cannot be obtained by iterations of the value function and therefore cannot represent the value of an optimal policy (Stokey and Lucas (1989, Chapter 4)). Henceforth, we shall consider only the root satisfying $f'(x) < 1$.

To find the roots of equation (C.15) it is convenient to rewrite (C.14):

$$CB + AD - (C + D)x = \frac{x(B - x)}{x - 1} \equiv g(x). \tag{C.16}$$

Under assumptions A1 and A2 in the text, $A > 0$, $C < 0$, $D < 0$ and $B - A < 0$. Second-order conditions (i.e. negative-definiteness of the matrix in (C.8)) imply that $B < x < 1$. It follows from these restrictions that $g(x)$ is strictly convex. Furthermore, $g(0) = g(B) = 0$, $g'(0) = -B$ and $g'(B) = -B/(B - 1)$.

Associated with the value of S' which solves (C.16) there is a corresponding value s' which is the slope of the boundary curve between the trigger sets T_i, $i = 1, 2$, and C. This relation is obtained by differentiating (8.33) in the text, yielding

$$s' = \frac{S' - A}{B - A}. \tag{C.17}$$

Note that since $B < S'$, by second-order conditions, $s' < 1$.

Consider a small perturbation around this path $a'b'd'$ in Figure 8.2. Let S' denote the slope of the reaction curve evaluated at the staggered steady-state (i.e. at $(S, S - gt)$). Similarly, let s' denote the slope of the boundary of the trigger sets T_i, $i = 1, 2$, and C, evaluated at the staggered steady state (i.e. at $(S - gt, S - gt)$). For sufficiently small perturbations these slopes can be taken as constant. Let δ be the difference between the two paths along the reaction curve for the first good, measured in units of z_2. It can be seen in Figure 8.2, and rigorously proved, that the initial δ translates into a difference $(S' - 1/1 - s')\delta$ along the trigger boundary for the second good and a difference of $(S' - 1/1 - s')^2\delta$ along the trigger boundary for the first good. Thus, if and only if

$$\left|\frac{S'-1}{1-s'}\right| < 1, \tag{C.18}$$

will the perturbed path return to the first good's curve, closer to the original point a. We therefore conclude that the necessary and sufficient condition for local stability of the staggered steady-state is condition (C.18).

It follows from (C.17) that if $S' < 0$, then $s' > 0$ and hence $|S' - 1/1 - s'| > 1$, i.e., the staggered steady-state is unstable. It remains to examine the case in which $S' > 0$. By the properties of $g(x)$, this can only occur if $AB + CD > 0$ and $B < 0$. It can be shown that

$$S' > \frac{A}{1-B+A} \quad \Leftrightarrow \quad g\left(\frac{A}{1-B+A}\right) < CB + AD - \frac{(C+D)A}{1-B+A}. \tag{C.19}$$

It remains to discuss the case of negative interactions, where $F_{12} \leqq 0$. In this case $C \geqq 0$, $A \leqq 0$ and $B < 0$. In contrast to the case with $F_{12} > 0$, (C.17) does *not* imply that if $S' < 0$ then $s' > 0$. Therefore, we need to consider the case $CB + AD < 0$ associated with negative S'. For this case too, it can be shown that (C.19) has to be satisfied. The condition in (C.19) can be simplified to

$$A + C < CB + AD, \tag{C.20}$$

which is the necessary and sufficient condition for local stability.

Appendix D

In this Appendix we prove Proposition 3 in the text.

Consider a quadratic profit function given by (8.36). The necessary conditions for a staggered steady state, (8.32)–(8.33), are now:

$$-2gt(a - (2b - c)(S - gt)) + r\beta = 0, \tag{D.1}$$

and

$$(a - (2b - c)S) \int_0^{2t} e^{-rx} \, dx + g(2b - c) \int_0^{2t} e^{-rx} x \, dx$$

$$+ cgt\left[\int_t^{2t} e^{-rx} \, dx - \int_0^t e^{-rx} \, dx\right] = 0, \tag{D.2}$$

where $S = S_b^*$ in the text.

Equations (D.1) and (D.2) uniquely determine the steady-state values for t and S. Given these values, one can calculate all the elements of the stability condition (C.20). In particular:

$$F_1(S - gt, S - 2gt) = \Delta + (2b - c)gt,$$

$$F_2(S - gt, S - 2gt) = \Delta + (4b - c)gt,$$

$$F_2(S - gt, S) = \Delta - cgt,$$

(D.3)

$$F_1(S - gt, S) = \Delta + 2bgt,$$

where $\Delta = a - (2b - c)S$. Using the definitions (C.13) in Appendix C,

$$F_2(S - gt, S)A = -2cgt,$$

$$F_2(S - gt, S)B = \Delta + (4b - 3c)gt,$$

(D.4)

$$F_2(S - gt, S)C = gc \int_0^t e^{-rx}\,dx,$$

$$F_2(S - gt, S)D = e^{-rt}(\Delta + (4b - c)gt).$$

The stability condition (C.20), $CB + AD > A + C$ is thus equivalent to:

$$(\Delta + (4b - 3c)gt) \int_0^t e^{-rx}\,dx - 2te^{-rt}(\Delta + (4b - c)gt)$$

$$> \left(-2t + \int_0^t e^{-rx}\,dx\right)(\Delta - cgt).$$

(D.5)

Substituting for Δ from (D.2) into (D.4) we obtain, after some manipulations, that (D.5) is equivalent to

$$c(2b + c) < 0.$$

(D.6)

The concavity requirements $b > 0$ and $4b^2 - c^2 > 0$ imply that $2b + c > 0$ for all c. Hence, (D.6) always holds when $c < 0$ and never holds when $c > 0$. This proves Proposition 3.

Appendix E

The purpose of this Appendix is to prove Proposition 4 in the text and its corollary.

Consider the staggered steady-state path starting at point b in Figure 8.2. At this point the staggered policy calls for a move to c. The value of the staggered steady-state path starting at c is given by

$$V_b = \frac{1}{1 - e^{-rt}} \left[\int_0^t e^{-rx} F(S_b^* - gt - gx, S_b^* - gx) \, dx - \beta e^{-rt} \right]. \tag{E.1}$$

If, instead, the monopolist would move to point e and follow thereafter the synchronized steady-state path, the value associated with this alternative path is

$$V_a = \frac{1}{1 - e^{-r\varepsilon}} \left[\int_0^\varepsilon e^{-rx} F(S_a^* - gx, S_a^* - gx) \, dx - 2\beta e^{-r\varepsilon} \right]. \tag{E.2}$$

where (S_b^*, t) and (S_a^*, ε) are the solutions of (8.32)–(8.33) and (8.30)–(8.31), respectively. By our assumptions, a move from b to c costs β while a move to e costs 2β. Therefore, a necessary condition for the optimality of the staggered programme is that

$$V_b - \beta > V_a - 2\beta. \tag{E.3}$$

Multiplying (E.3) by r, and taking the limit as $r \to 0$, the requirement is

$$\frac{1}{t} \left[\int_0^t F(S_b^* - gt - gx, S_b^* - gx) \, dx - \beta \right]$$

$$> \frac{1}{\varepsilon} \left[\int_0^\varepsilon F(S_a^* - gx, S_a^* - gx) \, dx - 2\beta \right]. \tag{E.4}$$

Using (8.31) and (8.33) in the text, (E.4) can be written

$$F(S_b^* - gt, S_b^*) > g \int_0^t F_1(S_a^* - gt - gx, S_a^* - gx) \, dx + F(S_a^*, S_a^*). \tag{E.5}$$

Substituting the quadratic formula (8.36) in the text into (E.5) and using (8.38)–(8.42) in the text, condition (E.5) is seen to be equivalent to

$$\left[\frac{2b - c}{2b + \dfrac{c}{2}} \right]^{1/6} > 1. \tag{E.6}$$

This inequality holds if, and only if, $c < 0$.

Notes

Acknowledgement. Sheshinski's research was partially supported by NSF grant SES-8821925 at Stanford University. The authors wish to thank Eyal Sulganik and two anonymous referees for helpful comments.

1. A number of recent studies have analysed the dynamic interaction of pricing policies in oligopolistic markets (Maskin and Tirole (1988), Gertner (1986) and Benabou and Gertner (1992)). However, these studies take the time pattern as exogenous, and focus on the equilibrium price configuration.

The issue of staggering vs. synchronization has been taken up by Ball and Cecchetti (1988), Ball and Romer (1989) and by McMillan and Zinde-Walsh (1987). The approach of Ball and Cecchetti emphasizes the informational gains from staggered pricing policies. McMillan and Zinde-Walsh consider a closed-loop equilibrium in an oligopolistic market for a homogeneous good. The homogeneity assumption eliminates price variation across products. Ball and Romer (1989) extend a model of Blanchard (Blanchard-Fischer (1989)), allowing each firm to choose whether to change prices at odd or even periods. This formulation permits both staggered and synchronized equilibria. The duration of the fixed price period is assumed to be determined exogeneously. In contrast, we treat the timing and the chosen real prices as endogenous.

2. A sufficient condition for the existence of $\bar{z}$ are that the quantity demanded of both goods drops to zero at sufficiently high, finite, prices. Sufficient conditions for the existence of $\underline{z}$ are that finite quantities are demanded at all positive prices and that marginal costs are strictly positive. For example, linear demands and constant marginal costs satisfy these assumptions. However, isoelastic demand is excluded.

3. We would like to thank Avner Bar-Ilan for the references to Bensoussan, Crouhy and Proth (1983), Bensoussan and Proth (1982), and Sulem (1986).

4. For a reference on the methodology, see Stokey and Lucas (1989).

5.

$$F(z_1, z_2) = F(z_1, z_1) + \int_{z_1}^{z_2} F_2(z_1, x)\, dx.$$

Using symmetry,

$$F(z_1, z_2) = F(z_2, z_2) - \int_{z_1}^{z_2} F_1(x, z_2)\, dx = F(z_2, z_2) - \int_{z_1}^{z_2} F_2(z_2, x)\, dx.$$

Adding up the above equalities we get

$$2F(z_1, z_2) = F(z_1, z_1) + F(z_2, z_2) + \int_{z_1}^{z_2} [F_2(z_1, x) - F_2(z_2, x)]\, dx.$$

Assuming $F_{12} > 0$, the integral of the difference in marginal profits must be negative, which establishes the claim.

6. The derivatives of V at a point (z, z) on the diagonal just below k are

$$V_i(z, z) = \int_0^{t^*(z, z)} e^{-rx} F_i(z - gx, z - gx)\, dx, \quad i = 1, 2.$$

Note that by symmetry, $V_1(z, z) = V_2(z, z)$. By the optimality of S_a^*, we have

$$V_i(S_a^*, S_a^*) = \int_0^{t^*(S_a^*, S_a^*)} e^{-rx} F_i(S_a^* - gx, S_a^* - gx)\, dx = 0, \quad i = 1, 2.$$

But $t^*(z, z) > t^*(S_a^*, S_a^*)$ and $F(z_1, z_2)$ is strictly quasi-concave. Hence, $V_i(S_a^*, S_a^*) = 0 \Rightarrow V_i(z, z) < 0$, for $i = 1, 2$. To locate the boundary points between C and T_i^-, $i = 1, 2$, we cannot use equations (8.23)–(8.25), since these do not hold with equality. Instead of marginal conditions we require that the firm be indifferent between holding prices constant for a non-negligible length of time, and changing prices instantly. For instance, on the diagonal,

$$V(z, z) = \int_0^{t^*(z, z)} e^{-rx} F(z - gx, z - gx) \, dx - e^{rt^*(z, z)}(V^* - 2\beta) = V^* - 2\beta.$$

The solution to this equation is point k in Figure 1.

7. Consider z_2 in the neighbourhood of S_a^*, which triggers a change to $S(z_2)$. Observe that $S(z_2)$ is also in the neighbourhood of S_a^*. From the properties of T_0^{++}, it follows that the subsequent price change at $t^*(S(z_2), z_2)$, will be a joint price increase. Hence,

$$(t^*, S(z_2)) = \operatorname{argmax}_{t, S} \int_0^t e^{-rx} F(S - gx, z_2 - gx) \, dx + e^{-rt}(V^* - 2\beta).$$

Differentiating the F.O.C. w.r.t. z_2, evaluating the derivatives at (S_a^*, S_a^*), we obtain

$$S'(S_a^*) \left[\int_0^{t^*} e^{-rx} F_{11}(S_a^* - gx, S_a^* - gx) \, dx + \frac{e^{-rt^*} F_1(S_a^* - gt^*, S_a^* - gt^*)}{2g} \right]$$

$$+ \int_0^{t^*} e^{-rx} F_{12}(S_a^* - gx, S_a^* - gx) \, dx + \frac{e^{-rt^*} F_1(S_a^* - gt^*, s_a^* - gt^*)}{2g} = 0$$

By second-order conditions, the term in square brackets is negative. The F.O.C. imply that $F_1(S_a^* - gt^*, S_a^* - gt^*) > 0$. Hence, with $F_{12} > 0$, $S'(S_a^*) > 0$.

8. Differentiating the "valuation formula", (8.15), we obtain

$$F_1(S(z_2), z_2) = g V_{11}(S(z_2), z_2) + g V_{12}(S(z_2), z_2).$$

Since, $F_1(S(z_2), z_2) < 0$, $V_{11}(S(z_2), z_2) < 0$ and $V_1(S(z_2), z_2) = 0$ for all z_2, we obtain

$$S'(z_2) = -\frac{V_{21}(S(z_2), z_2)}{V_{11}(S(z_2), z_2)} < 1.$$

Similarly, whenever V is differentiable at the boundary, the "valuation formula" implies

$$F_1(s(z_2), z_2) = g V_{11}(s(z_2), z_2) + g V_{12}(s(z_2), z_2).$$

Since $F_1(s(z_2), z_2) > 0$, $V_{11}(s(z_2), z_2) > 0$ and $V_1(s(z_2), z_2) = 0$ for all z_2, we obtain

$$s'(z_2) = \frac{V_{21}(s(z_2), z_2)}{V_{11}(s(z_2), z_2)} < 1.$$

References

Akerlof, G. and Yellen, J. (1985), "Can Small Deviations from Rationality Make Significant Differences to Economic Equilibria?", *American Economic Review*, 75, 708–721.

Ball, L. and Cecchetti, S. (1988), "Imperfect Information and Staggered Price Setting" *American Economic Review*, 78, pp. 999–1018.

Ball, L. and Romer, D. (1989), "The Equilibrium and Optimal Timing of Price Changes", *Review of Economic Studies*, 56, 179–198.

Benabou, R. (1988), "Search, Price Setting and Inflation," *Review of Economic Studies*, 55, 353–376.

Benabou, R. and Gertner, R. (1992), "Search with Learning from Prices: Does Increased Inflationary Uncertainty lead to Higher Markup" *Review of Economic Studies*, Forthcoming.

Bensoussan, A. and Proth, J. (1982), "On Some Impulse Control Problems with Concave Costs", *IEEE*, Decission and control, 1, 452–457.

Bensoussan, A., Crouhy, M. and Proth, J. (1983) *Mathematical Theory of Production Planning* (Amsterdam: North Holland).

Blanchard, O. (1983), "Price Asynchronization and Price Level Inertia", in Dornbusch, R. and Simonsen, M. (eds.), *Inflation, Debt and Indexation* (Cambridge: M.I.T. Press).

Blanchard, O. and Fischer, S. (1989) *Lectures on Macroeconomics* (Cambridge: M.I.T. Press).

Caplin, A. and Spulber, D. (1987), "Menu Costs and the Neutrality of Money", *Quarterly Journal of Economics*, 102, 703–726.

Constantinides, G. and Richard, S. (1978), "Existence of Optimal Single Policies for Discounted-Cost Inventory and Cash Management in Continuous Time", *Operations Research*, 26, 620–636.

Fishman, A. (1987) *Price Rigidities and Adjustment Costs in an Inflationary Economy with Monopolistic Markets* (Ph.D. dissertation, Hebrew University of Jerusalem).

Gertner, R. (1986), "Dynamic Duopoly with Price Inertia" (mimeo, University of Chicago).

McMillan, J. and Zinde-Walsh, V. (1987), "Inflation and the Timing of Price Changes" (Technical Report No. 15, Centre for Decision Sciences and Econometrics, University of Western Ontario).

Maskin, E. and Tirole, J. (1988), "A Theory of Dynamic Oligopoly II: Price Competition, Kinked Demand Curves and Edgeworth Cycles", *Econometrica*, 56, 571–600.

Sheshinski, E. and Weiss, Y. (1977), "Inflation and Costs of Price Adjustment", *Review of Economics*, 44, 287–303.

Sheshinski, E. and Weiss, Y. (1983), "Optimum Pricing Policy Under Stochastic Inflation", *Review of Economic Studies,* 50, 513–529.

Sheshinski, E. and Weiss, Y. (1989), "Staggered and Synchronized Price Policies Under Inflation: The Multiproduct Monopoly Case" (Discussion Paper No. 1428, Harvard Institute of Economic Research, Harvard University).

Stokey, N. and Lucas, R. (1989) *Recursive Methods in Economic Dynamics* (Cambridge: Harvard University Press).

Sulem, A. (1986), "Explicit Solution of a Two-Dimensional Deterministic Inventory Problem", *Mathematics of Operations Research*, 11, 134–146.

Taylor, J. (1980), "Aggregate Dynamics and Staggered Contracts", *Journal of Political Economy*, 88, 1–23.

IV AGGREGATION AND THE EFFECTS OF MONEY ON AGGREGATE OUTPUT

9 Menu Costs and the Neutrality of Money

Andrew S. Caplin and Daniel F. Spulber

I. Introduction

Historically determined nominal prices can lead to inertia in the aggregate level of prices, leaving room for monetary shocks to influence real variables. Formal models connecting the microeconomic behavior of nominal prices with aggregate price stickiness include models with staggered price and wage decisions [Fischer, 1977; Taylor, 1980; Blanchard, 1983; Parkin, 1986], models with partial adjustment of prices (e.g., Rotemberg [1982]), and the more recent "menu cost" models of Akerlof and Yellen [1985], Blanchard and Kiyotaki [1985], and Mankiw [1985]. We present an alternative aggregate model with microeconomic price stickiness that emphasizes the importance of endogenous timing of price adjustments. The model provides conditions under which money shocks have no real effects.

A number of macroeconomic models of price stickiness have a common microeconomic base: infrequent but large changes in nominal variables are assumed to be more economical than frequent small changes.[1] The models also share the assumption that the time between successive price revisions is preset, and hence unresponsive to shocks to the economy. This assumption is questionable both at the microeconomic level and in the aggregate. Formal microeconomic models (e.g., Sheshinski and Weiss [1983]) strongly suggest that more rapid inflation will shorten the time between price revisions. Empirical evidence against the fixed timing assumption is presented by Cecchetti [1986] and Liebermann and Zilberfarb [1985]. At the aggregate level large monetary shocks may increase the number of agents revising their nominal prices in a given period. This in turn reduces the extent of price level inertia. An important open question remains: what are the real effects of monetary shocks with endogenous timing of price revisions?

The present chapter assumes that individual firms adjust their prices using (s, S) pricing policies of Sheshinski and Weiss [1977, 1983]. To model asynchronization, we make a cross-sectional assumption on initial prices. The price level is derived endogenously by aggregating across firms. Aggregate price stickiness then vanishes despite the presence of nominal price rigidity and imperfectly synchronized price revisions.

The presence of *relative price variability* as a consequence of inflation is also observed endogenously through aggregation of cross-sectional price data. A simple formula is derived linking nominal price adjustment by firms with cross-sectional variability of inflation rates.

The basic model is outlined in Section II. The neutrality proposition is presented in Section III. In Section IV the model is applied to study relative price variability. Section V provides further discussion of the model and its assumptions. Conclusions are given in Section VI.

II. The Model

The Aggregate Setting

We provide an aggregate model of price dynamics with individual firms pursuing asynchronous (s, S) pricing policies. The structure of the aggregate model is kept as simple as possible to highlight the distinction between our model and others with asynchronous price and wage decisions. These alternative models frequently assume a staggered pattern of timing (e.g., Akerlof [1969], Fischer [1977], Taylor [1980], and Blanchard [1983]).

Money growth is subject to continuous shocks. The stochastic process governing monetary growth is taken as exogenous by all firms in the economy.[2] Let $M(t)$ denote the logarithm of the money supply at time t, where time is measured continuously. We assume that the money supply process is increasing over time and does not make discrete jumps.

ASSUMPTION 1. *Monotonicity and Continuity.* The money supply does not decrease over time, $M(t_2) \geq M(t_1)$ for $t_2 \geq t_1$. Also, the money supply process is continuous in the time parameter t. Normalize such that $M(0) = 0$.

The monotonicity assumption will rule out periods of deflation. The continuity assumption allows a simple characterization of firm pricing policies. The assumption also plays a role in analyzing the cross-sectional behavior of prices. This issue is taken up below. The monetary process is sufficiently general as to accommodate feedback rules. We shall consider particular examples of monetary processes below.

There is a continuum of firms in the economy indexed by $i \in [0, 1]$. All firms face identical demand and cost conditions. The assumed microeconomic structure is based on the menu cost model of Sheshinski and Weiss [1977, 1983]. Let $q_i(t)$ and $Q(t)$ represent firm i' *nominal price* and the *aggregate price index*, respectively, with $p_i(t)$ and $P(t)$ their respective logarithms. The aggregate price index, $P(t)$, is derived endogenously below from individual firm prices. It is convenient to express firm i's *real price*, $q(t)/Q(t)$, in log form, $r_i(t)$,

$$r_i(t) \equiv p_i(t) - P(t) = \ln[q_i(t)/Q(t)], \qquad (9.1)$$

for all $i \in [0, 1]$. We take $r_i(0)$ as given.

The *aggregate price index* $Q(t)$ is determined endogenously by aggregating individual firms' nominal prices $q_i(t)$. The index is assumed to depend only on the frequency distribution over nominal prices. Because firms have menu costs of price adjustment, prices may remain dispersed in the long run. Thus, the set of observed prices at any date may be described by a time-dependent frequency distribution function, say $G_t(q)$. The index is assumed also to satisfy homogeneity; when nominal prices double, so does the index.[3]

ASSUMPTION 2.   *Symmetric Price Index.*   The aggregate price index $Q(t)$ depends only on the frequency distribution of nominal prices and satisfies homogeneity:

$$Q(t) = Q(G_t(q)), \text{ where } G_t(q) \text{ is the proportion of firms}$$
$$i \in [0, 1] \text{ such that } q_i(t) \le q, \quad (9.2)$$

$$\text{if } G_{t_1}(q) = G_{t_2}(\lambda q) \text{ for all } q, \quad \text{then } \lambda Q(t_1) = Q(t_2), \text{ for any } t_1, t_2 \ge 0.$$
$$(9.3)$$

This condition is satisfied by a wide variety of common price indices.[4] An example of a price index that satisfies Assumption 2 is a simple *average* of nominal prices based on their frequency distribution, $Q(t) = \int q \, dG_t(q)$. More generally, let $Q(t) = \int w(q, G_t(\cdot)) q \, dG_t(q)$, where $w(q, G)$ represents weights as a function of prices q and the distribution of nominal prices G. The assumption requires the weights to satisfy $w(q, G_{t_1}) = w(\lambda q, G_{t_2})$ when $G_{t_1}(q) = G_{t_2}(\lambda q)$ for all q. An example of such a set of weights is $w(q, G) = q/\int q \, dG(q)$.

The Market Setting

Consumer demand is assumed to depend only on the firm's real price and on real money balances. Writing the arguments in log form, *consumer demand* faced by firm i, Γ_i, is defined by

$$\Gamma_i(t) \equiv \Gamma(r_i(t), M(t) - P(t)), \tag{9.4}$$

where $r_i(t)$ and $M(t) - P(t)$ are the log of firm i's price and the log of real balances, respectively.[5] One rationale for this is to assume that real balances enter consumer utility functions, as in, for example, Rotemberg [1982, 1983]. Note also that all firms can have some positive demand even though prices are dispersed. This may arise if the commodities are imperfect substitutes. It may also be that consumer search across firms is costly and that consumers do not recall prices posted by firms in earlier periods (see Benabou [1985b]).

Costs are assumed to be fixed in real terms. Production at rate $X_i(t)$ gives rise to real flow costs, $C(X_i(t))$. This assumption rules out stickiness in nominal input prices, including contractual wages. This prevents us from addressing the relationship between price stickiness and wage stickiness, a topic of independent interest (see Blanchard [1983]).[6] Additional study of the present model with input price stickiness is clearly desirable. All profits are distributed to consumers, and firm costs accrue to consumers as income.[7]

The good is assumed to be nonstorable, so that the firm's output is supplied at the same date it is produced. This removes intertemporal linkages embodied in inventories. As a result, the only variables that influence the firm's *flow rate of real profits* $B_i(t)$ are the instantaneous real price and the level of real money balances:[8]

$$B_i(t) \equiv B[r_i(t), M(t) - P(t)]$$

$$= \max_{X_i(t) \le \Gamma_i(t)} [e^{r_i(t)} X_i(t) - C(X_i(t))]. \tag{9.5}$$

Thus, the *output* of firm i, $X_i(t)$, is a function of its real price and the level of real money balances which solves the problem in equation (9.5):

$$X_i(t) = X(r_i(t), M(t) - P(t)). \tag{9.6}$$

Let $X(t)$ represent the constant dollar value of *aggregate output*:

$$X(t) \equiv \int_0^1 (q_i(t)/Q(t)) X_i(t) \, di = \int_0^1 e^{r_i(t)} X_i(t) \, di.$$

In the absence of menu costs, the firm picks its instantaneous price $r_i(t)$ to maximize flow profits $B(r_i(t), M(t) - P(t))$.[9] Nominal price stickiness is

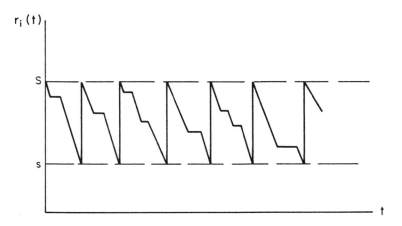

Figure 9.1

introduced into the model in the form of a real *menu cost*, β, which is incurred each time the firm changes its nominal price.[10] This fixed transaction cost results in price stickiness at the level of the individual firm. Rather than responding smoothly and continuously to changes in the overall price level the firm responds only occasionally, and with discrete price jumps.

We consider a firm that continuously monitors the price level, and pursues an (s, S) *pricing policy*, as introduced by Sheshinski and Weiss. The impact of this policy on the dynamics of the firm's real price is illustrated in Figure 9.1. The instant the log of the real price $r(t)$ hits the fixed lower limit s, the firm adjusts its nominal price, returning the log of the real price to its upper limit S. Let $D \equiv S - s$ represent the size of the firm's price increase. Then, the changes in the firm's nominal price within any time period $[0, t]$ are always an integer multiple of the price range, $p(t) - p(0) = k(t)D$, where $k(t) \geq 0$ is an integer. Noting that $r_i(0) = p_i(0)$ and using the definition of the firm's real price in equation (9.1), we may formally characterize the (s, S) pricing policy as follows: $r_i(t) \in (s, S]$ and

$$r_i(t) - r_i(0) = (p_i(t) - p_i(0)) - (P(t) - P(0))$$

$$= k_i(t)D - (P(t) - P(0)). \tag{9.7}$$

Hence, changes in the log of the firm's real price are an integer multiple of D minus the log of the price level.

Two important requirements are necessary for (s, S)-type policies to be optimal. One requirement is stationarity of real balances over time—$M(t) - P(t) = -P(0)$, so that demand Γ_i is stationary. We shall demonstrate that in equilibrium this requirement is satisfied. The other requirement concerns restrictions on the form of the anticipated inflation process. Conditions for optimality of (s, S) pricing policies in a stochastic setting have been considered by Sheshinski and Weiss [1983], Danziger [1984], and more recently by Caplin and Sheshinski [1987].[11] Danziger considers a world with discrete inflationary shocks. He demonstrates that when inflationary shocks arrive one at a time with exponentially distributed interarrival times, then the optimal pricing policy is of the (s, S) variety.[12] With general inflationary processes, the optimal pricing policy may take a more complex form.

The central qualitative feature of (s, S) pricing policies is that they make the time between successive price revisions endogenous: prices change more frequently when inflation is rapid than when it is slow. Alternative models of asynchronous price setting involve fixed decision times regardless of ensuing shocks to the economy. Seen in this light, one may be less concerned with the precise optimality of (s, S) pricing policies.[13] Rather, they may be seen as a simple and tractable alternative to the assumption of a predetermined pattern of price revisions.

Analysis of the time path of aggregate prices in our framework requires specification of the initial distribution of prices across firms in the economy. It is assumed that firms' initial real prices $r_i(0)$ are uniformly distributed over the range $(s, S]$. For ease of exposition we restate the uniformity assumption with a frequency distribution $F_0(p)$ which defines the proportion of firms with the logs of their initial prices $p_i(0)$ no higher than p.

ASSUMPTION 3.   *Uniformity.*   The frequency distribution over initial real prices satisfies

$$F_0(p) = \begin{cases} 0 & \text{for } p \leq s, \\ b/D & \text{for } p = s + b, \text{ with } 0 \leq b \leq D, \\ 1 & \text{for } p \geq S. \end{cases} \tag{9.8}$$

The uniform initial distribution of prices across the price range $(s, S]$ is the analogue in prices of the standard assumption of uniformly staggered price changes over time. Indeed, Assumption 3 is equivalent to an assumption of uniform staggered timing in the special case where inflation is constant at some rate $\lambda > 0$. However, it will be apparent that in a stochastic setting a uniform distribution of initial prices has significantly different implications.

In a fundamental sense Assumption 3 may be viewed as a statement about the endogenous tendency of prices to become uniformly distributed after a long history of inflationary shocks and pursuit of fixed (s, S) policies. This lies outside the current framework, since firms pursuing identical (s, S) policies in the face of inflation retain forever the initial difference in their real prices. However, if firms pursue slightly distinct (s, S) policies, or randomize on their trigger price s (as in Benabou [1985a]), their real prices become statistically independent of one another with the passage of time. A related result for inventories states that, absent degeneracies, firms that pursue (s, S) inventory policies have inventory levels that are independent in the long run [Caplin, 1985].

III. Neutrality

We address the connection between asynchronous price decisions and aggregate price stickiness. To what extent is the individual firm stickiness in nominal prices reflected in aggregate price inertia? The central result of the chapter is that *real balances and aggregate output are invariant to monetary shocks*. Price stickiness disappears in the aggregate. Given (s, S) pricing rules, the initial distribution of real prices is invariant and remains uniform. The aggregate nominal price index exactly reflects nominal money shocks. Consumer demand as a function of real prices and real balances remains stationary. This results in constant aggregate output.

In the absence of real shocks to the economy, money neutrality is appropriately defined as follows.

DEFINITION 1.   Money is *neutral* if aggregate real output is invariant to monetary shocks, $X(t) = X(0)$, for all $t \geq 0$.

Monetary policy may influence the *distribution* of real prices across firms in our model as will be seen in Section IV. However, these distributional effects cancel out in the aggregate.

Suppose that firms follow (s, S) policies in anticipation of constant real balances. That is, firms expect that $P(t) = M(t)$. Then, by the description

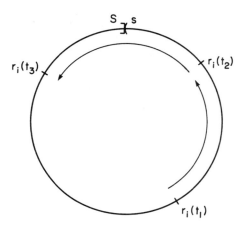

Figure 9.2

of (s, S) pricing policies in equation (9.7), we may calculate each firm's nominal price as a function of cumulative money growth and the firm's initial price:

$$p_i(t) = k_i(t)D + p_i(0), \tag{9.9}$$

where $k_i(t)$ is an integer determined by the requirement that $r_i(t) \in (s, S]$. Proposition 1 verifies that aggregation of these nominal prices yields a price level equal to cumulative money growth at each time t, so that money is neutral.

The neutrality result may be understood by observing that the (s, S) policy moves real prices around a circle. The method of proof is easily illustrated using Figure 9.2. Points on the circle represent the range of the log of the firm's real prices. At the apex of the circle, the outer limits of the range are adjacent. At time t_1, $r_i(t_1)$ is firm i's real price. Inflation occurring between time t_1 and t_2 reduces the real price to $r_i(t_2)$ as indicated by the counterclockwise motion. Between time t_2 and t_3, inflation drives the real price down to s, the price is then readjusted up to S and further inflation drives the real price to $r_i(t_3)$. It is critical to note that the rotation engendered by monetary growth is invariant to the location of the initial real price on the circle, thus preserving the initial uniformity of real prices.

PROPOSITION 1.   Given Assumptions 1 to 3, money is neutral if firms follow (s, S) pricing policies in anticipation of constant real balances.

Proof of Proposition 1. Let money growth be written as an integer multiple of D and a remainder $b(t)$:

$$M(t) = k(t)D + b(t), \tag{9.10}$$

where $k(t) \geq 0$ and $b(t) \geq 0$ are chosen such that $b(t) < D$. If firms follow (s, S) pricing policies and anticipate constant real balances, then by equation (9.9), the log of each firm i's nominal price can be expressed in terms of the components of money supply growth in equation (9.10):

$$p_i(t) = \begin{cases} p_i(0) + k(t)D, & \text{for } p_i(0) > s + b(t), \\ p_i(0) + [k(t) + 1]D, & \text{for } p_i(0) \leq s + b(t). \end{cases} \tag{9.11}$$

Equation (9.11) shows that if $s + b(t) < p_i(0) \leq S$, then $s + M(t) < p_i(t) \leq s + M(t) + D - b$. Also if $s < p_i(0) \leq s + b(t)$, then $s + M(t) + D - b < p_i(t) \leq S + M(t)$. By uniformity of initial real prices (Assumption 3), it follows that $p_i(t) - M(t)$ is uniform over the interval $(s, S]$, or equivalently,

$$F_t(p) = \begin{cases} 0 & \text{for } p \leq s + M(t), \\ b/D & \text{for } p = s + M(t) + b, \text{ with } 0 \leq b \leq D, \\ 1 & \text{for } p \geq S + M(t). \end{cases} \tag{9.12}$$

The frequency distribution over nominal prices is then given by $G_t(q) \equiv F_t(\ln q)$. Note that $G_t(q)$ is defined over $(e^{s+M(t)}, e^{S+M(t)}]$. Thus, we may define $G_t(e^{M(t)}x)$ over (e^s, e^S) so that $G_t(e^{M(t)}x) = G_0(x)$ for $x \in (e^s, e^S)$. Therefore, by the assumption of a symmetric price index, $Q(t) = e^{M(t)}Q(0)$. Thus, we have verified that endogenously derived inflation matches monetary growth and real balances are constant: $Q(t)/e^{M(t)} = Q(0)$. Furthermore, since $r_i(t) = p_i(t) - P(t = p_i(t) - M(t)$ is uniform over $(s, S]$ for $t \geq 0$, we have

$$X(t) = \int_0^1 e^{r_i(t)} X(r_i(t), P(0)) \, di = \int_0^1 e^{r_i(0)} X(r_i(0), P(0)) \, di, \tag{9.13}$$

so $X(t) = X(0)$.   Q.E.D.

Consider an illustrative example. Note first that since $p_i(t)$ is uniformly distributed on $(s + M(t), S + M(t))$, $q_i(t)$ is distributed on $(e^{sM(t)}, e^{SM(t)})$ with distribution $G_t(q) = (\ln q)/D$. If we use the simple arithmetic mean as our symmetric price index, the price level is then

$$Q(t) \equiv \left(\frac{1}{D}\right) \int_{e^{sM(t)}}^{e^{SM(t)}} dq = e^{M(t)} \frac{e^S - e^s}{D} = e^{M(t)} Q(0).$$

The central feature of Proposition 1 is that it provides a simple framework in which there are monetary shocks, asynchronous nominal price revisions, but no stickiness in the aggregate price level. In fact, $P(t) - M(t) = P(0)$. Thus it contrasts strongly with monetary models with a fixed staggered pattern of price and wage revisions, which can generate significant aggregate price stickiness (e.g., Akerlof [1969], Blanchard [1983], and Fischer [1977]). In qualitative terms, the difference between the results can be simply explained. In the staggered timing framework, large monetary shocks draw a response from a fixed fraction of the population, with the remainder pursuing an unchanged policy. The size of the predetermined pool of decision makers will influence the extent of price revision by those currently free to decide: on average, agents' prices adjust only partially to large monetary shocks. In contrast, the (s, S) model makes the fraction of firms that revise prices in any given period endogenous. Hence rapid growth of the money supply causes an increase in the number of price increases in a given period. Surprisingly, our simple form of endogenous timing completely removes aggregate inertia.

The result also provides a new perspective on the emerging study of menu costs and monetary policy in a *static* setting (e.g., Akerlof and Yellen [1985], Blanchard and Kiyotaki [1985], Mankiw [1985]). Here, Akerlof and Yellen [1985] argue that the presence of a small menu cost may make it optimal for an individual firm to maintain a fixed nominal price in the face of a monetary shock. This may lead to a welfare loss larger than the menu cost itself. The extension from the case of a single firm to the economy as a whole is based on a representative agent framework. Since one firm fails to adjust its price, so do all firms, and as a result the open market operation can have a significant real impact.

Taken literally, such reasoning can only be applied for the first monetary shock to an economy that had never before been out of static equilibrium. Even the second monetary shock may have a different effect, since after the first shock, the hypothesis that the initial real price is at its equilibrium level fails. Proposition 1 presents a simple setting where the presence of menu costs indeed prevents many firms from revising prices. However, those who do adjust their price do so discontinuously. Although only a few firms may adjust their prices, they adjust their prices by a large amount. The net result is that monetary shocks are absorbed with no real impact.

Proposition 1 also provides a positive answer to a question posed by Sheshinski and Weiss [1983] for their model of (s, S) pricing policies. They are concerned with providing a consistent aggregate version of their model. They consider identical firms facing exogenous inflationary shocks, uniformly distributed with respect to the time of their last price increase. Sheshinski and Weiss [1983, p. 523] note that:

large and/or closely spaced shocks may lead to synchronization and hence change the distribution. There is thus no simple correspondence between the process of exogenous shocks and the process followed by the aggregate price level.

Proposition 1 demonstrates that with identical firms, consistent aggregation requires that firms be uniformly distributed in terms of the log of their *initial real price* levels rather than the time of their last price change. The distinction is that in a stochastic setting uniformity in timing is unstable, while uniformity in real prices is continuously sustained.[14]

IV. Menu Costs and Relative Price Variability

In this section we develop formulae linking inflation and firm pricing policies to relative price variability. These formulae can be seen as stochastic generalizations of the deterministic price dispersion models of Rotemberg [1981], and Cecchetti [1985], which are based on staggered price setting. Our results also clarify the relationship between price variability and the time period between successive observations of the economy.[15]

The association between inflation and relative price variability has been widely investigated; see Fischer [1981] for a survey. The empirical research suggests a positive association between relative price variability and both the mean and the variance of the overall rate of inflation.[16] One important line of research into inflation and relative prices originates with Barro [1976]. Here it is inflationary variability rather than the rate of inflation per se that drives relative price variability. As the variability of inflation increases, individual firm estimates of inflation become more widely dispersed, driving apart firms' preset prices.[17] Barro's approach is further developed by Cukierman [1979], Cukierman and Wachtel [1982], Hercowitz [1981], and Parks [1978].

An alternative theory holds that inflationary variations in relative prices can be caused by nominal price inflexibility [Cecchetti, 1985; Mussa, 1981; Rotemberg, 1983].[18] Our formulae lie in this alternative tradition, stressing the costs of changing nominal prices.

The basic characterization of relative price variability to be given here is based on repeated observations of the economy, with successive observations separated by a fixed time period of arbitrary length $\tau > 0$. With this discrete pattern of observations, cumulative inflation during the tth time period is denoted $\Pi^\tau(t)$. Proposition 1 allows us to identify the inflation rate with the (stochastic) growth of the money supply:

$$\Pi^\tau(t) \equiv P[\tau(t + 1)] - P[\tau t] = M[\tau(t + 1)] - M[\tau t]. \tag{9.14}$$

Our results of this section require only that $\Pi^\tau(t)$ is a stationary stochastic process. It is also convenient to restrict attention to inflation or money supply processes that are regularly behaved.

ASSUMPTION 1A.   *Stationarity.*   For any $\tau > 0$, the process $\Pi^\tau(t)$ of equation (9.14) is a stationary stochastic process, with long-run probabilities specified by the density function $\phi^\tau(\Pi)$. The density of $\phi^\tau(\Pi)$ is assumed to be non-atomic, with compact support.

As in the proof of Proposition 1, it is useful to separate inflation into an integer multiple of D and a residual.[19] Definition 2 provides the appropriate formalization.

DEFINITION 2.   With cumulative inflation measured over periods of length $\tau > 0$, the *residual inflation process* $b^\tau(t)$ is defined as $\Pi^\tau(t)$ taken modulo D.

In light of Assumption 1A, the residual process $b^\tau(t)$ is itself stationary and has compact support, with long-run probabilities specified by the density function $\eta^\tau(b)$ satisfying,

$$\eta^\tau(b) = \sum_{k=0}^{\infty} \phi^\tau(kD + b). \tag{9.15}$$

Individual firm price increases are also measured at intervals of length τ:

$$\Pi_i^\tau(t) \equiv p_i[\tau(t + 1)] - p_i(\tau t). \tag{9.16}$$

To measure inflation, we use a specific price index. This is the standard *Divisia* index of inflation, with equal expenditure shares for distinct firms $i \in [0, 1]$:

$$\Pi^\tau(t) \equiv \int_0^1 \Pi_i^\tau(t)\,di. \tag{9.17}$$

The Divisia index is a standard employed in empirical studies of relative price variability (e.g., Fischer [1981], Hercowitz [1981], Parks [1978], and Vining and Elwertowski [1976]). The Divisia index is symmetric. By Proposition 1, it follows that the endogenous inflation measure in equation (9.17) is consistent with monetary growth in equation (9.14).

Relative price variability $V^\tau(t)$ is measured as the dispersion of individual firm inflation rates around the aggregate rate of inflation:

$$V^\tau(t) \equiv \int_0^1 [\Pi_i^\tau(t) - \Pi^\tau(t)]^2\,di. \tag{9.18}$$

We are interested in the statistical properties of $V^\tau(t)$, and in particular the influence of D, the size of individual price increases. Intuition suggests that increases in D may raise the general level of relative price variability. A precise characterization of the expected level of relative price variability is contained in Proposition 2.

PROPOSITION 2. Expected relative price variability is related to price changes D and the residual inflation process $b^\tau(t)$, as follows:

$$E[V^\tau(t)] = E\{b^\tau(t)[D - b^\tau(t)]\}, \tag{9.19}$$

with $b^\tau(t)$ as in Definition 2.

Proof of Proposition 2. To simplify notation, the superscript τ is suppressed throughout the proof. We first separate period t inflation in the standard manner,

$$\Pi(t) = k(t)D + b(t), \tag{9.20}$$

with $k(t)$ a nonnegative integer, and $0 \le b(t) < D$. The (s, S) pricing policies imply that individual firm price increases obey

$$\Pi_i(t) = \begin{cases} k(t)D & \text{for } r_i(t) > s + b(t), \\ [k(t) + 1]D & \text{for } r_i(t) \le s + b(t). \end{cases} \tag{9.21}$$

Hence $(\Pi_i(t) - \Pi(t))^2$ takes value b^2 for $r_i(t)$ above $s + b(t)$, $(D - b)^2$ otherwise. But from Proposition 1 we know that real prices $r_i(t)$ are distributed uniformly over $(s, S]$ for $t \ge 0$. Hence, using the definition of $V(t)$, we have

$$V(t) = \left(\frac{D - b(t)}{D}\right)b^2(t) + \left(\frac{b(t)}{D}\right)[D - b(t)]^2$$

$$= b(t)(D - b(t)). \tag{9.22}$$

Finally, Assumption 1A implies that $b(t)$ is a stationary process, allowing us to take expectations in (9.22).   Q.E.D.

Proposition 2 shows that the range of individual price variation D is a central determinant of the variability of individual price increases. However, interpretation of the result is complicated by the presence of the residual process, $b^\tau(t)$. While the formula does suggest a positive association between D and relative price variability, examples with a negative association are readily constructed.[20]

By changing the time interval between observations, it is possible to greatly simplify the formulae of Proposition 2. The results are stated for a restricted class of inflation processes introduced in Assumption 1B.[21] The restriction is imposed to simplify proofs: the analysis may incorporate more general conditions.

ASSUMPTION 1B. *Two-rate inflation process.* Monetary growth (and hence inflation) can take place at one of two distinct rates, g_H and g_L with $g_H > g_L \geq 0$. The time spent with inflation of g_H (respectively, g_L) is distributed exponentially with parameter λ_H (respectively, λ_L).

A desirable feature of the two-rate inflation processes of Assumption 1B is that their simple Markovian structure is inherited by the discretely observed process $\Pi^\tau(t)$. The state of the system at time t comprises a specification of all firms' instantaneous real prices $r_i(t)$, and the current inflation rate, H or L. State transitions in the ensuing interval depend only on cumulative inflation over the interval, and the level of inflation at the end of the interval. Such state transitions are then Markovian, since information available prior to t is irrelevant to the probabilistic progress of the system.[22]

With this background, we can provide the simple formulae of Proposition 3 which apply, respectively, to "widely spaced" and to "closely spaced" observations of the economy. The Proposition is proved in the Appendix.

PROPOSITION 3. Given Assumptions 1B, 2, and 3, if firms follow (s, S) pricing policies and τ is the period of observation, then expected relative price variability satisfies the following:

$$\lim_{\tau \to \infty} EV^\tau(t) = D^2/6, \tag{a}$$

$$\lim_{\tau \to 0} \left[\frac{EV^\tau(t)}{E\Pi^\tau(t)} \right] = D. \tag{b}$$

The surprising feature of part (a) of Proposition 3 is that with widely separated observations, relative price variability depends only on D. It may be that the formula is roughly appropriate for semiannual data where firms change prices at intervals ranging from one to three months. The applicability of part (b) of Proposition 3 is harder to gauge: the observation period must be considerably shorter than the time between successive price revisions.

Sheshinski and Weiss [1983] provide useful formulae for assessing the impact of parameter changes on $D = S - s$, the range of the log of real prices.[23] For $g_L = 0$, they establish that the range D is increasing in the price adjustment cost β and increasing in the certainty-equivalent rate of inflation $\bar{g}$, where $\bar{g} = (\lambda_L + \rho)g_H/(\lambda_L + \lambda_H + \rho)$ and where ρ is the rate of interest. Changes in parameter values λ_L, λ_H, ρ, and g_H will affect the price range and thus relative price variability as defined in Proposition 3a. However, it is difficult to establish a direct relation between the mean and variance of inflation and relative price variability.

It is possible to determine the effects of menu costs on relative price variability. Because (s, S) policies may not be optimal, we assume that firms choose the *best* (s, S) bounds. Then, we use a time period $\tau \leq D/g_H$. Since $\Pi(t) = k(t)D + b(t)$ from equation (9.20), the number of nominal price changes within the time period under observation is always zero so that $\Pi(t) = b(t)$. Then, we may write expected relative price variability, using Proposition 2, as follows:

$$E[V^\tau(t)] = E\{\Pi(t)[D - \Pi(t)]\}. \tag{9.23}$$

The inflation process $\Pi(t)$ is independent of adjustment costs, and the range of prices is increasing in β. Thus, if firms follow the best (s, S) pricing policy, expected relative price variability is increasing in the menu costs of price adjustment β.

V.   Interpretation of Assumptions

The neutrality of money in our model is particularly dependent on the (s, S) form of firm pricing policies. For firms to follow (s, S) policies, the monetary process must at least exhibit monotonicity and continuity. These requirements may be quite restrictive.

When the monetary process is nonmonotone, it will sometimes be necessary for the firm to *lower* its nominal price. The one-sided (s, S) pricing policies must be replaced by two-sided pricing policies, as analyzed by Barro [1972].[24] With the two-sided pricing policies, the neutrality proposition no longer holds: it may even be that unusually rapid monetary expansion is associated with increased real balances and vice versa.[25] A theoretical difficulty in modeling two-sided policies is that their properties under aggregation appear highly complex. Specifically, it is not possible to specify an initial cross-sectional distribution of prices which survives shocks.[26] In economic terms, this implies that a second positive shock to the money supply may have very different effects than the first positive shock. Such effects may well have non-intuitive implications: for example, after two successive positive shocks, output may be higher in response to a negative than in response to a third positive shock to the money supply. In the absence of a fully developed model, such comments remain speculative.

The assumed continuity of the money supply process has two roles. First, it gives rise to the simple form of the individual firm equations for price transitions. In particular, (9.7) no longer holds in the absence of continuity, since if the real price falls by a discrete amount at any given instant, then it may at some point fall strictly below s. The immediate response of increasing the real price to S then involves a discrete jump in the real price in excess of $D \equiv S - s$, contradicting (9.7). Sample path continuity plays an additional role in relation to the uniformity Assumption 3. Jumps in the price level act as a coordinating device, pulling many firms in the economy to adjust at the same instant, and eliminating uniformity. The uniform distribution over initial prices, however, is the only distribution that is invariant to shocks.

Finally, there are conditions under which alternative pricing policies may be optimal. Significant alterations in the monetary process may lead agents to revise trigger points.[27] One possibility is that a sudden increase in the rate and variability of money growth causes all agents to broaden their trigger range, raising S and lowering s. In this case, real balances may rise in the short run as firms find insufficient benefit from a price change. This increase in real balances corresponds to the effect noted in the literature on the impact of menu costs in a static setting, as in Akerlof and Yellen [1985]. Once again, note that the short-run expansionary impact of monetary policy is not stable. When real balances have risen enough, a sudden burst of price increases may be triggered as all firms go to the very top of their real price range. This process will result in a reduction of real balances to below their initial level, and a corresponding slowdown in activity.

The neutrality result depends on firms anticipating constant real money balances. What would happen if firms anticipated systematic changes in real money balances? For example, if firms expect real money balances, and therefore demand, to increase, this may trigger an earlier price increase, thus counteracting the rise in real balances. A formal analysis of this possibility is of interest.

It is worthwhile noting a concern about the exogenous demand functions Γ_i—particularly in evaluating comparative dynamics. It would, of course, be desirable to construct the demand functions endogenously from consumer utility functions with either differentiated products or consumer search. Ball and Romer [1986] derive such demand functions in a general equilibrium model with differentiated products. With endogenous search activity, demand at a real price of $r_i(t) > 0$ may be zero if all other firms have identical prices $r_j(t) = 0$, but positive if other firms have widely dispersed prices. Hence the functions $\Gamma[r_i(t), M(t) - P(t)]$ must be treated as conditional on the levels of S and s in the rest of the economy. Benabou [1985b] provides a thorough treatment of the interaction between search and menu costs.

VI. Conclusion

The chapter presents a model in which inflation is derived endogenously through price adjustment by firms. If firms pursue (s, S) price adjustment policies and the log of real prices are initially uniformly dispersed, then money shocks are shown to be neutral. Thus, nominal changes, such as monetary growth, do not have aggregate real effects despite the presence of menu costs of price adjustment. Although money is neutral, we observe the presence of relative price variability.

The model illustrates that individual firm price stickiness and staggered timing need not lead to aggregate price stickiness. This suggests that real effects of money shocks may depend more on fixed-length contracts than simply on asynchronous nominal price adjustment. Overall, the analysis highlights the importance of cross-sectional timing assumptions in macroeconomic models.

Appendix

Proof of Proposition 3

To prove part (a) in light of Proposition 2 requires only that

$$\lim_{\tau \to \infty} \{E[b^{\tau}(t)(D - b^{\tau}(t))]\} = D^2/6, \tag{9A.1}$$

with $b^{\tau}(t)$ as in Definition 2. Let $H^{\tau}(x)$ denote the long-run cumulative distribution of $b^{\tau}(t)$:

$$H^{\tau}(x) = \int_0^x \eta^{\tau}(b) \, db. \tag{9A.2}$$

The heart of the proof of part (a) is contained in Lemma 1.

LEMMA 1.   For $0 \le b \le D$, $\lim_{\tau \to \infty} H^{\tau}(x) = b/D$.

Proof.   With the simple two-level inflation process of Assumption 1(6), the individual firm's discretely observed real price behavior is ergodic, with a unique stationary density $\psi(r_i(t))$ which is uniform over $(s, S]$. Ergodicity can be proved by applying the procedure of Caplin and Spulber [1985, Proposition 1]. The trivial amendment concerns the fact that g_H and g_L may both be positive in the current case: in the earlier version $g_L = 0$. The existence of this simple ergodic distribution implies that

$$\lim_{\tau \to \infty} P\{r_i(t + \tau) \in (S - b, X) | r_i(t) = S\} = b/D. \tag{9A.3}$$

But $r_i(t) \in [s, S]$ and equation (9.7) show that the events $\{r_i(t + \tau) \in (S - b, S) | r_i(t) = S\}$ and $\{b^{\tau}(t) \le b | r_i(t) = S\}$ are equivalent. An identical argument applies conditions on other initial prices. This allows the conditioning to be removed so that

$$\lim_{\tau \to \infty} P\{b^\tau(t) \le b\} = b/D, \tag{9A.4}$$

as claimed.   Q.E.D.

Lemma 1 demonstrates that for $0 \le b \le D$, $F^m(b) \to b/D$ in distribution. Application of Proposition 8.12 of Breiman [1968] allows us to take limiting expectations using the uniform density:

$$\lim_{\tau \to \infty} \{E[b^\tau(t)(D - b^\tau(t))]\} = \frac{1}{D} \int_0^D b(D - b)\, db$$

$$= \frac{1}{D}\left[\frac{Db^2}{2} - \frac{b^3}{3}\right]_0^D = \frac{D^2}{6}, \tag{9A.5}$$

as claimed.

To establish part (b), it must be shown that for τ sufficiently small,

$$1 \ge \frac{E[b^\tau(t)(D - b^\tau(t))]}{DE(\Pi^\tau(t))} \ge 1 - \varepsilon \tag{9A.6}$$

for any given $\varepsilon \in (0, 1)$. To confirm this, pick a time interval τ below $\varepsilon(D/g_H)$, so that the maximal inflation rate in any given period is below εD. Then,

$$E[b^\tau(t)(D - b^\tau(t))] = E[\Pi^\tau(t)(D - b^\tau(t))] < DE(\Pi^\tau(t)). \tag{9A.7}$$

In addition,

$$E[b^\tau(t)(D - b^\tau(t))] \ge E[\Pi^\tau(t)(D - \varepsilon D)] = (1 - \varepsilon)DE[\Pi^\tau(t)]. \tag{9A.8}$$

Together, (9A.7) and (9A.8) establish part (b).   Q.E.D.

Notes

We thank Andrew Abel, Roland Benabou, Olivier Blanchard, Dennis Carlton, Stanley Fischer, Benjamin Friedman, Barry Nalebuff, William Nordhaus, David Romer, Julio Rotemberg, Eytan Sheshinski, John Veitch, and an anonymous referee for valuable comments. Spulber's research was supported by the National Science Foundation under Grant No. SES-82-19121. The paper was presented at the Fifth World Congress of the Econometric Society, Cambridge, MA, 1985, and at the NBER Program in Economic Fluctuations Conference, October, 1985.

1. An exception is Rotemberg [1983] who considers instead increasing marginal costs of nominal price revisions.

2. In general, the money growth process may be set as a feedback rule based on the history of output.

3. Individual firms set s and S taking the price level as exogenously given. However, for given levels s and S, the index endogenously determines $P(0)$: will the exogenous and endogenous indices be consistent? The answer is generally no: however, if we associate higher real balances with higher levels of s and S, there will be some initial specification of real balances guaranteeing this static consistency, since higher real balances raise the desired average real price, raising the endogenous level of $P(0)$ relative to the exogenous level.

4. Blanchard and Kiyotaki [1985] and Ball and Romer [1986] derive symmetric price indices based on an underlying symmetric utility framework.

5. The assumption that demand is independent of future prices rules out consumer speculation. Benabou [1985a] presents an analysis of optimal pricing policies in the face of consumer storage and speculation. In principle, the future path of real money balances may also influence real demand. For present purposes, Proposition 1 will allow us to ignore this potentially complex dependence.

6. Gordon [1981] finds evidence for price stickiness for periods with widely different forms of labor contract. This suggests that there are important sources of price stickiness other than the behavior of input prices.

7. By Walras' law, market clearing in the commodity market implies market clearing in the money market; see, for example, Rotemberg [1982].

8. The present formulation allows the firm to ration its customers. The case without rationing can also be handled by the model; see Sheshinski and Weiss [1983].

9. With standard assumptions, increases in real money balances that increase demand for the commodity will also raise the firm's optimal real price.

10. There is an issue here concerning the proper treatment of menu costs. If these are indeed real costs, they should be explicitly included as part of output. Hence a closed model of the economy should properly include a sector of variable size dedicated to the production of menus. This is ignored in our formulation.

11. Sheshinski and Weiss [1983] employ a special form of the stochastic inflation process. Caplin and Sheshinski [1987] present a discrete time formulation with i.i.d. inflationary shocks.

12. While the discrete nature of Danziger's inflation process contradicts Assumption 1, our analysis including the neutrality proposition nevertheless applies.

13. Even in the inventory literature, Arrow, Harris, and Marschak [1951] study (s, S) policies because of their relative simplicity. The first general proof of optimality is due to Scarf [1959]. Further, stationary (s, S) policies are frequently analyzed and applied in situations where they are undoubtedly suboptimal (such as in multi-echelon inventory systems [Schwarz, 1981] and in more general nonstationary environments [Karlin and Fabens, 1959].

14. In a deterministic world with constant inflation, the two forms of uniformity are equivalent.

15. As Cecchetti [1985] notes in a nonstochastic setting, there is no cross-sectional variance of inflation rates when the observation period is an integer multiple of the period between price revisions.

16. Early studies include Graham [1930] and Mills [1927]. More recent work includes Vining and Elwertowski [1976]; Pagan, Hall, and Trivedi [1983]; Balk [1985], and Marquez and Vining [1984].

17. According to this approach, the apparent association between the level of inflation and relative price variability is a statistical artifact, resulting from an actual association between the mean level of inflation and the variability of inflation. This relationship is explicitly investigated by Taylor [1981].

18. See also Carlton [1978] and Hubbard and Weiner [1985], who consider markets with both spot transactions and nominal contracting.

19. The formal identification between (s, S) policies and the modulo arithmetic also plays a role in the inventory literature (see Caplin [1985]).

20. For example with $\Pi^\tau(t)$ uniform over [9, 10] an increase in D from 8 to 9 reduces $EV^\tau(t)$ from $9\frac{2}{3}$ to $4\frac{1}{6}$.

21. Assumption 1B represents a slightly more general form of the inflation process studied by Sheshinski and Weiss [1983].

22. Note that transitions in the rate of inflation between observations are not independent of cumulative inflation. High cumulative inflation is associated with an ensuing inflation rate of g_H. Hence transition probabilities for the Markov process are nonseparable between real price transitions and transitions in the inflation rate.

23. The related (s, S) inventory literature suggests that increases in the mean and variance of sales will raise order size. The well-known Wilson lot-size formula (more familiar as the square-root formula for money demand) expresses the relationship in simple form. The more recent approximation formula of Ehrhardt [1979] has similar properties.

24. An analogous model of money holding with both inflows and outflows is due to Miller and Orr [1966].

25. A suggestive example is presented in Blanchard and Fischer [1985].

26. This will, of course, invalidate the neutrality proposition.

27. Blinder [1981] examines the related issue of changing trigger points and their impact on aggregate inventory behavior.

References

Akerlof, George A., "Relative Wages and the Rate of Inflation," *Quarterly Journal of Economics*, LXXXIII (1969), 353–74.

Akerlof, George A., and Janet Yellen, "A Near-Rational Model of the Business Cycle, with Wage and Price Inertia," *Quarterly Journal of Economics*, C (1985), 823–38.

Arrow, Kenneth J., Thomas Harris, and Jacob Marschak, "Optimal Inventory Policy," *Econometrica*, XIX (1951), 250–72.

Balk, B. M., "Inflation Variability and Relative Price Change Variability in the Netherlands, 1951–1981," *Economics Letters*, XIX (1985), 27–30.

Ball, Laurence, and David Romer, "Are Prices Too Sticky," Princeton University, Department of Economics, mimeo, August 1986.

Barro, Robert J., "A Theory of Monopolistic Price Adjustment," *Review of Economic Studies*, XXXIX (January 1972), 17–26.

Barro, Robert J., "Rational Expectations and the Role of Monetary Policy," *Journal of Monetary Economics*, II (1976), 1–32.

Benabou, Roland, "Optimal Price Dynamics and Speculation with a Storable Good," mimeo, 1985a, MIT.

Benabou, Roland, "Searchers, Price Setters and Inflation," mimeo, 1985b, MIT.

Blanchard, Olivier, "Price Asynchronization and Price Level Inertia," in R. Dornbusch and M. Simonsen, eds., *Indexation, Contracting and Debt in an Inflationary World* (Cambridge, MA: MIT Press, 1983).

Blanchard, Olivier, and Stanley Fischer, "Notes on Advanced Macroeconomic Theory," Chapters 9 and 10, mimeo, 1985.

Blanchard, Olivier, and N. Kiyotaki, "Monopolistic Competition, Aggregate Demand Externalities and Real Effects of Nominal Money," NBER Working Paper No. 1770, 1985, National Bureau of Economic Research.

Blinder, Alan S., "Retail Inventory Investment and Business Fluctuations," *Brookings Papers on Economic Activity*, II (1981), 443–505.

Breiman, Leo, *Probability* (Reading, MA: Addison-Wesley, 1968).

Caplin, Andrew S., "The Variability of Aggregate Demand with (S, s) Inventory Policies," *Econometrica*, LIII (November 1985), 1395–1410.

Caplin, Andrew S., and Eytan Sheshinski, "Optimality of (s, S) Pricing Policies," mimeo, 1987.

Caplin, Andrew S., and Daniel F. Spulber, "Inflation, Menu Costs and Relative Price Variability," Harvard Institute of Economic Research Discussion Paper No. 1181, 1985.

Carlton, Dennis W., "Market Behavior with Demand Uncertainty and Price Inflexibility," *American Economic Review*, LVIII (1978), 571–87.

Cecchetti, Steven, "The Frequency of Price Adjustment: A Study of the Newsstand Prices of Magazines," *Journal of Econometrics*, XXXI (1986), 255–74.

Cecchetti, Steven, "Staggered Contracts and the Frequency of Price Adjustment," *Quarterly Journal of Economics*, C (1985), 935–60.

Cukierman, Alex, "The Relationship Between Relative Prices and the General Price Level, A Suggested Interpretation," *American Economic Review*, LXIX (September 1979), 595–609.

Cukierman, Alex, and Paul Wachtel, "Relative Price Variability and Nonuniform Inflationary Expectations," *Journal of Political Economy*, XC (1982), 146–57.

Danziger, Leif, "Stochastic Inflation and the Optimal Policy of Price Adjustment," *Economic Inquiry*, XXII (1984), 98–108.

Ehrhardt, R. A., "The Power Approximation for Computing (s, S) Inventory Policies," *Management Science*, XXV (1979), 777–86.

Fischer, Stanley, "Long Term Contracts, Rational Expectations, and the Optimal Money Supply Rule," *Journal of Political Economy*, LXXXV (1977), 191–205.

Fischer, Stanley, "Relative Shocks, Relative Price Variability, and Inflation," *Brookings Papers on Economic Activity* (1981), 381–431.

Graham, Frank D., *Exchange, Prices and Production in Hyper-Inflation: Germany 1920–1923* (Princeton, NJ: Princeton University Press, 1930).

Gordon, Robert J., "Output Fluctuations and Gradual Price Adjustment," *Journal of Economic Literature*, XIX (1981), 493–530.

Hercowitz, Zvi, "Money and the Dispersion of Relative Prices," *Journal of Political Economy*, LXXXIX (April 1981), 328–56.

Hubbard, Robert G., and Robert J. Weiner, "Nominal Contracting and Price Flexibility in Product Markets," NBER Working Paper No. 1738, National Bureau of Economic Research, 1985.

Karlin, Samuel, and A. Fabens, "A Stationary Inventory Model with Makovian Demand," in K. Arrow, S. Karlin, and P. Suppes, eds., *Mathematical Methods in the Social Sciences* (Stanford, CA: Stanford University Press, 1959).

Liebermann, Y., and B. Z. Zilberfarb, "Price Adjustment Strategy Under Conditions of High Inflation: An Empirical Examination," *Journal of Economics and Business*, XXXVII (1985), 253–65.

Mankiw, N. Gregory, "Small Menu Costs and Large Business Cycles: A Macroeconomic Model of Monopoly," *Quarterly Journal of Economics*, C (1985), 529–39.

Marquez, John, and Daniel R. Vining, "Inflation and Relative Price Behavior: A Survey of the Literature," in M. Ballabou, ed., *Economic Perspectives*, Vol. 3 (New York: Harwood Academic Publishers, 1984).

Miller, M., and D. Orr, "A Model of the Demand for Money by Firms," *Quarterly Journal of Economics*, LXXX (1966), 413–35.

Mills, Frederick C., *The Behavior of Prices* (New York: Arno Press, 1927); National Bureau of Economic Research, reprint, 1975.

Mussa, Michael, "Sticky Prices and Disequilibrium Adjustment in a Rational Model of the Inflationary Process," *American Economic Review*, LXXI (December 1981), 1020–27.

Pagan, A. R., A. D. Hall, and P. K. Trivedi, "Assessing the Variability of Inflation," *Review of Economic Studies*, L (October 1983), 585–96.

Parkin, Michael, "The Output-Inflation Tradeoff When Prices Are Costly to Change," *Journal of Political Economy*, XCIV (1986), 200–24.

Parks, Richard W., "Inflation and Relative Price Variability," *Journal of Political Economy*, LXXXVI (February 1978), 79–95.

Rotemberg, Julio, "Monopolistic Price Adjustment and Aggregate Output," *Review of Economic Studies*, XLIX (October 1982), 517–31.

Rotemberg, Julio, "Aggregate Consequences of Fixed Costs of Price Adjustment," *American Economic Review*, LXXIII (June 1983), 433–36.

Rotemberg, Julio, "Fixed Costs of Price Adjustment and the Costs of Inflation," Sloan School of Management, mimeo, December 1981.

Scarf, Herbert E., "The Optimality of (s, S) Policies in the Dynamic Inventory Problem," Chapter 13 in K. J. Arrow, S. Karlin, and P. Suppes, eds., *Mathematical Methods in the Social Sciences* (Stanford: Stanford University Press, 1959).

Schwarz, L. B., ed., *Multi-Level Production/Inventory Control Systems: Theory and Practice* (Amsterdam: North-Holland, 1981).

Sheshinski, Eytant, and Yoram Weiss, "Inflation and Costs of Price Adjustment," *Review of Economic Studies*, LIV (1977), 287–303.

Sheshinski, Eytant, and Yoram Weiss, "Optimum Pricing Policy Under Stochastic Inflation," *Review of Economic Studies*, L (July 1983), 513–29.

Taylor, John B., "Aggregate Dynamics and Staggered Contracts," *Journal of Political Economy*, LXXXVIII (1980), 1–23.

Taylor, John B., "On the Relation Between the Variability of Inflation and the Average Inflation Rate," in Karl Brunner and Allen H. Meltzer, eds., *The Costs and Consequences of Inflation*, Carnegie-Rochester Conference Series on Public Policy, Vol. 15 (Amsterdam: North-Holland, 1981), pp. 57–85.

Vining, Daniel R., Jr., and Thomas C. Elwertowski, "The Relationship Between Relative Prices and the General Price Level," *American Economic Review*, LXVI (September 1976), 699–708.

10 Dynamic (S, s) Economies

Ricardo J. Caballero
Eduardo M.R.A. Engel

1 Introduction

In recent years there has been a surge in the application of formal micro-economic models of discontinuous and lumpy adjustment—originally developed in the early 50's for retail inventories—to a variety of topics in economics, such as cash balances, labor demand, investment, entry and exit, prices, durable goods and technology upgrade. Yet the possibility of explaining *aggregate* economic phenomena based on these models has remained largely unexplored, primarily because of the technical difficulties involved. Since aggregate data do not look as discontinuous and lumpy as their microeconomic counterparts, in order to apply these models to macroeconomic data aggregation has to be modeled explicitly. This is hard to do when shocks are not purely idiosyncratic but also have a common (or, equivalently, aggregate) component. The few results existent in the literature have provided important insights, but have been limited either to numerical simulations (Blinder 1981) or to steady state analysis (Caplin 1985, Caplin and Spulber 1987).[1] This chapter's main contribution is to provide a framework within which the out-of-steady-state aggregate dynamics of an economy with lumpy adjustment at the microeconomic level can be studied analytically.

We simplify the mathematics substantially by only considering a particular, but widely used, adjustment policy: the one sided (S, s) rule. In the last section we argue that many of this chapter's insights either carry over directly to more general forms of adjustment rules or provide the natural foundation for their study.

One of the appealing characteristics of (S, s) rules is their simplicity: an individual agent allows his state variable (e.g. inventories) to fall freely until it reaches a certain critical level s; at this point abrupt action takes place and the state variable is reset to an upper value S from where the cycle starts again. Examples where the optimality of fixed (S, s) rules has ben established go back to the problem of inventories management (Scarf, 1959); a more recent example is price setting in the presence of menu-costs (Sheshinski and Weiss, 1983; Caplin and Sheshinski, 1987). Moreover, the fixed (S, s) model has also been extensively used in the Operations Research and Economics literatures as an approximation for more complex optimal rules (e.g. Arrow, Harris and Marschak, 1951; Karlin and Fabens, 1959; Blinder, 1981; Ehrhardt, Schultz and Wagner, 1981; Blanchard and Fischer, 1989, p. 405).

Whenever microeconomic units adjust discretely and by large amounts, the issue of heterogeneity acquires high priority. The similarity between the economy's aggregate path and the discontinuous and lumpy path of microeconomic units grows with the degree of synchronization of units' actions. In the limit, when all units are identical and act simultaneously (the symmetric equilibria assumption), the aggregate path is indistinguishable from that of an individual unit. On the other hand, if units' actions exhibit little synchronization, the aggregate may depart substantially from the behavior of any single (representative) unit. The framework developed in this chapter addresses precisely the process of endogenous synchronization and staggering of individual units, and studies the aggregate implications of such phenomena.

We consider a dynamic economy where agents differ in their initial positions within their bands and face both *stochastic* and *structural* heterogeneity; where the former refers to the presence of (unit specific) idiosyncratic shocks, and the latter to differences in the widths of units' (S, s) bands and their response to aggregate shocks. We study the evolution of the economy's aggregate and the evolution of the difference between this aggregate and that of an economy without microeconomic friction, where the latter pertains to a situation where individual units adjust with no delay to all shocks. We also examine the sensitivity of this difference to common shocks. For example, in the retail inventory problem the aggregate deviation and sensitivity to common shocks correspond to the aggregate inventory level and its sensitivity to aggregate demand shocks, respectively.

In Section 2 we determine conditions under which the microeconomic effect of lumpy adjustment rules has no aggregate impact. Section 3 begins the study of the economy's aggregate (out-of-steady-state) dynamics by discussing the summary variables we use to describe the economy over time. In Section 4 we consider the effect of stochastic heterogeneity on the economy's dynamic aggregate behavior when no structural differences are present. We show that the economy's aggregate converges to that of its counterpart without friction when idiosyncratic shocks spread out without bound over time, and that the speed of convergence increases with the rate at which dispersion occurs; we also show that common shocks play no role in aiding convergence. Structural heterogeneity is incorporated into the analysis in Section 5; we show that it can lead to convergence by itself, that the speed of convergence grows with the degree of structural heterogeneity, and that common shocks aid convergence when structural differences are present. Section 6 shows that, paradoxically, the interaction between both forms of heterogeneity may actually slow down convergence. Section 7 presents final remarks. An extensive appendix follows.

2   Basic Model and Steady State

We consider an economy composed of a large number of units, and approximate this large number by a continuum, indexed by $i \in [0, 1]$. We let $z_i(t)$ denote the difference between $x_i(t)$, the actual value of unit i's state variable at time t when an (S, s) policy is followed, and $x_i^*(t)$, the value of the same variable if there was no friction. For example, consider the retail inventory problem, where firms decide on their optimal inventory holding in the presence of uncertain demand and fixed replenishment costs. In this case $x_i^*(t)$ and $x_i(t)$ are accumulated sales and accumulated inventory orders, and $z_i(t)$ is the level of inventories.

We express every frictionless (optimal) variable, $x_i^*(t)$, as the sum of an idiosyncratic component, $v_i(t)$, and the unit's response to an aggregate shock $a(t) \equiv \int x_i^*(t) \, di$:

$$x_i^*(t) = \theta_i a(t) + v_i(t), \tag{10.1}$$

where θ_i is unit i's sensitivity to the common shock.[2] For example, in the retail inventory problem $da(t)$ denotes aggregate demand shocks and θ_i the sensitivity of sector i's demand to these shocks. We normalize the sensitivity parameters so that $\int_0^1 \theta_i \, di = 1$; this implies that by construction $\int_0^1 v_i(t) \, di = 0$ for all t.

We assume that, for each unit i, $z_i(t)$ decreases monotonically and continuously until it reaches the unit specific trigger barrier, s_i; at this point finite control is exerted on x_i to bring z_i back to the unit specific target barrier S_i.[3]

ASSUMPTION 1.   *Stationarity, symmetry, monotonicity and continuity.*

1. The variable $z_i(t)$ is controlled according to a stationary, fixed band, one sided, unit specific (S, s) policy.

2. The (S, s) rules are symmetric: $S_i = -s_i$.[4]

3. The variable $z_i(t)$ decreases monotonically during time periods where no control is exerted.[5]

4. The sample paths of $v_i(t)$ are continuous and those of $a(t)$ are continuous, increasing and unbounded.

This framework can accommodate many well known problems, apart from the retail inventory problem mentioned above. A few of them are:

• The Pricing Problem, where firms pay a menu-cost when they adjust their nominal prices. In this case $x_i^*(t)$ is the frictionless optimal price and $x_i(t)$ the actual price charged.

• The Cash-Balance Problem, where consumers decide on the optimal level of cash holdings when adjusting their cash-balances is costly. In this case, $x_i^*(t)$ and $x_i(t)$ are accumulated expenditures and accumulated withdrawals, and $z_i(t)$ is the current cash balance.

• The Technology Update Problem, where firms decide on whether to scrap their current machines and update them or not. In this case, $x_i^*(t)$ and $x_i(t)$ are desired and actual state of technology, and $z_i(t)$ is the gap between them.

• The Durable Goods Problem, where consumers decide when to buy a durable good and adjusting the stock they have is costly. In this case, $x_i^*(t)$ and $x_i(t)$ are desired and actual levels of the stock of durable goods, and $z_i(t)$ is the gap between them. In this problem, the sensitivity parameters could correspond to the marginal propensities to consume.

• The Capital Stock Adjustment Problem, where firms decide when to adjust their capital stock when there are non-convex costs of adjustment. In this case, $x_i^*(t)$ and $x_i(t)$ are desired and actual levels of the stock of capital, and $z_i(t)$ is the gap between them.[6]

The main goal of this chapter is to examine the behavior of the variable we call "the aggregate," defined as the integral of the $x_i(t)$'s over all i's and denoted by $X(t)$. Using the definition of the $z_i(t)$'s, and letting $Z(t) \equiv \int_0^1 z_i(t)\, di$, leads to the following expression for $X(t)$:

$$X(t) = a(t) + Z(t). \tag{10.2}$$

When there is no microeconomic friction, all the z_i's are identically zero, thus $X(t) = X^*(t) = a(t)$. As we are interested in the effects of microeconomic (S, s) policies on the departure of $X(t)$ from $X^*(t)$, we focus on the mean of the cross-section distribution of individual departures, $Z(t)$.[7] The entire analysis carried out in this chapter—in particular the computation of the latter mean—is conditional on the actual path of the aggregate shock $a(t)$. It turns out that the results we derive do not depend on any particular features of this path, as long as $a(t)$ is continuous, increasing and tends to infinity (see Assumption 1). We therefore do not need to specify the stochastic mechanism underlying common shocks. The fact that we consider the dynamic path of the actual cross-section distribution—and not that of the joint distribution of all units—in spite of the presence of aggregate shocks, is one of the building blocks of the methodology we develop in this chapter. Its usefulness is best appreciated when we consider convergence issues in Sections 4 and 5. We therefore postpone discussing its importance until the final section.

Instead of working directly with $z_i(t)$, it is notationally convenient to describe the problem in terms of the fraction unit i has covered of its (S, s) band at time t, $c_i(t)$. We therefore define:

$$c_i(t) \equiv \frac{1}{2} - \frac{z_i(t)}{\lambda_i}, \tag{10.3}$$

where $\lambda_i \equiv S_i - s_i$ denotes unit i's bandwidth. The variable $c_i(t)$ takes values in $[0, 1)$; it starts its cycle when $c_i(t) = 0$ (i.e. when $z_i(t) = S_i$) and ends it when $c_i(t)$ reaches one (i.e. when $z_i(t)$ reaches s_i). Substituting $x_i(t) - x_i^*(t)$ for $z_i(t)$ in (10.3) yields:

$$c_i(t) \equiv \left(\frac{1}{2} - \frac{x_i(t) - x_i^*(t)}{\lambda_i} \right).$$

Substituting $x_i^*(t)$ by (10.1), adding and subtracting $c_i(0)$, and noting that $(x_i(t) - x_i(0))/\lambda_i$ is always an integer, yields:

$$c_i(t) = \left(c_i(0) + \frac{\theta_i a(t) + v_i(t)}{\lambda_i} \right) (\text{mod } 1), \tag{10.4}$$

where x (mod 1) denotes the difference between the real number x and its integer part and we set $a(0)$ and $v_i(0)$ equal to zero without loss of generality.

We let c_t, v_t, Θ and Λ denote random variables with a joint *probability* distribution identical to that of the joint *cross-section* distribution of the $c_i(t)$'s, the $v_i(t)$'s, the θ_i's and the λ_i's.[8] Thus, we have that:

$$c_t = \left(c_0 + \frac{\Theta a(t) + v_t}{\Lambda} \right) (\text{mod } 1). \tag{10.5}$$

An expression for the aggregate deviation, $Z(t)$, can be obtained directly in terms of the variables we defined above. All that is needed to determine $Z(t)$ is the value of the current aggregate shock, $a(t)$, and the cross-section distribution of the random vector $(c_0, v_t, \Lambda, \Theta)$.

PROPOSITION 1   *Suppose assumption 1 holds. Then $Z(t) = g(a(t), t)$ and $X(t) = a(t) + g(a(t), t)$, where*

$$g(a, t) \equiv \frac{1}{2} E(\Lambda) - E\left[\Lambda \left\{ \left(c_0 + \frac{\Theta a + v_t}{\Lambda} \right) (\text{mod } 1) \right\} \right].$$

Proof.   Follows directly from equations (10.3), (10.4) and (10.5).   ■

The intermittent and lumpy microeconomic behavior is irrelevant at the aggregate level when—for any realization of the stochastic mechanism underlying aggregate and idiosyncratic shocks—$Z(t)$ remains constant over time. Without loss of generality we suppose that the constant aggregate deviation is equal to zero in what follows.

DEFINITION 1   The aggregate deviation of an economy satisfying Assumption 1 *is at its steady state at time $t = 0$ if $g(a, t) = 0$ for all $a \geq a(0) \equiv 0$ and all $t \geq 0$, with $g(a, t)$ defined in Proposition 1.*

Whether the economy's aggregate deviation is at its steady state or not depends on the stochastic mechanism underlying the model. There are various sets of conditions under which the aggregate deviation remains equal to zero as time passes. In this chapter we consider conditions that can be expressed only in terms of *the cross-section distributions* defined above. In the following proposition—which is an extension of Proposition 1 in Caballero and Engel (1989b)—we show that when units' initial positions within their cycle are distributed uniformly on $[0, 1)$ and independent from the remaining sources of heterogeneity, the economy's aggregate deviation is at its steady state.

PROPOSITION 2 (*Caballero and Engel, 1989b*)   *Given Assumption 1, the economy's aggregate deviation is at its steady state at time $t = 0$ if c_0 is uniform on $[0, 1)$ and independent from Λ, Θ and v_t for all $t > 0$. Furthermore, c_t is uniform on $[0, 1)$ for all $t > 0$.*

This result shows that when units' positions within their cycle are independent from the sources of structural and stochastic heterogeneity, there exists a cross-section (or empirical) distribution of the c_i's that is invariant under continuous, monotone, aggregate shocks. This distribution is uniform. It follows—from equation (10.3)—that there also exists a cross-section distribution of the z_i's that is invariant under the same class of shocks. This distribution is determined by the probability distribution of Λ; it is uniform only when bandwidths do not vary across units.

Proposition 2 presents an economy with strong forms of microeconomic rigidity that has an aggregate behavior indistinguishable from that of an economy without friction. This is a generalization of the insightful result in Caplin and Spulber (1987). They consider the case where all units have the same bandwidth, no idiosyncratic shocks are present, and common shocks have the same impact on all units' $x_i^*(t)$'s. None of these conditions are required for Proposition 2 to hold. In addition, the scenario described in Proposition 2 has a realistic feature that is absent in an economy without structural or stochastic heterogeneity: the relative positions of units within their cycle change over time. The order in which units adjust their state variable does not repeat itself from one cycle to another.

Proposition 2 assumes that the initial cross-section distribution of the c_i's is independent from the joint distribution of idiosyncratic shocks, bandwidths and sensitivity parameters. If this is not the case, the cross-section distribution of the c_i's generally does not remain uniform on $[0, 1)$ and the aggregate deviation, $Z(t)$, does not remain constant. This happens, for example, when units with smaller bandwidths—or larger sensitivity parameters—are initially concentrated at the beginning of their cycle, as is further illustrated in Section 5.

3   Description of Non-Steady-State Dynamics

There are many reasons why Assumption 1 may be momentarily violated and the (S, s) economy's aggregate deviation be forced away from the steady state described in Proposition 2. For example, in the case of the pricing problem, a finite (discrete) change in $a(t)$, like an oil shock or a large monetary shock, bunches a fraction of units at the beginning of their cycle. Alternatively, a widening of units' bands—due, for example, to an increase in the rate of core inflation in an economy where bands are set optimally—leaves a fraction of the new state space initially with no units. In the time period following any one of these "structural changes," the aggregate deviation typically does not remain constant and the economy therefore is not at its steady state anymore.

In the following three sections we study the dynamic behavior of the economy outside of its steady state. We consider idiosyncratic shocks and structural heterogeneity as possible sources of convergence; the latter meaning differences in bandwidths and sensitivity parameters. For expository simplicity, we study the effects of these factors separately before considering their interaction.

Proposition 1 characterizes the dynamic path of the difference of the aggregates from economies with and without frictions. For example, it can be used to determine the evolution of the average level of inventories after an oil shock. Yet we may not only be interested in the level of aggregate inventories at a given point in time, but also in the potential impact of a small aggregate demand shock on this aggregate. This impact on $Z(t)$ is equal to the (partial) derivative of the function g—defined in Proposition 1—with respect to a, evaluated at $(a(t), t)$. We denote this derivative by $J(t) \equiv \partial g / \partial a$.

The relation between $J(t)$ and the cross-section distribution of firms' positions within their cycle is best understood if we look at the effect of a small common shock, Δa, on the aggregate deviation, $Z(t)$, when sensitivity parameters do not vary across units ($\Theta \equiv 1$). We begin with the units that are forced to start a new cycle. The common shock forces a unit with bandwidth λ to adjust only if it has covered a fraction larger than or equal to $1 - (\Delta a / \lambda)$ of its cycle before the shock. The fraction of units with bandwidth λ that reach their trigger point is proportional to $\Delta a \cdot f_{(c_t | \Lambda = \lambda)}(1^-) / \lambda + O((\Delta a)^2)$,[9] where $f_X(\lambda)$ denotes the density of the random variable X. Other things equal, this fraction is smaller the larger the common bandwidth. This effect is exactly offset by the fact that $Z(t)$ grows more when a unit with a larger bandwidth restarts its cycle. Thus, the contribution to the aggregate deviation of those units that adjust and have bandwidth equal to λ is proportional to $\Delta a \cdot f_{(c_t | \Lambda = \lambda)}(1^-) f_\Lambda(\lambda)$; the total increase in $Z(t)$ due to units reaching their trigger point is then equal to $\Delta a \cdot \int f_{(c_t | \Lambda = \lambda)}(1^-) f_\Lambda(\lambda) \, d\lambda = \Delta a \cdot f_{c_t}(1^-)$. Next we consider those units that do not start a new cycle after the aggregate shock. Every unit that does not adjust decreases its contribution to $Z(t)$ by Δa; their total contribution is equal to Δa (minus a term of order $(\Delta a)^2$ that accounts for the fact that not all units belong to the group that does not start a new cycle). We have therefore shown that $\Delta g / \Delta a$ is equal to $f_{c_t}(1^-) - 1 + O(\Delta a)$. Letting Δa approach zero we conclude that $J(t) = f_{c_t}(1^-) - 1$.

It is apparent from the previous paragraph and Proposition 1 that both $J(t)$ and $Z(t)$ may be equal to zero even when the economy's aggregate deviation is "far away" from its steady state. On the one hand, $J(t)$ is equal to zero every time $f_{c_t}(1^-)$ is equal to one;[10] on the other hand, Proposition 1 implies that $Z(t) = 0$ every time $\int \lambda E(c_t | \Lambda = \lambda) f_\Lambda(\lambda) d\lambda = 0$. Therefore $Z(t) = 0$ whenever the weighted average of the "sectoral" aggregates is equal to zero; where the latter are defined as the aggregates conditional on a common bandwidth. Since these sectoral aggregates may evolve in rather arbitrary ways, there is no reason why their average should remain equal to zero in the future.

It is tempting to argue, based on Proposition 2, that the economy's aggregate deviation is at its steady state every time the cross-section distribution of units within their cycle, c_t, is uniform on $[0, 1)$. This intuition is supported by the fact that $Z(t) = E\{\Lambda(\frac{1}{2} - c_t)\}$ is equal to zero when c_t is uniform on $[0, 1)$ and independent form Λ. Yet this argument is not correct, since c_0 is generally not independent from Λ. For example, consider the case where a fraction of units is bunched at the beginning of their cycle after the economy is perturbed away from its steady state. Other things equal, units with larger bandwidths move a smaller fraction of their cycle in a given period of time, so that the correlation between Λ and c_t is negative in the time period following the perturbation. We conclude that although $Z(t)$, $J(t)$ and the shape of the cross-section distribution of units' positions within their cycle are interesting summary variables of the economy's aggregate deviation at any particular instant in time, neither of them has the property of capturing how much the economy's aggregate behavior differs from that of its counterpart without frictions. Next we consider two indices that do have this property:

$$Z^*(t) \equiv \sup_{\{a \geq a(t), s \geq t\}} |g(a, s)|,$$

and

$$J^*(t) \equiv \sup_{\{a \geq a(t), s \geq t\}} \left| \frac{\partial g(a, s)}{\partial a} \right|.$$

The definition of these indices is now illustrated by describing how one of them, $Z^*(t)$, is evaluated at a given instant in time, t_0. Suppose that accumulated common shocks at time t_0 are equal to a_0. Consider all possible future paths of the aggregate shock, $\{a(s), s \geq t\}$, that satisfy Assumption 1 and have $a(t_0) = a_0$, and calculate the maximum (absolute) aggregate deviation for every one of them. The index $Z^*(t)$ then is equal to the largest among these maxima. The aggregate deviation and its sensitivity to small aggregate shocks have (absolute) values that are bounded from above by $Z^*(t)$ and $J^*(t)$ for any future trajectory of the common shock that satisfies Assumption 1.[11]

Once the economy's aggregate deviation departs from the steady state, it typically never exactly returns there. There usually is no instant in time t_0 at which the economy's aggregate deviation has actually reached its steady state again (in the sense of Definition 1). This implies that there always exists the possibility that the aggregate deviation's sensitivity to common shocks, $J(t)$, be relatively large at some instants in time, even if $Z^*(t)$ converges to zero. The aggregate effect of microeconomic frictions is not being washed away in this case. This justifies requiring that $J^*(t)$ also tends to zero for microeconomic frictions to become irrelevant at the macroeconomic level. Motivated by the discussion above we define "*convergence of the economy's aggregate to that of its counterpart with no friction*" as follows:

DEFINITION 2   The aggregate of an economy that satisfies Assumption 1 *converges* to that of its frictionless counterpart if $Z^*(t)$ and $J^*(t)$ tend to zero as t tends to infinity.[12]

In sum, we describe the dynamic behavior of an (S, s) economy using four summary variables. We look at the economy's aggregate deviation from the frictionless counterpart, at the sensitivity of this index to common shocks, and at the suprema of these indices over all possible realizations of the underlying stochastic mechanism.

4   Convergence and Idiosyncratic Shocks

4.1   Convergence

In this section we isolate stochastic heterogeneity as the only source of convergence by assuming that all units have the same bandwidth ($\lambda_i \equiv \lambda$) and the same sensitivity parameters ($\theta_i \equiv 1$).

There are many ways in which the economy's aggregate may converge to that of its frictionless counterpart. For example, convergence takes place if idiosyncratic shocks are correlated with c_0 in such a way that they exactly fill in the gaps between the density of c_t and a density uniform on $[0, 1)$ in finite time and, after this happens, become independent of units' positions within their cycle so that c_t remains uniform on $[0, 1)$ (see Proposition 2). This way of achieving convergence is rather far-fetched; there exist other scenarios where convergence takes place that are even more arbitrary. In this section we consider conditions that ensure convergence when there is no systematic relation between c_0 and the realizations of the idiosyncratic shocks.

ASSUMPTION 2 *Independence.* The random variables c_0 and v_t are independent for all $t > 0$, or, equivalently, dv_t is independent from c_s, for all $s \leq t$.

Under the independence assumption, convergence is not achieved by filling in the gaps in finite time, but by making initial conditions irrelevant as time passes. This happens when the cross-section distribution of idiosyncratic shocks, v_t, *folded back into the unit interval*, converges to a distribution uniform on $[0, 1)$ and thereby "washes away" the initial cross-section distribution of units' positions within their cycle. An example is useful at this point. Suppose that the process generating any unit's idiosyncratic shocks, $(v_i(t), t \geq 0)$, is Gaussian with variance $\sigma^2(t)$ growing as time passes. Since these processes are independent across units, the cross-section distribution of idiosyncratic shocks, v_t, also is normal and has the same variance. This follows from the Glivenko-Cantelli Theorem, see e.g. Billingsley (1986). Figure 10.1a illustrates how the cross-section density of idiosyncratic shocks flattens out; the corresponding evolution of the density of c_t is illustrated in Figure 10.1b—where we have abstracted from the value of the common shock $a(t)$—for the case where c_0 is a spike at 0.5. Since the expected value of c_t approaches one half, $Z(t)$ tends to zero, and since the cross-section density of c_t is approaching one, $J(t) = f_{c_t}(1^-) - 1$ tends to zero. Furthermore, since bandwidths and sensitivity parameters are the same across units, aggregate shocks do not act as a unit separating mechanism; all they do is move units around their cycle. Figure 10.1c illustrates this by showing how the density of c_t varies for different values of the common shock at a fixed instant in time ($t = 1.0$). It follows that $Z^*(t)$ and $J^*(t)$ both tend to zero. Thus Figure 10.1 suggests that all summary variables converge to zero when the cross-section density of idiosyn-

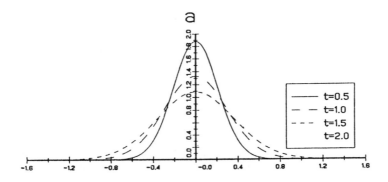

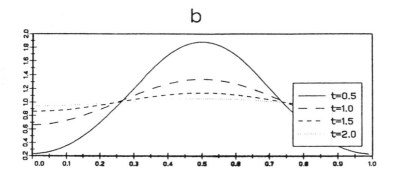

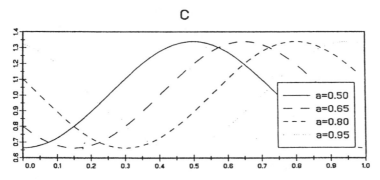

Figure 10.1

cratic shocks flattens out as time passes. This assumes that densities are unimodal, or at least that they do not oscillate too much. The following assumption makes these intuitive conditions on the density of the v_t's precise.

ASSUMPTION 3 *Flattening out of densities.* The total variation of the density of v_t tends to zero as t tends to infinity.[13]

Assumption 3 holds when the density of v_t is unimodal and its largest value tends to zero as t tends to infinity. Two situations where this happens are when the v_t's are normal and their variance tends to infinity, and when the v_t's are absolutely continuous and have independent increments or, more generally, are an integrated process. The proposition that follows provides general conditions under which convergence occurs.

PROPOSITION 3   *Suppose idiosyncratic shocks and differences in units' initial positions within their cycle are the only sources of heterogeneity and Assumptions 1–3 hold. Then the economy's aggregate converges to that of its counterpart without friction and c_t converges to a distribution uniform on* [0, 1).

Proof.   See the appendix. ∎

The assumptions of Proposition 3 are on the cross-section distribution of idiosyncratic shocks, not on the processes generating individual units' shocks. Since we have a continuum of units, the Glivenko-Cantelli Theorem (see Billingsley, 1986) provides a link between assumptions on the $v_i(t)$'s and assumptions on v_t. For example, if idiosyncratic shocks are i.i.d. across units, then the cross-section distribution of idiosyncratic shocks is equal to the probability distribution generating individual shocks. Another example is when the $v_i(t)$'s are of the form $\gamma_i w_i(t)$, with the $w_i(t)$'s i.i.d. across units and γ_i a fixed, unit specific parameter (that could depend on θ_i and λ_i). In this case v_t has the same probability distribution as the product of the independent random variables Γ and w_t, where Γ corresponds to the cross-section distribution γ_i's, and w_t to the common distribution of $w_i(t)$'s.

4.2   Speed of Convergence

Figure 10.1 suggests that convergence is faster when the variance of idiosyncratic shocks, relative to the common bandwidth, is larger. It also shows that the speed at which the economy's aggregate behavior approaches that of an economy with no friction—as measured by $Z^*(t)$ and $J^*(t)$—does not depend on the sample path of the common shock $a(t)$. We illustrate these issues with an example.

Suppose the economy's aggregate deviation is at its steady state, when an increase in the variance of shocks leads all units to increase their bandwidths by 50%, and that the new idiosyncratic shocks follow a Brownian motion with instantaneous standard deviation equal to 5%. From the symmetry assumption it follows that c_0 is uniform on $[1/4, 3/4]$. Figure 10.2a shows the resulting paths of the aggregate deviation $Z(t)$ for two economies which only differ in the realizations of the common shock, $a(t)$. The explicit dependence of $g(a(t), t)$ on t (via v_t) is reflected in the dampening of the oscillations of the sample paths of $Z(t)$. The dependence of g on $a(t)$ determines the speed at which the actual sample paths oscillate; the number of oscillations grows with the speed at which common shocks accumulate. Figure 10.2b illustrates the corresponding paths of $J(t)$.

The convergence mechanism we consider in this section ensures that the cross-section distribution of units' positions within their cycle converges to a distribution U uniform on $[0, 1)$. It is therefore not surprising that the summary variables $Z^*(t)$ and $J^*(t)$ are closely related to particular notions of distance between c_t and U. Since the corresponding relation for $J^*(t)$ can be derived intuitively, we only consider this case. From our discussion in Section 3, we have that $J(t)$ is equal to $f_{c_t}(1^-) - 1$. The index $J^*(t)$ is obtained by maximizing $\partial g / \partial a$ over all values of $a \geq a(t)$ and all values of $s \geq t$. Modifying the value of a for a fixed instant in time s rotates the density of c_s without affecting its shape; for this see Figure 10.1c and imagine joining both ends of the x-axis to form a circular diagram, as in Caplin and Spulber (1987). It follows that $\sup_a |\frac{\partial g}{\partial a}(a, s)|$ is equal to $\sup_a |f_{c_s}(a) - 1|$. The latter expression is the sup-distance between the densities of c_s and U, which we denote by $R(c_s, U)$. It is equal to the largest relative error made when approximating the distribution of c_s by a distribution uniform on $[0, 1)$.[14] We therefore have that $J^*(t) = \sup_{s \geq t} R(c_s, U)$. Figure 10.1b indicates that it is quite likely that $R(c_s, U)$ decreases monotonically over time. This is indeed true when the v_t's have independent increments, as is shown in Proposition A4 in the Appendix. It then follows that $J^*(t) = R(c_t, U)$, that is, that the largest (percentage) error made when approximating the probability of an event under c_t by the corresponding

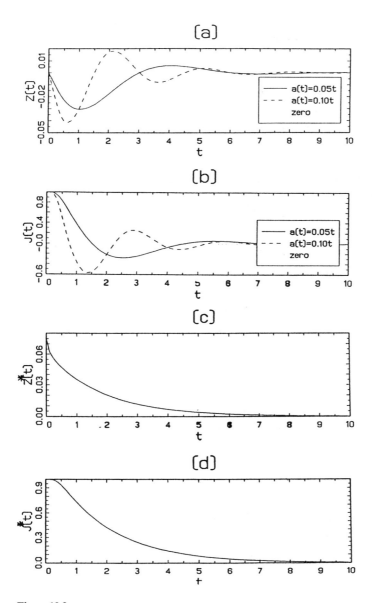

Figure 10.2

probability under U is equal to the largest sensitivity of the aggregate deviation to small common shocks over all possible future sample paths of $a(t)$.

Figures 10.2c and 10.2d show the trajectories of $Z^*(t)$ and $J^*(t)$ that correspond to Figures 10.2a and 10.2b. These do not depend on the particular paths of $a(t)$. It follows from the formulas we derive for the summary statistics in the appendix that the speed of convergence increases with the relative importance of idiosyncratic shocks compared with the common bandwidth. For example, if in the experiment of Figure 10.2 $x_i(t)$ an $x_i^*(t)$ are the logarithms of economically meaningful variables and time is measured in years, then it takes about 18 years before $J^*(t)$ is below 5 percent when σ/λ is equal to 0.1; if σ/λ is equal to 0.5 it takes only about 9 months.[15]

In Proposition A1 in the Appendix, we provide general expressions for the indices used to construct these figures. They are all expressed in terms of the Fourier coefficients of v_t, and show that, loosely speaking, the smaller the Fourier coefficients, the faster all indices converge to zero. This can be understood in terms of the example given in Figure 10.1 above, since Fourier coefficients measure how fast v_t spreads out.[16] Moreover, in the particular case where idiosyncratic shocks have independent increments, all the indices converge to zero at the same rate as $|k|^t$, where k denotes the first non-trivial Fourier coefficient of v_1/λ that differs from zero.[17] Hence speed of convergence is faster, the smaller the first non-trivial Fourier coefficient of v_1/λ. For example, when idiosyncratic shocks follow a Brownian motion with instantaneous variance σ^2, we have that $|k| = \exp(-2\pi^2\sigma^2/\lambda^2)$. Since the variance of the random variable that is folded back into the unit interval (see equation (10.4)) is $(\sigma/\lambda)^2$, it is not surprising that convergence is faster when this ratio is larger.

5 Convergence and Structural Heterogeneity

Structural heterogeneity—namely, differences in bandwidths and sensitivity parameters—is a second source of convergence. It ensures convergence by itself, even if no idiosyncratic uncertainty is present. It also adds various new features to the analysis of convergence and speed of convergence. Most prominently, aggregate shocks stop being irrelevant—as was the case in Section 4—and become the driving force behind convergence.

In this section we isolate structural heterogeneity as a source of convergence, by assuming that there are no idiosyncratic shocks. We consider both sources of convergence simultaneously in Section 6. We find it convenient to study separately the cases where differences in bandwidths and differences in sensitivity parameters are the only sources of convergence. We begin with the former case.

5.1 Heterogeneous Bandwidths

When structural heterogeneity due to different bandwidths is present, equation (10.3) may be used to show that:

$$Z(t) = \int \lambda f_\Lambda(\lambda) \{ \tfrac{1}{2} - C(t|\lambda) \} \, d\lambda, \tag{10.6}$$

where $f_\Lambda(\lambda)$ denotes the probability density of bandwidths and $C(t|\lambda)$ the average position within their cycle of the "sector" of the economy formed by units with bandwidths equal to λ.

Equation (10.6) shows that, as mentioned in Section 3, units with a larger bandwidth have a larger weight when determining the deviation of the aggregate from its frictionless counterpart. The weight is proportional to both the size of the bandwidth and the size of the sector. This equation also shows that the aggregate path of the economy may converge to that of its frictionless counterpart in one of two ways. First, convergence takes place if units within each sector approach a distribution uniform on their common bandwidth. Each sector then behaves as in a frictionless economy, and adding over all sectors shows that the economy's aggregate mimics that of its frictionless counterpart. Convergence occurs in this way when the density of idiosyncratic shocks spread out without limit as time passes (see Section 4). Yet convergence may take place even when the aggregate deviation of units with the same bandwidth does not converge at all, but synchronization among the aggregate deviations of different bandwidths breaks down over time. This is the case with sufficient differences in bandwidths.

Convergence We start our discussion of convergence by presenting an example where differences in bandwidths are the only source of convergence. All θ_i's are the same, there are no idiosyncratic shocks, and all units start off at the beginning of their cycle. We consider a cross-section distribution of the inverse-bandwidths—the $1/\lambda_i$'s—that is uniform on $[10, 20]$

and assume that the x_i's and x_i^*'s are the logarithms of economically meaningful variables. Bandwidths therefore vary between 5 and 10 percentage points. Since there are no idiosyncratic shocks, and all units start off at the beginning of their cycle, we may imagine that there is only one unit in each sector. The deviation of any given sector does not approach zero; it exhibits cycles that do not dampen out over time.

As common shocks begin to accumulate, units with different bands move in a fully synchronized manner within their bandwidths until they start completing their first cycle (at $t = 0.05$). The times at which units complete their cycles vary because bandwidths differ across units; this is the source of convergence in this example.

From equation (10.5) we have that $c_t = (a(t)/\Lambda)(\text{mod } 1)$, therefore the distribution of c_t is uniform on $[0, 1)$ every time accumulated common shocks are equal to a multiple of 0.1. It departs from this distribution after every visit, yet every time by less. A visit to the uniform distribution is characterized by the fact that the correlation between units' positions within their cycle and their bandwidths decreases when compared to the previous visit. Figures 10.3a and 10.3b show the paths of $Z(t)$ and $J(t)$. The discontinuities in $J(t)$ are due to the fact that the density of $1/\Lambda$ is not continuous at its endpoints. Modifying this density slightly at these points would lead to the same qualitative behavior without jumps. The Figure shows that the aggregate deviation, $Z(t)$, and its sensitivity to small common shocks, $J(t)$, oscillate on their way to zero.

When there is no stochastic heterogeneity, both $Z(t)$ and $J(t)$ only depend on time through the current value of $a(t)$; $g(a, t) \equiv g(a)$ remains constant as t varies (see Proposition 1). Hence the path of $Z^*(t) = \sup_{a \geq a(t)} |g(a)|$ and $J^*(t) = \sup_{a \geq a(t)} |g'(a)|$ are both equal to the envelopes of the sample path of $Z(t)$ and $J(t)$. Figures 10.3c and 10.3d show how $Z^*(t)$ and $J^*(t)$ evolve over time. This example also serves to show that convergence may take place even if units' initial positions within their cycles are highly correlated with their bandwidths. Structural heterogeneity achieves convergence by breaking down the correlation between the aggregates of different sectors.

Consider any cross-section distribution of $1/\Lambda$ that has a sufficiently smooth density. Partition the set of possible bandwidths into a finite number of intervals, and approximate the cross-section distribution of bandwidths within each interval by a uniform distribution. The argument given above applies to the sector composed of units with bandwidths in any one

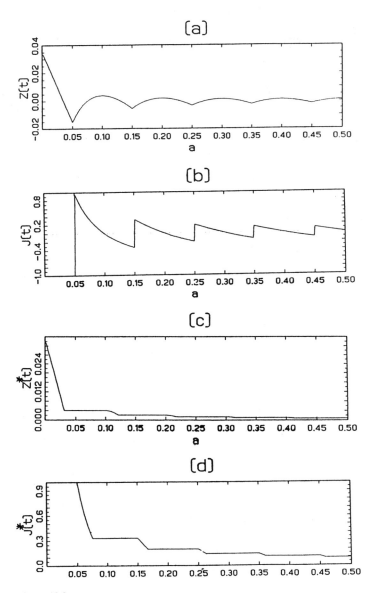

Figure 10.3

interval; these units' aggregate deviation therefore converges. It follows that the behavior of the entire economy's aggregate converges to that of its counterpart without friction. This argument explains why, when differences in bandwidths are the only source of heterogeneity, convergence takes place when the inverse of units' bandwidths has a smooth density. Since our model has a continuum of units, this is a relatively weak assumption.

The previous argument is based on assuming that c_0 is constant; it can be extended to the case where c_0 and Λ are not "perfectly" correlated by requiring that the density of $1/\Lambda$, *conditional on any value of c_0*, be sufficiently smooth.

ASSUMPTION 4 *Smoothness (1)*.   The random variable Λ has finite expectation and the density of $1/\Lambda$, conditional on any value of c_0, has bounded variation $V(\Lambda^{-1}|c_0)$ such that $E_{c_0}V(\Lambda^{-1}|c_0)$ is finite.

Below we provide a proposition generalizing and formalizing the insights of this example.

PROPOSITION 4   *Suppose that differences in bandwidths and units' initial positions within their cycle are the only source of heterogeneity, and that Assumptions 1 and 4 hold. Then the economy's aggregate behavior converges to that of its counterpart with no friction and c_t converges to a distribution uniform on the interval* $[0, 1)$.

Proof.   See the Appendix.   ∎

Speed of Convergence   The example above shows that the rate at which the common shock $a(t)$ grows—which is irrelevant in the case of only stochastic heterogeneity—is crucial when heterogeneity in bandwidths is the only source of convergence. The mechanism that leads to convergence in this case is not based upon spreading units out, but on having them move around their cycles at different speeds. This mixing effect grows with $a(t)$.

The example above also shows that the distance betwen the cross-section distribution of units' positions within their cycle and a distribution uniform on $[0, 1)$ does not decrease monotonically over time. Even though the distribution of units within their cycle approaches a distribution uniform on $[0, 1)$, there are periods when units "catch up" with each other and the distance between c_t and its limiting distribution increases. This differs from what we saw in Section 4; since the distance between c_t and a distribution uniform on $[0, 1)$ decreases monotonically over time when stochastic heterogeneity is the only source of convergence and idiosyncratic shocks have independent increments.

When there is no stochastic heterogeneity, $Z^*(t)$ and $J^*(t)$ depend on t only through the value of $a(t)$; it follows that the speed of convergence grows with the rate at which aggregate shocks accumulate. It is shown in the Appendix that, under the assumptions of Proposition 4, $J^*(t)$ is bounded from above by $k/a(t)$ for some constant k that depends on how smooth the corresponding densities are. This bound cannot be improved upon, it is sharp when the cross-section distribution of units' bandwidths within their cycle is uniform.

5.2 Heterogeneous Sensitivity Parameters

When different sensitivity parameters are the only source of convergence, equation (10.3) may be used to show that:

$$Z(t) = \lambda \int \{\tfrac{1}{2} - C(t|\theta)\} f_\Theta(\theta) \, d\theta, \tag{10.7}$$

where $f_\Theta(\theta)$ denotes the probability density of sensitivity parameters and $C(t|\theta)$ the average position within their cycle of the "sector" of the economy formed by units with sensitivity parameter equal to θ. As in the case with different bandwidths, when differences in sensitivity parameters are the only source of heterogeneity, aggregate shocks achieve convergence by gradually eliminating the synchronization between sectoral aggregates instead of by having every sectoral aggregate deviation converge.

When all bandwidths are the same (without loss of generality $\lambda_i \equiv 1$) and there are no idiosyncratic shocks, equation (10.5) implies that $c_t = (c_0 + a(t)\Theta)(\mathrm{mod}\ 1)$; hence c_t converges to a distribution uniform on $[0, 1)$ because $a(t)\Theta$ flattens out without bound as aggregate shocks accumulate. The correlation between the position within their cycle of units and different sensitivity parameters decreases over time, since common shocks affect them differently and these differences accumulate.[18] As long as Θ has a sufficiently smooth density, conditional on any value of c_0, the economy's aggregate deviation converges to that of its frictionless counterpart.

ASSUMPTION 5 *Smoothness (2)*.   The random variable Θ has a density $f_\Theta(\theta)$ such that $f_\Theta(\theta)$ and $\theta f_\theta(\theta)$, conditional on any value of c_0, have bounded variation $V(f_\Theta(\theta)|c_0)$ and $V(\theta f_\Theta(\theta)|c_0)$; and $E_{c_0} V(f_\Theta(\theta)|c_0)$ and $E_{c_0} V(\theta f_\Theta(\theta)|c_0)$ are both finite.

PROPOSITION 5 *Suppose that differences in sensitivity parameters and units' initial positions within their cycle are the only source of heterogeneity, and that Assumptions 1 and 5 hold. Then the economy's aggregate behavior converges to that of its counterpart with no friction and c_t converges to a distribution uniform on the interval* [0, 1).

Proof. See the Appendix. ∎

The speed at which the economy's aggregate converges to that of its frictionless counterpart increases with the rate at which $a(t)$ grows; it is shown in the Appendix that $Z^*(t)$ and $J^*(t)$ are both bounded from above by $k/a(t)$, where k depends on how smooth the corresponding densities are. This bound is sharp when sensitivity parameters have a uniform distribution.

The mechanism that leads to convergence in this case combines those present when either idiosyncratic shocks or differences in bandwidths are the sole source of heterogeneity. On the one hand, aggregate shocks are the main determinant of convergence, on the other, these shocks achieve convergence by spreading out indefinitely the $x_i^*(t)$'s, as idiosyncratic shocks did in Section 4.

6 Interactions

We have found conditions under which stochastic and structural heterogeneity yield convergence separately. It follows that convergence is more likely to occur when both sources of heterogeneity are present. We formalize this intuition at the end of Section A2 in the Appendix.

The results on the speed of convergence are, however, far less transparent. There is a broad set of parameters for which the intuitive assertion that when a second mechanism is added, convergence speeds up, is valid; surprisingly, however, this is not universally true.

Figure 10.4 presents an example of this paradox. It shows that adding structural heterogeneity to stochastic heterogeneity may slow down the speed of convergence. In this example, idiosyncratic shocks follow a Brownian motion (with instantaneous variance equal to 0.4 and $1/\Lambda$ is normal with mean 0.4 and variance η^2). All units have the same sensitivity

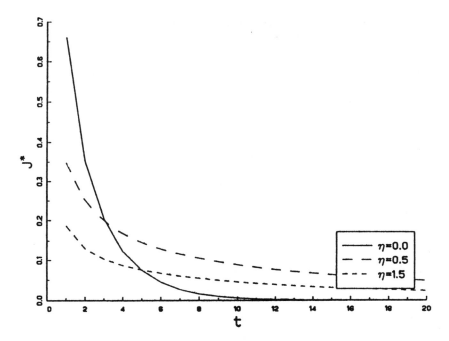

Figure 10.4

parameters and their initial distribution within their cycle is uniform on $[0, 0.2]$. Figure 10.4 shows the path of $J^*(t)$ for three values of the parameter η. It is apparent that—beyond a certain time threshold—convergence is faster when stochastic heterogeneity is the only source of convergence ($\eta = 0$) than when structural heterogeneity is also present ($\eta > 0$).[19]

Figure 10.4 is best understood by comparing the aggregate deviation without structural heterogeneity, $Z(t)$, with the aggregate deviation of a sector composed of units with a common bandwidth larger than average after structural heterogeneity is added. When structural heterogeneity is added to idiosyncratic uncertainty, the sectoral aggregates corresponding to larger bandwidths converge slower than $Z(t)$, since structural heterogeneity reduces the variance of their idiosyncratic shocks relative to their bandwidths and it is this ratio that determines the speed of convergence (see Section 4). For the same reason the sectoral aggregates corresponding to smaller bandwidths converge faster than $Z(t)$. Figure 10.4 shows an example where the slowdown of units with bandwidths larger than average dominates over the combined effect of the acceleration of units with bandwidths smaller than average and the decrease in synchronization between sectoral aggregates (see Section 5).

Perverse interactions may also be present when we add stochastic heterogeneity to an economy where structural heterogeneity—in the form of differences in bandwidths—leads to convergence by itself. This is best understood when we consider the case where there are no differences in sensitivity parameters and we group units into sectors according to the value of their idiosyncratic shock at time t, $v_i(t)$. Since the effect of $v_i(t)$ on units *within a sector* is the same as the effect of having a common shock equal to $a(t) + v_i(t)$ instead of $a(t)$, the discussion in Section 5 shows that sectors with positive $v_i(t)$'s are typically nearer to their steady state than they would be if there were no idiosyncratic shocks, while sectors with negative realizations are farther away. When adding sectoral aggregate deviations, structural heterogeneity decreases the degree of synchronization, yet it may happen that units with negative shocks determine the overall speed of convergence. We have constructed examples where this is the case.[20]

Finally, we consider the case where idiosyncratic shocks interact with differences in sensitivity parameters. For simplicity we suppose that bandwidths are the same across units. If the $v_i(t)$'s are i.i.d. across units and independent from Θ, then adding idiosyncratic shocks speeds up convergence (this follows form Proposition A4 in the Appendix). Yet when $v_i(t)$ depends on θ_i, there are cases where adding structural heterogeneity—in the form of differences in sensitivity parameters—slows down the speed at which an economy with stochastic heterogeneity converges.

7 Final Remarks

In this chapter we study the dynamic behavior of an (S, s) economy where units face idiosyncratic shocks and differ in both their bandwidths and their responses to aggregate shocks. We develop a framework that provides a meaningful characterization of the out-of-steady state dynamics of an (S, s) economy, and study its convergence properties and the speed at which this occurs.

The major building block in our approach is to work with the *cross-section distribution* of units' positions within their cycle, *conditional on the sample path of the aggregate shock.* This distribution, combined with that of structural differences and sensitivity parameters, describes the actual state of the economy at a given instant in time and—if the number of units is sufficiently large—does not depend on the value taken by every particular agent's idiosyncratic shock but only on the common distribution function originating them. This insight follows from the Glivenko-Cantelli Theorem (see Billingsley, 1986); it allows us to apply results from probability theory when studying convergence and speed of convergence. Although we work with (S, s) rules, the summary variables $Z(t)$, $J(t)$, $Z^*(t)$ and $J^*(t)$ should be applicable to a much broader set of circumstances where microeconomic frictions influence aggregate dynamics.

An important methodological contribution of our approach is that it substantially reduces the dimensionality of the problem. An alternative approach would be to characterize the joint behavior of n units, in terms of the joint distribution function describing units' positions at time t based upon information available at time $t = 0$ (e.g. Caplin, 1985). Within this approach, however, convergence means that given information available at time $t = 0$, our best forecast of the n-dimensional random vector describing agents' positions within their cycle at time t approaches a distribution uniform on the unit hypercube, $[0, 1]^n$. In this case speed of convergence slows down as the number of agents grows, since demanding that all agents be within a given distance from their uniform distribution becomes more stringent. This differs from the steady state we consider in this chapter, where the cross-section distribution of units' positions within their cycle is uniform on the interval $[0, 1]$. Considering statistics derived from the cross-section distribution—such as its mean and sensitivity to common shocks—and realizing that it does not depend on the actual realization of every agents' idiosyncratic shock simplifies the analysis considerably and provides ground for optimism about future research in this area.

We have implicitly assumed in our analysis that the redefinition of initial conditions—i.e. whatever moves the economy away from its steady state—occurs infrequently enough so that the economy has time to converge back to its steady state; the insights developed here, however, apply even when this is not the case (see Caballero and Engel, 1989a, and the working paper version of this chapter). In general, there is a permanent tension between the natural tendency for the economy's aggregate deviation to converge back to the steady state and the impact of repeated large (finite) aggregate shocks. Given any process generating the latter, the *average* distance of the economy from the steady state decreases with an increase in the importance of stochastic and structural heterogeneity (with the caveats of Section 6).

The techniques developed here have already found applications beyond the framework of this chapter. For example, Caplin and Leahy (1989) use them to prove convergence (up to a location parameter) in the context of a fully symmetric two sided (S, s) economy where heterogeneity is negligible; and Caballero and Engel (1989b) have used the concept of synchronization developed here to show that when strategic interactions are present, multiple equilibria can be ruled out once the cross-section distribution is sufficiently close to its steady state.

To conclude, we stress that the principle of conditioning on the aggregate in order to keep track of the evolution of the cross-section distribution is far more general than the framework of this chapter. This may be one of the building blocks of future work on aggregation of heterogeneous units in the presence of non-vanishing correlation across units.

Appendix

A1.   Exact Formulas for the Summary Variables

DEFINITION A1.   Given non-negative real numbers a and t, we define the random variables $C(a, t)$ and $Y(a, t)$ as follows:

$$C(a, t) = \left(c_0 + \frac{a\Theta + v_t}{\Lambda} \right), \tag{10.8}$$

$$Y(a, t) = [C(a, t)] \,(\mathrm{mod}\ 1); \tag{10.9}$$

with c_0, v_t, Θ and Λ as in Section 2. We then have that the function $g(a, t)$ defined in Section 2 is equal to $\frac{1}{2}E\Lambda - E\{\Lambda Y(a, t)\}$.

The following three propositions provide expressions to calculate $g(a, t)$ and $\partial g/\partial a$ when only *one* of the three sources of heterogeneity considered in this paper—idiosyncratic shocks, differences in bandwidths and differences in sensitivity parameters—is present, and all units have the same initial position within their cycle. Following these results we show how a simple conditioning argument extends them to the case where more than one source of convergence is present and units differ in their initial positions within their cycle.

LEMMA A1.   *Let X be a random variable whose density $f(x)$ has bounded variation. Then X (mod 1) also has a density, $f_1(x)$, and $f_1(x) = \sum_k f(x + k)$.*

Proof.   This is a well known result in probability theory; for a proof under the assumptions made above see Proposition 3.1 in Engel (1991). ∎

LEMMA A2.   Let X denote a random variable whose characteristic function $\hat{f}(z)$ satisfies $\sum_{k \geq 1} |\hat{f}(2\pi k)| < +\infty$. Then:

$$E[X(\text{mod } 1)] = \frac{1}{2} - \frac{1}{\pi} \sum_{k \geq 1} \frac{1}{k} \Im[\hat{f}(2\pi k)], \tag{10.10}$$

where $\Im[z]$ denotes the imaginary part of the complex number z and x (mod 1) the difference between x and the largest integer less than or equal to x.

Proof.   The Fourier coefficients of X and $X(\text{mod } 1)$ are the same (see e.g. Lemma 3.1 in Engel, 1992); hence the Fourier coefficients of $X(\text{mod } 1)$ are summable and $X(\text{mod } 1)$ has a continuous density, $f_1(x)$, with bounded variation. Applying Poisson's Summation Formula (see Butzer and Nessel, 1971, p. 202, for the version being used here) we then have that $f_1(x) = \sum_k \hat{f}(2\pi k)e^{-i2\pi k x}$. Substituting this expression for $f_1(x)$ in $E[X(\text{mod } 1)] = \int x f_1(x)\,dx$, interchanging the order of integration and summation,[21] and integrating the resulting terms, leads to equation (10.10). ∎

PROPOSITION A1.   *Suppose that $c_0 \equiv c$, $\Lambda \equiv 1$,[22] and $\Theta \equiv 1$ in equation (10.10), and assume that the density of v_t has a characteristic function, $\hat{f}_t(z)$, that satisfies $\sum_{k \geq 1} |\hat{f}_t(2\pi k)| < +\infty$. Then:*

$$g(a, t) = \frac{1}{\pi} \sum_{k \geq 1} \frac{1}{k} \Im[\hat{f}_t(2\pi k)e^{i2\pi k(c+a)}], \tag{10.11}$$

$$\frac{\partial g}{\partial a}(a, t) = 2 \sum_{k \geq 1} \Re[\hat{f}_t(2\pi k)e^{i2\pi k(c+a)}]; \tag{10.12}$$

where $\Re[z]$ and $\Im[z]$ denote the real and imaginary parts of the complex number z.

Proof. The expression for $g(a, t)$ follows directly from equation (10.10) in Lemma A1, letting $c + a + v_t$ play the role of X.

The expression for $\partial g / \partial a$ can be derived formally by differentiating the sum in (10.11) term by term. The change in the order of summation and differentiation is made rigorous by applying Lebesgue's Dominated Convergence Theorem (see e.g. Billingsley, 1986) and using the assumption that the Fourier coefficients of v_t are summable. ∎

PROPOSITION A2.   *Suppose that $c_0 \equiv c$ with $c \in [0, 1)$, $v_t \equiv 0$ and $\Theta \equiv 1$, that $E\Lambda$ is finite, and that $\lambda f_\Lambda(\lambda)$ has finite total variation, where $f_\Lambda(\lambda)$ denotes the density of Λ. Then:*

$$g(a, t) = (\tfrac{1}{2} - c)E\Lambda - a + \sum_{k \geq 1} \int_0^{a/(k-c)} \lambda f_\Lambda(\lambda)\, d\lambda, \tag{10.13}$$

$$\frac{\partial g}{\partial a}(a, t) = -1 + \sum_{k \geq 1} \frac{a}{(k - c)^2} f_\Lambda\left(\frac{a}{k - c}\right). \tag{10.14}$$

Proof. The expression for $g(a, t)$ follows from:

$$
\begin{aligned}
E[\Lambda Y(a, t)] &= \int \lambda \left[\left(c + \frac{a}{\lambda}\right)(\bmod 1)\right] f_\Lambda(\lambda)\, d\lambda \\
&= \sum_{k \geq 1} \int_{a/(k+1-c)}^{a/(k-c)} \lambda\left(c + \frac{a}{\lambda} - k\right) f_\Lambda(\lambda)\, d\lambda + \int_{a/(1-c)}^{+\infty} \lambda\left(c + \frac{a}{\lambda}\right) f_\Lambda(\lambda)\, d\lambda \\
&= c E\Lambda + a - \sum_{k \geq 1} k \int_{a/(k+1-c)}^{a/(k-c)} \lambda f_\Lambda(\lambda)\, d\lambda \\
&= c E\Lambda + a - \sum_{k \geq 1} \int_0^{a/(k-c)} \lambda f_\Lambda(\lambda)\, d\lambda.
\end{aligned}
$$

The expression for $\partial g / \partial a$ is obtained by differentiating the latter expression. The assumption that $\lambda f_\Lambda(\lambda)$ has bounded variation is used when interchanging the order of differentiation and summation. ∎

PROPOSITION A3.   *Suppose that $c_0 \equiv c$ with c in $[0, 1)$, $v_t \equiv 0$, and $\Lambda \equiv 1$, and that $\theta f_\Theta(\theta)$ has bounded variation, where $f_\Theta(\theta)$ denotes the density of Θ. Then:*

$$g(a, t) = \tfrac{1}{2} - a + \sum_k (k - c)\left\{F_\Theta\left(\frac{k + 1 - c}{a}\right) - F_\Theta\left(\frac{k - c}{a}\right)\right\},$$

$$\frac{\partial g}{\partial a}(a, t) = -1 + \frac{1}{a^2} \sum_k (k - c) f_\Theta\left(\frac{k - c}{a}\right),$$

where $F_\Theta(\theta)$ denotes the cumulative distribution function of Θ.

Proof. The expression for $g(a, t)$ is obtained using Lemma A1 as follows:

$$\mathrm{E}[(c + a\Theta)(\mathrm{mod}\ 1)] = \frac{1}{a} \sum_k \int_0^1 x f_\Theta\left(\frac{x + k - c}{a}\right) dx$$

$$= \sum_k \int_{(k-c)/a}^{(k+1-c)/a} (ua - k + c) f_\Theta(u)\, du$$

$$= a\mathrm{E}\Theta - \sum_k (k - c) \int_{(k-c)/a}^{(k+1-c)/a} f_\Theta(u)\, du$$

$$= a - \sum_k (k - c) \left\{ F_\Theta\left(\frac{k + 1 - c}{a}\right) - F_\Theta\left(\frac{k - c}{a}\right) \right\}.$$

The expression for $\partial g/\partial a$ is obtained by differentiating the latter expression; the assumption that $\theta f_\Theta(\theta)$ has bounded variation is used when interchanging the order of summation and differentiation. ∎

Generalizations When more than one source of convergence is present, we obtain expressions for $g(a, t)$ and $\partial g/\partial a$ by calculating $\mathrm{E}[\Lambda Y(a, t) | X = x]$—and the corresponding derivative—for an appropriately chosen random vector X using one of the above propositions, and then taking expected value with respect to X. This argument is based on the fact that $\mathrm{E}[f(X, Y)] = \mathrm{E}_X[f(X, Y) | X = x]$. It requires that the corresponding proposition's regularity conditions hold conditional on $X = x$ for any x, and, when calculating $\partial g/\partial a$, that they hold uniformly in x. Next we show explicitly how to apply this argument for every one of the propositions derived above.

1. If we want to apply Proposition A1 we let $(\frac{v_t}{\lambda}|c_0 = \bar{c}, \Lambda = \lambda, \Theta = \theta)$ play the role of v_t and $\bar{c} + (a\theta/\lambda)$ the role of c. This leads to the following expressions:

$$g(a, t) = \frac{1}{\pi} \sum_{k \geq 1} \frac{1}{k} \mathfrak{J}[\mathrm{E}_\Lambda\{\Lambda e^{i2\pi k C(a, t)} | \Lambda = \lambda\}],$$

$$\frac{\partial g}{\partial a}(a,t) = 2 \sum_{k \geq 1} \Re[E_\Theta\{\Theta e^{i2\pi k C(a,t)} | \Theta = \theta\}],$$

with $C(a,t)$ defined in (10.8).

2. If we want to apply Proposition A2 we let $(\Lambda | c_0 = \bar{c}, \Theta = \theta, v_t = v)$ play the role of Λ, $a\theta + v$ that of a and $\bar{c}$ that of c.

3. If we want to apply Proposition A3 we let $(\Theta | c_0 = \bar{c}, \Lambda = \lambda, v_t = v)$ play the role of Θ, $\bar{c} + (v/\lambda)$ that of c, and (a/λ) that of a.

A2   Convergence

LEMMA A3.   Let X denote a random variable that has a density, $f(x)$, with finite total variation equal to $V(f)$. Denote the density of $X(\text{mod } 1)$ by $f_1(x)$, and the sup-distance between $X(\text{mod } 1)$ and a distribution uniform on $[0,1]$ by $R(X(\text{mod } 1), U)$. Then:

$$|E[X(\text{mod } 1)] - \tfrac{1}{2}| \leq \tfrac{1}{2}R(X(\text{mod } 1), U), \tag{10.15}$$

$$R(X(\text{mod } 1), U) \leq \tfrac{1}{2}V(f). \tag{10.16}$$

Proof.   Equation (10.15) follows from:

$$|E[X(\text{mod } 1)] - \tfrac{1}{2}| = \left| \int_0^1 (f_1(x) - 1)x\,dx \right|$$

$$\leq \int_0^1 |f_1(x) - 1|x\,dx$$

$$\leq \int_0^1 R(X(\text{mod } 1), U)x\,dx$$

$$= \tfrac{1}{2}R(X(\text{mod } 1), U).$$

For a proof of equation (10.16), which is due to Kemperman, see Proposition 3.3.c in Engel (1992). ∎

LEMMA A4

1. Suppose that X and Y are random variables such that $(X | Y = y)$ has a density with finite total variation $V(X | Y = y)$ for all values of y and $E_Y V(X | Y = y)$ is finite. Then X has a density with finite total variation $V(X)$ and $V(X) \leq E_Y V(X | Y = y)$.

2. Let $f(x)$, $f_a(x)$ and $f_c(x)$ denote the densities of the random variables X, aX and $X + c$, with $a > 0$, and suppose that $f(x)$ has finite total variation $V(f)$. Then $f_a(x)$ and $f_c(x)$ also have finite total variation and $V(f_a) = V(f)/a$; $V(f_c) = V(f)$.

Proof. The proof of the first statement is analogous to that of Proposition 4.3 in Engel (1992). The proof of the second statement is trivial. ■

Proof of Proposition 3 Let $R(c_t, U)$ denote the sup-distance between c_t and a distribution uniform on the unit interval, and $V(X)$ denote the total variation of the density of the random variable X. From Lemma A3 it follows that $R(c_t, U) \leq \frac{1}{2}V(c_0 + (v_t/\lambda))$; Lemma A4 and Assumption 2 then imply that $R(c_t, U) \leq \frac{1}{2}V(v_t/\lambda) = \frac{1}{2}V(v_t)$. Assumption 3 now implies that c_t converges—in the sup-distance—to U. Since $J^*(t) = \sup_{s \geq t} R(c_s, U)$ (see Section 4), this is equivalent to having $J^*(t)$ converge to zero. That $Z^*(t)$ also tends to zero follows from the fact that, due to Lemma A3, it is bounded by $\sup_{s \geq t} R(c_s, U)$. ■

Proof of Proposition 4 We begin by noting that, since in this case c_t only depends on t through the value of $a(t)$, convergence of $Z^*(t)$ and $J^*(t)$ to zero is equivalent to convergence of $Z(t)$ and $J(t)$ to zero. The same holds for Proposition 5.

Let $R(c_t, U)$ denote the sup-distance between c_t and a distribution uniform on the unit interval and $V(X)$ denote the total variation of the density of the random variable X. From Lemma A3 it follows that $R(c_t, U) \leq V(c_0 + (a(t)/\Lambda))$. Using Lemma A4 we then have that $R(c_t, U) \leq E_{c_0}V(\Lambda^{-1}|c_0)/2a(t)$; therefore c_t converges to U and $J^*(t)$ converges to zero at a rate that is bounded from above by $1/a(t)$.

Theorem 4.2—due to Hopf—in Engel (1991) shows that (c_t, Λ) converges in the weak-star topology to (U, Λ), with Λ independent from U. It follows that $E(c_t \Lambda)$ converges to $\frac{1}{2}E\Lambda$, and therefore $Z(t)$ converges to zero. ■

Proof of Proposition 5 It follows from Lemmas A3 and A4 that $R(c_t, U) \leq k/a(t)$, with $k = E_{c_0}V(f_\Theta|c_0)/2$; therefore c_t converges to a distribution uniform on $[0, 1)$ and $Z(t)$ converges to zero.

To show that $J(t)$ converges to zero, we first consider the case where $c_0 \equiv c$. That $J(t)$ converges to zero in this case follows from the expression we derived for $\partial g/\partial a$ in Proposition A3 and the fact that $\sum_k \frac{k-c}{a^2}f_\Theta(\frac{k-c}{a})$

converges to $\int \theta f_\Theta(\theta)\,d\theta \equiv E\Theta$ because $\theta f_\Theta(\theta)$ is Riemann–integrable. Furthermore, since $E\Theta = 1$ we have:

$$|J(t)| = \left| \sum_k \frac{k-c}{a^2} f_\Theta\left(\frac{k-c}{a}\right) - \sum_k \int_{(k-c)/a}^{(k+1-c)/a} \theta f_\Theta(\theta)\,d\theta \right|$$

$$\leq \frac{1}{a}\sum_k \left| \frac{k-c}{a} f_\Theta\left(\frac{k-c}{a}\right) - \theta_k f_\Theta(\theta_k) \right|;$$

with $(k-c)/a \leq \theta_k \leq (k+1-c)/a$. It follows that $J(t) \leq V(\theta f_\Theta(\theta))/a(t)$; therefore the speed of convergence of $J^*(t)$—and, due to Lemma A3 that of $Z^*(t)$ too—is bounded from above by $1/a(t)$.

The case where c_0 is not equal to a spike follows from the previous argument by conditioning on the value of c_0 and using the hypotheses according to which $E_{c_0} V(\theta f_\Theta(\theta)|c_0)$ is finite. ∎

Generalizations Propositions 3, 4 and 5 can be extended easily to the case where more than one source of heterogeneity is present using a conditioning argument analogous to the one we used at the end of Section A1. ∎

PROPOSITION A4. *Suppose that X and Y are independent random variables such that the density of X has bounded variation. Then the sup-distance between $(X + Y)(\mathrm{mod}\ 1)$ and a distribution U uniform on $[0, 1]$ is less than or equal to the sup-distance between $(X \bmod 1)$ and U.*

Proof. Let $f_X(u)$ and $f_{X+Y}(u)$ denote the densities of $X(\mathrm{mod}\ 1)$ and $(X + Y)(\mathrm{mod}\ 1)$, and $F_Y(u)$ the cumulative distribution function of $Y(\mathrm{mod}\ 1)$. From Lemma A1 and the independence assumption it follows that $f_{X+Y}(u) = \int f_X(u - v)\,dF_Y(v)$. Hence:

$$|f_{X+Y}(u) - 1| = \left| \int_0^1 f_X(u-v)\,dF_Y(v) - 1 \right|$$

$$= \left| \int_0^1 (f_X(u-v) - 1)\,dF_Y(v) \right|$$

$$\leq \int_0^1 |f_X(u-v) - 1|\,dF_Y(v)|$$

$$\leq \int_0^1 R(X(\mathrm{mod}\ 1), U).$$

The desired conclusion follows by taking the supremum over all u in $[0, 1]$. ∎

Notes

We thank Roland Benabou, Olivier Blanchard, Andrew Caplin, Peter Diamond, Mohamad Hammour, Esteban Jadresic, Keith Head, Robert Porter, four anonymous referees and seminar participants at Columbia, MIT and Princeton for very useful comments. Ricardo Caballero acknowledges financial support from NSF through Grant SES-9010443.

1. Others have performed comparative statics experiments in models with no aggregate (continuous) shocks (e.g. Akerlof, 1979; Tsiddon, 1989).

2. Of course, studying the determination of the $x_i^*(t)$'s themselves can be, and has been, a topic in itself.

3. We assume that the (S, s) rules followed by units are given exogenously. This has two consequences. First, we do not consider the relation between the economy's aggregate behavior and the determinants of the (S, s) policies' optimal target and trigger points. This can be done easily, yet doing so is beyond the scope of this chapter. Second, the results we derive also apply in a broader class of problems, where (S, s) rules are not optimal but can be justified as either simple rules that approximate more complex first best rules or, perhaps equivalently, as arising from near rational behavior.

4. The only reason for having this assumption is that it simplifies some of the algebraic expressions. It is easy to work without it, as we did in preliminary versions of this chapter. For example, this implies that in the retail inventory problem z_i represents the inventory level in deviation from its long run average.

5. This assumption requires that the sum of changes in aggregate and idiosyncratic components always be positive: $\theta_i da(t) + dv_i(t) \geq 0$. We assume that $a(t)$ grows sufficiently fast—compared to the rate at which idiosyncratic shocks disperse—for this assumption to hold. On some occasions, however, calculations are simpler if we consider distributions generating idiosyncratic shocks that have infinite tails. Our model is appropriate in this case if the fraction of units violating the monotonicity assumption is small.

6. The monotonicity assumption is appropriate in the inventory problem when returns are dominated by new sales and the holding cost does not vary much; in the pricing problem, when core inflation is sufficiently large; in the cash balance problem, when expenditures dominate the interest rate variability; and in the technology, consumer durables, and investment problems, when the obsolescence and depreciation rates dominate the uncertainty faced by firms and consumers.

7. To reconstruct $X(t)$ based on $Z(t)$ we need to know the value of $a(t)$. This is usually obtained from a theoretical model for the frictionless economy.

8. Note that Θ and Λ do not have time subindices, indicating that units' sensitivity parameters and bandwidths do not change over time.

9. The 1^- is used in place of 1 to remind us that there are no units with $c_i(t) = 1$, since this is a trigger point. Strictly speaking, this notation is unnecessary since the density of an absolutely continuous random variable is determined up to a set of Lebesgue measure zero. What we have in mind is a continuous version of this density.

10. This assumes that all sensitivity parameters are the same across units. The expression for $J(t)$ is extended to the general case as follows. We apply the argument given in the text with the density of c_t conditional on the value of Θ instead of f_{c_t}, and take expectation with respect

to Θ, concluding that $J(t) = E_{\Theta}[\theta f_{(c_t|\Theta=\theta)}(1^-)] - 1$. The assertion that $J(t_0) = 0$ does not imply that $J(t)$ remains equal to zero is still valid.

11. Considering suprema in the definitions above is just one possible choice. We could work with a weighted average—over all possible values of $a \geq a(t)$ and $s \geq t$—where the weights reflect the likelihood of different sample paths of the common shock and the time discount rate.

12. Strictly speaking, we should consider higher derivatives of $Z(t)$ with respect to $a(t)$; we do not see any economic motivation for doing this.

13. The total variation of a function $f(x)$ is equal to $\sup \sum_k |f(x_{k+1}) - f(x_k)|$, where the supremum is taken over all finite increasing sequences $x_1 < x_2 < x_3 < \cdots$. It follows directly from this definition (see e.g. Proposition 3.4 in Engel, 1992) that the total variation of a unimodal function is equal to twice the maximum value it attains. More generally, if $f(x)$ is piecewise continuously differentiable, with jumps of absolute magnitude $\delta_1, \delta_2, \ldots$, then its total variation is equal to $\sum \delta_k + \int |f'(x)| \, dx$.

14. Formally:

$$R(c_s, U) = \sup_A \left| \frac{\Pr\{c_s \in A\}}{\Pr\{U \in A\}} - 1 \right|,$$

where the supremum is taken over all Borel sets with positive Lebesgue measure. The proof may be found in Caballero and Engel (1989a).

15. We have limited our attention to cases where the economy converges to the steady state, but the same approach can be used when this does not happen. In Caballero and Engel (1989b) we show that when the $v_i(t)$'s are stationary, the synchronizing features of large aggregate shocks can only be partially undone by stationary idiosyncratic shocks.

16. Given a random variable X, the real and imaginary parts of its first Fourier coefficient are equal to the expected value of $\cos(2\pi X)$ and $\sin(2\pi X)$. Since the sine and cosine functions are periodic, these expectations are equal to those of $\cos(2\pi X(\mathrm{mod}\ 1))$ and $\sin(2\pi X(\mathrm{mod}\ 1))$ and therefore measure how near to a uniform distribution the random variable X is after being folded back onto the unit interval.

17. When we say that $g(t)$ converges to zero at the same rate as a positive decreasing function $h(t)$, we mean that

$$0 < \lim_{t \to +\infty} \left(\limsup_{u \geq t} |g(u)|/h(t) \right) < +\infty.$$

18. Looking at a particular example—say, $c_0 \equiv 0$, $\Lambda \equiv 1$ and Θ uniform on $[1/2, 3/2]$-helps building the intuition behind how convergence takes place in this case. Since such an analysis is entirely analogous to the one we made in Section 5.1, we omit it.

19. A similar phenomenon takes place for $Z^*(t)$.

20. The argument given above assumes that units' idiosyncratic shocks are independent from their bandwidths. If v_t and Λ are correlated, the perverse effect described above may still happen. One exception, though, is when the $v_i(t)$'s are identically distributed except for a scale parameter that is proportional λ_i; in this case adding idiosyncratic shocks to differences in bandwidths always speeds up convergence. This follows from Proposition A4 and the Glivenko–Cantelli Theorem.

21. This step is based on Fubini's Theorem. It is here where we use the assumption that the Fourier coefficients of X are summable.

22. If $\Lambda \equiv \lambda$ we let v_t/λ play the role of v_t.

References

Akerlof, G. A.: "Irving Fisher on his Head: The Consequences of Constant Threshold-Target Monitoring of Money Holdings," *The Quarterly Journal of Economics*, 93-2 (1979), 169–187.

Arrow, K. J., T. Harris, and J. Marshack: "Optimal Inventory Policy," *Econometrica*, 19 (1951), 250–272.

Benabou, R.: "Optimal Price Dynamics and Speculation with a Storable Good," *Econometrica* 57-1 (1989), 41–81.

Billingsley, P.: *Probability and Measure*, 2nd Ed. John Wiley, New York, 1986.

Blanchard, O. J., and S. Fischer: *Lectures on Macroeconomics*, Cambridge, Mass.: MIT Press, 1989.

Blinder, A. S.: "Retail Inventory Investment and Business Fluctuations," *Brookings Papers on Economic Activity*, 2 (1981), 443–505.

Butzer, P. L., and R. J. Nessel: *Fourier Analysis and Approximation Vol. 1 One-Dimensional Theory*, Academic Press, New York, 1971.

Caballero, R. J., E. M. R. A. Engel: "The S-s Economy: Aggregation, Speed of Convergence and Monetary Policy Effectiveness," Columbia Univ. Working Paper #420, (1989a).

Caballero, R. J., and E. M. R. A. Engel: "Heterogeneity and Output Fluctuations in a Dynamic Menu Cost Economy," Columbia Univ. Working Paper #453, (1989b).

Caballero, R. J., and E. M. R. A. Engel: "Dynamic (S, s) Economies: Aggregation, Heterogeneity and Coordination," Columbia Univ. Working Paper #476, (1990).

Caplin, A. S.: "The Variability of Aggregate Demand with (S, s) Inventory Policies," *Econometrica*, 53 (1985), 1395–1410.

Caplin, A. S., and E. Sheshinski: "Optimality of S, s Pricing Policies," mimeo (1987).

Caplin, A. S., and D. Spulber: "Menu Costs and the Neutrality of Money," *Quarterly Journal of Economics*, 102-4 (1987), 703–725.

Caplin, A. S., and J. Leahy: "State-Dependent Pricing and the Dynamics of Money and Output," Columbia WP #448, October (1989).

Engel, E. M. R. A.: *A Road to Randomness in Physical Systems*, Lecture Notes in Statistics, Springer Verlag, New York, 1992.

Ehrhardt, R. A., C. Schulz, and H. Wagner: "(s, S) Policies for a Wholesale Inventory System," in Schwartz, L. B. (ed.), *Multi-Level Production/Inventory Control Systems: Theory and Practice*. Amsterdam: North Holland, 1981, 145–161.

Karlin, S., and A. Fabens: "A Stationary Inventory Model with Markovian Demand," Chapter 11 in *Mathematical Methods in the Social Sciences*, ed. by K. J. Arrow, S. Karlin and P. Suppes. Stanford: Stanford University Press, 1959.

Scarf, H. E.: "The Optimality of (S, s) Policies in the Dynamic Inventory Problem," Chapter 13 in *Mathematical Methods in the Social Sciences*, ed. by K. J. Arrow, S. Karlin and P. Suppes. Stanford: Stanford University Press, 1959.

Sheshinski, E., and Y. Weiss: "Inflation and Costs of Price Adjustment," *Review of Economic Studies*, 44 (1977), 287–303.

Sheshinski, E., and Y. Weiss: "Optimum Pricing Policy under Stochastic Inflation," *Review of Economic Studies*, 50 (1983), 513–529.

Tsiddon, D.: "The (Mis)Behavior of the Aggregate Price Level," mimeo (1989).

11 State-Dependent Pricing and the Dynamics of Money and Output

Andrew Caplin and John Leahy

I. Introduction

There is a long tradition in macroeconomics of attributing the real effects of nominal demand shocks to nominal price stickiness. In this view, if there is no change in prices when nominal demand rises, then quantities must bear the burden of adjustment. Hence nominal price rigidity provides the friction needed for nominal demand shocks to be transmitted to the real economy.

Standard models of this transmission mechanism, such as Fischer [1977] and Taylor [1980], are based on the assumption that each firm leaves its price unchanged for a fixed amount of time. The main reason for considering such time-dependent pricing rules is their analytic tractability. Constraining firms to adjust their prices at prespecified times both simplifies the derivation of equilibrium strategies and allows the use of powerful time series techniques to analyze aggregate dynamics. The main disadvantage of the time-dependent approach is that between price adjustments firms are not allowed to respond even to extreme changes of circumstance. This makes it difficult to know whether the qualitative effects of money in these models are the result of nominal rigidities per se or of the exogeneously imposed pattern of price changes.

An alternative approach to modeling price stickiness is to allow the price-setting decision to depend on the actual state of the economy, not just the date.[1] Microeconomic models of state-dependent pricing were introduced by Barro [1972] and Sheshinski and Weiss [1977, 1983]. They derived optimal policies for a firm facing a fixed cost of adjusting its nominal price, and found these policies to be of the (s, S) variety: a firm should change its price discretely each time it deviates a certain amount from its optimal value.

As yet, little is known about the macroeconomic implications of state-dependent pricing. The best understood example is due to Caplin and Spulber [1987]. Their model reveals the surprising possibility that price stickiness may disappear altogether at the aggregate level. With a continuously increasing path of the money supply, one-sided (s, S) pricing rules and a uniform initial distribution of prices, shocks to the money supply feed immediately into prices, and nominal shocks have no real effects.

Caballero and Engel [1989] show that while the strict neutrality result is lost with arbitrary price distributions, the unconditional correlation between money and output remains zero. Beyond these special cases the macroeconomic implications of state-dependent price rigidity are not well understood.[2]

In this chapter we provide the first example of a dynamic economy with state-dependent pricing in which monetary shocks have systematic effects on output. We find a method of aggregating individual price changes that allows a simple characterization of the money-output-price process when nominal shocks are symmetrically distributed. This characterization allows us to examine the statistical properties of the model. We confirm that some of the qualitative results of time-dependent models, such as a positive money-output correlation and an empirical Phillips curve, generalize to our state-dependent framework. Our model also has distinctive features. For example, we show that monetary expansion is more effective in expanding output when output is currently low, while monetary contraction is more effective in reducing output when output is currently high. Overall, the model points to a natural connection between state-dependent microeconomics and state-dependent macroeconomics.

We present the basic model in Section II. In Section III we use geometric reasoning to characterize the joint money-output-price process. Section IV addresses the contemporaneous relation between money and output. Section V establishes the existence of an empirical Phillips curve, and studies other features of the price process such as inflationary inertia. In Section VI we extend results of Caballero and Engel [1989] to rationalize an earlier assumption on the initial distribution of prices. Finally, Section VII discusses the sensitivity of the results to various alterations in the assumptions.

II. The Model

We follow Blanchard and Kiyotaki [1987] in focusing on a monopolistically competitive economy with fixed costs of price adjustment. There is a continuum of price-setting firms indexed by $i \in (0, 1]$. Each firm treats the current level and future evolution of the price index as independent of its own pricing decisions. At all times $t \geq 0$, the log of the price level, $p(t)$, is determined as the simple geometric mean of individual nominal prices:

$$p(t) = \int p_i(t)\, di. \tag{11.1}$$

The aggregate relationship between money, output, and prices is captured by the quantity equation:

$$m(t) = p(t) + y(t), \tag{11.2}$$

where $m(t)$ denotes the log of the money supply and $y(t)$ the log of output.

The final three components of the model are less standard and are given a fuller introduction below. The first assumption specifies the precise form of the monetary disturbance. The second assumption focuses on the pricing policies. The final assumption concerns the initial conditions.

The Money Supply Process

As in standard menu cost models, monetary disturbances are the only source of uncertainty.[3] Previous theoretical work on the aggregate implications of fixed adjustment costs has focused exclusively on the case in which the state variable changes in only one direction. In this chapter we provide a first approach to the case with two-sided shocks. We make the strong assumption that increases and decreases in the money supply are equally likely.

ASSUMPTION A1.   The process $m(t)$ is a Brownian motion with zero drift.

The consideration of symmetric shocks reflects a natural evolution in the macroeconomic literature on state-dependent pricing and parallels the development of the original microeconomic literature. The (s, S) inventory model of Arrow, Harris, and Marschak [1951] involves a one-sided shock to the inventory. Similarly, the model of monopoly pricing with inflation due to Sheshinski and Weiss [1983] rules out deflation. Early models with nonmonotone shocks include the model of a firm's demand for money due to Miller and Orr [1966] and the model of monopoly pricing with cost shocks due to Barro [1972]. In both cases the underlying shock is modeled as a symmetric random walk.

The Strategies

Following Barro [1972] and Sheshinski and Weiss [1983], the standard approach to state-dependent pricing is to consider a firm that pays an explicit real resource cost each time it changes its nominal price. We adopt this "menu cost" approach, viewing it as a valuable shortcut in deriving sensible state-dependent pricing strategies.

When it is costly to change nominal prices, the optimal pricing policy must balance the loss due to nonadjustment against the cost of changing price. In static menu cost models the cost of nonadjustment is often captured by a profit function that depends on a linear combination of real balances and the relative price:[4]

$$(m - p) - b(p_i - p). \tag{11.3}$$

Here the level of real balances influences profits through its effect on the level of aggregate demand, while the relative price influences the division of aggregate demand among firms. Changes in the money supply affect profits directly through the level of real money balances and indirectly by inducing changes in relative prices.

In order to reduce the number of state variables, we consider the special case in which the effect of a change in the money supply on the firm's profitability is independent of the aggregate price level. In the static models this assumption corresponds to setting $b = 1$ in equation (11.3). In this case the effect of money is the same whether it is transmitted through a change in real balances or through a change in the price level, thus removing the firm's need to keep track of the price level as an independent state variable. The firm's profits and pricing strategy depend only on its price relative to the money supply. It is convenient to define firm i's state as

$$\alpha_i(t) \equiv m(t) - p_i(t), \tag{11.4}$$

so that in the absence of price adjustment, increases in the money supply cause the state variable increase.

Given that the firm's profitability depends only on α_i, we may impose enough symmetry and regularity on the profit function that the firm finds it optimal to pursue a symmetric two-sided (s, S) policy.

ASSUMPTION A2.   Each firm adopts a symmetric two-sided (s, S) strategy in the state variable $\alpha_i(t)$, adjusting it to zero each time $|\alpha_i(t)|$ reaches S.

We do not pursue the issue of optimality here and instead regard this assumption as a simple state-dependent alternative to time-dependent pricing rules.

While the reduction to a single state variable plays a valuable simplifying role, it can in fact be dispensed with. When real balances and relative prices influence profits separately, the price process will influence the firm's choice of strategies. Equilibrium requires consistency between the pricing strategies and price process to which they give rise. Although this is in general a difficult problem, the single state formulation points the way to an essentially identical model with two state variables. This extension is outlined in Section VII and is given a complete treatment in Caplin and Leahy [1991a].

The Initial Conditions

We close the model with a specific assumption on the initial distribution of prices across firms and the initial level of the money supply.

ASSUMPTION A3.   Initial nominal prices satisfy

$p_i(0) = (\frac{1}{2} - i)$.

The initial money supply $m(0)$ is a random variable distributed uniformly on $(-S/2, S/2]$.

Assumption A3 implies that at time $t = 0$ the α_i are distributed uniformly over an interval of length S which is randomly placed in the range $(-S, S]$. The most important feature of the assumption is that the initial distribution of nominal prices across firms is uniform on $(-S/2, S/2]$. Starting with the initial money supply uniform on $(-S/2, S/2]$ merely serves to start output off in its long-run distribution, as shown in Section III.

To understand the value of this assumption, it is instructive to contrast it with the case in which the initial distribution of nominal prices across firms is triangular on $(-S, S]$. This cross-sectional distribution is appealing because over the long run, individual prices spend more time near the return point than near the adjustment barriers.[5] The problem with the triangular distribution, however, is that as soon as there is a shock the distribution across firms is no longer triangular. For example, a reduction in the money supply will empty a region of the state space as the high α_i firm is pulled below S. Further analysis then requires the consideration of other cross-sectional distributions, so that tracking the evolution of the economy becomes tremendously complicated. In contrast, we show below that our initial distribution has an invariance property which greatly simplifies aggregate dynamics.

There are two arguments that support Assumption A3 in addition to its analytic convenience. In Section VI we show that these initial conditions arise as a natural limit in a series of models with idiosyncratic as well as common shocks. Furthermore, in Section VII we use A3 as a stepping-stone in the study of arbitrary initial conditions.

III.   The Money-Output-Price Process

In this section we provide a complete characterization of the joint money-output-price process. This characterization follows from one fundamental observation: with Assumption A3 the distribution of prices across firms remains forever uniform over an interval of length S.

To see this, picture the initial distribution of the α_i variables as an elevator of height S moving inside an elevator-shaft of height $2S$, as in Figure 11.1a. The elevator starts at a random position in the shaft. Until the elevator has either risen to the top or fallen to the base of the shaft, the nominal prices of all firms remain unchanged. During this time the elevator moves precisely with the money supply. Only when the elevator seeks to go through the top or the base of the shaft is its motion constrained.

It is when the elevator reaches one of the barriers that the invariance property is in evidence. For example, if the money supply decreases when the elevator is at the base, firms are simply rotated around the range $(-S, 0]$. The *distribution* of the α variables is unchanged, as in the one-

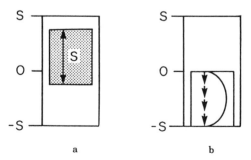

Figure 11.1

sided (s, S) story of Caplin and Spulber. The firms that lower their prices simply fill in the space vacated by firms pulled below the origin as in Figure 11.1b.

Note that the invariance property depends critically on the symmetry of the model. If price increases and decreases were of a different size, then the Brownian shocks would produce a continual and chaotic bunching and shattering of the price distribution.

The formal argument for the maintenance of uniformity in the symmetric case requires only that the path of the monetary process is continuous.

PROPOSITION 1.   Assume that A2 holds, that the variables $\alpha_i(0)$ are uniformly distributed over an interval of length S contained on $(-S, S]$, and that the path of the money supply is continuous. Then, at any given time $t \geq 0$, the variables $\alpha_i(t)$ remain uniformly distributed over an interval of length S contained in $(-S, S]$.

Proof.   First, we show that at any given time t, the distribution of $\alpha_i(t)$ taken modulo S is uniform. The proof is completed by showing that at any time t all values $\alpha_i(t)$ lie within a length S subset of $(-S, S]$.

With A2 all nominal price adjustments are of identical magnitude S. Since multiples of S are irrelevant to the modulo arithmetic, we arrive at the equation,

$$\alpha_i(t)(\text{mod } S) = [m(t) - p_i(t)](\text{mod } S)$$

$$= [m(t) - p_i(0)](\text{mod } S). \tag{11.5}$$

The distribution of $p_i(0)(\text{mod } S)$ across firms is uniform by assumption. Equation (11.5) guarantees that this uniformity property is inherited by the distribution of $\alpha_i(t)$, since the addition of the constant $m(t)$ does not disturb uniformity modulo S.

To complete the proof, we show that at any given time t, no two firm's real prices differ by more than S:

$$|\alpha_i(t) - \alpha_j(t)| \leq S \qquad \forall i, j \in (0, 1]. \tag{11.6}$$

This holds by assumption when $t = 0$. The only time that the difference between two firm's prices alters is when one of them changes its price. But at these times one firm adjusts to $\alpha_i(t) = 0$, so that equation (11.6) continues to apply.   Q.E.D.

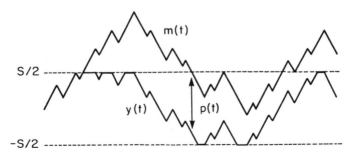

Figure 11.2

It is now straightforward to study the evolution of prices and output. From the quantity equation and the definitions of $p(t)$ and $\alpha_i(t)$, it follows that output corresponds to the mean of the distribution of the α_i variables:

$$y(t) = m(t) - \int p_i(t)\,di = \int \alpha_i(t)\,di.$$

With Proposition 1 the mean is simply the midpoint. To follow the output process, it is sufficient to keep track of the midpoint of the "price-elevator," as in Figure 11.2. Conversely, output is a sufficient statistic for the cross-sectional distribution of the state variables $\alpha_i(t)$, and hence for the overall state of the economy.

While all prices are in the interior of the range $(-S, S]$, changes in the money supply leave all nominal prices unchanged and feed directly into output. When output reaches $S/2$, the price elevator is at the top of the elevator shaft. Further increases in the money supply feed directly into prices and leave output unchanged, while decreases feed into output. When output is at $-S/2$, decreases in the money supply feed directly into prices, while increases feed into output. Formally, these properties define output as a regulated version of the money process, in the sense of Harrison [1985].[6]

PROPOSITION 2. Given the assumptions of Proposition 1, the output process is identical to the money process regulated at $S/2$ and $-S/2$.

Proof. It is immediate from Proposition 1 that $y(t)$ is always in the range $[-S/2, S/2]$. We define functions $u(t)$ and $l(t)$ as, respectively, the gross cumulative inflation and deflation in the aggregate price index up until time t. Note that $u(t)$ and $l(t)$ are increasing functions, and they also inherit continuity from $m(t)$. By the quantity equation,

$$y(t) = m(t) - p(t) = m(t) - u(t) + l(t).$$

Finally, it follows from Proposition 1 and Assumption A2 that increases in $u(t)$ require $y(t) = S/2$. Similarly, $l(t)$ increases only when $y(t) = -S/2$. Hence, $y(t)$ satisfies the conditions for a regulated process [Harrison, 1985, p. 22].   Q.E.D.

Proposition 2 places the analysis of money and output in a standard mathematical context: the theory of the regulated Brownian motion. An immediate implication is that the long-run distribution of output is uniform on $(-S/2, S/2]$.[7] This confirms that taking $m(0)$ to be uniform on $(-S/2, S/2]$ in Assumption A3 indeed starts the model in its long-run distribution. The fact that output is ergodic implies a form of monetary neutrality in the long run. This is, however, not the standard form of long-run neutrality in which the effect of an individual shock, as measured by an impulse response function, falls to zero as time passes. In our model, all shocks are permanent: in the absence of further shocks, the economy would remain forever at rest at the resulting level of output. It is only the cumulative effects of later shocks which ensure that expected output eventually returns to zero.

With Proposition 2 it is clear that output dynamics in this model are far more intricate than in the one-sided model. The model is a hybrid of the static menu cost model of Mankiw [1985] and the one-sided dynamic menu cost model of Caplin and Spulber [1987]. While output is in the interior of the range $[-S/2, S/2]$, small changes in the money supply feed directly into output, just as in the static model. The one-sided neutrality result emerges only at extreme levels of output. There is a clean separation between inflationary and noninflationary states of the economy.[8]

IV. The Interaction of Money and Output

We now turn to the statistical properties of the model. We show that our model with state-dependent pricing strategies produces novel predictions concerning the impact of money on the economy. In contrast to the one-sided model, there is a systematic relationship between monetary shocks and output: the overall correlation of money and output is positive. In

contrast to time-dependent models, the effect of money on the economy is
closely tied to the state of the economy, as reflected in the level of output.
For example, monetary expansion is more effective in expanding output
when output is currently low, while monetary contraction is more effective
in reducing output when output is currently high.

The relationship between output and the effects of monetary shocks
follows directly from an analysis of an arbitrary path of the money supply.
Figure 11.3 illustrates the paths of output associated with two different
initial levels of output. The figure shows that for a given path of the money
supply a higher level of initial output raises the entire path of output. The
paths associated with different levels of initial output may join, but they
can never cross. The figure also shows that the expected increment to
output is a decreasing function of the current output level, so that money
growth is less expansionary when output is already high. A higher initial
output both increases the cumulative amount of inflation and reduces the
amount of deflation. Geometrically, this corresponds to the declining distance between the output paths as time passes, so that an increase in initial
output leads to a less than one-for-one increase in final output. These
results are presented in Proposition 3.

It is useful to note that we lose no generality in fixing the initial time at
zero in the study of all correlations since we have started the model with
output in its long-run distribution.

PROPOSITION 3.   For a given path of the money supply, consider the paths
of output given two different initial output levels, $\tilde{y}(0) \geq y(0)$. Then at all
times $t \geq 0$, $\tilde{y}(t) \geq y(t)$, and $\tilde{y}(t) - \tilde{y}(0) \leq y(t) - y(0)$.

Another natural issue is the effect of money growth on expected future output. It appears reasonable that a higher rate of money growth
will result in a higher level of output. However, this is not universally

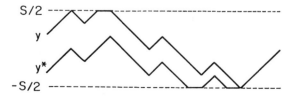

Figure 11.3

true. Note that a given change in the money supply over any period, $m(t) - m(0) \equiv \Delta m(t)$, is consistent with many different *paths* of the money supply. It is readily confirmed that knowing the initial level of output and the change in the money supply is not enough to pin down the level of final output. Furthermore, Example 1 shows that it is possible to raise the *entire* path of the money supply and yet dramatically lower final output. If there is a relationship between money and output, it is certainly not apparent from the analysis of isolated paths of the money supply.

EXAMPLE 1.   Given $y(0)$, consider the following two alternative paths for the money supply. In the first case the money supply m increases monotonically by an amount S between 0 and t, so that $y(t) = S/2$. In the second case the money supply m^* initially rises more rapidly: the maximal increase exceeds $2S$. Having risen monotonically to this maximum, m^* then decreases monotonically by S. Final output in this case is at a minimum $y^*(t) = -S/2$, despite the fact that this path lies everywhere above the first path, as in Figure 11.4.[9]

In spite of the possibility of a perverse relationship between money and output on individual paths, there is a simple overall statistical relationship. By averaging across paths, we show that larger increases in the money supply are associated with larger increases in output. This result is stated in Proposition 4. The proof makes heavy use of probabilistic reasoning, and is presented in Caplin and Leahy [1991b].

PROPOSITION 4.   For all $t \geq 0$ the conditional expectation of output, given initial output and the change in the money supply, $E\{y(t)|y(0), \Delta m(t)\}$ is increasing in $\Delta m(t)$.

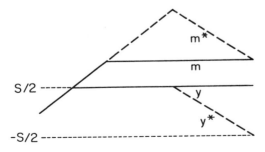

Figure 11.4

Proposition 4 allows an easy demonstration that the correlation between money and output is positive.

PROPOSITION 5.   The correlation between money and output is positive:

$\rho(y(t), \Delta m(t)) > 0.$

Proof.   Since $Ey(t) = E\Delta m(t) = 0,$

$\text{cov}(y(t), \Delta m(t)) = Ey(t)\Delta m(t)$

$$= E\{\Delta m(t) \cdot E\{y(t)|\Delta m(t)\}\}.$$

Note that $E\{y(t)|\Delta m(t)\}$ is increasing in $\Delta m(t)$, since the result in Proposition 4 survives when we remove the conditioning on the initial level of output. In addition, as a direct consequence of the symmetry of the model, $E\{y(t)|\Delta m(t) = 0\} = 0$. It follows that $E\{y(t)|\Delta m(t)\}$ has the sign of $\Delta m(t)$, establishing the result.   Q.E.D.

While the results in this section are derived for a very special model of state-dependent pricing, this is a general moral. State-dependent policies tend to produce state-dependence in the effect of macroeconomic shocks. Testing such models will require nonlinear estimation techniques in which the estimated parameters are allowed to depend on the state of the economy.

V.   Prices and Output

In continuous time the price level increases only when output is at its maximum value. This is reminiscent of the old-style Keynesian treatment of prices, with inflation occurring only at "full employment." Due to the accumulation of shocks, however, the discrete time data will not reveal such a simple relation. High *net* inflation over a discrete time period does not necessarily imply high output. For example, if money rises monotonically by some multiple of S and then falls by S, output will be at a minimum even though only price increases have been observed.

Once again, a probabilistic approach clarifies the issue. Proposition 6 establishes that the sign of the coefficient in a regression of output on inflation is positive, implying the presence of an empirical Phillips Curve. This result is proved in Caplin and Leahy [1991b].

PROPOSITION 6.   The correlation between inflation and output is positive:

$\rho(y(t), \Delta p(t)) > 0$.

A second important issue is the presence of inflationary inertia. Even though shocks to the money supply are independent and identically distributed over time, changes in the price level follow a far more complex pattern. In fact, the inflation rate displays positive autocorrelation, since inflation during period $t - 1$ is associated with above average final output $y(t - 1)$, which in turn makes inflation more likely in period t. Hence there are both inflationary and deflationary spells in the economy.

Finally, the model also has implications for the much investigated topic of the relationship between inflation and relative price variability. Note that the steady state distribution of $p_i - p$ is uniform over $(-S/2, S/2]$. Thus, the relative price formula is identical to that found for the one-sided model of (s, S) aggregation. This implies, for example, that in widely separated observations the variance of individual inflation rates around the economywide inflation rate approaches $S^2/6$ [Caplin and Spulber, 1987, pp. 717–18].

VI.   Convergence

In this section we provide some justification for the assumption that the $\alpha_i(0)$ are distributed uniformly over an interval of length S. We show that this distribution arises as a natural limiting case in models with idiosyncratic as well as common shocks.

We introduce the idiosyncratic shock in a way that does not alter the economic environment from the individual firm's perspective. Let $x_i(t)$ be an idiosyncratic shock to the profits of firm i, and suppose that firms' profits depend on the new state variable $z_i(t)$.

$z_i(t) \equiv m(t) - p_i(t) + x_i(t)$.

We assume that all idiosyncratic shocks and the money process are independent, mean zero Brownian motions. We further assume that the infinitesimal variance of the idiosyncratic shocks is ε^2, and that of the money supply is $\sigma^2 - \varepsilon^2$. Standard results on the Brownian motion then ensure that the evolution of $z_i(t)$ does not depend on the variance of the idiosyncratic shock. We therefore assume that the firm's pricing policy is to adjust $z_i(t)$ to zero when it deviates by S, regardless of the size of the idiosyncratic shock.

We are interested in the long-run behavior of the distribution of the $z_i(t)$ across firms. In Proposition 7 we show that for small enough values of ε the cross-sectional distribution of the $z_i(t)$ converges over time to a distribution arbitrarily close to a uniform distribution with support of length S.[10] The proposition is proved in the Appendix.

PROPOSITION 7. Assume that all firms pursue symmetric (s, S) policies in the variables $z_i(t)$, and that the path of the money supply is continuous. Then for any given cross-sectional distribution of the $z_i(0)$ on $(-S, S]$, there are small enough values of ε and large enough values of t so that the cross-sectional distribution of the $z_i(t)$ is arbitrarily close to a distribution uniform over a range S within $(-S, S]$ with an arbitrarily high probability.

The demonstration of convergence follows from logic similar to that used in the proof of Proposition 1. There, in the absence of idiosyncratic shocks, uniformity of the distribution taken modulo S and a support of the distribution of length S were sufficient to prove the invariance property. To prove Proposition 7, we show that each of these observations has an analog in models with idiosyncratic shocks.

While it is no longer true that the distribution of the $z_i(t)$ taken modulo S is always uniform, the distribution of the $z_i(t) \pmod{S}$ does converge over time to the uniform distribution irrespective of the size of the idiosyncratic shock. This result follows directly from an adaptation of Theorem 1 of Caballero and Engel [1989, p. 14]. They show that in a one-sided (s, S) model the cross-sectional distribution approaches uniformity over $(0, S]$ in the long run for all values of ε. Our two-sided model taken modulo S is equivalent to their one-sided model. In both models all changes in price are of size S and are therefore irrelevant to the distribution taken modulo S.

In the absence of idiosyncratic shocks, the only force affecting the distance between nominal prices was price adjustment, which itself placed all firms within S of one another. While price adjustment still pulls firms together in the present case, the idiosyncratic shocks tend to pull them apart. We can no longer guarantee that all firms lie within a range S. Lemma 2 in the Appendix, however, shows that with a small enough idiosyncratic shock we can ensure that most of the time most of the firms lie within a range close to S. Lemma 2 points to an important source of nonneutrality in two-sided (s, S) models. Since adjustment is to some point in the interior of the range of inaction, common shocks tend to group firms together. This suggests that the more important the common shock, the greater is the bunching and the greater is the nonneutrality of money.[11]

VII. Relaxing the Assumptions

We now consider the consequences of relaxing the assumptions of Section II. We show that many of the characteristics of the basic model survive in richer settings.

The Initial Conditions

When we allow for nonuniform price distributions, output is no longer a regulated Brownian motion, but is instead the sum of a regulated Brownian motion and an independent error term. Thus, alternative initial conditions simply add noise to the output dynamics.

To see this, first note that the assumption that the support of the initial distribution is of length S is innocuous. Without idiosyncratic shocks there is no force other than price adjustment that affects the difference between two firms' prices, and this always works to bring these prices within S of one another. After all firms have adjusted their price once, all the α_i will always lie in an interval of length S.

We may now confine our attention to initial distributions on $(0, S]$.[12] We wish to compare the output dynamics associated with an arbitrary initial distribution to the output dynamics under the uniform distribution.

Once again, a geometric approach is illuminating. Since both distributions have a support of length S, we may superimpose them in the elevator shaft of Figure 11.1 and analyze their evolution under a specific path of the money supply. Let $y^*(t)$ denote output with the new initial distribution, and let $y(t)$ denote output under the uniform initial distribution. In each case output is equal to the mean value of the respective α distribution. While the distributions are in the interior of the shaft, money supply shocks affect $y(t)$ and $y^*(t)$ equally. At the top and the bottom of the shaft price adjustment occurs. Price adjustment leaves $y(t)$ constant, but changes $y^*(t)$ by rotating the distribution of prices.

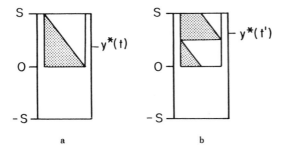

Figure 11.5

Figure 11.5 illustrates output dynamics in the nonuniform case. The density of firms at prices inside the lift is represented by the amount of shading. At both times t and t' the price-lift is at the top of the shaft. The only difference is that the distribution has been rotated by an amount $S/2$ between t and t'. As a result, $y^*(t)$ has risen, while $y(t)$ has remained at $S/2$.

In general, the difference between $y(t)$ and $y^*(t)$ is a function of the amount by which the initial density has been rotated:

$$y^*(t) - y(t) = f(r(t)).$$

Here the rotation is captured by the relative position of the firm initially at the base of the distribution, which we denote by $r(t)$.

The next result formalizes the sense in which arbitrary initial distributions add noise to $y(t)$.

PROPOSITION 8.   In the long run, $E\{f(r(t))|y(t)\} = 0$.

Proof.   Let $G(a)$ denote the initial distribution on $a \in [0, S)$. Then in the long run,

$$E\{f(r(t))|y(t)\} = E\{y^*(t)|y(t)\} - y(t)$$

$$= E\left\{\int_0^{S-r(t)} (a + r(t)) \, dG(a)\right.$$

$$\left. + \int_{S-r(t)}^S (a + r(t) - S) \, dG(a)\right\} - \frac{S}{2}$$

$$= Ea + Er(t) - ES(1 - G(S - r(t))) - \frac{S}{2}.$$

Since the long-run distribution of $r(t)$ is independent of $y(t)$ and is uniform on $(0, S]$, the second term in the final expression is $S/2$. A straightforward change of variable shows that the third term equals the mean of a.   Q.E.D.

Proposition 8 shows that in the long run $y^*(t)$ is a mean-preserving spread of $y(t)$. Not only does this result imply that $y(t)$ may provide a good approximation for $y^*(t)$, but it also allows us to apply many of our earlier results directly to arbitrary distributions. For example, altering the initial distribution does not alter the correlation of money and output, since in the long run the added noise in output is independent of the money supply.[13]

The Money Supply Process

Recent developments in the microeconomic literature on fixed adjustment costs point to possible future developments in the literature on aggregation. There is an emerging literature on optimal control against asymmetric two-sided processes.[14] Frequently, the optimal strategy is to adjust the state variable to an intermediate level from asymmetrically placed upper and lower boundaries. While this strategy is closely related to the symmetric strategy, the loss of symmetry makes distributional dynamics prohibitively complex. This undermines our ability to track macroeconomic aggregates analytically. Fortunately, there are important topics that can be understood without explicit reference to the distribution of prices.

For example, consider the covariance between changes in the money supply and output:

$$E\{y(t)\Delta m(t)\} = E\{(m(t) - p(t))\Delta m(t)\}.$$

Note that since $m(t) - p(t) = \int_0^1 \alpha_i(t)\, di$, it follows by Fubini's theorem that,

$$E\{y(t)\Delta m(t)\} = E\{\alpha_i(t)\Delta m(t)\}. \tag{11.7}$$

Hence the covariance between money and α_i is the same as the covariance between money and output. We may therefore be able to calculate the covariance between money and output from firm data even though we are unable to characterize the output process.

Note that this approach can only work in the case with a single state variable. With two state variables one cannot escape the need to follow the

entire distribution of prices over time, since this determines the evolution
of the price level and hence influences the choice of strategies.

The Single State Variable

So far, we have avoided the potentially separate influence that real balances and relative prices may exert on the firm's pricing decision. Allowing
$m - p$ and $p_i - p$ to play distinct roles appears to require a fundamental
change of perspective. We must now face head-on issues such as the determination of complex strategies in two state variables and the consistency
between these strategies and the resulting price processes. Our single state
model, however, provides a shortcut.

We first examine why the model as it stands is not well suited to the
presence of two state variables. When a firm is only concerned with the
future evolution of the money supply, the economy always looks the same
at all points of price adjustment. The firm therefore chooses the same
value of α_i regardless of whether it is increasing or decreasing its price. But,
with the firm interested in both the money supply and the price level, it no
longer makes sense for the firm to choose the same value of α_i when
increasing and decreasing its price, since in the former case the firm is
expecting inflation, while in the latter deflation.

The simplest alteration in the basic model that incorporates these considerations is to assume a constant size of price adjustment, which we shall
denote by D, and an initial distribution of prices that is uniform over an
interval of length D. These amendments preserve the invariance property
of the original model, and hence the simple characterization of the joint
money-output-price process. The only difference from the earlier analysis
is that the price-lift need not be half the length of the shaft, as illustrated
in Figure 11.6.

These simple amendments are indeed consistent with a separate role for
real balances and the relative price. This is confirmed in Caplin and Leahy
[1991a]. Here we provide a sketch of the argument. Under general conditions the firm with the highest relative price, $D/2$ will be the first firm
to lower its price. For any given beliefs concerning the probability law
governing the future evolution of money and prices, there is a critical value
of $(m - p)^*$ that will trigger this firm to adjust its price. Equilibrium requires only that expectations are rational and that the size of the price
adjustment precisely equals D. The invariance property then ensures that
all firms will act in an identical fashion when theirs is the highest relative

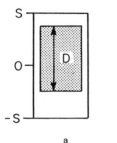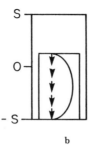

Figure 11.6

price, while symmetry ensures that the same arguments apply for the firm with the lowest real price.

Thus, there is a substantively identical model consistent with real money balances and relative prices having separate influences on profits. In equilibrium, output is a regulated Brownian motion with range $2(m - p)^*$, and the price level is the difference between m and y. All the Propositions in Sections III–VI of the chapter apply without alteration. Allowing for two state variables complicates the microeconomics, but leaves the macroeconomics intact.

VIII. Concluding Comments

We construct a simple dynamic menu cost model in which monetary disturbances have real effects. In our example money is a Brownian motion, and output is a regulated Brownian motion. This characterization allows us to fully analyze the interaction between money, prices, and output. As in static menu cost models, the proximate cause of nonneutrality is the bunching of firms' real prices. When all agents' real prices are close together, there will be long periods in which the price level does not change in response to monetary disturbances.

There are now two macroeconomic models with state-dependent pricing with radically different implications for aggregate price inertia. In contrast to the symmetric two-sided (s, S) model considered here, money and output are unrelated in the one-sided model of Caplin and Spulber [1987]. It is remarkable that the presence or absence of neutrality hinges on such an apparently orthogonal issue as the one-sided or two-sided nature of the shocks. The basic difference is that in the two-sided model a prolonged fall in the money supply ensures that all firms will be in the lower half of the state space. In the one-sided story there is no pattern of monetary disturbances that coordinates prices in this way.

The model also shows that state-dependent pricing models imply aggregate dynamics very different from those encountered in time-dependent models. In time-dependent models, the evolution of output is often captured by an ARMA process in which the coefficients on the shocks are constant over time. With state-dependent pricing the effect of money on output will depend on the state of the economy. In our model increases and decreases in the money supply have different effects depending on whether output is high or low. At higher output levels the expansionary effects of increases in the money supply are diminished, while the contractionary effects of decreases in money are enhanced.

The techniques and results of this chapter can be developed in several directions. For example, the model may be used to analyze such issues as the connection between the variance of monetary growth and the slope of the Phillips curve, investigated in Lucas [1973]. In addition the techniques we use to analyze the statistical properties of the regulated Brownian motion can be applied to other areas in which transactions costs play a role. These developments are contained in Caplin and Leahy [1991a, 1991b].

At a more general level our approach to dynamic macroeconomics discards the fiction of a representative agent. Instead, we view the economy as a collection of heterogeneous agents who allow their control variables to drift away from their optimal values. The important object of analysis is then the cross-sectional distribution of these control variables. In this chapter we find conditions under which the dynamic strategies of the individual agents aggregate to yield simple and interesting macroeconomic conclusions. It is clear that further study of distributional dynamics is vital in the many areas of macroeconomics in which transactions costs play a role.

IX. Appendix

Formal Treatment of Convergence

We now provide a formal proof of Proposition 7, which shows how the distribution in A3 arises as a limiting case in models with idiosyncratic shocks. To measure the distance between two distributions F and G, we use the variation distance,

$$d(F, G) = \frac{1}{2} \int_{-S}^{S} |f(x) - g(x)| \, dx,$$

where f and g denote the densities corresponding to F and G, respectively.

As in the proof of Proposition 1, two observations combine to give the overall result. The first, contained in Lemma 1, involves the distribution of $z_i(t)$ taken modulo S.

LEMMA 1.   At time t consider the distribution of $z_i(t)$, $i \in (0, 1]$, taken modulo S. For all $\varepsilon > 0$, this distribution converges over time to a distribution uniform on $(0, S]$.

Proof.   Apply Theorem 1 in Caballero and Engel [1989] to the z_i taken modulo S.   Q.E.D.

The second observation states that as we consider models with smaller and smaller idiosyncratic shocks, the bulk of the firms tend to gather within an interval of length S.

LEMMA 2.   For small enough values of ε and large enough values of t, there is an arbitrarily high probability that an arbitrarily large proportion of the firms have values of $z_i(t)$ within a range arbitrarily close to S.

Proof.   Fix α, β, and $\gamma \in (0, 1)$. We pick $\bar{\varepsilon}$ and $\bar{t}$ such that $\varepsilon < \bar{\varepsilon}$ and $t > \bar{t}$ imply that the probability that a proportion $(1 - \gamma)$ of the $z_i(t)$ lie within $S(1 + \beta)$ of each other is at least $(1 - \alpha)$.

To define $\bar{t}$, let $b(t)$ be a mean zero Brownian motion with infinitesimal variance $\sigma^2/2$ and $b(0) = 0$. We set $\bar{t}$ such that

$$\Pr\{\max |b(\bar{t})| > 2S + S\beta\} > 1 - \alpha. \tag{11.A1}$$

Note that $\bar{t}$ is finite almost surely.

To define $\bar{\varepsilon}$, we first choose $\hat{\varepsilon}$ so that

$$\Pr\left\{ \max_{t \in (0, \bar{t})} |x(t)| < \frac{S\beta}{4} \right\} > 1 - \gamma. \tag{11.A2}$$

We then define $\bar{\varepsilon} \equiv \min\{\hat{\varepsilon}, \sigma/\sqrt{2}\}$.

We now consider an idiosyncratic shock of standard deviation $\varepsilon < \bar{\varepsilon}$ and a time $t > \bar{t}$ as prescribed. Since $\varepsilon < \sigma/\sqrt{2}$, the infinitesimal variance of the common monetary shock $m(t)$ is greater than $\sigma^2/2$. Our choice of $\bar{t}$ then implies that at all times $t > \bar{t}$,

$$\max_{s \in (0, \bar{t})} |m(t) - m(t - s)| > 2S + S\beta, \qquad (11.A3)$$

with probability greater than $1 - \alpha$.

On the set of paths for which inequality (11.A3) holds, the money supply has either risen or fallen by $2S + S\beta$ at some time in the interval $[t - \bar{t}, t]$. Thus, in the absence of idiosyncratic shocks all firms would lie within S of one another. The only forces that may prevent firms from being within S of one another are the idiosyncratic shocks. We use the fact that $\varepsilon < \bar{\varepsilon}$ to bound the amount of divergence caused by the idiosyncratic shocks.

Inequality (11.A2) shows that for any firm i,

$$\Pr \left\{ \max_{s \in (0, \bar{t})} |x_i(t) - x_i(t - s)| < \frac{S\beta}{4} \right\} > 1 - \gamma.$$

Since the idiosyncratic shocks are independent and identically distributed across firms, the Glivenko-Cantelli lemma implies that this inequality also applies to a proportion $1 - \gamma$ of firms.[15] Let $\mathscr{A} \subset [0, 1]$ be the set of firms for which

$$\max_{s \in (0, \bar{t})} |x_i(t) - x_i(t - s)| < S\beta/4. \qquad (11.A4)$$

To complete the proof, we show that for all firms i and j in $\mathscr{A}$, $|z_i(t) - z_j(t)| < S(1 + \beta)$ whenever (11.A3) holds.

In combination, inequalities (11.A3) and (11.A4) show that for all firms in $\mathscr{A}$, the variable z has traveled over a range larger than $2S$ over the period $[t - \bar{t}, t]$. Therefore, all firms in $\mathscr{A}$ have adjusted their price during this period. Given firms i and j in $\mathscr{A}$, consider the last time $\hat{t} \in [t - \bar{t}, t]$ at which one of them adjusted their price. Note that $|z_i(\hat{t}) - z_j(\hat{t})| \leq S$, and that in the period $(\hat{t}, t]$ only the idiosyncratic shocks have separated these firms. But inequality (11.A4) shows that the most the idiosyncratic shock has moved either of them since $\hat{t}$ is $S\beta/2$. They therefore lie within $S(1 + \beta)$ of one another at time t, and the proof is complete.   Q.E.D.

We are now in a position to prove the main result.

PROPOSITION 7.   Assume that all firms pursue symmetric (s, S) policies in the variables $z_i(t)$, and that the path of the money supply is continuous. Then for any given cross-sectional distribution of the $z_i(0)$ on $(-S, S]$, there are small enough values of ε and large enough values of t so that the cross-sectional distribution of the $z_i(t)$ is arbitrarily close to a distribution uniform over a range S within $(-S, S]$ with an arbitrarily high probability.[16]

Proof.   Fix α, $\delta \in (0, 1)$. We pick $\bar{\varepsilon}$ and $\bar{t}$ such that $\varepsilon < \bar{\varepsilon}$ and $t > \bar{t}$ imply that

$$\Pr\{d(F_t, G) < \delta\} > 1 - \alpha,$$

where F_t is the distribution of the $z_i(t)$ and G is a distribution uniform over a range S within $(-S, S]$.

We now pick positive numbers β, γ, and ξ, such that,

$$\beta/S + \gamma + \xi < \delta.$$

With Lemma 1 we find a time t_1 such that for $t > t_1$,

$$\int_0^S \left| f(x) + f(x - S) - \frac{1}{S} \right| dx < \xi.$$

With Lemma 2 we can find t_2 and $\bar{\varepsilon}$ such that for $t > t_2$ and $\varepsilon < \bar{\varepsilon}$ a proportion $1 - \gamma$ of the z_i lie in a range $S + \beta$ with probability $(1 - \alpha)$.

Let $\bar{t} = \max(t_1, t_2)$. We now confirm that for $t > \bar{t}$ and $\varepsilon < \bar{\varepsilon}$,

$$\Pr\{d(F_t, G) < \delta\} > 1 - \alpha.$$

Consider a realization in which at least $1 - \gamma$ of the z_i lie within a set of length $S + \beta$, which we denote as $(a, a + S + \beta]$. We shall compute the distance between F_t and the uniform distribution on $(a + \beta, a + S + \beta]$. Without loss of generality take $a = -\beta$.[17] In this case G is uniform on $(0, S]$, and $d(F_t, G)$ can be decomposed as

$$2d(F_t, G) = \int_{-S}^{-\beta} f(x)\, dx + \int_{-\beta}^{0} f(x)\, dx$$

$$+ \int_0^{S-\beta} \left| f(x) - \frac{1}{S} \right| dx + \int_{S-\beta}^{S} \left| f(x) - \frac{1}{S} \right| dx.$$

The first term is bounded above by γ, the maximum proportion of firms in the range $(-S, -\beta]$. The third term is bounded using the triangle inequality,

$$\int_0^{S-\beta} \left| f(x) - \frac{1}{S} \right| dx \leq \int_0^{S-\beta} f(x-S)\, dx + \int_0^{S-\beta} \left| f(x) + f(x-S) - \frac{1}{S} \right| dx$$

$$< \gamma + \xi,$$

where the second inequality follows from the γ population in $(-S, -\beta]$ and Lemma 1 which bounds the distance between the distribution of $z_i \pmod S$ and the uniform distribution. Finally, note from Lemma 1 that

$$\int_{S-\beta}^{S} \left| f(x) + f(x-S) - \frac{1}{S} \right| dx < \xi.$$

Hence we can place an upper bound on the total population in the union of the regions $(S - \beta, S]$ and $(-\beta, 0]$,

$$\int_{S-\beta}^{S} f(x) + f(x-S)\, dx < \xi + \frac{\beta}{S}.$$

To maximize $\int_{-\beta}^{0} f(x)\, dx + \int_{S-\beta}^{S} |f(x) - 1/S|\, dx$ subject to this population constraint, we place all the population in the region $(-\beta, 0]$ to arrive at

$$\int_{-\beta}^{0} f(x)\, dx + \int_{S-\beta}^{S} \left| f(x) - \frac{1}{S} \right| dx < \xi + \frac{\beta}{S} + \frac{\beta}{S}.$$

This completes the proof.   Q.E.D.

Notes

We thank Olivier Blanchard and Ricardo Caballero for valuable comments. We acknowledge research support from the Olin Foundation and from the Sloan Foundation.

1. Blanchard and Fischer [1989] discuss the distinction between time- and state-dependent pricing rules.

2. Tsiddon [1988] considers the impact of a once-and-for-all change in the rate of growth of the money supply. Blanchard and Fischer [1989] construct a two-period example with symmetric monetary shocks (see Section II).

3. For example, see Rotemberg [1982], Caplin and Spulber [1987], and Blanchard and Fischer [1989].

4. For example, see Blanchard and Kiyotaki [1987].

5. This distribution is the long-run state occupancy probability for a single firm following a symmetric two-sided (s, S) policy, and is employed by Blanchard and Fischer [1989, p. 411] in a two-period example.

6. There is an interesting analogy between multi-agent menu cost models and a model with a single price-setting agent facing a linear cost of adjusting prices. Just as in Figure 11.2, linear adjustment costs lead to a range of inaction and regulation at the boundaries. Note that the analogy applies equally to the one-sided case. Regulation against an increasing process leads to the state variable being kept at the top of the range: hence the nominal price adjusts precisely in line with money increases, as in Caplin and Spulber [1987].

7. See Harrison [1985, p. 90].

8. Of course, addition of realistic elements such as idiosyncratic shocks and heterogeneity in menu costs and alternative price distributions will soften the boundary between inflationary and noninflationary states. We consider some of these elements in Section VII.

9. This example illustrates why two-sided (s, S) policies are so much more complex than one-sided (s, S) policies. The process of averaging is trivial in the case of one-sided policies with a monotonic money supply, since knowledge of $\alpha_i(0)$ for all i, $m(0)$, and $m(t)$ fully determines all $\alpha_i(t)$, and therefore the level of output. Contrary to Example 1, output dynamics are not influenced by the path of the money supply between 0 and t.

10. We use the variation norm to measure the distance between densities f and g, $\frac{1}{2}\int_{-S}^{S}|f(x) - g(x)|\,dx$.

11. Our result is a limit result as the idiosyncratic shock is removed. The dynamic implications of two-sided (s, S) policies in the presence of both idiosyncratic and common shocks are studied in Bertola and Caballero [1990].

12. Assuming that this distribution has all of its mass at a single point corresponds to a single firm following a two-sided (s, S) policy, so that the following results naturally apply to a representative agent model.

13. A related result is shown by Caballero and Engel [1989] for the one-sided (s, S) model, p. 27.

14. For example, Dixit [1989], Grossman and Laroque [1990], and Harrison, Sellke, and Taylor [1983] consider the geometric Brownian motion. Tsiddon [1987] derives the stationary density for an individual firm's prices with an asymmetric two-sided (s, S) policy.

15. We adopt the conventional treatment in which a continuum of independent random variables is treated as an idealized limit of the large finite case.

16. This is a form of convergence in probability. Let ε_n and t_n denote any pair of sequences converging to zero and infinity, respectively. Define the random variable X_n as the distribution of the z_i at time t_n in a model in which the initial distribution is F_0 and the variance of the idiosyncratic shock is ε_n. We prove

$$\lim_{n \to \infty} \Pr\{d(X_n, \operatorname{argmin}_G d(X_n, G)) > \delta\} = 0,$$

where G is chosen from the class of distributions that are uniform over an interval of length S.

17. This choice simplifies the notation. The basic point is that there are three regions to consider: $(-S, a) \cap (a + S + \beta, S)$, $(a + \beta, a + S)$, and $(a, a + \beta) \cap (a + S, a + S + \beta)$. These regions correspond to the three cases considered below.

References

Arrow, K. J., T. Harris, and J. Marschak, "Optimal Inventory Policy," *Econometrica*, XIX (1951), 205–72.

Barro, R., "A Theory of Monopolistic Price Adjustment," *Review of Economic Studies*, XXXIV (1972), 17–26.

Bertola, G., and R. Caballero, "Kinked Adjustment Costs and Aggregate Dynamics," *NBER Macroeconomics Annual* (1990), pp. 237–295.

Blanchard, O., and S. Fischer, *Lectures on Macroeconomics* (Cambridge: MIT Press, 1989).

Blanchard, O., and N. Kiyotaki, "Monopolistic Competition and the Effects of Aggregate Demand," *American Economic Review*, LXXVII (1987), 647–66.

Caballero, R., and E. Engel, "The *S-s* Economy: Aggregation, Speed of Convergence and Monetary Policy Effectiveness," Columbia University Discussion Paper No. 420, 1989.

Caplin, A., and J. Leahy, "A Dynamic Equilibrium Model of State-dependent Pricing," mimeo, Harvard University, 1991a.

Caplin, A., and J. Leahy, "Statistical Properties of the Regulated Brownian Motion," mimeo, Harvard University, 1991b.

Caplin, A., and D. Spulber, "Menu Costs and the Neutrality of Money," *Quarterly Journal of Economics*, CII (1987), 703–25.

Dixit, A., "Entry and Exit Decisions under Uncertainty," *Journal of Political Economy*, XCVII (1989), 620–38.

Fischer, S., "Long-Term Contracts, Rational Expectations, and the Optimal Money Supply Rule," *Journal of Political Economy*, LXXXV (1977), 163–90.

Grossman, S., and G. Laroque, "Asset Pricing and Optimal Portfolio Choice in the Presence of Illiquid Durable Consumption Goods," *Econometrica*, LVIII (1990), 25–51.

Harrison, J. M., *Brownian Motion and Stochastic Flow Systems* (New York: Wiley, 1985).

Harrison, J. M., T. M. Sellke, and A. J. Taylor, "Impulse Control of Brownian Motion," *Mathematics of Operations Research*, VIII (1983), 454–66.

Lucas, R. E. "Some International Evidence on Output-Inflation Tradeoffs," *American Economic Review*, LXIII (1973), 326–34.

Mankiw, N. G., "Small Menu Costs and Large Business Cycles: A Macroeconomic Model of Monopoly," *Quarterly Journal of Economics*, C (1985), 529–39.

Miller, M., and D. Orr, "A Model of the Demand for Money by Firms," *Quarterly Journal of Economics*, XXC (1966), 413–35.

Rotemberg, J., "Monopolistic Price Adjustment and Aggregate Output," *Review of Economic Studies*, IL (1982), 517–31.

Sheshinski, E., and Y. Weiss, "Inflation and the Costs of Price Adjustment," *Review of Economic Studies*, XLIV (1977), 287–303.

Sheshinski, E., and Y. Weiss, "Optimum Pricing Policy under Stochastic Inflation," *Review of Economic Studies*, L (1983), 513–29.

Taylor, J., "Aggregate Dynamics and Staggered Contracts," *Journal of Political Economy*, LXXXVIII (1980), 1–24.

Tsiddon, D., "The (Mis)behavior of the Aggregate Price Level," mimeo, Columbia University, 1987.

Tsiddon, D., "On the Stubbornness of Sticky Prices," Hebrew University Working Paper No. 174, 1988.

V SEARCH AND THE WELFARE COSTS OF INFLATION

12 Search, Price Setting and Inflation

Roland Benabou

Introduction

Price dynamics in imperfectly competitive markets result from the interplay of sellers' and buyers' strategies. Understanding the microeconomic determinants of price setting and their welfare or macroeconomic implications—such as the role of frictions in monopolistic competition or the effects of inflation—therefore requires an analysis which incorporates the decision problems of both types of agents. With this in mind, this chapter brings together two hitherto separated, but highly complementary, strands of the imperfect competition literature, namely optimal price adjustment and search models.

In the literature on price dynamics, sellers, be they monopolistic competitors (Phelps and Winter (1970)), monopolists (Barro (1972), Sheshinski and Weiss (1977), (1982), Rotemberg (1980)), or oligopolists (e.g. Green and Porter (1984), Maskin and Tirole (1988), Gertner (1985), Rotemberg and Saloner (1985), Sheshinski and Weiss (1987)) are endowed with complex optimization problems and sophisticated strategies (optimal control, repeated or Markov games etc.), while the purchasing side of the market is generally oversimplified as an exogenous, instantaneous demand curve.[1] Conversely, the literature on consumer search has mostly ignored price dynamics (important exceptions are Diamond (1971) and Rothschild (1973)), concentrating instead either on characterizing optimal search rules in complex situations (with learning or bargaining, several markets etc.) but where the determination of prices is unspecified, or on obtaining price dispersion in a market equilibrium where price-setting is optimal but static (Rob (1985), Stiglitz (1985), von zur Muehlen (1980)) or follows some *ad hoc* dynamic rule ("experimental behaviour": Axell (1977)).

A more balanced model of a dynamic, imperfectly competitive market is constructed in this chapter, with a double objective: to shed light on certain market frictions underlying monopolistic competition, and to provide a theoretical basis for the empirical relationship linking higher inflation rates to increased price dispersion. It uses as an important building block the Sheshinski and Weiss (1977) model, which shows that a monopolist who must keep pace with inflation in the rest of the economy, but faces a fixed cost of changing his price, will optimally follow an (S, s) real price policy. In other words, he adjusts his nominal price so as to achieve a real value of S every time this real value has been eroded down to $s < S$. This result was established under two important and related assumptions, both of which substantially restrict the opportunity set of buyers: the first is that the good is not storable (so there is no possibility of buying at today's low real price instead of tomorrow's high real price), the second that there is no competition through customers searching between different firms (hence there is no possibility of buying from a firm charging a low real price instead of one charging a high real price).

Lifting either of these restrictions on substitution by buyers between purchases at different points of the (S, s) cycle yields important insights into the relationship between inflation and price uncertainty. In Bénabou (1989), storage is introduced, and the optimal price policy shown to be a stochastic (S, s) rule, where the bounds are state-dependent random variables, appropriately chosen to try and deter speculation. Inflation—even perfectly regular and anticipated—thus generates price uncertainty at the individual firm level. In the present chapter, consumer search is introduced and a causal relationship between inflation and another type of price uncertainty, namely the dispersion of prices which searchers face in the market, is established.

In equilibrium, firms find it optimal—given inflation and consumers' search behaviour—to follow (S, s) price rules, while consumer search is optimal given the price policies. Inflation generates price dispersion which makes search potentially profitable, thereby increasing competition, and this phenomenon generates many interesting comparative statics and dynamics results. For instance, the bounds S and s decrease, and price dispersion between them increases, with the rate of inflation and with price adjustment costs; higher consumer search costs, on the other hand, lead to higher equilibrium prices and allow more price dispersion. Indeed, the whole equilibrium varies continuously from the competitive (Bertrand) to the monopolistic (Diamond (1971)) end of the spectrum; the latter's paradoxical monopoly-price result is easily explained as the limit of a smoother, monopolistically competitive equilibrium—with optimal search, price dynamics and entry—when frictions on firms' side of the market (price adjustment costs) but not on consumers' (search costs) tend to zero.

The model is presented in Section 1, and the existence of a unique equilibrium (satisfying appropriate conditions) established in Section 2.

Section 3 examines the effects of frictions (search and adjustment costs) on the equilibrium, while Section 4 focuses on inflation and its relationship to price uncertainty. Finally, Section 5 discusses and relates the model's results to those of the existing literature. Most proofs are given in the appendix.

1. The Model

1.1. Tastes and Technologies

Firms: A homogeneous good is produced and sold by a continuum of identical and infinitely-lived firms, with discount rate r. Production (or presence in the market) involves a fixed cost of $h \geq 0$[2] units of labour per unit of time, and a constant marginal cost of c units of labour. Firms will thus enter or exit the market until the remaining ones' intertemporal profits (measured in terms of labour) are equal to h/r. The (endogenous) density of consumers per firm in the market will be denoted as $x \in (0, +\infty)$; an increase in x corresponds to the exit of firms, a decrease to the entry of new ones.[3] Firms can implement a change in their nominal price at any time, but such a decision is costly: goods must be relabelled, new price lists and catalogues must be printed and sent, etc. Following Barro (1972), Mussa (1976), Sheshinski and Weiss (1977), (1982) and Rotemberg (1983), it will be assumed that any price adjustment requires a fixed amount $\beta > 0$ of labour.[4]

Consumers During each interval of time of length dt, a continuum of consumers with total mass $1 \cdot dt$ enter the market, with a utility function:

$$U(y, l) = (L - l) + Z \min(y, 1)$$

where $L > Z > c$ is the individual's endowment of labour and y his consumption of the good, which can be thought of as a durable (only one unit is desired over a lifetime). Consumers do not know how much each seller charges and must therefore search for an acceptable price. Search is instantaneous (or requires a length of time of order smaller than dt)[5] and consumers cannot postpone their consumption; thus within dt they all search, buy and exit the market, to be replaced by a similar generation of "instantaneous" consumers an instant later. Costless recall of previous offers is allowed, but since utility is linear and there is no limit to the number of searches a consumer can conduct,[6] optimal search is the same with and without recall, as shown in Lippman and McCall (1976). A first price quotation is received for free,[7] but each subsequent search requires τ units of labour, with $0 < \tau < L - Z$.

1.2. Inflation and the Distribution of Prices

It will be assumed that the whole economy is on a steady inflationary path: all *aggregate* nominal quantities, and in particular the nominal opportunity cost of labour (which can be thought of as the wage on a competitive labour market), grow at a rate of $g > 0$. All real prices will be expressed in terms of labour. Unlike the cost of labour, any index of the prices charged by firms results from their endogenous strategies; these must therefore replicate, as an aggregate, the inflationary process in response to which they arose (consistent aggregation). Caplin and Spulber (1987) showed that (S, s) rules possess this important property; Lemma 1 below follows from a more general proposition of theirs:

LEMMA 1. *If a continuum of price setters follow identical (S, s) rules with respect to some index inflating at a constant rate g, the only cross-sectional distribution of their real prices which is invariant over time is log-uniform over $[s, S]$. Under this invariant distribution, any index of firms' nominal prices P_t^i which is of the form $G[\int w(P_t^i) \, di]$ and is homogeneous of degree one, grows at the rate of g.*[8]

In simpler terms, if firms' prices are initially distributed log-uniformly over $[s, S]$—equivalently, if their last price adjustment dates are uniformly distributed over $[-\mathrm{Log}(S/s)/g, 0]$—this will remain the case forever. The intuition behind these results is simple (for details and formal proofs, see Caplin and Spulber (1987)). The logarithm $\mathrm{Log}(p_t^i)$ of firm i's real price at time t is transformed at time $t + \delta$ (where $\delta < T \equiv \mathrm{Log}(S/s)/g$) into $\mathrm{Log}(p_t^i) - g\delta$ if $\mathrm{Log}(p_t^i) \in (\mathrm{Log}(s) + g\delta, \mathrm{Log}(S)]$, and into $\mathrm{Log}(p_t^i) + g(T - \delta)$ if $\mathrm{Log}(p_t^i) \in [\mathrm{Log}(s), \mathrm{Log}(s) + g\delta]$. Thus, time simply rotates, at the constant speed g, firms' log-real prices along the circle of circumference gT obtained by connecting the extremities of the segment $[\mathrm{Log}(s), \mathrm{Log}(S)]$. Such a rotation preserves the uniform distribution over the circle (and only this one), or equivalently the log-uniform distribution of real prices on $[s, S]$, and thus keeps constant any average of the type $\int w(p_t^i) \, di$.

1.3. The Equilibrium Concept

The equilibrium of the good's market is a fixed point: individual price rules generate a cross-sectional distribution, which in turn determines optimal search, hence demand and thereby optimal price strategies; finally, the density of participating firms must leave each of them with zero profits. More formally, an equilibrium will be defined by the following four conditions:

E1. Symmetric (S, s) Nash equilibrium in price strategies: given that all other firms follow a common (S, s) rule, and given consumers' search strategy, a firm's optimal price policy is that same (S, s) rule.

E2. Steady-state distribution: real prices are initially distributed over $[s, S]$ according to the invariant distribution (log-uniform).

E3. Optimal sequential search: consumers search optimally, given firms' price strategies.

E4. Free entry: each firm's real intertemporal profits are zero.

It should be noted that E1 only restricts attention to a specific class of equilibria (symmetric (S, s)), but within the most general price strategy space. As to condition E2, it is justified (or even required) by the following three arguments of optimality, macroeconomic consistency, and stability. As indicated by Lemma 1, the invariant distribution is the only one which is preserved over time by the combination of inflation and (S, s) policies. Any other initial conditions will lead to a time-varying distribution, generally resulting in non-stationary search and demand, which in turn destroy the optimality of an (S, s) rule. Even if such is not the case, a time-varying distribution of real prices implies that any aggregate index of firms' nominal prices does not grow at the constant rate g (in particular, if all firms start at the same price, they remain synchronized and any such index is discontinuous); thus, even if the market by itself can be in such an equilibrium, it cannot be a consistent component of a smoothly inflating economy. Finally, for any initial cross-sectional distribution of real prices, convergence to the steady-state distribution occurs (exponentially) if the bounds (S, s) differ slightly between firms (as mentioned in Caplin and Spulber (1987)), or are randomized so as to limit storage by speculators (as in Bénabou (1989)).[9] Related results arise in the literature on time-contingent price (or wage) adjustment (e.g. Fethke and Policano (1986),

Ball and Romer (1989)), showing that firm-specific shocks tend to make staggered (respectively, synchronized) price setting stable (respectively, unstable).

2. The Equilibrium

The distribution of real prices resulting from $E2$ is:

$$(\forall p \in [s, S]) \left(d\mu(p) = \frac{dp/p}{\text{Log}(S/s)} \right). \tag{12.1}$$

It will be convenient to measure the dispersion of prices in the market by $(S - s)/s = 1/\sigma - 1$, where $1/\sigma = S/s$ is the ratio of the highest to the lowest price, which is here equivalent to the standard measure of dispersion:

LEMMA 2.1.   *The coefficient of variation* $(\text{Var}[p])^{1/2}/E[p]$ *of the distribution* $d\mu$ *depends only on* $1/\sigma = S/s$, *and is a strictly increasing function of this variable.*

Proof.   See appendix.   ‖

2.1. Search and Demand

The equilibrium distribution $d\mu$ of real prices in the market is constant over time and known to searchers; optimal sequential search is therefore determined by a real cutoff price R: a consumer keeps searching until he encounters a real price no greater than R, where:[10]

$$R = \tau + E[\min(R, p)]$$

which expresses indifference between stopping when R is offered and doing one more search, with the possibility of coming back to R if a higher price is encountered. Equivalently:

$$\tau = E[R - \min(R, p)] = \int_s^{\min(R,S)} (R - p) \, d\mu(p). \tag{12.2}$$

A consumer's purchasing decision is thus characterized by his effective reservation price $Q = \min(Z, R)$, which is the minimum of the two cutoff prices Z and R, derived respectively from *preferences* and optimal *search*: he buys if and only if $p \leq \min(Z, R)$. Since consumers are identical, they have the same Z, R and Q. Moreover, when sampling stores, they do so at random, so that each firm is visited by the same number of searchers, and (the density of) demand per firm is therefore:

$$d(p) = x \cdot \mathbb{1}_{\{p \leq \min(Z,R)\}} \tag{12.3}$$

where $\mathbb{1}_{\{.\}}$ denotes the indicator function, equal to 1 if the inequality between brackets holds, and to zero otherwise.

2.2. The Firm's Optimization Problem

Together with adjustment costs, this stationary demand function determines the optimal price policy of individual firms (which take Q and x as given).[11]

THEOREM 2.1.   *Assume that $\beta \leq Qx/(r + g)$. The optimal price policy of a representative firm is an (S, s) rule with $S = Q$ and $s/S = \sigma^*(r, g, \beta/Qx)$, determined as the unique solution to:*

$$rV = x(s - c) = x(Q\sigma - c)$$

where V denotes real intertemporal operating profits, equal to:

$$V = \frac{\int_\sigma^1 x(Qu - c)u^{-1+r/g}\, du - \beta g}{g(1 - \sigma^{r/g})}.$$

Moreover, σ^* is continuously differentiable in all its arguments, and decreasing in β/Qx (resp. in g) from a limit of 1 (resp. of $1 - r\beta/Qx$) at zero. The firm operates and implements this policy if and only if $rV \geq h$, or: $\sigma^*(r, g, \beta/Qx) \geq (c + h/x)/Q$.

Proof.   See appendix.   ‖

An alternative parametrisation of s and V is provided by the periodicity of price adjustments $T \equiv \text{Log}(S/s)$:

$$V = \frac{\int_0^T x(Qe^{-gt} - c)e^{-rt}\, dt - \beta}{(1 - e^{-rT})}.$$

It is never profitable to overshoot the real reservation price Q: the adjustment cost would be postponed, but so would the whole path of net future revenues, which is larger ($V \geq h/r$). The optimality condition $x(s - c) = rV$ is also quite intuitive: delaying adjustment by dt brings a marginal revenue of $x(s - c)\, dt$, but the maximum valuation is achieved only after

dt, hence an opportunity cost of $rV\,dt$. Because of the adjustment cost, the real intertemporal profits resulting from the optimal policy are the same as those the firm would earn if it sold the good at its minimum real price of s forever ($V = x(s - c)/r$).

It should also be noted that when the inflation rate g converges to zero, the optimal time between adjustments $T^*(r, g, \beta/Qx)$ goes to $+\infty$, as suggested by intuition, but the ratio $s/S = \sigma^*(r, g, \beta/Qx)$ remains bounded away from 1. This is in fact a general, but previously unnoticed, feature of (S, s) models: for the seller to be willing to change his price, the increase in revenue gained by adjusting from s to S must be large enough to compensate for the discrete cost of adjustment. The implications of this phenomenon will be examined in Section 4.

Finally, in equilibrium, both Q and x are endogenous and influence each firm's price dynamics through the size of its sales relative to its adjustment cost (β/Qx). In particular, there is a crowding externality among firms: a lower x (entry) causes a more than proportional decrease in profits, because the optimal s also decreases, as a small market share is not worth frequent price adjustments (cf. Theorem 2.1).[12]

The existence and uniqueness of the equilibrium will now be established in two steps, to which the next two subsections correspond. First, implicit equations characterizing the two possible equilibrium configurations of S are derived. These are then brought together with the conditions expressing free entry and the optimality of individual price adjustments into a single implicit equation, which is finally solved.

2.3. Characterization of the Equilibrium

The density x of consumers and their effective reservation price Q determine firms' optimal price dynamics (cf. Theorem 2.1); the resulting bounds (S, s) in turn characterize the invariant price distribution which consumers use to compute their search cutoff price R, and finally $Q = \min(R, Z)$. This closes the fixed-point loop. Moreover, it is clear that an equilibrium can be one of two types, depending on whether price-setters' monopolistic power is effectively constrained by preferences ($Q = Z$) or by competition through search ($Q = R$).

A-binding Preferences   Assume first that $Z \leq R$. By Theorem 2.1, $S = Z$ and $s = Z\sigma^*(r, g, \beta/Zx)$. In such an equilibrium, firms are able to adjust their price to the maximum value $S = Z$ permissible by consumers' intrinsic willingness to pay for the good. This maximum price is below consumers' optimal cutoff price from search, R, so that no one engages in search. The optimal stopping rule (12.2) defining R becomes:

$$R = \tau + E[\min(R, p)] = \tau + E[p] = \tau + \int_s^S p \, d\mu(p)$$

$$= \tau + \frac{S - s}{\text{Log}(S/s)} = \tau + \frac{Z(1 - \sigma)}{\text{Log}(1/\sigma)}$$

which by assumption must be no smaller than Z, so that:

$$Z \leq \frac{\tau}{1 - (1 - \sigma)/\text{Log}(1/\sigma)}. \tag{12.4a}$$

Although this inequality implicitly depends on x and even Z (because $\sigma = \sigma^*(r, g, \beta/Zx)$), it gives the right intuition: preferences are binding in equilibrium when search costs are sufficiently large with respect to Z, and when price dispersion in the market ($1/\sigma$), which makes search attractive, is not too important (the R.H.S. of (12.4a) is increasing in σ). Note that for a given maximum price S, price dispersion $1/\sigma$ and the average real price $(S - s)/\text{Log}(S/s) = S(1 - \sigma)/\text{Log}(1/\sigma)$ are negatively related, so that the two search-inducing effects of a lower average price and increased dispersion coincide here.

B-binding Search   Assume now that $Z > R$. By Theorem 2.1, $S = R$ and $s = S\sigma^*(r, g, \beta/Sx)$. Firms can only adjust to a maximum real price $S = R < Z$, because any higher price would trigger search and result in zero demand. The optimal stopping rule now becomes:

$$S = \tau + E[p] = \tau + \frac{S - s}{\text{Log}(S/s)}$$

or

$$S = \frac{\tau}{1 - (1 - \sigma)/\text{Log}(1/\sigma)} < Z. \tag{12.4b}$$

Again, S and x are implicit in the middle term (because $\sigma = g^*(r, g, \beta/Sx)$), but (12.4b) correctly suggests that search is binding in equilibrium when search costs are not too large with respect to Z, and there is sufficient price dispersion in the market. For all positive S and x, denote:

$$\frac{1}{\theta(r, g, \beta/Sx)} \equiv 1 - \frac{1 - \sigma^*(r, g, \beta/Sx)}{\text{Log}(1/\sigma^*(r, g, \beta/Sx))}.$$

Then (12.4a) and (12.4b) can be summarized as:

$$S = \min\{Z, \tau\theta(r, g, \beta/Sx)\}. \tag{12.4c}$$

2.4. Existence and Uniqueness

In equilibrium, each firm chooses its minimum price $s = S\sigma$ (or equivalently, the timing of its adjustments) optimally, equating (by Theorem 2.1):

$$s = c + \frac{rV}{x} = \frac{rS\left[\int_{er}^1 u^{r/g} \, du - \beta g/Sx\right]}{g(1 - \sigma^{r/g})},$$

or

$$\sigma = \frac{r[1 - \beta(r + g)/Sx - \sigma^{1+r/g}]}{(r + g)(1 - \sigma^{r/g})}. \tag{12.5}$$

Moreover, entry or exit has taken place until the remaining firms' profits $V - h/r = (x(s - c) - h)/r$ are equal to zero, or:

$$s = c + h/x \tag{12.6}$$

Using (12.6) and $S = s/\sigma$ to eliminate S from condition (12.5) which expresses the *optimal timing* of price adjustments yields:

$$\Phi(\sigma, x) \equiv (r + g)\sigma - g\sigma^{1+r/g} - r\left[1 - \frac{(r + g)\beta\sigma}{cx + h}\right] = 0. \tag{12.7}$$

Similarly, (12.4c) which determines the type of the equilibrium, becomes:

$$\sigma = \max\left[\frac{c + h/x}{Z}, \frac{c + h/x}{\tau\theta}\right]. \tag{12.8}$$

By definition of θ, $\sigma = (c + h/x)/\tau\theta$ if and only if:

$$\tau\sigma = \left(c + \frac{h}{x}\right)\left(1 - \frac{1 - \sigma}{\text{Log}(1/\sigma)}\right),$$

so that *search is binding* in equilibrium when:

$$\Psi(\sigma, x) \equiv \frac{1 - \sigma}{\text{Log}(1/\sigma)} + \frac{\tau\sigma}{c + h/x} - 1 = 0. \tag{12.9}$$

The solutions to the implicit equations (12.7) and (12.9) will now be examined.

LEMMA 2.2.   *For all $x > 0$, there exists a unique $(\sigma_0(x), \sigma_1(x))$ in $(0, 1)^2$ such that $\Phi(\sigma_0(x), x) = 0$ and $\Psi(\sigma_1(x), x) = 0$. Moreover, σ_0 is strictly increasing, and σ_1 strictly decreasing, in x.*

Proof.   See appendix.   ‖

Since $\partial\Psi(\sigma, x)/\partial\sigma > 0$ (cf. proof of the Lemma), preferences are binding, i.e. $\sigma > (c + h/x)/\tau\theta$, or $\Psi(\sigma, x) > 0$, if and only if $\sigma > \sigma_1(x)$. The equilibrium conditions (12.7) and (12.8) are therefore equivalent to:

$$\sigma = \sigma_0(x) \tag{12.10}$$

$$\sigma = \max\{\sigma_1(x), (c + h/x)/Z\} \tag{12.11}$$

or finally, defining: $\sigma_2(x) \equiv (c + h/x)/Z$ and eliminating σ:

$$\sigma_0(x) = \max\{\sigma_1(x), \sigma_2(x)\}. \tag{12.12}$$

The curves σ_0, σ_1 and σ_2 are plotted on Figure 12.1. Since (12.6) was incorporated into each of them, they are iso (zero) profit lines, along which $rV = h$.

The σ_0 curve represents the optimal periodicity of price adjustments: entry (a lower x) increases a firm's adjustment cost relative to its market share (β/Sx), making less frequent adjustment—i.e. a lower σ—optimal; the curve is therefore upward sloping. The σ_2 curve represents the binding preferences condition ($S = Z$): for profits to remain constant in spite of entry (a decrease in x), the lower bound $s = c + h/x$ must increase; thus $\sigma = s/Z$ must also increase, so that σ_2 is downward-sloping. Finally, σ_1 represents the binding search condition ($S = \tau\theta$). Here again, entry's depressing effect on profits must be compensated by a higher s, here equal to $\tau\theta\sigma$. Hence σ must increase ($d\theta/d\sigma > 0$), and σ_1 also slopes downwards: more frequent adjustments reduce price dispersion and the potential for search, allowing firms to charge higher maximum $S = \tau\theta$ and minimum $s = \tau\sigma\theta$ real prices.

An equilibrium is an intersection (x^*, σ^*) of the increasing σ_0 and decreasing $\sigma_3 \equiv \max(\sigma_1, \sigma_3)$, of which there always is one and only one. Moreover, search is binding if and only if σ_0 cuts σ_1 above σ_2. Let $(\tilde{x}, \tilde{\sigma})$ be the intersection of σ_0 and σ_2 (equilibrium with binding preferences), and define:

$$\tilde{\tau} \equiv Z\left[1 - \frac{1 - \tilde{\sigma}}{\text{Log}(1/\tilde{\sigma})}\right]. \tag{12.13}$$

Thus $\tilde{\tau}$ is the unique value for which the σ_1 curve cuts σ_0 and σ_2 at their common point $(\tilde{x}, \tilde{\sigma})$ (cf. Figure 12.1), i.e. such that $S = Z = R$. As τ decreases below $\tilde{\tau}$, the σ_1 curve pivots up and cuts σ_0 above σ_2, so search is and becomes increasingly binding, with σ^* and x^* increasing (less price dispersion, exit of firms). As τ increases above $\tilde{\tau}$, on the other hand, the σ_1 curve pivots down, cutting σ_0 below σ_2; hence the solution x^* to $\sigma_0(x) = \sigma_3(x)$ remains equal to $\tilde{x}$ and σ^* to $\tilde{\sigma}$ (binding preferences). More formally:

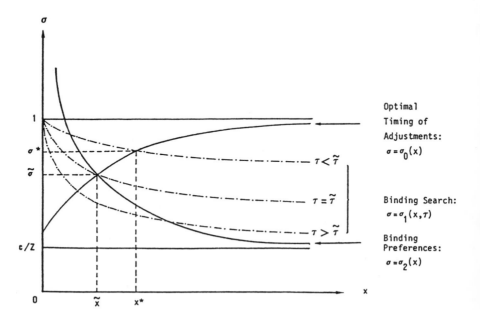

Figure 12.1
Determination of the equilibrium

THEOREM 2.2.   *There exists a unique market equilibrium, with a density* $1/x > 0$ *of firms following a common* (S, s) *pricing rule and earning zero profits. The real price bounds satisfy*:

$$S = \min\left\{Z, \frac{\tau}{1 - (S - s)/\mathrm{Log}(S/s)}\right\}; \qquad s/S = \sigma^*(r, g, \beta/Sx)$$

with the function σ^* *defined as in Theorem 2.1. Moreover, there exists* $\tilde{\tau} > 0$ *such that search is binding in equilibrium* $(S < Z)$ *if and only if* $\tau < \tilde{\tau}$.

Proof.   See appendix.   ‖

The equilibrium is represented as a function of τ in Figures 12.2(a) and 12.2(b). When search costs are large $(\tau \geqq \tilde{\tau})$, searching is not worthwhile, and only inflation combined with adjustment costs prevents sellers from enjoying their full monopoly power $(S = Z)$. When search costs are small, on the contrary $(\tau < \tilde{\tau})$, a new type of equilibrium emerges, in which the threat of consumer search effectively *imposes competition* among firms: at the price $S = \tau\theta$, consumers are just indifferent between buying and searching further, so that any adjustment to a higher real price—such as the monopoly level Z—would result in zero demand.

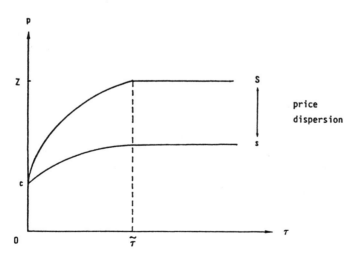

Figure 12.2a
The effect of search costs on real prices

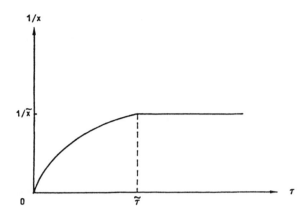

Figure 12.2b
The effect of search costs on the density of firms in the market

3. Market Frictions and the Diamond Paradox

A significant part of the search literature has been devoted to obtaining equilibrium price dispersion. This involves getting around the rather counterintuitive result (Diamond (1971)) which is generated by the basic search model where there are identical firms and consumers: if search is free, all firms must charge the competitive price, but if it is not, the unique equilibrium is for all firms to charge the monopoly price, no matter how high it is, how small the search cost, and how many firms there are.[13] As described by Stiglitz (1985), "search costs, even small search costs, have an enormous effect on the nature of the equilibrium." This result contradicts the economic intuition of "the dependence of equilibrium prices on the abilities of traders to find alternatives" (Diamond (1987a)), which in the present context means that equilibrium prices should be continuous and decreasing functions of search costs. The following result (illustrated in Figures 12.2(a) and 12.2(b) shows that as soon as even very small amounts of inflation and price adjustment costs are introduced, the equilibrium acquires this fundamental property.

PROPOSITION 3.1.   *The equilibrium is a continuous, monotonic and differentiable (except at $\tilde{\tau}$) function of the search cost τ. As τ decreases from $\tilde{\tau}$ to zero, the real price bounds (S, s) decrease from their monopoly levels $(Z, Z\tilde{\sigma})$*

*to the competitive price c, while the periodicity of price adjustment, price
dispersion and the density $1/x$ of firms in the market all decrease to zero.*

Proof. See appendix. ‖

This result is particularly interesting because it shows how the monopolistically competitive equilibrium with price dispersion becomes
increasingly competitive as search costs decrease, covering a spectrum
which ranges from the purely monopolistic case (*Diamond*) to the purely
competitive one (*Betrand*): the mounting competitive pressure generated
by search forces sellers to charge real prices which are both lower and
more in line with one another, and reduces the number of firms which
can profitably operate in the market. In the limit, a discrete number of
firms with negligible fixed costs (compared to market size: $h/x = \beta/x = 0$)
charge the marginal cost. The presence of frictions in the functioning of the
market on firms' side (costly price adjustment) as well as on consumers'
side (costly search) thus restores the balance which the original model
lacked and ensures a smoother, more realistic outcome. In this more symmetric light, Diamond's result is easily understood as one of the two polar
limiting cases where frictions on one side vanish: if search is free but price
adjustment costly, the market is totally biased against sellers and the competitive price prevails (Proposition 3.1); if price adjustment is free but
search costly, the market is totally biased against buyers and all purchases
take place at the monopoly price:

PROPOSITION 3.2. *The equilibrium is a continuous and monotonic function
of the adjustment cost β, and there exists $\tilde{\beta} > 0$ such that search is binding
if and only if $\beta > \tilde{\beta}$; the equilibrium is differentiable except at $\tilde{\beta}$. As β
decreases to zero, the real price bounds (S, s) increase to the monopoly price
Z; price dispersion and the periodicity of price adjustment decrease to zero,
while the density $1/x$ of firms increases to the maximum value $(Z - c)/h$
sustainable by the market.*

Proof. See appendix. ‖

This proposition is illustrated in Figures 12.3(a) to 12.3(c).[14] The first
two depict the equilibrium as a function of β, for a given value of τ; the last
one illustrates how the continuous function, associating to any $\tau \geq 0$ the
corresponding average price in the market $E[p]$, converges from below to

A.

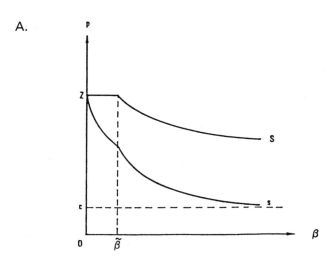

Figure 12.3a
The effect of adjustment cost on real prices

B.

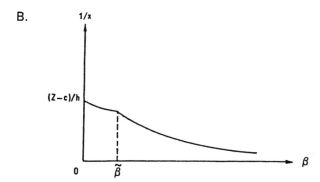

Figure 12.3b
The effect of adjustment costs on the density of firms in the market

C.

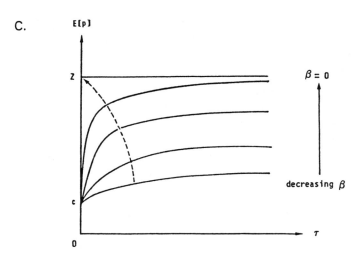

Figure 12.3c
The effect of adjustment and search costs on the average price

the discontinuous static equilibrium function $[\tau \to c + (Z - c)\mathbb{1}_{\{\tau > 0\}}]$ as β tends to zero (the graphs for S and s would be similar).

These results are quite intuitive: as it becomes less costly to change prices, firms do it more frequently, thereby reducing (for any given maximum real price) the amount of price dispersion and raising the average price in the market; this in turn decreases consumers' willingness to search, allowing firms to adjust to a higher maximum level and generating entry. When prices become perfectly flexible, all equilibrium prices converge to the monopoly level Z (as long as $\tau > 0$) and search disappears altogether, so that the Diamond (1971) result is obtained in the limit.[15] The limiting density of firms is that which leaves each of them with profits of $((Z - c)x - h)/r = 0$ when all charge the monopoly price Z forever.

4. Inflation, Price Dispersion, and Competition

There is considerable evidence that higher rates of inflation—even perfectly regular and anticipated ones—are associated with (and probably the cause of) greater relative price dispersion and uncertainty (see in particular Fischer (1981), (1984) and the references therein). The Sheshinski and Weiss (1977) model features a relationship between inflation and relative price variability at the individual firm level, while Caplin and Spulber (1986) establish a relationship between inflation and relative price dispersion by aggregating a continuum of independent (S, s) policies. Competition between sellers, however, constrains the amount of price variation—the (S, s) range—sustainable in the market, and should be explicitly incorporated into the analysis. This is done here through search, and the following proposition establishes a causal relationship between the aggregate rate of inflation and the amount of price dispersion—translating for buyers into price uncertainty—in the market. This relationship is robust to the effects of competition and entry, each of which works in the other direction.

PROPOSITION 4.   *The equilibrium is a continuous and monotonic function of the inflation rate g, and there exists $\tilde{g} \geq 0$ such that search is binding if and only if $g > \tilde{g}$; the equilibrium is differentiable except at $\tilde{g}$. As g decreases to zero, the equilibrium bounds (S, s) increase to limits $(\underline{S}, \underline{s})$, while price dispersion decreases to $(\underline{S} - \underline{s})/\underline{s} > 0$ and the density of firms increases to a limit of $1/\underline{x} < (Z - c)/h$.*[16] *Moreover, this limiting equilibrium, as a function of τ, possesses all the properties listed in Proposition 3.1; in particular, search is binding ($\underline{S} < Z$ and $d\underline{S}/d\tau > 0$) if and only if:*

$$\tau < \tilde{\underline{\tau}} \equiv Z\left[1 - \frac{1 - \tilde{\underline{\sigma}}}{\text{Log}(1/\tilde{\underline{\sigma}})}\right], \qquad \text{where } \tilde{\underline{\sigma}} \equiv \frac{h + r\beta c/Z}{h + r\beta}.$$

Proof.   See appendix.   ‖

This result is illustrated in Figures 12.4(a) and 12.4(b).[17] Figure 12.3(c) applies to variations in g as well as β, except that the limiting curve as g tends to zero is continuous and strictly below the static one.

In the presence of frictions, inflation is thus far from neutral; not only does it impose costly price adjustments, but also:

(a) It erodes the monopoly power of price setters by driving their real prices away from the profit-maximizing level; this is the usual Sheshinski–Weiss result (working here only in the downward direction because of the reservation-price nature of demand).

(b) It generates *price dispersion*, which makes search potentially profitable (a credible threat) and thereby *increases price competition*, resulting in lower real prices on the market and the exit of some firms.

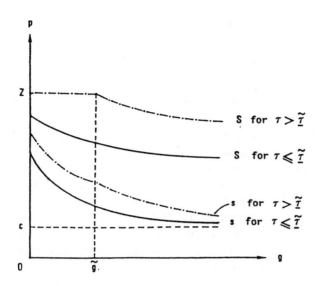

Figure 12.4a
The effect of inflation on real prices

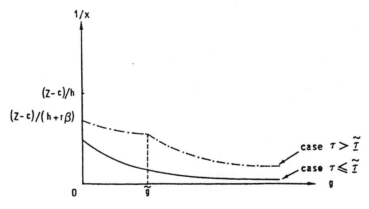

Figure 12.4b
The effect of inflation on the density of firms in the market

(c) At the *macroeconomic* level, *inflation alters the relative prices* of the different sectors—here labour and the good—even though these aggregate prices are growing at the same rate (cf. Lemma 1).[18]

Unlike the case of β, the monopoly price result is not even approximated by economies with arbitrarily small but positive inflation rates: as g converges to zero, s stays bounded away from S (see Theorem 2.1), so that there remains a finite amount of price dispersion in the market; this generates competition if search costs are lower than some finite limit. Thus it is more the presence of the cost of price adjustment than that of significant inflation which ensures a smooth functioning of the market— the latter essentially amplifies the effect of the former. One could even consider a static model in which there happened to be some price dispersion ($\sigma < 1$); given a cost of price adjustment β such that $x(S - s)/r < \beta$, or $\sigma > 1 - r\beta/Sx$, and a search cost low enough for search to be binding, this price dispersion would constitute an equilibrium. Of course, the notion of adjustment cost is intrinsically a dynamic one, and the reason for the initial dispersion and its exact form would have to be made explicit, as they are here through inflation.

5. Discussion

5.1. Search and Price Dispersion

The most common approach used by previous authors to circumvent the unsatisfactory monopoly price result of the basic model with identical consumers and firms is to allow for consumer heterogeneity. More precisely, it is assumed that buyers have different search costs (an exception is Diamond (1987b) where they differ in their valuations of the good). Even in this context, any improvement over the single-price result is conditional upon additional assumptions about either: (a) the existence of "enough" consumers with infinitesimal search cost, in the sense of a mass-point of the distribution at zero (von zur Muehlen (1980)), or a positive density in the neighbourhood of zero (Rob (1985), Stiglitz (1985)); (b) the elasticity of demand or unit costs; (c) the "experimental behaviour" of firms who try to discover their demand curve (Axell (1977)). Reinganum (1979), on the other hand, introduced heterogeneity among firms instead of consumers by assuming different unit costs and hence different monopoly prices. A price dispersion equilibrium is thus generated, in which all firms with cost below some critical level charge their monopoly price, while all others bunch (into an atom of the price distribution) at the monopoly price corresponding to this critical cost. In the terms of this chapter, it could be said that search is binding on the more inefficient firms, while only preferences (the elasticity of demand) limit the prices which the more efficient ones can charge.[19] The Reinganum model, however, still falls short of completely reconciling equilibrium price dispersion with search and providing a fully realistic description of monopolistic competition: indeed, for the firms among which price dispersion exists, search has no effect and the monopoly price result remains; conversely, there is no price dispersion among the firms for which search matters. Moreover, each firm is earning a different level of profits. In the long run, efficient technologies can be replicated, generating entry and exit and shifting the market structure towards the classical limit, where there remain only identical, efficient firms—and thus no price dispersion.

The model presented here is much closer than those mentioned just above to the original paradoxical case, since it involves identical consumers and firms, inelastic demand and constant unit costs. It clearly shows that the heart of the problem is *not heterogeneity* versus homogeneity, but the relative sizes of the *frictions*[20] that affect both sides of the market. Elastic demand, decreasing returns to scale or any arbitrary distribution of search costs could be added, but are not necessary. Similarly, using the results of Sheshinski and Weiss (1982) and Caplin and Spulber (1987), the rate of inflation could be made stochastic without affecting the results.

5.2. Other Equilibria

Condition E1, which restricts attention to a particular class of equilibria (not strategies), could be considered arbitrarily selective. The existence result is not in question, but uniqueness may not hold any more once other types of equilibria are allowed: there might be asymmetric (S, s) equilibria, non-(S, s) equilibria, etc. Perhaps this plethora is the best justification for focusing on a class which one judges to be both sensible (not to mention tractable), and well suited to the idea of monopolistic competition.

Even in the class of symmetric (S, s) equilibria, however, there exists another member which was excluded by condition E2: if all firms start at the same price and remain synchronized, there is no price dispersion, no search, and the simultaneous adjustment thus takes place to Z. This equilibrium replicates the monopoly price result and therefore shares none of the attractive comparative statics and limiting properties of the one selected by E2. It is therefore worth recalling that it was not excluded arbitrarily, but for several important reasons: inconsistency with the assumed aggregate inflationary process, and instability with respect to heterogeneity among firms, arising from slightly different costs, idiosyncratic shocks, or randomisation (see Section 1.3). The invariant distribution equilibrium studied here and this synchronized equilibrium in fact exhaust the class of symmetric (S, s) equilibria: any initial distribution which involves price dispersion will generate search—if search costs are low enough; if it is not invariant over time, search behaviour and therefore demand will not be stationary, destroying the optimality of (S, s) policies.

5.3.   Inflation and Welfare

Because of the simplifying assumption made about consumers' preferences, inflation here is entirely to their advantage and to the detriment of firms. With a more elastic demand curve, the upper real price bound S would be greater than the static monopoly price, so that inflation's pressure on real prices would not be downward only. Welfare conclusions would then be ambiguous, but the nature and comparative static properties of the equilibrium would most likely remain the same. In a stochastic setting, inflation could also lead to a deterioration in consumers' knowledge of the price distribution, thereby decreasing the profitability of search and reinforcing sellers' monopoly power, as in Gertner's (1987) static model of duopoly with search. Another important concern that one may have over the effect of inflation on welfare is the idea that if increased inflation generates increased price dispersion (as is the case here), it will also cause more resources to be spent on search. In this respect, the present model lacks both realism and predictive power: search is essentially a credible threat, which consumers faced with the maximum price in the market are just indifferent between carrying out and not carrying out. In Bénabou (1986), the model is therefore generalized to heterogeneous consumers, generating active search in equilibrium; these results are extended in Bénabou (1992) and used to analyse the relationships between inflation, the resources spent on search, and welfare.

Conclusion

The (S, s) pricing model has been extended to monopolistic competition by endogenously determining firms' demand curve from consumer search. The resulting equilibrium embodies optimal price-setting, sequential search and entry, and features a causal relationship between anticipated inflation and price dispersion. It also leads to the conclusion that Bertrand competition and the monopoly price result of Diamond (1971) are polar limiting cases of a smoother, monopolistically competitive equilibrium with frictions (search and price adjustment costs) on both sides of the market. It should still be possible, however, to incorporate additional and more complex features into the model, so as to further increase its realism and macroeconomic relevance.

Appendix

Proof of Lemma 2.1. Since $d\mu(p) = dp/[p \operatorname{Log}(S/s)]$:

$$E[p] = \left(\int_s^S p \cdot dp/p \right) \Big/ (\operatorname{Log}(S/s) = (S - s)/\operatorname{Log}(S/s);$$

$$E[p^2] = \left(\int_s^S p^2 \cdot dp/p \right) \Big/ (\operatorname{Log}(S/s) = (S^2 - s^2)/(2 \operatorname{Log}(S/s));$$

thus

$$\operatorname{Var}[p]/E[p]^2 = [(S + s)/(S - s)](\operatorname{Log}(S/s)/2) - 1$$

$$= \operatorname{Log}(1/\sigma)[(1/\sigma + 1)/(1/\sigma - 1)]/2 - 1 \equiv h(1/\sigma)$$

where, for all $y > 1$: $y(y - 1)^2 h'(y) = y^2 - 1 - 2y \operatorname{Log}(y) \equiv m(y)$, with: $m'(y) = 2(y - 1 - \operatorname{Log}(y)) > 0$ and $m(1) = 0$; thus $m(y) > 0$, or $h'(y) > 0$, for all $y > 1$. ‖

Proof of Theorem 2.1. The proof of the optimality of a recursive—i.e. (S, s)—real price policy given in the appendix of Sheshinski and Weiss (1977) relies only on the stationarity—and not on the functional form— of the demand curve. Their characterisation of the optimal (S, s) through first-order conditions, however, no longer holds here because the reservation-price nature of demand imposes a boundary constraint $S \leq Q$ on the optimization problem. This results in a non-interior solution for S.

Consider a feasible (S, s) rule where $S < Q$, and let $T = \text{Log}(S/s)/g$. Real intertemporal profits (gross of the fixed cost h/r) are:

$$V = -\beta + \int_0^T x(Se^{-gt} - c)e^{-rt}\, dt + Ve^{-rT}.$$

Now let the firm deviate at some time when a price change is called for, adjusting to Q instead of S, then readjusting to S after a time T and resuming (S, s) from there on. This perturbation yields:

$$W = -\beta + \int_0^T x(Qe^{-gt} - c)e^{-rt}\, dt + Ve^{-rT} > V$$

because $Q > S$. Therefore, a policy with $S < Q$ cannot be optimal.

Similarly, consider an (S, s) rule where $S > Q$. After an adjustment to S, sales are zero during a time $\delta = \text{Log}(S/Q)/g > 0$; note that $\delta < T = \text{Log}(S/s)/g$ if any sales are to be made. Moreover:

$$V = -\beta + \int_\delta^T x(Qe^{-g(t-\delta)} - c)e^{-rt}\, dt + Ve^{-rT}$$

Now let the firm deviate at some time when a price change is called for, adjusting to Q instead of S, then resuming the same (S, s) policy (the next adjustment thus takes place at s, after a time $T - \delta$); this yields:

$$W = -\beta + \int_0^{T-\delta} x(Qe^{-gt} - c)e^{-rt}\, dt + Ve^{-r(T-\delta)}$$

$$= -\beta + \left[\int_\delta^T x(Qe^{-g(t-\delta)} - c)e^{-rt}\, dt + Ve^{-rT}\right]e^{r\delta}$$

so that $W + \beta = e^{r\delta}(V + \beta)$, hence $W > V$, and $S > Q$ cannot be optimal.

Given that the optimal S is Q, profits (gross of fixed costs h/r) as a function V_T of $T = \text{Log}(Q/s)/g$ are:

$$V_T = \left[\int_0^T x(Qe^{-gt} - c)e^{-rt}\, dt - \beta\right]\Big/(1 - e^{-rT})$$

or

$$V_T = -cx/r + Qx[1 - \beta(r + g)/Qx - e^{-(r+g)T}]/[(r + g)(1 - e^{-rT})]. \tag{12.A1}$$

Alternatively, as a function of σ (let $u = e^{-gt}$):

$$V(\sigma) = -cx/r + Qx\left[\int_\sigma^1 u^{r/g}\,du - \beta g/Qx\right]\Big/[g(1 - \sigma^{r/g})]. \qquad (12.\text{A}2)$$

Hence

$$V'(\sigma)(1 - \sigma^{r/g})g = -\sigma^{-1+r/g}x[\sigma Q - r(V(\sigma)/x + c/r)],$$

so that

$$\text{sgn}\{V'(\sigma)\} = \text{sgn}\{rV(\sigma) - x(s - c)\} \qquad (12.\text{A}3)$$

where sgn$\{z\}$ denotes the sign of z. Thus $V'(\sigma) \geqq 0$ if and only if:

$$\sigma \leqq (rV(\sigma)/x + c)/Q = r\left[\int_\sigma^1 u^{r/g}\,du - \beta g/Qx\right]\Big/[g(1 - \sigma^{r/g})]$$

$$= r[1 - (r + g)\beta/Qx - \sigma^{1+r/g}]/[(r + g)(1 - \sigma^{r/g})]$$

or

$$f(\sigma) \equiv (r + g)\sigma - g\sigma^{1+r/g} - r[1 - (r + g)\beta/Qx] \geqq 0. \qquad (12.\text{A}4)$$

For all $\sigma \in (0, 1)$: $f'(\sigma) = (r+g)(1-\sigma^{r/g}) > 0$, $f(0) = -r(1-(r+g)\beta/Qx) < 0$ by hypothesis, and $f(1) = r(r+g)\beta/Qx > 0$. Therefore f has a unique zero— i.e. by (12.A3) $V(\sigma)$ has a unique global maximum—$\sigma \equiv \sigma^*(r, g, \beta/Qx) \in (0, 1)$. Equivalently, V_T has a unique maximum $T^*(r, g, \beta/Qx) \in (0, +\infty)$, with $\sigma^* = e^{-gT^*}$. Moreover, by (12.A3), $s = \sigma^*Q$ satisfies: $x(s - c) = rV_T$.

Let us now turn to the comparative statics of σ with respect to β and g. Since f is parametrized by r, g, and $\beta' \equiv \beta/Qx$, and continuously differentiable in these parameters, so is $\sigma = \sigma^*(r, g, \beta')$, and:

$$\partial\sigma/\partial\beta' = -(\partial f/\partial\beta')/(\partial f/\partial\sigma) = -r/(1 - \sigma^{r/g}) < 0;$$

$$\partial\sigma/\partial g = -(\partial f/\partial g)/(\partial f/\partial\sigma) < 0, \quad \text{because } \partial f/\partial\sigma > 0$$

and

$$\partial f/\partial g = \sigma[1 - \sigma^{r/g}(1 - (r/g)\,\text{Log}(\sigma))] + r\beta/Qx > 0$$

since

$$\text{Log}(1/\sigma^{r/g}) < 1/\sigma^{r/g} - 1.$$

Thus σ is decreasing in both β' and g, and therefore has finite limits $\underline{\sigma}'$ and $\underline{\sigma}$ as these parameters go to zero. Taking limits in: $f(\sigma; r, g, \beta') = 0$ as $\beta' = \beta/Qx$ tends to zero yields: $(r + g)\underline{\sigma}' - g(\underline{\sigma}')^{1+r/g} = r$, to which the only solution is $\underline{\sigma}' = 1$. Similarly, taking limits as g tends to zero yields: $r\underline{\sigma} = r(1 - r\beta/Qx)$, hence a limit $\underline{\sigma} = 1 - r\beta/Qx$. $\quad \|$

Proof of Lemma 2.2. By definition (equations (12.7) and (12.9) in the text):

$$\Phi(\sigma, x; r, g, \beta, h) = (r + g)\sigma - g\sigma^{1+r/g} - r[1 - (r + g)\beta\sigma/(cx + h)] \quad (12.\text{A}5)$$

$$\Psi(\sigma, x; \tau, h) = (1 - \sigma)/\text{Log}(1/\sigma) + \tau\sigma/(c + h/x) - 1 \quad (12.\text{A}6)$$

for all $\sigma \in (0, 1)$ and $x \in (0, +\infty)$. Hence:

$$\partial\Phi(\sigma, x)/\partial\sigma = (r + g)(1 - \sigma^{r/g}) + r(r + g)\beta/(cx + h) > 0;$$

$$\partial\Phi(\sigma, x)/\partial x = -r(r + g)\beta\sigma c/(cx + h)^2 < 0;$$

$$\Phi(0, x) = -r < 0; \Phi(1, x) = r(r + g)\beta/(cx + h) > 0;$$

and

$$\partial\Psi(\sigma, x)/\partial\sigma = [1/\sigma - 1 - \text{Log}(1/\sigma)]/\text{Log}(\sigma)^2 + \tau(c + h/x) > 0;$$

$$\partial\Psi(\sigma, x)/\partial x = \tau\sigma h/(cx + h)^2 > 0;$$

$$\Psi(0, x) = -1 < 0; \Psi(1, x) = \tau/(c + h/x) > 0.$$

The rest of the lemma follows immediately from the Implicit Function Theorem. Moreover, $\sigma_0'(x) > 0 > \sigma_1'(x)$ and the limiting equalities: $\Phi(1, +\infty) = 0 = \Psi(1, 0) = 0$ imply the following useful result:

$$\sigma_0(0) < \sigma_0(+\infty) = 1 = \sigma_1(0) > \sigma_1(+\infty). \quad \| \quad (12.\text{A}7)$$

Proof of Theorem 2.2. An equilibrium is a solution to (equation (12.12) in the text):

$$\sigma_0(x) = \max\{\sigma_1(x), \sigma_2(x)\} \equiv \sigma_3(x). \quad (12.\text{A}8)$$

By Lemma 2.2, $\sigma_0 - \sigma_3$ is increasing on $(0, +\infty)$. Moreover, by (12.A7): $\sigma_0(0) < \sigma_3(0)$ and $\sigma_0(+\infty) = 1 > \max(\sigma_1(+\infty), c/Z) = \sigma_3(+\infty)$. There exists therefore a *unique solution* x^* to (12.A8), defining the equilibrium:

$$(x^*, \sigma^* = \sigma_0(x^*) = \sigma_3(x^*), s^* = c + h/x^*,$$

$$S^* = \min\{Z, (c + h/x^*)/\sigma_1(x^*)\} = \min\{Z, \tau\theta(r, g, \beta/S^*x^*)\} \tag{12.A9}$$

by equation (12.4c) in the text.

It now remains to examine the values of τ for which search is binding in equilibrium. The function $\sigma_0 - \sigma_2$ is increasing on $(0, +\infty)$, with limiting values of $-\infty$ at $x = 0^+$ and $1 - c/Z$ at $x = +\infty$ (by (12.A7)). Therefore:

$$(\exists! \tilde{x} > 0) \quad (\sigma_0(\tilde{x}) = \sigma_2(\tilde{x})). \tag{12.A10}$$

Consider now, for any x, the equation defining $\sigma_1(x)$:

$$\Psi(\sigma, x; \tau, h) = (1 - \sigma)/\text{Log}(1/\sigma) + \tau\sigma/(c + h/x) - 1 = 0. \tag{12.A11}$$

For a given x, it can be viewed as an implicit equation in τ and σ; the solution $\sigma_1(x)$ is therefore also a function of τ, which will be made clear by writing it as $\sigma_1(x, \tau)$. Moreover:

$$\partial\sigma_1(x, \tau)/\partial\tau = -(\partial\Psi(\sigma_1, x; \tau)/\partial\tau)/(\partial\Psi(\sigma_1, x; \tau)/\partial\sigma);$$

$$\partial\Psi(\sigma_1, x; \tau)/\partial\sigma > 0 \quad \text{by Lemma 2.2;}$$

$$\partial\Psi(\sigma_1, x; \tau)/\partial\tau = \sigma_1/(c + h/x) > 0; \quad \text{therefore}$$

$$\partial\sigma_1(x, \tau)/\partial\tau < 0. \tag{12.A12}$$

It is clear from (12.A11) that $\sigma_1(x, 0) = 1$ for any $x > 0$, while as τ tends to $+\infty$, $\sigma_1(x, \tau) \approx (c + h/x)/\tau \approx 0$. Taking in particular $x = \tilde{x}$: $\sigma_1(\tilde{x}, \cdot)$ decreases from 1 to 0 on $[0, +\infty)$, while $\sigma_0(\tilde{x}) \in (0, 1)$. Hence:

$$(\exists! \tilde{\tau} > 0) \quad (\sigma_1(\tilde{x}, \tilde{\tau}) = \sigma_0(\tilde{x}) = \sigma_2(\tilde{x})). \tag{12.A13}$$

It will now be shown that search is binding (i.e. $\sigma_1(x^*, \tau) > \sigma_2(x^*)$) if and only if $\tau < \tilde{\tau}$. By definition of $\tilde{\tau}$:

(a) For $\tau \geq \tilde{\tau}$: $\sigma_1(\tilde{x}, \tau) \leq \sigma_2(\tilde{x})$ hence: $\sigma_0(\tilde{x}) = \sigma_3(\tilde{x}, \tau) = \sigma_2(\tilde{x})$ by (12.A8) and (12.A10); thus $\tilde{x}$ is still the equilibrium, and S is equal to $(c + h/\tilde{x})/\sigma_2(\tilde{x}) = Z$ (preferences binding).

(b) For $\tau < \tilde{\tau}$: $\sigma_1(\tilde{x}, \tau) > \sigma_2(\tilde{x})$ hence: $\sigma_0(\tilde{x}) = \sigma_2(\tilde{x}) < \sigma_3(\tilde{x}, \tau)$. Since $\sigma_3 - \sigma_0$ is decreasing, its zero—the equilibrium—must occur at some:

$$x^* > \tilde{x}, \quad \sigma^* = \sigma_0(x^*) > \tilde{\sigma}. \tag{12.A14}$$

This implies, by (12.A10): $\sigma_2(x^*) < \sigma_0(x^*) = \sigma_3(x^*, \tau)$, which in turn requires: $\sigma_3(x^*, \tau) = \sigma_1(x^*) > \sigma_2(x^*)$ (search binding). $\|$

Proof of Proposition 3.1.   By Theorem 2.2, when $\tau \geq \tilde{\tau}$, preferences are binding:

$$S = Z, \quad x = \tilde{x}, \quad \sigma = \sigma_0(\tilde{x}) = \sigma_2(\tilde{x}), \quad s = c + h/\tilde{x} \tag{12.A15}$$

so that the equilibrium is independent of τ. When $\tau < \tilde{\tau}$, search is binding and: $\sigma = \sigma_0(x) = \sigma_1(x, \tau)$; differentiation yields:

$$[\sigma_0'(x) - \partial\sigma_1(x, \tau)/\partial x](dx/d\tau) = \partial\sigma_1(x, \tau)/\partial\tau < 0$$

by (12.A12). Hence, since $\sigma_0'(x) > 0 > \partial\sigma_1(x, \tau)/\partial x$ by Lemma 2.2:

$$dx/d\tau < 0. \tag{12.A16}$$

Then: $\sigma = \sigma_0(x)$, $s = c + h/x$ and $S = s/\sigma$ imply:

$$d\sigma/d\tau < 0, \quad ds/d\tau > 0, \quad dS/d\tau > 0. \tag{12.A17}$$

As τ goes to zero, x and σ increase to limits $\hat{x}$ and $\hat{\sigma}$. Taking limits in (12.A11) (binding search condition) yields: $(1 - \hat{\sigma})/\text{Log}(1/\hat{\sigma}) = 1$, or $\hat{\sigma} = 1$. Taking now limits in $\Phi(\sigma, x) = 0$ (cf. (12.A5)) yields $\hat{x} = +\infty$, implying finally that both $s = c + h/x$ and $S = s/\sigma$ converge to c. $\parallel$

Proof of Proposition 3.2.   *Monotonicity.*   The direct dependence of σ_0 on β (in addition to the indirect one through x) will be made clear by denoting it as $\sigma_0(x, \beta)$. To examine how the equilibrium varies with β, we will first focus on the threshold levels $\tilde{x}$ and $\tilde{\tau}$. Denoting as $\tilde{\sigma}$ the quantity $\sigma_2(\tilde{x}) = \sigma_0(\tilde{x}, \beta)$, (cf. (12.A10)), and differentiating with respect to β:

$$[\partial\sigma_0(\tilde{x}, \beta)/\partial x - \sigma_2'(\tilde{x})](d\tilde{x}/d\beta) = -\partial\sigma_0(\tilde{x}, \beta)/\partial\beta.$$

But since

$$\partial\sigma_0(\tilde{x}, \beta)/\partial\beta = -(\partial\Phi(\tilde{\sigma}, \tilde{x}; \beta)/\partial\beta)/(\partial\Phi(\tilde{\sigma}, \tilde{x}; \beta)/\partial\sigma)$$

$$= -r(r + g)\tilde{\sigma}/[(c\tilde{x} + h)(\partial\Phi(\tilde{\sigma}, \tilde{x}; \beta)/\partial\sigma)] < 0, \tag{12.A18}$$

$$d\tilde{x}/d\beta > 0. \tag{12.A19}$$

Similarly, $\tilde{\tau}$ is defined in (12.A13) by: $\sigma_1(\tilde{x}, \tilde{\tau}) = \tilde{\sigma} = \sigma_2(\tilde{x})$, so

$$[\partial\sigma_1(\tilde{x}, \tilde{\tau})/\partial x - \sigma_2'(\tilde{x})](d\tilde{x}/d\beta) = -(\partial\sigma_1(\tilde{x}, \tilde{\tau})/\partial\tau)(d\tilde{\tau}/d\beta).$$

Therefore, by (12.A12) and (12.A19), $d\tilde{\tau}/d\beta$ has the sign of $\partial\sigma_1(\tilde{x}, \tilde{\tau})/\partial x - \sigma_2'(\tilde{x})$, which is that of:

$$-\partial\Psi(\tilde{\sigma}, \tilde{x}; \tilde{\tau})/\partial x - \sigma_2'(\tilde{x})\partial\Psi(\tilde{\sigma}, \tilde{x}; \tilde{\tau})/\partial\sigma$$

$$= (h/Z\tilde{x}^2)[k'(\tilde{\sigma}) + \tilde{\tau}\tilde{x}/(c\tilde{x} + h)] - \tilde{\tau}h\tilde{\sigma}/(c\tilde{x} + h)^2$$

where for all $\sigma \in (0, 1)$, one defines:

$$k(\sigma) \equiv (1 - \sigma)/\mathrm{Log}(1/\sigma). \tag{12.A20}$$

$$k'(\sigma) = [1/\sigma - 1 - \mathrm{Log}(1/\sigma)]/[\mathrm{Log}(1/\sigma)^2] > 0. \tag{12.A21}$$

Moreover, leaving out the term in $k'(\tilde{\sigma})$ in the above expression yields:

$$\tilde{\tau}h/[(c\tilde{x} + h)Z\tilde{x}] - \tilde{\tau}h\tilde{\sigma}/(c\tilde{x} + h)^2,$$

which is proportional to

$$c\tilde{x} + h - Z\tilde{x}\tilde{\sigma} = h - \tilde{x}(Z\tilde{\sigma} - c) = h - \tilde{x}(Z\sigma_2(\tilde{x}) - c) = 0$$

by the definitions of $\tilde{\sigma}$ and $\sigma_2(\cdot)$. Therefore:

$$\partial\sigma_1(\tilde{x}, \tilde{\tau})/\partial x - \sigma_2'(\tilde{x}) > 0 \tag{12.A22}$$

$$d\tilde{\tau}/d\beta > 0. \tag{12.A23}$$

Consider now any β and β', with $\beta > \beta' > 0$. Equilibrium values corresponding to β' will be denoted by a prime. By (12.A23), $\tilde{\tau} > \tilde{\tau}'$, so three cases arise:

(a) For $\tau \geqq \tilde{\tau} > \tilde{\tau}'$, preferences are binding in both the equilibrium with search cost τ and adjustment cost β, and in that with τ and β'. Thus: $x = \tilde{x} > \tilde{x}'$ by (12.A19); $\sigma = \sigma_2(\tilde{x}) < \sigma_2(\tilde{x}') = \sigma'$;

$$s = c + h/\tilde{x} < c + h/\tilde{x}' = s', \qquad S = Z = S'.$$

(b) For $\tilde{\tau} > \tau \geqq \tilde{\tau}'$, preferences are binding with β' and search with β, so: $x > \tilde{x} > \tilde{x}' = x'$ by (12.A14) and (12.A19); $\sigma = \sigma_1(x) < \sigma_1(x') < \sigma_2(x') = \sigma'$;

$$s = c + h/x < c + h/\tilde{x}' = s'; \qquad S < Z = S'.$$

(c) For $\tilde{\tau} > \tilde{\tau}' > \tau$, search is binding in both cases; this is also true for any $\beta'' \in (\beta', \beta)$, because $\tau < \tilde{\tau}' < \tilde{\tau}''$. Thus, for any such $\beta'': \sigma_0(x'', \beta'') = \sigma_1(x'')$, and differentiation yields:

$$[\partial\sigma_0(x'', \beta'')/\partial x - \sigma_1'(x'')](dx''/d\beta) = -\partial\sigma_0(x'', \beta'')/\partial\beta > 0$$

by (12.A18). This in turn implies: $dx''/d\beta > 0$ for all $\beta'' \in (\beta', \beta)$ or:

$$dx/d\beta > 0 \tag{12.A24}$$

$$ds/d\beta < 0, \quad d\sigma/d\beta < 0, \quad d\theta/d\beta < 0; \quad dS/d\beta = d(\tau\theta)/d\beta < 0 \tag{12.A25}$$

on the interval (β', β). Finally, these inequalities imply:

$$S < S', \quad s < s', \quad \sigma < \sigma', \quad x > x', \tag{12.A26}$$

which concludes the proof of the equilibrium's monotonicity in β.

Limits. As β tends to zero, the monotone functions $\tilde{x}$, $\tilde{\sigma}$, $\tilde{\tau}$, S, s, σ and x possess limits $\underline{\tilde{x}}$, $\underline{\tilde{\sigma}}$, $\underline{\tilde{\tau}}$, $\underline{S}$, $\underline{s}$, $\underline{\sigma}$ and $\underline{x}$. Since $\tilde{\sigma} = \sigma_0(\tilde{x}, \beta)$: $\Phi(\tilde{\sigma}, \tilde{x}) = 0$; taking limits as β goes to zero yields (cf. (12.A5)): $(r + g)\underline{\tilde{\sigma}} - g\underline{\tilde{\sigma}}^{1+r/g} - r = 0$, so $\underline{\tilde{\sigma}} = 1$. But $z\underline{\tilde{\sigma}} = z\sigma_2(\underline{\tilde{x}}) = c + h/\underline{\tilde{x}}$, hence: $\underline{\tilde{x}} = h/(Z - c)$. Similarly, $\tilde{\sigma} = \sigma_1(\tilde{x}, \beta; \tilde{\tau})$, so $\Psi(\tilde{\sigma}, \tilde{x}; \tilde{\tau}) = 0$; taking limits as β tends to zero yields (cf. (12.A6)): $1 + \underline{\tilde{\tau}}/Z - 1 = 0$, so that:

$$\underline{\tilde{\sigma}} = 1, \quad \underline{\tilde{x}} = h/(Z - c), \quad \underline{\tilde{\tau}} = 0. \tag{12.A27}$$

Thus, for any $\tau > 0$: $\tilde{\beta} \equiv \min\{\beta > 0 | \tilde{\tau} \geq \tau\} > 0$ is well defined and positive, and $\tau > \tilde{\tau}$ for $\beta < \tilde{\beta}$. Preferences are then binding: $S = Z$, $x = \tilde{x}$, $\sigma = \sigma_2(\tilde{x})$, $s = Z\sigma_2(\tilde{x})$. Taking limits as β goes to zero:

$$\underline{S} = Z, \quad \underline{x} = h/(Z - c), \quad \underline{\sigma} = 1, \quad \underline{s} = Z. \quad \| \tag{12.A28}$$

Proof of Proposition 4. Monotonicity. As was done with β, σ_0 will be denoted here as $\sigma_0(x, g)$. First for all positive g and x:

$$\partial\sigma_0(x, g)/\partial g < 0 \tag{12.A29}$$

because it has the opposite sign of:

$$\partial\Phi(\sigma_0, x; g)/\partial g = (\sigma_0)^{1+r/g}\{[(\sigma_0)^{-r/g} - 1 + (r/g)\operatorname{Log}(\sigma_0)] + r\beta\sigma_0/(cx + h)\} > 0.$$

Replacing β by g in the monotonicity proofs of Proposition 3.2 yields by exactly the same calculations:

$$d\tilde{x}/dg > 0, \quad d\tilde{\tau}/dg > 0 \tag{12.A30}$$

$$dx/dg > 0, \quad d\sigma/dg < 0, \quad ds/dg < 0, \quad dS/dg \leq 0, \tag{12.A31}$$

with the last inequality being strict (search binding) when $\tau < \tilde{\tau}$, which by (12.A30) is equivalent to: $g > \tilde{g} \equiv \inf\{g > 0 | \tilde{\tau} \geq \tau\} \geq 0$.

Limits. The limiting equilibrium $(\underline{\tilde{x}}, \underline{\tilde{\sigma}}, \underline{\tilde{\tau}}; \underline{x}, \underline{\sigma}, \underline{s}, \underline{S})$ as g tends to zero is different from that obtained as β tends to zero. Taking limits in $\Phi(\tilde{\sigma}, \tilde{x}; g) =$

0 (because $\tilde{\sigma} = \sigma_0(\tilde{x}, g)$) yields (cf. (12.A5)):

$$\underline{\tilde{\sigma}} + r\beta\underline{\tilde{\sigma}}/(c\underline{\tilde{x}} + h) - 1 = 0.$$

But:

$$\underline{\tilde{\sigma}} = \sigma_2(\underline{\tilde{x}}) = (c + h/\underline{\tilde{x}})/Z;$$

finally, eliminating $\underline{\tilde{\sigma}}$:

$$\underline{\tilde{x}} = (h + r\beta)/(Z - c), \qquad \underline{\tilde{\sigma}} = (h + r\beta c/Z)/(h + r\beta). \tag{12.A32}$$

Similarly, $\tilde{\sigma} = \sigma_1(\tilde{x}, g; \tilde{\tau})$ or $\Psi(\tilde{\sigma}, \tilde{x}; \tilde{\tau}, g) = 0$; taking limits (cf. (12.A6)) leads to: $\underline{\tilde{\tau}}\,\underline{\tilde{\sigma}}/(c + h/\underline{\tilde{x}}) = 1 - (1 - \underline{\tilde{\sigma}})/\mathrm{Log}(1/\underline{\tilde{\sigma}})$ or:

$$\underline{\tilde{\tau}} = Z[1 - (1 - \underline{\tilde{\sigma}})/\mathrm{Log}(1/\underline{\tilde{\sigma}})] > 0 \tag{12.A33}$$

because $\underline{\tilde{\sigma}} \in (0, 1)$ by (12.A32). Formulas (12.A32) and (12.A33) should be contrasted to (12.A27). It will now be shown that the limiting equilibrium has search binding when $\tau < \underline{\tilde{\tau}}$.

(a) For $\tau > \underline{\tilde{\tau}}$: when g is small enough, $\tau > \tilde{\tau}$ by (12.A30), and preferences are binding: $S = Z$, $x = \tilde{x}$, $\sigma = \sigma_2(\tilde{x})$, $s = Z\sigma = Z\sigma_2(\tilde{x})$. Taking limits as g tends to zero yields: $S = Z$, $x = \underline{\tilde{x}} > h/(Z - c)$, $\underline{\sigma} = \underline{\tilde{\sigma}} < 1$ and $\underline{s} = Z\underline{\tilde{\sigma}} < Z$.

(b) For $\tau \leq \underline{\tilde{\tau}}$: for all $g > 0$, $\tau < \tilde{\tau}$ by (12.A30), and search is binding: $S = \tau\theta < Z$, and $x > \tilde{x}$ (by (12.A14)). Taking now limits as g goes to zero in $\Psi(\sigma_1(x, g), x; \tau, g) = 0$ yields: $k(\underline{\sigma}) + \tau\underline{\sigma}/(c + h/\underline{x}) = 1$; since $\underline{x} \geq \underline{\tilde{x}} > 0$ by (12.A32), this requires $\underline{\sigma} < 1$. Hence:

$$\underline{x} \geq \underline{\tilde{x}} > h/(Z - c); \qquad \underline{\sigma} < 1; \qquad \underline{s} = \underline{S}\underline{\tilde{\sigma}} \leq Z\underline{\sigma} < Z. \tag{12.A34}$$

$$\underline{S} = \tau/[1 - (1 - \underline{\sigma})/\mathrm{Log}(1/\underline{\sigma})] \leq Z. \tag{12.A35}$$

It only remains to show that (12.A35) holds with strict inequality, and implies that $dS/dg < 0$, when $\tau < \underline{\tilde{\tau}}$ (note that $\underline{\sigma}$ depends on τ, hence (12.A35) is implicit in this parameter), i.e. that $\underline{S}$ possesses the same properties that were established for any S corresponding to $g > 0$ in Proposition 3.1. Since that proof relied only on the fact that:

$$\partial\sigma_0(x, g)/\partial x > 0 > \partial\sigma_1(x, \tau)/\partial x \quad \text{and} \quad \partial\sigma_1(x, \tau)/\partial\tau < 0$$

and since the function σ_1 is independent of g, it suffices to show that $\sigma_0(x, 0)$ is strictly increasing in x. But (cf. proof of Lemma 2.2):

$$\partial\sigma_0(x, 0)/\partial x = r\beta\sigma_0 c/[(cx + h)(cx + h + r\beta)] > 0. \quad \|$$

Notes

This paper is a revised and abridged version of Chapter Two of my 1986 Ph.D. dissertation at MIT. I wish to thank Olivier Blanchard, Peter Diamond and Jean Tirole for helpful comments. I remain responsible for all errors and inaccuracies.

1. A very notable exception is the literature on durable goods: Stokey (1981), Bulow (1982), Sobel (1984), Conlisk, Gestner and Sobel (1984), Gul, Sonnenschein and Wilson (1985), etc.

2. The proofs (cf. appendix) will actually be carried out with $h > 0$ for convenience; the case where $h = 0$ is obtained as a limit. Note that entry is treated here in a long-term, or comparative statics sense, since its dynamic process is left unspecified.

3. All the chapter's results would remain essentially unchanged if the number of firms in the market was fixed instead of endogenous (cf. Bénabou (1986)).

4. In Bénabou (1986) the model is also solved with different specifications of the price adjustment cost, which is allowed to depend on the number of customers or on the firm's new price (this last case corresponds to sales lost because of resources—i.e. labour—diverted to changing prices). All results are robust to the choice of specification.

5. This assumption is convenient but inessential; the results remain unchanged when each search requires a finite length of time, provided it is assumed that consumers have no discount rate and, most importantly, no possibility of recalling past offers.

6. Because search is instantaneous, time is no limit on the number of searches; footnote 10 below will make clear that neither is wealth.

7. This standard assumption ensures that no consumer is kept out of the market because the surplus he can expect from optimal search is smaller than the cost of the first sampling.

8. Caplin and Spulber (1987) deal more generally with any continuous and monotonic inflationary process. For the subcase of constant inflation, see also Rotemberg (1983). Note that among the indexes covered by the Lemma are the arithmetic and geometric averages, and the Divisia index.

9. The invariant distribution in these cases is not exactly log-uniform any more, but what really matters for the problem at hand are its invariance and non-degeneracy, not its precise functional form.

10. Lippman and McCall (1976) show that, with recall allowed, (the same) R characterizes the optimal decision rule:
(a) in the infinite horizon problem where the constraint imposed by finite wealth (here, labour) on the number of searches is disregarded.
(b) until the last period of the finite horizon problem where this constraint (here $N \leq (L - Z)/\tau$) is taken into account.
Following most of the literature, the chapter will implicitly deal with case (a); the model and results derived here, however, are fully robust to the incorporation of the wealth constraint, because (as will be seen below) in equilibrium the maximum real price in the marekt S is no greater than R. Thus: (1) No search actually takes place (hence the constraint is not binding) in equilibrium; (2) In game-theoretic terms, consumers' threat of rejecting, and not coming back to, any price greater than R, which sustains the equilibrium, is credible even off the equilibrium path. Indeed: (i) they can search at least once, since $\tau < L - Z$; by (b) above, it is thus optimal to reject $p > R$; (iii) since $S \leq R$, they immediately find another price $p' < R$, hence never come back to p.

11. This optimisation problem differs from the one covered by Sheshinski and Weiss (1977) because the demand curve is rectangular, so that the optimal S is not an interior but a corner solution and because they do not explicitly impose that profits be non-negative.

12. This externality is robust to the specification of an adjustment cost $\beta(x)$ increasing in the number of customers, as long as there are increasing returns to scale in this technology

($\beta(x)/x$ is decreasing); cf. Bénabou (1986). Another such externality would be for search costs to vary with x: more firms make search easier, as in Diamond (1982). Since the first effect is already embodied in the model while the second one involves additional assumptions about the search technology, attention is restricted here to the former.

13. Indeed, if all firms do so, search is pointless, so there is no competition and no firm has any incentive to change its price; conversely, in an equilibrium no firm can charge a price above consumers' common reservation price, or else it gets zero demand; thus there is no search either and all firms must be charging the monopoly price.

14. The curves are drawn for $\tau < \tilde{\tau}_\infty \equiv Z[(1 - (1 - c)/Z)/\text{Log}(Z/c)]$, which ensures that $\tilde{\beta} < +\infty$ (search binding for $\beta = +\infty$). When $\tau \geqq \tilde{\tau}_\infty$: $S = Z$ for all β. The decrease in the slopes of s and $1/x$ at $\tilde{\beta}$ results from equation (12.A22).

15. Most of Diamond's (1971) paper involves a fixed number of firms; cf. note 3 above.

16. As in Sheshinski and Weiss (1977), the sign of the derivative of the periodicity of adjustment T^* with respect to g is generally ambiguous.

17. The same remarks as in note (14) apply, replacing $\tilde{\beta}$ by $\tilde{g}$ (in the case $\tau > \tilde{\tau}$).

18. Section 5.3 discusses an extension of the model (Bénabou (1986), (1992)) in which inflation generates active search and therefore has an additional resource cost.

19. I am grateful to Peter Diamond for pointing out this analogy. One can also be drawn with Diamond (1987b), where firms which specialize in serving high valuation consumers are constrained by the threat of search, which prevents them from charging these customers their full valuation; firms specializing in low valuation consumers, on the other hand, are constrained only by the latter's preferences (valuations).

20. Another type of friction or market imperfection is the fixed cost h; comparative statics and dynamics exercises similar to those presented here for β and g can be performed with respect to h (cf. Bénabou (1986)).

References

Axell, B. (1977), "Search Market Equilibrium," *Scandinavian Journal of Economics*, 79, 20–40.

Ball, L. and Romer, D. (1989), "The Equilibrium and Optimal Timing of Price Changes", Review of Economic Studies, 56, 179–198.

Barro, R. (1972), "A Theory of Monopolistic Price Adjustment," *Review of Economic Studies*, 39, 17–26.

Bénabou, R. (1986), "Optimal Price Dynamics, Speculation and Search under Inflation" (Ph.D. Dissertation, Massachusetts Institute of Technology, Chapter Two).

Bénabou, R. (1989), "Optimal Price Dynamics and Speculation with a Storable Good," *Econometrica*, 57, 41–81.

Bénabou, R. (1992), "Inflation and Efficiency in Search Markets", Review of Economic Studies, 59, 299–329.

Bulow, J. (1982), "Durable Goods Monopolists," *Journal of Political Economy*, 90, 314–332.

Caplin, A. and Spulber, D. (1987), "Menu Costs and the Neutrality of Money," *Quarterly Journal of Economics*, 102, 703–725.

Conlisk, J. Gestner, E. and Sobel, J. (1984), "Cyclical Pricing by a Durable Goods Monopoly," *Quarterly Journal of Economics*, 99, 489–505.

Diamond, P. (1971), "A Model of Price Adjustment," *Journal of Economic Theory*, 3, 156–168.

Diamond, P. (1982), "Aggregate Demand Management in Search Equilibrium," *Journal of Political Economy*, 90, 881–894.

Diamond, P. (1987a), "Search Theory," *New Palgrave Dictionary of Economics* (London: Macmillan).

Diamond, P. (1987b), "Consumer Differences and Prices in a Search Model," *Quarterly Journal of Economics*, 102, 429–436.

Fethke, G. and Policano, A. (1986), "Will Wage Setters ever Stagger Decisions?" *Quarterly Journal of Economics*, 101, 867–877.

Fischer, S. (1981), "Relative Shocks, Relative Price Variability, and Inflation," *Brookings Papers on Economic Activity*, 381–432.

Fischer, S. (1984), "The Benefits of Price Stability", (MIT Working Paper no. 352).

Gertner, R. (1985), "Dynamic Duopoly with Price Inertia", (mimeo, MIT).

Gertner, R. (1987), "Inflation and Monopoly Power in a Duopoly Model with Search" (mimeo, University of Chicago, Graduate School of Business).

Green, E. and Porter, R. (1984), "Noncooperative Collusion under Imperfect Information," *Econometrica*, 52, 87–100.

Gul, F., Sonnenschein, H. and Wilson, R. (1985), "Dynamic Foundation of Monopoly and the Coase Conjecture," *Journal of Economic Theory*, 39, 155–190.

Lippman, S. and McCall, J. (1976), "The Economics of Job Search: A Survey," *Economic Inquiry*, 14, 155–189.

Maskin, E. and Tirole, J. (1988), "Models of Dynamic Oligopoly II: Price Competition, Kinked Demand Curves, and Edgeworth Cycles." *Econometrica*, 56, 571–600.

Mussa, M. (1976), "The Welfare Cost of Inflation and the Role of Inflation as a Unit of Account," *Journal of Money, Credit and Banking*, 9, 276–286.

Phelps, E. and Winter, S. (1970), "Optimal Price Policy under Atomistic Competition," in E. Phelps et.al., *Microeconomic Foundations of Inflation and Unemployment Theory*, (New York: Norton), 309–337.

Reinganum, J. (1979), "A Simple Model of Equilibrium Price Dispersion," *Journal of Political Economy*, 87, 851–858.

Rob, R. (1985), "Equilibrium Price Distributions," *Review of Economic Studies*, 52, 487–504.

Rotemberg, J. (1980), "Monopolistic Price Adjustment and Aggregate Output," *Review of Economic Studies*, 49, 517–531.

Rotemberg, J. (1983), "Aggregate Consequences of Fixed Costs of Price Adjustment," *American Economic Review*, 73, 433–436.

Rotemberg, J. and Saloner, G. (1985), "A Supergame-Theoretic Model of Business Cycles and Price Wars During Booms," *American Economic Review*, 76, 390–407.

Rothschild, M. (1973), "Models of Market Organization with Imperfect Information: A Survey," *Journal of Political Economy*, 81, 1283–1308.

Sheshinski, E. and Weiss, Y. (1977), "Inflation and Costs of Price Adjustment," *Review of Economic Studies*, 44, 287–304.

Sheshinski, E. and Weiss, Y. (1982), "Optimum Pricing Policy and Stochastic Inflation," *Review of Economic Studies*, 50, 513–529.

Sheshinski, E. and Weiss, Y. (1987), "Optimal Price Adjustment under Inflation; the Duopoly Case", (mimeo, Hebrew University of Jerusalem).

Sobel, J. (1984), "The Timing of Sales," *Review of Economic Studies*, 51, 353–368.

Stiglitz, J. (1985), "Competitivity and the Number of Firms in a Market: Are Duopolies More Competitive Than Atomistic Markets?" (IMSSS Technical Report no. 476, Stanford University).

Stokey, N. L. (1981), "Rational Expectations and Durable Goods Pricing," *Bell Journal of Economics*, 12, 112–128.

Von zur Muehlen, P. (1980), "Monopolistic Competition and Sequential Search," *Journal of Economic Dynamics and Control*, 2, 257–281.

13 Inflation and Efficiency in Search Markets

Roland Benabou

Introduction

Because higher inflation tends to be associated with greater dispersion of prices, households and businesses will devote more resources to searching for the lowest price when inflation is high.... Although this activity is productive from the point of view of the individual, from society's point of view it represents a waste because the resources are not being used to produce real goods and services.... For [this] reason, resources will not be allocated efficiently.
—Economic Report of the President (1990)[1]

This policy concern reflects what Fischer (1984) identified as "a persistent theme in the inflation literature," namely that inflation distorts the allocative role of the price system. Prominent in the standard list of potential inefficiencies is the connection described above between inflation, increased price dispersion, and the resources spent on search.

There is a fair amount of empirical evidence that higher rates of inflation are associated with increased variability and dispersion of relative prices. However, there is no theoretical model (nor empirical assessment) of the presumed link between this dispersion and the social cost of search.[2]

This chapter provides such a model; more generally, it examines how anticipated inflation affects market efficiency, output and social welfare. This requires taking into account what all informal arguments, including the above quotation, omit: the impact of search on equilibrium prices and entry. Indeed, if increased search makes markets more competitive, then it may in fact not be a net waste from society's point of view.

Previous models have captured some aspects of the interaction between inflation and market efficiency, but still miss others which are central to the issues at hand.[3] Benabou (1988) showed that in a search market with costs of price adjustment the increased price dispersion caused by inflation can intensify competition, reduce real prices and increase welfare (entry equalizes profits to zero). Diamond (1992), using different assumptions about search and price adjustment technologies, obtains similar effects for moderate inflation rates; but at higher rates, the exit of firms causes a worsening of the "thin-market" externality, and welfare declines as sellers become harder to find. These insights are useful, but restricted by two strong assumptions which both models share: buyers are identical and have unit demands below a certain valuation for the good. The first restriction implies that in equilibrium buyers search only once, making the resource cost of search a non-issue. The second means that the only allocative role of prices is through entry. Moreover, because firms cannot overshoot consumers' reservation value, there is a sense in which the chosen specification of preferences makes it easier for inflation to decrease real prices than to increase them.

To address these issues, this chapter generalizes Benabou (1988) in two directions:

(i) *Heterogeneity* among buyers accounts for search in equilibrium; the corresponding resource cost can then be linked to inflation.

(ii) Buyers with quite *general preferences* allow prices to play their full allocative role in the determination of output and welfare. Inflation can now potentially increase or reduce monopoly power and output, and the slope of this Phillips curve can be related to market structure.

In fact, one worthwhile purpose that this chapter might serve is to dispel any (incorrect) perception that models of (S, s) pricing and search tend to imply that inflation is beneficial. With some of the specifications used, it can be quite harmful.

The generalizations described above make the equilibrium fairly complex. Firms follow staggered (S, s) rules, while buyers search sequentially. Those with a low search cost seek and find sellers which have not revised their nominal price recently, while those with higher cost search less and buy more dearly. Correspondingly, a firm's sales increase while its nominal price remains fixed, and fall after each adjustment.

We prove the existence of equilibrium and identify the different components of welfare which are affected by inflation. In the case where costs of price adjustment are small, we show that inflation increases price dispersion and the resource cost of search, as traditionally asserted. For more general comparative statics, in particular those concerning output and welfare, we must resort to simulations. These confirm that the resource cost of search always rises with inflation, but also reveal that it remains quite small. The intuition is that the increased search by low search-cost buyers and the exit of firms both act as negative feed-backs which limit equilibrium price dispersion and total search. The output and welfare simulations indicate that what really matters is the way in which inflation alters monopoly power and the distribution of transaction prices. Two forces are at work there.

The first one is strategic complementarity between firms' prices, which reinforces the impact which inflation would have on a single monopolist's average price and output. This effect in turn can be positive or negative, depending on the form of consumers' preferences (Naish (1986), Konieczny (1990a)). The second force is increased price dispersion, which always raises the return to search—particularly for low search-cost types. This tends to reduce monopoly power. Therefore, in markets where search is inexpensive (compared to consumer surplus from the good), welfare will not fall very much, and may even rise with inflation. When search is more costly, however, inflation can significantly decrease output and welfare.

The general conclusion of the chapter is that formal analysis cuts both ways with respect to the conventional wisdom. It provides a rigorous basis for the idea that higher inflation results in more resources devoted to search, but also brings to light several more significant effects. These show that standard claims about the distortions which inflation causes in the price system cannot be taken at face value; nor is the usual type of evidence on price dispersion sufficient to assess them. The theory points instead to the need for more focussed empirical studies, paying particular attention to inflation's impact on markups, the entry or exit of firms, and market structure in general.

Section 1 presents the model. Section 2 derives optimal strategies and entry. The existence of an equilibrium and some of inflation's effects are established in Section 3. Section 4 analyzes the different components of welfare, and their variation with inflation is examined through simulations in Section 5. Throughout the paper the reader might want to refer to Figure 13.1.

1. The Model

1.1. Overview

It might be helpful to start with a general overview of the model's structure; specific assumptions will follow. We consider a monopolistically competitive search market under inflation. Its basic elements are illustrated in Figure 13.1, which is meant to serve as a road map throughout

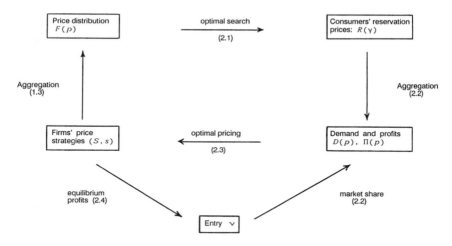

Figure 13.1
The structure of equilibrium. The numbers refer to the corresponding sections of the paper.

the chapter; indeed, each segment of the diagram corresponds to one of the sub-sections.

Firms set nominal prices, following staggered (S, s) price strategies. These generate a real price distribution $F(p)$, which determines an optimal reservation price $R(\gamma)$ for each buyer γ. These search rules aggregate to a demand curve $D(p)$ and profit function $\Pi(p)$, which in equilibrium must validate the original (S, s) price strategy as optimal for each firm. Finally, firms enter or exit the market until a marginal entrant's net present value of profits is zero.

We now describe in more detail the supply and demand sides of the market, as well as the inflationary process.

1.2. Description of the Market

A homogeneous good is produced by a continuum of identical firms, using labour as the sole input. These firms are infinitely-lived, with discount rate ρ. During each unit of time, production requires a fixed cost $h \geq 0$ and a marginal cost $c > 0$ per unit of output. Both are real costs, expressed in units of labour. Entry determines the measure $v \in (0, +\infty)$ of firms operating in equilibrium.

The demand side consists of a continuous flow of buyers who enter the market to make a one-time purchase of the good—for instance a durable.

During a period of length dt, a measure $1 \cdot dt$ of them arrive. Their surplus or indirect utility from buying the good at a real price p is $V(p)$; so when they do buy at p, they purchase $z(p) = -V'(p)$ units. Since $z(p)$ is the demand they would address to a monopolist, it will be called monopoly demand.

ASSUMPTION 1. Consumer surplus $V(p)$ is decreasing, convex and twice-continuously differentiable inside its support $[0, M]$, $c < M \leq +\infty$. Monopoly demand $z(p) \equiv -V'(p)$ has non-decreasing elasticity on $(0, M)$. If surplus is positive at any price $(M = +\infty)$, then $\lim_{p \to \infty} [-pz'(p)/z(p)] > 1$.

Assumption 1 is quite weak, and satisfied by all usual demand functions (and associated surplus $V(p) = \int_p^\infty z(u) \, du$): reservation price, linear, iso-elastic, exponential, etc.[4] It implies the following well-known property:

PROPOSITION 1. *The monopoly profit function* $\pi(p) = (p - c)z(p)$ *is strictly quasi-concave on its support, with a maximum at a finite* $p^m \in (c, M]$.

We consider, however, a market where buyers face many sellers whose prices they do not know, but among which they can search. Firms' demand and profit functions are then endogenous, and not equal to $z(p)$ and $\pi(p)$; Proposition 1 will nonetheless remain useful.

It is assumed that search is instantaneous and that buyers cannot postpone consumption; thus within the interval dt, all $1 \cdot dt$ of them arrive, search, buy, and leave the market. They are replaced by a similar generation of instantaneous consumers an instant later.[5] A first quotation is received for free but each subsequent search requires the expenditure of γ units of labour.[6] Consumers' labour endowment is assumed to be large enough for income effects from search costs to be neglible. Thus each one maximizes the expectation of $V(p_k) - k \cdot \gamma$, where p_k is the (random) real price at which he ends up buying, after k costly searches. Consumers differ only by their search costs, and for simplicity we assume:

ASSUMPTION 2. Buyers' search costs are uniformly distributed on the interval $[\underline{\gamma}, \bar{\gamma}]$, with $0 \leq \underline{\gamma} < \bar{\gamma}$.

1.3. Inflation and (S, s) Policies

Money is used as the unit of account, so that firms must set their prices in nominal terms. We consider a regime of steady, perfectly anticipated inflation, in which all aggregate prices grow at a constant rate $g > 0$. This is true in particular of the nominal wage, with respect to which real prices are defined; a fixed nominal price thus means a real price falling at the rate g. Firms can change their nominal price at any time, but doing so entails a real fixed cost $\beta > 0$. This may stem from decision costs, changing price tags, issuing and sending new price lists and catalogues, etc. But β can also be viewed as a proxy for any adverse reactions of customers to a price increase, not captured by the model (say, reputation effects); these need not be small.[7]

A firm's optimal price policy in such an environment is generally an (S, s) rule: it adjusts its nominal price so as to achieve a real value of S, every time this real value has been eroded down to $s < S$.[8] Our focus will therefore be on equilibria where firms' optimal strategy is a common (S, s) rule; a more formal definition is given below.

The set of equilibria under consideration will be narrowed down further by the requirement that the cross-sectional distribution of firms' real prices be invariant over time. With a constant rate of inflation this corresponds to price adjustments which are uniformly staggered (Rotemberg (1983)), and the invariant distribution is log-uniform on $[s, S]$ (Caplin and Spulber (1987)):[9]

$$dF(p) = \frac{dp}{p \, \mathrm{Ln}(S/s)} \quad \text{for all } p \text{ in } [s, S]. \tag{13.1}$$

There are three reasons for this stationarity requirement. The first one is microeconomic consistency: a time-varying (non-degenerate) price distribution would result in non-stationary search rules, demand and profit functions.[10] This in turn would make stationary (S, s) price strategies suboptimal. The second one is macroeconomic consistency: only if the distribution of firms' real prices is stationary will their nominal prices aggregate back into an index which grows smoothly, at the same rate g as the rest of the (macro) economy. The third reason is long-run stability. Almost any source of heterogeneity in firms' adjustment times, such as idiosyncratic cost or demand shocks, will cause the cross-sectional distribution of prices to converge to the steady-state distribution.[11]

1.4. Entry

In steady-state, the net present value of real profits for a potential entrant must be zero. As an entrant must pay β to set its first price (to S optimally), it is in the same position as a firm at s, about to start a new cycle. We can thus summarize the requirements illustrated on Figure 13.1 as follows:

Definition. A stationary, symmetric equilibrium is a triplet (S, s, v) and a sequential search strategy for each buyer such that: (a) there are v firms in the market, following identical, uniformly staggered (S, s) rules; (b) these price strategies and buyers' search strategies form a *subgame-perfect* equilibrium; (c) firms earn zero net discounted profits over each price cycle.

2. Search, Demand, and Pricing in Equilibrium

2.1. Search

We start by deriving each buyer's optimal search rule, given the distribution of prices (13.1) generated by firms' staggered (S, s) policies; see the upper part of Figure 13.1. For a buyer with search cost γ, the best strategy consists of accepting offers up to a real reservation price r at which he is indifferent between buying and searching again:[12]

$$V(r) = -\gamma + \int_s^r V(p)F(p)\,dp + \int_r^s V(r)F(p)\,dp, \tag{13.2}$$

assuming for now that this equation has a solution. Equivalently, the reservation price equates the cost and expected benefit of the marginal search:

$$\Gamma(r) \equiv \int_s^r [V(p) - V(r)]\,dF(p) = \int_s^r z(p)F(p)\,dp = \gamma. \tag{13.3}$$

The return $\Gamma(r)$ to searching rather than accepting a price r is increasing and continuously differentiable on $[s, M)$. Therefore, for a consumer with $\gamma < \Gamma(M)$, i.e. who would rather search than accept an offer leaving him with zero surplus, (13.3) has a unique solution $r = R(\gamma) \equiv \Gamma^{-1}(\gamma)$, with $s \leq r < M$; this is his optimal reservation price. As seen from (13.2), the expected surplus of such a consumer in this market is $V(r) + \gamma$.

For a consumer with $\gamma > \Gamma(M)$, on the other hand, any offer below M is preferable to search, so let $R(\gamma) = M$. Of course in equilibrium no firm ever charges more than M, since this would lead to zero demand; thus $S \leq M$ (this is formally proved in Section 2.3). The consumer will therefore accept the first offer encountered, and his expected surplus is just the market average:

$$\bar{V}(S, s) \equiv \int_s^S V(u)\,dF(u) = \int_s^M V(u)\,dF(u) = \int_s^M z(u)F(u)\,du = \Gamma(M)$$

(13.4)

where we used $S \leq M$ and $V(M) = 0$. Summarizing both cases, a buyer with search cost γ rejects offers above his reservation price $r = R(\gamma)$:

$$R(\gamma) = \sup\left\{ r \in (s, M)\,\bigg|\, \Gamma(r) = \int_s^r z(p)F(p)\,dp \leq \gamma \right\}$$

(13.5)

which embodies both his preferences and search prospects. When faced with an offer $p \leq R(\gamma)$, he accepts it and buys $z(p)$ units. The value of this optimal strategy is $V(R(\gamma)) + \Gamma(R(\gamma))$.[13] The highest and lowest reservation prices in the population, $R(\bar{\gamma})$ and $R(\underline{\gamma})$, will be denoted as $\bar{r}$ and $\underline{r}$.

2.2. Demand and Profits

We now proceed to aggregate the search rules of individual buyers into the demand curve faced by firms, as indicated on Figure 13.1. Since no one buys above $\bar{r}$, we can focus attention on prices below $\bar{r}$. Moreover, intuition suggests that pricing above $\bar{r}$ is never optimal, so that $S \leq \bar{r} \leq M$; this is formally shown in the next section.

There are $1/(\bar{\gamma} - \underline{\gamma})$ buyers with given search cost γ. They search at random until they find one of the $v \cdot F(R(\gamma))$ firms charging a price $p \leq R(\gamma)$, i.e. such that the marginal return to search $\Gamma(p)$ is less than their search cost γ. As a result, each of these firms will eventually retain $1/(v \cdot (\bar{\gamma} - \underline{\gamma}) \cdot F(R(\gamma)))$ such buyers, and each of them will buy $z(p)$ units. The demand for a firm charging a real price p is therefore:

$$D(p) = \frac{z(p)}{v}\cdot\left[\int_{\Gamma(p)}^{\bar{\gamma}} \frac{1}{F(R(\gamma))}\cdot\frac{d\gamma}{\bar{\gamma} - \underline{\gamma}}\right]$$

(13.6)

It is useful—and perhaps more intuitive—to express $D(p)$ in terms of the distribution of buyers' reservation prices. Consider first consumers with reservation price $r < M$; by (13.3), there are $\Gamma'(r)/(\bar{\gamma} - \underline{\gamma}) = z(r) \cdot F(r)/(\bar{\gamma} - \underline{\gamma})$ of them, and their probability of success in each round of search is $F(r)$. A given firm will therefore be visited by $z(r) \cdot F(r)/(v(\bar{\gamma} - \underline{\gamma}))$ of these buyers on their first search, $z(r) \cdot F(r)(1 - F(r))/(v(\bar{\gamma} - \underline{\gamma}))$ on their second search, $z(r) \cdot F(r)(1 - F(r))^{k-1}/(v(\bar{\gamma} - \gamma))$ on their k-th search, etc.; hence a total of $z(r)/(v(\bar{\gamma} - \gamma))$ consumers with reservation price r. Summing up over those who accept the firm's price, and adding the non-searchers ($r = M$, or $\gamma \geq \Gamma(M)$), of which each firm gets a share $1/v$, we have:[14]

$$D(p) = \frac{z(p)}{v(\bar{\gamma} - \gamma)} \left[\int_p^M z(r)\,dr + \int_{\Gamma(M)}^{\bar{\gamma}} d\gamma \right] \quad \text{for } p \geq \underline{r}, \tag{13.7}$$

or:

$$D(p) = \frac{1}{\bar{\gamma} - \gamma} \frac{z(p)}{v} [V(p) + \bar{\gamma} - \Gamma(M)] \quad \text{for } p \geq \underline{r}. \tag{13.8}$$

For $p < \underline{r}$, $V(p)$ is replaced by $V(\underline{r})$: charging less than the lowest reservation price does not attract any more customers, since it does not affect the price distribution $F(p)$ on which search decisions are based. At prices $p \geq \underline{r}$, search makes $D(p)$ more elastic than monopoly demand $z(p)$. Although this elasticity need not be increasing, the equilibrium demand function has the following fundamental property:[15]

PROPOSITION 2. *If $\underline{r} \leq p^m$, the equilibrium profit function $\Pi(p) = (p - c)D(p)$ is strictly quasi-concave on its support $[0, \bar{r}]$, with a maximum at some $p^* \leq p^m$.*

Proof. See appendix. ‖

As in Caplin and Nalebuff (1988), the aggregation of heterogeneous individuals' demand functions results in a (strictly) quasi-concave profit function.[16] This property will play a crucial role in the existence of an equilibrium, ensuring both that a firm's optimal strategy is an (S', s') rule, and the continuity of this best response in (S, s) space.

2.3. Price Strategies

We now close the price-search loop of Figure 13.1, by deriving a firm's best response to the (S, s) strategy of its competitors and buyers' search rules, as embodied in $D(p)$.

First, the strict quasi-concavity of the profit function $\Pi(p)$ is both necessary and sufficient to ensure that the optimal price strategy is a unique, stationary (S', s') rule (Zinde-Walsh (1987), Caplin and Sheshinski (1987)).[17] The firm's intertemporal real operating profits are therefore:

$$W(S', s') = \frac{\int_0^{T'} \Pi(S'e^{-gt})e^{-\rho t}\,dt - \beta}{1 - e^{-\rho T'}} \quad \text{with } T' = \frac{\text{Ln}(S'/s')}{g}. \quad (13.9)$$

T' is the duration of a real price cycle between S' and s', i.e. the length of time that the nominal price remains fixed. The firm chooses (S', s') or (S', T'), so as to maximize W. If there exists an interior optimum, it solves the first-order conditions $\partial W/\partial S' = 0$, $\partial W/\partial s' = 0$, or:

$$\Pi(s') = \rho W(S', s') \quad (13.10)$$

$$\Pi(S') - \Pi(s') = \rho\beta. \quad (13.11)$$

Condition (13.10) equates the benefit and opportunity cost of delaying adjustment when s' is reached: extra profits $\Pi(s') \cdot dt$ are earned, but the present value W is deferred by dt. Integrating (13.9) by parts, condition (13.11) can be rewritten as equating discounted marginal profits over the price cycle $\int_0^{T'} \Pi'(S'e^{-gt})e^{-(\rho+g)t}\,dt$ to zero. In general the optimum need not be interior, that is, we may have $S' = M$.[18] It is shown in the appendix that the appropriate, more general form of the first-order conditions is:

$$\Pi(s') = \rho W(S', s') \quad (13.12)$$

$$\Pi(S') - \Pi(s') \geq \rho\beta \quad \text{with equality unless (w.e.u.) } S' = M. \quad (13.13)$$

Conversely, if (13.12)–(13.13) have a solution, it is unique and is an interior optimum (Sheshinski and Weiss (1977)). In equilibrium, an individual price-setter's best response (S', s') must coincide with the (S, s) implemented by its competitors. It follows from the above discussion, and in particular from the uniqueness of the best response, that this fixed-point property is equivalent to the requirement that the original (S, s) pair solve (13.12)–(13.13). In particular, (13.13) requires $S' \leq \bar{r}$, validating our previous claim that $S \leq \bar{r} \leq M$.

2.4. Entry

The last requirement for a monopolistically competitive equilibrium is that firms' operating profits (net of adjustment costs) just cover their fixed costs h/ρ:

$$\rho W(S, s) = h, \quad (13.14)$$

or

$$\Pi(s) = h \tag{13.15}$$

by (13.12) with $(S', s') = (S, s)$. It is worth noting from (13.15) that operating profits always cover fixed and variable costs, so firms are always willing to operate and satisfy demand. To illustrate the role played by entry and exit, suppose for instance that fixed costs h or adjustment costs β become large. Some firms then leave, increasing the remaining ones' market share $1/v$. As a result, the profits $\Pi(p) = (1/v) \cdot \pi(p)[V(p) + \bar{\gamma} - \Gamma(M)]/(\bar{\gamma} - \underline{\gamma})$ which they make at *any* price $p < \bar{r}$ rise, and so does the present value W given in (13.9). This continues until profits cover all costs.[19]

We can now express all equilibrium conditions in terms of $E \equiv (S, s, v, \underline{r}, \bar{r})$ only. In order to avoid rewriting the complicated expressions for the return to search, equilibrium profits and value from an (S', s') strategy, we shall simply make these functions' dependence on E explicit, by denoting them as $\Gamma_E(p)$, $\Pi_E(p)$, and $W_E(S', s')$ respectively. Γ_E is defined from (13.1) and (13.3); Π_E results from (13.8); finally, given Π_E, W_E is given by (13.9).

PROPOSITION 3.   *An equilibrium is a quintuple* $E \equiv (S, s, v, \underline{r}, \bar{r})$, *with* $s < S < +\infty, 0 < v < +\infty$, *and* $\underline{r} \leq p^m$, *which solves:*[20]

$$\Gamma_E(\underline{r}) \leq \underline{\gamma}, \qquad w.e.u. \quad \underline{r} = M. \quad (Optimality\ of\ \underline{r}) \tag{13.16}$$

$$\Gamma_E(\bar{r}) \leq \bar{\gamma} \qquad w.e.u. \quad \bar{r} = M. \quad (Optimality\ of\ \bar{r}) \tag{13.17}$$

$$\Pi_E(s) = h. \qquad (Optimality\ of\ s) \tag{13.18}$$

$$\Pi_E(S) \geq h + \rho\beta, \qquad w.e.u. \quad S = M. \quad (Optimality\ of\ S) \tag{13.19}$$

$$W_E(S, s) = h/\rho. \qquad (Entry) \tag{13.20}$$

This system of five equations in five unknowns is the analytical counterpart to Figure 13.1. It summarizes the entry, pricing strategies and search decisions of all firms and buyers in the market. The fixed-point nature of an equilibrium is apparent from the fact that E appears as both parameter and argument.

3.   Equilibrium

We first briefly examine a market with identical buyers. This simple case reveals most clearly an important mechanism by which inflation can pro-

mote competition via increased price dispersion. It also provides a robust
intuition for the more complex case of heterogeneous buyers, which is
considered next. In that case the dispersion effect is counterbalanced and
possibly dominated by other effects, but still plays an important role.

3.1. Identical Buyers

Let buyers have the same search cost $\bar{\gamma} = \underline{\gamma} \equiv \gamma$ and unit demand, i.e.
$V(p) = \max(M - p, 0)$. Since they have the same reservation price $\underline{r} =
\bar{r} \equiv r$, the demand curve which firms face is just a step function:[21]

$$D(p) = 1/v \quad \text{for } p \leq r, \qquad D(p) = 0 \quad \text{for } p > r. \tag{13.21}$$

Since demand is inelastic below r and zero above, firms optimally set
$S = r$.[22] Equation (13.17) then becomes: $S - \int_s^S p \, dF(p) \leq \gamma$ (w.e.u. $S = M$),
so, with (13.18):

$$S = \min\left\{M, \gamma + \frac{S-s}{Ln(S/s)}\right\}; \qquad s = c + \frac{h}{v}. \tag{13.22}$$

The highest price is constrained by the minimum of consumers' willingness to pay and the average price in the market, plus the search cost;
the lowest price reflects production costs and market share. Entry (13.20)
determines v. This is the model analyzed in detail in Benabou (1988); in
particular:

THEOREM 1. *If buyers have the same search cost and inelastic demand,
there is a unique equilibrium. A higher inflation rate increases price dispersion S/s but reduces real prices S and s and the number of firms v. Inflation
improves consumer surplus and (at least when ρ is not too large) social
welfare.*[23]

The basic intuition is very simple. In equilibrium all buyers accept the
first price offered, but search matters as a credible threat constraining S.
By increasing price dispersion and the return to search, a higher rate of
inflation creates more competitive pressure on firms, forcing a lowering of
the whole (S, s) price range and an increase in consumer surplus.[24] Due to
staggering, the aggregate of net profits per unit of time is just v times a
single firm's net average profits over the cycle; when ρ is small, this is close
to its net discounted profits over the cycle, which are zero due to entry.
Thus total welfare increases as well.

To show that inflation can also *lower* welfare by increasing monopoly power and generating a resource cost of search, we now turn back to the general model. The reader who wishes to skip the derivation of the equilibrium can go directly to Theorem 2 below.

3.2. Heterogeneous Buyers

Let us revert to the case of different buyers with general preferences satisfying Assumption 1, and simplify the problem by assuming that $\gamma = 0$. Condition (13.16) then gives $\underline{r} = s$, which must be no greater than p^m. Condition (3.17) is unchanged and determines the maximum reservation price $\underline{r}$ as a function of (S, s). Condition (3.18) gives the equilibrium number of firms:

$$v = \frac{\pi(s)}{h\bar{\gamma}} [V(s) + \bar{\gamma} - \bar{V}(S, s)] \tag{13.23}$$

where $\bar{V}(S, s) = \Gamma(M)$ by (13.4). Substituting v into (13.19) and (13.20) then leads to a system in the two unknowns (S, s) only:[25]

$$\pi(S)[V(S) + \bar{\gamma} - \bar{V}(S, s)] \geq \left[1 + \frac{\rho\beta}{h}\right]\pi(s)[V(s) + \bar{\gamma} - \bar{V}(S, s)],$$

$$\text{w.e.u.} \quad S = M; \tag{13.24}$$

$$\int_s^S \frac{\pi(u)[V(u) + \bar{\gamma} - \bar{V}(S, s)]}{\pi(s)[V(s) + \bar{\gamma} - \bar{V}(S, s)]} u^{\delta-1} \, du = \left[\frac{g\beta \cdot S^\delta}{h} + \frac{S^\delta - s^\delta}{\delta}\right] \tag{13.25}$$

where $\delta \equiv \rho/g$. This system completely determines the equilibrium, provided $s \leq p^m$ and the right-hand side of (13.24) is positive. It shows that equilibrium prices depend on the market frictions only through the ratios β/h of adjustment costs to fixed costs, and $\bar{\gamma}/V(\cdot)$ of search costs relative to consumer surplus. We shall come back to these intuitive properties when interpreting the simulations of Section 5.

Using in particular the strict quasi-concavity of Π established in Proposition 2 and the properties of $z(p)$ from Assumption 1, we prove:

THEOREM 2. *When $\gamma = 0$, there exists an equilibrium; buyers search actively and each firm's sales are cyclical.*

Proof. See appendix. ‖

This result is of some independent interest because it provides a parallel, for search and dynamic price-setting, to the general existence results of

Caplin and Nalebuff (1988) for static models of imperfect competition. In both cases the equilibrium rests on the property that the demands of individuals with appropriately distributed characteristics aggregate to a quasi-concave profit function, so that firms' best-reply correspondence is continuous.

In general one cannot establish the uniqueness of the (symmetric) equilibrium analytically, but numerical simulations strongly suggest that such is the case.[26] In any event, all equilibria share the same basic features: buyers with low search actively seek firms which have not revised their nominal price recently—and are thus at a low point of their (S, s) cycle. Buyers whose search cost is higher search less and do not fare as well. As a result, a firm's sales increase while its nominal price remains fixed, and fall after each adjustment.

3.3.   The Resource Cost of Search

We can now evaluate total search expenditures by consumers C_s, and see whether they rise with inflation. To compute C_s, note that each buyer with cost γ searches on average $1/F(R(\gamma))$ times; since the first one is free, we have[27]

$$C_s = \int_{\underline{\gamma}}^{\bar{\gamma}} \gamma \cdot \left[\frac{1}{F(R(\gamma))} - 1 \right] \frac{d\gamma}{\bar{\gamma} - \underline{\gamma}} = \int_{\underline{r}}^{\bar{r}} \Gamma(r) \left[\frac{1}{F(r)} - 1 \right] \Gamma'(r) \frac{dr}{\bar{\gamma} - \underline{\gamma}},$$

or[28]

$$C_s = \int_{\underline{r}}^{\bar{r}} z(r)\Gamma(r) \frac{dr}{\bar{\gamma} - \underline{\gamma}} - \frac{\bar{\gamma} + \underline{\gamma}}{2} \tag{13.26}$$

We now show that price dispersion and the cost C_s increase with the inflation rate, assuming the costs of price adjustment are small. Consider first the case where prices are perfectly flexible, i.e. $\beta = 0$. The equilibrium then reduces to a single real price $S = s = p_*$. By Proposition 2, p_* is the unique maximizer of $\Pi_*(p) = \pi(p)[V(p) + \bar{y} - V(p_*)]$, since $\bar{V}(p_*, p_*) = V(p_*)$. Note that the threat of search generally forces $p_* < p^m$. Now, for small $\rho\beta/h$ and $g\beta/h$, third-order Taylor expansions allow us to show:

PROPOSITION 4.   *Assume that price adjustment costs are small ($\beta \ll \min\{h/\rho, h/g\}$), and $\gamma = 0$. A higher rate of inflation then results in more frequent price adjustments, increased real price dispersion and more resources spent on search. Specifically:*

$$\frac{S - p_*}{p_*} \approx \frac{p_* - s}{p_*} \approx \frac{gT}{2} \approx \left[\frac{g\beta}{ah}\right]^{1/3} \tag{13.27}$$

$$C_s \approx \left[\frac{g\beta}{bh}\right]^{2/3} \tag{13.28}$$

where p_* is the real price when $\beta = 0$, $a = -2p_*^2 \cdot \Pi_*''(p_*)/(3\Pi^*(p_*))$ reflects the concavity of equilibrium profits near p_*, and $b = a \cdot (6\bar{\gamma})^{3/2}/(p_* \cdot z(p_*))^3$.

Proof. See appendix. ∥

This result is interesting because one often thinks of costs of price adjustment as not being very large. While the approximations require in principle that $(g\beta/h)^{1/3}$ and $(\rho\beta/h)^{1/3}$ be small, hence $g\beta/h$ and $\rho\beta/h$ very small, simulations show that they remain reliable up to $\beta/h \leq 0.1$ and $g \leq 50\%$.[29] On the other hand, this still leaves out interesting cases, such as free entry ($h = 0$); more generally, realism only requires β to be small compared to gross revenue $p \cdot D(p)$, not to operating profits ($p - c)D(p)$, or $h = (s - c)D(s)$.

In any case, the resources spent on search are only one of the components of welfare; we now turn to the others, proceeding in two stages. In Section 4 output, surplus, profits and welfare are computed as functions of the equilibrium $E = (S, s, \bar{r}, \underline{r}, v)$; this brings to light the different channels through which inflation operates. As the model is too complicated to do comparative statics and assess the importance of the various effects analytically, simulations are then performed in Section 5.

4.   Inflation and Welfare

Welfare is defined as the sum of aggregate consumer and producer surplus, and not in any Paretian sense. Indeed it will be clear that inflation causes substantial redistributions between firms and consumers, as well as among consumers with different search costs. Turning to buyers first, their welfare per unit of time is simply the value of their search strategies:

$$B_c = \int_{\underline{\gamma}}^{\bar{\gamma}} [V(R(\gamma)) + \Gamma(R(\gamma))] \frac{d\gamma}{\bar{\gamma} - \underline{\gamma}} \tag{13.29}$$

which depends only on the equilibrium (S, s) bounds. In particular, if buyers have unit demands, as in Benabou (1988) or Diamond (1992), all that matters is their common reservation price, i.e. the highest price in the market. A more fruitful decomposition of B_c is the difference between the gross surplus from all transactions and the total resource cost of search C_s:

$$B_c = \int_s^S V(p)N(p)\,dF(p) - C_s \tag{13.30}$$

where $N(p) = D(p)/z(p) = \min(V(p), V(\underline{r})) + \bar{y} - \bar{V}(S, s)$ is the total number of transactions at a price p, and $N \cdot dF$ sums to one on $[s, S]$.[30] Aggregate output is given by the same expression as gross surplus $B_c + C_s$, but with $V(p)$ replaced by $z(p)$. Clearly, inflation will affect surplus and output both through F, the *distribution of prices* in the market, and through N, the *distribution of transactions* across prices. This latter effect is accompanied by a change in the total amount of search and its cost C_s, given by (13.26).

In the absence of discounting, B_c would represent total social welfare. Indeed, as price revisions are uniformly staggered, aggregate profits per unit of time coincide with a given firm's average profits over the (S, s) cycle, times the number of firms v; when $\rho = 0$, these average profits, net of fixed and menu costs, are equalized by entry to zero (let $\rho \to 0$ in (13.9) and (13.14)).

When $\rho > 0$, undiscounted profits over the cycle are larger than discounted profits; since it is the latter (net of fixed costs) which are zero, total profits per unit of time are positive, and can be decomposed into:

$$B_f = \int_s^S (p - c)z(p)N(p)\,dF(p) - v\left[h + \frac{\beta}{T}\right]. \tag{13.31}$$

The first term is operating profits from the $N(p)$ transactions at each firm; the second one is total fixed costs; the last one is total adjustment costs, since a proportion $1/T = g/\mathrm{Ln}(S/s)$ of firms adjust per unit of time.[31] Summing up, social welfare equals *aggregate gains from trade*, minus the resources spent on the three types of *market frictions*: search, price adjustment, and fixed operating costs:

$$B = \int_s^S [(p - c)z(p) + V(p)]N(p)\,dF(p) - C_s - v\left[h + \frac{\beta}{T}\right]. \tag{13.32}$$

The first term reflects the allocative role played by prices through production, search and consumption decision. With unit consumer demand it becomes a constant. In general, however, the equilibrium (S, s) price cycles can either worsen or alleviate the inefficiency of monopolistic pricing, and this term will thus be affected by inflation.

The second term reflects the resources spent on search for better prices, and will generally rise with inflation. It vanishes in models with identical buyers, since all accept the first offer received.[32] The third effect of inflation will be to tend to reduce the number of firms in the market (by forcing them to charge less profitable real prices and adjust more often), and with it the inefficient duplication of fixed costs which characterizes monopolistic competition when $h > 0$. Finally, this induced exit will partially offset the increase in adjustment costs per operating firm (last term).

5.   Simulations

We now turn to simulations of the model. Their purpose is not to match actual data, but simply to help explore the various channels through which inflation operates in equilibrium, and provide a sense of the magnitudes involved. Two specifications of preferences are used, corresponding to isoelastic ($z(p) = p^{-\alpha}$, $M = +\infty$) and linear ($z(p) = M - p$) monopoly demand. The inflation rate g ranges from zero to fifty per cent a year. A large number of parameter values were explored, but only a dozen representative outcomes are reported. The reference set of parameters is $c = 1$, $\gamma = 0$, $\bar{\gamma} = 0.10$, $\beta = h = 10$, $\rho = 0.05$, $\alpha = 4.1$ or $M = 8$; alternative values are explored in Figures 13.2(a) to 13.8(c). The parameters were chosen so as to yield plausible values of the duration of prices, price dispersion, and adjustment costs as a fraction of revenues over a cycle.[33]

5.1   Price Dispersion, Search, and Exit

Three very *robust results* come out of the simulations, holding across all preference specifications and parameter values. They show in particular that the conclusions of Proposition 4 hold quite generally, and not just for very small price adjustment costs.

RESULT 1.   *As the rate of inflation increases, so does real price dispersion, although prices are changed more frequently.*

For the isoelastic specification (Figure 13.2(a)), both price dispersion and its rate of increase with inflation are quite significant: for g equal to

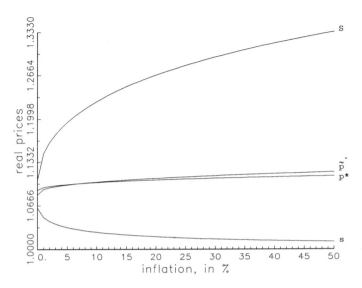

Figure 13.2a
Inflation and real prices: $c = 1$, $\beta = h = 10$, $\bar{y} = .10$, $\rho = .05$, $z(p) = p^{-\alpha}$, $\alpha = 4.1$

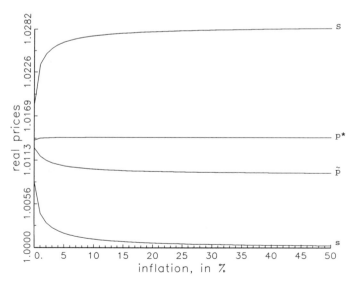

Figure 13.2b
Inflation and real prices: $c = 1$, $\beta = h = 10$, $\bar{y} = .10$, $\rho = .05$, $z(p) = M - p$, $M = 8$

1%, 10% and 50%, $S/s - 1$ is respectively 9.3%, 19.5% and 31.7%. This accords well with the empirical evidence that higher rates of inflation are associated with greater price dispersion, such as Fischer (1981), Domberger (1987), or Danziger (1987b). The linear specification, on the contrary, leads to a very weak relationship (Figure 13.2(b)): price dispersion only rises from 1.9% at $g = 1\%$ to 2.8% at $g = 50\%$, while the decrease in T is very fast: for $g = 1\%$, 10% and 50%, prices are revised every 20.6, 5.7 and 0.7 months, versus every 97.0, 21.2 and 6.6 months under the isoelastic specification. This is consistent with Kashyap's (1987) findings of very small price adjustments (2–3% for certain goods). Cecchetti (1986) also shows that for magazine prices, higher inflation is accompanied by more frequent but not significantly larger adjustments. In his case, however, $S/s - 1$ is always large (25%); this type of behaviour seems more difficult to account for with the type of (S, s) model considered here.

Figures 13.2(a) and 2(b) also show firms' desired price p^* and the average transaction price $\tilde{p}$, which indicates how effective searchers are in finding the "bargains" which inflation creates in the market.[34,35]

The next result, illustrated in Figures 13.3(a) and 13.3(b), confirms the idea of a cost of inflation due to increased search, but with an important caveat.

RESULT 2. *As the rate of inflation increases, so do the total number of searches and the total resources spent on search. This cost, however, remains small.*

The basic mechanism is clear: although inflation may cause prices to be higher or lower on average (see p^* and $\tilde{p}$), it always increases dispersion, and thereby results in increased search and more resources spent on search.[36]

There is, however, an opposing force at work: while more price dispersion generates more search, more search intensifies price competition and allows less price dispersion.[37] This is why C_s increases rapidly with inflation rates of up to about 20%, then tapers off. As a result, the total cost of search remains rather small; on average consumers search only a couple of times. This result is very robust to variations in $\bar{y}$ and other parameters, and perhaps not as surprising as one would initially think. If search costs are high, increased price dispersion at higher inflation rates is sustainable, but only because few consumers can take advantage of it; if search costs

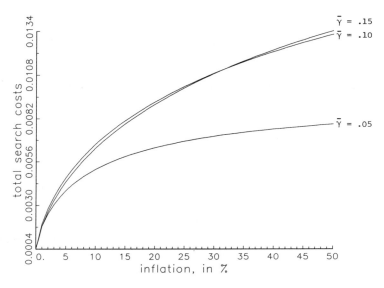

Figure 13.3a
Inflation and the resource cost of search: $c = 1$, $\beta = h = 10$, $\rho = .05$, $z(p) = p^{-\alpha}$, $\alpha = 4.1$

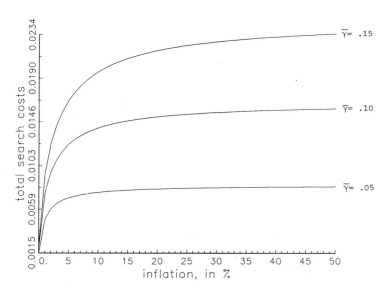

Figure 13.3b
Inflation and the resource cost of search: $c = 1$, $\beta = h = 10$, $\rho = .05$, $z(p) = M - p$, $M = 8$

are low, firms will not allow large price dispersion even at high inflation, so as to limit the amount of search by buyers.

The next result (and Figures 13.4(a)–13.4(b) shows that the exit of firms constitutes a second feedback which limits the impact of inflation on real prices. In fact, the effects of search and exit as dampening forces are visible on all equilibrium variables (most curves become fairly flat above $g = 20\%$). Because informal arguments fail to take them into account, they may well overestimate both the costs and benefits of inflation.

RESULT 3. *As the rate of inflation increases, the number of firms in the market decreases.*

Higher inflation forces each firm to widen its price range around p^* (Result 1); this always lowers profits, as do the more frequent menu costs. Equilibrium profits are restored by the exit of some firms; the remaining ones' increased market share now makes it profitable for them to revise their prices more often. This constitutes the second limiting force on price dispersion and search.

The model's implication that inflation results in markets which are more concentrated (but not necessarily less competitive, as will be seen below) could be tested by checking whether prolonged inflationary periods are associated with greater numbers of bankruptcies and mergers. The elimination of firms from a monopolistically competitive market promotes efficiency by reducing rent dissipation, i.e. the duplication of fixed and pricing costs. On the other hand, bankruptcies entail economic and political costs (reorganization, unemployment) which might realistically offset this efficiency gain, at least from an elected policy-maker's point of view.

We now turn to the effects of inflation on output (or on the average transaction price $\tilde{p}$) and on the different components of welfare. Unlike the preceding ones, they turn out to be very sensitive to the specification of consumers' *preferences* and the values of the *market frictions* $\bar{\gamma}$, β and h.

5.2. The Inflation-Output Relationship

Naish (1986) and Konieczny (1990a) have examined whether inflation increases or lowers the average price and output of a monopolistic firm over its (S, s) cycle. The answer unfortunately depends on two somewhat unintuitive factors: the skewness of the (log) profit function, which determines whether S increases faster or slower than s decreases as inflation

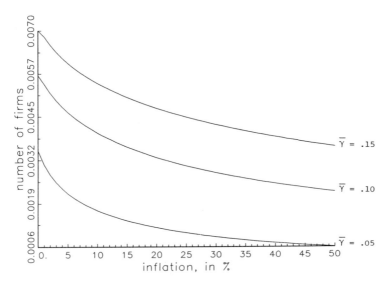

Figure 13.4a
Inflation and the number of firms: $c = 1$, $\beta = h = 10$, $\rho = .05$, $z(p) = p^{-\alpha}$, $\alpha = 4.1$

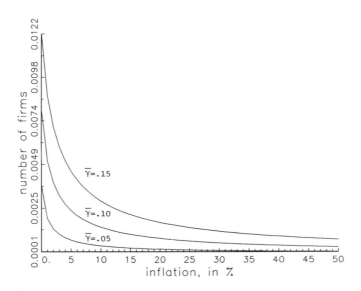

Figure 13.4b
Inflation and the number of firms: $c = 1$, $\beta = h = 10$, $\rho = .05$, $z(p) = M - p$, $M = 8$

rises, and the curvature of the demand function, which determines the output consequences of these changes (through Jensen's inequality). With constant marginal cost, inflation tends to decrease output if demand is isoelastic, and to increase it if demand is linear (Naish (1986)). This sensitivity in itself justifies modelling preferences with enough generality.

Under monopolistic competition, demand and profit functions are endogenous, and therefore affected by inflation; this makes skewness and curvature more elusive concepts. It remains true, however, that the functional form of $z(p)$ strongly influences demand $D(p)$ and profits $\Pi(p)$; see (13.8). There is unfortunately no more economic intuition to be gained here than in the monopoly case. But equally important are other firms' pricing and buyers' purchasing decisions, embodied in the number of buyers at a price p, namely $D(p)/z(p) = [V(p) + \bar{\gamma} - \bar{V}(S, s)]/(v\bar{\gamma})$. These decisions reflect in turn the whole market structure, i.e. the costs of search, price adjustment, and entry. It is on these equilibrium aspects of the inflation-output relationship that the model will deliver some new results and intuitions.

Figures 13.5(a)–13.5(b) and 13.6(a)–13.6(b) plot *percentage* deviations of output from its zero inflation level. They confirm that the monopoly results need no longer hold, but only provide a reasonable "first guess." With the isoelastic specification, the effect of inflation can be *strongly negative*: a rise in g from zero to 5% a year reduces output by 4.0%; from 5% to 10% there is a further decrease of 3.5% (Figure 13.5(a) for $\bar{\gamma} = 0.15$). With a lower α, the slope of the Phillips curve becomes slightly positive; for $\alpha = 1.1$, a 10% inflation rate raises output by 0.5% (Figure 13.6(a)). With the linear specification, the impact of inflation is less than 2% either way (Figures 13.5(b) and 13.6(b)); as mentioned before, it mostly translates into a rapid decrease in T and v.

To understand the intuition for what determines the average price and output in equilibrium, assume first that in response to an increase in inflation, firms re-set their (S, s) bands as monopolists, not taking into account the fact that their profit and demand functions will be different in the new equilibrium. The (S, s) band widens, and the average price moves up or down, depending on the form of the old $\Pi(p)$. But both these effects have equilibrium consequences. First, if firms now have higher prices on average, then any one of them can shift its price band up a little without losing too many customers; this in turn encourages other firms to move still a little higher, and so on. The same holds true for downward move-

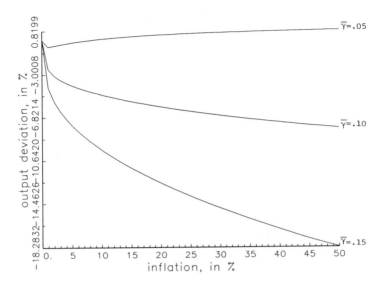

Figure 13.5a
Inflation, output, and search costs: $c = 1$, $\beta = h = 10$, $\rho = .05$, $z(p) = p^{-\alpha}$, $\alpha = 4.1$

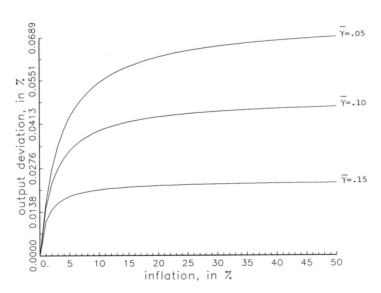

Figure 13.5b
Inflation, output, and search costs: $c = 1$, $\beta = h = 10$, $\rho = .05$, $z(p) = M - p$, $M = 8$

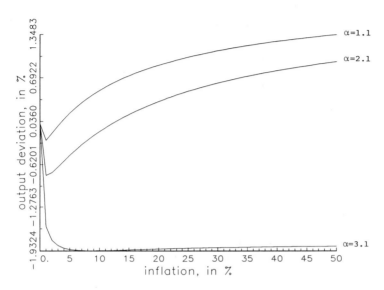

Figure 13.6a
Inflation, output, and preferences: $c = 1$, $\beta = h = 10$, $\bar{\gamma} = .10$, $\rho = .05$, $z(p) = p^{-\alpha}$

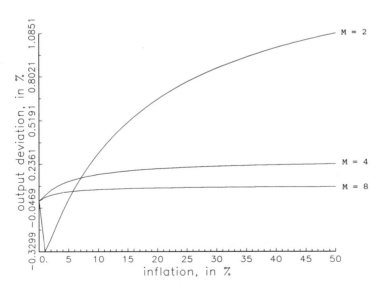

Figure 13.6b
Inflation, output, and preferences: $c = 1$, $\beta = h = 10$, $\bar{\gamma} = .10$, $\rho = .05$, $z(p) = M - p$

ments. Thus *strategic complementarity* reinforces a single firm's incentive to shift its (S, s) band in either direction. Secondly, the increased dispersion per se always raises the return to search, as in Theorem 1, and this works to lower prices. The relative strength of these two forces depends in particular on how easy it is to search, and on how much surplus is derived from finding a lower price. This intuition is confirmed by the simulations shown on Figures 13.5(a)–13.5(b).

RESULT 4.   *A higher rate of inflation can increase or decrease output. The slope of this Phillips curve depends on preferences and market structure. If search costs are low (respectively, high) relative to consumer surplus, inflation tends to raise (respectively, lower) output.*

Indeed, the more desired the good (low α or high M) and the easier it is to search (low $\bar{\gamma}$), the more demand and profits are determined by search as opposed to tastes, as more buyers try to take advantage of increased price dispersion to find low prices. In the converse situation, severe stagflation is possible. The model thus delivers positive results in spite of the

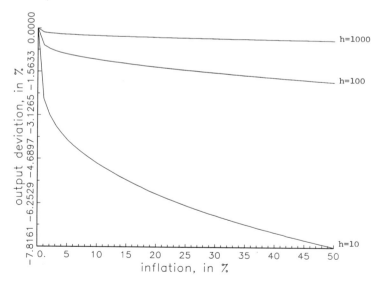

Figure 13.7
Inflation, output, and fixed costs: $c = 1$, $\beta = 10$, $\bar{\gamma} = .10$, $\rho = .05$, $z(p) = p^{-\alpha}$, $\alpha = 4.1$

sensitivity of the Phillips curve to the functional form of consumer surplus (itself a reminder of the risks of drawing conclusions from convenient but restrictive specifications). In particular, the implication that inflation has a differential impact on markups and output across markets with different degrees of friction or competitiveness should be empirically *testable*.

As shown by Figure 13.7, the entry cost h also significantly affects the slope of the output-inflation locus. Higher fixed costs imply fewer operating firms; their larger market shares then justify more frequent price revisions, and this reduces real prices' sensitivity to inflation.

5.3. Surplus, Profits, and Welfare

Figures 13.8(a)–13.8(b) illustrate the typical results emerging from welfare simulations. Social welfare generally varies like its main component, gross consumer surplus, which in turn follows output. It is possible, however, that increased search costs reverse this relationship (Figure 13.8(c) for g between 1% and 4%). The original concern with this cost of inflation thus had some validity, although the numbers here remain quite small. For firms, gross profits vary inversely with output (as does the average transaction price $\bar{p}$). The resources spent on fixed costs decrease as firms are forced out of the market, but the total cost of price adjustments increases. In fact, net profits always decrease (when $\rho > 0$), subtracting from total welfare. As before, the effects are much larger with isoelastic than with linear $z(p)$: in Figure 13.8(a) a rise in g from 0% to 10% (respectively from 10% to 20%) decreases B by a substantial 6.6% (respectively 8.6%), but in Figure 13.8(b) it increases it by only 0.02% (respectively by 0.03%).

RESULT 5.   *Whether inflation is beneficial or harmful to social welfare depends on preferences and market structure, and in particular, on whether search costs are low or high relative to consumer surplus. The variations of welfare most often mirror those of total output, but increased search expenditures may sometimes cause it to fall in spite of rising output.*

6. Conclusion

This chapter has examined the functioning of a monopolistically competitive search market under inflation. It has formalized the idea that inflation increases the amount of resources spent on search, and more generally

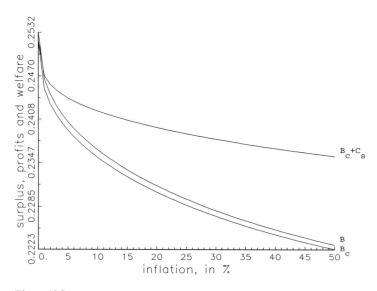

Figure 13.8a
Inflation and welfare: $c = 1$, $\beta = h = 10$, $\bar{y} = .10$, $\rho = .05$, $z(p) = p^{-\alpha}$, $\alpha = 4.1$
$B_C + C_S$ = gross consumer surplus; B_C = consumer surplus, net of search costs;
$B - B_C$ = net profits; B = social welfare

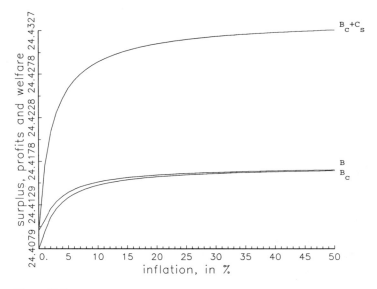

Figure 13.8b
Inflation and welfare: B_C, C_S, and B defined as on Figure 13.8a; $c = 1$, $\beta = h = 10$, $\bar{y} = .10$,
$\rho = .05$, $z(p) = M - p$, $M = 8$

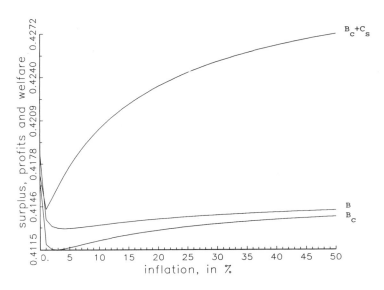

Figure 13.8c
Inflation and welfare: B_C, C_S, and B defined as on Figure 13.8a; $c = 1$, $\beta = h = 10$, $\bar{\gamma} = .10$, $\rho = .05$, $z(p) = M - p$, $M = 8$

has developed a micro-theoretic framework to examine several channels through which inflation affects competition, output and welfare.

While inflation increases price dispersion and the resources devoted to search, it also has a long-run benefit, by reducing the number of firms and rent dissipation. But most importantly, it alters both the distribution of equilibrium prices and the distribution of buyers across prices. This effect can potentially alleviate or worsen the inefficiency of monopolistic pricing, as follows. In markets where search is inexpensive relative to the surplus derived from the good, welfare will not fall very much, and may even rise with inflation, as most buyers take advantage of the increased price dispersion. When search is costly, on the contrary, inflation can significantly reduce output and welfare.

It is interesting to relate these results to those obtained by Benabou and Gertner (1992) for the effects of *unanticipated* inflation, i.e. of the price level's variance rather than its trend. Once it is recognized that agents can not only engage in signal extraction (as in Lucas (1973), Cukierman (1979, 1983) or Hercowitz (1981)), but also acquire additional information through search, similar conclusions emerge: whether inflation uncertainty impairs or promotes efficiency depends on the size of informational costs.

Clearly, inflation's impact on search and competition is only one of its many consequences. Numerous other potential costs identified by Fischer and Modigliani (1978) lie outside the scope of this chapter. Its aim, however, was only to examine a certain conventional wisdom about the distortions inflicted by inflation to the price system. In that respect, it shows that assessing the validity of such claims will in fact require empirical studies which go beyond simple measures of price dispersion, but pay particular attention to markups, entry or exit, and market structure.

Appendix

Proof of Proposition 2. The equilibrium profit function is (see equation (13.8) and footnote (14))

$$\Pi(p) = \frac{1}{\bar{\gamma} - \underline{\gamma}} \frac{\pi(p)}{v} [\min(V(p), V(\underline{r})) + \underline{\gamma} - \max(\underline{\gamma}, \overline{V}(S, s))] \tag{13.A1}$$

with $\pi(p) = (p - c)z(p)$ and $\overline{V}(S, s) = \Gamma(M)$. To simplify the notation, let $K \equiv \bar{\gamma} - \max(\underline{\gamma}, \overline{V}(S, s))$, and $\Delta(p) \equiv z(p)(V(p) + K)$, for all p. Finally, we denote the elasticity of monopoly demand $z(p)$ as $\alpha_z(p) \equiv -pz'(p)/z(p)$.

On the interval $(0, \underline{r}]$, $\Pi(p)$ is proportional to monopoly profits $\pi(p)$; given Proposition 1, it is therefore increasing, provided $\underline{r} \le p^m$.

On the interval $[\underline{r}, \bar{r}]$, $D(p)$ is proportional $\Delta(p)$ and $\Pi(p)$ to $\Pi_\Delta(p) \equiv (p - c)\Delta(p)$, which will now be shown to be strictly quasi-concave on its support $[c, \bar{r}] \subset [c, M]$. There are two cases to consider.

Case 1. When $K < 0$, or $\bar{r} < M$, we show the stronger property that $\Delta(p)$ has increasing elasticity $\alpha_\Delta(p)$. Proposition 1 will then yield strict quasi-concavity of $\Pi_\Delta(p)$. On $(0, \bar{r})\Delta(p)$ has elasticity:

$$\alpha_\Delta(p) = \alpha_z(p) + \frac{pz(p)}{V(p) + K} > \alpha_z(p) \tag{13.A2}$$

and:

$$\alpha'_\Delta(p) = \alpha'_z(p) + \frac{z(p)(1 - \alpha_z(p))(V(p) + K)) + p \cdot z(p)^2}{(V(p) + K)^2} \tag{13.A3}$$

where we used the fact that:

$$\frac{d(p \cdot z(p))}{dp} = z(p)(1 - \alpha_z(p)). \tag{13.A4}$$

But this same equality yields:

$$p \cdot z(p) - \bar{r} \cdot z(\bar{r}) = - \int_p^{\bar{r}} z(u)(1 - \alpha_z(u)) \, du$$

$$= (V(\bar{r}) + K)(1 - \alpha_z(\bar{r})) - (V(p) + K)(1 - \alpha_z(p))$$

$$+ \int_p^{\bar{r}} (V(u) + K) \cdot \alpha_z'(u) \, du.$$

The numerator of the second term in (13.A3) thus becomes:

$$z(p) \left[\bar{r} \cdot z(\bar{r}) + \int_p^{\bar{r}} (V(u) + K) \cdot \alpha_z'(u) \, du - (V(\bar{r}) + K)(\alpha_z(\bar{r}) - 1) \right]. \tag{13.A5}$$

By definition of $\bar{r}$ and K, $\bar{r} < M$ implies $V(\bar{r}) + K = 0$, so the last term cancels out, while the remaining two are positive; hence the result.

Case 2. The case where $K \geq 0$, or $\bar{r} = M$ is more difficult, because the last term in (13.A5) is generally negative. Consider marginal profits on $[0, M]$:

$$\Pi_\Delta'(p) = \Delta'(p)[p(1 - 1/\alpha_\Delta(p)) - c] \equiv \Delta'(p)[h(p) - c] \tag{13.A6}$$

where $\alpha_\Delta(p) > \alpha_z(p)$ was defined in (13.A2). By Assumption 1, α_z is non-decreasing, so there exists an $m_z \in [0, M]$ such that $\alpha_z(p) \leq 1$ on $(0, m_z]$ and $\alpha_z(p) \geq 1$ on $[m_z, M)$; one of these intervals may be empty, but when $M = +\infty$, $\alpha_z(+\infty) > 1$ implies $m_z < +\infty$.

On $(0, m_z)$, $\alpha_z(p) \leq 1$ and (13.A4) imply that the function $p \cdot z(p)$ is non-decreasing. Therefore, by (13.A2) and (13.A3) α_Δ is strictly increasing on $[0, m_z]$, so there exists a unique $m_\Delta \in [0, m_z]$, such that $\alpha_\Delta(p) \leq 1$ on $(0, m_\Delta]$ and $\alpha_\Delta(p) > 1$ on $[m_\Delta, M)$.

On $[0, m_\Delta]$, $\alpha_\Delta(p) \leq 1$, so $h(p) \leq 0$ by (13.A6), or $\Pi_\Delta'(p) > 0$. We shall now examine the variations of $h(p)$ on $[m_\Delta, M]$.

(i) On $(m_\Delta, m_z]$, $\alpha_\Delta(p)$ is increasing and $1 - 1/\alpha_\Delta(p) > 0$, so $h(p)$ is increasing.

(ii) On $(m_z, M]$ (when it is not empty) $\alpha_\Delta(p)$ need not be monotonic but we shall prove that $h(p)$ is.

Indeed:

$$\alpha_\Delta(p)^2 \cdot h'(p) = \alpha_\Delta(p)^2 - \alpha_\Delta(p) + p \cdot \alpha_\Delta'(p).$$

But multiplying (13.A3) by p and substituting in (13.A2) yields:

$$p \cdot \alpha_\Delta'(p) = p \cdot \alpha_z'(p) + (1 - \alpha_z(p))(\alpha_\Delta(p) - \alpha_z(p)) + (\alpha_\Delta(p) - \alpha_z(p))^2$$

$$\geq (\alpha_\Delta(p) - \alpha_z(p))(1 + \alpha_\Delta(p) - 2\alpha_z(p))$$

so that (omitting the dependence on p):

$$\alpha_\Delta^2 \cdot h' \geq \alpha_\Delta^2 - \alpha_\Delta + (\alpha_\Delta - \alpha_z)(1 + \alpha_\Delta - 2\alpha_z)$$

$$= \alpha_z(\alpha_z - 1) + (\alpha_\Delta - \alpha_z)(\alpha_\Delta + \alpha_z - 1 + 1 + \alpha_\Delta - 2\alpha_z)$$

$$= \alpha_z(\alpha_z - 1) + (\alpha_\Delta - \alpha_z)(2\alpha_\Delta - \alpha_z) > 0$$

since $\alpha_\Delta > \alpha_z > 1$. Thus $h(p)$ increases on $(m_\Delta, M]$ and is non-positive on $[0, m_\Delta]$. As a result, there exists a unique $p^* \in (m_\Delta, M]$, such that $h(p) < c$, i.e. $\Pi_\Delta'(p) > 0$ on $(0, p^*)$ and $h(p) > c$, i.e. $\Pi_\Delta'(p) < 0$ on $(p^*, M]$. Moreover, $\Pi_\Delta'(p^*) = 0$ if $p^* < M$, which always is the case when $M = +\infty$, because $\alpha_\Delta(+\infty) \geq \alpha_z(+\infty) > 1$ implies $h(+\infty) = +\infty$.   ‖

Proof of Proposition 3. Let us first rewrite $W(S', s')$ by eliminating T' from (13.9). Denoting $\delta \equiv \rho/g$ and $u = S'e^{-gt}$, we have:

$$W(S', s') = \frac{\displaystyle\int_{s'}^{S'} \Pi(u)u^{-1+\delta}\,du - \beta g S'^{\delta}}{g(S'^{\delta} - s'^{\delta})}. \tag{13.A7}$$

Straightforward algebra gives the first-order conditions (FOC) for an interior optimum. Given the possible kink at $\bar{r}$ when $\bar{r} = M$, the most general condition for S' is: $\partial W(S'^{-}, s')/\partial S' \geq 0 \geq \partial W(S'^{+}, s')/\partial S'$, with equality unless $S' = \bar{r} = M$. But for $S' > \bar{r}$, $\partial W(S', s')/\partial S' = -\delta S'^{\delta-1}(\beta + W(S', s'))/(S'^{\delta} - s'^{\delta}) < 0$. Therefore $S' > \bar{r}$ is never optimal, and the first-order condition is simply $\partial W(S'^{-}, s')/\partial S' \geq 0$, i.e. $\Pi(S') - \Pi(s') \geq \rho\beta$, with equality unless $S' = \bar{r} = M$. Since $\Pi(S') \geq \rho(W + \beta) > 0$ requires $S' \leq \bar{r} \leq M$, this is equivalent to (13.13). The property that the FOC have at most one solution, and that, if it exists, it satisfies the second-order conditions and characterizes the optimum, follows from Sheshinski and Weiss (1977) and Zinde-Walsh (1987).   ‖

Proof of Theorem 2. Given v, an equilibrium (S, s) is fixed point of firms' best reply functions. With endogenous entry, however, it is a solution to (13.24)–(13.25), which corresponds to a fixed point of a somewhat different mapping, with a less straightforward economic interpretation.

1. *Preferences with bounded support:*
Assume first that $M < +\infty$, so that the non-empty set:

$$K \equiv \{(S, s) \in R^2 | c \leq s \leq p^m, s \leq S \leq M\} \tag{13.A8}$$

is not only convex but also compact. For all (S, s) in K, define as before the average surplus $\overline{V}(S, s)$ by:

$$\overline{V}(S, s) = \int_s^S \frac{V(u)}{u} \cdot \frac{du}{\text{Ln}(S/s)} \tag{13.A9}$$

for $s < S$, and by $\overline{V}(s, s) = V(s)$ (l'Hôpital's rule). Clearly:

$$V(S) \leq \overline{V}(S, s) \leq V(s) \tag{13.A10}$$

with strict inequality unless $S = s$. Define now, for all (S, s) in K and any $p \in [c, M]$:

$$\Pi_{(S,s)}(p) \equiv \pi(p) \cdot \max\{V(u) + \bar{\gamma} - \overline{V}(S, s), 0\} \tag{13.A11}$$

which is, up to a constant, the profit function of a firm in an (S, s) equilibrium. From Proposition 1, we know that $\Pi_{(S,s)}(p)$ is strictly quasi-concave (and clearly continuous) on its support, which is $[c, \bar{r}]$. Note that if $s < M$, $\Pi_{(S,s)}(p) > 0$ for p just above s, while if $s = M$, then $S = s = M$ so $\Pi_{(S,s)}(p) = \bar{\gamma}\pi(p) > 0$ for p just above c. Thus $\Pi_{(S,s)}$ never has trivial support ($\bar{r} > c$).

Next, define for all (S, s) in K:

$$J(S, s) = \int_s^S \Pi_{(S,s)}(u) \frac{u^{\delta-1}}{(S^\delta - s^\delta)/\delta + g\beta S^\delta/h} du. \tag{13.A12}$$

$J(S, s)$ is a weighted average of a firm's discounted profits in an (S, s) equilibrium, i.e. of $\rho W(S, s)$, given by (13.12), and of h; with entry, $\rho W(S, s) = h$, so $J(S, s) = \rho W(S, s) = h$.

Denoting by $p^*_{(S,s)} \leq p^m$ the unique maximum of the function $\Pi_{(S,s)}$, and by $\Pi^*_{(S,s)}$ its maximal value, we have:

$$0 \leq J(S, s) < \Pi^*_{(S,s)} \cdot \frac{(S^\delta - s^\delta)/\delta}{(S^\delta - s^\delta)/\delta + g\beta S^\delta/h} < \frac{\Pi^*_{(S,s)}}{1 + g\beta/h} \tag{13.A13}$$

with the first inequality being strict unless $S = s$ (since $S < +\infty$). The strict quasi-concavity of $\Pi_{(S,s)}(p)$ and (13.A13) imply:

$\forall (S, s) \in K$, $\exists !(s', S') \in [c, p^*_{(S,s)}) \times (p^*_{(S,s)}, M] \subset K$ such that

$$\Pi_{(S,s)}(s') = J(S, s);$$

$$\Pi_{(S,s)}(S') \geqq (1 + \rho\beta/h)J(S, s); \tag{13.A14}$$

$$[\Pi_{(S,s)}(S') - (1 + \rho\beta/h)J(S, s)](M - S) = 0.$$

Moreover, note that: $s' > c$ unless $J(S, s) = 0$, i.e. unless $S = s$. We shall denote the solution to (13.A14), given (S, s), by $(S', s') = \Psi(S, s)$.

The functions appearing in (13.A14) are clearly continuous in $(S, s; S', s')$. Together with the *uniqueness* of the solution (S', s'), this implies that Ψ is continuous in (S, s) on K. Indeed, if $(S_n, s_n)_{n \in N}$ converges to $(S, s) \in K$, then the corresponding sequence $(S'_n, s'_n)_{n \in N}$ is in the compact set K, so it must have at least one accumulation point (S'', s''). But writing down (13.A14) for $(S_n, s_n; S'_n, s'_n)$ and taking limits implies that $(S, s; S'', s'')$ verifies (13.A14). The uniqueness of the solution, given (S, s) implies that any such accumulation point (S'', s'') must equal (S', s'); thus $(S'_n, s'_n)_{n \in N}$ converges to (S', s').

The function Ψ, which maps the convex, compact set K into itself, must have a fixed point $(S^*, s^*) = \Psi(S^*, s^*) = (S^{*\prime}, s^{*\prime})$. Moreover, by (13.A14), $s^{*\prime} < p^*_{(S,s)} < S^{*\prime}$, so: (i) $s^* < p^m$; (ii) $s^* < S^*$, hence $J(S^*, s^*) > 0$ and $s^* > c$. This ensures that $v \in (0, +\infty)$. Similarly, if $z(M) = 0$, then necessarily $S < M$. This concludes the proof in this case.

2. *Preferences with unbounded support*:

Assume now that $z(p)$ and $V(p)$ have support $(0, +\infty)$. For each finite $M > p^m$, consider the truncated demand function $z_M(p)$ (or surplus $V_M(p)$) which coincides with $z(p)$ (or $V(p)$) on $(0, M]$, and is zero afterwards. Since z_M still satisfies Assumption 1, the above result guarantees the existence of an equilibrium (S^*_M, s^*_M) for these modified preferences. The equilibrium (S^*, s^*) for the infinite-support problem will be constructed as a limit of (S^*_M, s^*_M) for a sequence of values of M going to $+\infty$. In order to do so, it must be proved that S^*_M remains bounded even as M tends to $+\infty$. We shall start by proving:

LEMMA 1.   *There exists $B > p^m$, such that for all $s \in [c, p^m]$, and all $S > B$:*

$$\frac{J(S, s)}{\Pi_{(S,s)}(S)} > \frac{1}{1 + \rho\beta/h}. \tag{13.A15}$$

Moreover, the same inequality holds, when $B < S < M$, for the functions $\Pi^M_{(S,s)}(p)$ and $J^M(S,s)$ associated by (13.A9)–(13.A11)–(13.A12) to any finite truncation of preferences at $M > B$.

This result will prove that for all $M > B$, $S^*_M \leq B$, or else the second condition of (13.A14), for the corresponding functions $\Pi^M_{(S,s)}(p)$ and $J^M(S,s)$, would not hold for $S^{*\prime}_M = S^*_M$. Note that since $V(p)$ is decreasing and $s > 0$:

$$\frac{J(S,s)}{\Pi_{(S,s)}(S)} = \int_s^S \frac{\pi(u)(V(u) + \bar{\gamma} - \bar{V}(S,s))}{\pi(S)(V(p) + \bar{\gamma} - \bar{V}(S,s))} \cdot \frac{\delta u^{\delta-1}}{S^\delta(1 + \rho\beta/h) - s^\delta} du$$

$$> \int_s^S \frac{\pi(u)}{\pi(S)} \cdot \frac{\delta u^{\delta-1} \, du}{S^\delta(1 + \rho\beta/h)}.$$

The same holds true in any truncated problem, so that it suffices to prove

LEMMA 2.   *There exists $B > p^m$, such that for all $s \in [c, p^m]$ and all $S > B$:*

$$\int_s^S \frac{\pi(u)}{\pi(S)} \frac{\delta u^{\delta-1}}{S^\delta} du > 1. \tag{13.A16}$$

Moreover, the same inequality also holds, for $B < S < M$, for the function $\pi^M(p) = (p - c)z^M(p)$ associated to any truncation of preferences at $M > B$.

Proof.   For $M > S > B$, the left-hand-side of (13.A16) remains unchanged when preferences are truncated at M, so that attention can be confined to the untruncated case. Under Assumption 1, there exists $A > p^m$ and $\alpha > 1$ such that, for all $p \geq A$: $z'(p)/z(p) > -\alpha/p$. Integrating over $[u, S]$ for $u < S$:

$$\frac{z(S)}{z(u)} < \left[\frac{S}{u}\right]^{-\alpha} \tag{13.A17}$$

The left-hand-side of (13.A16) is therefore bounded from below by:

$$\int_A^S \frac{(u - c)}{(S - c)} \cdot \frac{u^{\delta-\alpha+1}}{S^{\delta-\alpha}} du = \frac{\delta}{s^{\delta-\alpha}(S - c)} \left[\frac{S^{\delta-\alpha+1} - A^{\delta-\alpha+1}}{\delta - \alpha + 1} - \frac{S^{\delta-\alpha} - A^{\delta-\alpha}}{\delta - \alpha}\right] \tag{13.A18}$$

where we have assumed, for now, that $\delta - \alpha \notin \{0, -1\}$.

Case 1. $\delta - \alpha + 1 > 0$; as S tends to $+\infty$, the terms in $S^{\delta-\alpha+1}$ dominate the above expression, which therefore tends to $\delta/(\delta - \alpha + 1) > 1$, hence the result.

Case 2. $\delta - \alpha + 1 < 0$; the term in brackets is always positive, and in the limit both $S^{\delta-\alpha+1}$ and $S^{\delta-\alpha}$ tend to zero; since the first term is equivalent to $\delta/S^{\delta-\alpha+1}$, the above expression tends to $+\infty$ with S, hence the result.

Case 3. $\delta - \alpha + 1 = 0$; the right-hand side of (13.A18) must then be replaced by $[\delta S/(S - c)][\mathrm{Ln}(S/A) + c \cdot (1/A - 1/S)]$, which also tends to $+\infty$ with S.

Case 4. $\alpha - \delta = 0$; the right-hand side of (13.A18) must then be replaced by $\delta[(S - A)/(S - c) - c \cdot \mathrm{Ln}(S/A)/(S - c)]$, which also tends to $+\infty$ with S. ‖

This concludes the proof of Lemma 2, in all cases. Consider now a sequence of truncations at $M = n$, for $n \in N$, $n > B$, with corresponding equilibria (S_n^*, s_n^*). By definition, $(S_n^*, s_n^*; S_n^*, s_n^*)$ satisfy (13.A14), for the functions $\Pi_{(S,s)}^n(p)$ and $J^n(S, s)$. By Lemma 1, the sequence $(S_n^*, s_n^*)_{n \in N}$ remains in the compact set $[c, p^m] \times [p^m, B]$, so there exists a subsequence which converges to some limit (S^*, s^*); taking limits in (13.A14) for that subsequence easily yields the result that $(S^*, s^*; S^*, s^*)$ satisfies (13.A14) for the untruncated functions $z(p)$ and $V(p)$, so that (S^*, s^*) is an equilibrium for the original preferences with unbounded support. ‖

Proof of Proposition 4. Define the function $\varphi(u) = \varphi_{(S,s)}(u) \equiv \pi(u)[V(u) + \bar{\gamma} - \bar{V}(S, s)]$; the subscript (S, s) will be omitted when no confusion results. Denote also $\Psi(u) \equiv \pi(u)[V(u) + \bar{\gamma} - V(p_*)]$, where p_* is the equilibrium price when $\beta = 0$; Ψ corresponds to Π_* defined in the main text. By definition, $\varphi(p_*) = \Psi(p_*) = \bar{\gamma} \cdot \pi(p_*)$ and $\Psi'(p_*) = 0$. We shall abbreviate $\Psi(p_*)$ as Ψ_*, $\Psi''(p_*)$ as Ψ''_*, $V(p_*)$ as V_*, etc. Let us start by rewriting (13.24)–(13.25) as:

$$\varphi(S) - \varphi(s) = \varepsilon \cdot \varphi(s) \tag{13.A19}$$

$$\int_s^S [\varphi(u) - \varphi(p_*)]u^{\delta-1}\, du = \varepsilon \cdot \varphi(s) \cdot S^\delta/\delta + [\varphi(s) - \varphi(p_*)](S^\delta - s^\delta)/\delta \tag{13.A20}$$

where $\varepsilon \equiv \rho\beta/h \ll 1$. We shall neglect all terms of order higher than ε, denoted as $o(\varepsilon)$; the system then becomes:

$$\varphi(S) - \varphi(s) = \varepsilon \cdot \Psi_* + o(\varepsilon) \tag{13.A21}$$

$$\int_s^S [\varphi(u) - \varphi(p_*)]u^{\delta-1}\, du - \Psi_* \cdot p_*^\delta \cdot \varepsilon/\delta + [\varphi(s) - \varphi(p_*)](S^\delta - s^\delta)/\delta. \tag{13.A22}$$

Moreover, $\varphi(u) = \Psi(u) - \pi(u)[\bar{V}(S,s) - V_*]$. Next, define $X \ll 1$ and $x \ll 1$ by $S = p_*(1 + X)$, $s = p_*(1 - x)$, and expand $\bar{V}(S,s) - V_*$, $\varphi(u) - \varphi(p)$, and finally the whole system (13.A21)–(13.A22) up to the third order in (X, x); higher-order terms are denoted $o(3)$. Tedious but straightforward calculations (available from the author upon request) lead to:

$$(X + x)[A_1(X - x) + A_2(X^2 - Xx + x^2) + A_3(X - x)^2] + o(3)$$
$$= \varepsilon \cdot \Psi_* + o(\varepsilon) \tag{13.A23}$$

$$(X + x)[B_1(2x^2 - X^2 + Xx) + B_2 X(X - x)] + o(3) = \varepsilon \cdot \Psi_*/\delta + o(\varepsilon) \tag{13.A24}$$

where

$$A_1 \equiv p_*^2 \cdot \Psi_*''/2 - \phi_1 \cdot p_* \cdot \pi_*' \qquad A_2 \equiv p_*^3 \cdot \Psi_*'''/6 - \phi_2 \cdot p_* \cdot \pi_*'$$

$$A_3 \equiv -\phi_1 \cdot p_*^2 \cdot \Psi_*''/2 \qquad B_1 = -p_*^2 \cdot \Psi_*''/6 \qquad B_2 \equiv -\phi_1 \cdot p_* \cdot \pi_*'$$

$$\phi_1 = -p_* \cdot z_*/2 \qquad \phi_2 \equiv 2p_* \cdot z_* - p_*^2 \cdot z_*'$$

Now let η be the highest of the orders of X and x in ε: $X = \omega \cdot \varepsilon^\eta + o(\varepsilon^\eta)$, $x = \sigma \cdot \varepsilon^\eta + o(\varepsilon^\eta)$, with $\omega + \sigma > 0$. The system becomes:

$$\varepsilon^{2\eta} \cdot (\omega + \sigma)[A_1(\omega - \sigma) + A_2(\omega^2 - \omega\sigma + \sigma^2) + A_3(\omega - \sigma)^2] + o(\varepsilon^{2\eta})$$
$$= \varepsilon \cdot \Psi_* + o(\varepsilon) \tag{13.A25}$$

$$\varepsilon^{3\eta} \cdot (\omega + \sigma)[B_1(2\sigma^2 - \omega^2 + \omega\sigma) + B_2\omega(\omega - \sigma)] + o(\varepsilon^{3\eta}) = \varepsilon \cdot \Psi_*/\delta + o(\varepsilon) \tag{13.A26}$$

Equation (13.A26) implies that $\eta = 1/3$. Equation (13.A25) then requires that $\omega - \sigma = 0$ (and that $X - x$ be of order ε), so that (13.A26) becomes $4 \cdot B_1 \cdot \sigma^3 = \Psi_*/\delta$, which proves (13.27) in Proposition 4.

We now turn to C^s, assuming first $\bar{r} < M$. With $\gamma = 0$ (13.26) becomes:

$$\bar{\gamma}[C_s + \bar{\gamma}/2] = \int_s^{\bar{r}} z(r)\Gamma(r)\,dr$$

$$= [(\bar{V}(S,s) - V(r))\Gamma(r)]_s^{\bar{r}} - \int_s^{\bar{r}} (\bar{V}(S,s) - V(r))z(r)F(r)\,dr$$

$$= (\bar{V}(S,s) - V(\bar{r}))\cdot\bar{\gamma} - [(\bar{V}(S,s) - V(r))^2/2]_s^{\bar{r}}$$

$$- \int_s^S (\bar{V}(S,s) - V(r))z(r)F(r)\,dr$$

But

$$\bar{V}(S,s) = \Gamma(M) = \Gamma(\bar{r}) + \int_{\bar{r}}^M z(r)\,dr = \bar{\gamma} + V(\bar{r}),$$

so

$$\bar{\gamma}\cdot C_s = (\bar{V}(S,s) - V(S))^2/2 - \int_s^S (\bar{V}(S,s) - V(r))z(r)F(r)\,dr. \qquad (13.A27)$$

When $\bar{r} = M$, similar calculations show that (13.A27) remains unchanged. Finally, Taylor expansions of second order in $x = X$ (using the previous results) yield:

$$(\bar{V}(S,s) - V(S))^2/2 = z_*^2\cdot p_*^2\cdot x^2/2 + o(x^2)$$

$$\int_s^S (\bar{V}(S,s) - V(r))z(r)F(r)\,dr = z_*^2\cdot p_*^2\cdot x^2/3 + o(x^2)$$

hence the result in (13.27).   ∥

Notes

I am grateful to George Akerloff, Ben Bernanke, Peter Diamond, Ariel Halperin, Jean Tirole and two anonymous referees for helpful remarks; to Leonardo Felli for assistance with the simulations; and to the NSF for financial support. I remain responsible for all errors and inaccuracies.

1. Chapter 3, "The Costs of Inflation and Recession," page 79. The order of the first two sentences was inverted for clarity of the excerpt.

2. Fischer (1981) and Cukierman (1983) provide surveys of the literature on inflation and price dispersion across goods. Domberger (1987) and Danziger (1987b) show similar effects within markets for homogeneous goods. Fischer (1981) and Driffill, Mizon and Ulph (1989)

review the main theories which could account for these correlations. The latter paper also reexamines some of the traditional evidence and questions whether it reliably establishes such links.

3. In focussing on the effects of inflation in a search market, we are leaving aside a parallel literature where imperfect competition arises instead from product differentiation (Danziger (1988), Konieczny (1987)). In these models as well, the net effect of inflation on welfare depends critically on consumer preferences and market structure.

4. When $M < +\infty$, $z(p)$ may be discontinuous at M, or have an elasticity smaller than one on $[0, M]$.

5. Search is thus very fast with respect to real price erosion. This is the converse of the assumption in Cassella and Feinstein (1990), where inflation alters real prices faster than bargaining offers can be made. Indeed, theirs is a model of hyperinflation, while here we deal with moderate to high rates of inflation. We could also assume that search takes place in real time, but that consumers retain no memory of previous offers (whose current real value would otherwise be computable), so that they keep searching from the same distribution. Memory and intertemporal arbitrage would introduce a whole set of interesting but very complex issues into the model; see Benabou (1989) for some of them.

6. This standard assumption ensures that no consumer is kept out of the market because his expected surplus from search is less than the cost of the first sampling.

7. Although such costs generally increase with the size of price changes, the form of the optimal policy remains the same as long as the average cost $\beta(\Delta p)/\Delta p$ is decreasing; see Konieczny (1990b).

8. See Sheshinski and Weiss (1977), Caplin and Shesinski (1987). The full specification of the strategy involves an additional trigger point $\hat{s} > S$, such that if $p > \hat{s}$, the firm adjusts down to S, but if $S < p < \hat{s}$ it lets inflation gradually do the job. Following the literature, we simply refer to the strategy as an (S, s) rule, although it implicitly includes an $\hat{s}$ which is relevant to describe out-of-equilibrium behaviour.

9. We thus focus on certain types of equilibria, namely staggered symmetric (S, s) equilibria, but do not impose any restriction on strategies. These equilibria are subgame-perfect, i.e. such that no firm ever wants to change the nature or timing of its price decisions, as long as no positive measure of firms or buyers has deviated. Other equilibria, e.g. synchronized (S, s), exist but do not satisfy macroeconomic consistency and feature no search.

10. For any distribution of search costs with low enough γ.

11. Convergence occurs if firms are subject to cumulative idiosyncratic shocks or use different (S, s) bounds (Tsiddon (1987), Caballero and Engel (1991)), or if they randomize their price adjustments to deter storage by speculators (Benabou (1989)). While these results do not directly apply to an equilibrium model as (S, s) rules are generally not optimal on the convergence path, their common intuition seems quite robust.

12. Since utility is linear in search expenditures and there is no limit to the number of searches a consumer can conduct (we shall return to this question later), optimal search is the same with and without recall.

13. If the first search was costly, the consumers with $\gamma > \Gamma(M)$ would stay out of the market. One might therefore be tempted to restrict attention to the case where $\Gamma(M) > \bar{\gamma}$, which also simplifies most equations and proofs. Such an equilibrium, however, does not always exist.

14. The argument leading to (13.7) implicitly assumes $\gamma \leqq \Gamma(M) \leq \bar{\gamma}$ when $\Gamma(M) > \bar{\gamma}$, the bracketed term is just $\int_p^{\bar{r}} z(r)\, dr = V(p) - V(\bar{r})$. But $\Gamma(M) - \bar{\gamma} = \Gamma(M) - \Gamma(\bar{r}) = \int_{\bar{r}}^{M} z(r) F(r)\, dr = V(\bar{r})$ since $\bar{r} \geqq S$; hence (13.7) still holds. The general formula, including the case $\Gamma(M) < \gamma$, is given by equation (13.A1) in appendix.

15. Note also that $D(p)$ may be discontinuous at $\bar{r}$ when $\bar{r} = M$, i.e. $\Gamma(M) < \bar{\gamma}$ and $z(M^-) > 0$ (e.g. unit demand below M); this implies $D(\bar{r}^-) > 0$.

16. In spite of the similarity, there is no obvious mapping of this search problem into a product differentiation model which would allow their powerful aggregation theorem to be used. A direct proof is thus required.

17. There are two additional wrinkles. First, profits must tend to zero as the price tends to $+\infty$; this holds under Assumption 1. Secondly, profits along this $(S's')$ path must remain positive, or else the firm will not always meet demand, as was implicitly assumed, and may even shut down. For a monopolist, a strategy with these properties (even one leading to a non-negative value of the firm) does not always exist—say if price adjustment costs are too large. Here, however, the entry or exit of firms will ensure that it always does.

18. In particular, when $\bar{r} = M$, $D(p)$ and $\Pi(p)$ may be discontinuous at $\bar{r}$ (see (13.8)), hence W not differentiable in S' at that point.

19. Equivalently, all fixed costs become smaller with respect to demand. There are some pricing costs (e.g. labelling goods) which increase with the volume of sales. But as long as the average cost per unit is decreasing, meaning that changing prices involves increasing returns, the results remain unaffected.

20. That $\underline{r} \leq p^m$ is required in Proposition 2 for quasi-concavity; (3.18) and (3.19) imply $s \geq c$ and $S \leq \bar{r}$. The same system describes the equilibrium for a market without entry, if one fixes v and lets h vary instead; such an equilibrium may fail to exist, i.e. (13.16)–(13.20) with a given v may entail $h < 0$.

21. Formally, replace $V(p)$ by $M - p$ in (13.8) and use l'Hôpital's rule to show that $(\bar{r} - \underline{r})/(\bar{\gamma} - \underline{\gamma})$ tends to $\Gamma'(r) = z(r)F(r) = 1$ as $[\bar{\gamma}, \underline{\gamma}]$ shrinks to $\{\gamma\}$ and $\bar{r}$ and $\underline{r}$ tend to a common limit $\bar{r}$, with $\Gamma(r) = \gamma \leq \Gamma(M)$.

22. In this limiting case, (13.19) becomes $(S - c)/v \geq h + \rho\beta$, w.e.u. $S = \bar{r}$, and one can show that (13.18) and (13.20) require that the inequality be strict.

23. Price dispersion is measured by $S/s - 1$. Benabou (1988) shows that the log-uniform distribution's coefficient of variation is a monotonic function of S/s. Danziger (1987a) proves a similar result for the distribution of purchase-weighted prices of a monopolist with iso-elastic demand.

24. A decrease in γ also lowers S, s and v but reduces price dispersion S/s.

25. These conditions assume $\delta > 0$ and $h > 0$. Similar ones hold when there is no discounting or no fixed costs. When $\rho \to 0$, $(S^\delta - s^\delta)/\delta$ tends to $\mathrm{Ln}(S/s) = T/g$, and firms maximize profits per unit of time, i.e. the limit of ρW, as given by (13.9). When $h = 0$, (13.18) implies that $s = c$.

26. There may also be non-symmetric equilibria, where different groups of firms use different (S, s) bands and equilibrium profits are not strictly quasi-concave; these lie outside the scope of this chapter.

27. Because of his budget constraint, each buyer's labour endowment L should cover his search costs. This cannot be ensured with probability one, but the probability that a buyer runs out of resources before finding $p \leq R(\gamma)$ is very small if $L \gg \gamma[1/F(R(\gamma)) - 1]$. For all $r \geq s$, (13.3) implies $\Gamma(r) \leq (V(s) - V(r))F(r)$, so that $\gamma/F(R(\gamma)) \leq V(s)$ and it suffices to assume that $L \gg V(c)$.

28. For simplicity, it is assumed that $\bar{r} < M$. Otherwise, the last term in (13.26) must be replaced by $(\Gamma(M)^2 - \underline{\gamma}^2)/(2(\bar{\gamma} + \underline{\gamma}))$.

29. Dixit (1991), examining models of (S, s) behaviour under uncertainty, also finds Taylor approximations to be fairly reliable.

30. The equality of (13.29) and (13.30) follows from (13.26) and the definition of Γ.

31. Alternatively, each firm's intertemporal profits, starting from s, are zero; but they are positive until it reaches s from its initial position, i.e. until its first adjustment. Thus (equality with (13.31) rests on (13.1) and (13.20)):

$$B_f = v \int_s^S \int_0^{\theta(p)} [\Pi(pe^{-gt}) - h]e^{-\rho t} \, dt \, dF(p) \quad \text{where } \theta(p) = \text{Ln}(p/s)/g.$$

32. In Diamond (1992) there is a cost of involuntary search, which also depends on inflation. Impatient consumers must wait for buying opportunities, whose arrival rate depends on the stock of goods produced but yet unsold; the latter is determined by a zero-profit condition. It is as if the first term of (13.32) were multiplied by an increasing function of v. We could incorporate a similar thin-market effect here by having the distribution of search costs shift up as v falls.

33. The latter vary between 7% at $g = 0\%$ and 0.05% at $g = 50\%$. Since $\beta/h = 1$, the same holds for fixed costs. This small value of h is meant to reflect monopolistic competition; higher values are explored in the simulations.

34. In $\bar{p}$, prices are weighted by the number of buyers who end up paying them, but not by the quantity bought. A purchase-weighted average would essentially vary inversely with output, which is examined later.

35. The equilibrium without inflation is also noteworthy. When $g = \rho = 0$, firms adjust once and for all to the unique p_* which maximizes profits per unit of time. Since $S = s = p_*$ there is no search, but the threat of search by buyers with low γ forces $p_* < p^m$. When $\rho > 0$, there is a discontinuity at $g = 0^+$: because the discrete cost β must be compensated by a discrete increase in discounted profits, S and s remain bounded away from one another, generating price dispersion and search; indeed, (13.13) requires that $S > s$.

36. Buyers with low search cost can be shown to always search more; the behaviour of those with high search costs is ambiguous, but all simulations show that the total number of searches increases with inflation, in a manner similar to the total cost of search.

37. This interaction was noted by Paroush (1986) in his discussion of the effects of inflation.

References

Benabou, R. (1988), "Search, Price Setting and Inflation," *Review of Economic Studies*, 55, 353–373.

Benabou, R. (1989), "Optimal Price Dynamics and Speculation with a Storable Good," *Econometrica*, 57, 41–81.

Benabou, R. and Gertner, R. (1992), "Search with Learning from Prices: Does Increased Inflationary Uncertainty Lead to Higher Markups?" Forthcoming, Review of Economic Studies.

Caballero, R. and Engel, E. (1991), "Dynamic (S, s) Economics," *Econometrica*, 59, 1659–1686.

Caplin, A. and Nalebuff, B. (1988), "After Hotelling: Existence of Equilibrium for an Imperfectly Competitive Market" (Mimeo, Princeton University).

Caplin, A. and Spulber, D. (1987), "Menu Costs and the Neutrality of Money," *Quarterly Journal of Economics*, 102, 703–725.

Caplin, A. and Sheshinski, E. (1987), "Optimality of (S, s) Pricing Policies" (Mimeo, Harvard University).

Cassella, A. and Feinstein, J. (1990), "Economic Exchange During Hyperinflation," *Journal of Political Economy*, 98, 1–27.

Cecchetti, S. (1986), "The Frequency of Price Adjustment: A Study of the Newsstand Price of Magazines," *Journal of Econometrics*, 31, 225–274.

Cuckierman, A. (1979), "The Relationship Between Relative Prices and the General Price Level: A Suggested Interpretation," *American Economic Review*, 69, 444–447.

Cuckierman, A. (1983), "Relative Price Variability and Inflation: A Survey and Further Results," *Carnegie Rochester Conference Series on Public Policy*, 19, 103–158.

Danziger, L. (1987a), "On Inflation and Relative Price Variability," *Economic Inquiry*, 25, 285–298.

Danziger, L. (1987b), "Inflation, Fixed Costs of Price Adjustment, and the Measurement of Relative Price Variability," *American Economic Review*, 77, 704–713.

Danziger, L. (1988), "Costs of Price Adjustment and the Welfare Economics of Inflation and Disinflation," *American Economic Review*, 78, 633–646.

Diamond, P. (1992), "Search, Sticky Prices, and Inflation" Forthcoming in *Review of Economic Studies*.

Dixit, A. (1991), "Analytical Approximations in Models of Hysteresis," *Review of Economic Studies*, 58, 141–152.

Domberger, S. (1987), "Relative Price Variability and Inflation: A Disaggregated Analysis," *Journal of Political Economy*, 95, 547–566.

Driffill, J., Mizon, G. and Ulph, A. (1989), "Costs of Inflation" (Centre for Economic Policy Research, Discussion Paper No. 293).

Economic Report of the President (1990) (Washington, D.C.: United States Government Printing Office).

Fischer, S. (1981), "Relative Shocks, Relative Price Variability, and Inflation," *Brookings Papers on Economic Activity*, 2, 381–432.

Fischer, S. (1984), "The Benefits of Price Stability" (M.I.T. Working Paper No. 352).

Fischer, S. and Modigliani, F. (1978), "Towards an Understanding of the Real Costs of Inflation," *Weltwirtschaftliches Archiv*, 114, 810–833.

Hercowitz, Z. (1981), "Money and the Dispersion of Relative Prices," *Journal of Political Economy*, 89, 328–356.

Kashyap, A. (1987), "Sticky Prices: Some New Evidence from Retail Catalogs" (unpublished Ph.D. dissertation, MIT, Chapter 1).

Konieczny, J. (1987), "On the Role of Money as a Unit of Account and the Welfare Costs of Inflation" (Mimeo, Wilfrid Laurier University).

Konieczny, J. (1990a), "Inflation, Output and Labor Productivity When Prices Are Changed Infrequently," *Economica*, 57, 201–218.

Konieczny, J. (1990b), "Variable Price Adjustment Costs" (Mimeo, Wilfrid Laurier University).

Lucas, R. Jr. (1973), "Some International Evidence on Output-Inflation Tradeoffs," *American Economic Review*, 63, 326–334.

Naish, H. (1986), "Price Adjustment Costs and the Output-Inflation Tradeoff," *Economica*, 53, 219–230.

Paroush, J. (1986), "Inflation, Search Costs and Price Dispersion," *Journal of Macroeconomics*, 8, 329–336.

Rotemberg, J. (1983), "Aggregate Consequences of Fixed Costs of Price Adjustment," *American Economic Review*, 73, 433–436.

Sheshinski, E. and Weiss, Y. (1977), "Inflation and Costs of Price Adjustment," *Review of Economic Studies*, 44, 287–304.

Tsiddon, D. (1987), "The (Mis)Behavior of the Aggregate Price Level" (Mimeo, Hebrew University of Jerusalem).

Zinde-Walsh, V. (1987), "On the Periodicity of Solutions to Dynamic Problems of Costly Price Adjustment under Inflation," *Economic Letters*, 23, 365–369.

14 Search, Sticky Prices, and Inflation

Peter A. Diamond

Search theory has been developed in response to the observation that resource allocation is a time-consuming, costly process and the possibility that explicit modeling of the resource allocation process would result in a somewhat different picture of the workings of the economy. By and large, search theoretic models have been real models. Yet money exists as a transactions medium precisely to economize on transactions costs. Moreover, there are costs to selecting and adjusting nominal prices. Just as transaction costs are a necessary part of the coordination of trade, so some degree of price stickiness is a necessary part of a realistic transactions technology. These costs of price adjustments have been recognized in the literature on (S, s) pricing, following Barro (1972) and Sheshinski and Weiss (1977). More recently, Benabou (1988) combined consumer search with (S, s) pricing policy by firms. He followed standard practice in the sticky price literature by assuming that a change in price by a firm affects all transactions by that firm after that date.

This chapter explores an alternative simple assumption: that nominal prices are attached to individual units of commodities. The prices attached to newly produced goods are continuously adjusted. Prices attached to previously produced commodities can be changed at a cost. Thus there is a sticker cost rather than a menu cost. This alternative reflects actual practice for some commodities where there is a large distribution of units of inventory available for inspection with prices attached. For example, it is common in secondhand book stores in the United States. It was common for many supermarkets before electronic scanners. Moreover, this assumption avoids a difficult problem in equilibrium modeling with the standard alternative assumption: the relative timing of price changes of different firms.[1] By assuming a constant cost per commodity for which the price is changed, all firms will behave the same, continuously repricing the lowest price goods in inventory. This chapter explores the comparative statics of steady economywide inflation in a market with consumer search and optimal price setting by firms. The first part of the chapter examines the case where the cost of adjusting prices is sufficiently large that adjustments do not happen. In Section 7 the model is extended to (S, s) pricing and to include inventory carrying costs.

The model has continuous time with a continuous flow of identical new consumers into the market, each of whom seeks to purchase one unit, provided the real price does not exceed the utility value of the good. There is utility discounting but no explicit cost of search. On the firm side there is free entry with identical firms and optimal price setting. The optimal price for a newly produced good is the maximum that consumers searching in an inflationary environment are willing to pay. Inflation produces the possibility of bargains from finding previously priced goods that have not yet been sold or repriced. The model assumes that the nominal interest rate rises one for one with the inflation rate. This assumption, appropriate for credit card purchases, is in contrast with a situation in which no interest is earned on the purchasing power being carried during the search process. It is assumed that the rate of meeting between customers and inventory is a constant returns-to-scale function of the stocks of customers and inventory, with the probability of a contact being the same for each individual.

In steady-state equilibrium the flow of newly produced goods equals the exogenous flow of new customers. However, the stocks of goods in inventory and of searching customers adjust in response to the zero expected profit condition arising from free entry. With no repricing, the greater the inflation rate, the greater the stock of customers and the smaller the stock of inventories (the smaller the transaction rate for customers and the greater the transaction rate for commodities). The real price placed on a newly produced good is not monotonic in the inflation rate. Since utility of consumption minus this price is also the expected utility of consumers, consumers are better off with some inflation than with none. The gain from moderate inflation comes from the dilution of the market power created by the costs of search. When inflation becomes large enough, the decrease in entry offsets the direct gain from reducing market power. Calculations are presented giving the price of newly produced goods as a function of the inflation rate.

Implicit in the introduction above is the assumption that at each location there is just a single unit of the good for sale, and that unit is instantaneously replaced when sold. In this setting, it is interesting to contrast the menu and sticker cost approaches. With menu costs, the cost of changing the price is the same at any time. Thus there would be no relationship between the timing of price changes and the timing of sales. With steady inflation, the former would be determinate, while the latter is stochastic with random matching. With sticker costs there is no cost to selecting a different price when the new unit of inventory arrives, but there is a cost of changing the price while a unit remains in inventory. Thus, with sticker costs the prices change whenever the good is sold and may also change at other times. It is interesting to extend the model to delays in restocking stores (which continue to have inventory capacities of one unit). This makes no change in the sticker cost model (although one might want to incorporate the length of delay into the search and matching process for comparative static purposes). The possibility of stockouts makes the standard menu cost solution no longer correct. No store would bear the cost of changing its price at a time when it was stocked out. Thus repricing would become stochastic.

Another situation to consider is batch reordering of inventory. Assume that two units arrive instantaneously after the last item in inventory is sold. Both models are robust to some versions of this; both models are not robust to all versions. Consider menu costs first. If there could be two sales at the same moment of time (not a Poisson assumption), then the incentive to reprice would depend on the size of inventories and we would not get standard menu cost results. Next consider sticker costs. If the costless pricing of goods could be done at any time, only one unit would be priced when the two goods arrive, the other being priced when it is put on display for consumers. This is the same as the basic model. If they had to be priced at the same time (or bear an additional cost), then we are in a more complicated model where the two simultaneously arriving goods would be given two different prices, one the reservation price of shoppers at that time and one a higher price. While this would be more complicated than the analysis done, it seems likely to me that it would have the same qualitative characteristics of equilibrium. More complicated stories arise when the acquisition of inventory is more opportunistic than simply ordering from a supplier, as with secondhand books.

1. Matching Technology

It is assumed that there is a continuous flow of size x of new customers into this market. Each customer seeks to purchase one unit of the commodity as long as the real price does not exceed u. We denote by X the stock of customers actively searching in the market. Similarly, we denote by y the flow of newly produced commodities into inventory, and by Y the stock of goods available in inventory. There is a matching technology that determines the flow rate of matches as a continuously differentiable function of the stocks of customers and inventory, $m(X, Y)$. We assume that m has constant returns to scale with a strictly positive marginal contribution by each factor, $m_1 > 0$, $m_2 > 0$, provided there are positive levels of both factors.

In steady-state equilibrium the flow of matches equals both the endogenous flow of inventory and the exogenous flow of new customers (since there is no reason for a meeting not to result in a purchase). Taste differences that would endogenize the purchase probability below 1 are not examined.[2] Thus we have:

$$x = y = m(X, Y). \tag{14.1}$$

We assume that each individual experiences the same flow probability of a match and so experiences the arrival of a transaction opportunity as a Poisson process. We denote these arrival rates of transactions for customers and inventory by a and b. From (14.1), we see that in steady-state equilibrium the Poisson arrival rates satisfy:

$$a = m(X, Y)/X = x/X, \tag{14.2a}$$

$$b = m(X, Y)/Y = x/Y. \tag{14.2b}$$

With constant returns to scale, from (14.1) and (14.2), we have

$$1 = m(a^{-1}, b^{-1}). \tag{14.3}$$

2. The Distribution of Prices

As we will note below, firms will price newly produced goods at the reservation price of customers. There is no reason for a distribution of prices of newly produced goods. Thus the distribution of prices on goods currently in the market reflects the constant arrival of goods whose real prices decay exponentially at the inflation rate,[3] π ($\pi > 0$), with the quantity of goods still remaining on the market at any given price also declining exponentially at the arrival rate of transactions, b. Thus at any time the distribution of real prices in the market has positive density between 0 and p, the price set on newly produced goods. Consider any real price, s, in this interval. Purchases reduce the stock of goods with prices below s at the rate $bF(s)Y$, where F is the distribution of prices. Inflation adds to the stock of goods with real prices below s at the rate $\pi s f(s) Y$, where f is the density of prices. Equating these two flows and solving the resulting differential equation, the steady-state density of real prices on commodities in inventory satisfies:

$$f(s) = \left(\frac{b}{\pi p}\right)\left(\frac{s}{p}\right)^{b/\pi - 1} \qquad 0 \le s \le p. \tag{14.4}$$

This distribution is homogeneous of degree 0 in b and π since proportional changes in both variables are equivalent to a change in the units in which time is measured. The mean and coefficient of variation of the prices of goods on the market (and so of transactions) satisfy

$$\bar{p} = \frac{bp}{b + \pi}, \tag{14.5a}$$

$$\sigma/\bar{p} = \pi/[b(b + 2\pi)]^{1/2}. \tag{14.5b}$$

3. Consumer Search

We assume that the purchasing power held by customers while searching is earning the going rate of interest in the economy and that the real rate of interest in the economy is independent of the inflation rate. Thus we assume that the nominal rate increases point for point with the inflation rate:

$$i = \pi + r, \tag{14.6}$$

where i and r are the nominal and real interest rates, respectively. This assumption fits with payment by check or credit card rather than currency. We denote by V the asset value of being a customer in the search market. This is an endogenous variable depending on the distributions of prices and of waiting times until purchase. We assume that the real rate of utility discount on the utility from consuming this good is equal to the real rate of interest in the economy earned on purchasing power. We also assume that utility is linear in income available to spend on other goods. Thus we can use the standard dynamic programming framework for describing consumer search. Denoting by p^* the reservation price of a consumer, we have

$$rV = a \int_0^{p^*} [u - V - s] f(s) \, ds. \tag{14.7}$$

The reservation price is equal to the utility from consuming the commodity less the value of continuing to search for later consumption:

$$p^* = u - V. \tag{14.8}$$

Since, as will be argued below, firms never set real prices above real willingness to pay, p^* coincides with p, the price of newly produced commodities. Thus, we can write (14.7) as:

$$rV = a(u - V - \bar{p}). \tag{14.9}$$

Substituting for the mean price from (14.5a), and dropping the distinction between the price and the reservation price, we have:

$$r(u - p) = ap \left(\frac{\pi}{b + \pi} \right). \tag{14.10}$$

The combination of a positive inflation rate and the only cost of search being delay in gratification implies that the reservation price is strictly less than the utility value of the good, u. The addition of an explicit search cost would raise the possibility that u is the reservation price rather than a value derived from the comparison of purchasing today with purchasing in the future.

4.   Pricing and Entry

We assume that the real cost of producing the unit for sale is c, with $c < u$. This cost is rising in nominal terms at the rate π. We assume that there is no setup cost to entering this market. With free entry and identical firms, the expected real discounted profit from producing a good for sale in this market will equal c. When the firm produces a unit of the good, it attaches a nominal price to the unit and is not allowed to revise that price in the future. No firm will set a price higher than the common reservation price of customers. To do so would simply introduce a period when a good was sitting in inventory, not available for sale. This would lose the real interest rate on the real cost of production that has already taken place, even though there was no loss from inflation while waiting for the reservation price to rise to the level of price that had been set on the commodity.

Thus, consumers always buy from the first seller they encounter. Search is a threat that is not carried out in equilibrium but affects pricing behavior. With a fixed nominal price on a unit of inventory, we can calculate the expected present discounted value of profit from the sale of this commodity, using the usual dynamic programming approach. For this commodity the profit opportunities are stationary in nominal terms, given that the commodity has not yet been sold. Thus the equation is stated in nominal terms. W is used to denote the value of a newly produced commodity for sale:

$$iW = b(p - W). \tag{14.11}$$

With free entry W must equal the cost of production, c. Converting the nominal interest rate into a real rate plus the inflation rate, the zero profit condition can be written as:

$$bp = (r + \pi + b)c. \tag{14.12}$$

The markup over cost depends upon the real interest rate, the inflation rate, and the arrival rate of transactions. Combining (14.5a) and (14.12), we see that the mean real transactions price satisfies

$$\bar{p} = \left(1 + \frac{r}{b + \pi}\right)c = \left(\frac{b + i}{b + \pi}\right)c. \tag{14.13}$$

5. Equilibrium

The model can be stated in terms of the three endogenous variables a, b, and p, with the variables determined by (14.3), (14.10), and (14.12). Eliminating the price from (14.10) and (14.12), we get the condition

$$\frac{u}{c} = \left(1 + \frac{r + \pi}{b}\right)\left(1 + \frac{a\pi}{rb + r\pi}\right). \tag{14.14}$$

We can now solve for a and b from (14.3) and (14.14). To examine the solution, we first note that (14.3) is independent of the inflation rate, with a decreasing in b. In (14.14), a is an increasing convex function of b. Moreover, in (14.14), b is increasing in π. Thus, when there is an equilibrium with positive production, it is unique and increases in π increase b and

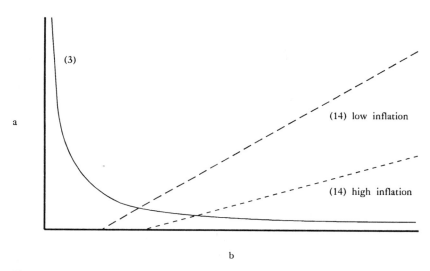

Figure 14.1
Equilibrium

decrease a.[4] This is illustrated in Figure 14.1, which shows equation (14.3) as well as equation (14.14) for two levels of inflation. There will be an equilibrium with positive production if the matching function is such that at some values of the stocks of inventory and customers, one has a value of b at least as large as the critical value that satisfies (14.14) with a equal to zero. This critical value is equal to $(r + \pi)/(u/c - 1)$. Thus there will be equilibria with positive production at all inflation rates if there is no upper bound to achievable b. For example, this will be true with the Cobb-Douglas matching function. If there is an upper limit to b, it is not possible to break even if the inflation rate is sufficiently large.

To understand the effects of inflation, consider first the zero inflation equilibrium. In this case, the price is equal to the utility of the good, u, independent of the matching function (Diamond, 1971). At this price the arrival rate of sales is determined so that the present discounted value of receiving the price is equal to the cost of the good; thus, a does not enter (14.14). Once there is inflation, the reservation price of consumers depends on a as well as on the inflation rate, and with price equal to the reservation price, the break-even condition depends on a as well as on b. All three endogenous variables, a, b, and p, are affected by the inflation rate. As we will see, p is not monotonic in the inflation rate. Nevertheless,

a and b are monotonic. Thus the sign of the effect of higher inflation is correctly described by the simple direct impact: inflation lowers the expected profit of a sale at a given arrival rate of sales, requiring a rise in the arrival rate of sales to satisfy the zero profit condition. Given the matching technology, a rise in the arrival rate of sales goes with a fall in the arrival rate of purchases.

The relationship between the real price of newly produced goods and the inflation rate depends upon the nature of the search technology. This can be seen by using (14.10) and (14.12) to eliminate a and b from (14.3):

$$1 = (p - c)m\left(\frac{\pi p}{r(u - p)(rc + \pi p)}, \frac{1}{(r + \pi)c}\right).$$ (14.15)

Equation (14.15) can be differentiated implicitly to examine how p varies with different parameters. For this calculation, it is useful to have a symbol for the share of customers in the marginal value of contributions to matching. Remembering that m has constant returns to scale and is evaluated at the point (a^{-1}, b^{-1}), we define α by

$$\alpha = \frac{X m_1(X, Y)}{m(X, Y)} = \frac{m_1(a^{-1}, b^{-1})}{a m(a^{-1}, b^{-1})}.$$ (14.16)

If the matching function is Cobb-Douglas, α is the coefficient on customers. Differentiating (14.15) with respect to u, we have

$$\frac{dp}{du} = \alpha\left(\frac{u - p}{p - c} + \alpha \frac{urc + \pi p^2}{prc + \pi p^2}\right)^{-1}$$ (14.17)

For p closer to c than u, dp/du is smaller than $\alpha/(1 + \alpha)$. This is in sharp contrast with the no inflation case where $p = u$.

Differentiating (14.15) implicitly with respect to π, we have

$$\frac{dp}{d\pi} = \frac{-(p - c)\left[\left(\dfrac{prc}{r(u - p)(rc + \pi p)^2}\right)m_1 - \left(\dfrac{1}{c(r + \pi)^2}\right)m_2\right]}{m + (p - c)\left(\dfrac{\pi(urc + \pi p^2)}{r(u - p)^2(rc + \pi p)^2}\right)m_1}$$

$$= \frac{-(p - c)\left[\dfrac{\alpha rc}{\pi(rc + \pi p)} - \dfrac{1 - \alpha}{r + \pi}\right]}{1 + (p - c)\alpha\left[\dfrac{urc + \pi p^2}{p(u - p)(rc + \pi p)}\right]}.$$ (14.18)

The denominator is positive. Thus the sign of $\frac{dp}{d\pi}$ can be written as

$$\operatorname{sign}\frac{dp}{d\pi} = \operatorname{sign}\left(\frac{1-\alpha}{\alpha} - \frac{rc(r+\pi)}{\pi(rc+p\pi)}\right). \tag{14.19}$$

From (14.19), one can see that p is decreasing in π at $\pi = 0$ and increasing in π for π sufficiently large. Thus, at low inflation rates, the real price on newly produced goods declines as inflation with sticky prices decreases the market power of suppliers. As inflation gets large enough, the decline in inventory relative to customers increases the real price on newly produced goods. Thus, the rate of inflation that minimizes the real price of newly priced goods is positive. This result can also be seen from the fact that with no inflation, the price is equal to the utility of consumers, $p = u$. Since consumers will never buy at a real price above u, inflation can only lower p. As π rises without limit, so does b. If m is continuous at zero inventory, as π rises without limit, a goes to zero and p goes to u. If we allow a discontinuity at zero inventory, a can have a positive limit and so p a limit below u.

Since p is endogenous, the price-minimizing inflation rate cannot be read directly from (14.19). For the Cobb-Douglas case, we note from (14.19) that the inflation rate that minimizes p is less than $\frac{\alpha}{1-\alpha}$ times the real rate of interest. Using (14.15), the equilibrium price as a function of the inflation rate has been calculated for the Cobb-Douglas search technology, $m = A^{-1}X^{\alpha}Y^{1-\alpha}$. Some of the results are shown in Figures 14.2–14.4. The figures show the u-shaped pattern of real price as a function of the inflation rate, the effect of greater search speed in lowering price, and the small impact of the utility of the good on the equilibrium price. Since price falls sharply with the inflation rate in the neighborhood of zero inflation, the figures do not contain inflation rates all the way to zero.

6. Welfare Analysis

Since the model has been solved only for the steady-state equilibrium, it is not possible, with the equations on hand, to analyze the effects of changing the inflation rate. But it is easy to compare welfare in alternative steady states. The free entry-zero profit condition implies that suppliers are in the same position in all steady states. Thus, for welfare analysis, it suffices to consider only the position of buyers. The expected utility of

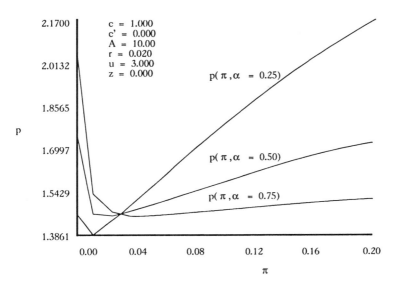

Figure 14.2
Real price on newly produced goods relative to inflation, varying matching technologies

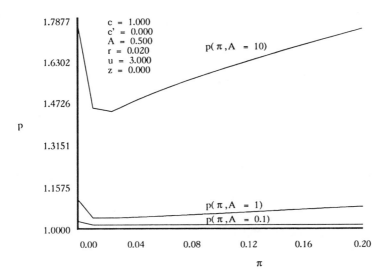

Figure 14.3
Real price on newly produced goods relative to inflation, varying speed of search

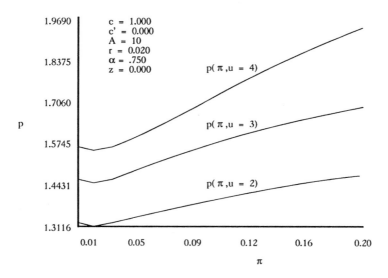

Figure 14.4
Real price on newly produced goods relative to inflation, varying utility

each of the newly arriving consumers was given in (14.8), which we repeat here:

$$V = u - p^*. \tag{14.8'}$$

That is, the expected utility of a new entrant is the utility of instantaneous consumption of the good less the maximum price the consumer is willing to pay to avoid delay in consumption, forgoing also the opportunity to buy at a better price. (Since the consumer's problem is stationary, V is also the expected discounted utility of shoppers who entered earlier and have not yet purchased.) In equilibrium, the price set on newly priced goods is equal to the reservation price of consumers. Thus there is an inverse one-to-one map across steady states between the expected utility of consumers and the price of newly priced goods, and there is an optimal inflation rate (in the sense of steady-state comparisons) that is positive. With zero inflation, the price is set to extract all of consumer surplus from purchasers. Thus it is not surprising that positive inflation can only improve consumer welfare relative to zero inflation by cutting into market power.[5] Similarly, deflation will result in higher expected utility than zero inflation (Diamond and Felli, 1990). With two consumer types, differing only in the utility of purchasing the good, the expected utility of those with low utility is increasing in the inflation rate at rates near zero. However, the expected utility of those with high utility may be increasing or decreasing in the inflation rate at rates near zero (Diamond, 1991).

7. Price Adjustment

We now generalize the model by assuming that the price of a single unit of the commodity can be changed at a cost c'. For $c' \geq c$, no one would ever bother to change the price, since it is cheaper to produce a new unit. For $c' < c$, some price adjustment will take place. We denote by p' the real price at which the price change is made. The price will be changed to p, the reservation price of consumers, which is also the price placed on newly produced goods. The price change occurs if the unit remains on the market long enough for the real price to fall from p to p'. The length of time, t, satisfying this condition is equal to $(\ln(p/p'))/\pi$. A good stays on the market this long with probability

$$e^{-bt} = \left(\frac{p'}{p}\right)^{b/\pi}.$$

(14.20)

The Distribution of Prices

The density of prices in the market is a truncated (and proportionally increased) adjustment of the density in (14.4):

$$f(s) = \frac{b}{\pi} s^{b/\pi - 1} (p^{b/\pi} - (p')^{b/\pi})^{-1} \qquad p' \leq s \leq p.$$

(14.21)

The mean price of goods in the market now satisfies

$$\bar{p} = \left(\frac{b}{b + \pi}\right)\left(\frac{p^{b/\pi + 1} - (p')^{b/\pi + 1}}{p^{b/\pi} - (p')^{b/\pi}}\right).$$

(14.22)

Consumer Search

As before, the value of search satisfies

$$rV = a \int_{p'}^{p} (u - V - s)f(s)\, ds$$

$$= a(u - V - \bar{p}).$$

(14.23)

Solving for the reservation price, p, $(=u - V)$, we have

$$p = \frac{ru + a\bar{p}}{r + a}.$$
(14.24)

Pricing and Entry

Turning to the supply side of the market, we need to evaluate the real value, W, of a good with real price p that will be repriced to p when the price falls to p'. From the analysis above, (14.11), a good priced at p and left on the market indefinitely is worth $bp/(r + \pi + b)$. With probability e^{-bt}, at time t, the good is repriced, forgoing the expected profit $bp'/(r + \pi + b)$, bearing the repricing cost c', and restoring value. Thus

$$W = \frac{bp}{r + \pi + b} - e^{-bt}e^{-rt}\left(\frac{bp'}{r + \pi + b} + c' - W\right)$$

$$= \frac{bp}{r + \pi + b} - \left(\frac{p'}{p}\right)^{(b+r)/\pi}\left(\frac{bp'}{r + \pi + b} + c' - W\right).$$
(14.25)

Solving (14.25), we have

$$W = \frac{\dfrac{bp}{r + \pi + b} - \left(\dfrac{p'}{p}\right)^{(b+r)/\pi}\left(\dfrac{bp'}{r + \pi + b} + c'\right)}{1 - \left(\dfrac{p'}{p}\right)^{(b+r)/\pi}}.$$
(14.26)

Equation (14.26) gives W for any p'. To find the optimal p', we maximize (14.26) with respect to p'. Implicitly differentiating (14.25) and setting $\partial W/\partial p'$ equal to zero, we have

$$W - c' = \frac{bp'}{b + r}.$$
(14.27)

As before, free entry sets the value of a newly priced good equal to the cost of production,

$$W = c.$$
(14.28)

Equilibrium

The model can now be described in terms of the endogenous variables a, b, X, Y, W, p, p', and $\bar{p}$. These variables solve equations (14.1), (14.2a),

(14.2b), (14.22), (14.24), (14.26), (14.27), and (14.28). Eliminating W, X, and Y, the equations can be written as

$$1 = m(a^{-1}, b^{-1}),$$

$$a = r(u - p)/(p - \bar{p}),$$

$$b = \frac{r(c - c')}{p' + c' - c},$$

(14.29)

$$\bar{p} = \left(\frac{b}{b + \pi}\right)\left(\frac{p - (p'/p)^{b/\pi}p'}{1 - (p'/p)^{b/\pi}}\right),$$

$$c = \frac{bp}{r + b + \pi} - \left(\frac{p'}{p}\right)^{(b+r)/\pi}\left(\frac{bp'}{r + b + \pi} + c' - c\right).$$

Solving out for a, b, and $\bar{p}$, (14.29) becomes a two-equation system in p and p'. For the Cobb-Douglas case $m = A^{-1}X^{\alpha}Y^{1-\alpha}$, some calculated values are shown in Figures 14.5–14.7. Again, the figures do not contain values for inflation rates close to zero. As above, at $\pi = 0$, $p = u$. For the Cobb-Douglas case, as π rises without limit, a goes to zero and p goes to

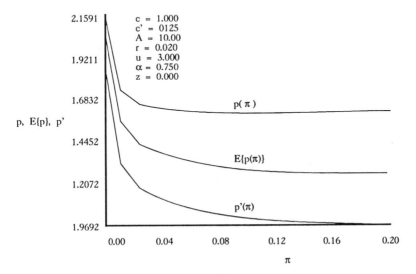

Figure 14.5
Maximum, mean, and minimum real prices relative to inflation

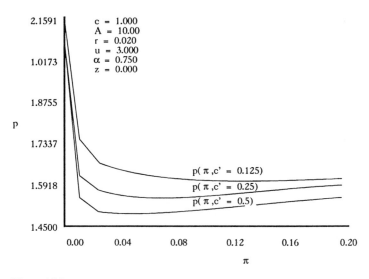

Figure 14.6
Real price on newly produced goods relative to inflation, varying repricing cost

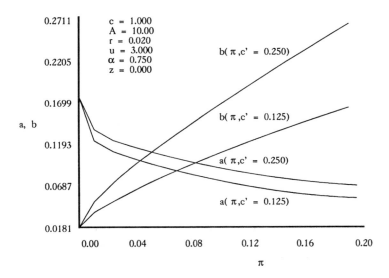

Figure 14.7
Transaction arrival rates relative to inflation

u. Figure 14.5 shows minimum, mean, and maximum prices as a function of the inflation rate. Figure 14.6 shows the relation of price to inflation for different costs of price adjustment. Greater adjustment costs give lower prices. Also, the welfare gain from higher inflation extends to higher values of inflation with lower costs of adjustment. Figure 14.7 shows the equilibrium arrival rates for both sides of the market. The greater the inflation rate, the more rapid the rate of sales and the slower the rate of purchase.

Inventory Carrying Costs

It is straightforward to add a real carrying cost, z, for holding the good in inventory. Since the probability of sale is independent of price, we can distinguish a gross of carrying cost value of a unit of inventory, W, and a net value, W':

$$W - W' = \frac{z}{b + r}. \tag{14.30}$$

The zero profit condition, (14.28), now becomes

$$W' = c,$$

or   (14.31)

$$W = c + \frac{z}{b + r}.$$

Since (14.27) and (14.28) are the only equations containing W in the set of equations determining equilibrium, we can calculate the equilibrium values by replacing c in (14.29) with $c + \frac{z}{b+r}$. Doing this, the changed equations in (14.29) become

$$b = \frac{r(c - c') + z}{p' + c' - c},$$

$$c = \frac{bp}{r + b + \pi} - \left(\frac{p'}{p}\right)^{(b+r)/\pi} \left(\frac{bp'}{r + b + \pi} + c' - c\right) - \left(1 - \left(\frac{p'}{p}\right)^{(b+r)/\pi}\right)\left(\frac{z}{b + r}\right). \tag{14.32}$$

For the Cobb-Douglas case, some calculated values are shown in Figures 14.8–14.11. Again, the figures do not contain values for inflation rates close to zero. Figure 14.8 relates the price of newly priced goods to the

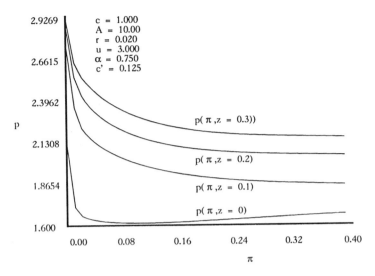

Figure 14.8
Real price on newly produced goods relative to inflation, varying inventory carrying costs

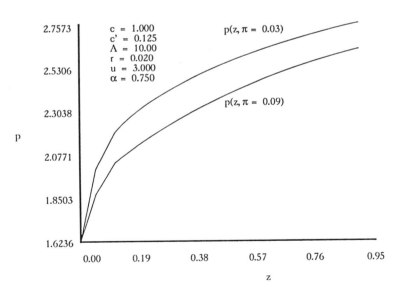

Figure 14.9
Real price on newly produced goods relative to inventory carrying costs, varying inflation

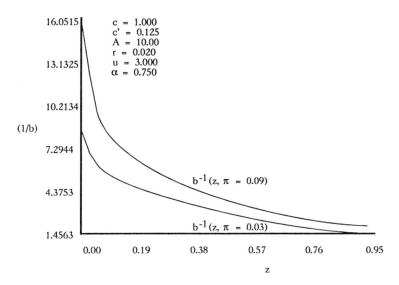

Figure 14.10
Expected time in inventory relative to inventory carrying costs, varying inflation

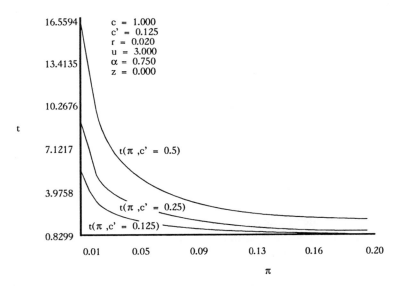

Figure 14.11
Time to repricing relative to inflation, varying repricing cost

inflation rate for different levels of carrying cost. Note that the horizontal scale has been doubled to show the wide range over which welfare is rising with inflation for high z values. Figures 14.9 and 14.10 relate the price and the expected time in inventory to the carrying cost for .03 and .09 inflation rates. Figure 14.11 relates the length of time before repricing to the inflation rate for different costs of repricing. As noted in the derivation of (14.20), this time satisfies

$$t = \frac{\ln(p/p')}{\pi}.$$ (14.33)

It would be interesting to explore analytically the monotonicities that have shown up in the calculated examples.

8. Conclusion

Search theory has been developed to explore the implications for trade coordination of the fact that there does not exist a costless, instantaneous trade coordination mechanism. Money is used as a method of holding down transactions costs. In the absence of a costless and perfect indexing mechanism, nominal rigidities are a necessary part of realistic descriptions of trade coordination. Nominal rigidities come in a variety of forms associated with different technologies for arranging trades. This chapter adds to the ongoing literature by examining the implications of one such nominal rigidity for the allocation process.

A central aspect of this model is the presence of market power in the absence of inflation. Thus, the interaction of inflation and market power plays a central role in the welfare analysis of inflation. This central role seems appropriate to me, although the modeled interactions are very special. In addition to the obvious choice of a sticker cost approach rather than menu costs or finite-length contracts, and of the assumed lack of an inflation cost while carrying purchasing power, the model assumed perfect knowledge and understanding of inflation by shoppers. I suspect that memory limitations and only partial understanding of the inflation process are important parts of the response of allocation to different inflation rates.

The model analyzed was also special in that demand was for a single unit and all consumers had the same utility functions. This ruled out the possibility of initial prices in excess of the monopoly price in anticipation of a declining real price, as in Sheshinski and Weiss (1977). To examine the behavior of equilibrium in a more interesting setting, one would want differing reservation utilities across consumers or demands that vary with price, taking on more than just two different values. These are natural directions for extending the model.

Notes

I am grateful to Peter Howitt, anonymous referees, an editor, and participants in the Harvard-MIT Theory Workshop for valuable comments; to Leonardo Felli for research assistance; and to NSF for research support.

1. For discussions of the timing issue with many firms, see Caplin and Spulber (1987), Caballero and Engel (1991), and Caplin and Leahy (1991).

2. For a model with two types of consumers so that some meetings do not result in purchases, see Diamond (1991).

3. For analysis of the case of deflation, see Diamond and Felli (1990).

4. Thus increases in the inflation rate increase the stock of shopping customers and decrease the stock of inventory. Moreover, from (14.13), the mean price is increasing in the inflation rate.

5. Benabou (1992) finds that welfare can rise or fall relative to inflation depending on parameters

References

Barro, R. (1972), "A Theory of Monopolistic Price Adjustment," *Review of Economic Studies*, 39, 17–26.

Benabou, R. (1988), "Search, Price Setting and Inflation," *Review of Economic Studies* 55, 353–376.

Benabou, R. (1992), "Inflation and Efficiency in Search Markets," *Review of Economic Studies* 59, 299–329.

Caballero, R., and E. Engel (1991), "Dynamic (*S-s*) Economies," *Econometrica* 59, 1659–1686.

Caplin, A., and J. Leahy (1991), "State-Dependent Pricing and the Dynamics of Money and Output," *Quarterly Journal of Economics*, 106, 683–708.

Caplin, A., and D. Spulber (1987), "Menu Costs and the Neutrality of Money," *Quarterly Journal of Economics*, 102, 703–725.

Diamond, P. (1971), "A Model of Price Adjustment," *Journal of Economic Theory*, 3, 156–168.

Diamond, P. (1991), "Search, Sticky Prices, and Inflation with Consumer Differences," MIT Working Paper 573.

Diamond, P., and L. Felli (1990), "Search, Sticky Prices, and Deflation," unpublished ms., MIT.

Sheshinski, E., and Y. Weiss (1977), "Inflation and Costs of Price Adjustment," *Review of Economic Studies*, 44, 287–304.

VI PRICING POLICIES UNDER INFLATION: THE EMPIRICAL EVIDENCE

15 Why Are Prices Sticky? Preliminary Results from an Interview Study

Alan S. Blinder

Those of us who teach Keynesian economics (an increasing number these days) attach great importance to the phenomenon of wage and/or price "stickiness." It explains, for example, why recessions cure themselves only slowly and why changes in the money supply have real effects. In fact, Keynesian economics is sometimes characterized as the economics of nominal rigidities. Yet, more than a half-century after Keynes published *The General Theory*, the phenomenon itself remains poorly understood. Just why are wages or prices sticky?

It is not that economists have ignored these questions. One could literally fill many volumes with good empirical studies of wage and price stickiness, and many more with clever theories purporting to explain these phenomena. Yet, despite all this work, the range of admissible theories is wider than ever, and new theories continue to crop up faster than old ones are rejected. This lack of scientific progress makes one wonder about the basic research strategy that economists have been pursuing. Is there a better way?

In Section I, I argue that traditional research strategies may be unpromising vehicles for learning about why prices are sticky; the time may have come to entertain new and unorthodox approaches. Section II defends the notion that interviews, in particular, can be a useful research tool in this area. Sections III and IV then describe the design of and summarize some preliminary findings from a large-scale interview study currently underway at Princeton. This chapter is very much a progress report since the interviewing still has 9–12 months to go.

I. Why Interviews?

The standard program of scientific research in economics is to (a) develop a theory of some phenomenon, (b) formulate it in econometric terms, and then (c) test it with actual data. The theory is then either rejected or provisionally accepted, that is, allowed to survive to the next test. Unfortunately, this program has been singularly unsuccessful in the area of wage-price stickiness. Most economists would, I think, agree that we know next to nothing about which of several dozen theories of wage-price stickiness are valid and which are not. We might have expected statistical tests to have weeded out the weaker theories by now, especially since many of them have been around a long time. But, in fact, the survivorship rate rivals that of congressional elections. Why?

Part of the reason, no doubt, is that economists are fonder of building theories than of testing them. But I think the main reason is that most of the theories are *empty* in the following specific sense: Either they involve unobservable variables in an essential way, or they carry no real implications other than that prices are "sluggish" in some unmeasurable sense, or both. This makes econometric modeling a blunt, perhaps even useless, investigative tool. Let me illustrate.

To begin with, think about what we mean when we say that a theory predicts that prices are "sticky": Often nothing more than that prices adjust less rapidly than Walrasian market-clearing prices. But since equilibrium price movements often go unmeasured, it is hard to know whether actual prices are moving faster or slower than this norm. More important, all the theories share *exactly the same* prediction: that prices are sticky in this sense. So how are we to discriminate among them? It seems difficult even to imagine what a decisive test would look like, much less to carry one out.

A natural idea is to use each theory to derive other, auxiliary predictions, and then test these. Unfortunately, often there are no such predictions—or at least none that can be checked against actual data. One reason is that many of the theories are based on variables that are *unobservable* either in principle or in practice.

As an example of the former, consider the theory that firms hesitate to cut prices because they fear that customers will interpret a price cut as a signal that quality has been reduced—*when, in fact, there has been no quality reduction.* Clearly, the theory is predicated on the existence of *unobservable* quality differences for, if consumers could observe quality readily, price would not play a signalling role. As an example of the latter, consider the so-called menu cost theory. In principle, fixed costs of changing prices can be observed and measured. In practice, such costs take disparate forms in different firms, and we have no data on their magnitude. So the theory can be tested at best indirectly, at worst not at all.[1]

One might argue that theories that make identical predictions are, in an operational sense, the same theory; so it does not matter which theory is correct. In fact, however, it does matter. It matters for the value of economics as a descriptive science; and it matters for the conduct of macroeconomic policy because not all sources of price rigidity open the door to welfare-improving policies.

If it really matters which theory is correct, but conventional modes of economic inquiry cannot ajudicate the dispute, economic science would appear to be in deep trouble. Fortunately, one other common characteristic of the theories suggests a way out: Virtually every theory of price rigidity *describes a chain of reasoning which allegedly leads the firm to conclude that a change in price is inadvisable.*

That is what gave me the idea for an interview study. If actual decision makers really think the way one of these theories says, they ought to know that they do. If you ask them open-ended questions like, "Why don't you cut your prices when sales decline?," you may get shrugs or incoherent answers. But, if you confront them with the chain of reasoning they actually follow, they ought to recognize and agree with it. Conversely, if they explicitly deny the relevance or validity of a particular argument, then it is probably not governing their behavior. At least that is my methodological precept.

II.   But Aren't Interviews Unreliable?

Economists are skeptical that you can learn much by asking people. We are trained to study behavior by watching what people *do* (usually in markets), not by listening to what they *say*. For example, critics will point out that subjects of interviews have no incentive to respond truthfully or thoughtfully; so *homo economicus* might refuse to cooperate or even give misleading answers. If the respondent has reason to conceal the truth or mislead the interviewer, this objection is probably a show stopper. But, in the case of price stickiness, people have no particular reason to conceal the truth. As long as people are not pathological liars, interviews may elicit useful information.

The thoughtfulness problem goes deeper. We all know the billiard ball analogy: A good pool player makes excellent use of the laws of physics without understanding them, and certainly without being able to articulate them. For this reason, many economists doubt that much can be learned by asking "economic players" about how they play the game. But I believe that more pointed questions, posed in plain English, can elicit useful answers. For example, if you ask a skilled billiards player whether he bases his shots on the principle that the angle of incidence equals the angle of reflection, he will probably look at you quizzically. But, if you take him to the table and, pointing to the proper angles, ask: "Do you try to make this angle the same as that angle?," I imagine he would respond in the affirmative.

Legitimate questions can also be raised about the size and representativeness of interview samples. Detailed case studies of two or three companies can, at most, provide anecdotes, not useful statistical information. And samples that are unrepresentative of the underlying population give no basis for drawing inferences about population statistics. But these are familiar problems, well known to any user of data. They are not reasons to reject interview evidence out of hand.

We should remember that theory and econometrics have their limitations, too. Theoretical deductions are often untested or, worse yet, *untestable*. Econometric evidence is often equivocal and/or subject to methodological dispute. The imperfect knowledge we can pick up from interviews and questionnaires should therefore not be compared to some epistemological ideal, but to the imperfect knowledge that nonexperimental scientists can deduce theoretically or glean from econometric studies. By this more reasonable standard of evidence, data culled from interviews certainly look admissible.

III.   The Research Design

Along with a team of Princeton graduate students, I have now been in the business of interviewing executives about their pricing strategies since August 1988. Let me briefly describe the research strategy and some of the tactics.

Designing the Questionnaire

The first step, obviously, was to decide which theories were to be tested and then to turn them into questions that ordinary people can understand. This selection process was not entirely objective; nor could it have been. In scouring the intellectual waterfront, I excluded theories that sounded silly or that actually *were* silly, or that seemed too complicated to be explained tersely in plain English. These omissions were not particularly costly; they did not disqualify any of the major competing theories.

Translating the equations and diagrams into English proved to be easy. My first stab at a questionnaire was tried out on many "guinea pigs" (including economists, business people, and a few scholars involved in survey research) and altered in literally hundreds of ways. But, in general, the current version of the questionnaire bears a striking resemblance to my original draft. Translating from technical journalese into English simply proved not to be very difficult. I took this to be a good omen.

However, one important caveat should be entered. Not infrequently, a question must be rephrased on the spot to make the respondent understand it. To do so successfully, an interviewer must be reasonably articulate, must be able to think on his or her feet, and, most importantly, must understand the economics well enough to paraphrase a question without changing its meaning. Thus professional pollsters will not do. Instead, my interviewers are carefully selected Princeton graduate students.

Eliciting Cooperation from Businesses

The next problem was getting our feet in the door and getting our questions answered by the right people. A low response rate would obviously raise fears of selectivity bias.

A small-scale pilot study was used both to estimate the likely response rate in a large-scale study and to polish our questionnaire and interviewing techniques. We randomly selected 16 firms in the northeastern United States and wrote each an introductory letter requesting an interview. We then followed up with phone calls and/or further mailings as necessary and, after considerable efforts, successfully interviewed 8 companies. (These 8 companies are *not* included in the data reported below.) The estimated 50 percent response rate struck me as high enough to merit proceeding to the full study. So far, the response rate in the full study is running above 60 percent.

In addition, we had no trouble making connections with the person or persons in each company who could answer our questions. The number of "I don't know" responses has been small, and almost never do we hear, "You're asking the wrong person." Once in the door, we have found people more than willing to talk frankly. They find the questions interesting, mostly understandable, and not invasive of privacy.[2] Our experience, in fact, is that people are often eager to tell us things about which we would never have dared ask for fear that we would appear to be prying. We do, of course, promise confidentiality.

Getting Economists to Pay Attention

The hardest problem may yet lie ahead: Getting economists to pay attention to the results. Several concrete steps have been taken to increase the believability of the ultimate findings, whatever they may be. First, I wrote letters to the originators or major proponents of each theory. The letters explained the nature of the study, included a copy of the relevant portion of the questionnaire, asked for suggested improvements in the questions, and asked the "theorists" to suggest other testable implications of their theories. Most responded, sometimes offering useful ideas for modifying the questionnaire, which were adopted. Interestingly, however, not one person suggested a single further implication that could be tested in the questionnaire. This underscores the point I made earlier about the theories being empty.

Second, and much more important, we have taken great pains to ensure that the sample of firms is (a) large enough for serious statistical analysis, (b) randomly selected, and (c) representative of the private, for-profit GNP. To my knowledge, this is the first time anything like this has ever been attempted in an interview study. Since it is what makes the study unique, it is worth describing in some detail.

We purchased a tape listing firms with annual sales over $10 million in the northeastern United States, an area which accounts for 40–45 percent of U.S. GNP. From this sampling universe, we eliminated government enterprises and nonprofits on the grounds that the theories we wanted to test were all about profit-seeking firms; this left almost 25,000 firms. We then assigned a sampling weight to each firm proportional to its value-added and drew a random sample of 400 firms, seeking to complete 200 interviews. (Remember, the estimated response rate was 50 percent.)

Notice that we excluded any company with annual sales under $10 million, even though they employ nearly half the labor force. Why? Because there are so many of them, and the expense of reaching any sizable portion would be prohibitive. Clearly, an optimal experimental design would balance the value of the information obtained against the costs of obtaining it and would, therefore, undersample very small companies.[3] We approximated this crudely by not sampling any companies below the $10 million threshold. Analogous cost considerations motivated the geographical truncation: costs depend on distance from Princeton, NJ; benefits do not.

These two exclusions, however, might compromise the representativeness of the sample. So we remedied them as follows. Suppose pricing behavior varies geographically only because industrial structure differs across states, not because, say, California firms are inherently different from New Jersey firms. Then we can (and did) create a *synthetic national sample* by reweighting each firm in the Northeast to reflect national, rather than regional, shares in value-added. Firms in industries that are overrepresented in the Northeast, like banking, were appropriately undersampled; and firms in industries underrepresented in the region, like gas and oil extraction, were correspondingly oversampled. Thus, the industrial structure of our sampling frame matches that of the nation as a whole.

While we were adjusting sampling weights, it was a simple matter to reduce the potential bias from omitting small firms. For example, any sample that excludes firms with annual sales under $10 million will underweight retailing. We simply oversampled the remaining retail firms enough to assign retailing its proper national weight—and similarly for every other two-digit industry. In this way, we eliminate from our sample the portion of any "large-firm bias" that stems from the different industrial structures of small versus large firms. However, to the extent that small firms really differ from large firms *in the same industry*, the bias remains.

IV. Preliminary Results

The interviewing is now in progress. Given the limited clerical and interviewer resources at my disposal, we are conducting them in eight waves of approximately 50 letters (25 interviews) each over a period of about 18 months. As of this writing, the first three waves are nearly complete and we have just begun the fourth.

The results reported here are based on tabulations of the 72 interviews completed as of mid-November 1990. Since this partial sample is too small to permit much useful disaggregation, I restrict my attention to national averages here. Once the full sample of 200 is available, however, there will be a great deal of information about, for example, how the validity of different theories varies by industry.

The questionnaire comes in two parts and usually takes about 45–60 minutes to administer. The first part gathers a variety of factual information about each firm, while the second inquires directly about the theories.

The factual data will eventually be used for disaggregation, in cross tabulations, and as right-hand variables in regressions explaining the validity of the various theories. I make little use of these data in this chapter, but one issue is important enough to deal with right now: Just how "sticky" are prices in the U.S. economy?

To find out, we ask each firm, "How often do the prices of your most important products change in a typical year?" The distribution is shown in panel A of Table 15.1. These results offer cheer for Keynesians who model prices as, say, rigid for one period or more. I like to joke that in macroeconomic theory we know that the length of "the period" is one quarter. According to these data, less than 15 percent of the GNP is repriced more frequently than quarterly, and fully 55 percent is repriced no more often than once per year. If we had to pick a single abstraction to represent the whole economy, annual price change (the median response) would appear to be the "right" model.

From the point of view of macroeconomic theory, frequency of price change may not be the right question to ask, for it depends as much on the frequency of shocks as on firms' pricing strategies. We are more interested

Table 15.1
Measures of price stickness

A. Frequency of price change[a]	Percent of companies
More than 12	10.1
4.01 to 12	4.3
2.01 to 4	10.1
1.01 to 2	20.3
1.0	37.7
Less than 1.0	17.4

B. *Question*: How much time normally elapses after a significant ____ before you raise (reduce) your prices?

Event	Mean lag[b]	Standard deviation
Increase in demand	3.23	2.93
Decrease in demand	3.60	3.93
Increase in costs	3.17	2.90
Decrease in costs	3.97	4.47

Based on 72 interviews completed as of mid-November 1990.
a. Times per year.
b. In months.

to know how long price adjustments lag behind shocks to demand and cost. Panel B summarizes the results from a series of questions of the form, "How much time normally elapses after a significant____before you raise [reduce] your prices?" We inquire about four events: an increase in demand, a decrease in demand, an increase in cost, and a decrease in cost. The table shows that, while the distributions are quite spread out, the mean lags cluster in the 3–4 month range. There is precious little evidence that prices increase faster than they decrease, and virtually none that firms respond to cost shocks more quickly than to demand shocks.

The bulk of the questionnaire inquires about the twelve theories themselves. We begin each section by succinctly summarizing one of the theories and then posing a question like, "How important is this in explaining the speed of price adjustment in your company?"[4] Respondents answer freely in their own words, but interviewers code the responses on the four-point scale indicated at the bottom of Table 15.2.

While the scale resembles the typical grading system used at universities, we should expect the "grades" to be more compressed. At the high end, no theory is ever going to score a perfect 4.0. A theory rated "very important" by half the firms and "of minor importance" by the other half would be a fine theory indeed. So I would interpret a score of 3.0 as excellent. At the low end, a score of 1.0 would mean that every firm in the

Table 15.2
Summary evaluation of theories

Rank	Theory	Mean score[a]	Percentage "3" or higher
1	Delivery lags/service	2.86	65
2	Coordination failure	2.85	66
3	Cost-based price	2.72	57
4	Implicit contracts	2.52	56
5	Explicit nominal contracts	2.29	40
6	Costs of price adjustment	2.28	43
7	Procyclical elasticity	1.97	36
8	Pricing points	1.97	33
9	Inventories	1.72	28
10	Constant marginal cost	1.56	19
11	Hierarchies	1.54	18
12	Judging quality by price	1.45	12

Based on 72 interviews completed as of mid-November 1990.
a. Based on the following scale: 1 = totally unimportant; 2 = of minor importance; 3 = moderately important; 4 = very important; N = don't know or cannot answer.

sample dismissed the theory out of hand. This is not a grade of D, but a kind of super F. Indeed, any score below 1.5 is a remarkably poor performance.

If the respondent says a particular idea is "totally unimportant" to the speed of price adjustment, we ask no further questions about that theory. Otherwise, we ask a variety of follow-up questions (sometimes many, sometimes few) geared specifically to each theory. In this interim report, I ignore follow-up questions and concentrate on the main questions about the perceived validity of each theory.

Table 15.2 summarizes the central results on the validity of the twelve theories, as perceived by actual decision makers, ranked in order of popularity. The second column names the theories briefly, and sometimes cryptically. (Explanations follow.) The third column records the mean score on the four-point scale; remember that we expect most theories to score in the 1.5–3.0 range. We can interpret a rating of 1 or 2 as meaning that the firm rejects the theory as an explanation of price rigidity, and a rating of 3 or 4 as meaning that the firm accepts it. So the fourth column gives the percentage of respondents that rate the theory as 3 or higher—an indicator of the fraction of the private, for-profit GNP to which this theory applies. The two alternative ways of ranking the theories agree closely. Ranked from best to worst by mean score, the theories are:

1) *Delivery lags/service*:[5] The idea here is that price is but one of several elements that matter to buyers. Rather than cut (raise) prices when demand is low (high), firms might prefer to shorten (lengthen) delivery lags or provide more (less) auxiliary services. The mean score for this theory so far is a healthy 2.86. Seventy-six percent of the firms accept the premise, and 65 percent say it is an important factor in slowing down price adjustments.

2) *Coordination failure*: This very old idea has been revived and formalized in recent New Keynesian theorizing. The notion is that firms might like to raise or lower prices, but hesitate to do so unless and until other firms move first. Once other firms move, they follow quickly. The mean score for this theory of 2.85 and its "acceptance rate" of 66 percent are quite high indeed.

3) *Cost-based pricing* connotes another old Keynesian idea: that prices are based on costs and do not rise until costs rise. Well over half the firms in our sample so far rate this a moderately or very important factor in explaining the speed of price adjustment; the mean score is 2.72.

4) *Implicit contracts* connotes the "invisible handshake" theory that firms have implicit understandings with their customers which proscribe price increases when markets are tight. Though this theory obtains an average score of 2.52, it elicits strikingly bimodal responses. Sixty-one percent of the sample accepts the premise that implicit contracts exist and, within this subsample, respondents generally think such contracts are an important source of price stickiness: the mean response within this group is a stunning 3.42.

5) *Explicit nominal contracts* refers to the naive Keynesian idea that written contracts prohibit price adjustments while they remain in force. Most firms have such contracts, for at least some of their products; but discounting appears to be common. Our rough estimate is that this is an important factor in price stickiness for only about 40 percent of the economy. The mean score (counting firms with no explicit contracts as 1's) is 2.29.

6) A number of theorists have suggested that firms incur special *costs of price adjustment* whenever they change prices. Both menu costs and convex costs are lumped together under this rubric, but follow-up questions distinguish between the two. About 70 percent of all firms report that they have such costs. But fewer than half think them an important factor in slowing down price responses. The average score is 2.28.

7) According to a very old idea revived in the mid-1980's, demand curves become less elastic when they shift in. Such *procyclical behavior of elasticity* would lead to countercyclical markups which would, in turn, rigidify prices. This is another case where the premise is often accepted (59 percent of the time), but the idea is thought to be a significant source of price rigidity in only 36 percent of the cases. The average score is just below 2, which connotes minor importance.

8) *Pricing points* refers to the idea that certain prices (such as $19.95 for a shirt) are psychological barriers that firms are reluctant to cross. This also scores 1.97 on average. Again, a majority of the firms (53 percent) accepts the premise; but only a third think it explains much price stickiness.

9) *Inventories* refers to the theory that, when demand rises (falls), firms draw down (build up) their inventories rather than increase (decrease) prices. Note that this question is not asked of service companies, so the sample size so far is only 33. Of these, however, fewer than a third think inventories a significant factor in deferring price adjustments. The average score is a low 1.72.

10) *Constant marginal cost* is shorthand for the notion that prices are sticky because both marginal costs and markups are constant over the business cycle. Since its ratings are so poor (a mean score of only 1.56 and an acceptance rate of just 19 percent), I should explain how we posed the question. First, we asked respondents how their "variable costs of producing additional units" (our plain-English translation of marginal cost) behave as output rises. Only 42 percent of the sample reported that their MC was constant. Among this minority, about 60 percent said that the constancy of MC was totally unimportant or of minor importance in explaining their speed of price adjustment.

11) *Hierarchies* is a code word for a "theory" that does not come from the academic literature. Rather, it was suggested to us by an executive of a large corporation. The simple idea is that price changes are slowed down by the difficulty of getting a large, hierarchical organization to take action. Its low average score of 1.54 may appear unsurprising, since it should apply only to giant companies. But, even among firms with annual sales over $100 million, its mean score is only 1.66.

12) The worst theory, according to our practitioners, is *judging quality by price*, a theory I have mentioned before. It obtains a paltry mean score of 1.45 and an acceptance rate of just 12 percent. Less than a quarter of the firms in the sample so far think their customers would "interpret a price cut as a signal that the quality of the product has been reduced." In our tabulations, we count the others as rating the theory "totally unimportant." However, among the minority of firms whose customers *do* judge quality by price, roughly 45 percent say it is a moderately or very important factor in discouraging price increases. Thus this theory may be of some importance within a narrow sector of the economy.

In summary, it seems to me that the theories divide themselves into three groups. The top four listed above distinguish themselves as especially promising and/or applicable to the U.S. economy. The leading theory (by a slim margin), delivery lags/service, has not received the attention it deserves. The other three look to me decidedly Keynesian. Cost-based pricing is, of course, old-fashioned Keynesian stuff. Coordination failure is a major strain of New Keynesian theorizing. And the "invisible handshake" is by now part of the Keynesian tradition.

At the bottom of the list, we find four theories that appear to be rejected by our respondents. Two of them have enjoyed great popularity in the

1980's. If practitioners are to be believed, marginal costs are constant in only a minority of industries. And judging quality by price appears to be neither a common nor an important phenomenon.

It is true that these results are based on only 36 percent of the ultimate sample. But I will be surprised if the rankings change dramatically as more data come in; 72 observations is sufficient to answer most questions about national averages. The payoff to a large sample will come later, when I have enough data to answer disaggregated questions like, "What kinds of firms make 'invisible handshakes' with their customers?" I will report information of that sort at a later date.

Notes

I owe many debts of gratitude: to the Russell Sage and Alfred P. Sloan Foundations for financial support; to Eric Wanner for persuading me to go ahead with the project; to Elie Canetti for extensive and excellent research assistance; to Phyllis Durepos for efficiently handling the considerable volume of office traffic; to my graduate student interviewers, Anthony Marcus, David Genesove, Katy Graddy, Dean Jolliffe, Harold Kim, John Leahy, Alec Levenson, John Penrod, Michael Quinn, Steve Schwartz, Tim Vogelsang, and David Zimmerman; to Bob Abelson, George Akerlof, Larry Ball, Olivier Blanchard, Elizabeth Bogan, Dennis Carlton, Russell Cooper, Bob Gordon, Bruce Greenwald, Glenn Hubbard, Tom Juster, Danny Kahneman, Anil Kashyap, Alan Krueger, David Romer, Julio Rotemberg, Bob Shiller, and Andy Weiss for helpful suggestions; and, especially, to the many business executives who took time out from their busy schedules to answer our questions.

1. For example, the menu cost theory predicts firms will never make "small" price changes, which appears to be a testable proposition. But does it rule out price increases of 1 percent or 10 percent? Without measuring the menu costs, we cannot answer this question.

2. Considerable effort was expended to guarantee the latter. For example, I abjured any questions that might conjure up images of the U.S. Department of Justice.

3. This presumes that the study aims to explain the behavior of the GNP deflator.

4. For many theories, there is a preliminary factual question. For example, before we ask whether judging quality by price deters price increases, we first ask whether the firm thinks its customers actually do judge quality by price.

5. Space constraints prohibit me from giving scholarly references for each of the theories. I apologize to those slighted.

16 The Frequency of Price Adjustment: A Study of the Newsstand Prices of Magazines

Stephen G. Cecchetti

1. Introduction

The effect of price stickiness on aggregate output fluctuations has been the subject of much recent macroeconomic research.[1] Models which assume that individual agents adjust their prices at discrete and overlapping intervals conclude that longer periods between price changes lead to greater serial correlation of output in response to unanticipated shocks. The presence of monopolistic competition at the level of the individual price setters is usually used to justify the price change technology imposed on the model. The descriptive power of these models depends on the accuracy of their characterization of the price change process. Consequently, describing the evolution of the price change frequency and identifying its determinants is important to the understanding of macroeconomic fluctuations.

The frequency of price adjustment is almost certainly dependent on the economic environment. In this context, two questions are of interest. First, what is the response of the frequency of adjustment to increases in general price inflation? And second, what is the structure of the cost of price adjustment? Theoretical models of price determination in the presence of monopolistic competition, including those in Sheshinski and Weiss (1977, 1983), Mussa (1981a, b) and Iwai (1981), offer no general answer to the first question. Regarding the second, they assume the cost of a nominal price change to be constant in real terms. These costs are believed to take two forms: administrative, the cost of determining and implementing a new price; and informational, the cost imposed on the firm's customers and associated with a possible loss of sales to competitors. Rotemberg (1982a, b) has suggested that in the presence of monopolistic competition where substitute goods are readily available, the costs may be proportional to the size of the real price change. He argues that customers prefer stable price paths which exhibit small adjustments to those with large infrequent jumps. Alternatively, the hypothesis that the cost of changing a nominal price may be a decreasing function of the frequency with which the price is changed yields similar price adjustment behavior.[2] But whether costs are invariant to the size or frequency of price change is an empirical question.

Studying price changes requires data of a type that is not normally available. Ideally one would like observations on the changes in the transactions price of a consistent product over a period of time long enough for there to have been substantial variation in economic conditions. In addition, the product price must not be the outcome of a continuous auction market mechanism. Auction prices change costlessly between each transaction.

Data on the newsstand or cover prices of magazines fit these requirements quite well. The prices exhibit the desired property of discrete and infrequent adjustment, suggesting that they are not the result of an auction mechanism. The data are readily available in libraries, and transactions actually occurred at these prices.

This chapter continues with a descriptive presentation of the data on the newsstand prices of thirty-eight American magazines over the period from 1953 to 1979. Section 3 describes a target–threshold model of a monopolistically competitive firm facing general price inflation, an uncertain future and costly nominal price adjustment. The model implies that the firm will develop a rule for changing prices which states that the firm's fixed nominal price is changed when it is far enough out of line with current conditions. A logistic specification of the probability of observing a magazine price change during a given time period is derived from the model. The estimation focuses on the econometric problems associated with the possibility that magazines have price change rules that change over time. These difficulties are addressed by employing a rarely used but very powerful fixed effects model developed by Chamberlain (1980, 1984) to deal with discrete panel data sets where unobservable effects vary both across time and across groups.[3] The fourth section presents estimates of the model and a discussion of their properties.

The chapter provides two conclusions. While in theoretical models where the relationship between aggregate inflation and the frequency of price change is ambiguous, the results for these data indicate that prices have changed more frequently during periods of higher inflation.[4] In addition, the data are inconsistent with a simple model where the cost of a price change is constant in real terms. The observed increases in frequency of price changes are too rapid given the changes in aggregate inflation. The implication of this is that the costs of changing prices decrease as either the frequency of adjustment increases or the size of a real price change decreases. This provides an empirical basis for the cost technologies assumed by Rotemberg (1982a, b) in his studies of the aggregate consequences of sticky prices.

2. Description of Magazine Price Data

Data were collected on the newsstand prices of thirty-eight magazines over the period from 1953 to 1979.[5] (The list of magazines included appears in the appendix.) For each magazine, the price of the first issue in each year was noted. If a magazine's price at the beginning of 1975 differed from the price at the beginning of 1976, then the magazine was assigned a price change during 1975. As a consequence of this procedure, the frequency of the data is annual.[6]

Before beginning the more rigorous statistical investigation of the properties of these data, it is useful to examine some simple summary statistics. These are presented in table 16.1. From the first two columns of the table it appears that a magazine is more likely to change its price when general price inflation is high. Closer examination gives the impression that increases in the number of price changes lag rises in inflation by roughly one year.

Table 16.1 also presents information on the experience of magazines whose price changed in a given year. As will be argued in the next section, it is the experience of a firm since its last price change that determines if a price changes. The three series reported are for the average time since the last change for those magazines that change price (the length of spells completed in a given year),[7] the average fixed price change actually observed, and the cumulative aggregate inflation during that period. Several interesting conclusions emerge from these data. First, over the entire sample period there was an increase in the number of changes along with a decrease in the average length of a completed spell. At the same time, the average size of the fixed price change remained remarkably stable, while the cumulative aggregate inflation first decreased in the 1960's and then increased in the 1970's. The actual quantity of general price inflation between price changes is quite striking. As inflation increased in the 1970's magazines allowed their real prices to erode by nearly one-quarter. This is evidence of incredible price stickiness which can only be associated with high costs of fixed price changes. It is very unlikely that the administrative costs of actually changing prices can explain this. The obvious explanation is that each magazine fears that if it 'moves' first to adjust its price for

Table 16.1
Magazine price changes, 1953–1979

	Number of magazines changing price	Current inflation	Average number of years since last change	Average fixed price change	Average inflation since last change
1953	1	0.2	6.0	14.3	15.7
1954	2	2.2	7.0	27.0	17.9
1955	4	2.8	6.5	21.9	16.4
1956	8	3.8	6.4	31.5	18.3
1957	12	2.3	8.3	22.9	22.6
1958	4	1.0	9.8	20.2	23.1
1959	2	2.4	3.0	22.5	5.7
1960	1	1.1	14.0	18.2	37.1
1961	3	0.4	3.3	26.1	4.3
1962	5	1.9	9.0	29.1	17.8
1963	12	1.2	8.0	22.7	14.3
1964	7	0.9	6.0	16.4	10.2
1965	5	1.7	7.4	26.4	10.8
1966	9	4.0	5.2	17.5	10.8
1967	11	2.8	4.6	28.2	9.8
1968	8	4.3	6.9	29.0	18.3
1969	9	4.9	5.8	21.7	17.2
1970	8	5.0	7.5	25.5	23.6
1971	4	3.4	6.3	28.0	22.2
1972	4	2.9	5.3	22.6	19.4
1973	8	5.2	5.9	27.3	22.9
1974	19	11.9	4.8	29.4	28.0
1975	11	7.5	3.6	25.2	24.3
1976	17	4.8	2.9	24.9	18.0
1977	13	5.4	3.5	26.3	20.3
1978	12	8.1	1.8	24.5	12.7
1979	12	8.1	3.1	19.1	22.2

Calculations using newsstand prices of magazines which changed price from first issue of year to first issue of following year. The magazines used are listed in the appendix. Inflation computations use the deflator for gross domestic non-farm product, excluding housing services. All changes are measured as percentages.

inflation, it will raise its relative price above that of the competition, losing sales. The degree of magazine price stickiness provides strong support for sticky price theories based on monopolistic competition.

3. Specification of the Model

Explicit modeling of the timing of a firm's price change is extremely difficult. The decision to change a price in the presence of adjustment costs and an uncertain future is the solution to a stochastic dynamic programming problem. The problem is complicated by the fact that a firm knows that it can update its expectations in later periods, correcting any mistakes it may have previously made. While the repeated nature of the problem simplifies it considerably, it allows only a characterization of long-term average behavior.

Iwai (1981) has examined the firm's price adjustment problem using a target–threshold model of the type developed by Miller and Orr (1966) in their study of the demand for money.[8] Faced with costs of charging a price different from the short-term profit-maximizing price, and costs of changing its nominal price, the firm develops a rule that governs its price changes. This rule states that when the fixed nominal price, $P(t)$, is far enough away from the short-term optimal price, $P^*(t)$, the price will be changed.[9] The short-term optimal price is the price that would be set if price change were costless and continuous.

The firm's price change rule can be characterized by the maximum distance $P^*(t)$ will be allowed to deviate from $P(t)$ before the price is changed. Define the firm's measure of disequilibrium $z_t = \log(P^*(t)/P(t))$, h_c to be the maximum value z_t can attain before the price is changed, the barrier, and h_0 to be the distance from $P^*(t)$ at which $P(t)$ is set when it is changed, the return point.[10]

To best understand how this works, take an example where the firm's environment is stable so that the price change rule is constant. Beginning with the observation of a price change at $t = 0$, the fixed price is set so that $z_0 = h_0$, or $\log P(0) = \log P^*(0) - h_0$. Under the usual circumstances with a positive aggregate inflation rate, the fixed price is set above P^* so h_0 is negative. As time proceeds, P^* grows steadily until it exceeds the level prescribed by the rule. When the change in P^* exceeds the distance from the return point to the barrier, so $\log P^*(t) - \log P^*(0) \geq$

$(h_c - h_0)$, the price is changed. The new price log $P(t)$ equals log $P^* - h_0 =$ log $P(0) + (h_c - h_0)$.[11]

It is clear from this exposition that the probability of observing a fixed price change corresponds to the probability that the measure of disequilibrium z_t, exceeds the barrier h_c, or that log P^* has traveled more than the distance $(h_c - h_0)$. In a stochastic steady state, Iwai has shown that the probability of seeing a price change depends on the long-run expected rate of change of the short-term optimal price and the volatility of sales (the drift and variance in P^*), as well as the cost of changing prices. But since an increase in inflation, for real adjustment costs fixed, leads to a change in the price change rule which is represented by a growth in the distance $(h_c - h_0)$, as well as an increase in the speed at which $P^*(t)$ moves, one cannot determine whether higher inflation leads to an increase in the probability of observing a price change. But Iwai does show unambiguously that as the cost of price change declines, the distance $(h_c - h_0)$, from the return point to the barrier, falls as well.

An empirical specification of the probability of seeing a magazine price change can be developed from this discussion. This can be done so as to yield information not only about the effects of inflation, but also about the price change rule itself. There are two approaches that can be taken. The first derives a specification directly from the theoretical work. The Iwai model is a characterization of behavior in a stochastic steady state. If one were in a stochastic steady state where the transition probabilities are constant, the probability of observing a price change would depend only on the expected rate of change in the short-term optimal price and the volatility of sales. The steady state assumption would make the probability of a particular firm changing its price independent of that firm's history. One would be able to collect data that were consistent with the interpretation of the model as representing long-term average behavior. With data on individual firm prices, this would suggest estimation of a probability model with inflation and sales volatility as the only independent variables.

If prices changed frequently relative to changes in the economic environment, the data on price changes would come from a sequence of steady states and this simple approach would be sensible. The reported results in section 4 include such a specification. But since the amount of short-term inflation, as reported in table 16.1, fluctuates dramatically relative to the time between magazine price changes, it is unlikely that the steady state model is appropriate. To make the point more explicitly, notice from table 16.1 that in 1970 eight magazines changed their prices after an average period of seven and one half years. During the seven years from 1963 to 1970, annual inflation fluctuated from 1% to 5%. This suggests that prices changed infrequently relative to changes in the economic environment and leads to the conclusion that the period under consideration is not made up of many different steady states.

An alternative procedure begins by noting that a firm's price change decision depends on the distance P^* has moved since its last price change, and the distance from the return point to the barrier as specified by the current rule. The probability of viewing a price change then depends on the realized path followed by P^* during the time the nominal price is unchanged. The problem that arises in this interpretation is that the rule may change over time. But as Iwai has suggested, in the short run, the firm's rule is probably an artifact of long-term expectations held some time in the past. The specification developed below is able to account for the type of gradual change this implies.

To proceed, define y_{it} to be one if magazine i changed price at time t, $\Delta \log P^*(i, t)$ to be the change in the short-term optimal price since the last nominal price change, and $[h_c(i, t), h_0(i, t)]$ to be the ith magazine's rule at time ι. Then,

$$\Pr(y_{it} = 1) = \Pr\{\Delta \log P^*(i, t) > h_c(i, t) - h_0(i, \tilde{t})\}, \tag{16.1}$$

where $\tilde{t}$ is the time of the last price change, so $h_0(i, \tilde{t})$ is the return point from the rule in effect when the price was last changed. Eq. (16.1) states that when the distance the short-term optimal price has traveled exceeds the distance from the previous return point to the current barrier, the firm changes its price.[12]

An approach similar to Rotemberg (1982a, b) can be used to develop a model for P^*. Assume that each firm i is a monopolistic competitor with demand and cost function of the following form:

$$Q^d(i, t) = [P(i, t)/\bar{P}(t)]^a X(t)^b, \tag{16.2}$$

and

$$C(Q(i, t)) = A e^{\delta t} Q(i, t)^\alpha w(t), \tag{16.3}$$

where $\bar{P}$ is the aggregate price level, $X(t)$ is total industry sales, $e^{\delta t}$ represents technological change, $w(t)$ is input prices, and a, b, A, and α are constants. Substituting (16.2) into (16.3) allows formation of the firm's profit function. Taking the derivative of profits with respect to the price, setting the result equal to zero and solving for $P(i, t)$, yields log $P^*(i, t)$. Then, assuming $\bar{P}$ and $w(t)$ change at the same constant rate π, and adding a stochastic error u_{it} to represent components of P^* not directly included in (16.2) and (16.3), Δ log $P^*(i, t)$ can be written as

$$\Delta \log P^*(i, t) = b_0 T_{it} + b_1 (\pi T)_{it} + b_2 \dot{X}_{it} + u_{it}, \tag{16.4}$$

where T_{it} is the time since the last price change for magazine i, $(\pi T)_{it}$ is cumulative inflation since the last price change, and $\dot{X}_{it}$ is the cumulative change in industry sales since the last price change for the ith magazine.[13] Included in the error term u_{it} are firm- and time-specific measures of costs and demand which are not readily observable.

Specification of eq. (16.1) for the purposes of estimation can be carried out by defining

$$S_{it} = \Delta \log P^*(i, t) - \{h_c(i, t) - h_0(i, \tilde{t})\}$$
$$= a_{it} + b_0 T_{it} + b_1 (\pi T)_{it} + b_2 \dot{X}_{it} + u_{it}. \tag{16.5}$$

The quantity a_{it} represents information about magazine i's price change rule at time t. Assuming u_{it} has a cumulative logistic distribution, then

$$\Pr(y_{it} = 1) = F(\bar{S}_{it}), \tag{16.6}$$

where F signifies the logistic function and $\bar{S}_{it} = S_{it} - u_{it}$.[14] Obviously for a_{it} to be identified, it cannot be permitted to change for each magazine for every time period. In what follows identification is achieved by assuming that the constant associated with a magazine takes on the same value in non-overlapping three-year periods.

Substituting eq. (16.5) into (16.6) yields the model for estimation. It has the characteristic that the probability of observing a magazine price change on a given day depends on a firm's history, or path, prior to that day. The model decomposes the probability of observing a price change into a component that can be explained by rule changes and a component that can be explained by changes in the movement of P^*. Changes in the constant term a_{it} in eq. (16.5) represent changes in the distance $(h_c(i, t) - h_0(i, \tilde{t}))$ both across magazines and over time. And the b_i's are related to the short-run changes in the probability of observing a price change, holding the price change rule fixed.

The model specified in (16.5) can be modified to include the information contained in the magazine's previous fixed price change, $\Delta \log P(i, \tilde{t})$. Note that

$$\Delta \log P(i, \tilde{t}) = h_c(i, \tilde{t}) - h_0(i, \tilde{t}), \tag{16.7}$$

so

$$a_{it} + \Delta \log P(i, \tilde{t}) = h_c(i, \tilde{t}) - h_c(i, t). \tag{16.8}$$

Then, defining $a_{it}^* = a_{it} + \Delta \log P(i, \tilde{t})$, and substituting the result into eq. (16.5), a new specification can be derived with the previous fixed price change added to the original set of right-hand-side variables. For this case (16.5) can be rewritten as

$$S_{it} = a_{it}^* - \Delta \log P(i, \tilde{t}) + b_0 T_{it} + b_1 (\pi T)_{it} + b_2 \dot{X}_{it} + u_{it}. \tag{16.9}$$

The new constant term, a_{it}^*, is a measure of the distance from the current ceiling barrier to the one implied by the previous price change.

In order to allow both the a_{it}'s and the a_{it}^*'s, and consequently the price change rule, to vary both across magazines and over time, a particular form of a logistic model is used. In his study of the analysis of covariance in discrete data models, Chamberlain (1980, 1984) describes a technique designed to handle what he calls fixed individual or group effects. Problems occur in panel data sets where small groups of observations are known to be related, having special characteristics that cannot be directly observed. This relationship is the fixed effect. Examples are readily apparent in applications using longitudinal data where a group is an individual or a family. As Chamberlain points out, when personal characteristics are correlated with the explanatory variables, standard estimation techniques fail to identify the coefficients related to these variables. He then proposes a practical way to control for these fixed effects thereby circumventing the problem.

In the framework of the magazine price model a 'group' is a series of adjacent years for a given magazine during which the price change rule is assumed not to change. One approach to dealing with this would be to allow the constant term to vary from group to group, including a dummy variable for each. When there are a large number of groups and only a small number of observations in each, this involves massive computation.

In the standard case, one would simply choose estimates of the a's and b's to maximize $\log L = \sum_i \sum_t \log F(\bar{S}_{it})$. Chamberlain notes that when F is a logistic function, the sum of the dependent variables within a group is a sufficient statistic for the fixed effect, or group-specific constant term. To see how this works, label a group of observations for magazine i over which the constant term is the same by j and its associated constant a_{ij}. Then the sum of the value of the dependent variable over the group, call this Φ_{ij}, is a sufficient statistic for a_{ij}. If, for example, a set of observations is one magazine for three years, then a_{ij} represents the constant for that portion of the panel data set and the sum Φ_{ij} is the number of price changes that occurred over that period. Chamberlain shows that maximizing $\log L$ is the same as maximizing the conditional likelihood $\log L^c = \sum_i \sum_t \log G(\bar{S}_{it})$ where $G(\bar{S}_{it}) = \Pr(y_{it}|\Phi_{ij})$ and the observation at time t is in group j. Some thought reveals that formulation of $\log L^c$ will entail throwing out any cells where all y_{it}'s are the same, so their sum is either zero or the size of the cell. These cells are degenerate; the likelihood of observing a particular outcome at a given time is completely determined given this sum.

It is important to understand the nature of the conditional likelihood function that is used in the fixed effects estimation. First, it is only a function of the slope parameters, the b's in eqs. (16.5) and (16.9), and not the fixed effects themselves. The a's, which are treated as nuisance parameters, are integrated out. They are never estimated. The conditional likelihood function and the unconditional likelihood function of the standard logit estimation are not comparable. They need not be of the same order of magnitude. In fact, whenever degenerate cells exist, the probability of observing the sum, $\Pr(\Phi_{ij})$, cannot be computed and calculation of the value of the unconditional likelihood will not be possible.

4. Empirical Results

The model developed in the last section was estimated using data on changes in the newsstand prices of magazines. The Chamberlain fixed effects logistic formulation was used. The constant term was allowed to change for each magazine every three years.[15] There are a total of 318 constant terms for the 954 observations in the sample. This is equivalent to allowing each magazine to revise its price change rule at most once in each three-year period, or up to nine times over the twenty-seven years covered in the sample.

Table 16.2 presents the estimates for five specifications of the model. All utilize the Chamberlain technique.[16] The results for each model include the parameter estimates, the $\hat{b}$'s, with their asymptotic t-statistics in the left half of each column, and the estimated slope of the probability at the regressor means, the $\hat{\gamma}$'s, in the second half. An individual $\hat{\gamma}_i$ is defined as the derivative of the probability with respect to X_i, evaluated at the mean of the data set, and equals $\hat{b}_i P(1 - P)$, where P is the average probability of observing a price change in the data set as a whole. The asymptotic t-statistics for the $\hat{\gamma}$'s are also reported.[17]

The first column of table 16.2 presents results for the steady state model that implies the probability of observing a price change should depend on inflation and sales volatility alone. This model was estimated using the fixed effects formulation both for comparability with the path-dependent versions and to allow differences across magazines. The log likelihood value of -181.30 is barely different from the value of -182.37 computed when the parameters are constrained to zero.[18] Along with the theoretical arguments in the previous section, this is evidence that the steady state model is inappropriate for the study of magazine price changes.

The second and third columns of table 16.2 report estimates based on the path-dependent model of eqs. (16.5) and (16.6). Column (3) includes $\Delta \log P(i, \tilde{t})$ as a right-hand-side variable. The fourth and fifth columns of the table combine the steady state and path-dependent models by adding current inflation and sales volatility to the variables representing $\Delta \log P^*$. The combined models are attempts to include the determinants of the price change rule directly in the specification to be estimated. They are a type of reduced form.[19] The values of the log likelihood function suggest that the four path-dependent models are substantially better at explaining the data than is the steady state model.[20] The estimates represent the short-run response of the probability to changes in the three variables in the model. These are short-run changes since the computations presume that the price change rule is fixed.

Several conclusions are immediately apparent. First, an increase in the time since the last price change by one year increases the probability of a price change by a substantial amount, between 0.13 and 0.18. This increase holds fixed the amount of cumulative inflation experienced over the period

Table 16.2
Estimated coefficients and slopes of the probability at the regressor means for the magazine price model

	(1)		(2)		(3)		(4)		(5)	
	$\hat{b}$	$\hat{\gamma}$	$\hat{b}$	$\hat{\gamma}$	$\hat{b}$	$\hat{\gamma}$	$\hat{b}$	$\hat{\gamma}$	$\hat{b}$	$\hat{\gamma}$
Time since last change (T)	—	—	1.12 (3.66)	0.18 (1.36)	1.14 (3.67)	0.19 (1.07)	0.76 (2.65)	0.13 (1.06)	0.79 (2.68)	0.13 (0.94)
Inflation since last change (πT)	—	—	11.57 (1.68)	1.90 (1.39)	11.83 (1.69)	1.95 (1.09)	24.14 (2.95)	3.97 (1.30)	24.18 (2.94)	3.98 (1.07)
Previous fixed price change ($\Delta \log P(\tilde{i})$)	—	—	—	—	-7.06 (1.67)	-1.16 (1.94)	—	—	-6.33 (1.50)	-1.04 (1.40)
Current inflation (π)	9.81 (1.45)	1.16 (1.02)	—	—	—	—	-29.47 (2.15)	-4.85 (1.54)	-27.60 (1.97)	-4.54 (1.14)
Industry sales growth (X)	—	—	5.85 (1.76)	0.96 (1.21)	5.49 (1.61)	0.90 (0.96)	7.96 (2.35)	1.31 (1.14)	7.93 (2.23)	1.30 (0.98)
Sales volatility	0.053 (0.86)	0.0087 (0.68)	—	—	—	—	0.14 (1.36)	0.22 (0.76)	0.15 (1.45)	0.024 (0.74)
Log likelihood	-181.30		-82.91		-81.39		-77.86		-76.67	

The numbers in parentheses are asymptotic t-statistics. The $\hat{b}$'s are the coefficient estimates and the $\hat{\gamma}$'s are estimates of the slopes of the probability. All estimates use the Chamberlain fixed effects conditional logit specification described in the text. The number of observations is 954 for all models. The current inflation and πT variables are computed using the implicit deflator for gross domestic non-farm product, excluding housing services, from the Department of Commerce. The derivation of the sales volatility measure is described in the appendix. Industry sales growth is the growth in single-copy sales divided by the total number of magazines.

since the last change, so it reflects technological change in production as well as secular demand shifts.

The evidence on the effect of inflation on the probability of observing a price change appears mixed. Models (2) and (3) predict that if a magazine experiences higher inflation for any year since its last price change, the probability of its price changing will increase unambiguously. In fact, a single year with just five percentage points more inflation will increase the probability by the $\hat{\gamma}$ for πT of 1.95, times 0.05, or nearly 0.1. But the estimates of models (16.4) and (16.5) tell a different story. They predict that a five percentage point increase in inflation for one year will initially lower the probability by 0.05 below where it would have been. (This is the sum of the $\hat{\gamma}$'s for πT and π times 0.05.) Then in the following year, the probability will rise 0.15 above where it would have been. According to the combined model, the time path of the inflation increases matters.

Use of the Chamberlain technique can be tested against several interesting alternatives. One might think that the structure of the constant term, and consequently that of the price change rule, might not be so complex. Two possibilities are that the constant may vary only across magazines, or that it might not vary at all. This suggests several dummy variable specifications against which to test the estimates from the more complex technique. The first containing one constant term, the same for all magazines and all time, and the second including thirty-eight constant terms, one for each magazine. Under normal circumstances, comparison of pairs of models is made possible by either a likelihood ratio statistic based on the value of the two unconditional likelihoods or a Wald statistic computed from the sets of parameter estimates and their estimated covariance matrices. But since the simpler models are estimated using the standard procedure which yields a value for the unconditional likelihood, log L, in the previous discussion, and the Chamberlain method only allows computation of the non-comparable conditional likelihood log L^c, tests of the first type cannot be performed. Furthermore, direct estimation of all of the fixed effects, the a's in the Chamberlain model, is not possible. But the various specifications of the constant can be compared using a Hausman (1979) test to examine the parameters of interest, the b_i's in table 16.2.[22] The test was run on the four path-dependent specifications and the results were all the same. The parameter vector from the estimation which utilized the Chamberlain technique is always significantly different from that obtained from either of the simpler constant term specifications. Test sta-

tistics with chi-squared distributions with 3, 4, or 5 degrees of freedom rise
as high as 60 and never fall below 40.

The Hausman tests indicate that for models (2) and (3) the constant
term, and consequently the price change rule, differs both across magazines and over time. The interpretation of the constant term in specifications (4) and (5) is not as clear-cut since it is the portion of the price change
rule not adequately captured by the current inflation and sales volatility
variables. So the rejection of the simple model based on the Hausman test
is not as informative. One conclusion is that the inclusion of a linear
function of current inflation and sales volatility to measure changes in the
price change rule is inappropriate. If it were correct the test would fail to
reject a simpler model. It can be argued that the variables as included in
(4) and (5) are misspecified. A careful reading of the theory shows that it
implies that the current distance $\{h_c(i, t) - h_0(i, t)\}$ is determined by the
long-run expectation of future inflation and volatility at the time of the
most recent rule revision. Modeling the price change rule using current
levels of inflation and sales volatility presumes that the rule changes every
year.[23] But in the path-dependent model prices change slowly and the rule
is an historical artifact. To specify the determinants of the rule correctly
one would have to formulate an explicit model of the timing of rule revisions. Only then, when one could specify the information available to
agents at the time of the revisions, would consideration of the determinants of $(h_c(i, t) - h_0(i, t))$ be possible. This argues for discounting (4) and
(5) completely.[24]

To study the price change rule, estimates of the average value of the
constant term, call this $\bar{a}_t$, were computed.[25] Recall that the constant term
is not estimated directly using the Chamberlain technique. Unfortunately,
the technique does not allow calculation of the actual value of the constant in every one of the 318 cells for which it theoretically exists. In those
cases where the sum of the y_{it}'s over the three-year period is either zero or
three, the probability of any individual y_{it} being zero or one is completely
determined given this sum. In these degenerate cases, the constant is either
positive or negative infinity. What can be computed is the value of the
constant at the mean of the data for the nine non-overlapping three-year
periods that comprise the data set. These are measures of the constant for
a representative average magazine. Changes in $\bar{a}_t$ are changes in the probability of observing a price change, holding the distance P^* has traveled
fixed, and suggest changes in the price change rule.

Table 16.3
Estimates of the average fixed effect ($\bar{a}_t$ and $\bar{a}_t^*$)

Period	$\bar{a}_t$	$\bar{a}_t^*$	$[\Delta \log \bar{P}(t) \times 100]$	Average inflation	Average number of price changes
1953–1955	−11.87	−9.83	21.1	1.7	2.3
	(8.16)	(5.71)			
1956–1958	−9.86	−7.94	25.8	2.4	8.0
	(7.05)	(4.83)			
1959–1961	−9.83	−8.08	23.6	1.3	2.0
	(6.80)	(4.94)			
1962–1964	−9.62	−7.84	22.2	1.3	8.0
	(5.39)	(4.18)			
1965–1967	−8.71	−6.94	24.0	2.8	8.3
	(6.13)	(4.33)			
1968–1970	−7.81	−5.97	25.3	4.7	8.3
	(7.69)	(4.28)			
1971–1973	−8.21	−6.40	26.3	3.8	5.3
	(8.23)	(4.71)			
1974–1976	−6.12	−4.18	26.8	8.0	15.7
	(5.82)	(2.85)			
1977–1979	−4.51	−2.77	23.4	7.2	12.3
	(6.00)	(2.21)			

Values in parentheses are asymptotic t-statistics. The first two columns are calculated using eq. (16.5) substituted into (16.6), and estimated parameters reported in columns (2) and (3) of table 16.2. The value for the average fixed effect is the log of the average odds during the period, less the sum of the average level of the independent variables weighted by the parameter estimates. The remaining columns are three-year averages from table 16.1.

The first column of table 16.3 reports the estimates of the average $\bar{a}_t$'s using model (2) of table 16.2, and the second column reports average $\bar{a}_t^*$'s using model (3). Asymptotic t-statistics are also reported. To understand how these are computed take an example. The estimated $\bar{a}_t$ for the 1965–1967 period is the log of the average odds over the period, less the sum of the average value of each independent variable weighted by its coefficient estimates, as reported in the column (2) of table 16.2.[26]

Changes in $\bar{a}_t$ are changes in the probability of observing a price change given the level of the right-hand-side variables in the model. One way to calibrate these changes is to compute how long a wait (years since the previous price change) produces an equivalent change in the probability. Using the estimates from model (2) and assuming steady 5% inflation, it can be shown that an increase in the constant from −9.8 to −6.1 increases the probability by the same amount as waiting an additional 2.2 years.[27]

Put differently, the rise of 2.3 in $\bar{a}_t$ decreases the time since the last change required to achieve a given probability by 2.2 years.

Increase in $\bar{a}_t$ represent a decrease in the distance from the previous return point to the current barrier.[28] Analogously, an increase in $\bar{a}_t^*$ can be interpreted as a lowering of the current ceiling, $h_c(t)$, relative to the previous one, $h_c(\tilde{t})$. These estimates, together with direct information on the average current fixed price change $\Delta \log \bar{P}(t)$ reported in the third column of table 16.3, yield an interesting picture of the evolution of the price change rule.[29] The table shows some large fluctuations in the a_t's, but only small changes in the $\Delta \log \bar{P}(t)$'s. The decreases in the a_t's during the entire sample suggest first a change in the symmetry of the price change rule, and then an actual decrease in the distance from the ceiling to the barrier. When $\bar{a}_t$ grows, but the actual price change remains the same, the new barrier and return point will both be below the previous ones. The growth in $\bar{a}_t^*$ signifies downward revisions of the ceiling barrier h_c. A higher $\bar{a}_t$ means that P^* is not allowed to travel as far above the fixed price before a change, and that the fixed price is reset further above P^* than it was before. It is interesting to speculate about the causes of this change in symmetry. Changes in uncertainty and attitudes towards it in recent years may be responsible.[30] When estimates of future inflation are imprecise and the costs of changing prices are high, it is reasonable to expect a risk-averse price setter to choose a fixed price that overshoots the current short-run optimal price by more than he or she would if future inflation were certain.

The series presented in table 16.3 can also be used to examine the adjustment cost structure. The theory described in section 3 predicts that when the real cost of a price change is constant, the distance from the return point to the barrier of the price change rule should grow with inflation. This means that the estimates of $\Delta \log \bar{P}(t)$ should increase with inflation, and that the $\bar{a}_t$'s should decrease (become more negative). This is clearly not the case. The evidence shows that the distance of the rule in nominal terms shrank slightly during the 1970's, a time when general price inflation was increasing. This is consistent with the fact that the average real fixed price change (nominal change less inflation since the last change) decreased substantially during the 1970's. Since the theory states that the distance from the return point to the barrier shrinks with adjustment costs, the results suggest that the cost of a nominal price change falls either when the size of a real price change decreases, as described by Rotemberg, or as the frequency of adjustment increases.[31]

5. Conclusion

The newsstand prices of magazines provide strong empirical support for sticky price models based on monopolistic competition. The data show that magazine prices exhibit substantial stickiness allowing their real prices to erode by as much as one-quarter before implementing a fixed price change. Further analysis demonstrates that the costs of nominal price changes decrease either with increases in the frequency of adjustment, or with decreases in the size of a real price change. The evidence supports the contention that customers faced with ready substitutes prefer stable price paths to those with large infrequent jumps.

Changes in the economic environment since the Korean War, most notably increases in the level of general price inflation, have led to an increase in the frequency of magazine price change. As average annual inflation rose from near 2% in the 1953–1965 period to almost 8% in the latter half of the 1970's, the average time between magazine price changes fell from seven and a half years to three and a quarter years. While this evidence is for prices in only one industry, it is extremely likely that the frequency of adjustment for all prices in the economy increased over this period.[32] The shortening of the time period between nominal price adjustments has been the result of two complementary and related factors. First, there has been an increase in the rate of change in the price a firm would charge in the absence of adjustment costs. This short-term optimal price has been moving more rapidly as a consequence of higher general price inflation. Second, contrary to the results of models that hold real adjustment costs fixed, the empirical results show that higher inflation was accompanied by relative constancy in the distance the optimal price has to move before the fixed price is changed. This finding implies both that price setters opt for more frequent price adjustment when inflation is higher, and that adjustment costs fall as changes become more frequent. There appears to be justification for the claim that an inflationary environment breeds a lowering of buyer resistance to price changes.

It is clear from this exercise that the frequency of price adjustment is a quantity determined endogenously in the economy. Any attempt to build a model of the inflation process and macroeconomic adjustment must take account of this endogeneity. Both the short-run and long-run effects of increases in inflation on the frequency of price adjustment appear to be sizable. The implication is that higher inflation leads to faster adjustment and less price stickiness.[33] Failure of staggered contracts models to take this into account could easily lead to false conclusions about the short-term impact and longevity of both government intervention and external shocks.

Appendix

A.1. Magazines

The data set is composed of magazines continuously published from January 1950 to January 1980 and available on a newsstand in the winter of 1982. Due to a lack of information on the size of the previous nominal price change, $\Delta \log P(\tilde{t})$, data used in the estimation of section 4 does not begin in 1953 for thirteen of the thirty-eight magazines. For four magazines, data were lost for three years, for eight they were lost for six years, and for one, data were lost for twelve years. This left a total of 954 observations. The data were collected at the Berkeley Public Library and at various libraries of the University of California. The magazines used were: *Antiques, Architectural Review, Atlantic, Audio, Better Homes and Gardens, Business Week, Commentary, Consumer Reports, Current History, Ebony, Esquire, Films in Review, Foreign Affairs, Good Housekeeping, Harper's Bazaar, Harper's Magazine, High Fidelity, House and Garden, House Beautiful, Interiors, Modern Photography, Motor Trend, Nation, The New Leader, The New Republic, New Yorker, Newsweek, Parents', Popular Mechanics, Popular Science, Road and Track, Science Digest, Scientific American, Sunset, Time, U.S. News and World Report, Vogue,* and *Yachting.*

A.2. The Sales Volatility Index

The sales volatility index used in the estimation reported in section 3, table 16.2, was generated as the three-year centered moving average of the squared residuals from a regression of the single-copy sales of all magazines on three past lags and the total number of magazines available in a given year.

The regression results are

$$ScS(t) = -9{,}758.280 + 1.123\ ScS(t-1) - 0.537\ ScS(t-2)$$
$$\quad\quad\quad\quad (1.79) \quad\quad\quad (6.96) \quad\quad\quad\quad\quad (1.92)$$

$$+\ 0.255\ ScS(t-3) + 1{,}591.6\ TM(t),$$
$$\quad (1.29) \quad\quad\quad\quad\quad\quad (2.18)$$

$$\bar{R}^2 = 0.94, \quad\quad D.W. = 1.94, \quad\quad S.E.R. = 2{,}522.000,$$

where $ScS(t)$ are the single-copy sales in year t and $TM(t)$ are the total magazines available in year t. The source of these data is the Magazine Publishers Association.

The sales volatility index used in the reported work was scaled by a factor of 10^{12}. The index represents the one-period-ahead uncertainty in industry sales conditional on sales during the past three years. The use of sales figures, indirectly to compute the volatility measure and directly in forming the past sales value, in an estimation based on prices may produce inconsistency. But given that it is industry-wide sales based on eighty to one hundred magazines that are used, and that there are only thirty-eight magazines in the sample, each magazine's sales are small relative to the total, so this is unlikely to be a serious problem.

Notes

This chapter is a revised version of the second essay of my Ph.D. dissertation completed in August 1982 at the University of California, Berkeley. Thanks are due especially to George Akerlof without whom this study would never have been started, to Bill Greene for providing help at every stage, and to Paul Ruud, Tom Rothenberg, Bob Cumby, George Sofianos, Peter Berck, Paul Wachtel, Keith Johnson and anonymous referees for comments. All remaining errors are mine.

1. The work of Taylor (1980) on staggered contracts, of Blanchard (1984) on price asynchronization and of Rotemberg (1983a, b) on sticky prices are examples.

2. These hypotheses are all variants of the Okun (1975, 1981) customer market hypothesis.

3. The choice of a logit model, as opposed to a duration model of the type studied in Kiefer (1985), provides substantial flexibility in dealing with fixed effects. In alternative approaches the inclusion of individual or group effects can be extremely difficult except in the simplest of cases.

4. In a study of the price of noodles and instant coffee in Israel over the period from 1965 to 1978, Sheshinski, Tishler and Weiss (1979) also conclude that increases in inflation led to more frequent price adjustments. But the nature of government intervention in the Israeli price system suggests that further research using market-determined prices is of interest.

5. While most magazines are sold by subscription, nearly one-third are sold as single copies. Data from the Magazine Publishers Association covering the period of the sample show that

an average of 218 million copies of magazines are sold annually. Of these, an average of 69 million were single-copy sales.

6. There are so few price changes that an increased observation frequency, say quarterly, would yield many time periods with no changes at all.

7. To facilitate this computation, for each magazine data was collected on the data of the price change prior to 1953.

8. Sheshinski and Weiss (1977, 1983) derive a general set of conditions under which it is optimal for a firm to adopt a target–threshold pricing policy, often referred to as (s, S).

9. For a rigorous and complete treatment, the reader is referred to Iwai (1982), particularly ch. 6, along with its appendices and supplement.

10. Depending on the firm's loss function and discount rate, h_0 may be set equal to zero.

11. The complete version of the model would include 'a floor barrier' in addition to the ceiling barrier h_c. But since no downward adjustments are observed in the data, this has been omitted.

12. This is exactly the same as stating that the proportional difference between $P^*(t)$ and $P(t)$ exceeds h_c.

13. The term in eq. (16.4) the time since the last price change, T_{it}, may represent a trend in demand as well as technological change. To see why, note that inclusion of an exponential time trend in (16.2) leads to exactly the same expression.

14. See Chamberlain (1980, 1984) for a discussion of the use of the logistic distribution in discrete data analysis.

15. The length of the period was chosen to be small enough to allow flexibility in the specification, large enough so that the remaining parameters could be estimated with precision, and because it is an integer divisor of twenty-seven, the number of years in the sample. Experimentation with two- and four-year periods yielded similar results.

16. Newton's method was used to obtain the estimates. See Greene (1983).

17. Note that since $P = F(Xb)$, computation of the standard errors is non-trivial.

18. An experiment was performed where current inflation was replaced by a three-year lagged moving average. The results were nearly identical.

19. As is discussed below, if the rule is truly linear in current inflation and sales volatility, then the Chamberlain technique would be unnecessary. The constant would not vary at least over time. Allowing the constant to vary allows the specification of the determinants of the rule to be more complex than a simple fixed linear function.

20. Statistical comparison of the steady state model with the other models in table 16.2 would require development of a test for non-nested limited dependent variable models. While it may be possible to work out a test for the case under consideration, it is beyond the scope of this chapter.

21. Using the model discussed in Cecchetti (1985) it can be shown that these estimates imply that an increase in inflation will lead to an increase in the dispersion of relative price inflation, even though the probability of seeing a price change increases. Hence an increase in inflation leads to a decrease in the informativeness of the price system.

22. The Hausman test examines two nested models, one with more parameters than the other. Under the hypothesis that the model with fewer parameters is not misspecified, the larger model yields consistent but asymptotically inefficient estimates of the parameters of interest. Hausman develops a procedure based on the variance–covariance matrices of the two estimators for testing whether the parameter vectors are significantly different.

23. Experimentation with lagged moving averages of inflation did not alter the results.

24. An alternative interpretation of the test results is that movements in the constant term in models (4) and (5) are an indication of non-linearity in the relationship of the price change rule to its determinants. If the function is seriously non-linear in the range of the data, movements in the constant term would reflect the differences between the correct relationship and the linear one estimated. In this case as well, interpretation of the constant term is difficult.

25. In light of the previous discussion, results are reported using only the pure path-dependent models (2) and (3). It is important to point out that the pattern of the estimated constant term for the combined models (4) and (5) is exactly the same as that presented.

26. So $\bar{a}_t = \log(P_t/(1 - P_t)) - \overline{X}_t b$, where P_t is the average probability over a three-year period.

27. The additional waiting time is $\Delta T = \Delta \bar{a}_t/(\hat{b}_1 + \hat{b}_2 \pi)$.

28. Under certain circumstances, problems can arise in the interpretation of the average values of the fixed effect, $\bar{a}_t$ and $\bar{a}_t^*$. To the extent that either systematic changes in the price change rule are correlated with variables included in the model of P^* or components causing movements in P^* have been omitted, the estimates may not accurately reflect changes in the distance from the return point to the barrier. But given the specification of the model it is difficult to see how this could be so.

29. $\Delta \log \overline{P}(t) = h_c(t) - h_0(t)$, the average current fixed price change, should not be confused with $\Delta \log P(i, \tilde{t})$, the previous fixed price change for an individual magazine.

30. Since the estimates of the a_t's from models (4) and (5) which include sales volatility show the same pattern as those in table 16.3, the uncertainty would have to arise from a source not specifically considered.

31. The slight increase in the estimates of the a_t's for the 1971–1973 period is consistent with the expectation that the Nixon wage–price controls raised adjustment costs.

32. Evidence is provided in Cecchetti (1985) that the average frequency of price change in the economy as a whole increased first in 1967 and again following the Nixon incomes policy in 1974.

33. As is noted above, the information content of the price system may decrease with inflation as relative price variation appears to increase. While adjustment is faster, knowledge about the current environment and P^* is less precise. This creates a type of inefficiency that is very different from that usually studied with sticky price models.

References

Blanchard, O. J., 1983, Price asynchronization and price level inertia, in: R. Dornbusch and M. H. Simonsen, eds. Inflation, debt and indexation (M.I.T. Press, Cambridge, MA).

Cecchetti, S. G., 1985, Staggered contracts and the frequency of price adjustment, Quarterly Journal of Economics 100, 925–959.

Chamberlain, G., 1980, Analysis of covariance with qualitative data, Review of Economic Studies 47, 225–238.

Chamberlain, G., 1984, Panel data, in: A. Griliches and M.D. Intriligator, eds., Handbook of econometrics, Vol. 2 (North-Holland, Amsterdam) 1247–1318.

Greene, W. H., 1983, LIMDEP, American Statistician 37, 170.

Hausman, J. A., 1978, Specification tests in econometrics, Econometrica 46, 1251–1271.

Iwai, K., 1981, Disequilibrium dynamics (Yale University Press, New Haven, CT).

Kiefer, N. M., ed., 1985, Econometric analysis of duration data, Annals 1985-1, Journal of Econometrics 28, 1–169.

Miller, M. H. and D. Orr, 1966, A model of the demand for money by firms, Quarterly Journal of Economics 80, 413–415.

Mussa, M., 1981a, Sticky individual prices and the dynamics of the general price level, in: K. Brunner and A. H. Meltzer, eds., The costs and consequences of inflation, Carnegie–Rochester Conference Series on Public Policy, Vol. 15 (North-Holland, Amsterdam).

Mussa, M., 1981b, Sticky prices and disequilibrium adjustment in a rational model of the inflationary process, American Economic Review 71, 1020–1027.

Okun, A. M., 1975, Inflation: Its mechanics and welfare costs, Brookings Papers on Economic Activity 2, 351–399.

Okun, A. M., 1981, Prices and quantities (The Brookings Institution, Washington, DC).

Rotemberg, J. J., 1982a, Monopolistic price adjustment and aggregate output, Review of Economic Studies 49, 517–531.

Rotemberg, J. J., 1982b, Sticky prices in the United States, Journal of Political Economy 90, 1187–1121.

Sheshinski, E., A. Tishler and Y. Weiss, 1979, Inflation, costs of adjustment and the amplitude of real price changes: An empirical analysis, Working paper 35-79 (Foerder Institute for Economic Research, Tel-Aviv University, Tel-Aviv).

Sheshinski, E. and Y. Weiss, 1977, Inflation and costs of adjustment, Review of Economic Studies 44, 281–303.

Sheshinski E. and Y. Weiss, 1983, Optimal pricing policy under stochastic inflation, Review of Economic Studies 51, 513–529.

Taylor, J. B., 1980, Aggregate dynamics and staggered contracts, Journal of Political Economy 88, 1–23.

17 The Behavior of Prices and Inflation: An Empirical Analysis of Disaggregated Price Data

Saul Lach and Daniel Tsiddon

I. Introduction

In the past decade, many empirical studies on the dispersion of prices reached the conclusion that price dispersion is positively correlated with the rate of inflation. Different mechanisms accounting for this correlation have been advanced in the literature. The approach of Lucas (1973), based on imperfect information, emphasizes the role of unexpected inflation and inflation variability in generating intermarket price dispersion (Hercowitz 1981; Cukierman 1984). Another approach builds on the presumption that nominal price changes are costly; that is, they are subject to menu costs. The optimal policy, in this case, is to set prices discontinuously according to an (S, s) pricing rule (Sheshinski and Weiss 1983). In choosing the target and the threshold, a price setter contemplates the future evolution of inflation. Therefore, the distribution of inflation and, in particular, expected inflation affects the dispersion of prices. Still another theory that leads to a positive relation between inflation and price dispersion is based on costly consumer search (Bénabou 1988). Stigler and Kindahl (1970) argue that the search process by itself is not sufficient to reduce price dispersion when consumers' information about prices erodes as a result of inflation. Van Hoomissen (1988a, 1988b) posits that information's obsolescence due to inflation reduces the optimal stock of price information that consumers wish to hold, thereby leading to greater price dispersion.

The high rates of inflation in the past two decades have prompted many economists to believe that there is something fundamentally wrong with inflation, beyond its intrinsic potential to surprise. Recent developments have shown that price dispersion or, more generally, its distribution is linked to a central question in macroeconomics: Does the aggregate price level lag behind money supply in such a way that it can be exploited by the monetary authority? Can expected changes in the money supply affect output? A series of recent papers that tackle this issue examine the relationship between the behavior of the aggregate price level and the distribution of prices (Caplin and Spulber 1987; Tsiddon 1988; Caballero and Engel 1989b). It follows, then, that different approaches posit different channels by which inflation affects the dispersion of prices and, implicitly or explicitly, emphasize different aspects of the inflationary process as the primary cause of such an effect. In addition, it is now recognized that the pattern of this dispersion may have important macroeconomic implications.

In this study we analyze these interrelated issues using disaggregated data on prices of foodstuffs in Israel during 1978–84. Inflation was not a new phenomenon in the Israel of 1978, and it persisted at very high rates until 1985. The price data were drawn from the sample used in the monthly computation of the consumer price index by the Central Bureau of Statistics. These are micro-level data, collected at the store level, and therefore most closely resemble the data envisioned by the cost of adjustment theory: price quotations at the level of the price setter.

We find that *expected inflation* has an important effect on price dispersion. We show that the effect of the expected component of inflation on intramarket price variability is stronger than the effect of the unexpected part of inflation. As the data show that over 80 percent of total price variability comes from the intramarket price variability, the effect of expected inflation on overall price variability is substantial.

We show that, even in times of high inflation, price quotations are not trivially short and price changes are not synchronized across firms. These facts, taken together, confirm that there is some staggering in the setting of prices. We find that the distribution of real prices is far from being uniform, as many menu cost-based models assume or conclude. In fact, as inflation increases to very high levels, this distribution is not even symmetric. Our results point toward the following description: when the annual inflation rate reaches 130 percent, there are equal chances of finding real prices above or below the market average, but upward deviations in the real price are further away from zero than downward ones. On the other hand, *extreme* deviations from the market average are more likely to be downward. Furthermore, as the annual inflation rate more than doubles from 60 to 130 percent, real prices are pushed toward both tails of the distribution.

The chapter is organized as follows. Section II describes the data, and Section III presents the results on the relationship between price dispersion and inflation. Section IV analyzes other aspects of the behavior of prices: the duration of price quotations and the size of price changes, the synchronization in the timing of price changes across firms, and the distribution of real prices. Section V presents conclusions.

II. Description of the Data

The data set consists of price quotations on 26 food products reported by a sample of stores. The data were collected by the Central Bureau of Statistics (CBS) for the purpose of computing the consumer price index (CPI). The 26 products satisfy the following criteria: they are homogeneous, they did not change substantially either in quality or in the structure of their markets, and their prices were not controlled by the government during the period investigated.

The periods for which most of the data are available are 1978–79, 1981–82, and the first nine months of 1984 (before the first stabilization program was launched). The data for 1980 and 1983 practically disappeared from the CBS archives. We have 1983 data for only three fish products and for rice; in the case of beef for soup, the data for 1978 were missing.

The data were collected by monthly visits to stores always in the same week of the month. Each week therefore reflects a different set of stores, and the same stores reappear every four weeks. Chain stores are not included in the sample, and the only information available, besides the price quotation, is the store's code number and the week, month, and year in which it was sampled.

Table 17.1 presents basic statistics. For each product there usually is a different number of reporting stores (col. 1), and of course the same store may report prices of several products. Unfortunately, the data set is not balanced: not only is the number of nonmissing observations per store different across stores, but the calendar period in which they were sampled is also different. In half of the 57 months, the number of stores with nonmissing data exceeds the figure in column 2; the median store coverage ratio is well above 50 percent for almost all products. Similarly, half of the reporting stores have data for at least the number of months appearing in column 4. Dividing the numbers in column 4 by 57 yields the median monthly coverage ratio appearing in column 5: with a few exceptions, 50 percent of the stores appear in well above 55 percent of the sample period. At least for the first 20 products, these figures suggest that although there are some changes over time in the identity of the sampled stores, there is a sizable core of stores constituting a more or less balanced set of data.

Table 17.1
Basic statistics for 1978–79, 1981–82, and 1984:1–1984:9

Product	Number of reporting stores (1)	Median number of stores per month (2)	Median store coverage ratio (col. 2 ÷ col. 1) (3)	Median number of months per store (4)	Median monthly ratio (col. 4 ÷ 57) (5)
1. Tea bags	31	22	.71	47	.82
2. Fresh beef	56	40	.71	47.5	.83
3. Frozen goulash	50	43	.86	54	.95
4. Challah bread	21	14	.67	49	.86
5. Cocoa powder	30	26	.87	54	.95
6. Fish fillet	30	20	.67	42	.74
7. Arrack	31	21	.68	47	.82
8. Buri fish	29	18	.62	39	.68
9. Codfish	28	19	.68	47.5	.83
10. Frozen breef liver	45	30	.67	40	.70
11. Fresh beef liver	45	26	.58	33	.58
12. Chicken breast	54	38	.70	48	.84
13. Chicken liver	53	36	.68	39	.68
14. Rice	26	22	.85	54	.95
15. Turkey breast	43	24	.56	37	.65
16. Steak	48	29	.60	38.5	.67
17. Beef for soup*	50	28	.56	28.5	.63
18. Chicken legs	48	29	.60	35.5	.62
19. White vermouth	27	11	.41	18	.32
20. Liquor	21	9	.43	12	.21
21. Champagne	22	11	.50	18	.32
22. Vodka	29	16	.55	30	.53
23. Red wine	31	19	.61	32	.56
24. Rosé wine	28	17	.61	35	.61
25. Hock wine	33	19	.58	33	.58
26. Sweet red wine	34	18	.53	34	.60

* Does not include data for 1978, so col. 5 equals col. 4 divided by four.

III. Relative Price Variability and Inflation

As mentioned in the Introduction, a number of not necessarily competing hypotheses have been advanced to explain the observed positive association between relative prices and some aspects of inflation. These theories usually emphasize the role of different characteristics of inflation—such as expected or unexpected inflation or its variability—in explaining this positive correlation.

At this stage it is convenient to clarify what we mean by relative price variability and price dispersion. The first concept refers to the tendency of relative prices to change over time and is usually proxied by the cross-sectional (i.e., across stores in this chapter) variance of the *rate of change* of price. We emphasize that relative prices here refer to the comparison of prices across the store dimension, with the product held fixed. On the other hand, price dispersion is a more static concept that looks at the cross-sectional variance of price *levels*. Clearly, these two concepts are different objects. In fact, they may even move in opposite directions. At the risk of creating a false dichotomy between the different models mentioned in the Introduction, we chose to elaborate on two, and by no means the only, particular approaches. The first approach underlies the positive effect of expected inflation on the dispersion of prices and is associated with menu cost models. The presence of fixed costs of adjustment in nominal prices induces the firm to change its nominal prices in a discontinuous fashion. If the inflation rate is nonnegative and if some other conditions are satisfied, the optimal policy is to change the nominal price only when the real price hits a lower threshold, s (Caplin and Sheshinski 1987). The nominal price is changed so that the new real price equals a higher return point, S. One feature of this optimal policy is that the characteristics of the inflationary process affect both the threshold and the return points. In particular, the distance between S and s increases with the *expected* value of inflation, and since, under further restrictions (Tsiddon 1988), such an increase is associated with a greater dispersion of prices, the relationship between them is positive. These models are usually concerned with the price-setting behavior of sellers of a single product. Hence, they have direct implications for *intramarket* dispersion of prices.

The second approach is based on the Lucas-type confusion between aggregate and relative shocks and emphasizes the positive effect of *unexpected* inflation on relative price variability. These models are constructed

in such a way that the relevant dimension along which prices are compared is the product dimension. One way of carrying on this comparison
in a meaningful fashion is to compare the rates of change in the products'
price. That is, the relevant concept is the dispersion of the products' own
inflation rates around an aggregate rate of inflation. According to the
terminology adopted in this chapter, this is the *intermarket* relative price
variability. This effect has been confirmed empirically by several studies
(Parks [1978], Fischer [1981], and Hercowitz [1981]; for a dissenting
view, see Jaffee and Kleiman [1977]).

The main topic of this section is the empirical relationship between the
variability of relative prices of a given product across stores, the *intramarket* price variability for short, and the expected and unexpected components of inflation.[1]

Before we discuss the empirical results, some comments on our measure
of price variability and expected inflation are in order. The unit of time
used in the analysis is 1 month. We therefore aggregate our weekly data
into a monthly measure of price variability.[2] Let P_{ijt} be the price of product i in store j during month t and N_{it} the number of stores quoting prices
of product i in month t. As mentioned above, relative price variability is
usually measured by the cross-sectional variance of the rates of change of
price (Domberger 1987; Van Hoomissen 1988a), and we do the same.
Denote the rate of change in the price of product i in store j between
month $t - 1$ and month t by $DP_{ijt} = \ln P_{ijt} - \ln P_{ijt-1}$. Their standard deviation across stores is

$$\text{SDP}_{it} = \left[\frac{1}{N_{it} - 1} \sum_j (DP_{ijt} - DP_{i.t})^2 \right]^{1/2}, \tag{17.1}$$

where $P_{i.t}$ is product i's monthly average inflation rate and equals
$(1/N_{it}) \sum_j DP_{ijt}$.[3]

Some of the advantages of working with rates of change are that they
eliminate possible store effects in price levels (which enter multiplicatively),
they may also help in taking care of possible nonstationarities in price
levels, and they facilitate aggregation over products and thus make the
results of our analysis comparable to other results obtained at more aggregate levels.

On the other hand, menu cost models have direct implications on the
relationship between inflation and intramarket price dispersion. In fact, as
Danziger (1987) points out, in a model with homogeneous firms and a

deterministic environment, relative price variability is not a monotone function of the rate of inflation. In his model, based on Rotemberg's (1983) approach, an increase in the inflation rate increases SDP at low levels of inflation but decreases it when inflation is too high. This occurs despite the fact that the *dispersion* of prices is always positively related to the inflation rate.

This suggests that one should look for the effects of expected inflation on a measure of price dispersion such as the cross-sectional coefficient of variation of price *levels*. The problems we run into while analyzing the relationship between this measure of price dispersion and inflation convinced us that we need a more structured and empirically oriented model to tackle this issue. Hence we do not present results on the effects of the components of inflation on the cross-sectional dispersion of price levels.[4]

While it is true that menu cost models do not imply a univocal relationship between price variability and inflation, is there still anything to be learned from the empirical finding that this relationship is positive? Our answer is also positive for two reasons. First, even in Danziger's stylized model, the association between SDP and inflation implied by menu cost models is positive provided that the period between successive price adjustments exceeds 1.5 months (Danziger 1987, p. 707). In our sample, the average duration of a price quotation is 1.9 months in 1978–79 and decreases to 1.5 months during 1982. From our empirical perspective, therefore, the nonmonotonicity of the SDP-inflation relationship may be relevant only in a small portion of the data (see n. 8). Second, the stores in our data are, of course, not homogeneous as the Rotemberg model assumes. In the Rotemberg model the distance of the (S, s) band is $k\pi^{1/3}$, where k is a constant whose value depends on the parameters of the model and π is the rate of inflation. One manifestation of store heterogeneity is, presumably, in heterogeneous values for k. In this case, the difference in the magnitude of the (S, s) band between two stores, $(k_1 - k_2)\pi^{1/3}$, is increasing in the inflation rate. Moreover, as shown in Appendix A, in most empirically relevant circumstances, DP_{ijt} is approximately equal to the length of the (S, s) band of product i sold by store j at some time between months $t - 1$ and t. Thus the preceding argument implies that the cross-sectional variance of DP_{ijt} is increasing in the inflation rate. Store heterogeneity opens up a new channel by which inflation affects price variability, a channel that is missing in theoretical models that assume a homogeneous environment.

In sum, while the direct implications of menu cost models are better cast in terms of the relationship between price dispersion as defined here and inflation, we have argued that, for our empirical purposes, a similar implication holds for the relationship between relative price variability and the rate of inflation.

The details on the construction of the expected and unexpected inflation series are provided in Appendix B. For each product, expected inflation is taken to be the predicted value from a regression of current own inflation rate on past own inflation rates, past aggregate inflation rates, and time-related variables. It should be pointed out that although the CPI inflation rate was very high in the sample period, its behavior was not particularly erratic. In fact, the inflationary process in Israel was characterized by "steps" (Liviatan and Piterman 1986). This feature gives meaning to the notion of (linearly) predicting the inflation rate. Since the model used for prediction is a very simple and intuitive one (see App. B), we are confident that the decomposition into expected and unexpected components is not an artificial one.[5]

For each of the 26 products, we constructed time series of the measure of intramarket relative price variability, SDP, and of expected and unexpected inflation. We estimated sets of regressions with SDP_{it} as the dependent variable, where $i = 1, \ldots, 26$ indexes products. The regression results are provided in table 17.2. In one set, SDP was regressed on the expected ($E\Pi_{it}$) and unexpected ($U\Pi_{it}$) inflation rates of each product (cols. 1 and 2); in the other case, the regressor was the actual inflation rate of each product, now denoted by Π_{it} (col. 6).[6] These regressions are to be interpreted as a summary of correlations or reduced-form associations only since we are not estimating a structural model. Since we are dealing with foodstuffs, which are strongly affected by seasonality, government policy, and other "common" shocks, the natural framework for estimation is a system of seemingly unrelated regressions (SUR), which allows for contemporaneous correlation across different products.[7] On average, the best results, in terms of goodness of fit and parsimony, were obtained when the explanatory variables entered linearly. Quadratic specifications, although significant in some individual products, do not change the overall picture and are not presented here.[8] Hence, the models being estimated in each case are

$$\text{SDP}_{it} = \beta_{i0} + \beta_{i1} E\Pi_{it} + \beta_{i2} U\Pi_{it} + \varepsilon_{it} \tag{17.2}$$

and

$$\text{SDP}_{it} = \alpha_{i0} + \alpha_{i1} \Pi_{it} + \mathbf{u}_{it}, \tag{17.2'}$$

where ε_t and $\mathbf{u}_t$ are 26×1 vectors of disturbances each of which is independently and identically distributed with zero mean and a possible nondiagonal covariance matrix.[9]

Table 17.2 clearly shows that in most products, expected inflation has a positive effect on price variability. In 24 out of the 26 products this coefficient is positive and significant. For unexpected inflation, b_2 is positive and significant in 22 products. In 17 products the estimated coefficient is higher in $E\Pi$ than in $U\Pi$, and this difference is statistically significant in nine cases.

In order to assess the explanatory power of the regression, we decompose the variation of SDP for each product into explained and unexplained parts. Since expected and unexpected inflation are orthogonal by construction, the explained part consists of $b_1^2 S_{ee} + b_2^2 S_{uu}$, where S_{ee} and S_{uu} are, respectively, the sum of squared deviations around their means of the expected and the unexpected inflation rates. Since the residuals are not orthogonal to the regressors, their covariance with $E\Pi$ and $U\Pi$ times their respective coefficient estimates is included in the unexplained part (see n. † in table 17.2). We define a goodness-of-fit measure for each product as the ratio of the explained sum of squares to the variance of SDP, which may exceed one. This is denoted by R^2 and is presented in column 3. Furthermore, this explained part can be attributed either to expected ($b_1^2 S_{ee}$) or to unexpected ($b_2^2 S_{uu}$) inflation. A comparison of columns 4 and 5 reveals that whatever the explanatory power of the regression is, this additional explanation is due to the expected component of inflation rather than to the unexpected one.[10]

The estimated coefficient of expected inflation averages 0.43 (standard error 0.15) over all products,[11] which is 20 percent higher than the average value of the coefficient of the unexpected rate of inflation, 0.36 (0.16), and very similar to the average coefficient of actual inflation, 0.41 (0.14).[12]

Two additional sets of regressions were run using different measures of inflation. Their results are provided in table 17.3. Columns 1–3 indicate that aggregate inflation matters. Aggregate inflation is defined by the rate of change of the CPI (see App. B). The estimates indicate a pattern similar to the one found when the product's own inflation rates were used: expected aggregate inflation ($E\Pi_{cpi}$) has a positive effect on intramarket

Table 17.2
Intramarket price variability (dependent variable: SDP)

Product	$E\Pi_i^*$ (1)	$U\Pi_i^*$ (2)	R^2 (3)	$E\Pi_i^\dagger$ Contribution (4)	$U\Pi_i^\dagger$ Contribution (5)	Π_i (6)
1	.68 (6.2)	.63 (3.0)	.36	.35	.08	.67 (6.5)
2	.28 (7.3)	.17 (3.4)	.32	.29	.05	.24 (7.5)
3	.21 (2.1)	.40 (3.4)	.09	.03	.07	.30 (4.0)
4	.50 (8.8)	.46 (5.7)	.60	.41	.17	.49 (11.5)
5	.54 (12.4)	.59 (7.0)	.77	.73	.19	.55 (13.5)
6	.34 (7.1)	.31 (5.3)	.45	.31	.15	.34 (8.9)
7	.40 (6.2)	.44 (5.4)	.33	.20	.12	.43 (8.6)
8	.49 (8.2)	.26 (3.4)	.48	.40	.06	.39 (8.5)
9	.41 (7.5)	.47 (8.5)	.59	.32	.32	.43 (10.8)
10	.54 (8.8)	.23 (1.9)	.37	.37	.01	.49 (8.5)
11	.36 (10.4)	.17 (2.6)	.55	.53	.03	.31 (10.2)
12	.67 (5.4)	.50 (3.2)	.20	.16	.04	.60 (6.6)
13	.46 (10.8)	.33 (7.2)	.46	.42	.15	.41 (12.0)
14	.63 (4.8)	.44 (2.4)	.17	.14	.03	.56 (5.9)
15	.49 (8.8)	.28 (3.5)	.42	.31	.04	.43 (10.5)
16	.51 (11.0)	.22 (3.7)	.58	.56	.05	.39 (9.7)
17	.27 (4.6)	.16 (1.9)	.38	.34	.06	.24 (4.7)
18	.08 (1.5)	.22 (3.7)	.15	.02	.11	.13 (3.5)
19	.46 (8.2)	.28 (3.7)	.36	.32	.05	.38 (8.2)

Table 17.2 (continued)

Product	$E\Pi_i^*$ (1)	$U\Pi_i^*$ (2)	R^2 (3)	$E\Pi_i^\dagger$ Contribution (4)	$U\Pi_i^\dagger$ Contribution (5)	Π_i (6)
20	.49 (6.4)	.06 (.5)	.24	.24	.00	.41 (6.1)
21	.40 (6.8)	.40 (4.2)	.43	.36	.12	.40 (7.8)
22	.36 (6.1)	.55 (7.6)	.41	.18	.22	.43 (9.4)
23	.46 (8.3)	.60 (10.5)	.51	.24	.29	.52 (12.6)
24	.28 (4.0)	.16 (3.1)	.17	.12	.05	.18 (4.6)
25	.23 (.9)	.43 (1.1)	.03	.01	.01	.38 (1.8)
26	.68 (11.9)	.58 (8.5)	.50	.46	.17	.68 (14.3)
Average‡	.43 (.15)	.36 (.16)				.41 (.14)

Note: The equations for each product were estimated jointly using the SUR procedure, with the exception of product 17, for which 1978 data were missing. t-values are in parentheses.
* Expected and unexpected inflation are defined in App. B.
† From eq. (17.2), the total variation of SDP_t around its sample mean, with the subscript i omitted, is given by

$$\sum_t (SDP_t - SDP_.)^2 = b_1^2 S_{ee} + b_2^2 S_{uu} + 2b_1 b_2 S_{eu} + \sum_t \hat{\varepsilon}_t^2 + 2b_1 \sum_t \hat{\varepsilon}_t E\Pi + 2b_2 \sum_t \hat{\varepsilon}_t U\Pi.$$

where $SDP_.$ is the sample mean of SDP_t; S_{ee} and S_{uu} are the sum of squared deviations around their means of expected and unexpected inflation, respectively; $S_{eu} = \Sigma_t (E\Pi_t - E\Pi) \times (U\Pi_t - U\Pi)$; $\hat{\varepsilon}_t$ is the generalized least squares residual from eq. (17.2); and b_1 and b_2 are the generalized least squares estimators appearing in cols. 1 and 2. Then R^2 is defined by

$$R^2 = \frac{b_1^2 S_{ee} + b_2^2 S_{uu} + 2b_1 b_2 S_{eu}}{\sum_t (SDP_t - SDP_.)^2},$$

and the contributions of $E\Pi$ and $U\Pi$ are $b_1^2 S_{ee}/\Sigma_t (SDP_t - SDP_.)^2$ and $b_2^2 S_{uu}/\Sigma_t (SDP_t - SDP_.)^2$, respectively.
‡ Averages across products of individual estimates and their standard errors (in parentheses).

Table 17.3
Intramarket price variability (dependent variable: SDP)

Product	$E\Pi^*_{cpi}$ (1)	$U\Pi^*_{cpi}$ (2)	R^2 (3)	$E\Pi^\dagger_i$ (4)	$\lvert U\Pi_i\rvert^\dagger$ (5)
1	.56 (2.7)	.20 (.39)	.12	.59 (5.0)	−.45 (−1.3)
2	.38 (5.3)	.33 (1.9)	.36	.18 (3.9)	.22 (2.3)
3	−.13 (−.58)	1.01 (1.94)	.08	.12 (1.1)	−.01 (−.1)
4	.43 (2.59)	1.23 (2.95)	.21	.49 (7.2)	−.30 (−1.6)
5	.53 (4.64)	.19 (.65)	.30	.43 (7.6)	.30 (1.75)
6	.44 (5.18)	−.07 (−.41)	.30	.38 (6.2)	−.3 (−2.5)
7	.55 (4.68)	−.39 (−1.3)	.34	.38 (4.9)	−.07 (−.6)
8	.23 (1.64)	.15 (.49)	.04	.56 (7.6)	−.14 (−.9)
9	.26 (2.22)	−.45 (−1.8)	.11	.40 (5.4)	−.23 (−2.0)
10	.96 (6.25)	1.71 (4.43)	.50	.47 (7.4)	−.18 (−1.0)
11	.41 (6.81)	.23 (1.57)	.48	.34 (9.8)	−.07 (−.7)
12	.83 (4.42)	.84 (1.79)	.29	.63 (4.3)	−.37 (−1.3)
13	.45 (5.93)	.58 (3.04)	.44	.39 (7.1)	−.15 (−1.9)
14	1.61 (5.79)	.33 (.57)	.35	.54 (3.6)	.30 (.9)
15	.64 (5.98)	.85 (3.2)	.45	.42 (7.4)	.63 (5.2)
16	.52 (6.08)	.59 (2.76)	.44	.44 (9.5)	.38 (4.2)
17	.24 (2.83)	.37 (1.84)	.21	.25 (4.0)	.15 (1.2)
18	.17 (1.85)	.32 (1.44)	.09	.09 (1.7)	.09 (1.0)
19	.50 (3.01)	.46 (1.11)	.16	.42 (6.8)	−.1 (−.7)
20	.31 (1.55)	.21 (.43)	.05	.46 (5.1)	−.04 (−.2)
21	.20 (1.24)	−.05 (−.14)	.03	.31 (4.6)	.02 (.1)

Table 17.3 (continued)

Product	$E\Pi_{\text{cpi}}^*$ (1)	$U\Pi_{\text{cpi}}^*$ (2)	R^2 (3)	$E\Pi_i^\dagger$ (4)	$|U\Pi_i|^\dagger$ (5)
22	.46 (3.07)	−.27 (.71)	.18	.31 (4.6)	.35 (3.1)
23	.55 (3.72)	.20 (.55)	.21	.27 (3.7)	.37 (3.3)
24	.42 (2.81)	.43 (1.14)	.14	.20 (2.5)	.04 (.5)
25	.89 (2.34)	.27 (.28)	.10	.16 (.6)	.04 (.1)
26	.68 (4.03)	.19 (.44)	.24	.52 (7.3)	−.17 (−1.4)
Average‡	.50 (.32)	.36 (.48)	.24 (.15)	.37 (.15)	.01 (.26)

Note: t-values are in parentheses.
* The equations were estimated separately by OLS since the regressors are identical across equations. There are 54 observations for all products except products 6, 8, 9, and 14. These have 66 observations corresponding to the additional year 1983. Expected and unexpected CPI inflation are defined in App. B.
† The equations for each product were estimated jointly using the SUR procedure, with the exception of product 17, for which 1978 data were missing. Expected and unexpected own-product inflation are defined in App. B.
‡ Averages across products of individual estimates and their standard errors (in parentheses).

price variability. On average, across products, the estimated coefficient of $E\Pi_{cpi}$ is 0.50 and that of $U\Pi_{cpi}$ is 0.36.[13] A comparison of the estimated coefficients across products in tables 17.2 and 17.3 indicates that these averages mask a more variable response to aggregate inflation across products than to own inflation. The estimated coefficient of $E\Pi$ is larger than that of $U\Pi$ in 16 products, but significantly so in only five products. Columns 4 and 5 present estimates of the coefficients in a regression in which the explanatory variables are $E\Pi_{it}$, as in table 17.2, and the absolute value of $U\Pi_{it}$, denoted by $|U\Pi_{it}|$. The motivation behind this specification is that $|U\Pi_{it}|$ may be used as a proxy for the variance of the inflation process.[14] In only four products is the coefficient of $|U\Pi_{it}|$ numerically larger than the coefficient of expected inflation. On average, $|U\Pi_{it}|$ has no discernible positive effect on relative price variability.

These results show that expected inflation affects *intramarket* relative price variability. They also suggest that the expected component of inflation has more explanatory power than the unexpected one. This, in turn, implies that using actual inflation data as an explanatory variable captures mostly the effect of expected inflation and not of Lucas-type confusion effects. In this sense, the results presented here are consistent with the predictions of menu cost models.

IV. The Behavior of Prices

There are at least two reasons why the characterization of the behavior of prices is extremely important for economic analysis: The first reason has to do with the welfare costs of inflation, and the other is concerned with the constraints put by the behavior of rational price setters on an active monetary policy. The second issue will guide us in our description of the behavior of prices. It can be defined more precisely by the following questions: Do prices lag behind money in a way that can be used by the government to pursue an active monetary policy? Can expected changes in the money supply affect output? In the following subsections we describe four aspects of price behavior that have a bearing on these questions: the duration of price quotations and the magnitude of price changes (subsection A), the synchronization of price changes (subsection B), and the shape of the distribution of real prices (subsection C). Although each aspect is important in itself, it is the interaction between them that is crucial for the proper understanding of nominal rigidities.

A. Duration of Price Quotations and the Size of Price Changes

Over all products and stores, the duration of a price quotation in 1978–79 was 1.9 months, and in 1981–82 it was 1.6 months.[15] That is, prices lasted approximately 20 percent less in 1981–82 than in 1978–79. This is not surprising if one takes into account that the CPI monthly inflation rate rose from 4.9 percent in 1978–79 to 6.6 percent in 1981–82, a 35 percent increase. In addition, this empirical observation is implied by theory: Menu costs models, assuming a not too asymmetric profit function, imply that prices change more frequently when expected inflation increases, even though the (S, s) band itself increases (Rotemberg 1983; Tsiddon 1991).

Table 17.4 presents several results on the direction and size of price changes and on the duration of price quotations for each product in two periods, 1978–1979:6 and 1982.[16] First, we ask the following question: Within each period, what proportion of all price quotations are changing from month to month? And, in which direction are they changing? For

Table 17.4 Duration and change of price quotations

	A. 1978–1979:6						B. 1982					
	Changes (%)*		Duration (months)			(S, s) Band (%):†	Changes (%)		Duration (months)			(S, s) Band (%):
Product	No (1)	Up (2)	50% (3)	75% (4)	Mean (5)	mean (6)	No (7)	Up (8)	50% (9)	75% (10)	Mean (11)	mean (12)
1	76	16	3	6	4.1	4.4	45	49	1	2	1.6	10.5
2	43	53	1	2	1.6	7.1	37	61	1	2	1.3	11.1
3	60	33	1	3	2.0	6.0	29	67	1	2	1.4	10.4
4	85	14	3	4	3.0	14.0	35	62	1	2	1.5	11.8
5	53	42	2	3	2.0	8.8	45	50	1	1	1.5	10.6
6	48	50	1	2	1.7	7.2	39	54	1	2	1.5	10.0
7	69	26	2	3	2.2	8.0	47	50	2	2	1.75	12.7
8	41	44	1	2	1.6	6.8	20	76	1	1	1.2	10.3
9	51	39	1	2	1.8	7.5	38	54	1	2	1.4	12.7
10	43	51	1	2	1.6	7.8	32	61	1	2	1.4	11.8
11	53	44	1	2	1.9	8.1	40	57	1	2	1.5	10.5
12	39	55	1	2	1.5	7.2	21	75	1	1	1.2	10.9
13	56	39	1	3	2.2	7.1	26	72	1	2	1.3	12.1
14	70	25	1	4.5	2.7	6.4	47	43	1	2	1.6	11.2
15	39	55	1	2	1.4	7.7	25	73	1	1	1.2	6.9
16	48	49	1	2	1.7	7.5	37	59	1	2	1.4	11.4
17‡	53	45	1	2	1.5	7.8	33	59	1	1	1.3	10.4
18	40	49	1	2	1.6	6.2	18	79	1	1	1.2	9.9
19	72	21	2	3	2.6	14.7	53	44	1	2	1.8	10.8
20	80	17	2	4	2.8	10.9	49	49	1	2	1.2	14.4
21	76	19	2	4	2.4	11.7	53	43	1	3	1.9	12.5
22	77	20	2	3	2.6	11.8	49	48	1	2	1.8	13.0
23	76	22	2	3.5	2.5	12.6	51	46	2	2	1.8	12.1
24	78	19	3	4	3.1	14.4	43	54	1	2	1.7	14.3
25	76	20	2	4	2.5	12.1	52	47	1	2	1.6	12.6
26	78	19	2	4	2.8	14.0	44	53	1.5	2	1.7	14.1
Average§	61	34	1.6	3	2.21	9.1	39	57	1.1	1.85	1.48	12.8
	(16)	(14)	(.7)	(1.1)	(.65)	(3.0)	(11)	(11)	(.3)	(.5)	(.21)	11.5
												(1.6)

* Percentage of all observations in which price quotations remained constant (No) or changed upward (Up). † Arithmetic mean of all nonzero DP_{jt}, by product. ‡ Since data for 1978 are not available, figures are for January to June 1979. § Average across products of individual estimates and, in parentheses, their standard errors.

each product, we classified all nonmissing observations, corresponding to each store-month combination, into one of three categories according to the direction in which the price changed from the previous month: it either decreased, remained constant, or increased. In columns 1, 2, 7, and 8, we present the percentage of all observations falling into the no change (No) and upward changes (Up) categories. The first striking observation is that during 1978–1979:6, in most products, prices are quite stable in the sense that in more than 50 percent of the opportunities recorded (number of stores times 18 months), stores opted not to change prices. Such stability is less common in 1982 but is still not negligible. The average over products of cases in which the price was not changed is 61 percent in the first period and decreases to 39 percent in 1982. These nontrivial figures can be taken to be evidence favorable to the menu cost approach. It is interesting to note that even when inflation is always positive there are instances in which prices are reduced in nominal terms. This could be taken to be indicative of the presence of idiosyncratic shocks affecting the stores (Tsiddon 1988). This, however, does not happen very often: 5 percent of all price quotations in both periods.

In computing the duration of a price quotation, we are faced with the problem that the observed values of durations are truncated at 1 month, the period of time between observations. Hence, all inferences on duration are made on the basis of its truncated distribution. In order to unravel the nontruncated moments, we would have to appeal to strong distributional assumptions. We do not proceed this way; instead we assume that the truncated distribution shifts between periods in the same way as the underlying nontruncated distribution. We believe that our inferences on the changes in the distribution of durations between periods would not be subject to such a severe truncation bias. In this fashion, we hope to capture the qualitative changes between periods of low and high inflation. Since, in both periods, the observed median duration is around one, this results in a very nonsymmetric distribution of observed durations. Hence, in columns 3–5 and 9–11 we present the second and third quartiles and the mean of the truncated distribution of durations. In both periods and in all products the first quartile is 1 month. A close look at the figures reveals that, although there is heterogeneity across products in the duration of prices, in almost all products, the high tail of the distribution is squeezed down. The average duration of a price quotation across products and stores was reduced by 40 percent between 1978–1979:6 and 1982, from 2.2 to 1.5 months, as can be seen in columns 5 and 11. This reduction reflects a decline in the average duration in each product, sometimes by as much as 40 percent (products 1, 4, 13, 14, 20, 24, and 26) and by as little as 12 percent (product 6).

Out of the 10 products whose price quotations had an average duration of over 2.5 months in 1978–1979:6, seven of them are wines and liquors.[17] These are also the products that exhibited the largest reduction in the average durations of their price quotations. This group of products seems to behave differently than the other food items. This will be seen more clearly shortly, when the magnitude of the price changes is analyzed. However, to understand the reasons that make these products different, a more thorough study is called for.

Since the monthly inflation (CPI during 1978–1979:6 was 3.9 percent, roughly speaking, the real price of the product eroded by 8.6 percent before the nominal price was changed. Correspondingly, with a CPI increase of 7.3 percent in 1982, the real price decreased, on average, by 11 percent before the store decided to revise it. These figures are quite large, especially when one takes into account that most products in the analysis are basic foodstuffs, products usually believed to have many substitutes. Yet their real price can change by about 8.5–11 percent before their nominal price is adjusted upward. The large magnitude of the real price erosion does not seem to be an isolated phenomenon of the particular data set utilized. Cecchetti (1986) reaches a similar conclusion using price data on American magazines: real prices erode by as much as 25 percent before they are adjusted upward. These results strongly suggest that nominal rigidities are a common phenomenon.

As shown in Appendix A, DP_{ijt} is approximately equal to the (S, s) band $(= S - s)$ of product i sold by store j at some time between t and $t - 1$, in percentage terms. Hence, averaging over all price changes provides an estimate of the average length of the (S, s) band, which should not differ much from the figure of 8.5–11 percent mentioned above. In columns 6 and 12 of table 17.4 we present this average change. We see, in fact, that the length of the (S, s) band was on average 9.1 percent in 1978–1979:6, when monthly inflation was 3.9 percent, and 11.5 percent in 1982 with a 7.3 percent monthly inflation rate. Most products, except wines and liquors, show substantial increases in their (S, s) band lengths. In the latter group, the average change of price did not change as much and actually decreased in some items (they were very high to begin with in 1978–

1979:6). The picture that emerges from the data shows that the response to inflation of stores selling wine and liquors is mainly to shorten the duration of the nominal price quotations; in other products, the elicited response is more like an increased magnitude of the nominal price change, the (S, s) band.

The preceding analysis did not differentiate between increases and decreases of the nominal price. Restricting ourselves to the upward changes only, which constitute 95 percent of the sample, we obviously find that the average change in price is larger in both periods. However, the increase in the average size of the change between the periods is somewhat smaller. On average, the increase in price amounted to 12.3 and 12.9 percent in each period, respectively. As before, wines and liquors behave differently, and, in fact, the average increase in their price was actually reduced between 1978–1979:6 and 1982.

Finally, one may ask whether the data indicate the presence of systematic differences across stores in the size of the price change and in their durations. In other words, are there store effects? Intuitively, we would expect to find that either there are no store effects at all, neither in the size of the price change nor in their duration, or, if there are any store effects in the size of the price change, they would have to be positively correlated with corresponding effects in the duration of nominal price quotations. For each product and in each period, we separately tested the equality of store-specific means of price change and of their duration, $X_{ij.} = (1/T_{ij})\Sigma_t X_{ijt}$, where X is either the change in price (DP) or the duration of the nominal price quotation and T_{ij} is the number of nonmissing observations of product i in store j. Regarding the magnitude of the price change, the F-test cannot reject the null hypothesis of equality among stores in basically all products.[18] Note that this is still consistent with possible store effects in the price *level*. The F-test results concerning the equality among stores in the average duration of their price quotations are more ambiguous. In 1978–1979:6, the null hypothesis is rejected in seven products, whereas in 1982 it is rejected on 12 occasions. These rejections should be taken with a grain of salt because they may be caused by a small group of stores that differ too much from the others.[19] In any case, the simple correlation between the mean change in price with the mean duration per store over all products is significantly different from zero: .33 in 1978–1979:6 and .60 in 1982.[20]

B. The (A)Synchronization of Price Changes

The preceding subsection reported that a substantial number of prices remain constant for at least 2 months. At the existing inflation rates, this is not a trivially short period of time. Thus whether the timing of price changes is synchronized across firms or not is an important issue for the analysis of the real effects of monetary policy.

Suppose that there is a monetary expansion that affects the demand faced by each store and that, in response, stores increase their prices. Suppose, further, that stores do not act simultaneously; that is, price changes are not fully synchronized across stores. Then on changing its price, each store must take into account the fact that other stores have not yet done so. Were the store to ignore this in setting its price, its price would be too high and it would lose customers. If price changes were fully synchronized, stores would still take into account the behavior of rival stores; in equilibrium, however, the aggregate price will immediately increase so as to leave real balances unchanged.[21]

In many models it is this lack of synchronization in the pricing decision across stores that makes the lag in the aggregate price level longer than the duration of an average price quotation.[22] This result is certainly not specific to the menu cost model; it can be equally generated by other forms of nominal rigidities.

In trying to assess the degree of synchronization in price changes with our data, we are faced with the problem that the period of observation is 1 month. As inflation increases, from 1981 onward, the duration of a price quotation is reduced and may be less than 1 month. This implies that we would observe a large proportion of firms changing prices each month, giving the impression of a high degree of synchronization across stores. For an annual rate of inflation of 130 percent in 1982, this interpretation is problematic.[23] We therefore proceed to analyze the relatively low-inflation period of 1978–79, which still had a 60 percent yearly inflation. For each month and for each product, we compute the proportion of reporting stores that changed their prices in that month.[24] These proportions appear in figure 17.1. For the 23 months between 1978:2 and 1979:12, this proportion averages .395, with a standard deviation of .113. This implies that each store changes its price every 2.5 months or that each month, on average, 40 percent of the stores change their prices. If price changes were fully synchronized, we would expect these proportions to

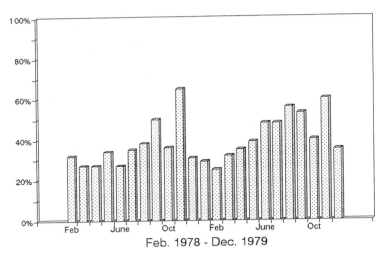

Figure 17.1
Proportion of price changes—(a)synchronization of price changes

vary considerably over time. In the extreme case, we should observe a sequence of zeros (no price changes) followed by a one (all stores change prices simultaneously), another sequence of zeros, and so on. A simple calculation shows that the standard deviation implied by such a pattern is four times as large as the estimated one.[25] Thus the relatively small variance in the estimated proportions is indicative of less than perfect synchronization; in other words, price changes are staggered. The pattern seems to be cyclical, perhaps because of seasonalities (observe the large November effect); starting in mid-1979, there also seems to have been, not surprisingly, a positive trend.

Another way of checking the degree of synchronization is by looking at the serial correlation among the estimated proportions. When prices change every 1.9 months on average, full synchronization implies some negative autocorrelation of order less than three; perfect staggering would imply no autocorrelation at all. None of the estimated autocorrelations is statistically significant, perhaps because of the small number of observations.[26] Nevertheless, the first three autocorrelations are positive, indicating that price changes are not fully synchronized.

Yet another confirmation of the lack of synchronization in price changes comes from the cross-correlations between changes in the money supply and the proportion of price changes. Since we do not know the speed at which changes in the money supply are transmitted to the food market, we look at cross-correlations between these two series, up to four lags. Intuitively, if there is full synchronization, some of these cross-correlations should be positive, but we find no evidence of this: all four cross-correlations are negative or very close to zero.[27]

These results indicate that in food markets, characterized by inexpensive and relatively homogeneous products, and in a period in which yearly inflation was 60 percent, price changes do not cluster. Stores do not coordinate the timing of their price changes, not even implicitly.

C.   The Distribution of Real Prices

We have shown that stores maintain constant their nominal prices for relatively long periods of time and that when they do update them they do not do so simultaneously. Do these two characteristics of firm behavior carry any macroeconomic implications? Specifically, suppose that there is a change in the money supply. Does the presence of lags in the adjustment of the nominal price at the firm level imply a lag in the adjustment of the aggregate price level? In order to draw any conclusions on the behavior of the aggregate price level, we must know the distribution of real prices. This is the topic investigated in this subsection.

In using our price data to determine the shape of the distribution of real prices, we must first define what we mean by real prices. The price data, after being transformed into natural logarithms, are denoted by lowercase letters. The real price of product i in store j during the tth month, Y_{ijt}, is the deviation of the log of the nominal price, p_{ijt}, from the log of the (geometric) mean of product i's prices across all stores sampled that month: $Y_{ijt} = p_{ijt} - p_{i.t}$, where $p_{i.t} = (1/N_{it})\sum_j p_{ijt}$. Thus Y_{ijt} is approximately equal to the percentage deviation of the store's price from the (geometric) mean price in month t.

The distribution of real prices in which we are interested is the cross-sectional (monthly) distribution of Y_{ijt}, for each product i. Suppose, first, that we concentrate on a single month for a particular product. Using data on Y_{ijt} to analyze its distribution may be problematic owing to the presence of store heterogeneity in the price level.[28] Heterogeneity of optimal prices across stores may result from different demand and supply conditions in different locations or, to a lesser extent, from the systematic differences in sampling dates over the month. It is first assumed that this heterogeneity is reflected only in a time-invariant mean real price for each store, $EY_{ijt} = \mu_{ij}$. Hence, we can write $Y_{ijt} = \mu_{ij} + \varepsilon_{ijt}$, where $\varepsilon_{ijt} = Y_{ijt} - EY_{ijt}$.[29] If theoretical models on pricing behavior ignore store heterogeneity, then their conclusions may be interpreted as saying something about the distribution of ε. In this case, one would like to recenter the data and analyze the deviations of each store's real price from its expected value, or the within-store real price variation, $Y_{ijt} - \mu_{ij}$. On the other hand, if one's goal is to compare distributions in different periods, these store effects do not have to be removed provided, of course, that the set of stores does not change much between the periods. This procedure has its advantages because the store effect formulation may not be satisfactory or because the store effects are believed to be partly endogenous and therefore not independent of the rate of inflation. In this case the data should be left uncentered.[30] We look at both possibilities.

Next, we address the time-series dimension of the data. The average number, over all products, of price quotations per month ranges from 10 to 44. The first nine months of 1984 are omitted from the analysis, so that only 48 months remain, corresponding to the years 1978–79 and 1981–82. This presents two problems: first, there are not enough data in each month for the results to be robust; second, the analysis and interpretation of 48 cross-sectional distributions for each of the 26 products are untractable. Thus we aggregated the data into the two subperiods analyzed previously corresponding to low and high inflationary steps, 1978–1979:6 and 1982. Here, aggregation means that in each case we look at the sum of frequency counts over 18 or 12 months. However, even if the distribution of $Y_{ijt} - \mu_{ij}$ has the same zero mean over time, it may not have the same variance over time if the latter is affected by the rate of inflation. Since there is still considerable variation in the inflation rates within each subperiod, it may be the case that the variance of Y_{ijt} is not constant over time. To handle this problem, we assume that, for each product i, the variance of Y_{ijt} changes over time but that in every month all stores have the same variance. Hence, for all j in N_{it}, $\text{var}(Y_{ijt}) = \sigma_{it}^2$. Thus to make sense of the time aggregation under this circumstance, we should look at the distribution of the following variable:

$$Z_{ijt} = \frac{Y_{ijt} - \mu_{ij}}{\sigma_{it}}. \tag{17.3}$$

Notice that the expected value and variance of the standardized real price,

Z, are the same across products. Provided that these two moments determine all other higher moments of the distribution of Z, one can go a step further and argue that aggregating again over products does not change the distribution.[31] Aggregation now means adding the frequency counts of Z over different products. This is the procedure adopted here.

For example, if the store's real price Y_{ijt} has expected value μ_{ij} and variance σ_{it}^2 and comes from a uniformly distributed population, then Z_{ijt} is also uniformly distributed on the interval $(-\sqrt{3}, \sqrt{3})$ for each product. Under this hypothesis, a plot of the frequency counts of all data points in all products should have an approximately rectangular shape over that interval; otherwise this would constitute evidence against the null hypothesis that real prices are uniformly distributed.

Since the parameters μ_{ij} and σ_{it}^2 are unknown, they have to be estimated. It can be shown that, as T and N tend to infinity, the estimators in equation (17.4) are consistent for μ_{ij} and σ_{it}^2.

$$Y_{ij.} = \frac{1}{T_{ij}} \sum_t Y_{ijt}, \quad STD_{it} = \left[\frac{1}{N_{it}} \sum_j (Y_{ijt} - Y_{ij.})^2 \right]^{1/2}, \tag{17.4}$$

where T_{ij} is the number of nonmissing price quotations of product i in store j.[32] Hence, the time-series dimension of the data is used to estimate the store effects and the cross-section dimension to estimate the variance of real prices.

In analyzing the distribution of real prices, we shall take the uniform distribution as a benchmark case since it has been the focus of recent research in aggregate (S, s) behavior. Caplin and Spulber (1987) derive the result that money is neutral in a model in which all price setters follow a constant (S, s) rule, the initial distribution of (the log of) real prices is uniform, and shocks to the money supply are nonnegative and have no idiosyncratic component. At any instant, the number of firms that change their prices, as they pass the threshold, multiplied by the change in their real price is just sufficient to compensate for the deterioration of real prices in all firms that do not change their prices. The average (aggregate) price level, therefore, equals the (normalized) quantity of money at every instant. This conclusion strongly depends on the distributional assumption on (the log of) real prices. This result was later strengthened by Caballero and Engel (1989b), who show that adding nonnegative idiosyncratic shocks makes the uniform distribution the unique stable equilibrium distribution, thereby dispensing with the arbitrary assumption of uniformity of the

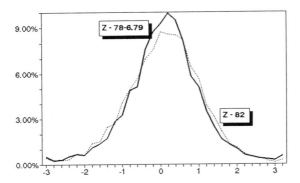

Properties of the Distribution of Real Prices - Z

Figure 17.2
The distribution of real prices—Z

initial distribution.[33] In equilibrium, then, discrete price adjustments at the firm level do not carry over and generate a lag in the response of the aggregate price level to changes in the money supply. If these models, or their assumptions, are approximately correct, then plots of the frequency counts of the standardized real price should be approximately rectangular over the interval $(-\sqrt{3}, \sqrt{3})$.

Figure 17.2 presents histograms of standardized real prices, Z_{ijt}, for all 26 products taken together, in each of the two periods (table 17.5 presents summary statistics). Recall that, by construction, Z_{ijt} has zero mean and unit variance. The histograms give us the impression that the distributions of standardized real prices are unimodal. One may even conjecture that they are symmetric or slightly skewed to the left. The apparent symmetry of the estimated quantiles and the low negative values of the skewness coefficients tend to confirm this. Formally, we use the observed moment ratio $b_1 = m_3/m_2^{3/2}$, where m_k is the kth sample moment about the sample mean, as a base for a symmetry test. The standardized value of b_1 has a limiting standard normal distribution, and its value is denoted by S (Gupta 1967). The results of the test imply that the data reject the hypothesis that the distribution is symmetric about zero in favor of the alternative that it is skewed to the left in 1982 but not in 1978–1979:6. Apparently, even the small observed differences in the quantiles cannot be supported under symmetry given the large number of observations used.[34] The fol-

Table 17.5
Properties of the distribution of real price—Z

Period	N	Skewness	Kurtosis	Max	95%	90%	75%	50%	25%	10%	5%	Min	S
1978–1979:6	10,965	−.06	1.58	6.27	1.61	1.16	.56	.028	−.56	−1.21	−1.67	−5.32	1.09
1982	7,080	−.13	.81	5.29	1.58	1.20	.63	.03	−.61	−1.25	−1.68	−4.72	2.90

Note: $-P > D_N < .01$ and $P > D_U < .01$.

Table 17.6
Properties of the distribution of real price—Y

Period	N	Var	Skewness	Kurtosis	Max	95%	90%	75%	50%	25%	10%	5%	Min	S
1978–1979:6	10,965	.027	.06	6.86	2.33	.24	.17	.09	.002	−.08	−.18	−.26	−1.07	.23
1982	7,080	.041	−.58	2.96	1.01	.3	.24	.12	.002	−.10	−.23	−.33	−1.16	6.7

Note: $-P > D_N < .01$ and $P > D_U < .01$.

lowing features of the distribution of real prices are worthwhile mentioning. First, the estimated median, for all practical purposes, coincides with the zero mean. Second, the left skewness means that there is a mass concentration, a hump, above zero that seems to occur between the 75 and the 95 percent quantiles. In other words, the upper tail is thinner than the lower tail. Note also that, in general, the third quartile is further away from zero than the first quartile. All this points toward the following: There are equal chances of finding real prices above or below the market average, but upward deviations in the real price are further away from zero than downward ones. On the other hand, *extreme* deviations from the market average are more likely to be downward. These features better describe the distribution of prices in 1982 than in 1978–1979:6. Visual inspection of the histograms indicates that, for all products taken together and in all periods, the distribution of (standardized) real prices is *not* uniform. Also, it is *not* normal as the Kolmogorov-Smirnov test results confirm (their respective tail probabilities are denoted by $P > D_u$ and $P > D_n$). Finally, the results of separate analysis of the histograms and related statistics for each of the 26 products for the four years 1978–79 and 1981–82 are consistent with the aggregate picture.

Figure 17.3 provides information on the nonstandardized real price Y_{ijt} (summary statistics appear in table 17.6). Examining Y_{ijt} serves two purposes: First, it reinforces our previous conclusions on the distribution of real prices in the sense that they are not a result of data manipulations. Second, it has the advantage that it lends itself to straightforward interpretation: 50 percent of the real prices lie within 8–10 percent of the average price, and 80 percent lie within 20–25 percent of it. These are nonnegligible differences. For a product with an average price of one, we have a 50 percent probability of paying less than 0.9 or more than 1.1. The summary statistics also confirm that the dispersion of real prices increases with inflation. First, the variance of the distribution increases by 50 percent. Second, in 1978–1979:6, with 3.9 percent monthly inflation, 25 percent of the prices are 8 percent below the mean and 25 percent are 9 percent above the mean. In 1982, when inflation per month is 7.3 percent, the first and third quartiles are −10 and 12 percent, respectively. In 1978–1979:6, the distribution is symmetric, but in 1982 it is skewed to the left. This means that, while in the low-inflation period deviations from the mean price in both directions have the same probability, by the time we

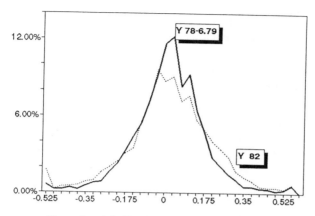

Properties of the Distribution of Real Prices - Y

Figure 17.3
The distribution of real prices—Y

reach 1982 with an inflation rate that is almost doubled, the probability of being 10 percent above the mean price is higher than that of being 10 percent below. In both periods, the distributions are neither uniform nor normal.

The empirical results show that real prices are not uniformly distributed. This conclusion is robust to different transformations of the raw price data.[35] To conclude, however, that it indicates that (S, s) behavior is not supported by the data is not warranted. The uniform distribution is the result of aggregate (S, s) behavior only under very specific assumptions. If these are not met, then the conclusion that the distribution of real prices is uniform does not have to follow. In fact, Tsiddon (1988) shows that if idiosyncratic and aggregate shocks follow a Brownian motion, implying positive and negative values, then the stationary equilibrium distribution is not uniform. If, in addition, shocks do not have zero mean, the distribution of real prices is not symmetric.[36] Two-sided menu cost models such as this provide additional predictions that can be tested by the data.

First, as expected inflation increases, real prices spend more time closer to the lower threshold, implying that we should observe a decrease in the lower quantiles, that is, a shift in the mass of the distribution toward the lower tail. Second, in these models, the distribution of the durations of price quotations is directly related to the distribution of real prices. In a sense, they are mirror images of each other: if the distribution of real prices becomes more humped to the left as inflation increases, so does the distribution of durations, and vice versa.[37]

Can we detect a shift in the distribution of real prices between 1978–1979:6 (3.9 percent monthly inflation) and 1982 (7.3 percent monthly inflation) in the direction predicted by the theory? The answer is a qualified yes. Figure 17.2 indicates that the interquartile range is larger in 1982 than in 1978–1979:6, meaning that prices were pushed to *both* tails of the distribution. The change in the distribution of Y in figure 17.3 seems to obey the same pattern as for Z. However, these changes in the shape of the distribution do not seem to be dramatic, and although not inconsistent with the theory, they are probably not strong enough to support any decisive answer. At this stage, therefore, we find the evidence on this issue only suggestive.

The other prediction from two-sided menu cost models is related to the distribution of durations. The theoretical results were derived for positive changes in price (Tsiddon 1988). Thus figure 17.4 and table 17.7 present statistics on the distribution of durations between upward changes of nominal prices only.[38] We address two issues: the asymmetry of the distri-

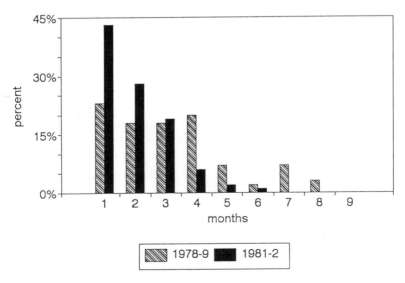

Figure 17.4
Durations of price quotations, products 1, 4, 7, and 19–26

Table 17.7
Summary statistics for figure 17.4

Period	N	Mean	Skewness	10%	25%	50%	75%	90%	Range
1978–79, 1981–82	2,077	2.4	1.55	1	1	2	3	4	10
1978–79	645	3.2	.86	1	2	3	4	7	10
1981–82	1,432	2.0	1.34	1	1	2	3	3	7

bution and the degree to which it changes between 1978–79 (low inflation) and 1981–82 (high inflation). Looking first at the four years together, we see that the distribution is clearly skewed to the right; it has a positive skewness coefficient. Comparing the two subperiods, we observe an increase in the coefficient of skewness from 0.86 to 1.34. This is a direct consequence of the flattening in the upper tail and the increase in the lower tail of the distribution: the upper 10 percent of the durations exceeded 7 months in 1978–79 but exceeded only 3 months in 1981–82; the lower 25 percent were up to 2 months in 1978–79 but only up to 1 month in 1981–82.[39] Thus the duration data are consistent with the prediction from two-sided menu cost models, and if one is willing to accept the theoretical results at face value, they imply that the distribution of real prices gets more humped to the left as the rate of inflation increases.

V. Conclusion

This chapter deals with the relationship between real prices and the rate of inflation using disaggregated price data on 26 Israeli foodstuffs, between January 1978 and September 1984. Inflation was not a new phenomenon in these markets, and although rates of inflation were high, this was not, for the most part, a period of hyperinflation.

We have shown that relative price variability is directly linked to expected inflation. Specifically, intramarket price variability is mostly affected by the expected component of inflation. Since our data show that intramarket variability contributes around 80 percent of total price variability, expected inflation is a more important variable in explaining price variability than its unexpected counterpart. We interpret this strong effect through the lens of menu cost models, but even if one objects to this kind of reasoning, the fact remains that the price system is not invariant to expected inflation.

The chapter discusses other aspects of price adjustments as well. When monthly inflation is around 3.9 percent in 1978–1979:6, real prices erode by 9 percent on average before they are changed. As the monthly rate of inflation climbs to 7.3 percent in 1982, the erosion in real prices is larger, 11.5 percent on average. This is accompanied by a shortening of the time between price adjustments. In fact, the average duration of a price quotation drops from 2.2 to 1.5 months between 1978–1979:6 and 1982. Fixed time-dependent rules, therefore, are not empirically validated by the data.

We also show that price changes are not synchronized across stores. At the store level, asynchronization must mean that the magnitude of the adjustment in the nominal price (when adjusted) is smaller, since other stores have not changed their prices yet. At the macro level, this asynchronization suggests that the aggregate price level does not adjust immediately to changes in the money supply. This suggestion is reinforced by the shape of the distribution of real prices. Models based on (S, s) pricing rules posit a relationship between the response of the aggregate price level to monetary shocks and the distribution of real prices across stores. Recall that the distribution of real prices is unimodal but not always symmetric about zero. It is neither normal nor uniform. A nonuniform distribution suggests, at least within the framework of discrete (S, s) pricing rules, that firms' discontinuous price adjustments *do* slow down the response of aggregate price to monetary shocks. Thus individual firm lags are transmitted into lags of the aggregate price level. The dynamic behavior of the aggregate price level is, therefore, affected by the dispersion of real prices.

This chapter is mostly descriptive and does not attempt to formally test discrete price adjustment rules. We plan to use our detailed data set to investigate this and other aspects of firms' pricing behavior in future work.

Appendix A.   Interpretation of DP_{ijt}

Suppose that time is measured by days, indexed by $v = 1, 2, \ldots$, and that a month always has 30 days. Thus beginnings of months correspond to values of v equal to 1, 31, 61, 91, and so on. This subsequence is generated by $1 + 30(t - 1)$, where $t = 1, 2, \ldots$ is understood to represent the beginning of the tth month. Since we deal with a single product, we omit the subscript i from this Appendix. The observed nominal price quotation of store j in month t is denoted by P_{jt}. It corresponds to the price observed when the store was sampled during month $t - 1$, say, at day c, with $1 + 30(t - 2) < c < 1 + 30(t - 1)$. It is, by definition, the *last* nominal price chosen by store j *prior* to being sampled during month $t - 1$. Suppose that this nominal price was chosen at day $v = \tau$, that is, $P_{jt} = P_{j\tau}$. At the time of the change in price, τ, the store's real price was $P_{j\tau}/P_{.\tau}$, where $P_{.\tau}$ is the average price across stores at time τ. If the store follows an (S, s) pricing policy, this real price is store j's upper bound at time τ, $S_{j\tau}$. On the other hand, just before the nominal price is adjusted, the real price in store j reaches the lower bound $s_{j\tau}$. This lower bound equals the previous nominal price divided by the average price level at time τ, $s_{j\tau} = P_{j\tau'}/P_{.\tau}$, where τ' is the date of the *last* change in the price level before time τ (i.e., the price remained unchanged between τ' and τ). A measure of the length of the (S, s) band at time τ is then given by $\log(S_{j\tau}/s_{j\tau}) = \log(P_{j\tau}/P_{j\tau'})$.

How do observed prices in months t and $t - 1$ relate to prices in days τ and τ'? Suppose that store j changes its price *once* between two consecutive sampling dates, $c' < c$. Then it must be the case that τ' is less than c', which is less than $1 + 30(t - 2)$; that is, the last change before day τ occurred before the sampling date in month $t - 2$. Thus the events occur in the following sequence: $\tau' < c' < 1 + 30(t - 2) < \tau < c < 1 + 30(t - 1)$, as shown in the first time line in figure 17.A1. Under these assumptions we get, in terms of observed prices, $P_{jt-1} = P_{j\tau'}$ and $P_{jt} = P_{j\tau}$. Hence, $DP_{jt} = \log(P_{jt}/P_{jt-1})$ is a measure of $\log(S/s)$ at day τ during month $t - 1$.

If the store did not change its price between c' and c, we cannot hope to measure the length of the (S, s) band from events (none) that occurred during month $t - 1$, and, in fact, DP_{jt} will be zero. If, on the other hand, the store changes its price more than once between c' and c, the matching with observed prices is not so clear-cut. Let τ' denote now the last time the

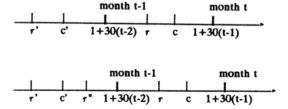

Figure 17.A1
Time lines

nominal price was changed before the beginning of month $t - 1$ and prior to being sampled during month $t - 2$. This implies that the observed price in month $t - 1$ is $P_{jt'}$. Let τ'' be the first time the price is changed *after* the sampling date in month $t - 2$, and let τ be as before. That is, $\tau' < c' < \tau'' < 1 + 30(t - 2) < \tau < c < 1 + 30(t - 1)$, as shown in the second time line in figure 17.A1. Then $DP_{jt} = \log(P_{jt}/P_{jt-1}) = \log(S_{jt}/P_{jt'}) + \log P_{.\tau} = \log(S_{jt}/s_{jt''}) + \log(P_{.\tau}/P_{.\tau''})$ since, by the same reasoning as before, $s_{jt''} = P_{jt'}/P_{.\tau''}$. Thus if prices change more than once between sampling dates, DP_{jt} is measuring the difference between the (S, s) bounds in different days that are at most 4 weeks apart and the inflation rate between these days. The bias is $DP_{jt} - \log(S_{jt}/s_{jt}) = \log(s_{jt}/s_{jt''}) + \log(P_{.\tau}/P_{.\tau''})$. The second term is usually positive but should be empirically negligible because the difference in the price level within a month is small compared to the size of DP_{jt}. If the lower bound decreases with expected inflation, as some models predict, the first term is negative. Hence, the approximation might not be too bad.

The outcome of all this is that the standard deviation of DP serves as an approximation to the standard deviation of the length of the (S, s) band in percentage terms.

Appendix B.   Inflation Forecasts

In this Appendix we explain how the monthly inflation forecasts were constructed for each of the 26 products and for the aggregate inflation rate. We restrict ourselves here to a 1-month-ahead forecast and ignore other possibilities.

The data utilized to calculate the inflation rates are the monthly price indexes for each product in 1977:1–1984:9. These indexes were computed by the Central Bureau of Statistics from virtually the same data used by us throughout our analysis. The difference stems mainly from the exclusion from our working sampling of stores that were infrequently sampled.

The different behavior of inflation between the earlier and later years of the sample period dictated that we perform separate forecasts for 1977:1–1979:12 and 1980:1–1984:9. The expected inflation of product i's price in month t is given by

$$E\Pi_{it} = \hat{\alpha} + \sum_{\tau=1}^{q} \hat{\delta}_\tau \Pi_{it-\tau} + \sum_{\tau=1}^{p} \hat{\beta}_\tau \Pi_{cpi,t-\tau} + \text{time}.$$

That is, product i's rate of inflation, Π_{it}, is forecasted by the last q values of its own inflation rates, $\Pi_{it-\tau}$; by the last p observations on aggregate inflation, as measured by changes in the monthly CPI, $\Pi_{cpi,t-\tau}$; and by time-related variables. These time-related variables were either monthly dummies, a linear time trend, or a dummy variable for the year 1984, the year in which inflation climbed to a higher step. The choices among these options followed F-test results. To make the choice of lag length manageable, we confine ourselves to choose from among zero, three, or six own lags and zero or three CPI lags. Again, on the basis of goodness-of-fit criteria, values of q were chosen from among these options (see cols. 1 and 2 in table 17.B1), while p was set at three. The estimates in the expected inflation equation were obtained from OLS regressions run on each product separately.[40] Their R^2 values are presented in columns 3 and 4 of table 17.B1.

In the first period, monthly dummies were added in all regressions. The R^2 statistics lie between .6 and .9 with two exceptions, products 6 and 9. The regression results, not presented here, indicate that the fit of the model is significantly diminished when the own inflation lags are excluded from the regression.

In the second period, the 1984 dummy variable coefficient was in general significantly positive. Not surprisingly, the predictive power in this period, as measured by the R^2, is between one-half and two-thirds of that in the first period.

Each forecasting regression was tested for serial correlation using the Lagrange multiplier test suggested by Breusch (1978) and Godfrey (1978) for testing the existence of autoregressive or moving average errors of order $p = 1$, 2 and for autoregressive conditional heteroscedasticity (ARCH) as in Engle (1982). In general, the null hypotheses of no serial correlation and conditional homoscedasticity cannot be rejected by the data.[41]

The expected aggregate inflation rate ($E\Pi_{cpi}$) was computed as the predicted value of Π_{cpi} given by a regression of current Π_{cpi} on its previous six lags and on monthly dummies from 1977:1 to 1984:9:

$$E\Pi_{cpi,t} = -.02 + .36\Pi_{cpi,t-1} + .08\Pi_{cpi,t-2} + .30\Pi_{cpi,t-3}$$
$$+ .04\Pi_{cpi,t-4} + .09\Pi_{cpi,t-5} + .24\Pi_{cpi,t-6}$$
$$+ \text{monthly dummies}; \quad R^2 = .78, \ T = 86.$$

Table 17.B1
Inflation forecasts

Product	Lags of own inflation*		R^2	
	1977–79[†] (1)	1980–84 (2)	1977–79 (3)	1980–84 (4)
1	6	3[‡]	.90	.48
2	3	3[§]	.64	.45
3	3	3[‡§]	.86	.27
4	6	3[§]	.74	.19
5	3	3[†‡§]	.69	.79
6	3	3[§]	.43	.54
7	3	3[§]	.83	.30
8	6	3[§]	.85	.42
9	3	3[†§]	.46	.43
10	6	6[†§]	.83	.71
11	3	6[†§]	.61	.66
12	3	3[‡]	.57	.38
13	3	3[†]	.83	.35
14	6	6[§]	.84	.60
15	3	6[§]	.70	.52
16	3	3[§]	.75	.39
17	3	3[§]	.71	.45
18	3	3[‡§]	.67	.32
19	3	3[†§]	.81	.44
20	3	3[†§]	.91	.41
21	3	6[†§]	.90	.49
22	6	3	.94	.20
23	3	3	.92	.13
24	3	3	.92	.09
25	3	3[†]	.90	.46
26	3	3[†]	.87	.42

* In addition, three lags of aggregate inflation, Π_{cpi}, were used in each product.
[†] Monthly dummies were added.
[‡] A linear time trend was added.
[§] A dummy for 1984 was added.

The resulting residuals are well behaved: the Lagrange multiplier test statistics for testing the existence of autoregressive or moving average errors of order $p = 1, 2, 3, 6$, and 12 are, respectively, 0.67, 3.10, 3.6, 4.36, and 17.28, which are significantly less than the χ_p^2 critical value at 5 and 10 percent significance levels. In addition, Engle's ARCH(p) disturbance model is also rejected by the data for $p = 1, 2, 4$, and 12: the corresponding test statistics (χ_p^2) are 0.04, 0.21, 0.68, and 7.20.

Notes

We would like to thank Miriam Zadik of the Central Bureau of Statistics for providing the data, Joram Mayshar and Shlomo Yitzhaki for helpful discussions, and Alan Zukerman for research assistance. The comments from seminar participants at Ben Gurion, Tel Aviv, and the Hebrew universities, at the 1990 NBER Summer Institute, and from two anonymous referees are gratefully acknowledged. This project was supported by a grant from the Israel Foundation Trustees and the Falk Institute for Economic Research in Israel.

1. Domberger (1987) also draws the distinction between intermarket and intramarket price variability. Until recently, however, empirical work on the latter was rarely conducted, presumably because of the lack of adequate data. Domberger (1987) and Van Hoomissen (1988a) are recent exceptions. The latter paper studies intramarket price variability in Israel using the same type of data we use, but for a smaller number of products during a longer period, 1971–84. Both papers, however, focus on issues different from the ones analyzed here.

2. There are two reasons for doing this. First, the data on inflation rates provided by the CBS come on a monthly basis, and, more important, the number of price quotations per week is quite low: its average ranges between 2.5 and 10.7 per product. On a monthly basis, however, the averages range between 10.3 and 42.8 price quotations per product.

3. Notice that between-week differences in inflation rates were not removed from (17.1. Were we measuring price dispersion, i.e., dispersion of price *levels*, this would constitute a problem since it implies a built-in positive correlation between the monthly variability measure and inflation. Thus the between-week effects of inflation have to be removed from measures of price dispersion such as the cross-sectional coefficient of variation of price levels. Regarding (17.1), between-week differences in inflation *rates* are not that significant, and it is not obvious in which direction these differences move as inflation changes over time. It should also be noted that this measure incorporates stores' inflation rates that were sampled at about 21 days apart, the length of time between the first and last weeks in the month.

4. The Durbin-Watson statistics from the regression of the coefficient of variation (CV) on expected ($E\Pi$) and unexpected ($U\Pi$) inflation indicated the presence of AR(1) disturbances in all products. In half of them, however, this was a result of "dynamic misspecification"; i.e., the nonlinear restriction imposed by the AR(1) model on the regression of CV against its own lagged value and current and lagged values of $E\Pi$ and $U\Pi$ was rejected by the data. In these cases, CV_{-1} was highly significant (t-values above 10), and $E\Pi$ and $U\Pi$ became insignificant. In the other half of the products, the evidence for position effects of expected and unexpected inflation was not that strong either: only about half of them had significant positive estimates.

5. Lach (1993) shows that errors in the decomposition of inflation into expected and unexpected components that, by construction, cancel each other do not affect the consistency of the ordinary least squares (OLS) estimator of the parameter of expected inflation but may under- or overestimate the parameter of the unexpected part of inflation depending on the

sign of $\beta_1 - \beta_2$ in eq. (17.2). The latter term's sign can be consistently estimated since the plim of the OLS estimator of $\beta_1 - \beta_2$ is proportional to the true difference $\beta_1 - \beta_2$. Hence, we can still draw unbiased inferences on the relative effects of expected vs. unexpected inflation based on OLS estimators.

6. The inflation rate Π_{it} is conceptually the same as $DP_{i.t}$. Since the former variable is taken directly from the CBS publications, it is not exactly equal to $DP_{i.t}$. See App. B for details.

7. This two-step procedure, first running actual inflation on a set of exogenous and predetermined variables and then using the predicted and residual values are regressors in an OLS regression of the SDP equation, provides consistent and efficient estimators of β_1 and β_2 in eq. (17.2), at least in the context of a single equation (Pagan 1984). The only problem lies in the computation of the variance of β_1, which is underestimated by standard OLS procedures. Notice, however, that this bias disappears under the null hypothesis: $\beta_1 = \beta_2$. Using an instrumental variable procedure to surmount this problem (Pesaran 1987) essentially produces the same numerical estimates as the two-step procedure, so that the downward bias in the variance estimator of β_1 is numerically insignificant. It is easy to show that the system-wide SUR estimators generated by the two-step procedure are still consistent. The main reason for not selecting the instrumental variable procedure is that the two-step procedure allowed us to use complete data from 1977:1 to 1984:9 to construct the expected and unexpected inflation and to run separate regressions for 1977–79 and 1980–84. This is technically more difficult to accomplish with the instrumental variable procedure since data for SDP in 1977, 1980, and 1983 are missing. For more details, see App. B.

8. In estimating the SUR equations, we did not allow for different numbers of observations in each product. The four products for which 1983 data exist were jointly estimated in a separate run. Their estimates are basically unchanged. The results presented in the tables correspond to the periods 1978–79, 1981–82, and 1984:1–1984:9. Quadratic specifications may be important because of Danziger's point discussed above. Regressing SDP against linear and quadratic expected inflation shows that the quadratic term is significantly negative in only three out of the 26 products. A simple calculation indicated that the estimated slope becomes negative in only a few months in late 1984, maybe because of the phenomenon pointed out by Danziger. Since this is a very minor portion of our data, we did not pursue this issue further, on the presumption that the overall results will not be affected.

9. There is a group of products (3, 5, 9, 10, 12, and 14) that exhibit first-order serial correlation and fourth-order autoregressive conditional heteroscedasticity of their error terms. Excluding them from the SUR procedure does not alter the results of the remaining products whose disturbances are serially uncorrelated and conditionally homoscedastic. Since even in the case in which the estimated variances of these six products are doubled the main conclusions are not affected, we chose to ignore this issue.

10. The reason that cols. 4 and 5 do not add up to col. 3 is that the orthogonality of the regressors is not satisfied because of our use of a sample period in these regressions different from the sample period used in the construction of these variables (see App. B). In most cases, the discrepancy is less than 1 percent of the total.

11. Here and in the rest of the chapter, the standard error refers to the standard deviation of individual product estimates around their average.

12. Restricting the same coefficients over all products results in almost identical estimates: 0.43 (0.012) for $E\Pi$ and 0.35 (0.016) for $U\Pi$. These restrictions are rejected by the data (F-value of 5.4 with [48, 1,275] degrees of freedom). As explained in the text, SDP may move in a direction opposite to that of a measure of the dispersion of price levels, and this happens because there are both positive and negative changes in prices. To partially cope with this problem, SDP was computed only for stores that had positive changes in prices (UPSDP). In this case (not presented here), the average coefficients of predicted and unpredicted inflation are quite similar, 0.24 (0.18) and 0.23 (0.19), respectively. Because of the large number of stores that do not change prices, especially at the beginning of the sample period, UPSDP is

sometimes missing and sometimes based on a small number of observations. Weighing the observations by the latter did not change the results, and the large number of nonoverlapping missing values made it inappropriate to try to improve efficiency by SUR methods. Hence, these results are based on individual OLS regressions and are significantly less accurate than the results in table 17.2. Because of the large standard errors, only 15 products have significantly positive coefficients for $E\Pi$, and $U\Pi$ is significantly positive in only nine products. In 14 products the estimated coefficient is larger for $E\Pi$ than for $U\Pi$, but this difference is significant in only three products.

13. These estimates were generated by the two-step procedure explained in Pagan (1984). An instrumental variable estimation method delivers estimates that are, numerically, very similar. See n. 7 for an assessment of this method.

14. We thank an anonymous referee for suggesting this point.

15. The duration of a price quotation is defined as the number of months that elapsed between two different price quotations, provided that there are no missing values in between.

16. These periods correspond to the two extremes of the sample in terms of the level of inflation. Restricting the first period to the year 1978 reduces the number of observations considerably, since in 1978 there were significantly fewer price changes. Hence, it was extended till June 1979, which corresponds to the same inflationary step. On the other hand, adding 1981 or parts of it to 1982 considerably increases the standard errors, presumably because of the reduction in duration from 1981 to 1982. In 1984 the duration recorded for most prices was 1 month. This is, of course, a result of the discrete feature of the data. In all likelihood, prices changed more than once a month. Although it may be possible to deal effectively with this type of truncation, we chose to exclude the observations for 1984 from the analysis in this section.

17. In nine of these 10 products, the median duration is greater than or equal to 2 months. All wines and liquors are made in Israel, and therefore their prices are not directly related to the exchange rate. The other three products are tea bags, sweet challah bread, and rice. One possible cause of this may be the different market structures of these products. If there are reasons to believe that, because of the greater possibility for product differentiation among wines and liquors, competition in these markets may be less stringent than in the markets for fresh chicken or beef, the reported differences in the duration of price quotations are not unexpected. Menu cost models imply that the less concave the profit function around the optimal price (i.e., the more monopoly power a price setter has), the wider the range of real prices he accepts without changing the nominal price (i.e., the longer is the duration of a price quotation).

18. In 1978–1979:6, in four products the null is rejected at the 5 percent but not at the 1 percent significance level. In 1982, the null hypothesis is rejected in only one case, product 8.

19. This is conceivable since the long tail of the truncated distribution of durations implies the presence of some extreme values. This means that, given a period of fixed length (18 or 12 months), the averages computed for the stores that have these long durations are based on a small number of observations. Hence, these extreme values may not be averaged out over time. The null hypothesis is rejected at the 5 percent significance level in products 1, 2, 3, 5, 9, 16, and 17 in 1978–1979:6 and in products 5, 7, 8, 12, 14, 16, 18, 19, and 21–24 in 1982. However, it cannot be rejected at the 1 percent significance level in products 14, 16, 21, and 22 in 1982.

20. At the individual product level, in the first period, in only two cases is this correlation negative, but not significantly so. In another eight products, the correlations are positive but also not significantly so. In 1982, all but two correlations are significantly positive.

21. Under ideal conditions, of course. It is implicitly assumed that a monetary expansion has an instantaneous effect on demands. As a referee pointed out, it takes time for money to change hands, and thus money supply may have real effects on relative prices.

22. See Fischer (1977). This statement is not always correct. In Caplin and Spulber (1987), e.g., there is no synchronization at all, and aggregate price adjusts immediately to changes in the money supply. Their assumption on the distribution of prices plays a key role in deriving this result (see subsection C).

23. It is not the same to have all firms changing their prices within a month when the monthly inflation is 1 percent as when it is 8 percent. This is not to say that synchronization does not increase with inflation. There are many reasons why this must be so. It is true of both menu cost–based (Tsiddon 1988) and information-based (Van Hoomissen 1988b) models, We merely say that the finding that most stores change prices within the month, as it occurs in the 1980s, should be interpreted with care.

24. We concentrate on only upward changes since we want to relate to the effects of an aggregate shock and downplay the role of idiosyncratic factors. Note, also, that we are not dealing with the interesting question of comovements in the prices of different products sold by the same store.

25. Suppose that prices change every 3 months (eight times in 2 years); the average proportion is then .333 with a standard deviation of .481.

26. The estimates of the first five autocorrelations are .29, .39, .03, -11, and $-.29$, with long standard errors on the order of .25.

27. The estimates for these cross-correlations are .09, $-.44$, $-.26$, $-.05$, and $-.11$ for the contemporaneous changes and four lags of changes in the money supply. Standard errors are approximately .20.

28. Recall that in the previous subsection we did not find significant store effects in price *changes*.

29. Since Y is the log of nominal price, this formulation implies that, for a given realization of ε, the price of product i in store j deviates by a fixed μ_{ij} percent from the (geometric) mean price. In terms of the nominal price (not in logs), we can write $P_{ijt} = \exp(p_{i.t} + \mu_{ij} + \varepsilon_{ijt})$.

30. We thank a referee for pointing out this issue.

31. This is satisfied, for example, by the normal and uniform distributions.

32. For Y_{ij} to be consistent, it is sufficient that $\{Y_{ijt}, t = 1, 2, \ldots\}$ be a stationary sequence with mean μ_{ij}, satisfying $\gamma(T_{ij}) \to 0$ as $T_{ij} \to \infty$, where γ is the autocovariance function of Y. For STD_{it} to be consistent, it is sufficient to require that $\{(Y_{ijt} - \mu_{ij})^2, j = 1, 2, \ldots\}$ be a stationary ergodic sequence with finite mean or that its elements be asymptotically uncorrelated.

33. They also qualify their result by showing that, when out of equilibrium, firms' lags are transmitted to the aggregate price level and that heterogeneity across firms speeds up convergence to equilibrium (Caballero and Engel 1989a).

34. One should be cautious with these formal tests since they assume independently and identically distributed variables.

35. For additional results, see Lach and Tsiddon (1990).

36. If shocks are two-sided, then there are two thresholds and one return point. The additional threshold emerges when the real price increases too much in the opposite direction to that of the trend. The shape of the stationary distribution in the case of Brownian motion without drift is triangular.

37. Specifically, if the evolution of the log of the real price can be represented by a Brownian motion (with drift) and if nominal prices are always increasing, then the duration of a price quotation is (asymptotically) distributed as an inverse Gauss variable. This distribution is humped to the left, and as the average real price deteriorates faster (i.e., as the rate of inflation increases), so does the asymmetry of this distribution.

38. The figures correspond to a group of 11 products (1, 4, 7, and 19–26) that are homogeneous in terms of the average durations (and variance) of their nominal prices. The nominal prices in these products lasted, on average, 3 months in 1978–79 but only 2 months in 1981–82. There are two reasons for concentrating on this subset of products: First, because of their homogeneity, we avoid the use of an arbitrary normalization to aggregate heterogeneous products, and, second, their long duration minimizes the left-censoring problem inherent to duration data.

39. It should be pointed out that a decrease in the mean duration does not necessarily imply an increase in the skewness of the distribution. Actually, a decrease in the mean duration can be accomplished by an increase in the symmetry of the distribution; i.e., average duration and skewness decline together.

40. We also experimented with data on aggregate money balances (M1) and with more sophisticated methods of estimation (autoregressive integrated moving average [ARIMA] estimation). Inclusion of M1 does not provide additional information when we use the CPI, and the ARIMA model did not yield significantly better results. The ARIMA procedure did not allow us to break the sample down into two subperiods because of the small number of observations.

41. Both in 1977–79 and in 1980–84, the null hypothesis of uncorrelated errors against the alternative AR(1)–MA(1) (AR(2)–MA(2)) cannot be rejected in 24 (23) products, at a 5 percent significance level. Engle's (1982) ARCH(p) disturbance model is rejected in all products for $p = 1$, 2, and 4 in the 1977–79 regressions. In 1980–84, however, conditional homoscedasticity is rejected in two to three products in favor of the ARCH(p) model.

References

Bénabou, Roland, "Search, Price Setting and Inflation," *Rev. Econ. Studies* 55 (July 1988): 353–76.

Breusch, T. S. "Testing for Autocorrelation in Dynamic Linear Models." *Australian Econ. Papers* 17 (December 1978): 334–55.

Caballero, Ricardo J., and Engel, Edward M. R. A. "Heterogeneity and Output Fluctuations in a Dynamic Menu Cost Economy." Discussion Paper no. 453. New York: Columbia Univ., 1989. (*a*)

Caballero, Ricardo J., and Engel, Edward M. R. A. "The $S - s$ Economy: Aggregation, Speed of Convergence and Monetary Policy Effectiveness." Manuscript. New York: Columbia Univ., 1989. (*b*).

Caplin, Andrew S., and Sheshinski, Eitan. "The Optimality of (S, s) Pricing Policies." Working Paper no. 166. Jerusalem: Hebrew Univ., 1987.

Caplin, Andrew S., and Spulber, Daniel F. "Menu Costs and the Neutrality of Money." *Q.J.E.* 102 (November 1987): 703–25.

Cecchetti, Stephen G. "The Frequency of Price Adjustment: A Study of the Newsstand Prices of Magazines." *J. Econometrics* 31 (April 1986): 255–74.

Cukierman, Alex. *Inflation, Stagflation, Relative Prices, and Imperfect Information.* Cambridge: Cambridge Univ. Press, 1984.

Danziger, Leif. "Inflation, Fixed Cost of Price Adjustment, and Measurement of Relative-Price Variability: Theory and Evidence." *A.E.R.* 77 (September 1987): 704–13.

Domberger, Simon. "Relative Price Variability and Inflation: A Disaggregated Analysis." *J.P.E.* 95 (June 1987): 547–66.

Engle, Robert F. "Autoregressive Conditional Heteroscedasticity with Estimates of the Variance in the United Kingdom Inflation." *Econometrica* 50 (July 1982): 987–1007.

Fischer, Stanley. "Long-Term Contracts, Rational Expectations, and the Optimal Money Supply Rule." *J.P.E.* 85 (February 1977): 191–205.

Fischer, Stanley. "Relative Shocks, Relative Price Variability, and Inflation." *Brookings Papers Econ. Activity*, no. 2 (1981), pp. 381–431.

Godfrey, Leslie G. "Testing against General Autoregressive and Moving Average Error Models When the Regressors Include Lagged Dependent Variables." *Econometrica* 46 (November 1978): 1293–1301.

Gupta, M. K. "An Asymptoticall Nonparametric Test of Symmetry." *Ann. Math. Statis.* 38 (June 1967): 849–66.

Hercowitz, Zvi. "Money and the Dispersion of Relative Prices." *J.P.E.* 89 (April 1981): 328–56.

Jaffee, Dwight M., and Kleiman, Ephraim. "The Welfare Implications of Uneven Inflation." In *Inflation Theory and Anti-Inflation Policy*, edited by Erik Lundberg. London: Macmillan, 1977.

Lach, Saul. "Decomposition of Variables and Correlated Measurement Errors." Forthcoming, *International Economic Review*, 1993.

Lach, Saul, and Tsiddon, Daniel. "The Behavior of Prices and Inflation: An Empirical Analysis of Disaggregated Data." Working Paper no. 224. Jerusalem: Hebrew Univ., 1990.

Liviatan, Nissan, and Piterman, Silvia. "Accelerating Inflation and Balance-of-Payments Crises, 1973–1984." In *The Israeli Economy: Maturing through Crises*, edited by Yoram Ben-Porath. Cambridge, Mass.: Harvard Univ. Press, 1986.

Lucas, Robert E., Jr. "Some International Evidence on Output-Inflation Tradeoffs." *A.E.R.* 63 (June 1973): 326–34.

Pagan, Adrian R. "Econometric Issues in the Analysis of Regressions with Generated Regressors." *Internat. Econ. Rev.* 25 (February 1984): 221–47.

Parks, Richard W. "Inflation and Relative Price Variability." *J.P.E.* 86 (February 1978): 79–95.

Pesaran, M. Hashem. *The Limits to Rational Expectations.* Oxford: Blackwell, 1987.

Rotemberg, Julio J. "Aggregate Consequences of Fixed Cost of Price Adjustment." *A.E.R.* 73 (June 1983): 433–36.

Sheshinski, Eytan, and Weiss, Yoram. "Optimum Pricing Policy under Stochastic Inflation." *Rev. Econ. Studies* 50 (July 1983): 513–29.

Stigler, George J., and Kindahl, James K. *The Behavior of Industrial Prices.* General series, no. 90. New York: Columbia Univ. Press (for NBER), 1970.

Tsiddon, Daniel, "The (Mis) Behavior of the Aggregate Price Level." Working Paper no. 182. Jerusalem: Hebrew Univ., 1988.

Tsiddon, Daniel, "On the Stubbornness of Sticky Prices." *Internat. Econ. Rev.* 32 (February 1991): 69–75.

Van Hoomissen, Theresa. "Price Dispersion and Inflation: Evidence from Israel." *J.P.E.* 96 (December 1988): 1303–14. (*a*)

Van Hoomissen, Theresa. "Search, Information and Price Dispersion in Inflationary Circumstances: Theory and Evidence." Manuscript. Stony Brook: State Univ. New York, 1988. (*b*)

18 Inflation and Relative Prices: Evidence from Argentina

Mariano Tommasi

Introduction

A look at the *Handbook of Monetary Economics* (1990) leaves one with the impression that inflation is a relatively minor problem. The prevailing wisdom that can be gleaned from any popular newspaper or magazine is quite different. Such a divergence of views can be explained by the different meanings given to the word "inflation." Most technical writings implicitly define inflation in a narrower sense than the general public does. The definition "a general increase in the price level" does not incorporate many characteristics of actual inflationary experiences, such as inflation uncertainty, relative price variability, inflation-proof activities, government measures to curb inflation, and many other distortions that tend to be correlated with higher rates of growth of the price level.

This chapter provides microeconomic evidence that furnishes a link between inflation as it is narrowly defined and some of the phenomena mentioned above. In particular, I try to describe a high-inflation environment from the perspective of a price-taking consumer. The main conclusion is that higher inflation is associated with a decreased durability of real-price information. In Tommasi (1991), I embed this finding in an equilibrium search model: a product market in which all the conditions for perfect competition are met, except for costless information. Search costs and agent heterogeneity induce price dispersion and local monopoly power for sellers. Inflation-related shocks, by lowering the durability of real prices, move the economy away from perfect competition by increasing monopoly power. This has the following welfare implications: (1) higher real prices paid by consumers, (2) lower productivity, and (3) survival of less efficient producers. All of these implications are consistent with popular (nontechnical) notions of inflation.

Those results contrast with the analysis in two related works: Benabou (1988) and Fischer (1986). Benabou, building on the work on adjustment costs by Sheshinski and Weiss (1977, 1983), predicts a positive effect of inflation on consumer welfare in a search market. Sheshinski and Weiss introduced the notion of "menu cost," that is, a cost of changing nominal prices. Such a cost makes the continuous adjustment of nominal prices (to maintain real ones constant) a suboptimal strategy. The optimal thing to do is to follow an (S, s) rule, allowing the real price to fall to s before adjusting the nominal price to reach the real level S. They show that the range $(S-s)$ is increasing in inflation. Their welfare analysis concentrates on sellers (they just postulate a demand curve), and the conclusion is that firms are hurt by being away from their profit-maximizing point due to inflation. Benabou (1988) closes their analysis by providing an explicit search-theoretic analysis of the consumer problem. The increase in price dispersion induces consumers to be more informed in equilibrium. This is a standard result in search theory: a spread is beneficial given the possibility of truncating the undesirable part of the distribution. The increased search intensity reduces prices on average (a fall in the price of this commodity relative to labor, the numeraire) and increases consumer welfare.

Consumers in Benabou's world are short-lived; they are in the market just once. For that reason one important effect of inflation is missing. Inflation affects relative price variability (rates of change of prices over time are more dispersed across markets and across sellers within a market), as I show in this chapter. Benabou (1988) concentrates on the contemporaneous cross-sectional effect of inflation, while my theoretical work concentrates on the intertemporal behavior of prices. The evidence in this chapter and in the empirical literature reviewed below tends to support the notion that the main dimension affected by inflation is the intertemporal one.

Even after recognizing the association between inflation and relative price variability, the welfare implications are not clear in the previous literature. It is a folk theorem among some economists that inflation-induced "excess" price variability generates inefficiencies in resource allocation. Fischer (1986, chs. 1–3) casts doubts on that claim. He shows that price variability can be welfare-improving. He exploits the quasi-convexity of the indirect utility function in the price vector: substitution toward goods whose prices are relatively low increases welfare. The analysis is carried out on the assumption of perfect information. As soon as we recognize that information is not a free good, it can be proved (Tommasi 1991) that the net effect of price variability can be welfare-decreasing in the case of variability across different goods, and that it is indeed welfare-decreasing in the case of variability across sellers of the same good.[1] In this way, the folk theorem is formalized.

Although this chapter is mainly directed to show the informational consequences of high inflation, the evidence here is also helpful in evaluating theories that try to explain the inflation-price variability relationship. The reason for not framing the study as a test of those theories is that none of the popular theories ("information" and "adjustment costs") has an unequivocal prediction for the inflation-variability (Danziger 1987) or inflation-dispersion[2] (Tommasi 1991) relationships. My own reading of the evidence below is that price-change technologies (and other transaction technologies) are really endogenous. In a high inflation country like Argentina, (inferior) technologies that save on "menu costs" are adopted. This endogeneity can be seen as reinforcing the explanation in Ball, Mankiw, and Romer (1988) for the steeper Phillips curve in these countries.[3]

The remainder of the chapter is organized in eight sections. Section 1 reviews the related empirical literature. Section 2 describes the data to be used. The empirical results for relative price variability and for intra-market price dispersion are presented in Sections 3 and 4. Section 5 shows that the degree of intertemporal correlation of real prices is diminishing in inflation. Section 6 presents some preliminary evidence on another effect of high inflation: the absence of advertised markdowns. Section 7 looks at the behavior of price changes, in particular the degree of synchronization in their timing across firms and across goods for a given firm. Section 8 concludes.

1.   Previous Empirical Studies

There is a huge literature, going back to Glejser (1965) and Parks (1978), that looks into the relation between inflation and the variability of relative prices across different goods. For an excellent recent survey see Palerm (1990). The main conclusion from those studies is that both expected and unexpected inflation are positively correlated to relative price variability (RPV), as measured by the standard deviation of the rates of change of individual prices around the average inflation rate.

More recently, inspired by Fischer (1981), there has been a move toward more disaggregated evidence. Domberger (1987) analyzes RPV *within* markets, defining markets as activity headings in the United Kingdom's SIC . His intragood analysis refers to different goods within one activity heading. There, once again, inflation and RPV appear positively correlated. The first study that takes prices of the same good across different stores is Van Hoomissen (1988a). Using monthly data from Israel, for the period 1971–1984, she also finds that RPV, this time at the intragood level, is increasing in inflation. This chapter reproduces those findings, intergood and intragood, with weekly data from Argentina in 1990. There are two problems with the theoretical argument in the Van Hoomissen paper, to be discussed in more detail later. She posits a search theoretic model in which inflation, by lowering consumers' information, will imply higher price dispersion in equilibrium. The problem with that argument is that it is based on another sort of folk result, which is not really general. It is shown in MacMinn (1980), Carlson and McAfee (1983), and Tommasi (1991) that there is no unambiguous implication from diminished consumer information to cross-sectional price dispersion. Also, Van Hoomissen's theoretical prediction is framed in terms of the cross-sectional dispersion of prices at one point in time but tested against RPV. A more adequate measure of price dispersion is used in her (1988b) paper, in Reinsdorf (1991), in Conklin (1989), and in this chapter. The findings in this area are inconclusive, but most of the studies (including this one) tend to suggest a positive but weak relationship.

This chapter looks directly into the informational assumptions present in Van Hoomissen (1988a) and Tommasi (1991). The findings here support their claim that higher inflations are associated with diminished informativeness of current prices about future ones.

2. Data Description and Variance Decomposition

The data set used for this study contains observations on the prices of 15 products in 5 supermarkets within the same neighborhood in the Federal District of Buenos Aires, collected by the Secretaria de Comercio. The frequency of observation is weekly (46 weeks from February to December 1990), a dimension not studied before, which is particularly useful for the analysis from the perspective of repeat buyers. The products are homogeneous groceries, each of them a particular brand/quality; for instance, "coffee" is a particular brand and size of instant coffee. Also, an independent measure of weekly inflation is used in order to verify that the results obtained using the within-sample measure are not induced by the small sample size. That measure is constructed from data provided by IPES, another institution that constructed its own price index in 1990, a high inflation year in Argentina, when there was demand for estimates of the inflation rate at frequencies higher than monthly. The correlation between

Table 18.1
Summary Statistics DPit: [average rate of price change], σit: [standard deviation of rates of change across stores], (45 weeks)

Good	DPit (mean)				σit (standard dev.)			
	Mean	St. D	Min	Max	Mean	St. D	Min	Max
Butter	.043	.100	−.169	.387	.051	.045	.000	.202
Coffee	.033	.086	−.102	.299	.059	.046	.000	.166
Deodorant	.034	.087	−.093	.361	.031	.042	.000	.126
Flour	.030	.155	−.282	.543	.084	.066	.000	.288
Laundry detergent	.038	.134	−.061	.621	.046	.047	.000	.213
Oil	.029	.107	−.166	.377	.050	.035	.000	.123
Orange juice	.045	.099	−.042	.456	.051	.043	.000	.185
Peas	.034	.113	−.139	.421	.072	.067	.000	.278
Powder milk	.035	.093	−.075	.527	.026	.030	.000	.119
Rice	.043	.143	−.211	.530	.063	.069	.000	.321
Soap	.036	.134	−.270	.628	.040	.056	.000	.254
Tea	.036	.146	−.336	.506	.083	.088	.000	.286
Tomato sauce	.037	.102	−.067	.438	.088	.070	.000	.323
Tuna (a)	.052	.133	−.103	.414	.077	.069	.000	.308
Yerba	.037	.095	−.065	.362	.042	.039	.000	.177

Note: (a) 25 weeks.

this measure of inflation and the one calculated from the sample was 0.89. Table 18.1 shows the latter (DP).

Let P_{ijt} be the price of good i at store j in time period t. There are I goods, and n_i is the number of stores selling good i. Let P_i be the average price of good i across the n_i stores carrying it.

$$P_{it} = \frac{1}{n_i} \sum_{j=1}^{n_i} P_{ijt} \tag{18.1}$$

Let P_t be the price index. I have looked at both weighted and unweighted measures, without significant changes in the findings, and only the latter is reported here:

$$P_t = \frac{1}{\sum_{i=1}^{I} n_i} \sum_{i=1}^{I} \sum_{j=1}^{n_i} P_{ijt} \tag{18.2}$$

It is clear from equation (18.2) that there are two dimensions of aggregation when constructing a price index: first across sellers of any given product, and then across products. We will analyze the behavior of panel data at the disaggregated level of the store, in particular its evolution over time across different inflationary regimes. To do that, it is helpful to decompose the variance of individual observations around the average, as follows:[4]

$$\sum_i \sum_j (P_{ijt} - P_t)^2 = \underbrace{\sum_i \sum_j (P_{ijt} - P_{it})^2}_{\text{WITHIN}} + \underbrace{\sum_i n_i (P_{it} - P_t)^2}_{\text{BETWEEN}} \tag{18.3}$$

This decomposition is analogous to the one in Domberger (1987). In that paper, i referred to a product within an activity heading j, rather than to a store selling a product j. The first term on the right of (18.3) is the variance *within* good: deviation of individual sellers' prices with respect to the product average. The second term captures the variance *between* goods: the deviation of individual products around the overall mean P_t. Equation (18.3) refers to the cross-sectional variance of prices at one point in time. The same decomposition is valid for the variance of rates of change over time; we only need to replace the P's by its growth rates[5]. This latter dimension is the one to be studied first.

3.   Relative Price Variability

This section looks at the variability of relative prices, both across goods and across sellers for any given good. Both dimensions are found to be positively related to inflation.

Let DP_{it} be the rate of growth of price i at time t:

$$DP_{it} = \ln(P_{it}) - \ln(P_{it-1}) \tag{18.4}$$

and DP_t the average (within sample) inflation rate across products:

$$DP_t = \frac{1}{I} \sum_i DP_{it}. \tag{18.5}$$

I use σ_t, the standard deviation of product-specific inflation rates around the mean, as a measure of interproduct price variability:

$$\sigma_t = \left[\frac{1}{I} \sum_i (DP_{it} - DP_t)^2 \right]^{1/2}. \tag{18.6}$$

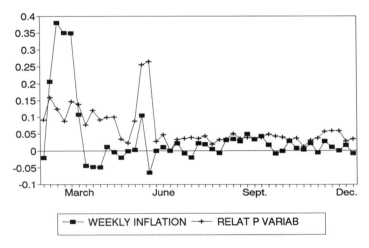

Figure 18.1
Inflation and RPV, 1990

Figure 18.1 shows the behavior of DP_t and σ_t for the sample period. Inflation averaged 4 percent per week in the 46 weeks of the sample, which includes episodes of deflation. We interpret this surprising behavior as part of the high inflation world. This is an environment of price uncertainty, where some overshooting occurs: Sellers overestimate the increase in nominal demand, and in the face of very low sales, have to adjust downward. For that reason, I explored specifications using the absolute value of inflation, to check whether price decreases also imply relative price variability. This is confirmed by the data.[6] The best-fitting relationship is given by

$$\text{VARIABILITY} = 0.024 + 1.65 \, |\text{INFLA}| - 3.84 \, \text{INFLA}^2 \qquad R^2 = .51$$
$$\qquad\qquad\qquad (0.28) \qquad\qquad (0.80)$$

where the numbers in parentheses are standard errors.

This confirms previous findings: inflation and RPV appear to be positively correlated. There are two additional features that will reappear at the more disaggregated level: (1) episodes of deflation are also associated with high relative price variability, and (2) plotting variability against inflation, we obtain a concave picture. The latter, also present in other studies (Van Hoomissen 1988a; Palerm 1990), suggests the presence of some unifying forces in pricing at very high inflation. I elaborate on this in the concluding section.

We now turn our attention to the more disaggregated analysis, of variability "within," that is, across individual stores carrying the same good. It is well known[7] that price differences above and beyond those justified by differential "service" do exist across sellers of homogeneous goods. The question we try to address is whether the pattern of intertemporal variability observed across goods as a function of inflation is also present at the intramarket level.

For each product i, P_{ijt} is the price in store j, DP_{ijt} is its rate of change, DP_{it} the average rate of change across stores, and σ_{it} the standard deviation of store-specific rate of price change around the product average.

$$DP_{ijt} = \ln(P_{ijt}) - \ln(P_{ijt-1}) \tag{18.7}$$

$$DP_{it} = \frac{1}{n_i} \sum_j DP_{ijt} \tag{18.8}$$

$$\sigma_{it} = \left[\frac{1}{n_i} \sum_j (DP_{ijt} - DP_{it})^2 \right]^{1/2}. \tag{18.9}$$

Summary statistics are given in Table 18.1.

It is likely that the error terms across equations are not independent (mainly because we have the same stores across goods). This suggests the use of seemingly unrelated regression (SUR) estimators. Such a procedure requires the same number of observations across equations. Since only 25 weeks of prices of tuna were available, this product was independently analyzed by OLS. The system containing the other 14 equations was estimated applying SUR. This had the expected effect of reducing the standard deviation of the estimates, thus increasing the significance of the coefficients.

As expected, the best results were obtained using the absolute value of inflation. The quadratic specification gives the best fit, with a negative coefficient on inflation squared.

The results are reported in the first columns of Table 18.2 and some representative plots are presented in Figure 18.2. As stated before, inflation has the effect of making *intramarket* relative prices more volatile; deflation episodes produce similar effects. Furthermore, there is some evidence of "concavity"[8] at very high inflation. Since a positive correlation

Table 18.2
Price variability across sellers [weekly data, Argentina, 1990; dependent variable STDEV(DPij)] (45 weeks)

Good	Seemingly unrelated regression estimates				OLS estimates		
	constant	|DPi|	DPi2	R2	constant	|infla|	R2
Butter	.022 (3.45)	.645 (4.46)	−.929 (−2.14)	.51	.020 (2.86)	.354 (5.26)	.38
Coffee	.017 (3.52)	1.406 (10.59)	−3.588 (−7.59)	.73	.046 (6.81)	.264 (4.00)	.25
Deodorant	.001 (.47)	1.285 (17.93)	−2.99 (−13.05)	.83	.021 (3.25)	.218 (3.53)	.21
Flour	.037 (4.90)	.793 (7.31)	−9.25 (−4.12)	.66	.059 (7.19)	.501 (6.25)	.46
Laundry detergent	.016 (4.15)	.853 (10.55)	−.976 (−7.16)	.76	.027 (4.85)	.363 (6.60)	.49
Oil	.029 (5.06)	.520 (4.00)	−.920 (−2.51)	.32	.025 (3.87)	.195 (3.13)	.17
Orange juice	.015 (2.84)	1.240 (9.96)	−2.54 (−8.24)	.60	.043 (7.59)	.721 (4.34)	.29
Peas	.026 (4.16)	.915 (11.16)	−.366 (−5.19)	.71	.052 (5.44)	.418 (4.56)	.31
Powder milk	.011 (2.96)	.356 (7.85)	−.228 −7.41	.51	.022 (4.94)	.364 (2.78)	.15
Rice	.017 (3.16)	.805 (9.47)	−.737 (−4.00)	.82	.007 (1.10)	.642 (9.80)	.68
Soap	.011 (2.82)	.830 (11.09)	−.860 (−6.30)	.80	.026 (4.43)	.172 (7.89)	.58
Tea	.017 (2.53)	1.308 (11.48)	−1.935 (−6.83)	.80	.033 (2.57)	.595 (4.70)	.32
Tomato sauce	.041 (5.27)	.936 (5.42)	−.768 (−1.78)	.73	.059 (8.22)	.586 (8.39)	.61
Tuna (a)	.029 (1.92)	.654 (2.14)	−.430 (−.56)	.61	.059 (3.84)	.234 (2.07)	.12
Yerba	.016 (2.85)	.986 (6.06)	−2.16 (−4.54)	.42	.033 (5.37)	.178 (2.97)	.15

Note: t-statistics are in parentheses
(a) OLS estimate. 25 weeks

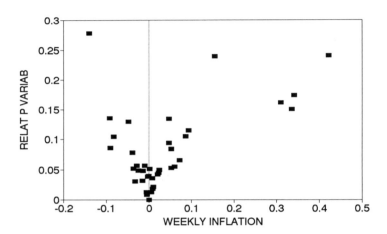

Figure 18.2a
Relative price variability across stores: Peas

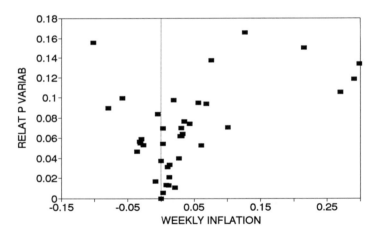

Figure 18.2b
Relative price variability across stores: Coffee

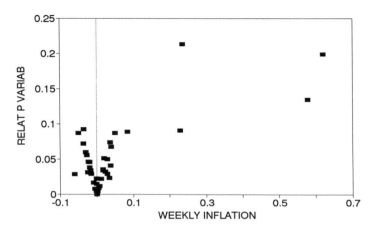

Figure 18.2c
Relative price variability across stores: Laundry detergent

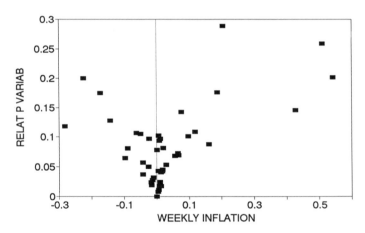

Figure 18.2d
Relative price variability across stores: Flour

between σ and DP as defined in (18.8) and (18.9) may result to some extent from having only five stores, I used the independent measure of inflation to check the validity of the results. Being the same regressor across equations, it prevents us from using SUR. The OLS estimates are in the last columns of Table 18.2. All of the coefficients except one are significant at the 1 percent level, which suggests that the relationship is not a spurious one.

4.   Cross-Sectional Dispersion of Prices

I look here into the association of inflation with the contemporaneous discrepancies between the prices offered by different sellers of the same good. I do not attempt to use these results as a test of a particular theory since, as explained, the two popular theories do not have unequivocal predictions in this matter. A positive relation *might* be predicted from a menu-cost model. The presence of a cost of adjusting nominal prices induces firms to maintain the nominal price unchanged (while real price declines) for a certain period. At higher inflation levels, the flotation band of real price widens. In a monopolistically competitive market, *if the timing of firms' price adjustment is independent*,[9] we should observe cross-sectional variance of real prices increasing in inflation. Another link between inflation and price dispersion is forwarded by Van Hoomissen (1988). Inflation causes information to depreciate more rapidly, thus inducing agents to hold smaller information stocks. From there, it is inferred that a wider dispersion will obtain. Along similar lines, Reinsdorf (1991) predicts that *surprise* inflation will reduce reservation prices and "hence" dispersion (the opposite conclusion).

Their implications hinge on a "missing link" that relates diminished information with price dispersion. That intuition seems to have originated from Stigler's (1961) seminal paper. That was a partial analysis of the buyers' side. Equilibrium search theory implies that real prices will be decreasing in the degree of consumer information, but that effect is not necessarily larger at the upper end of the distribution; hence there is no general conclusion with regard to cross-sectional dispersion.[10] With that caveat in mind, we proceed to the estimation.

The procedure here is very similar to the one in the previous section. The measure of price dispersion used is the coefficient of variation (CV_{it}) of prices p_{ijt}. Since in the Argentine case the price level "explodes" over cer-

Table 18.3
Price dispersion across sellers [weekly data, Argentina, 1990; dependent variable CVi]
(45 weeks)

Good	Seemingly unrelated regression estimates				OLS estimates		
	constant	|DPi|	DPi2	R2	constant	|infla|	R2
Butter	.035	.168	.26	.42	.021	.278	.34
	(7.07)	(1.52)	(.84)		(3.52)	(4.89)	
Coffee	.074	.178	.232	.23	.074	.221	.24
	(11.65)	(1.14)	(.40)		(12.68)	(3.88)	
Deodorant	.054	.491	−1.101	.19	.059	.140	.09
	(9.16)	(3.15)	(−2.19)		(9.39)	(2.31)	
Flour	.082	.024	.173	.10	.079	.192	.13
	(10.35)	(.22)	(.74)		(11.05)	(2.75)	
Laundry	.072	.273	−.332	.09	.070	.212	.25
detergent	(11.81)	(2.20)	(−1.60)		(12.80)	(3.98)	
Oil	.041	.409	−.904	.24	.027	.145	.10
	(9.77)	(4.43)	(−3.46)		(4.39)	(2.44)	
Orange	.065	.463	−1.19	0	.076	−.046	0
juice	(10.19)	(3.06)	(−3.22)		(14.16)	(−.29)	
Peas	.15	.064	.007	.01	.150	.278	.03
	(16.67)	(0.59)	(.08)		(16.63)	(4.89)	
Powder	.053	.200	−.142	.19	.055	.439	.23
milk	(12.19)	(3.73)	−3.91		(13.72)	(3.73)	
Rice	.070	.140	.092	.28	.021	.405	.54
	(10.20)	(1.25)	(.37)		(3.69)	(7.32)	
Soap	.053	.431	−.697	.18	.057	.588	.17
	(8.37)	(4.11)	(−3.67)		(9.07)	(3.18)	
Tea	.081	.175	.231	.32	.041	.407	.26
	(10.33)	(1.42)	(.74)		(4.04)	(4.04)	
Tomato	.084	.443	−.878	.07	.092	.172	.05
sauce	(7.87)	(2.07)	(−1.65)		(9.84)	(1.88)	
Tuna (a)	.112	−.341	1.610	.36	.099	.203	.15
	(7.18)	(−1.08)	(2.00)		(8.04)	(2.26)	
Yerba	.61	−.081	.515	.12	.057	.104	.14
	(15.64)	(−.82)	(1.76)		(15.19)	(2.86)	

Note: *t*-statistics are in parentheses
(a) OLS estimate. 25 weeks

tain periods, variances of goods' prices (across j) explode as well. Such movement does not capture real price dispersion but is an artifact of units of nominal prices. The coefficient of variation is the standard deviation as a percentage of the mean price of a good and does not have this problem:

$$CV_{it} = \frac{n_i^{1/2}}{\sum_j P_{ijt}} [\sum_j (P_{ijt} - P_{it})^2]^{1/2} \tag{18.10}$$

where $P_{it} = 1/n_i \sum_j P_{ijt}$.

The Zellner estimator is used for the same reason given in the section on RPV. The best-fitting equations are again those with the absolute value of inflation, and are reported in the left half of Table 18.3.[11] Representative plots are presented in Figure 18.3. Inflation does seem to have the effect of increasing price dispersion, and the squared term has a negative coefficient in the multiple regression. In this case, though, levels of significance are quite low. This is in line with the findings of Van Hoomissen (1988b) for Israel and Conklin (1989) for Argentina. Reinsdorf (1991) finds an inverse relation for the Volcker disinflation of 1980–82.

5.   Correlation of Real Prices over Time

The issue studied in this section is the effect of inflation on the correlation of real prices (product- and store-specific) over time. This is particularly important for the literature on repeat purchases. We try to test the assertion that the informativeness of current prices about future prices is diminished by inflation. Previous exploratory work on a small comparative sample between the United States and Argentina showed such a correlation being significantly higher for the United States. Here, I look at the time series from Argentina. I divide the 45 weeks of the 1990 sample into three 15-week periods: the first one of high inflation, and the other two of (by Argentine standards) low inflation. Weekly inflation averaged 8.8 percent during the first period, 0.8 percent in the second, and 1.2 percent at the end of the year.[12] If, consistent with the previous analysis, we want to consider deflation as part of the inflationary phenomenon, the *absolute* value of inflation averaged 11.3 percent, 2.1 percent, and 1.5 percent, respectively.

Let P_{ijt} be the price of good i in store j, P_{it} the product average, and z_{ijt} a measure of the real price (actually of the deviation from mean in real terms, a way of characterizing high- and low-priced stores)[13]

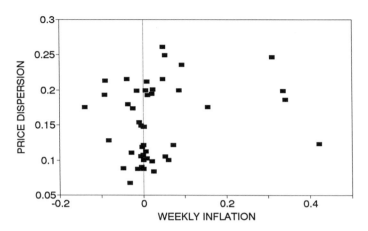

Figure 18.3a
Price dispersion: Peas

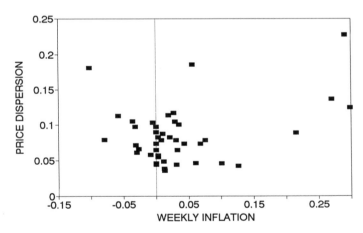

Figure 18.3b
Price dispersion: Coffee

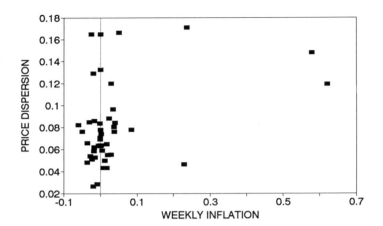

Figure 18.3c
Price dispersion: Laundry detergent

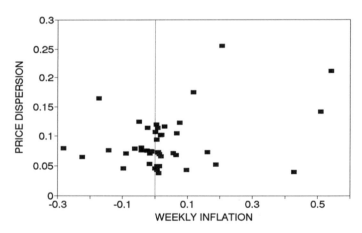

Figure 18.3d
Price dispersion: Flour

$$z_{ijt} = \frac{P_{ijt} - P_{it}}{P_{it}}.$$ (18.11)

The time series properties of the series z_{ijt} were analyzed by looking at the partial autocorrelations. This suggested describing its behavior by the AR(1) process:

$$z_{ijt} = \rho z_{ijt-1} + \varepsilon_{jt}.$$ (18.12)

Table 18.4 provides the values of ρ and t-statistics for each product-store pair in periods 1 (high inflation) and 3 (low inflation). Period 2 looks very similar to period 3 and is omitted (except for tuna) to make the table more readable. The last column gives an average of ρ per product across stores. These averages show that the correlation coefficients are higher for the low inflation period in all of the cases. The value of ρ is of the order of 30 percent at high inflation and of 65–70 percent at low inflation. The hypothesis that "inflation affects the stability of real prices and hence depreciates consumer information" is borne out by the data. Table 18.5 summarizes this information.

6.   The Absence of Sales

Economists from high inflation countries (like Argentina or Israel), when exposed to more stable economies (like the United States), are shocked to observe the amount of information consumers have about prices. The almost nonexistence of catalogs, price advertising, and markdown sales in high inflation situations is a manifestation of this phenomenon. It is also an indication that "menu costs" are really endogenous. In inflationary environments, technologies that minimize such costs are adopted.

The absence of sales at high inflation can be rationalized in two (complementary) ways. In relation to the model in Tommasi (1991), consumers have very little information about prices; hence it is harder to convey the message that you are offering a real bargain. In addition, it is very costly to compromise the maintenance of a nominal price for a long enough period to make a "sale" feasible.

It is true that, even in Argentina, stores can build a reputation for low prices. It is also clear that such a process is more difficult than in a stable environment. The information conveyed by the claim "We charge low

Table 18.4
Intertemporal correlation of prices [ρ in (18.12)]

Good		A	B	C	D	E	Mean
Butter	(1)	.18	.20	.42	−.18	.54	.23
		(.62)	(.72)	(1.60)	(−.64)	(2.30)	
	(2)	.48	.26	.35	.45	.25	.36
		(2.31)	(1.20)	(1.39)	(2.07)	(1.04)	
Coffee	(1)	.93	.85	.48	.42	.71	.68
		(7.86)	(5.69)	(1.97)	(1.63)	(3.64)	
	(2)	.91	.84	.83	.57	.56	.74
		(8.99)	(5.39)	(6.53)	(2.73)	(2.22)	
Flour	(1)	.39	.29	.48	.52	−.06	.32
		(1.50)	(1.40)	(1.91)	(2.28)	(−.19)	
	(2)	.89	.52	.69	.32	.15	.51
		(6.41)	(2.23)	(4.95)	(1.34)	(.63)	
Laundry detergent	(1)	.83	.68	.81	.42	.49	.65
		(5.81)	(3.42)	(5.80)	(1.94)	(2.41)	
	(2)	.88	.74	.87	.58	.50	.71
		(6.64)	(5.20)	(7.40)	(2.92)	(1.18)	
Oil	(1)	.28	.27	.16	.40	.51	.32
		(1.08)	(1.06)	(.65)	(1.74)	(2.16)	
	(2)	.87	.86	.72	.37	.08	.48
		(6.57)	(6.76)	(4.45)	(1.51)	(.32)	
Peas	(1)	.57	.37	.60	.67	.63	.57
		(2.47)	(1.45)	(2.59)	(3.05)	(2.89)	
	(2)	.25	1.02	.98	.40	.99	.72
		(1.07)	(14.60)	(12.17)	(1.35)	(10.25)	
Rice	(1)	.01	.02	.37	.34	.09	.17
		(.04)	(.08)	(1.45)	(1.33)	(.36)	
	(2)	.82	.80	.73	.25	.81	.68
		(5.62)	(4.94)	(3.93)	(1.05)	(5.16)	
Soap	(1)	.46	.43	.49	.05	.31	.35
		(.89)	(1.94)	(2.24)	(.20)	(1.36)	
	(2)	.95	.63	.34	.96	.60	.70
		(7.57)	(2.86)	(1.21)	(11.23)	(2.32)	
Tea	(1)	−.01	.08	−.05	.26	.25	.11
		(−.03)	(.28)	(−.20)	(.99)	(1.31)	
	(2)	.76	.83	.56	.57	.95	.73
		(9.49)	(5.29)	(3.64)	(3.81)	(7.14)	
Tomato sauce	(1)	−.31	.14	−.33	−.16	.06	−.12
		(−1.16)	(.52)	(−1.31)	(−.60)	(.23)	
	(2)	.78	.94	.79	.83	.87	.84
		(4.37)	(9.08)	(4.76)	(4.79)	(4.76)	
Tuna	(1)	.36	.43	.71	.52	.51	.51
		(1.12)	(1.47)	(3.18)	(1.93)	(1.53)	
	(*)	.75	.89	.88	.61	.87	.80
		(3.71)	(8.00)	(6.93)	(2.91)	(6.02)	
Yerba	(1)	.80	.47	.37	.58	.38	.52
		(4.89)	(1.90)	(1.44)	(2.55)	(1.49)	
	(2)	.85	.82	1.01	.62	.81	.82
		(6.95)	(6.45)	(10.47)	(4.09)	(5.13)	

Note: *t*-statistics are in parentheses.
(1) 15 weeks: January–May 1990.
(2) 15 weeks: August–December 1990.
(*) 15 weeks: May–August 1990.

Table 18.5
Argentina, 1990

	January–May	May–August	August–December
Average weekly inflation (%)	8.82	0.80	1.17
Average ρ	.30	.63	.67
% of cases where ρ is significant at .05	28	82	78

prices" is less convincing than the one of "We will charge x dollars for the next 2 weeks."

The sample that I am using states when the reported quotation is claimed to be "on sale." As a check, I verified that in all of the cases the reported prices represented the minimum prices in their cross section at the respective points in time, and also nominal price decreases from their previous level.

Figure 18.4 shows the number of sales, together with aggregate inflation for the period. As expected, there are no sales during the high inflation episode and they reappear after "stabilization."

Insofar as the presence of markdowns is welfare-improving for buyers, we have an additional instance where inflation alters the transaction technology and hence diminishes welfare.

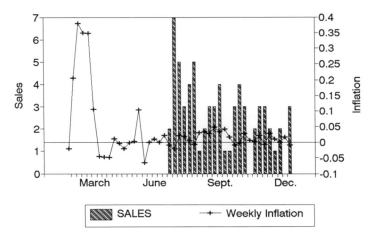

Figure 18.4
Markdown sales

7. Price Changes

Most of this chapter concentrates on the microeconomic description of a
high-inflation environment from the perspective of a buyer, as an input to
the search-theoretic literature. Only passing attention was given to the
seller price-setting decision, the main focus of the cost-of-adjustment literature. This section focuses on the size, frequency, and correlation of price
changes. This preliminary work tries to provide some evidence on the
nature of pricing at high inflation, in order to illuminate the relationship
between inflation in the macroeconomy and microbehavior.

For this section, I use a subsample of the 7 goods for which there was
not a single missing observation over the 46-week period. The information
for these 35 observations (5 stores) is summarized in Table 18.6. This table
shows how many of these prices increased, stayed unchanged, and decreased, together with the aggregate inflation rate in each week. The last
two columns show the average and the standard deviation of the distribution of price changes ($\ln P_t - \ln P_{t-1}$) for the case of price increases.

The number of nominal price reductions is substantial and the reductions are quite synchronized, at least during the first part of the year.
As explained before, this relates to the high macroeconomic uncertainty of
the period. The occurrence of these price decreases seems to indicate that
"menu costs," strictly interpreted, were relatively unimportant when compared with potential losses due to an inadequate relative price. This is not
surprising if we think that these costs are endogenous to the level and
variability of inflation. In such interpretation, Argentina should have one
of the most "efficient" price change technologies.

The price increase column provides information that could be used to
evaluate the literature on endogenous staggering. This is an important
question for the effects of monetary shocks (see ch. 8 in Blanchard and
Fischer 1989; Ball and Romer 1989; and references there). One measure of
the degree of synchronization (Lach and Tsiddon 1990) is given by the
standard deviation of the proportion of stores changing price each period.
At full synchronization it will be at its maximum (close to 0.5) and in full
staggering should be zero. The estimated value is 0.23. Taking into account that the high aggregate instability of the period induces a bias toward synchronization, this number can be interpreted as suggestive of
some staggering. Whether this is the outcome of Ss rules or of other ad-

Table 18.6
Price changes

		Number of				
Week	Weekly inflation	Price increases	No change	Price decreases	Average increase	St.dev. increase
1	−0.02	3	12	20	0.101	0.063
2	0.21	33	1	1	0.338	0.178
3	0.38	32	3	0	0.399	0.196
4	0.35	33	1	1	0.364	0.116
5	0.35	30	5	0	0.466	0.200
6	0.11	20	2	13	0.187	0.150
7	−0.04	3	19	13	0.125	0.043
8	−0.05	5	9	21	0.113	0.093
9	−0.05	4	15	16	0.203	0.106
10	0.01	8	10	17	0.102	0.061
11	0.00	16	5	14	0.099	0.065
12	−0.02	10	11	14	0.063	0.051
13	0.00	6	26	3	0.035	0.022
14	0.00	14	17	4	0.096	0.064
15	0.10	13	18	4	0.103	0.129
16	−0.06	12	20	3	0.054	0.032
17	0.00	6	23	6	0.055	0.027
18	0.01	15	10	10	0.072	0.044
19	0.00	0	35	0	—	—
20	0.02	12	19	4	0.099	0.087
21	−0.01	6	23	6	0.083	0.027
22	−0.02	5	17	13	0.068	0.020
23	0.02	13	18	4	0.077	0.047
24	0.02	6	20	9	0.088	0.067
25	0.00	8	22	5	0.068	0.039
26	−0.01	7	21	7	0.057	0.019
27	0.03	18	15	2	0.098	0.071
28	0.03	22	11	2	0.098	0.065
29	0.03	12	21	2	0.085	0.058
30	0.05	13	15	6	0.101	0.061
31	0.03	15	20	0	0.107	0.069
32	0.04	17	13	5	0.101	0.068
33	0.02	4	21	10	0.057	0.042
34	−0.01	5	25	5	0.053	0.015
35	0.00	5	21	9	0.079	0.030
36	0.03	13	17	5	0.104	0.060
37	0.01	11	21	3	0.090	0.076
38	0.00	8	24	3	0.059	0.040
39	0.02	18	9	8	0.049	0.052
40	−0.01	11	21	3	0.057	0.044
41	0.03	9	21	5	0.136	0.149
42	0.01	12	16	7	0.090	0.069
43	0.00	8	20	7	0.168	0.120
44	0.02	13	19	3	0.094	0.075
45	−0.01	4	27	4	0.099	0.069

Note: Total number of observations = 35 (5 stores × 7 products).

Table 18.7
Correlation of price changes across goods (per store)

Week	Weekly inflation	Store A (+)	Store A (−)	Store B (+)	Store B (−)	Store C (+)	Store C (−)	Store D (+)	Store D (−)	Store E (+)	Store E (−)
1	−0.02	0	3	0	4	1	4	0	6	2	3
2	0.21	6	0	6	0	7	0	7	0	6	1
3	0.38	4	0	7	0	7	0	7	0	6	0
4	0.35	6	0	7	0	7	0	5	1	7	0
5	0.35	6	0	7	0	6	0	7	0	3	0
6	0.11	2	3	3	4	4	2	4	3	7	0
7	−0.04	0	2	0	4	0	4	0	2	3	1
8	−0.05	0	4	0	4	2	4	1	4	2	4
9	−0.05	1	3	0	4	0	2	2	3	1	3
10	0.01	0	4	2	1	0	3	1	6	5	2
11	0.00	1	3	3	2	5	1	3	4	3	4
12	−0.02	3	0	1	4	2	0	2	4	1	6
13	0.00	2	0	1	2	1	1	1	0	1	0
14	0.00	4	1	4	0	2	1	2	0	2	2
15	0.10	2	1	2	0	3	2	3	1	3	0
16	−0.06	1	0	2	2	2	0	4	0	3	1
17	0.00	2	1	0	2	2	1	1	1	1	0
18	0.01	4	1	3	0	3	3	3	2	2	4
19	0.00	0	0	0	0	0	0	0	0	0	0
20	0.02	3	1	1	1	3	1	0	1	4	0
21	−0.01	0	1	1	2	1	1	3	2	1	0
22	−0.02	1	3	1	1	2	1	1	4	0	3
23	0.02	1	0	2	2	3	0	4	0	3	2
24	0.02	1	0	3	0	0	3	1	3	1	2
25	0.00	2	0	2	2	1	3	0	0	3	0
26	−0.01	1	1	1	0	1	0	2	4	1	2
27	0.03	3	0	2	0	4	0	3	1	5	1
28	0.03	5	0	2	1	3	1	7	0	4	0
29	0.03	2	0	3	0	2	1	3	0	2	1
30	0.05	2	0	2	2	3	1	3	3	2	0
31	0.03	2	0	3	0	3	0	2	0	4	0
32	0.04	3	2	2	0	4	1	5	1	2	1
33	0.02	1	2	1	1	1	2	0	2	1	3
34	−0.01	1	2	0	1	1	1	2	1	1	0
35	0.00	0	2	1	0	2	0	0	3	2	3
36	0.03	4	0	1	1	2	2	5	0	1	2
37	0.01	2	0	2	0	1	1	0	1	5	1
38	0.00	3	0	0	0	1	1	2	1	2	0
39	0.02	2	1	4	1	5	1	5	2	2	3
40	−0.01	1	0	2	0	3	1	1	0	3	2
41	0.03	3	1	1	1	1	1	3	2	1	0
42	0.01	1	1	2	3	3	1	0	1	5	1
43	0.00	1	1	2	0	2	2	0	2	3	1
44	0.02	0	1	3	0	2	0	4	1	3	1
45	−0.01	0	0	0	1	1	0	2	1	1	1

(+) number of price increases
(−) number of price decreases
Note: Total number of goods per store = 7.

justment cost, or is just related to the arrival of information, we cannot say at this point. The highly irregular intertemporal pattern of inflation makes the sample not very adequate to analyze the extant cost of adjustment models, which are formulated either for the constant inflation case (Sheshinski and Weiss 1977; Benabou 1988) or for very specific stochastic formulations (Sheshinski and Weiss 1983; Caplin and Sheshinski 1987). Lach and Tsiddon (1990) have a more stable inflation sample, so that they can better frame their analysis in terms of those theories. Further theoretical and empirical work is necessary to study an unstable experience like the Argentine one.

Another interesting cut into the data is given in Table 18.7. Since all the products were sold in the same stores (supermarkets), we can look into the correlation of price changes across goods sold in any store. Table 18.7 provides the weekly inflation rate together with the number of products whose price was increased and those whose price was decreased (out of seven goods in the sample), for each of the 5 stores. This is a helpful exercise in trying to better understand which is the nature of the "adjustment costs" that prevent a continuous adjustment of every price. Following Sheshinski and Weiss (1990), we can think of two extremes: "menu costs," where there are important economies of scale across products (you just print a new catalog or menu, so that the marginal cost of changing one more price is almost zero), or "decision costs," were the price change technology is linear in the number of goods. Menu costs will tend to induce bunching (synchronization) in pricing, while the CRS technology will tend to generate staggering. The analysis of Table 18.7 shows evidence of staggering,[14] favoring the "decision cost" interpretation. The appearance of bunching in the first part of the sample is again a consequence of the high aggregate variability.

8. Conclusion

This chapter provides evidence in support of the view that inflation diminishes the durability of price information. This is concluded from an analysis of the time-series properties of real prices at the store level. At higher inflation, forecast power diminishes substantially. Also, inflation is found to be positively correlated with inter- and intraproduct price variability and (weakly) with intraproduct price dispersion.

Interestingly, we find that the squared inflation term is negative in the regressions of dispersion and, mainly, variability. This could be a statistical artifact given the frequency of observation. At high inflation levels the observation period becomes "too long" when compared with the frequency of changes, and hence hides intraperiod price variability. Variability (at high inflation) tended to decrease as I tried using less frequent observations.[15] Yet the fact that we have few observations in the decreasing portion of the variability-inflation curve makes the evidence insufficient to draw a clear-cut conclusion.

This leaves open the possibility of a "genuine" tendency toward unification of prices at highest inflation levels. In Tommasi (1991) I provide reasons how inflation in the macroeconomy might be reflected as idiosyncratic shocks to the firms in a micromarket. There, the inflation-induced cost shock is the only information taken into account for pricing (aside from demand conditions). In a situation of very high inflation, the pace of price changes is faster than the availability of aggregate information, so that signal extraction problems of the Lucas type become more relevant. The intuition is that in those cases, the weights in the pricing decision will be shifted from the past idiosyncratic cost shocks to the expectations about future inflation (to avoid capital losses), and thus some predictor of inflation will be used. In an economy like Argentina, natural candidates are the evolution of the exchange rate, announcements about macroeconomic policies, and new information about the relative strength of different pressure groups. Since these signals are commonly observed, and since forward-looking behavior is relatively more important in high-inflation situations, firms' pricing decisions tend to be more similar.

Future work will try to formalize this idea in an empirically oriented way, in order to better understand the behavior of real price distributions in cases of high and unstable inflation such as the recent Argentine experience. In particular, further modeling is necessary to address the ways in which inflation affects price dispersion and the dynamic interaction between aggregate instability and microbehavior.

There are other directions in which this empirical effort should be pursued. An important one is the effect of macroeconomic instability on market structure and performance. A first step is taken in Benabou (1991), where the behavior of markups is analyzed with time series for the United States. Cross-sectional evidence will be useful in uncovering the long-run microeconomic effects of macroeconomic instability.

Notes

This chapter is based on Chapter 2 of my dissertation at the University of Chicago. I am indebted to Lester Telser and Yoram Weiss for valuable comments, and to Theresa Van Hoomissen, Angel Palerm, and Jim Conklin for allowing my access to their unpublished research. Thanks are also due to Gary Becker, Sherwin Rosen, Ken Sokoloff, and Mario Tommasi. The Bradley Foundation and the UCLA Academic Senate provided support. All errors are my own.

1. In our sample (weekly data from Argentina in 1990) intramarket variability represents 90 percent of overall variability.

2. Throughout this study the term "relative price variability" (RPV) refers to the tendency of relative prices to change over time, which is usually proxied by the cross-sectional standard deviation of *rates of change* of prices around an average inflation rate. This will be distinguished both theoretically and empirically from "dispersion," a cross-sectional dispersion of prices around an average price at a point in time. This latter measure is a meaningful concept only at the intraproduct level. As explained in the next section, there has been some confusion of the two concepts in both the empirical and the theoretical literature.

3. They exploit the endogenous timing of price changes in a staggered equilibrium, for a *given* cost of changing nominal prices.

4. $\sum_i \sum_j (P_{ij} - P)^2 = \sum_i \sum_j [(P_{ij} - P_i) + (P_i - P)]^2$

$$= \sum_i \sum_j (P_{ij} - P_i)^2 + \sum_i \sum_j (P_i - P)^2 + 2 \sum_i \sum_j (P_{ij} - P_i)(P_i - P).$$

But

$$\sum_i \sum_j (P_{ij} - P_i)(P_i - P) = \sum_i (P_i - P) \sum_j (P_{ij} - P_i).$$

Notice that, from (18.1):

$$\sum_j (P_{ij} - P_i) = 0 \qquad \text{for all } i.$$

So that

$$\sum_i \sum_j (P_{ij} - P)^2 = \sum_i \sum_j (P_{ij} - P_i)^2 + \sum_i n_i(P_i - P)^2.$$

5. The share of intragood (within) variability in the overall variability of DP_{ijt} is around 90 percent for our sample and seems to be increasing in the aggregate inflation rate, consistent with the findings in Lach and Tsiddon (1990).

6. For the intragood counterpart, see the V-shaped plots in Figure 18.2.

7. See Stigler (1961), Marvel (1976), Pratt et al. (1979), Mathewson (1983), Dahlby and West (1986), Van Hoomissen (1988b), and Abbott (1989).

8. At the highest inflation weeks, variability was not as high as a linear relation would predict. As explained in Section 8, this may be just a statistical artifact, given the endogenous frequency of price changes.

9. This relates to whether staggering or synchronization is the equilibrium outcome. See Ball and Romer (1989) and references there.

10. See MacMinn (1980), Carlson and McAfee (1983), and, for a specific application to inflation, Tommasi (1991).

11. Once again, the rest of the table provides a check using the independent series for inflation.

12. The averages were 9.3 percent 0.7 percent, and 1.1 percent, using the alternative inflation series.

13. Other, more aggregate, normalizations were explored without substantial changes in the findings.

14. The methodology consisted of looking at the correlation of each column, as in Lach and Tsiddon (1990).

15. A similar finding is reported in Palerm (1990).

References

Abbott, Thomas (1989). "Price Dispersion in US Manufacturing." Bureau of the Census, Center for Economic Studies Discussion Paper (October).

Ball, Laurence, and David Romer (1989). "The Equilibrium and Optimal Timing of Price Changes." *Review of Economic Studies* 56: 179–198.

Ball, Laurence, G. Mankiw, and D. Romer (1988). "The New Keynesian Economics and the Output-Inflation Trade-off." *Brookings Papers on Economic Activity* 1: 1–65.

Benabou, Roland (1988). "Search, Price Setting and Inflation." *Review of Economic Studies* 55: 353–376.

Benabou, Roland (1991). "Inflation and Markups: Theories and Evidence from the Retail Trade Sector." MIT Working paper 587 (August).

Blanchard, Olivier, and Stanley Fischer (1989). *Lectures on Macroeconomics.* Cambridge, Mass.: MIT Press.

Caplin, Andrew, and E. Sheshinski (1987). "The Optimality of (S, s) Pricing Policies." The Hebrew University Working Paper 166.

Carlson, John, and R. McAfee (1983). "Discrete Equilibrium Price Dispersion." *Journal of Political Economy* 91: 480–493.

Conklin, James (1989). "High Inflation, Information and Price Dispersion: Recent Evidence from Argentina." Mimeo, Stanford University.

Dahlby, Bev, and Douglas West (1986). "Price Dispersion in an Automobile Insurance Market." *Journal of Political Economy* 94: 418–438.

Danziger, Leif (1987). "Inflation, Fixed Cost of Price Adjustment, and Measurement of Relative Price Variability." *American Economic Review* 77: 704–713.

Domberger, Simon (1987). "Relative Price Variability and Inflation: A Disaggregated Analysis." *Journal of Political Economy* 95: 547–566.

Fischer, Stanley (1981). "Relative Shocks, Relative Price Variability, and Inflation." *Brookings Papers on Economic Activity* 2: 381–431.

Fischer, Stanley (1986). *Indexing, Inflation, and Economic Policy.* Cambridge, Mass.: MIT Press.

Glejser, H. (1965). "Inflation, Productivity and Relative Prices: A Statistical Study." *Review of Economics and Statistics* 47: 761–780.

Handbook of Monetary Economics (1990). B. Friedman and F. Hahn, eds. Amsterdam: North-Holland.

Lach, Saul, and Daniel Tsiddon (1990). "The Behavior of Prices and Inflation: An Empirical Analysis of Dissaggregated Price Data." This volume.

MacMinn, Richard (1980). "Search and Market Equilibrium." *Journal of Political Economy* 88: 308–327.

Marvel, Howard (1976). "The Economics of Information and Retail Gasoline Price Behavior: An Empirical Analysis." *Journal of Political Economy* 84: 1033–1059.

Mathewson, Frank (1983). "Information, Search and Price Variability of Individual Life Insurance Contracts." *Journal of Industrial Economics* 32: 131–148.

Palerm, Angel (1990). "Price Formation and Relative Price Variability in an Inflationary Environment: Mexico, 1940–1984." Ph.D. dissertation, University of California, Los Angeles.

Parks, Richard (1978). "Inflation and Relative Price Variability." *Journal of Political Economy* 86: 79–95.

Pratt, John, David Wise, and Richard Zeckhauser (1979). "Price Differences in Almost Competitive Markets." *Quarterly Journal of Economics* 93: 189–211.

Reinsdorf, Marshall (1991). "New Evidence on the Relation Between Inflation and Price Dispersion." Mimeo, Bureau of Labor Statistics (February).

Sheshinski, Eytan, and Yoram Weiss (1977). "Inflation and Costs of Price Adjustment." *Review of Economic Studies* 44: 287–304.

Sheshinski, Eytan, and Yoram Weiss (1983). "Optimum Pricing Policy Under Stochastic Inflation." *Review of Economic Studies* 50: 513–529.

Sheshinski, Eytan, and Yoram Weiss (1990). "Staggered and Synchronized Price Policies Under Inflation: The Multiproduct Monopoly Case." The Hebrew University Working Paper 234 (September).

Stigler, George (1961). "The Economics of Information." *Journal of Political Economy* 69: 213–225.

Tommasi, Mariano (1991). "The Consequences of Inflation: Effects of Price Instability on Search Markets." UCLA Working Paper 655.

Van Hoomissen, Theresa (1988a). "Price Dispersion and Inflation: Evidence from Israel." *Journal of Political Economy* 96: 1303–1314.

Van Hoomissen, Theresa (1988b). "Search, Information and Price Dispersion in Inflationary Circumstances: Theory and Evidence." Mimeo, SUNY Stony Brook.

Index

Adjustment costs, 11, 12, 14, 20, 23, 24, 41, 117–118, 119, 140n1, 172, 189, 190, 191, 192(table), 231, 293, 317, 320(figs.), 328, 336–337nn4, 12, 350, 401, 419, 428, 438
  changes in, 127–128
  and equilibrium, 319, 321
  and inflation rate, 135–136, 138
  and optimization problems, 311–312
  and pricing policies, 143, 180
  and profits, 147–148, 193
Adjustment policy, 241–242. *See also* Discontinuous adjustment; Lumpy adjustment
Aggregate behavior, 244–245
Aggregate deviation
  bandwidths, 263–264
  and steady state, 246–247, 249–250, 265–266
Aggregate shock, 247, 248–249, 250, 265, 273n5, 471
Aggregation, 193, 380n16, 467
  and convergence, 242–243
  deterministic, 21–23
  models of, 40–43
  one-sided, 26–31
  and price dynamics, 218–219
  stochastic, 23–26
  two-sided, 31–38
Allocation, of resources, 385
Allocative role of prices, 341, 342, 356
Argentina, 14, 489, 503, 505, 510
  price changes in, 506–509
  price dispersion in, 498–502
  price variability in, 490–498, 504(table)
ARMA process, 296
Asset demands, 41

Bandwidths, 266
  aggregate deviation and, 263–264
  convergence of heterogeneous, 257–261
  and idiosyncratic shock, 247, 248, 253–254, 262, 274n20
Barrier control, and Markov chains, 99–102
Basco Inc., 117
Benabou model, 21, 22, 23, 41
Bertrand competition, 327
Bertrand model, 182
Boundaries
  construction of, 87–90
  price adjustments, 181–182
Boundary conditions, 105
  Dirichlet, 63, 66, 69–70
  Neumann, 64, 66, 70

Bratten's condition, 51
Brownian motion, 97, 98, 111, 285, 291, 295, 296, 301n14, 484nn36, 37
  control policy and, 99, 100
  and idiosyncratic shocks, 262–263, 471
  money supply, 279, 289
Brownian shocks, 283
Buenos Aires, price variability in, 490–498
Buyers
  flow of, 344–345
  and goods valuation, 341–342
  heterogenous, 353–354
  identical, 351–353
  search costs of, 347–348, 380n27
  welfare and, 394, 396

Canada, 11, 14
Capital stock, 244
Carrying costs, inventory, 401–404
Cash balance, 241, 244
Cash management, 97
Catalogs, 117
CBS. *See* Central Bureau of Statistics
Central Bureau of Statistics (CBS), 447, 481n2
Certainty equivalence, 155
  and rate of inflation, 148–150, 152
Chamberlain fixed effects logistic formulation, 432–433, 435–436, 442n19
Cobb-Douglas matching function, 392, 394, 399, 401, 404
Common shocks, 34–35, 245, 248, 250, 254, 258, 291, 452
Comparative statics, 154–156, 165n4
Competition, 278–279, 322, 337n13, 359, 381n33, 423, 429–430
Competitors, 349–350
Complementarity, 174
Compound Poisson Process, 154
Consumer price index (CPI), 447, 461
Consumers, 324, 336n5, 337n19, 381n32, 405n4, 503
  behavior, 3, 307–308, 356–357, 391
  and markets, 22, 379nn6, 13, 385–386, 488
  reservation price, 348–349
  search by, 389–390, 397–398
  utility of, 394, 396
Consumer surplus, 137, 367
Continuation set, boundary determination of, 87–90
Continuity, 218, 243, 244
Contraction mapping, 176
Contract period, 9–10, 12
Contracts, 9, 10, 13, 419

Control. *See also* Impulse control
  continuous, 58–63
  mixed and one-sided, 111–112
  optimal, 65, 70, 72
  and value functions, 102–106
Control policy, and Markov chains, 99–102
Control theory, 57
  impulse, 58–63
Convergence, 248, 274n15, 312
  idiosyncratic shocks and, 296–300, 379n11
  money process, 289–291
  proposition proofs for, 270–272
  sources of, 266–270
  speed of, 253–256, 262, 265
  and stochastic heterogeneity, 250–253
  and structural heterogeneity, 256–262
Coordination, 418
Corporations, 21
Cost function, 109
Costs, 24, 98, 212n2, 243, 356, 380n19, 420.
    See also Adjustment costs; Search costs
  and aggregation models, 218–219
  and demand, 429–430
  fixed, 337n20, 366(fig.)
  and ordering policy, 50, 57, 111
  and price changes, 180, 379n7
Coupling, 91
CPI. *See* Consumer price index
Credit, 99, 111
Curvature, of demand function, 363

Decision costs, 170, 173
Deflation, 9, 396–397
Delivery
  lags in, 54–56, 418
  with zero time lag, 52–54
Demand, 77, 233, 241, 324, 356–357,
    380n23, 483n21
  and aggregate models, 218–219
  deterministic, 81–83
  elasticity of, 419
  and market, 344–345
  and price, 117, 219–220
  and profits, 348–349
  and search, 310–311, 327
Demand functions, 349, 363, 429–430
Demand shocks, 277, 417
  aggregate, 242, 243–244, 246
Densities, 261
  of idiosyncratic shock, 251–253
Deviations, price, 29, 30, 32, 33, 36, 38–39
Diffusion inventory system, 78–79
Dirac measure, 59
Discontinuous adjustment, 241, 242

Discount factor, zero, 83–84, 91, 92
Discrete adjustments, 98
Distribution, 324, 385
  of durations, 473, 475, 484n39
  and idiosyncratic shock, 467, 469
  money supply, 289–290
  of prices, 14, 15, 26–27, 29–30, 32, 157,
    222–223, 278, 281–282, 289–290, 291,
    292–293, 308, 310, 312, 346, 369,
    388–389, 397, 465–476, 483n22
  probability and cross-section, 245–246,
    296
Distribution functions, 132
Divisia index, 228–229, 336n8
Duopoly games, Bertrand, 169
Durations
  distribution of, 473–475, 483n19, 484n39
  of price quotations, 458–462, 482–
    483nn15, 17
Dynamic programming, 103
  and continuous control, 60–62

Economic value function, 59–60
Employment, 19, 41, 42, 98
Entry, 241, 346–347
  and firm equilibrium, 344, 350–351
  pricing and, 390–391, 398
Equilibrium, 41, 327, 337n13, 342, 344, 363,
    380n20
  and adjustment cost, 319, 321
  and entry, 350–351
  flow of goods and, 386, 388
  and heterogeneous buyers, 353–354
  and identical buyers, 351–353
  and inflation rates, 322, 324, 392–394
  of market, 309–310, 317
  monotonicity and, 332–335
  price adjustment, 398–400, 469, 484n33
  pricing policies, 12–14, 22, 312–317,
    330–331, 346, 376–378
  with production, 391–392
  profit function, 349, 370–378, 381n36
  and search cost, 318–319, 332
  symmetric, 325–326, 347, 379n9
Equilibrium modeling, 385
Equilibrium search model, 487
Exit, 241, 342, 361

Feedback, 22, 64
Firms, 4, 327, 362(figs.)
  behavior of, 3, 307
  density of, 318(fig.), 323(fig.)
  deviations of, 29, 30, 32, 38–39
  exit of, 342, 361

monopolistically competitive, 23–24
optimization problems of, 311–312
pricing policies of, 7–8, 314
Foodstuffs, prices of, 446, 447, 448(table),
  452, 468(fig.), 470(tables), 472(fig.),
  474(fig.), 475, 482–483n17
Fourier coefficients, 267
Frictions, 325
Fubini's Theorem, 274n21
Functional spaces, 67–68

Gamma density, 158–159
Gaussian process, 58, 94
Germany, 5, 7(fig.)
Glivenko-Cantelli Theorem, 251, 253, 265,
  274n20
Goods, 342, 386, 423, 501–502(figs.)
  durable, 19, 41, 97, 241, 244
  price variability, 490, 492, 496–497(figs.)
  stock of, 388–389
  as strategic complements, 173–174

Hausman test, 435, 436, 442n22
Heterogeneity, 342. See also Stochastic
  heterogeneity; Structural heterogeneity
Hierarchies, 420
Hiring costs, 98
History-dependence, 186
HJB equations (dynamic programming
  equation), 61–62, 65, 67
Holding costs, 49, 51
Hyperinflation, 5, 379n5

Idiosyncratic shocks, 35, 193, 242, 246, 248,
  273n5, 274n20, 301n8, 510
  Brownian motion of, 262–263, 471
  and convergence, 296–300, 379n11
  cross-section density of, 251–253
  distribution of, 247, 251, 264–265, 266
  and equilibrium distribution, 467, 469
  money process, 289–291
  speed of convergence and, 253–256
Implicit Function Theorem, 330
Impulse control, 57, 62–63, 99, 105, 112
  optimality of, 106–109, 110–111
  QVIs, 66–75
Indexation, 3, 10, 336n8
Inflation, inflation rates, 4, 10, 14, 21, 23,
  38, 39, 118, 192(table), 222, 236n15,
  237n22, 248, 308, 312, 317, 343, 379n8,
  440, 442nn19, 23, 446, 481nn2–6, 487
  adjustment costs and, 189, 193
  certainty equivalence and, 148–150
  Divisia index of, 228–229

endogenous, 233–234
and equilibrium, 392–394
expected, 144–145
forecasts of, 478–480
and interest rates, 128–132
and markets, 341, 404
and monopoly pricing, 279, 342, 357
and optimal pricing, 26, 143–148, 396
and output, 22, 38, 289, 361–367
and price adjustment, 11–12, 119,
  123–126, 135–136, 138, 154, 233–234,
  294, 441n4, 442n18
and price changes, 5, 167, 424, 425–427,
  433, 435, 436, 438, 439, 442n21, 482n16
and price dispersion, 6–9, 305, 321–322,
  341, 352, 357–361, 378–379n2, 445,
  498–500, 510
and prices, 20, 137–138, 169, 228, 288, 306,
  322–324, 358(figs.), 400(figs.), 402(figs.),
  483n23
and price variability, 218, 227, 236n17,
  449–458, 475, 488, 489, 490, 494, 498, 509
and profits, 126–127
real prices and, 395(figs.), 500, 503
as renewal process, 150–152
and sales, 503–505
and search, 337n18, 343–344, 370, 379n3
short-term, 428–429
and (S, s) policies, 345–346
and stocks, 386, 388–389, 405n4
and welfare, 3, 8, 326, 342, 353, 355–357,
  367–369, 458
zero, 396–397
Inflation process, 336n8, 445–446
  two-level, 234–235
  two-rate, 230–231
Instantaneous (barrier) control, 112
  and Markov chains, 99–102
  optimality of, 107, 109–110
  and value function, 105–106
Insurance, 11
Interest rate, 22, 118, 170
  and optimal pricing policy, 143–144
  and price adjustment policy, 128–132
Interviews
  questionnaire design in, 412–413
  reliability of, 411–412
  results of, 415–421
  sampling in, 414–415
Inventory, 82(fig.), 99, 243, 273n6
  and aggregate demand shocks, 243–244
  carrying costs of, 401–404
  fluctuations in, 419–420
  holding and shortage costs of, 49–51

Inventory (cont.)
  inflation and, 386, 388–389, 405n4
  price changes on, 386–387
Inventory control, 57, 97
  and QVIs, 75–92
Inventory system, 86–87, 92, 241
Investment, 19, 57, 97–98, 241
Israel, 3, 5(fig.), 8, 14, 446, 448(table)
Ito's formula, 60, 65–66
Iwai model, 428, 429

J. C. Penney Co., 117
Joint ordering, 85

Karlin's condition, 51
Kolmgorov-Smirnov test, 471

Labor, 22, 308
Law of motion, Markovian, 35
Lebesgue's Dominated Convergence
  Theorem, 268
Lipschitz properties, 58, 73–74
Lumpy adjustment, 241, 242

Macroeconomics, 19, 42
  costs of price adjustment, 20, 23–24
  theories in, 410–411, 416–417
Magazines, 440, 441–442n5
  price changes, 425–427, 428–429,
    432–435, 442n7
  price models for, 431–432, 439
Market frictions, 356
Markets, 236n7, 305, 336n10, 337n20,
  341, 342, 404, 424. *See also* Search
  markets
  consumers and, 22, 379nn6, 13, 385–386,
    488
  equilibrium of, 309–310, 317
  price variability in, 489–490
  structure of, 4, 367
Markov chains, 66
  and control policy, 99–102
  and optimal regulation, 98, 112
  two-state, 143, 154–156
Markovian control, 64, 65
Markovian structure, 230
Markov process, 30, 35
Menu costs, 170, 173, 221, 226, 241, 280,
  301n8, 410, 489
  and distribution of durations, 473, 475
  models of, 21–22, 450–451
  and price changes, adjustments, 234, 244,
    386–387, 487–488
  and relative price variability, 227–231

Microeconomics, 19, 42, 43, 241, 242, 246,
  247
Modulo equivalence, 35
Monetary expansion, 33, 39
Monetary policy, 226
Monetary shocks, 24, 30, 31, 223, 226–227,
  291, 298
  impacts of, 25–26, 27, 36, 37–38
  and output, 285–286
  and price levels, 217, 277, 278
  response to, 33–35
Money, 39, 232, 345, 404, 484n40
  and consumer demand, 219–220
  and output, 37, 285–288
Money growth, 31, 32, 33, 38, 218, 225,
  300n2
  and future output, 286–287
Money-output-price process
  characterization of, 282–285
  model of, 278–282
Money supply, 280, 281, 291, 296, 298,
  300n2, 445, 483n21
  drift in, 38–39
  paths of, 287, 299
  process of, 232–233, 279, 289–290,
    293–294
Monopolies, 169, 171, 172, 342
  optimal price policies, 173, 174–185,
    189–190
Montonicity, 145, 158, 218, 243
  and equilibrium, 332–335
  inventory and, 244, 273n6
  of pricing policies, 174, 199
Montgomery Ward & Co., 117

Nash equilibrium, 309
Neumann boundary condition, 78
Neutrality
  average, 26–29, 33
  monetary policy, 223–227
  and one-sided aggregation, 26–31
Newspapers, 5, 6(fig.), 7(fig.)
Nonneutrality, and two-sided aggregation,
  31–38

Oil shock, 248
One sided (S, s) rule. *See* (S, s) rules
Operations Research and Economics,
  241–242
Optimal control, conditions for, 106–111
Optimal cost function, 74, 75, 82(fig.), 86–87
Optimal ordering policy, 78, 85
Optimal pricing policy, 99, 143, 164n2, 173,
  222, 236n5, 280, 327–331

features of, 194–202
and inflation, 145–148
obtaining, 64–65
and real adjustment costs, 117–119
(S, s) policies, 157–164
and value function, 174–185
Optimal regulation, 98, 112
Optimal search rules, 305
Optimization problems, 305, 311–312
Option pricing, 98
Output, 13, 21, 284, 295, 423
and inflation, 22, 38, 289, 361–367
and money, 37, 285–288
price distribution and, 291, 292
prices and, 288–289, 381n34
and welfare, 342–343

Phillips curve, 278, 288, 296, 366–367
Poisson process, 154, 158, 388
Poisson's Summation Formula, 267
Pontryagin's maximum principle, 64
Precommitment policy, 153
Preferences, 342, 365(figs.), 367
binding, 312–313, 316
with bounded support, 373–374
with unbounded support, 374–376
Price adjustments, 4, 10, 20, 22, 140n4, 172,
173, 179, 278, 280, 291, 308, 315, 319, 341,
356, 417, 418, 424, 442n11, 461, 469, 475.
See also Adjustment costs
boundaries and, 181–182
frequency of, 423, 439–440
and inflation, 294, 359, 441n4
macroeconomics of, 23–24
menu costs of, 234, 244, 487–488
models of, 119–123, 397–404
money-output-price process, 283, 290
and rate of inflation, 123–126, 138
and real rate of interest, 128–132
and taxes, 133–135
timing of, 154, 190, 277, 309–310
upward, 27–28
Price changes, 179, 180, 213n7, 379n7, 423,
442–443nn6, 24, 29, 483n24
in Argentina, 506–509
distribution of, 475–476
duration of, 458–462
expected frequency of, 153–154, 483n23
nominal, 3, 4–6, 194–195
fixed costs of, 117, 305–306
frequency of, 118, 442n13, 483n25
and inflation, 148–149, 167, 425–427,
442n21, 482n16
in macroeconomic theory, 416–417

and menu costs, 386–387
modeling, 430–431, 432–439, 443nn25, 28
and optimal policy, 159, 194, 200
and real prices, 178, 461
real resource costs of, 279–280
short-term inflation and, 428–429
synchronization of, 190, 463–465
timing of, 10, 15, 169–170, 190, 427–428
value function and, 175, 176
Price cycles, 185
Price dispersion, 6–9, 380nn23, 24, 446,
449, 481n3, 501–502(figs.)
and equilibrium, 318, 319, 324–325
and inflation rates, 322, 341, 352, 357–361,
366, 378–379n2, 445, 452, 498–500, 509,
510
in menu cost models, 450–451
relative, 6–9
Price dynamics, 218, 305
Price increases, 180, 213n7, 229–230
Price indexes, 24, 40, 219, 225–226
Price intervals, 185, 189
Price levels, 19, 147, 217, 221, 227, 236n3
aggregate, 143, 157
and price index, 225–226
Price movement, 121
Price paths, 4, 172
Price quotations, duration of, 458–462,
474(fig.), 482–483nn15, 17
Price reductions, 180, 181
Price revisions, 217, 231
Price rigidity, 20, 411, 416
Prices, 28, 33, 132, 140n9, 155, 169, 170,
212n2, 241, 284, 305, 343, 352, 353,
385, 420, 484nn38, 39, 487,
504(table)
adjustment costs and, 320(fig.), 321(fig.)
competition, 322, 359
and consumer demand, 219–220
and discounted profits, 159–160
distribution of, 14, 15, 22, 26–27, 29–30,
32, 157, 222–223, 278, 281–282, 289–290,
291, 292–293, 308, 310, 312, 346, 356,
369, 388–389, 397, 465–476, 483n22
equilibrium bounds on, 22, 376–378
inflation rate and, 11–12, 137–138, 306,
322–324, 358(figs.), 395(figs.), 396(figs.),
400(fig.), 500, 503
nominal, 4–6, 171, 217, 224–225, 483n29
optimal, 20–21, 25, 386
and output, 288–289, 361–363
and real profits, 126–127
reduction of, 8, 11, 341
reservation, 348–349, 356, 389–390

Prices (cont.)
  single state variable and, 294–295
  utility functions and, 404–405
  variability in, 4, 21, 283, 321–322
Price-setting, 19, 241, 301n6, 305, 353–354
Price shocks, 24, 26
Price stickiness, 19, 20, 217, 223, 234, 236n6,
  409, 410, 416(table), 423, 425, 439
  nominal, 220–221, 277
Price strategies, 349–350
Price variability, 480n1
  and inflation, 236n17, 449–458, 488,
  489–490, 509, 510
  interpreting, 476–477
  relative, 227–231, 475, 492–498
Pricing, pricing policies, 3, 4, 117, 170, 177,
  218, 221, 227. See also Optimal pricing
  policy; Staggered steady state;
  Synchronized steady state
  aggregate deviation in, 247–248
  allocative role of, 341, 342
  consistency, 156–157
  cost-based, 418–419
  and entry, 390–391, 398
  equilibrium in, 12–14, 312–317
  increases and, 229–230
  and inflation, 7–8, 20, 143–144
  models of, 9–12
  monetary process, 232–233
  money supply, 289–290
  monopolistic, 279, 357
  one-sided, 28, 301n9
  optimization problems and, 311–312
  profits and, 171–172
  search costs and, 347–348
  (S, s), 305–306
  stability analysis of, 185–187
  state-dependent, 43–44, 277–278, 295–296
  two-sided, 20, 301nn5, 12
Pricing points, 419
Probability theory, 94–95
Production, 57, 307
  costs of, 136, 390–391
  equilibrium with, 391–392
Products, 7, 90–91
Profitability, 132, 173
Profit functions, 182, 190, 345
  equilibrium, 349, 370–378
  quadratic, 170–171, 186, 189, 191,
  208–209
  symmetry of, 175–176
Profits, 136, 179, 193, 220, 280, 281, 336n11,
  352, 361, 380nn17, 26, 31, 381n35
  and demand, 348–349

discounted real, 138–139, 159–160
  marginal, 131, 184–185, 212n5
  maximization of, 169, 380n25
  net value of, 344, 346
  and price adjustment, 22, 118, 119–123,
  147–148, 430
  and price strategies, 349–350
  and pricing policies, 171–172, 178, 314
  and real prices, 126–127, 145
Properties, asymptotic, 90–91

Quality, and price, 420, 421
Quasi-variational inequalities (QVIs), 57,
  65
  elliptic, 68–71
  first-order, 73–75
  and impulse control problems, 64, 66–75
  and inventory control problems, 75–92
  parabolic, 72–73
Questionnaires, design of, 412–413,
  415–416
QVIs. See Quasi-variational inequalities

Random walk, 37, 100, 101
Reaction functions, 178
Real estate, 3
Reinganum model, 325
Relative price variability (RPV), 511n2
  goods and sellers, 492–498
  and inflation, 489–490
Renewal processes, 143
  inflation as, 150–152
Representative agent case, 28–29
Rigidities, nominal, 3, 4, 5, 9, 14
Risk-dominance, 118, 131
RPV. See Relative price variability

Sales, 97, 243, 328, 428, 503, 505
Sales volatility index, 440–441, 442n19
Sampling, 414–415
SDP, and intramarket price variability,
  450–458, 482n12
Search, 356, 379nn5, 6, 13
  B-binding, 313–314
  consumer, 389–390, 391, 397–398
  and demand, 310–311
  and inflation, 337n18, 370
  resource cost of, 354–355
Search behavior, 22–23, 306, 327, 488
Search costs, 14, 321(fig.), 341, 364(figs.),
  381n32, 487
  buyers, 345, 347–348, 380n27
  and equilibrium, 318–319, 332
  and price dispersion, 324–325, 359–360

Search markets, 343–345, 379n3
Search theory, 385, 404
Sears Roebuck, 117
Seemingly unrelated regressions (SUR), 452, 481–482nn8, 9, 494
Sellers, 305, 487, 488, 492, 494, 495(table), 499(table)
Sensitivity parameters, heterogeneous, 261–262, 266
Sheshinski-Weiss model, 21, 22, 23
Shock processes, 39–40
Shocks, 10, 20, 218, 277, 484n36, 487. *See also* Aggregate shock; Common shock; Idiosyncratic shock
  exogenous, 19, 24
  inflationary, 9, 222
  one-sided, 279, 295
  two-sided, 31–32, 295–296
Shortage costs, 49, 51, 85
Skewness, 363
Smooth pasting conditions, 98, 108–109, 110
Social welfare. *See* Welfare
(S, s) models, 154, 155, 165n4
  applicability of, 10–11, 12, 13–14, 22, 23
  inflation and, 345–346
  optimality and uniqueness of, 157–164
  policies, 305–306
  price adjustment, 20, 156
  and steady state, 243–247
(S, s) rules, 241–242, 244, 273n3
Stability, global, 187
Stability analysis, pricing policy and, 185–187
Staggered steady state, 170–171, 172–173, 183, 184, 188, 189–190, 191, 193, 210, 212n1
  quadratic profit function and, 208–209
  stability of, 204–208
Staggering, 212n1, 242
State-dependent pricing, 42, 43–44, 277–278, 295–296, 306
  models of, 279–281, 296
State variables
  and money supply process, 293–294
  and prices, 294–295
Static monopoly models, 23
Stationarity, 145, 228–229, 243
Steady state, 274n15, 442n20. *See also* Synchronized steady state
  aggregate deviation and, 249–250, 265–266
  (S, s) model, 243–247

Stochastic heterogeneity, 242–243, 258, 262, 264
  of convergence, 250–253
Stochastic optimal control, 97, 98
Stocking, 387
Storage, 85, 137
Strategic complementarity, 366
Structural heterogeneity, 242–243, 248, 264
  and convergence, 256–262
Substitution, 306
Supermarkets, 385
  price variability in, 490–498
SUR. *See* Seemingly unrelated regressions
Surplus, 345, 347–348, 367
Symmetry, of (S, s) rules, 243, 244
Synchronization, 242, 264
  of price revisions, 217–218
  of pricing policies, 169–170, 174, 212n1
Synchronized steady state, 169–170, 171, 172, 183, 185, 186–189, 190, 191
  uniqueness of, 202–204

Taxes, and price adjustment policy, 133–135
Taylor expansions, 84, 354
Technologies, 325, 489
  cost, 424–425
  matching, 387–388
Technology upgrade (update), 241, 244
Theories
  evaluating, 415–418
  wage-price stickiness, 409–410
Theory of viscosity solutions, 66
Time lag
  in delivery, 54–56
  zero, 52–54
Transactions, 356, 388, 400(fig.)
Transactions costs, 385

Unions, 13
United States, 13, 14
Utility functions, 404–405

Valuation formulation, 184, 197
Value functions, 109
  and control, 102–106
  of optimal policy, 174–185, 195–197
Variational inequality (VI) problem, 66
VI. *See* Variational inequality problem
Viscosity solutions, 74–75

Wages, 3, 10, 13, 15
Wage stickiness, 409

Wald's Identity, 15
Wald statistic, 435
Walras' law, 236n7
Wealth, 97, 336n10
Weirstrass' Theorem, 195
Welfare, 7, 136, 305, 341
  analysis of, 394, 396–397
  inflation and, 23, 326, 342, 353, 355–357,
    367–369, 487, 505
Welfare costs, of inflation, 3, 5–6, 8, 458
Wiener process, 58, 76, 94, 99

Zero discount factor, 83–84, 91